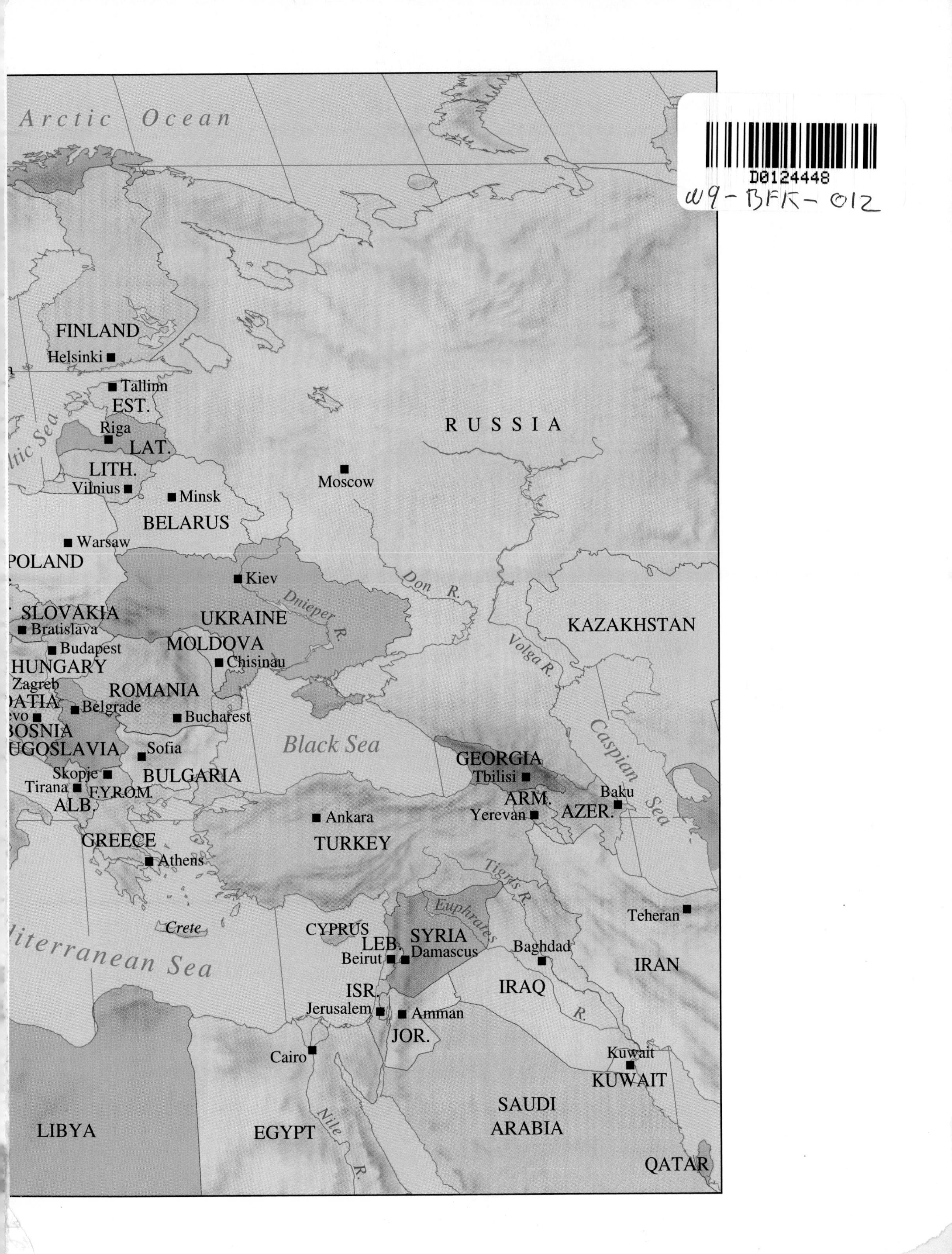

Arctic Ocean
FINLAND
Helsinki
Tallinn
EST.
Riga
LAT.
LITH.
Vilnius
Minsk
BELARUS
Warsaw
POLAND
RUSSIA
Moscow
Kiev
UKRAINE
Dnieper R.
Don R.
Volga R.
KAZAKHSTAN
SLOVAKIA
Bratislava
Budapest
HUNGARY
MOLDOVA
Chisinau
Zagreb
ROMANIA
Belgrade
Bucharest
BOSNIA
UGOSLAVIA
Sofia
BULGARIA
Skopje
Tirana
F.Y.R.O.M.
ALB.
Black Sea
Caspian Sea
GEORGIA
Tbilisi
ARM.
Baku
Yerevan
AZER.
Ankara
TURKEY
GREECE
Athens
Crete
literranean Sea
Tigris R.
Euphrates
CYPRUS
SYRIA
LEB.
Beirut
Damascus
Baghdad
IRAQ
Teheran
IRAN
ISR.
Jerusalem
Amman
JOR.
R.
Cairo
Kuwait
KUWAIT
SAUDI ARABIA
LIBYA
EGYPT
Nile R.
QATAR

FOURTH EDITION

Western Civilization

Volume B: 1300 to 1815

Jackson J. Spielvogel
The Pennsylvania State University

Australia • Canada • Denmark • Japan • Mexico • New Zealand
Philippines • Puerto Rico • Singapore • South Africa • Spain
United Kingdom • United States

History Publisher: *Clark Baxter*
Senior Development Editor: *Sharon Adams Poore*
Assistant Editor: *Cherie Hackelberg*
Editorial Assistant: *Melissa Gleason*
Marketing Manager: *Jay Hu*
Print Buyer: *Barbara Britton*
Permissions Editor: *Susan Walters*
Interior and Cover Designer: *Norman Baugher*
Production Service: *Jon Peck, Dovetail Publishing Services*
Copy Editor: *Patricia Lewis*

Photo Researcher: *Sarah Evertson, Image Quest*
Maps: *MapQuest.com, Inc.*
Compositor: *New England Typographic Service*
Printer/Binder: *World Color, Versailles*
Cover Printer: *Phoenix Color Corp.*
Cover and page ii image: *Meister des Marienlebens,* Koln, 1460/90 Geburt Mariae, Alte Pinakothek, Munich, Photo © Artothek
Photo Credits begin on page 599

Printed in the United States of America
2 3 4 5 6 7 03 02 01 00

ISBN: 0-534-56839-4

Wadsworth/Thomson Learning
10 Davis Drive
Belmont, CA 94002-3098
USA
www.wadsworth.com

International Headquarters
Thomson Learning
290 Harbor Drive, 2nd Floor
Stamford, CT 06902-7477
USA

UK/Europe/Middle East
Thomson Learning
Berkshire House
168-173 High Holborn
London WC1V 7AA
United Kingdom

Asia
Thomson Learning
60 Albert Street #15-01
Albert Complex
Singapore 189969

Canada
Nelson/Thomson Learning
1120 Birchmount Road
Scarborough, Ontario M1K 5G4
Canada

This book is printed on acid-free recycled paper.

About the Author

JACKSON J. SPIELVOGEL is associate professor of history at The Pennsylvania State University. He received his Ph.D. from The Ohio State University, where he specialized in Reformation history under Harold J. Grimm. His articles and reviews have appeared in such journals as Moreana, Journal of General Education, Catholic Historical Review, Archiv für Reformationsgeschichte, *and* American Historical Review. *He has also contributed chapters or articles to* The Social History of the Reformation, The Holy Roman Empire: A Dictionary Handbook, Simon Wiesenthal Center Annual of Holocaust Studies, *and* Utopian Studies. *His work has been supported by fellowships from the Fulbright Foundation and the Foundation for Reformation Research. At Penn State, he helped inaugurate the Western civilization courses as well as a popular course on Nazi Germany. His book* Hitler and Nazi Germany *was published in 1987 (third edition, 1996). He is the co-author (with William Duiker) of* World History, *published in January 1994 (second edition, 1998). Professor Spielvogel has won five major university-wide teaching awards. During the year 1988–1989, he held the Penn State Teaching Fellowship, the university's most prestigious teaching award. In 1996, he won the Dean Arthur Ray Warnock Award for Outstanding Faculty Member. In 1997, he became the first winner of the Schreyer Institute's Student Choice Award for innovative and inspiring teaching.*

To Diane,
whose love and support
made it all possible

Brief Contents

Detailed Contents

Maps

Chronologies

Preface

We are often reminded how important it is to understand today's world if we are to deal with our growing number of challenges. And yet that understanding will be incomplete if we in the Western world do not comprehend the meaning of Western civilization and the role Western civilization has played in the world. For all of our modern progress, we still greatly reflect our religious traditions, our political systems and theories, our economic and social structures, and our cultural heritage. I have written this history of Western civilization to assist a new generation of students in learning more about the past that has helped create them and the world in which they live.

As a teacher of Western civilization courses at a major university, I have become aware of the tendency of many textbooks to simplify the content of Western civilization courses by emphasizing an intellectual perspective or political perspective or, most recently, a social perspective, often at the expense of sufficient details in a chronological framework. This approach is confusing to students whose high school social studies programs have often neglected a systematic study of Western civilization. I have attempted to write a well-balanced work in which the political, economic, social, religious, intellectual, cultural, and military aspects of Western civilization have been integrated into a chronologically ordered synthesis. I have been especially aware of the need to integrate the latest research on social history and women's history into each chapter of the book rather than isolating it either in lengthy topical chapters, which confuse the student by interrupting the chronological narrative, or in separate sections that appear at periodic intervals between chapters. If the results of the new social and women's history are to be taken seriously, they must be fully integrated into the basic narrative itself.

Another purpose in writing this history of Western civilization has been to put the story back in history. That story is an exciting one; yet many textbooks, often the product of several authors with different writing styles, fail to capture the imagination of their readers. Narrative history effectively transmits the knowledge of the past and is the form that best aids remembrance. At the same time, I have not overlooked the need for the kind of historical analysis that makes students aware that historians often disagree in their interpretations of the past.

To enliven the past and let readers see for themselves the materials that historians use to create their pictures of the past, I have included in each chapter primary sources (boxed documents) that are keyed to the discussion in the text. The documents include examples of the religious, artistic, intellectual, social, economic, and political aspects of Western life. Such varied sources as a Roman banquet menu, a student fight song in twentieth-century Britain, letters exchanged between a husband on the battle front and his wife in World War I, the Declaration of the Rights of Woman and the Citizen in the French Revolution, and a debate in the Reformation era all reveal in a vivid fashion what Western civilization meant to the individual men and women who shaped it by their activities.

Each chapter has a lengthy introduction and conclusion to help maintain the continuity of the narrative and to provide a synthesis of important themes. Anecdotes in the chapter introductions convey more dramatically the major theme or themes of each chapter. Detailed chronologies reinforce the events discussed in the text while timelines at the end of each chapter enable students to review at a glance the major developments of an era. An annotated bibliography at the end of each chapter reviews the most recent literature on each period and also gives references to some of the older, "classic" works in each field. Extensive maps and illustrations serve to deepen the reader's understanding of the text. To facilitate understanding of cultural movements, illustrations of artistic works discussed in the text are placed next to the discussions. New to the fourth edition are chapter outlines and focus questions at the beginning of each chapter, which will help students with an overview and guide them to the main subjects of each chapter. Also new to the fourth edition are a glossary of important terms and a pronunciation guide.

As preparation for the revision of *Western Civilization*, I reexamined the entire book and analyzed the comments and reviews of many colleagues who have found the book to be a useful instrument for introducing their students to the history of Western civilization. In making revisions for the fourth edition, I sought to build upon the strengths of the first, second, and third editions and, above all, to maintain the balance, synthesis, and narrative qualities that characterized those editions. To keep up with the ever-growing body of historical scholarship, new or revised material has been added throughout the book on many topics, including, for example, civilization in Mesopotamia and Egypt; ancient Israel; Corinth, Sparta, and tyranny in ancient Greece; literature in the late Roman Republic; the late Roman Empire; women in early Christianity and the new Germanic kingdoms; the rise and spread of Islam; the Black Death; Catherine of Siena; Christine de Pizan; European discovery and expansion in the sixteenth and seventeenth centuries; the French Wars of Religion; Artemisia Gentileschi; Judith Leyster and Dutch realism; Louis XIV; nobility in the eighteenth century; female utopian socialists; women and work in the nineteenth century; women and the Paris commune; Impressionism; women reformers and the "new woman" in the nineteenth century; the history of Canada; the Great Depression; movies in the 1920s and 1930s; new attitudes toward sexuality in the 1920s; women in World War II resistance movements; history of the United States and Canada since 1945; gender issues in the welfare state; the women's liberation movement; and the war in Kosovo. Throughout the revising process I also worked to craft a book that I hope students will continue to find very readable. New subheadings were added in many chapters of the fourth edition in order to facilitate the reader's comprehension of the content of the chapters.

To provide a more logical arrangement of the material, I also made organizational changes in Chapters 1, 6, 14, 28, and 29. Chapters 9, 10, and 11 on the High Middle Ages were reorganized and condensed to form two new chapters entitled "The Recovery and Growth of European Society in the High Middle Ages" and "A New World of Cities and Kingdoms." Moreover, all "Suggestions for Further Reading" at the end of each chapter were updated, and new illustrations were added to every chapter.

The enthusiastic response to the primary sources (boxed documents) led me to evaluate the content of each document carefully and add new documents throughout the text, including "The Legal Rights of Women," "A Leader of the Paris Commune," "Hesse and the Unconcious," and "Margaret Thatcher: Entering a Man's World." For the fourth edition, the maps have been revised where needed and, as in previous editions, are carefully keyed to all text references. New maps have also been added, including "Religious Groups in the Eighteenth Century," "The Columbian Exchange," and "The Holocaust."

Because courses in Western civilization at American and Canadian colleges and universities follow different chronological divisions, a one-volume edition, two two-volume editions, and a three-volume edition of this text are being made available to fit the needs of instructors. Teaching and learning ancillaries include the following:

For the Instructor

Instructor's Manual with Test Bank Prepared by Kevin Robbins, Indiana University Purdue University Indianapolis. This new Instructor's Manual contains chapter outlines, suggested lecture topics, and discussion questions for the maps and artwork as well as the primary source documents located in the text. World-wide Web sites and resources, video collections, suggested student activities, and secondary sources for lecture preparation are also included. Exam questions include essays, identifications, and multiple-choice questions. Available in two volumes.

Thomson World Class Learning Testing Tools This fully integrated suite of test creation, delivery, and classroom management tools includes Thomson World Class Test, Test Online, and World Class Management software. Available for Windows and Macintosh.

Full Color Map Acetate Package This package includes maps from the text and from other sources. More than 100 four color images are provided in a handy three-ring binder. Map commentary is provided by James Harrison, Siena College.

Map Slides 100 full color map slides.

Lecture Enrichment Slides Prepared by Dale Hoak and George Strong, College of William and Mary. These 100 slides contain images of famous paintings, statues, architectural achievements, and interesting photos. The authors supply commentary for each slide.

History Video Library A completely new selection of videos to go with the fourth edition. Over 50 titles to choose from, with coverage spanning from "Egypt: A Gift to Civilization" to "Children of the Holocaust."

CNN Today Videos For *Western Civilization*, the perfect lecture launchers contain video clips ranging from one to five minutes long.

Sights and Sounds of History Videodisc and Video Short Uses focused video clips, photos, artwork, animations, music, and dramatic readings to bring history to life. The video segments average four minutes long and are available on VHS. These make excellent lecture launchers.

PowerPoint Features acetate map images in PowerPoint format. Available for Windows and Macintosh.

For the Student

Study Guide Prepared by James Baker, Western Kentucky University. Includes chapter outlines, chapter summaries, and seven different types of questions for each chapter. Available in two volumes.

Study Tips Prepared by James Baker, Western Kentucky University. Provides a brief study guide for students containing chapter outlines, study questions, and pronunciations. Available in two volumes.

Map Exercise Workbook This workbook, prepared by Cynthia Kosso, Northern Arizona University, has been thoroughly revised including new easier to read maps. Over 20 maps and exercises ask students to identify important cities and countries and answer critical thinking questions. Available in two volumes.

MapTutor CD ROM This interactive map tutorial helps students learn geography by having them locate geographical features, regions, cities, and sociopolitical movements. Each map exercise is accompanied by questions that test their knowledge and promote critical thinking. Animations vividly show movements such as the conquests of the Romans, the spread of Christianity, invasions, medieval trade routes, the spread of the Black Death, and more.

Document Exercise Workbook Prepared by Donna Van Raaphorst, Cuyahoga Community College. A collection of exercises based on primary sources. Revised for this edition, it now contains a web component that points students to museums and other useful sites. Available in two volumes.

Journey of Civilizations CD ROM This CD-Rom takes the student on 18 interactive journeys through history. Enhanced with QuickTime movies, animations, sound clips, maps, and more, the journeys allow students to engage in history as active participants rather than as readers of past events. Available for Windows.

WebTutor This customized online study supplement helps students succeed by taking the course beyond the classroom boundaries to a virtual environment. Professors can use *WebTutor* to provide virtual office hours, post their syllabi, set up threaded discussions, and track student progress with the quizzing material. For Students, *WebTutor* offers real-time access to a full array of study tools, including flashcards, practice quizzes and tests, online tutorials, exercises, discussion questions, web links, and a full glossary. Visit www.itped.com for a demonstration.

Hammond Historical Atlas of the World This atlas helps integrate dozens of maps into the course.

Internet Guide for History, 2/e Prepared by John Soares. Provides newly revised and up-to-date internet exercises by topic.

Western Civilization, Canadian Supplement Prepared by Maryann Farkus, Dawson College. Discusses Canadian history and culture in the context of Western Civilization.

Archer, Documents of Western Civilization Contains a broad selection of carefully chosen documents. Available in two volumes.

InfoTrac® College Edition Create your own collection of secondary readings from more than 900 popular and scholarly periodicals such as *Smithsonian*, *Historian*, and *Harper's* for four months. Students can browse, choose, and print any articles they want 24 hours a day.

Historic Times: The Wadsworth History Resource Center A web site just for history students. Features links to museums, documents, and other Web sites. http://history.wadsworth.com

Acknowledgements

I began to teach at age five in my family's grape arbor. By the age of ten, I wanted to know and understand everything in the world so I set out to memorize our entire set of encyclopedia volumes. At seventeen, as editor of the high school yearbook, I chose "Patterns" as its theme. With that as my early history, followed by twenty rich years of teaching, writing, and family nurturing, it seemed quite natural to accept the challenge of writing a history of Western civilization as I approached that period in life often described as the age of wisdom. Although I see this writing adventure as part of the natural unfolding of my life, I gratefully acknowledge that without the generosity of many others, it would not have been possible.

David Redles gave generously of his time and ideas, especially for Chapters 28 and 29. Chris Colin provided research on the history of music, while Laurie Batitto, Alex Spencer, Stephen Maloney, Shaun Mason, Peter Angelos, and Fred Schooley offered valuable editorial assistance. I deeply appreciate the valuable technical assistance provided by Dayton Coles. I am also thankful to the thousands of students whose questions and responses have caused me to see many aspects of Western civilization in new ways.

My ability to undertake a project of this magnitude was in part due to the outstanding European history teachers that I had as both an undergraduate and a graduate student. These included Kent Forster (modern Europe) and Robert W. Green (early modern Europe) at The Pennsylvania State University; and Franklin Pegues (medieval), Andreas Dorpalen (modern Germany), William MacDonald (ancient), and Harold J. Grimm (Renaissance and Reformation) at The Ohio State University. These teachers provided me with profound insights into Western civilization and also taught me by their examples that learning only becomes true understanding when it is accompanied by compassion, humility, and open-mindedness.

I would like to thank the many teachers and students who have used the first three editions of my *Western Civilization*. Their enthusiastic response to a textbook that was intended to put the story back in history and capture the imagination of the reader has been very gratifying. I especially thank the many teachers and students who made the effort to contact me personally to share their enthusiasm. I also want to thank Charmarie Blaisdell of Northeastern University for her detailed analysis of women's history in the third edition. Her suggestions were very valuable in preparing the fourth edition. Thanks to West/Wadsworth's comprehensive review process, many historians were asked to evaluate my manuscript and review the first, second, and third editions. I am grateful to the following for the innumerable suggestions that have greatly improved my work:

Paul Allen
University of Utah

Gerald Anderson
North Dakota State University

Letizia Argenteri
University of San Diego

Roy A. Austensen
Illinois State University

James A. Baer
Northern Virginia Community College—Alexandria

James T. Baker
Western Kentucky University

Patrick Bass
Morningside College

John F. Battick
University of Maine

Frederic J. Baumgartner
Virginia Polytechnic Institute

Phillip N. Bebb
Ohio University

Anthony Bedford
Modesto Junior College

F. E. Beemon
Middle Tennessee State University

Leonard R. Berlanstein
University of Virginia

Douglas T. Bisson
Belmont University

Charmarie Blaisdell
Northeastern University

Stephen H. Blumm
Montgomery County Community College

Hugh S. Bonar
California State University

Werner Braatz
University of Wisconsin—Oshkosh

Alfred S. Bradford
University of Missouri

Maryann E. Brink
College of William & Mary

Blaine T. Browne
Broward Community College

J. Holden Camp, Jr.,
Hillyer College, University of Hartford

Martha Carlin
University of Wisconsin —Milwaukee

Jack Cargill
Rutgers University

Elizabeth Carney
Clemson University

Eric H. Cline
Xavier University

Robert Cole
Utah State University

William J. Connell
Rutgers University

Nancy Conradt
College of DuPage

Marc Cooper
Southwest Missouri State

Richard A. Cosgrove
University of Arizona

David A. Crain
South Dakota State University

Michael F. Doyle
Ocean County College

James W. Ermatinger
University of Nebraska—Kearney

Porter Ewing
Los Angeles City College

Carla Falkner
Northeast Mississippi Community College

Steven Fanning
University of Illinois—Chicago

Ellsworth Faris
California State University—Chico

Gary B. Ferngren
Oregon State University

Mary Helen Finnerty
Westchester Community College

A. Z. Freeman
Robinson College

Marsha Frey
Kansas State University

Frank J. Frost
University of California —Santa Barbara

Frank Garosi
California State University — Sacramento

Richard M. Golden
University of North Texas

Manuel G. Gonzales
Diablo Valley College

Amy G. Gordon
Denison University

Richard J. Grace
Providence College

Hanns Gross
Loyola University

John F. Guilmartin
Ohio State University

Jeffrey S. Hamilton
Gustavus Adolphus College

J. Drew Harrington
Western Kentucky University

James Harrison
Siena College

A. J. Heisserer
University of Oklahoma

Betsey Hertzler
Mesa Community College

Robert Herzstein
University of South Carolina

Shirley Hickson
North Greenville College

Martha L. Hildreth
University of Nevada

Boyd H. Hill, Jr.
University of Colorado—Boulder

Michael Hofstetter
Bethany College

Donald C. Holsinger
Seattle Pacific University

Frank L. Holt
University of Houston

W. Robert Houston
University of South Alabama

Paul Hughes
Sussex County Community College

Richard A. Jackson
University of Houston

Fred Jewell
Harding University

Jenny M. Jochens
Towson State University

William M. Johnston
University of Massachusetts

Jeffrey A. Kaufmann
Muscatine Community College

David O. Kieft
University of Minnesota

Patricia Killen
Pacific Lutheran University

William E. Kinsella, Jr.
Northern Virginia Community College—Annandale

James M. Kittelson
Ohio State University

Doug Klepper
Santa Fe Community College

Cynthia Kosso
Northern Arizona University

Clayton Miles Lehmann
University of South Dakota

Diana Chen Lin
Indiana University, Northwest

Ursula W. MacAffer
Hudson Valley Community College

Harold Marcuse
University of California —Santa Barbara

Mavis Mate
University of Oregon

T. Ronald Melton
Brewton Parker College

Jack Allen Meyer
University of South Carolina

Eugene W. Miller, Jr.
The Pennsylvania State University—Hazleton

Thomas M. Mulhern
University of North Dakota

John Patrick Montano
University of Delaware

Rex Morrow
Trident Technical College

Pierce Mullen
Montana State University

Frederick I. Murphy
Western Kentucky University

William M. Murray
University of South Florida

Otto M. Nelson
Texas Tech University

Sam Nelson
Willmar Community College

John A. Nichols
Slippery Rock University

Lisa Nofzinger
Albuquerque Technical Vocational Institute

Chris Oldstone-Moore
Augustana College

Donald Ostrowski
Harvard University

James O. Overfield
University of Vermont

Matthew L. Panczyk
Bergen Community College

Kathleen Parrow
Black Hills State University

Carla Rahn Phillips
University of Minnesota

Keith Pickus
Wichita State University

Linda J. Piper
University of Georgia

Janet Polasky
University of New Hampshire

Charles A. Povlovich
California State University — Fullerton

Nancy Rachels
Hillsborough Community College

Charles Rearick
University of Massachusetts —Amherst

Jerome V. Reel, Jr.
Clemson University

Joseph Robertson
Gadsden State Community College

Jonathan Roth
San Jose State University

Constance M. Rousseau
Providence College

Julius R. Ruff
Marquette University

Richard Saller
University of Chicago

Magdalena Sanchez
Texas Christian University

Jack Schanfield
Suffolk County Community College

Roger Schlesinger
Washington State University

Joanne Schneider
Rhode Island College

Thomas C. Schunk
University of Wisconsin—Oshkosh

Kyle C. Sessions
Illinois State University

Linda Simmons
Northern Virginia Community College—Manassas

Donald V. Sippel
Rhode Island College

Glen Spann
Asbury College

John W. Steinberg
Georgia Southern University

Paul W. Strait
Florida State University

James E. Straukamp
California State University —Sacramento

Brian E. Strayer
Andrews University

Fred Suppe
Ball State University

Roger Tate
Somerset Community College

Tom Taylor
Seattle University

Jack W. Thacker
Western Kentucky University

Thomas Turley
Santa Clara University

John G. Tuthill
University of Guam

Maarten Ultee
University of Alabama

Donna L. Van Raaphorst
Cuyahoga Community College

Allen M. Ward
University of Connecticut

Richard D. Weigel
Western Kentucky University

Michael Weiss
Linn-Benton Community College

Arthur H. Williamson
California State University —Sacramento

Katherine Workman
Wright State University

Judith T. Wozniak
Cleveland State University

Walter J. Wussow
University of Wisconsin —Eau Claire

Edwin M. Yamauchi
Miami University

The editors at Wadsworth Publishing Company have been both helpful and congenial at all times. Hal Humphrey guided the overall production of the book with much insight. I especially wish to thank Clark Baxter, whose clever wit, wisdom, gentle prodding, and good friendship have added much depth to our working relationship. Sharon Adams Poore thoughtfully guided the preparation of outstanding teaching and learning ancillaries. Jon Peck, of Dovetail Publishing Services, was extremely cooperative and competent in the production of the book. Pat Lewis, an outstanding copyeditor, taught me much about the fine points of the English language. Sarah Evertson provided valuable assistance in obtaining new illustrations for the fourth edition.

We are grateful to the authors and publishers acknowledged here for their permission to reprint copyrighted material. We have made every reasonable effort to identify copyright owners of materials in the boxed documents. If any information is found to be incomplete, we will gladly make whatever additional acknowledgements might be necessary.

Above all, I thank my family for their support. The gifts of love, laughter, and patience from my daughters, Jennifer and Kathryn, my sons, Eric and Christian, and my daughter-in-law, Liz, were invaluable. My wife and best friend, Diane, contributed editorial assistance, wise counsel, and the loving support that made it possible for me to complete a project of this magnitude. I could not have written the book without her.

Introduction to Students of Western Civilization

Civilization, as historians define it, first emerged between 5,000 and 6,000 years ago when people began to live in organized communities with distinct political, military, economic, and social structures. Religious, intellectual, and artistic activities also assumed important roles in these early societies. The focus of this book is on Western civilization, a civilization that for most of its history has been identified with the continent of Europe. Its origins, however, go back to the Mediterranean basin, including lands in North Africa, and the Near East as well as Europe itself. Moreover, the spread of Europeans abroad led to the development of offshoots of Western civilization in other parts of the world.

Because civilized life includes all the deeds and experiences of people organized in communities, the history of a civilization must encompass a series of studies. An examination of Western civilization requires us to study the political, economic, social, military, cultural, intellectual, and religious aspects that make up the life of that civilization and show how they are interrelated. In so doing, we need also at times to focus on some of the unique features of Western civilization. Certainly, science played a crucial role in the development of modern Western civilization. Although such societies as those of the Greeks, the Romans, and medieval Europeans were based largely on a belief in the existence of a spiritual order, Western civilization experienced a dramatic departure to a natural or material view of the universe in the seventeenth-century Scientific Revolution. Science and technology have been important in the growth of a modern and largely secular Western civilization, although antecedents to scientific development also existed in Greek, Islamic, and medieval thought and practice.

Many historians have also viewed the concept of political liberty, the fundamental value of every individual, and the creation of a rational outlook, based on a system of logical, analytical thought, as unique aspects of Western civilization. Of course, Western civilization has also witnessed the frightening negation of liberty, individualism, and reason. Racism, violence, world wars, totalitarianism—these, too, must form part of the story. Finally, regardless of our concentration on Western civilization and its characteristics, we need to take into account that other civilizations have influenced Western civilization and it, in turn, has affected the development of other civilizations.

In our examination of Western civilization, we need also to be aware of the dating of time. In recording the past, historians try to determine the exact time when events occurred. World War II in Europe, for example, began on September 1, 1939, when Hitler sent German troops into Poland, and ended on May 7, 1945, when Germany surrendered. By using dates, historians can place events in order and try to determine the development of patterns over periods of time.

If someone asked you when you were born, you would reply with a number, such as 1980. In the United States, we would all accept that number without question because it is part of the dating system followed in the Western world (Europe and the Western Hemisphere). In this system, events are dated by counting backward or forward from the birth of Christ (assumed to be the year 1). An event that took place 400 years before the birth of Christ would be dated 400 B.C. (before Christ). Dates after the birth of Christ are labeled A.D. These letters stand for the Latin words anno Domini, which mean "in the year of the lord." Thus, an event that took place 250 years after the birth of Christ is written A.D. 250, or in the year of the lord 250. It can also be written as 250, just as you would not give your birth year as A.D. 1980, but simply 1980. Historians also make use of other terms to refer to time. A decade is 10 years; a century is 100 years; and a millennium is 1,000 years. The phrase fourth century B.C. refers to the fourth period of 100 years counting backward from 1, the assumed date of the birth of Christ. Since the first century B.C. would be the years 100 B.C. to 1 B.C., the fourth century B.C. would be the years 400 B.C. to 301 B.C. We could say, then, that an event in 350 B.C. took place in the fourth century B.C.

The phrase fourth century A.D. refers to the fourth period of 100 years after the birth of Christ. Since the first period of 100 years would be the years 1 to 100, the fourth period or fourth century would be the years 301 to 400. We could say, then, for example, that an event in 350 took place in the fourth century. Likewise, the first millennium B.C. refers to the years 1000 B.C. to 1 B.C.; the second millennium A.D. refers to the years 1001 to 2000. Some historians now prefer to use the abbreviations B.C.E. ("before the common era") and C.E. ("common era") instead of B.C. and A.D. This is especially true of world historians who prefer to use symbols that are not so Western or Christian oriented. The dates, of course, remain the same. Thus, 1950 B.C.E. and 1950 B.C. would be the same year. In keeping with current usage by many historians of Western civilization, this book will use the terms B.C. and A.D.

The dating of events can also vary from people to people. Most people in the Western world use the Western calendar, also known as the Gregorian calendar after Pope Gregory XIII who refined it in 1582. The Hebrew calendar, on the other hand, uses a different system in which the year 1 is the equivalent of the Western year 3760 B.C., considered by Jews to be the date of the creation of the world. Thus, the Western year 2000 will be the year 5760 on the Jewish calendar. The Islamic calendar begins year 1 on the day Muhammad fled Mecca, which is the year 622 on the Western calendar.

The beginnings of Western civilization can be traced back to the ancient Near East, where people in Mesopotamia and Egypt developed organized societies and created the ideas and institutions that we associate with civilization. The later Greeks and Romans, who played such a crucial role in the development of Western civilization, were themselves nourished and influenced by these older societies in the Near East. Around 3000 B.C., people in Mesopotamia and Egypt began to develop cities and wrestle with the problems of organized states. They developed writing to keep records and created literature. They constructed monumental architecture to please their gods, symbolize their power, and preserve their culture for all time. They developed new political, military, social, and religious structures to deal with the basic problems of human existence and organization. These first literate civilizations left detailed records that allow us to view how they grappled with three of the fundamental problems that humans have pondered: the nature of human relationships, the nature of the universe, and the role of divine forces in that cosmos. Although later peoples in Western civilization would provide different answers from those of the Mesopotamians and Egyptians, it was they who first posed the questions, gave answers, and wrote them down. Human memory begins with these two civilizations.

By 1500 B.C., much of the creative impulse of the Mesopotamian and Egyptian civilizations was beginning to wane. The entry of new peoples known as Indo-Europeans who moved into Asia Minor and Anatolia (modern Turkey) led to the creation of a Hittite kingdom that entered into conflict with the Egyptians. The invasion of the Sea Peoples around 1200 B.C., however, destroyed the Hittites, severely weakened the Egyptians, and created a power vacuum that allowed a patchwork of petty kingdoms and city-states to emerge, especially in the area of Syria and Palestine. These small states did not last, however. Ever since the first city-states had arisen in the Near East around 3000 B.C., there had been an ongoing movement toward the creation of larger territorial states with more sophisticated systems of control. This process reached a high point in the first millennium B.C. with the appearance of empires that embraced the entire Near East. Between 1000 and 500 B.C., the Assyrians, Chaldeans, and Persians all created empires that encompassed either large areas or all of the ancient Near East. The Assyrian Empire was the first to unite almost all of the ancient Near East. Even larger, however, was the empire of the Great Kings of Persia. Although it owed much to the administrative organization created by the Assyrians, the Persian Empire had its own peculiar strengths. Persian rule was tolerant as well as efficient. Conquered peoples were allowed to keep their own religions, customs, and methods of doing business. The many years of peace that the Persian Empire brought to the Near East facilitated trade and the general well-being of its peoples. It is no wonder that many Near Eastern peoples expressed their gratitude for being subjects of the Great Kings of Persia.

The Hebrews were one of these peoples. They created no empire and were dominated by the Assyrians, Chaldeans, and Persians in turn. Nevertheless, they left a spiritual legacy that influenced much of the later development of Western civilization. The evolution of Hebrew monotheism (belief in a single god) created in Judaism one of the world's greatest religions; it influenced the development of both Christianity and Islam. When we speak of the Judaeo-Christian heritage of Western civilization, we refer not only to the concept of monotheism, but also to ideas of law, morality, and social justice that have become important parts of Western culture.

On the western fringes of the Persian Empire, another relatively small group of people, the Greeks, were creating cultural and political ideals that would also have an important impact on Western civilization. The first Greek civilization, known as Mycenaean civilization, took shape around 1600 B.C. and fell to new Greek-speaking invaders around 1100 B.C. The ensuing so-called Dark Age (c. 1100–c. 750 B.C.) did witness the creation of a system of writing and the work of Homer, whose ideals formed the basis of Greek education for hundreds of years. By the eighth century B.C., the polis or city-state had become the chief focus of Greek life. Loyalty to the polis created a close-knit community, but also divided Greece into a host of independent states. Two of them, Sparta and Athens, became the most important. They were very different, however. Sparta created a closed, highly disciplined society while Athens moved toward an open, democratic civilization.

The classical age in Greece (c. 500–338 B.C.) began with a mighty confrontation between the Greeks and the Persian Empire. After their victory over the Persians, the Greeks began to divide into two large alliances, one headed by Sparta and the other by Athens. Athens created a naval empire and flourished during the age of Pericles, but fear of Athens led to the Great Peloponnesian War between Sparta and Athens and their allies. For all of their brilliant accomplishments, the Greeks were unable to rise above the divisions and rivalries that caused them to fight each other and undermine their own civilization.

The accomplishments of the Greeks formed the fountainhead of Western culture. Socrates, Plato, and Aristotle established the foundations of Western philosophy. Herodotus and Thucydides created the discipline of history. Our literary forms are largely derived from Greek poetry and drama. Greek notions of harmony, proportion, and beauty have remained the touchstones for all subsequent Western art. A rational method of inquiry, so important to modern science, was conceived in ancient Greece. Many of our political terms are Greek in origin, and so too are our concepts of the rights and duties of citizenship, especially as they were conceived in Athens, the first great democracy the world had seen. Especially during their classical period, the Greeks raised and debated the fundamental questions about the purpose of human existence, the structure of human society, and the nature of the universe that have concerned Western thinkers ever since.

While the Greek city-states were continuing to fight each other, to their north a new and powerful kingdom—Macedonia—emerged in its own right. Under King Philip II, the Macedonians defeated a Greek allied army in 338 B.C. and then consolidated their control over the Greek peninsula. Although the independent Greek city-states lost their freedom when they were conquered by the Macedonians, Greek culture did not die. Under the leadership of Alexander the Great, son of Philip II, both Macedonians and Greeks invaded and conquered the Persian Empire. In the conquered lands, Greeks and non-Greeks established a series of kingdoms (known as the Hellenistic kingdoms) and inaugurated the Hellenistic era.

The Hellenistic period was, in its own way, a vibrant one. New cities arose and flourished. New philosophical ideas captured the minds of many. Significant achievements occurred in art, literature, and science. Greek culture spread throughout the Near East and made an impact wherever it was carried. In some areas of the Hellenistic world, queens played an active role in political life, and many upper-class women found new avenues for expressing themselves.

But serious problems remained. Hellenistic kings continued to engage in inconclusive wars. The gulf between rich and poor was indeed great. Much of the formal culture was the special preserve of the Greek conquerors whose attitude of superiority kept them largely separated from the native masses of the Hellenistic kingdoms. Although the Hellenistic world achieved a degree of political stability, by the late third century B.C., signs of decline were beginning to multiply. Some of the more farsighted perhaps realized the danger presented to the Hellenistic world by the growing power of Rome.

Sometime in the eighth century B.C., a group of Latin-speaking people built a small community called Rome on the Tiber River in Italy. Between 509 and 264 B.C., this city expanded and united almost all of Italy under its control. Even more dramatically, between 264 and 133 B.C., Rome expanded to the west and east and became master of the Mediterranean Sea.

After 133 B.C., however, Rome's republican institutions proved inadequate for the task of ruling an empire. In the breakdown that ensued, ambitious individuals saw opportunities for power unparalleled in Roman history and succumbed to the temptations. After a series of bloody civil wars, peace was finally achieved when Octavian defeated Antony and Cleopatra. Octavian's real task was at hand: to create a new system of government that seemed to preserve the Republic while establishing the basis for a new system that would rule the empire in an orderly fashion. Octavian, who came to be known by the title of Augustus, proved equal to the task.

After a century of internal upheaval, Augustus established a new order that began the Roman Empire, which experienced a lengthy period of peace and prosperity between 14 and 180. During this era, trade flourished and the provinces were governed efficiently. In the course of the third century, however, the Roman Empire came near to collapse due to invasions, civil wars, and economic decline. Although the emperors Diocletian and Constantine brought new life to the so-called Late Empire at the beginning of the fourth century, their efforts only shored up the empire temporarily. In the course of the fifth century, the empire divided into western and eastern parts, and in 476, the Roman Empire in the west came to an end with the ouster of Emperor Romulus Augustulus.

The Roman Empire was the largest empire in antiquity. Using their practical skills, the Romans made achievements in language, law, engineering, and government that were bequeathed to the future. The Romance languages of today (French, Italian, Spanish, Portuguese, and Romanian) are based on Latin. Western practices of impartial justice and trial by jury owe much to Roman law. As great builders, the Romans left monuments to their skills throughout Europe, some of which, such as aqueducts and roads, are still in use today. Aspects of Roman administrative practices survived in the Western world for centuries. The Romans also preserved the intellectual heritage of the ancient world.

During its last two hundred years, a slow transformation of the Roman world took place with the spread of Christianity. The rise of Christianity marked an important break with the dominant values of the Roman world. Christianity began as a small Jewish sect, but under the guidance of Paul of Tarsus it became a world religion that appealed to both Jews and non-Jews. Despite persecution by Roman authorities, Christianity grew and became widely accepted by the fourth century. At the end of that century, it was made the official state religion of the Roman Empire.

The period that saw the disintegration of the western part of the Roman Empire also witnessed the emergence of a new European civilization in the Early Middle Ages. The early medieval civilization that arose out of the collapse of the Western Roman Empire was formed by the coalescence of three major elements: the Germanic peoples who moved into the western part of the empire and established new kingdoms; the continuing attraction of the Greco-Roman cultural legacy; and the Christian church. Politically, a new series of Germanic kingdoms emerged in western Europe. Each fused Roman and Germanic elements to create a new society. The Christian church (or Roman Catholic church as it came to be called in the west) played a crucial role in the growth of the new European civilization. The church developed an organized government under the leadership of the pope. It also assimilated the classical tradition and through its clergy brought Christianized civilization to the Germanic tribes. Especially important were the monks and nuns who led the way in converting the Germanic peoples in Europe to Christianity.

At the end of the eighth century, a new kingdom—the Carolingian Empire—came to control much of western and central Europe, especially during the reign of Charlemagne. The pope's coronation of Charlemagne, descendant of a Germanic tribe that had converted to Christianity, as Roman emperor in 800 symbolized the fusion of the three chief components of the new European civilization: the German tribes, the classical tradition, and Christianity. In the long run, the creation of a western empire fostered the idea of a distinct European identity and marked the shift of power from the south to the north. Italy and the Mediterranean had been the center of the Roman Empire. The lands north of the Alps now became the political center of Europe, and increasingly, Europe emerged as the focus and center of Western civilization.

Building upon a fusion of Germanic, classical, and Christian elements, the medieval European world first became visible in the Carolingian Empire of Charlemagne. His empire was well governed, but was ultimately held together by personal loyalty to a strong king. The economy of the eighth and ninth centuries was based almost entirely on farming, however, and this proved inadequate to maintain a large monarchical system. As a result, a new political and military order—known as feudalism—subsequently evolved to become an integral part of the political world of the Middle Ages. The feudal order was characterized by a decentralization of political power, in which lords exercised legal, administrative, and military power. The practice of feudalism transferred public power into many private hands and seemed to provide the security sorely lacking in a time of weak central government.

European civilization began on a shaky and uncertain foundation, however. In the ninth century, Vikings, Magyars, and Muslims posed threats that could easily have stifled the new society, but the new European civilization managed to meet these challenges. The Vikings and Magyars were assimilated, and recovery slowly began to set in. By 1000, European civilization was ready to embark upon a period of dazzling vitality and expansion.

The new European civilization that had emerged in the ninth and tenth centuries began to come into its own in the eleventh and twelfth centuries as Europeans established new patterns that reached their high point in the thirteenth century. The High Middle Ages (1000–1300) was a period of recovery and growth for Western civilization, characterized by a greater sense of security and a burst of energy and enthusiasm. Climatic improvements that produced better growing conditions, an expansion of cultivated land, and technological changes combined to enable Europe's food supply to increase significantly after

1000. This increase in agricultural production helped sustain a dramatic rise in population that was physically apparent in the expansion of towns and cities.

The development of trade and the rise of cities added a dynamic new element to the civilization of the High Middle Ages. Trading activities flourished first in northern Italy and Flanders and then spread outward from these centers. In the late tenth and eleventh centuries, this renewal of commercial life led to a revival of cities. Old Roman sites came back to life while new towns arose at major crossroads or natural harbors favorable to trading activities. By the twelfth and thirteenth centuries, both the urban centers and the urban population of Europe were experiencing a dramatic expansion. The revival of trade, the expansion of towns and cities, and the development of a money economy did not mean the end of a predominantly rural European society, but they did open the door to new ways to make a living and new opportunities for people to expand and enrich their lives. Eventually, they created the foundations for the development of a predominantly urban industrial society. Commerce, cities, and a money economy also helped to undermine feudal institutions while strengthening monarchical authority.

During the High Middle Ages, European society was dominated by a landed aristocracy whose primary function was to fight. These nobles built innumerable castles that gave a distinctive look to the countryside. Although lords and vassals seemed forever mired in endless petty conflicts, over time medieval kings began to exert a centralizing authority and inaugurated the process of developing new kinds of monarchical states. By the thirteenth century, European monarchs were solidifying their governmental institutions in pursuit of greater power. The nobles, whose warlike attitudes were rationalized by labeling them the defenders of Christian society, continued to dominate the medieval world politically, economically, and socially. But quietly and surely, within this world of castles and private power, kings gradually began to extend their public powers and developed the machinery of government that would enable them to become the centers of political authority in Europe. Although they could not know it then, the actions of these medieval monarchs laid the foundation for the European kingdoms that in one form or another have dominated the European political scene ever since.

During the High Middle Ages, the power of both nobles and kings was often overshadowed by the authority of the Catholic church, perhaps the dominant institution of the High Middle Ages. In the Early Middle Ages, the Catholic church had shared in the challenge of new growth by reforming itself and striking out on a path toward greater papal power, both within the church and over European society. The High Middle Ages witnessed a spiritual renewal that led to numerous and even divergent paths: revived papal leadership, the development of centralized administrative machinery that buttressed papal authority, and new dimensions to the religious life of the clergy and laity. A wave of religious enthusiasm in the twelfth and thirteenth centuries led to the formation of new religious orders that worked to provide for the needs of the people, especially their concern for achieving salvation.

The economic, political, and religious growth of the High Middle Ages also gave European society a new confidence that enabled it to look beyond its borders to the lands and empires of the east. Only a confident Europe could have undertaken the crusades, the military effort to recover the Holy Land of the Near East from the Muslims. The crusades gave the revived papacy of the High Middle Ages yet another opportunity to demonstrate its influence over European society.

Western assurance and energy, so crucial to the crusades, were also evident in a burst of intellectual and artistic activity. New educational institutions known as universities came into being in the twelfth century. New literature, written in the vernacular language, appealed to the growing number of people in cities or at courts who could read. The study of theology, "queen of the sciences," reached a high point in the work of Thomas Aquinas. At the same time, a religious building spree—especially evident in the great Romanesque and Gothic cathedrals of the age—left the landscape bedecked with churches that were the visible symbols of Christian Europe's vitality.

Growth and optimism seemed to characterize the High Middle Ages, but underneath the calm exterior lay seeds of discontent and change. Dissent from church teaching and practices grew in the thirteenth century, leading to a climate of fear and intolerance as the church responded with inquisitorial instruments to enforce conformity to its teachings. Minorities of all kinds suffered intolerance and, worse still, persecution at the hands of people who worked to maintain the image of an ideal Christian society. The breakdown of the old agricultural system and the creation of new relationships between lords and peasants led to local peasant uprisings in the late thirteenth century. The crusades ended ignominiously with the fall of the last crusading foothold in the east in 1291. By that time, more and more signs of ominous troubles were appearing. The fourteenth century would prove to be a time of crisis for European civilization.

CHAPTER

11

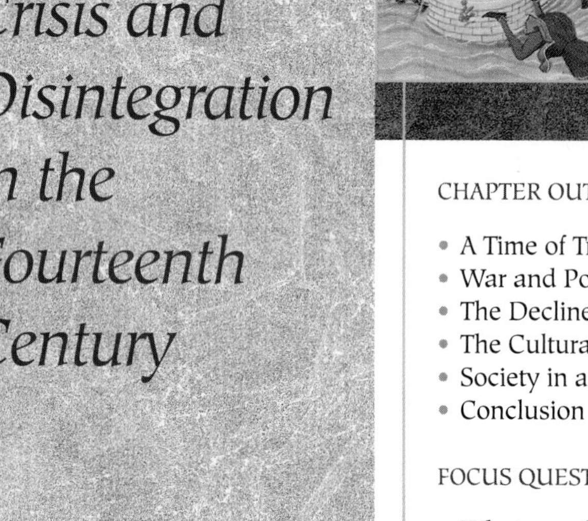

The Late Middle Ages: Crisis and Disintegration in the Fourteenth Century

CHAPTER OUTLINE

- A Time of Troubles: Black Death and Social Crisis
- War and Political Instability
- The Decline of the Church
- The Cultural World of the Fourteenth Century
- Society in an Age of Adversity
- Conclusion

FOCUS QUESTIONS

- What was the Black Death, and what was its impact on European society?
- What major problems did European states face in the fourteenth century?
- How and why did the authority and prestige of the papacy decline in the fourteenth century?
- What were the major developments in art and literature in the fourteenth century?
- How did the adversities of the fourteenth century affect urban life and medical practices?

THE HIGH MIDDLE AGES of the eleventh, twelfth, and thirteenth centuries had been a period of great innovation, evident in significant economic, social, political, religious, intellectual, and cultural changes. And yet, by the end of the thirteenth century, certain tensions had begun to creep into European society. In the course of the next century, these tensions became a torrent of troubles. At mid-century, one of the most destructive natural disasters in history erupted—the Black Death. One contemporary observer named Henry Knighton, a canon of Saint Mary-of-the-Meadow Abbey in Leicester, England, was simply overwhelmed by the magnitude of the catastrophe. Knighton began his account of the great plague with these words: "In this year [1348] and in the following one there was a general mortality of people throughout the whole world." Few were left untouched; the plague struck even isolated monasteries: "At Montpellier, there remained out of a hundred and forty friars only seven." Animals, too, were devastated: "During this same year, there was a great mortality of sheep everywhere in the kingdom; in one place and in one pasture, more than five thousand sheep died and became so putrefied that neither beast nor bird wanted to touch them." Knighton was also stunned by the economic and social consequences of the Black Death. Prices dropped: "And the price of everything was cheap, because of the fear of death; there were very few who took any care for their wealth, or for anything else." Meanwhile laborers were scarce, so their wages increased: "In the following autumn, one could not hire a reaper at a lower wage than eight pence with food, or a mower at less than twelve pence with food. Because of this, much grain rotted in the fields for lack of harvesting." So many people died that some towns were deserted and some villages disappeared altogether: "Many small villages and hamlets were completely deserted; there was not one house left in them, but all those who had lived in them were dead." Some people thought the end of the world was at hand.

Plague was not the only disaster in the fourteenth century. Signs of disintegration were everywhere: famine, economic depression, war, social upheaval, a rise in crime and violence, and a decline in the power of the universal Catholic church. Periods of disintegration, however, are often fertile grounds for change and new developments. Out of the dissolution of medieval civilization came a rebirth of culture that many historians have labeled the Renaissance.

◆ A Time of Troubles: Black Death and Social Crisis

Well into the thirteenth century, Europe had experienced good harvests and an expanding population. By the end of the thirteenth century, however, a period of disastrous changes had begun.

Famine and Population

By the end of the thirteenth and beginning of the fourteenth century, there were noticeable changes in weather patterns as Europe entered a period that has been called a "little ice age." A small shift in overall temperature patterns resulted in shortened growing seasons and disastrous weather conditions, including heavy storms and constant rain. Between 1315 and 1317, northern Europe experienced heavy rains that destroyed harvests and caused serious food shortages, resulting in extreme hunger and starvation. The great famine of 1315–1317 in northern Europe became an all-too-familiar pattern. Southern Europe, for example, seems to have been struck by similar conditions, especially in the 1330s and 1340s. Hunger became widespread, and the scene described by this chronicler became common:

> We saw a larger number of both sexes, not only from nearby places but from as much as five leagues away, barefooted and maybe even, except for women, in a completely nude state, together with their priests coming in procession at the Church of the Holy Martyrs, their bones bulging out, devoutly carrying bodies of saints and other relics to be adorned hoping to get relief.[1]

Some historians estimate that famine killed 10 percent of the European population in the first half of the fourteenth century.

Europe had experienced a great increase in population in the High Middle Ages. By 1300, however, indications are that Europe had reached the upper limit of its population, not in an absolute sense, but in the number of people who could be supported by existing agricultural production and technology. Virtually all productive land was being farmed, including many marginal lands that needed intensive cultivation and proved easily susceptible to changing weather patterns. We know that there was also a movement from overpopulated rural areas to urban locations. Eighteen percent of the people in the village of Broughton in England, for example, migrated between 1288 and 1340. There is no certainty that these migrants found better economic opportunities in urban areas. We might, in fact, conclude the opposite based on the reports of increasing numbers of poor people in the cities. In 1330, for example, one chronicler estimated that of the 100,000 inhabitants of Florence, 17,000 were paupers. Moreover, evidence suggests that because of the increase in population, individual peasant holdings by 1300 were shrinking in size to an acreage that could no longer support a peasant family. Europe seemed to have reached an upper limit to population growth, and the number of poor appeared to have increased noticeably.

Although the extent to which famine contributed to the decline of population in the early fourteenth century is unclear, some historians have pointed out that it could have had other effects on the surviving population. Famine may have led to chronic malnutrition, which in turn contributed to increased infant mortality, lower birthrates, and higher susceptibility to disease since malnourished people are less able to resist infection. This, they argue, helps to explain the high mortality of the great plague known as the Black Death.

The Black Death

The Black Death of the mid-fourteenth century was the most devastating natural disaster in European history. It ravaged Europe, wiping out 25 to 50 percent of the population and causing economic, social, political, and cultural upheaval. Contemporary chroniclers lamented that parents abandoned their children; one related the words: "Oh father, why have you abandoned me? . . . Mother, where have you gone?"[2] People were horrified by an evil

MASS BURIAL OF PLAGUE VICTIMS. The Black Death spread to northern Europe by the end of 1348. Shown here is a mass burial of victims of the plague in Tournai, located in modern Belgium. As is evident in the illustration, at this stage of the plague, there was still time to make coffins for the victims' burial. Later, as the plague intensified, the dead were thrown into open pits.

force they could not understand and by the subsequent breakdown of all normal human relations.

The Black Death was all the more horrible because it was the first major epidemic disease to strike Europe since the seventh century, an absence that helps explain medieval Europe's remarkable population growth. This great plague originated in central Asia. It was spread, it is believed, both by the Mongols as they expanded across Asia and by central Asian rodents that moved westward when ecological changes made their homeland inhospitable.

Bubonic plague, which was the most common and most important form of plague in the diffusion of the Black Death, was spread by black rats infested with fleas who were host to the deadly bacterium *Yersinia pestis*. Symptoms of bubonic plague included high fever, aching joints, swelling of the lymph nodes, and dark blotches caused by bleeding beneath the skin. Bubonic plague was actually the least toxic form of plague, but nevertheless killed 50 to 60 percent of its victims. In pneumonic plague, the bacterial infection spread to the lungs, resulting in severe coughing, bloody sputum, and the relatively easy spread of the bacillus from human to human by coughing. Fortunately, this more deadly form of the plague occurred less frequently than bubonic plague. Very rare was septicemic plague, which was carried by insects. It was extremely lethal—a victim usually died within one day of the initial infection.

The plague reached Europe in October of 1347 when Genoese merchants brought it from the Black Sea to the island of Sicily off the coast of southern Italy. It spread quickly, reaching southern Italy and southern France and Spain by the end of 1347. Usually, the diffusion of the Black Death followed commercial trade routes. In 1348, the plague spread through France and the Low Countries and into Germany. By the end of that year, it had reached England, which it ravaged in 1349. By the end of 1349, it had expanded to northern Europe and Scandinavia. Eastern Europe and Russia were affected by 1351, although mortality rates were never as high in eastern Europe as they were in western and central Europe.

Mortality figures for the Black Death were incredibly high. Italy was especially hard hit. As the commercial center of the Mediterranean, Italy possessed scores of ports where the plague could be introduced. Italy's crowded cities, whether large, such as Florence, Genoa, and Venice with populations near 100,000, or small, such as Orvieto and Pistoia, suffered losses of 50 to 60 percent (see the box on p. 300). France and England were also particularly devastated. In northern France, farming villages suffered mortality rates of 30 percent, while cities such as Rouen were more severely affected and experienced losses of 30 to 40 percent. In England and Germany, entire villages simply disappeared from history. In Germany, of approximately 170,000 inhabited locations, only 130,000 were left by the end of the fourteenth century. Overall, however, Germany suffered less than France and England.

It has been estimated that the European population declined by 25 to 50 percent between 1347 and 1351. If we accept the recent scholarly assessment of a European population of 75 million in the early fourteenth century, this means a death toll of 19 to 38 million people in four years. Moreover, the plague did not end in 1351. There were major outbreaks again in 1361–1362 and 1369 and then recurrences every five or six to ten or twelve years depending on climatic and ecological conditions during the remainder of the fourteenth century and all of the fifteenth century. Recent estimates are that the European population declined between 60 and 75 percent between 1347 and 1450 and did not begin to recover until the end of the fifteenth century; not until the mid-sixteenth century did Europe begin to regain its thirteenth-century population levels. Even then, recurrences of the plague did not end until the beginning of the eighteenth century.

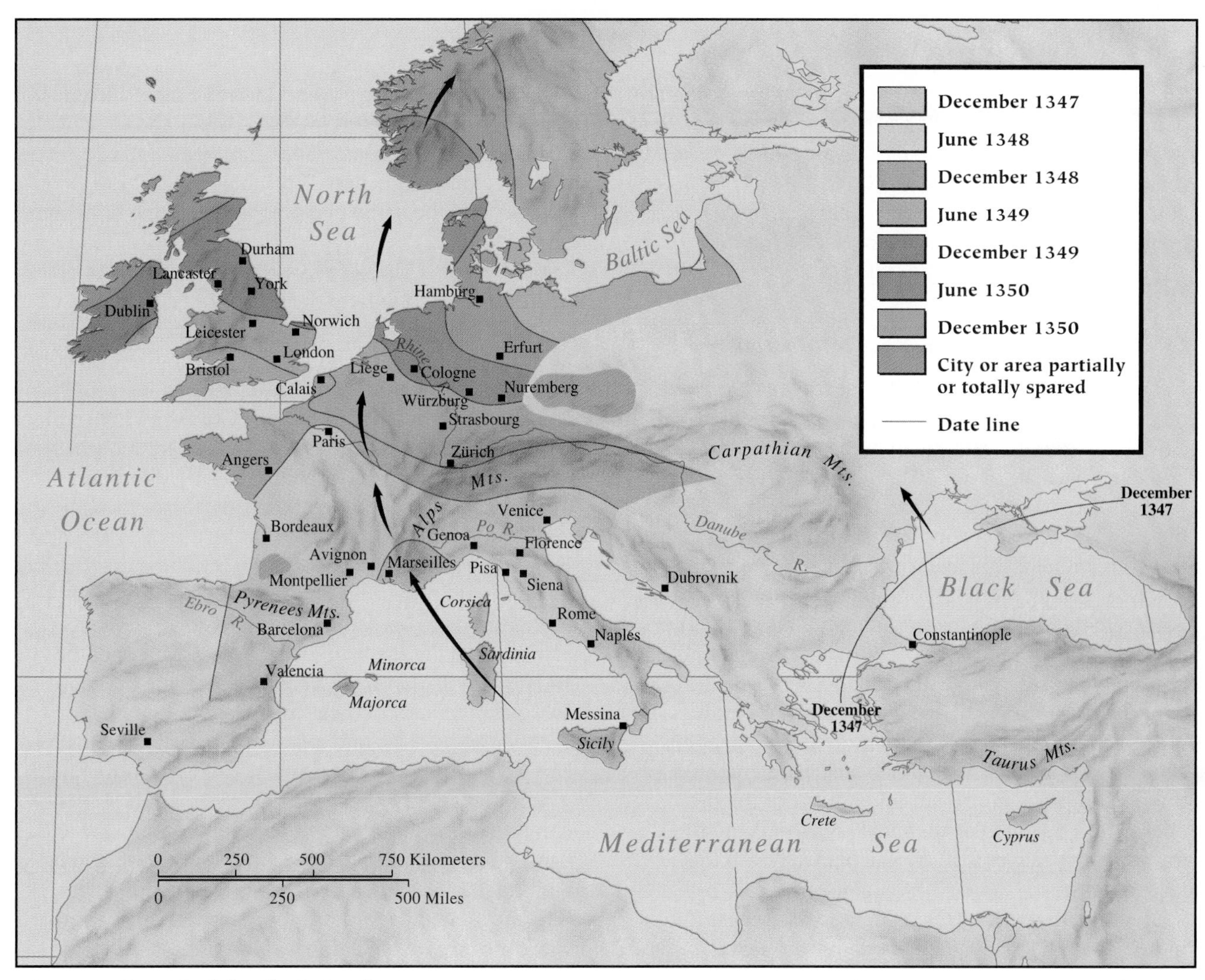

MAP 11.1 Spread of the Black Death.

LIFE AND DEATH: REACTIONS TO THE PLAGUE

Natural disasters of the magnitude of the great plague produce extreme psychological reactions. There were acts of heroism and great courage. Stories abound of priests and nuns who stayed with the suffering until they themselves died of the plague. Many other clergymen fled for their lives as fast as they could. Living for the moment, some people threw themselves with abandon into sexual and alcoholic orgies. The fourteenth-century Italian writer Giovanni Boccaccio gave a classic description of this kind of reaction to the plague in Florence in the preface to his famous work *The Decameron:*

> Others, arriving at a contrary conclusion, held that plenty of drinking and enjoyment, singing and free living and the gratification of the appetite in every possible way, letting the devil take the hindmost, was the best preventative of such a malady; and as far as they could, they suited the action to the word. Day and night they went from one tavern to another drinking and carousing unrestrainedly. At the least inkling of something that suited them, they ran wild in other people's houses, and there was no one to prevent them, for everyone had abandoned all responsibility for his belongings as well as for himself, considering his days numbered.[3]

Wealthy and powerful people fled to their country estates, as Boccaccio recounted: "Still others . . . maintained that no remedy against plagues was better than to leave them miles behind. Men and women without number . . . caring for nobody but themselves, abandoned the city, their houses and estates, their own flesh and blood even, and their effects, in search of a country place."[4]

The attempt to explain the Black Death and mitigate its harshness led to extreme sorts of behavior. To many, the plague had either been sent by God as a punishment for humans' sins or caused by the devil. Some resorted to extreme asceticism to cleanse themselves of sin and gain God's forgiveness. Such were the flagellants who became a popular movement in 1348, especially in Germany. Groups of flagellants, both men and women, wandered from town to town, flogging themselves with whips to win the forgiveness of a God whom they felt had

The Black Death

The Black Death was the most terrifying natural calamity of the entire Middle Ages. It has been estimated that 25 to 50 percent of the population died as the plague spread throughout Europe between 1347 and 1351. This contemporary description of the great plague in Florence is taken from the preface to The Decameron *by the fourteenth-century Italian writer Giovanni Boccaccio.*

Giovanni Boccaccio, *The Decameron*

In the year of Our Lord 1348 the deadly plague broke out in the great city of Florence, most beautiful of Italian cities. Whether through the operation of the heavenly bodies or because of our own iniquities which the just wrath of God sought to correct, the plague had arisen in the East some years before, causing the death of countless human beings. It spread without stop from one place to another, until, unfortunately, it swept over the West. Neither knowledge nor human foresight availed against it, though the city was cleansed of much filth by chosen officers in charge and sick persons were forbidden to enter it, while advice was broadcast for the preservation of health. Nor did humble supplications serve. Not once but many times they were ordained in the form of processions and other ways for the propitiation of God by the faithful, but, in spite of everything, toward the spring of the year the plague began to show its ravages. . . .

It did not manifest itself as in the East, where if a man bled at the nose he had certain warning of inevitable death. At the onset of the disease both men and women were afflicted by a sort of swelling in the groin or under the armpits which sometimes attained the size of a common apple or egg. Some of these swellings were larger and some smaller, and were commonly called boils. From these two starting points the boils began in a little while to spread and appear generally all over the body. Afterwards, the manifestation of the disease changed into black or livid spots on the arms, thighs, and the whole person. In many these blotches were large and far apart, in others small and closely clustered. Like the boils, which had been and continued to be a certain indication of coming death, these blotches had the same meaning for everyone on whom they appeared.

Neither the advice of physicians nor the virtue of any medicine seemed to help or avail in the cure of these diseases. Indeed, . . . not only did few recover, but on the contrary almost everyone died within three days of the appearance of the signs—some sooner, some later. . . . The virulence of the plague was all the greater in that it was communicated by the sick to the well by contact, not unlike fire when dry or fatty things are brought near it. But the evil was still worse. Not only did conversation and familiarity with the diseased spread the malady and even cause death, but the mere touch of the clothes or any other object the sick had touched or used, seemed to spread the pestilence. . . .

More wretched still were the circumstances of the common people and, for a great part, of the middle class, for, confined to their homes either by hope of safety or by poverty, and restricted to their own sections, they fell sick daily by thousands. There, devoid of help or care, they died almost without redemption. A great many breathed their last in the public streets, day and night; a large number perished in their homes, and it was only by the stench of their decaying bodies that they proclaimed their death to their neighbors. Everywhere the city was teeming with corpses. . . .

So many bodies were brought to the churches every day that the consecrated ground did not suffice to hold them, particularly according to the ancient custom of giving each corpse its individual place. Huge trenches were dug in the crowded churchyards and the new dead were piled in them, layer upon layer, like merchandise in the hold of a ship. A little earth covered the corpses of each row, and the procedure continued until the trench was filled to the top.

sent the plague to punish humans for their sinful ways. One contemporary chronicler described a flagellant procession:

> The penitents went about, coming first out of Germany. They were men who did public penance and scourged themselves with whips of hard knotted leather with little iron spikes. Some made themselves bleed very badly between the shoulder blades and some foolish women had cloths ready to catch the blood and smear it on their eyes, saying it was miraculous blood. While they were doing penance, they sang very mournful songs about the nativity and the passion of Our Lord. The object of this penance was to put a stop to the mortality, for in that time . . . at least a third of all the people in the world died.[5]

The flagellants attracted attention and created mass hysteria wherever they went. The Catholic church, however, became alarmed when flagellant groups began to kill Jews and attack the clergy who opposed them. Some groups also developed a millenarian aspect, placing their emphasis on the coming end of the world, the return of Jesus, and the establishment of a thousand-year kingdom under his governance. Pope Clement VI condemned the flagellants in October 1349 and urged the public authorities to crush them. By the end of 1350, most of the flagellant movements had been destroyed.

An outbreak of virulent anti-Semitism also accompanied the Black Death. Jews were accused of causing the

THE FLAGELLANTS. Reactions to the plague were extreme at times. Believing that asceticism could atone for humankind's sins and win God's forgiveness, flagellants wandered from town to town flogging themselves with whips, as in this illustration.

plague by poisoning town wells. Although Jews were persecuted in Spain, the worst pogroms against this helpless minority were carried out in Germany; more than sixty major Jewish communities in Germany had been exterminated by 1351 (see the box on p. 302). Many Jews fled eastward to Russia and especially to Poland where the king offered them protection. Eastern Europe became home to large Jewish communities.

The prevalence of death because of the plague and its recurrences affected people in profound ways. Some survivors apparently came to treat life as something cheap and passing. Violence and violent death appeared to be more common after the plague than before. Postplague Europe also demonstrated a morbid preoccupation with death. In their sermons, priests reminded parishioners that each night's sleep might be their last. Tombstones were decorated with macabre scenes of naked corpses in various stages of decomposition with snakes entwined in their bones and their innards filled with worms.

Economic Dislocation and Social Upheaval

The population collapse of the fourteenth century had dire economic and social consequences. Economic dislocation was accompanied by social upheaval. Between 1000 and 1300, Europe had been relatively stable. The tripartite division of society into the three estates of clergy (those who pray), nobility (those who fight), and laborers (those who work) had already begun to disintegrate in the thirteenth century, however. In the fourteenth century, a series of urban and rural revolts rocked European society.

NOBLE LANDLORDS AND PEASANTS

Both peasants and landlords were affected by the demographic crisis of the fourteenth century. Most noticeably, Europe experienced a serious labor shortage that caused a dramatic rise in the price of labor. At Cuxham manor in England, for example, a farm laborer who had received two shillings a week in 1347 was paid seven in 1349 and almost eleven by 1350. At the same time, the decline in population depressed or held stable the demand for agricultural produce, resulting in stable or falling prices for output (although in England prices remained high until the 1380s). The chronicler Henry Knighton observed: "And the price of everything was cheap. . . . For a man could buy a horse for half a mark [six shillings], which before was worth forty shillings."[6] Since landlords were having to pay more for labor at the same time that their rents or income were declining, they began to experience considerable adversity and lower standards of living. In England, aristocratic incomes dropped more than 20 percent between 1347 and 1353. The wealthiest aristocrats could still afford their privileged lifestyle, but lesser lords faced impoverishment.

Aristocrats responded to adversity by seeking to lower the wage rate. The English Parliament passed the Statute of Laborers (1351), which attempted to limit wages to preplague levels and to forbid the mobility of peasants as well. Although such laws proved largely unenforceable, they did keep wages from rising as high as they might have in a free market. Overall, the position of landlords continued to deteriorate during the late fourteenth and early fifteenth centuries. At the same time, the position of peasants improved, though not uniformly throughout Europe.

The decline in the number of peasants after the Black Death accelerated the process of converting labor services to rents, freeing peasants from the obligations of servile tenure and weakening the system of manorialism. But there were limits to how much the peasants could advance. They faced the same economic hurdles as the lords. Moreover, peasants were faced with the attempts of lords to impose wage restrictions, reinstate old forms of labor service, and create new obligations. New governmental taxes also hurt. Peasant complaints became widespread and soon gave rise to rural revolts.

PEASANT REVOLTS

In 1358, a peasant revolt, known as the *Jacquerie,* broke out in northern France. The destruction of normal order by the Black Death and the subsequent economic dislocation

A Medieval Holocaust: The Cremation of the Strasbourg Jews

In their attempt to explain the widespread horrors of the Black Death, medieval Christian communities looked for scapegoats. As at the time of the crusades, the Jews were blamed for poisoning wells and hence spreading the plague. This selection by a contemporary chronicler, written in 1349, gives an account of how Christians in the town of Strasbourg in the Holy Roman Empire dealt with their Jewish community. It is apparent that financial gain was also an important motive in killing the Jews.

Jacob von Königshofen, "The Cremation of the Strasbourg Jews"

In the year 1349 there occurred the greatest epidemic that ever happened. Death went from one end of the earth to the other. . . . And from what this epidemic came, all wise teachers and physicians could only say that it was God's will. . . . This epidemic also came to Strasbourg in the summer of the above-mentioned year, and it is estimated that about sixteen thousand people died.

In the matter of this plague the Jews throughout the world were reviled and accused in all lands of having caused it through the poison which they are said to have put into the water and the wells—that is what they were accused of—and for this reason the Jews were burnt all the way from the Mediterranean into Germany. . . .

[The account then goes on to discuss the situation of the Jews in the city of Strasbourg.]

On Saturday . . . they burnt the Jews on a wooden platform in their cemetery. There were about two thousand people of them. Those who wanted to baptise themselves were spared. [About 1,000 accepted baptism.] Many small children were taken out of the fire and baptized against the will of their fathers and mothers. And everything that was owed to the Jews was canceled, and the Jews had to surrender all pledges and notes that they had taken for debts. The council, however, took the cash that the Jews possessed and divided it among the working-men proportionately. The money was indeed the thing that killed the Jews. If they had been poor and if the feudal lords had not been in debt to them, they would not have been burnt. . . .

Thus were the Jews burnt at Strasbourg, and in the same year in all the cities of the Rhine, whether Free Cities or Imperial Cities or cities belonging to the lords. In some towns they burnt the Jews after a trial, in others, without a trial. In some cities the Jews themselves set fire to their houses and cremated themselves.

It was decided in Strasbourg that no Jew should enter the city for 100 years, but before 20 years had passed, the council and magistrates agreed that they ought to admit the Jews again into the city for 20 years. And so the Jews came back again to Strasbourg in the year 1368 after the birth of our Lord.

were important factors in causing the revolt, but the ravages created by the Hundred Years' War also affected the French peasantry (see War and Political Instability later in this chapter). Both the French and English forces followed a deliberate policy of laying waste to peasants' lands while bands of mercenaries lived off the land by taking peasants' produce as well. Thus, the *Jacquerie* was a revolt of desperation; it was linked to the political ambitions of townspeople in Paris who were also upset with the conduct of the war and wished to limit monarchical power. The leader of the peasants was actually a bourgeois draper, Etienne Marcel.

Peasant anger was also exacerbated by growing class tensions. Landed nobles were eager to hold onto their politically privileged position and felt increasingly threatened in the new postplague world of higher wages and lower prices. Aristocrats looked upon peasants with utter contempt. A French tale told to upper-class audiences contained this remarkable passage:

> Tell me, Lord, if you please, by what right or title does a villein [peasant] eat beef? . . . Should they eat fish? Rather let them eat thistles and briars, thorns and straw and hay on Sunday and peapods on weekdays. They should keep watch without sleep and have trouble always; that is how villeins should live. Yet each day they are full and drunk on the best wines, and in fine clothes. The great expenditures of villeins come as a high cost, for it is this that destroys and ruins the world. It is they who spoil the common welfare. From the villein comes all unhappiness. Should they eat meat? Rather should they chew grass on the heath with the horned cattle and go naked on all fours.[7]

The peasants reciprocated this contempt for their so-called social superiors.

The outburst of peasant anger led to savage confrontations. Castles were burned and nobles murdered (see the box on p. 303). Such atrocities did not go unanswered, however. The *Jacquerie* soon failed as the privileged classes closed ranks, savagely massacred the rebels, and ended the revolt.

The English Peasants' Revolt of 1381 was the most famous of all. It was a product not of desperation but of rising expectations. After the Black Death, the condition of the English peasants had improved as they enjoyed greater freedom and higher wages or lower rents. Aristocratic landlords had fought back with legislation to depress wages and attempted to reimpose old feudal dues. The most immediate cause of the revolt, however, was the monarchy's attempt to raise revenues by imposing a poll tax or a flat charge on each adult member of the popula-

A Revolt of French Peasants

In 1358, French peasants rose up in a revolt known as the Jacquerie. *The relationship between aristocrats and peasants had degenerated as a result of the social upheavals and privations caused by the Black Death and the Hundred Years' War. This excerpt from the chronicle of an aristocrat paints a horrifying picture of the barbarities that occurred during the revolt.*

Jean Froissart, *Chronicles*

There were very strange and terrible happenings in several parts of the kingdom of France. . . . They began when some of the men from the country towns came together in the Beauvais region. They had no leaders and at first they numbered scarcely 100. One of them got up and said that the nobility of France, knights and squires, were disgracing and betraying the realm, and that it would be a good thing if they were all destroyed. At this they all shouted: "He's right! He's right! Shame on any man who saves the gentry from being wiped out!"

They banded together and went off, without further deliberation and unarmed except for pikes and knives, to the house of a knight who lived nearby. They broke in and killed the knight, with his lady and his children, big and small, and set fire to the house. Next they went to another castle and did much worse; for, having seized the knight and bound him securely to a post, several of them violated his wife and daughter before his eyes. Then they killed the wife, who was pregnant, and the daughter and all the other children, and finally put the knight to death with great cruelty and burned and razed the castle.

They did similar things in a number of castles and big houses, and their ranks swelled until there were a good 6,000 of them. Wherever they went their numbers grew, for all the men of the same sort joined them. The knights and squires fled before them with their families. They took their wives and daughters many miles away to put them in safety, leaving their houses open with their possessions inside. And those evil men, who had come together without leaders or arms, pillaged and burned everything and violated and killed all the ladies and girls without mercy, like mad dogs. Their barbarous acts were worse than anything that ever took place between Christians and Saracens. Never did men commit such vile deeds. They were such that no living creature ought to see, or even imagine or think of, and the men who committed the most were admired and had the highest places among them. I could never bring myself to write down the horrible and shameful things which they did to the ladies. But, among other brutal excesses, they killed a knight, put him on a spit, and turned him at the fire and roasted him before the lady and her children. After about a dozen of them had violated the lady, they tried to force her and the children to eat the knight's flesh before putting them cruelly to death.

tion. Peasants in eastern England, the wealthiest part of the country, refused to pay the tax and expelled the collectors forcibly from their villages.

This action sparked a widespread rebellion of both peasants and townspeople led by a well-to-do peasant called Wat Tyler and a preacher named John Ball. The latter preached an effective message against the noble class, as recounted by the French chronicler Froissart:

> Good people, things cannot go right in England and never will, until goods are held in common and there are no more villeins and gentlefolk, but we are all one and the same. In what way are those whom we call lords greater masters than ourselves? How have they deserved it? Why do they hold us in bondage? If we all spring from a single father and mother, Adam and Eve, how can they claim or prove that they are lords more than us, except by making us produce and grow the wealth which they spend?[8]

The movement developed a famous jingle based on Ball's preaching: "When Adam delved and Eve span, who was then a gentleman?"

The revolt was initially successful as the rebels burned down the manor houses of aristocrats, lawyers, and government officials and murdered several important

PEASANT REBELLION. The fourteenth century witnessed a number of revolts of the peasantry against noble landowners. Although the revolts were initially successful, they were soon crushed. This fifteenth-century illustration shows nobles massacring the rebels in the French *Jacquerie* of 1358.

HARBOR SCENE AT HAMBURG. This illustration from a fifteenth-century treatise on the laws of Hamburg shows a busy port with ships of all sizes. At the left, a crane is used to unload barrels. In the building at the right, customs officials collect their dues. Merchants and townspeople are shown talking at dockside.

officials, including the archbishop of Canterbury. Peasants from Kent and Essex marched on London, demanding an end to serfdom and immunity from prosecution for acts undertaken during the rebellion. The young king Richard II, aged fifteen, promised to accept the rebels' demands if they returned to their homes. They accepted the king's word and dispersed, but the king reneged and with the assistance of the aristocrats arrested hundreds of the rebels. The poll tax was eliminated, however, and in the end most of the rebels were pardoned.

REVOLTS IN THE CITIES

Revolts also erupted in the cities. Commercial and industrial activity suffered almost immediately from the Black Death. An oversupply of goods and an immediate drop in demand led to a decline in trade after 1350. Some industries suffered greatly. Florence's woolen industry, one of the giants, produced 70,000 to 80,000 pieces of cloth in 1338; in 1378, it was yielding only 24,000 pieces. In Ypres, Flanders, cloth production fell an incredible 85 percent. Bordeaux wine exports fell by 50 percent. Bourgeois merchants and manufacturers responded to the decline in trade and production by attempting to restrict competition and resist the demands of the lower classes.

In urban areas where capitalist industrialists paid low wages and managed to prevent workers from forming organizations to help themselves, industrial revolts broke out throughout Europe. Ghent experienced one in 1381, Rouen in 1382. Most famous, however, was the revolt of the *ciompi* in Florence in 1378. The *ciompi* were wool workers in Florence's most prominent industry. In the 1370s, not only was the woolen industry depressed, but the wool workers saw their real wages decline when the coinage in which they were paid was debased. Their revolt won them some concessions from the municipal government, including the right to form guilds and be represented in the government. But their newly won rights were short-lived. Government authorities brought an end to *ciompi* participation in the government by 1382.

The urban and rural revolts of the fourteenth century contained some common elements. As a result of the Black Death, both workers and peasants had sustained some basic improvements in wages and living conditions. The privileged classes, whether noble landlords or wealthy bourgeoisie, wished to retain their old advantages and deny workers and peasants their newfound gains. Peasants and workers fought back. They did so at a time when normal law and order were breaking down anyway as a result of the upheaval fostered by the Black Death and the war in France.

Although the revolts sometimes resulted in short-term gains for the participants, it is also true that the uprisings were quickly crushed and their gains lost. Geographically dispersed, rural and urban revolters were not united and had no long-range goals. Immediate gains were uppermost in their minds. Accustomed to ruling, the established classes easily combined and crushed dissent when faced with social uprisings. But after the fourteenth century, the harmony theoretically implicit in the medieval hierarchy of the classes was never the same again. The rural and urban revolts of the fourteenth century ushered in an age of social conflict that characterized much of later European history.

◆ War and Political Instability

Famine, plague, economic turmoil, social upheaval, and violence were not the only problems of the fourteenth century. War and political instability must also be added to the list. Of all the struggles that ensued in the fourteenth century, the Hundred Years' War was the most famous and the most violent.

Causes of the Hundred Years' War

In 1259, the English king, Henry III, had relinquished his claims to all the French territories previously held by the English monarchy except for one relatively small possession known as the duchy of Gascony. As duke of Gascony, the English king pledged loyalty as a vassal to the French king. But this territory gave rise to numerous disputes between the kings of England and France. By the thirteenth century, the Capetian monarchs had greatly increased their power over their more important vassals, the great lords of France. Royal officials interfered regularly in the affairs of the vassals' fiefs, especially in matters of justice. Although this policy irritated all the vassals, it especially annoyed the king of England who considered himself the peer of the French king.

An economic problem involving the county of Flanders was a second factor contributing to the Hundred Years' War. Urban revolts in Flanders pitted artisans against wealthy merchants and threatened to disrupt the lucrative shipments of English wool to Flanders. Flanders was England's chief market for raw wool, and the English king received huge revenues from export duties on wool. When the French monarchy began to intervene in Flanders on the side of the merchants, the English felt threatened. If the French were to gain control of Flanders, they could play havoc with the wool trade. Accordingly, the English king began to support the Flemish artisans.

A dispute over the right of succession to the French throne also complicated the struggle between the French and the English. In the fourteenth century, the Capetian dynasty failed to produce a male heir for the first time in almost 400 years. In 1328, the senior branch of the Capetian dynasty became extinct in the male line with the death of Charles IV. As the son of the daughter of King Philip IV, King Edward III of England (1327–1377) had a claim to the French throne as a close male relative. French practice, however, emphasized descent through the male line, and a cousin of the Capetians, Philip, duke of Valois, became king as Philip VI (1328–1350).

The immediate cause of the war between France and England was yet another quarrel over Gascony. In 1337, when Edward III, the king of England and duke of Gascony, refused to do homage to Philip VI for Gascony, the French king seized the duchy. Edward responded by declaring war on Philip, the "so-called King of France." There is no doubt that the personalities of the two monarchs also had much to do with the outbreak of the Hundred Years' War. Both Edward and Philip loved luxury and shared a desire for the glory and prestige that came from military engagements. Both were only too willing to use their respective nation's resources to satisfy their own desires. Moreover, for many nobles, the promise of plunder and territorial gain was an incentive to follow the disruptive path of their rulers.

Conduct and Course of the War

The Hundred Years' War began in a burst of knightly enthusiasm. Knights were trained to be warriors; they viewed the clash of battle as the ultimate opportunity to demonstrate their chivalric qualities. The Hundred Years' War proved to be an important watershed, however, for the feudal way of life was on the decline. This would become most evident when peasant foot soldiers instead of knights determined the outcomes of the chief battles of the Hundred Years' War.

CHRONOLOGY

The Hundred Years' War

Outbreak of hostilities	1337
Battle of Crécy	1346
Battle of Poitiers	1356
Peace of Brétigny	1359
Death of Edward III	1377
Twenty-year truce	1396
Henry V (1413–1422) renews the war	1415
Battle of Agincourt	1415
French recovery under Joan of Arc	1429–1431
End of the war	1453

It was the English, more than the French, who moved beyond the traditional feudal levy. The French army of 1337 with its heavily armed noble cavalry resembled its twelfth- and thirteenth-century forebears. The noble cavalry considered themselves the fighting elite and looked with contempt upon the foot soldiers and crossbowmen because they were peasants or other social inferiors. Such attitudes cost the French dearly in the early battles.

The English army, however, had evolved differently and had included peasants as paid foot soldiers since at least Anglo-Saxon times. Armed with pikes, many of these foot soldiers had also adopted the longbow, invented by the Welsh. The longbow had a more rapid speed of fire than the more powerful crossbow. Although the English made use of heavily armed cavalry, they relied even more on large numbers of foot soldiers.

Edward III's early campaigns in France achieved little. When Edward renewed his efforts in 1346 with an invasion of Normandy, Philip responded by raising a large force to crush the English army and met Edward's forces at Crécy, just south of Flanders. Although historians disagree on the numbers involved, the undoubtedly larger French army followed no battle plan but simply attacked the English lines in a disorderly fashion. The arrows of the English archers devastated the French cavalry. As the chronicler Froissart described it, "[with their longbows] the English continued to shoot into the thickest part of the crowd, wasting none of their arrows. They impaled or wounded horses and riders, who fell to the ground in great distress, unable to get up again [because of their heavy armor] without the help of several men."[9] It was a stunning victory for the English. Edward followed up his victory by capturing the French port of Calais to serve as a staging ground for future invasions.

The Battle of Crécy was not decisive, however. The English simply did not possess the resources to subjugate all of France. Truces, small-scale hostilities, and some

The Hundred Years' War

In his account of the Hundred Years' War, the fourteenth-century French chronicler Jean Froissart described the sack of the fortified French town of Limoges by the Black Prince, Edward, the prince of Wales. It provides a vivid example of how noncombatants fared during the war.

Jean Froissart, *Chronicles*

For about a month, certainly not longer, the Prince of Wales remained before Limoges. During that time he allowed no assaults or skirmishes, but pushed on steadily with the mining. The knights inside and the townspeople, who knew what was going on, started a countermine in the hope of killing the English miners, but it was a failure. When the Prince's miners who, as they dug, were continually shoring up their tunnel, had completed their work, they said to the Prince: "My lord, whenever you like now we can bring a big piece of wall down into the moat, so that you can get into the city quite easily and safely."

The Prince was very pleased to hear this. "Excellent," he said. "At six o'clock tomorrow morning show me what you can do."

When they knew it was the right time for it, the miners started a fire in their mine. In the morning, just as the Prince had specified, a great section of the wall collapsed, filling the moat at the place where it fell. For the English, who were armed and ready waiting, it was a welcome sight. Those on foot could enter as they liked, and did so. They rushed to the gate, cut through the bars holding it and knocked it down. They did the same with the barriers outside, meeting with no resistance. It was all done so quickly that the people in the town were taken unawares. Then the Prince, the Duke of Lancaster, the Earl of Cambridge, Sir Guichard d'Angle, with all the others and their men burst into the city, followed by pillagers on foot, all in a mood to wreak havoc and do murder, killing indiscriminately, for those were their orders. There were pitiful scenes. Men, women, and children flung themselves on their knees before the Prince, crying: "Have mercy on us, gentle sir!" But he was so inflamed with anger that he would not listen. Neither man nor woman was heeded, but all who could be found were put to the sword, including many who were in no way to blame. I do not understand how they could have failed to take pity on people who were too unimportant to have committed treason. Yet they paid for it, and paid more dearly than the leaders who had committed it.

There is no man so hard-hearted that, if he had been in Limoges on that day, and had remembered God, he would not have wept bitterly at the fearful slaughter which took place. More than 3,000 persons, men, women, and children, were dragged out to have their throats cut. May God receive their souls, for they were true martyrs.

BATTLE OF CRÉCY. This fifteenth-century manuscript illustration depicts the Battle of Crécy, the first of several military disasters suffered by the French in the Hundred Years' War, and shows why the English preferred the longbow to the crossbow. At the left, the French crossbowmen stop firing and prime their weapons by cranking the handle, while English archers continue to fire their longbows (a skilled archer could fire ten arrows a minute).

major operations were combined in an orgy of seemingly incessant struggle. The English campaigns were waged by Edward III and his son Edward, the prince of Wales, known as the Black Prince. The Black Prince's campaigns in France were devastating (see the box above). Avoiding pitched battles, his forces deliberately ravaged the land, burning crops and entire unfortified villages and towns and stealing anything of value. For the English, such campaigns were profitable; for the French people, they meant hunger, deprivation, and death. When the army of the Black Prince was finally forced to do battle, the French, under their king John II (1350–1364), were once again defeated. This time even the king was captured. This Battle of Poitiers (1356) ended the first phase of the Hundred Years' War. Under the Peace of Brétigny (1359), the French agreed to pay a large ransom for King John, the English territories in Gascony were enlarged, and Edward renounced his claims to the throne of France in return for John's promise to give up any feudal control over English lands in France. This first phase of the war made it clear that, despite their victories, the English were not really strong enough to subdue all of France and make Edward III's claim to the French monarchy a reality.

Monarchs, however, could be slow learners. The Treaty of Brétigny was never really enforced. In the next

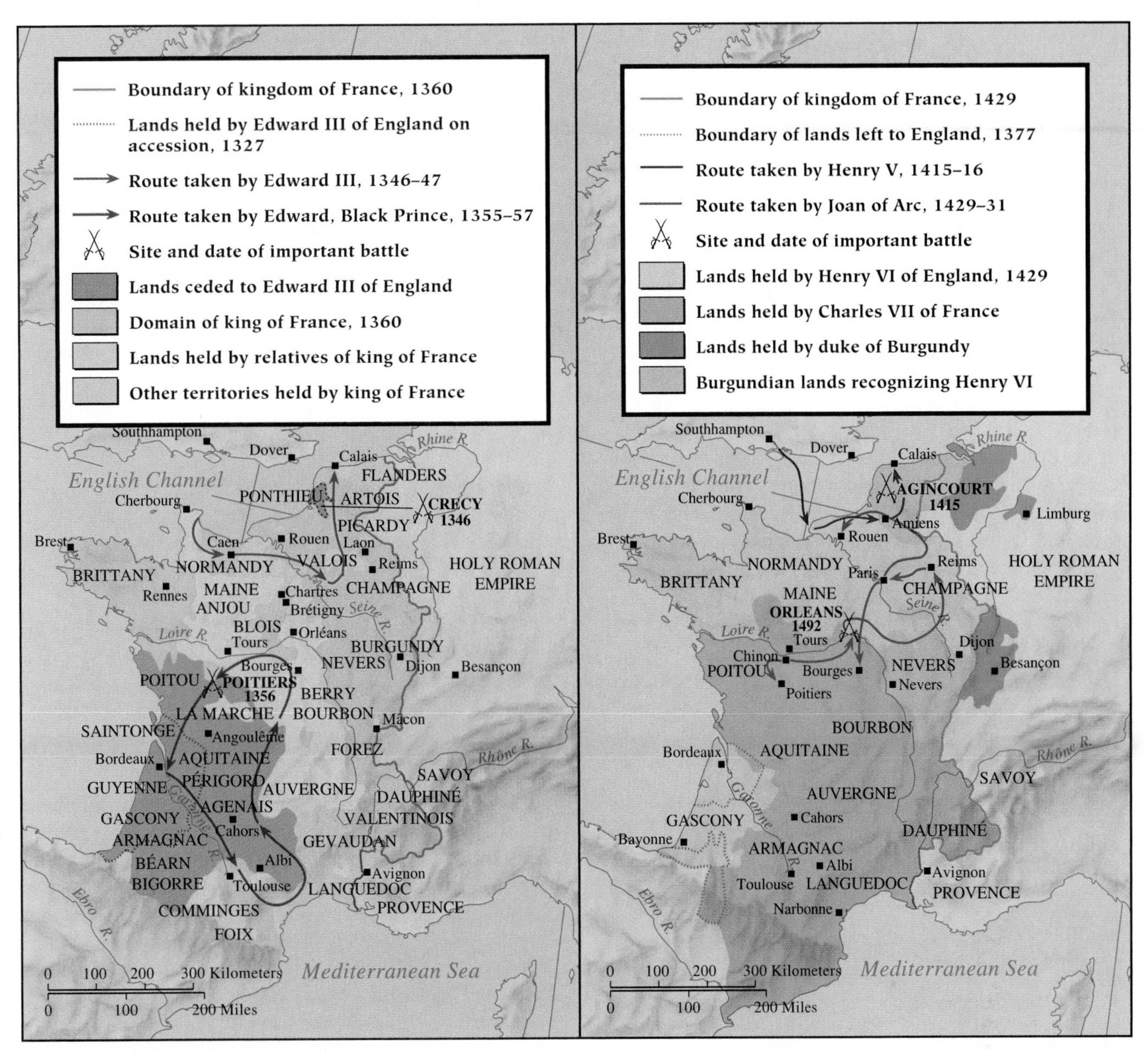

MAP 11.2 **The Hundred Years' War.**

phase of the war, under the capable hands of John's son Charles V (1364–1380), the French recovered what they had previously lost. The English returned to plundering the French countryside and avoiding pitched battles. That pleased Charles, who did not want to engage in set battles, preferring to use armed bands to reduce the English fortresses systematically. By 1374, the French had recovered their lost lands, although France itself continued to be plagued by "free companies" of mercenaries, who, no longer paid by the English, simply lived off the land by plunder and ransom. Nevertheless, for the time being, the war seemed over, especially when a twenty-year truce was negotiated in 1396.

In 1415, however, the English king, Henry V (1413–1422), renewed the war. At the Battle of Agincourt (1415), the French suffered a disastrous defeat and 1,500 French nobles died when the heavy, armor-plated French knights attempted to attack across a field turned to mud by heavy rain. Henry went on to reconquer Normandy and forge an alliance with the duke of Burgundy, making the English masters of northern France.

The seemingly hopeless French cause fell into the hands of Charles the dauphin (the title given to the heir to the throne), who governed the southern two-thirds of French lands from Bourges. Charles was weak and timid and was unable to rally the French against the English, who, in 1428, had turned south and were besieging the city of Orléans to gain access to the valley of the Loire. The French monarch was saved, quite unexpectedly, by a French peasant woman.

Joan of Arc was born in 1412, the daughter of well-to-do peasants from the village of Domrémy in Champagne. Deeply religious, Joan experienced visions and came to believe that her favorite saints had commanded her to free France and have the dauphin crowned as king. In February 1429, Joan made her way to

The Trial of Joan of Arc

Feared by the English and Burgundians, Joan of Arc was put on trial on charges of witchcraft and heresy after her capture. She was condemned for heresy and burned at the stake on May 30, 1431. This excerpt is taken from the records of Joan's trial, which presented a dramatic confrontation between the judges, trained in the complexities of legal questioning, and a nineteen-year-old woman who relied only on the "voices" of saints who gave her advice. In this selection, Joan describes what these voices told her to do.

The Trial of Joan of Arc

Afterward, she declared that at the age of thirteen she had a voice from God to help her and guide her. And the first time she was much afraid. And this voice came toward noon, in summer, in her father's garden. . . . She heard the voice on her right, in the direction of the church; and she seldom heard it without a light. This light came from the same side as the voice, and generally there was a great light. . . .

Asked what instruction this voice gave her for the salvation of her soul: she said it taught her to be good and to go to church often. . . . She said that the voice told her to come, and she could no longer stay where she was; and the voice told her again that she should raise the siege of the city of Orléans. She said moreover that the voice told her that she, Joan, should go to Robert de Baudricourt, in the town of Vaucouleurs of which he was captain, and he would provide an escort for her. And the said Joan answered that she was a poor maid, knowing nothing of riding or fighting. She said she went to an uncle of hers, and told him she wanted to stay with him for some time; and she stayed there about eight days. And she told her uncle she must go to the said town of Vaucouleurs, and so her uncle took her.

Then she said that when she reached Vaucouleurs she easily recognized Robert de Baudricourt, although she had never seen him before; and she knew him through her voice, for the voice had told her it was he. . . . The said Robert twice refused to hear her and repulsed her; the third time he listened to her and gave her an escort. And the voice had told her that it would be so.

JOAN OF ARC. **Pictured here in a suit of armor, Joan of Arc is holding aloft a banner that shows Jesus and two angels. This portrait dates from the late fifteenth century; there are no portraits of Joan made from life.**

the dauphin's court, where her sincerity and simplicity persuaded Charles to allow her to accompany a French army to Orléans. Apparently inspired by the faith of the peasant woman who called herself "the Maid," the French armies found new confidence in themselves and liberated Orléans, changing the course of the war. Within a few weeks, the entire Loire valley had been freed of the English. In July 1429, fulfilling Joan's other task, the dauphin was crowned king of France and became Charles VII (1422–1461). In accomplishing the two commands of her angelic voices, Joan had brought the war to a decisive turning point.

Joan, however, did not live to see the war concluded. She was captured by the Burgundian allies of the English in 1430. Wishing to eliminate the "Maid" for obvious political reasons, the English turned Joan over to the Inquisition on charges of witchcraft (see the box above). In the fifteenth century, spiritual visions were thought to be inspired either by God or the devil. Since Joan dressed in men's clothing, it was easy for her enemies to believe that she was in league with the "prince of darkness." She was condemned to death as a heretic and burned at the stake in 1431, at the age of nineteen. To the end, as the flames rose up around her, she declared "that her voices came from God and had not deceived her." Twenty-five years later, a new ecclesiastical court exonerated her of these charges. In 1920, she was made a saint of the Roman Catholic church.

Joan of Arc's accomplishments proved decisive. Although the war dragged on for another two decades, defeats of English armies in Normandy and Aquitaine led to French victory. The ability of the French to use artillery, which had first made its appearance in Europe in the fourteenth century, played a role in their success. But the deaths of England's best commanders and the instability of the English government under King Henry VI (1422–1461) contributed to England's defeat. By 1453, the only part of France that was left in England's hands was the coastal town of Calais, which remained English for another century.

Political Instability

The fourteenth century was a period of adversity for the internal political stability of European governments. Although government bureaucracies grew ever larger, at the same time the question of who should control the bureaucracies led to internal conflict and instability. This instability was part of a general breakdown of customary feudal institutions. Traditional feudal loyalties were disintegrating rapidly and had not yet been replaced by the national loyalties of the future. Like the lord and serf relationship, the lord and vassal relationship based on land and military service was being replaced by a contract based on money, as money payments called scutage were increasingly substituted for military service. Monarchs welcomed this development because they could now hire professional soldiers who tended to be more reliable anyway. At the same time, nobles began to form factions that looked for opportunities to advance their power and wealth at the expense of other noble factions and of their monarchs. Related to the rise of factions were two other developments that added to the instability of governments in the fourteenth century.

First, dynasties of the fourteenth century seemed unable to produce direct male heirs. By the mid-fifteenth century, reigning monarchs in many European countries were actually not the direct male descendants of those ruling in 1300. The founders of these new dynasties had to struggle for their positions as factions of nobles vied to gain material advantages for themselves. At the end of the fourteenth century and beginning of the fifteenth, there were two claimants to the throne of France, and two aristocratic factions fought for control of England; in Germany, three princes struggled to be recognized as emperor.

Fourteenth-century monarchs, whether of old or new dynasties, found themselves with financial problems as well. The shift to using mercenary soldiers left monarchs perennially short of cash. Traditional revenues, especially rents from property, increasingly proved insufficient to meet their needs. Monarchs attempted to generate new sources of revenues, especially through taxes, which often meant going through parliaments. This opened the door for parliamentary bodies to gain more power by asking for favors first. Although unsuccessful in most cases, the parliaments simply added another element of uncertainty and confusion to fourteenth-century politics. By turning now to a survey of some western and central European states (eastern Europe will be examined in Chapter 12), we can see how these disruptive factors worked in each country.

The Growth of England's Political Institutions

In the fourteenth century, the fifty-year reign of Edward III (1327–1377) was an important one for the evolution of English political institutions. Parliament increased in prominence and developed its basic structure and functions during Edward's reign. Because of his constant need for money to fight the Hundred Years' War, Edward came to rely upon Parliament to levy new taxes. In return for regular grants, Edward made several concessions, including a commitment to levy no direct tax without Parliament's consent and to allow Parliament to examine the government accounts to ensure that the money was being spent properly. By the end of Edward's reign, Parliament had become an important component of the English governmental system. Indeed, Parliament even impeached and condemned several royal ministers for acting contrary to its wishes.

During this same period, Parliament began to assume the organizational structure it has retained to this day. The Great Council of barons became the House of Lords and evolved into a body composed of the chief bishops and abbots of the realm and aristocratic peers whose position in Parliament was hereditary. The representatives of the shires and boroughs, who were considered less important than the lay and ecclesiastical lords, held collective meetings and soon came to be regarded as the House of Commons. Together, the House of Lords and House of Commons constituted Parliament. Although the House of Commons did little beyond approving measures proposed by the Lords, during Edward's reign the Commons did begin the practice of drawing up petitions, which, if accepted by the king, became law. Although the king and the Lords could amend or reject these petitions, this new procedure marked the beginning of the Commons' role in initiating legislation.

After Edward III's death, England began to experience the internal instability of aristocratic factionalism that was wracking other European countries. The early years of the reign of Edward's grandson, Richard II (1377–1399), began inauspiciously with the Peasants' Revolt that ended only when the king made concessions. Richard's reign was troubled by competing groups of nobles who sought to pursue their own interests. One faction, led by Henry of Lancaster, defeated the king's forces and then deposed and killed him. Henry of Lancaster became King Henry IV (1399–1413). In the fifteenth century, factional conflict would lead to a devastating series of civil wars.

The Problems of the French Kings

At the beginning of the fourteenth century, France was the most prosperous monarchy in Europe. By the end of the fourteenth century, much of its wealth had been dissipated, and rival factions of aristocrats had made effective monarchical rule a virtual impossibility.

The French monarchical state had always had an underlying, inherent weakness that proved its undoing

RICHARD II. Richard II faced a baronial revolt that led to his deposition as king of England. Richard commissioned this life-size portrait of himself in the early 1390s to be placed in Westminster Abbey. The artist's use of realistic details in the portrayal of the face produced a genuine (though artificially youthful) likeness of the king.

in difficult times. Although Capetian monarchs had found ways to enlarge their royal domain and extend their control by developing a large and effective bureaucracy, the various feudal territories that made up France still maintained their own princes, customs, and laws. The parliamentary institutions of France provide a good example of France's basic lack of unity. The French parliament, known as the Estates-General and composed of representatives of the clergy, nobility, and the Third Estate (everyone else), usually represented only the north of France, not the entire kingdom. The southern provinces had their own estates while local estates existed in other parts of France. Unlike the English Parliament, which was evolving into a crucial part of the English government, the French Estates-General was simply one of many such institutions.

When Philip VI (1328–1350) became involved in the Hundred Years' War with England, he found it necessary to devise new sources of revenue, including a tax on salt known as the *gabelle* and a hearth tax eventually called the *taille*. These taxes weighed heavily upon the French peasantry and middle class. Consequently, when additional taxes had to be raised to pay for the ransom of King John II after his capture at the Battle of Poitiers, the middle-class inhabitants of the towns tried to use the Estates-General to reform the French government and tax structure.

At the meeting of the Estates-General in 1357, under the leadership of the Parisian provost Etienne Marcel, representatives of the Third Estate granted taxes in exchange for a promise from King John's son, the dauphin Charles, not to tax without the Estates-General's permission and to allow the Estates-General to meet on a regular basis and participate in important political decisions. After Marcel's movement was crushed in 1358, this attempt to make the Estates-General a functioning part of the French government collapsed. The dauphin became King Charles V (1364–1380) and went on to recover much of the land lost to the English. His military successes underscored his efforts to reestablish strong monarchical powers. He undermined the role of the Estates-General by getting them to grant him taxes with no fixed time limit. Charles's death in 1380 soon led to a new time of troubles for the French monarchy, however.

The insanity of Charles VI (1380–1422), which first became apparent in 1392, opened the door to rival factions of French nobles aspiring to power and wealth. The dukes of Burgundy and Orléans competed to control Charles and the French monarchy. Their struggles created chaos for the French government and the French people. Many nobles supported the Orléanist faction while Paris and other towns favored the Burgundians. By the beginning of the fifteenth century, France seemed hopelessly mired in a civil war. When the English renewed the Hundred Years' War in 1415, the Burgundians supported the English cause and the English monarch's claim to the throne of France.

The German Monarchy

The Holy Roman Empire, whose core consisted of the lands of Germany, had already begun to fall apart in the High Middle Ages. Northern Italy, which the German emperors had tried to include in their medieval empire, had been free from any real imperial control since the end of the Hohenstaufen dynasty in the thirteenth century. In Germany itself, the failure of the Hohenstaufens ended any chance of centralized monarchical authority, and Germany became a land of hundreds of virtually independent states. These varied in size and power and included princely states, such as the duchies of Bavaria and Saxony; free imperial city-states (self-governing cities directly under the control of the Holy Roman Emperor rather than a German territorial prince), such as Nuremberg; modest territories of petty imperial knights; and ecclesiastical states, such as the archbishopric of Cologne. In the latter states, an ecclesiastical official, such as a bishop, archbishop, or abbot, served in a dual capacity as an administrative official of the Catholic church and secular lord over the territories of his ecclesiastical state. Although all of the rulers of these different states had some obligations to the German king and Holy Roman Emperor, increasingly they acted independently of the German ruler.

Because of its unique pattern of development in the High Middle Ages, the German monarchy had become established on an elective rather than hereditary basis. This principle of election was standardized in 1356 by the Golden Bull issued by Emperor Charles IV (1346–1378). This document stated that four lay princes (the count palatine of the Rhine, the duke of Saxony, the margrave of Brandenburg, and the king of Bohemia) and three ecclesiastical rulers (the archbishops of Mainz, Trier, and Cologne) would serve as electors with the legal power to elect the "king of the Romans and future emperor, to be ruler of the world and of the Christian people."[10] "King of the Romans" was the official title of the German king; after his imperial coronation, he would also have the title emperor. The Golden Bull effectively eliminated any papal influence from the election of an emperor.

In the fourteenth century, the electoral principle further ensured that kings of Germany were generally weak. Their ability to exercise effective power depended upon the extent of their own family possessions. Two different families held the title of emperor in the fourteenth century; at the beginning of the fifteenth century, three emperors claimed the throne. Although the dispute was quickly settled, Germany entered the fifteenth century in a condition that verged on anarchy. Princes fought princes and leagues of cities. The emperors were virtually powerless to control any of them.

CHRONOLOGY

The States of Western and Central Europe

England	
Edward III	1327–1377
Richard II	1377–1399
Henry IV	1399–1413
France	
Philip VI	1328–1350
John II	1350–1364
Capture at Poitiers	1356
Crushing of the *Jacquerie* and Etienne Marcel	1358
Charles V	1364–1380
Charles VI	1380–1422
The German monarchy	
Golden Bull	1356
Italy	
Florence	
Ordinances of Justice	1293
Venice	
Closing of Great Council	1297
Milan	
Visconti established themselves as rulers of Milan	1322
Giangaleazzo Visconti purchases title of duke	1395

The States of Italy

By the fourteenth century, Italy, too, had failed to develop a centralized monarchical state. Papal opposition to the rule of the Hohenstaufen emperors in northern Italy had virtually guaranteed that. Moreover, southern Italy was divided into the kingdom of Naples, ruled by the French house of Anjou, and Sicily, whose kings came from the Spanish house of Aragon. The center of the peninsula remained under the rather shaky control of the papacy. Lack of centralized authority had enabled numerous city-states in northern Italy to remain independent of any political authority.

In the fourteenth century, then, Italy was divided into a host of petty states operating independently of one another. The numerous northern city-states engaged in constant quarrels and petty wars as cities fought each other for control of trade routes or other commercial advantages. Within the cities, classes and parties fought for control of the government. In the midst of this confusion, two general tendencies can be discerned in the fourteenth century: the replacement of republican governments by tyrants and the expansion of the larger city-states at the expense of the less powerful ones.

Nearly all the cities of northern Italy began their existence as free communes with republican governments. But in the fourteenth century, intense internal strife led city-states to resort to temporary expedients, allowing rule by one man with dictatorial powers. Limited rule, however, soon became long-term despotism, as tyrants proved willing to use force to maintain themselves in power. Eventually, such tyrants tried to legitimize their power by purchasing titles from the emperor (still nominally ruler of northern Italy as Holy Roman Emperor). In this fashion, the Visconti became the dukes of Milan and the d'Este, the dukes of Ferrara.

Another change of great significance was the development of larger, regional states as the larger states expanded at the expense of the smaller ones. To fight their battles, city-states came to rely on mercenary soldiers, whose leaders, called *condottieri,* sold the services of their bands to the highest bidder. These mercenaries wreaked havoc on the countryside, living by blackmail and looting when they were not actively engaged in battles. Many were foreigners who flocked to Italy during the periods of truce of the Hundred Years' War. By the end of the fourteenth century and beginning of the fifteenth, three major states came to dominate northern Italy, the despotic state of Milan and the republican states of Florence and Venice.

Located in the rich land of the Po valley where the chief trade routes from Italian coastal cities to the Alpine passes crossed, Milan was one of the richest city-states in Italy. Politically, it was also one of the most agitated. Constant rivalry between the nobles who possessed rich estates in the surrounding countryside and the wealthy merchant class within the city enabled a family known as the Visconti to enhance their own power. Already by 1322, the Visconti had established themselves as hereditary despots of Milan. Giangaleazzo Visconti, who ruled from 1385 to 1402, transformed this despotism into a hereditary duchy by purchasing the title of duke from the emperor in 1395. Under Giangaleazzo's direction, the duchy of Milan extended its power over all of Lombardy and even threatened to conquer much of northern Italy until the duke's untimely death before the gates of Florence in 1402.

Florence, like the other Italian towns, was initially a free commune dominated by a patrician class of nobles known as the *grandi*. But the rapid expansion of Florence's economy made possible the development of a wealthy merchant-industrialist class known as the *popolo grasso*—literally the "fat people." In 1293, the *popolo grasso* assumed a dominant role in government by establishing a new constitution known as the Ordinances of Justice. It provided for a republican government controlled by the seven major guilds of the city, which represented the interests of the wealthier classes. Executive power was vested in the hands of a council of elected priors (the *signoria*) and a standard-bearer of justice called the *gonfaloniere*, assisted by a number of councils with advisory and overlapping powers. Near the mid-fourteenth century, revolutionary activity by the *popolo minuto*, the small shopkeepers and artisans, won them a share in the government. Even greater expansion occurred briefly when the *ciompi*, or industrial wool workers, were allowed to be represented in the government after their revolt in 1378. Only four years later, however, a counterrevolution brought the "fat people" back into virtual control of the government. After 1382, the Florentine government was controlled by a small merchant oligarchy that manipulated the supposedly republican government. By that time, Florence had also been successful in a series of wars against its neighbors. It had conquered most of Tuscany and established itself as a major territorial state in northern Italy.

The other major northern Italian state was the republic of Venice, which had grown rich from commercial activity throughout the eastern Mediterranean and into northern Europe. A large number of merchant families became extremely wealthy. In the constitution of 1297, these patricians took control of the republic. In this year, the Great Council, the source of all political power, was closed to all but the members of about 200 families. Since all other magistrates of the city were either chosen from or by this council, these families now formed a hereditary patriciate that completely dominated the city. Although the doge (or duke) had been the executive head of the republic since the Early Middle Ages, by 1300 he had become largely a figurehead. Actual power was vested in the hands of the Great Council and the legislative body known as the Senate, while an extraordinary body known as the Council of Ten, first formed in 1310, came to be the real executive power of the state. Venetian government was respected by contemporaries for its stability. A sixteenth-century Italian historian noted that Venice had "the best government of any city not only in our own times but also in the classical world."[11]

In the fourteenth century, Venice also embarked on a policy of expansion. By the end of the fourteenth century, it had created a commercial empire by establishing colonies and trading posts in the eastern Mediterranean and Black Sea as well as continuing its commercial monopolies in the Byzantine Empire. At the same time, Venice began to conquer the territory adjoining it in northern Italy.

◆ The Decline of the Church

The papacy of the Roman Catholic church reached the height of its power in the thirteenth century. Theories of papal supremacy included a doctrine of "fullness of power" as the spiritual head of Christendom and claims to universal temporal authority over all secular rulers. But papal claims of temporal supremacy were increasingly out of step with the growing secular monarchies of Europe and ultimately brought the papacy into a conflict with these territorial states that it was unable to win. Papal defeat, in turn, led to other crises that brought into question and undermined not only the pope's temporal authority over all Christendom, but his spiritual authority as well.

Boniface VIII and the Conflict with the State

The struggle between the papacy and the secular monarchies began during the pontificate of Pope Boniface VIII (1294–1303). One major issue appeared to be at stake between the pope and King Philip IV (1285–1314) of France. In his desire to acquire new revenues, Philip claimed the right to tax the French clergy. Boniface VIII responded that the clergy of any state could not pay taxes to their secular ruler without the pope's consent. Underlying this issue, however, was a basic conflict between the claims of the papacy to universal authority over both church and state, which necessitated complete control over the clergy, and the claims of the king that all subjects, including the clergy, were under the jurisdiction of the crown and subject to the king's authority on matters of taxation and justice. In short, the fundamental issue was the universal sovereignty of the papacy versus the royal sovereignty of the monarch.

Boniface VIII's Defense of Papal Supremacy

One of the more remarkable documents of the fourteenth century was the exaggerated statement of papal supremacy issued by Pope Boniface VIII in 1302 in the heat of his conflict with the French king Philip IV. Ironically, this strongest statement ever made of papal supremacy was issued at a time when the rising power of the secular monarchies made it increasingly difficult for the premises to be accepted. Not long after issuing it, Boniface was taken prisoner by the French. Although freed by his fellow Italians, the humiliation of his defeat led to his death a short time later.

❋ Pope Boniface VIII, *Unam Sanctam*

We are compelled, our faith urging us, to believe and to hold—and we do firmly believe and simply confess—that there is one holy catholic and apostolic church, outside of which there is neither salvation nor remission of sins. . . . In this church there is one Lord, one faith and one baptism. . . . Therefore, of this one and only church there is one body and one head . . . Christ, namely, and the vicar of Christ, St. Peter, and the successor of Peter. For the Lord himself said to Peter, feed my sheep. . . .

We are told by the word of the gospel that in this His fold there are two swords—a spiritual, namely, and a temporal. . . . Both swords, the spiritual and the material, therefore, are in the power of the church; the one, indeed, to be wielded for the church, the other by the church; the one by the hand of the priest, the other by the hand of kings and knights, but at the will and sufferance of the priest. One sword, moreover, ought to be under the other, and the temporal authority to be subjected to the spiritual. . . .

Therefore if the earthly power err it shall be judged by the spiritual power; but if the lesser spiritual power err, by the greater. But if the greatest, it can be judged by God alone, not by man, the apostle bearing witness. A spiritual man judges all things, but he himself is judged by no one. This authority, moreover, even though it is given to man and exercised through man, is not human but rather divine, being given by divine lips to Peter and founded on a rock for him and his successors through Christ himself whom he has confessed; the Lord himself saying to Peter: "Whatsoever you shall bind, etc." Whoever, therefore, resists this power thus ordained by God, resists the ordination of God. . . .

Indeed, we declare, announce and define, that it is altogether necessary to salvation for every human creature to be subject to the Roman pontiff.

Boniface VIII attempted to assert his position by issuing a series of papal bulls or letters, the most important of which was *Unam Sanctam*, issued in 1302. It was the strongest statement ever made by a pope on the supremacy of the spiritual authority over the temporal authority (see the box above). Its statements, such as "The temporal authority ought to be subject to the spiritual power," and "If the earthly power errs it shall be judged by the spiritual power," made clear papal claims to temporal supremacy. When it became apparent that the pope had decided to act upon these principles by excommunicating Philip IV, the latter decided to preempt the pope's action.

To resolve the conflict, Philip had the French clergy issue a summons for Boniface VIII to appear on charges of heresy. A small contingent of French forces under the royal lawyer William de Nogaret was sent to capture Boniface and bring him back to France for trial. The pope was captured in Anagni, although Italian nobles from the surrounding countryside soon rescued him from Nogaret's clutches. The shock of this experience, however, soon led to the pope's death. Philip's strong-arm tactics had produced a clear victory for the national monarchy over the papacy since no later pope dared renew the extravagant claims of Boniface VIII. To ensure his position and avoid any future papal threat, Philip IV brought enough pressure

POPE BONIFACE VIII. The conflict between church and state in the Middle Ages reached its height in the struggle between Pope Boniface VIII and Philip IV of France. This fourteenth-century miniature depicts Boniface VIII presiding over a gathering of cardinals.

to bear on the college of cardinals to achieve the election of a Frenchman as pope in 1305, Clement V (1305–1314). Using the excuse of turbulence in the city of Rome, the new pope took up residence in Avignon on the east bank of the Rhône River. Although Avignon was located in the Holy Roman Empire and was not a French possession, it lay just across the river from the territory of King Philip IV. Clement may have intended to return to Rome, but he and his successors remained in Avignon for the next seventy-two years, which created yet another crisis for the church.

The Papacy at Avignon (1305–1377)

The residency of the popes in Avignon for almost three-quarters of the fourteenth century led to a decline in papal prestige and a growing antipapal sentiment. The city of Rome was the traditional capital of the universal church. The pope was the bishop of Rome, and his position was based upon being the successor to the apostle Peter, traditionally considered the first bishop of Rome. It was quite unseemly that the head of the Catholic church should reside in Avignon instead of Rome. Although the Avignonese popes frequently announced their intention to return to Rome, the political turmoil in the Papal States in central Italy always gave them an excuse to postpone their departure. In the decades of the 1330s, the popes began to construct a stately palace in Avignon, a clear indication that they intended to stay for some time.

Other factors also led to a decline in papal prestige during the Avignonese residency. It was widely believed that the popes at Avignon were captives of the French monarchy. Although questionable, since Avignon did not belong to the French monarchy, it was easy to believe in view of Avignon's proximity to French lands. Moreover, during the seventy-two years of the Avignonese papacy, of the 134 new cardinals created by the popes, 113 of them were French. Understandably, then, others viewed the papacy as captive to French interests. It would appear, however, that papal policy in the fourteenth century was consistent in itself and not simply an instrument of the kings of France.

The papal residency at Avignon was also an important turning point in the church's attempt to adapt itself to the changing economic and political conditions of Europe. Like the growing monarchical states, the popes centralized their administration by developing a specialized bureaucracy. In fact, the papal bureaucracy in the fourteenth century became the most sophisticated administrative system in the medieval world. Under the leadership of the pope and college of cardinals, it was divided into four major units: the papal penitentiary oversaw ecclesiastical discipline and issued papal pardons; the chancery prepared and sent out papal letters and documents; the Roman rota was responsible for judicial affairs and served as a court of appeals for cases referred to it by the pope; and the papal chamber or treasury encompassed the various departments dealing with the collection and dispersal of the vast revenues of the church. Together, these administrative units constituted an increasingly specialized and efficient bureaucratic machine.

At the same time, the popes extended their right of provision, or the power to appoint officials to vacant benefices. A benefice was a church position that consisted of a sacred office and the right of the holder to the annual revenues from the endowment. The Avignonese popes enlarged the categories of benefices reserved for papal provision to include most major elective offices (archbishops, bishops, abbots) and a large number of lesser offices (canons and parish rectors). This right of provision came to be used in a manipulative way and led to serious abuses. Popes paid cardinals for their services by giving them a number of benefices (a practice known as pluralism). Since pluralists were frequently absent and simply paid substitutes to perform their duties, the practice led to low levels of performance. Widespread pluralism and absenteeism caused a decline in effective pastoral work.

The right of papal provision was closely related to the raising of new revenues. Popes streamlined tax collection by dividing Christendom into districts and instituted new taxes as well. Although steady revenues from ecclesiastical offices meant a drastic increase in papal income, such taxes and payments were often hard on the clergy, especially in light of fourteenth-century economic conditions. Nevertheless, payment of the taxes was enforced by the threat of excommunication.

The use of excommunication to force clerics to pay taxes did not improve people's opinion of the pope's use of his spiritual authority. Furthermore, the splendor in which the pope and cardinals were living in Avignon led to highly vocal criticism of both clergy and papacy in the fourteenth century. Avignon had become a powerful symbol of abuses within the church, and many people began to call for the pope's return to Rome. One of the most prominent calls came from Catherine of Siena (c. 1347–1380), whose saintly demeanor and claims of visions from God led the city of Florence to send her on a mission to Pope Gregory XI (1370–1378) in Avignon. She told the pope: "Because God has given you authority and because you have accepted it, you ought to use your virtue and power; if you do not wish to use it, it might be better for you to resign what you have accepted; it would give more honor to God and health to your soul."[12]

The Great Schism

Catherine of Siena's admonition seemed to be heeded in 1377, when at long last Pope Gregory XI, perceiving the disastrous decline in papal prestige, returned to Rome. He died soon afterward, however, in the spring of 1378. When the college of cardinals met in conclave to elect a new pope, the citizens of Rome, fearful that the French majority would choose another Frenchman who would return the papacy to Avignon, threatened that the cardinals would not leave Rome alive unless a Roman or Ital-

CHRONOLOGY

The Decline of the Church

Pope Boniface VIII	1294–1303
Unam Sanctam	1302
The papacy at Avignon	1305–1377
Pope Gregory XI returns to Rome	1377
The Great Schism begins	1378
Pope Urban VI	1378–1389
Failure of Council of Pisa to end schism; election of Alexander V	1409
Council of Constance	1414–1418
End of schism; election of Martin V	1417

ian were elected pope. Indeed, the guards of the conclave warned the cardinals that they "ran the risk of being torn in pieces" if they did not choose an Italian. Wisely, the terrified cardinals duly elected the Italian archbishop of Bari, who was subsequently crowned as Pope Urban VI (1378–1389) on Easter Sunday. Five months later, a group of dissenting cardinals—the French ones—declared Urban's election null and void and chose one of their number, a Frenchman, who took the title of Clement VII and promptly returned to Avignon. Since Urban remained in Rome, there were now two popes, initiating what has been called the Great Schism of the church. Europe's loyalties became divided: France, Spain, Scotland, and southern Italy supported Clement, while England, Germany, Scandinavia, and most of Italy supported Urban. These divisions generally followed political lines and reflected the bitter division between the English and the French in the Hundred Years' War. Since the French supported the Avignonese pope, so did their allies; their enemies, particularly England and its allies, supported the Roman pope. The need for political support caused both popes to subordinate their policies to the policies of these states.

The Great Schism lasted for nearly forty years and had a baleful effect upon the Catholic church and Christendom in general. The schism greatly aggravated the financial abuses that had developed within the church during the Avignonese papacy. Two papal administrative systems (with only one-half the accustomed revenues) worked to increase taxation. At the same time, the schism badly damaged the faith of Christian believers. The pope was widely believed to be the leader of Christendom and, as Boniface VIII had pointed out, held the keys to the kingdom of heaven. Since both lines of popes denounced the other as the Antichrist, such a spectacle could not help but undermine the institution that had become the very foundation of the church.

New Thoughts on Church and State and the Rise of Conciliarism

As dissatisfaction with the papacy grew, so also did the calls for a revolutionary approach to solving the church's institutional problems. One of the most systematic was provided by Marsiglio of Padua (1270?–1342), rector of the University of Paris and author of the remarkable book, *Defender of the Peace.*

Marsiglio denied that the temporal authority was subject to the spiritual authority as popes from Innocent III to Boniface VIII had maintained. Instead, he argued that the church was only one element of society, part of the secular state with respect to temporal affairs, and must confine itself solely to spiritual functions. Furthermore, Marsiglio argued, the church was a community of the faithful in which all authority is ultimately derived from the entire community. The clergy hold no special authority from God, but serve only to administer the affairs of the church on behalf of all Christians. Final authority in spiritual matters must reside not with the pope but with a general church council representing all members. As Marsiglio stated it: "Doubtful sentences of divine law, especially on those matters which are called articles of the Christian faith, . . . must be defined only by the general council of the believers, . . . no partial group or individual person of whatever status [the pope], has the authority to make such definitions."[13]

The Great Schism led large numbers of serious churchmen to take up the theory of conciliarism in the belief that only a general council of the church could end the schism and bring reform to the church in its "head and members." The only serious issue left to be decided was who should call the council. Church law held that only a pope could convene a council. Professors of theology argued, however, that since the competing popes would not do so, either members of the church hierarchy or even secular princes, especially the Holy Roman Emperor, could convene a council to settle all relevant issues.

In desperation, a group of cardinals from both lines of popes finally heeded these theoretical formulations and convened a general council on their own. This Council of Pisa, which met in 1409, deposed the two popes and elected a new one, Alexander V. The council's action proved disastrous when the two deposed popes refused to step down. There were now three popes, and the church seemed more hopelessly divided than ever.

Leadership in convening a new council now passed to the Holy Roman Emperor Sigismund. As a result of his efforts, a new ecumenical church council met at Constance from 1414 to 1418. Ending the schism proved to be the Council of Constance's easiest task. After the three competing popes either resigned or were deposed, a new conclave elected Cardinal Oddone Colonna, a member of a prominent Roman family, as Pope Martin V (1417–1431). The Great Schism had finally been ended.

Popular Religion in an Age of Adversity

The concern of popes and leading clerics with finances and power during the struggles of Boniface VIII, the Avignonese papacy, and the Great Schism could not help but lead to a decline in prestige and respect for the institutional church, especially the papacy. At the same time, in the fourteenth century, the Black Death and its recurrences made an important impact on the religious life of ordinary Christians by heightening their preoccupation with death and salvation. The church often failed to provide sufficient spiritual comfort as many parish priests fled from the plague. In some English dioceses, for example, as many as 20 percent of the parish clergy abandoned their parishes.

Christians responded in different ways to the adversities of the fourteenth century. First of all, there was a tendency to stress the performance of good works, including acts of charity, as a means of assuring salvation. This was visible in wills where bequests to hospitals and other charitable foundations increased. In London, 5 percent of the wills registered in court before 1348 left a bequest to hospitals. From 1350 to 1360, 15 percent did so, while the average bequest increased by 40 percent. Another sign of the heightened concern for salvation was the establishment of family chapels served by priests whose primary responsibility was to say masses for the good of the deceased's soul. These became even more significant as the importance of purgatory rose. Purgatory was defined by the church as the place in which souls existed after death so that they could be purged of the punishment due to the consequences of sin. In effect, the soul was purified in purgatory before it ascended into heaven. It was believed that, like indulgences, prayers and private masses for the dead could shorten the amount of time souls spent in purgatory.

All of these developments are part of a larger trend—a new emphasis in late medieval Christianity on a mechanical path to salvation. Chalking up good deeds to ensure salvation was done in numerous ways, but was nowhere more evident than in the growing emphasis on indulgences. We should also note that pilgrimages, which became increasingly popular, and charitable contributions were good works that could be accomplished without the involvement of clerics, a reflection of the loss of faith in the institutional church and its clergy and another noticeable feature of popular religious life. But while there was an evident loss of faith in the hierarchical or institutional church, interest in Christianity itself did not decline. Indeed, people sought to play a more active role in their own salvation. This is particularly evident in the popularity of mysticism and lay piety in the fourteenth century.

MYSTICISM AND LAY PIETY

The mysticism of the fourteenth century was certainly not new, for Christians throughout the Middle Ages had claimed to have had mystical experiences. Mysticism did have a particularly strong impact in the fourteenth century, however, especially along the Rhine River in Germany and in the Low Countries.

Simply defined, mysticism is the immediate experience of oneness with God. It is this experience that characterized the teaching of Meister Eckhart (1260–1327), who sparked a mystical movement in western Germany. Eckhart was a well-educated Dominican theologian who wrote learned Latin works on theology, but he was also a popular preacher whose message on the union of the soul with God was typical of mysticism. According to Eckhart, such a union was attainable for those who pursued it wholeheartedly. He referred to this spiritual encounter as the "birth of Christ" in the soul.

Eckhart's mystical teachings were carried on by his disciples and pupils. One in particular, Johannes Tauler (c. 1300–1361), was significant in channeling German mysticism into a practical direction as an inspiration to inner piety or an inwardness of religious feeling. Tauler's sermons concentrated on the same idea of the union of the soul with God, but they also focused on the need to prepare the soul for the mystical encounter by expressing the love of God in the ordinary activities of everyday life. Tauler's ideas deepened the religious life of clerics and lay folk and connected mysticism to the development of the lay piety that became more visible as Eckhart's and Tauler's movement spread from Germany into the Low Countries.

In the Low Countries, German mysticism was transformed into a new form called the Modern Devotion, whose founder was Gerard Groote (1340–1384). After a religious conversion, Groote entered a monastery for several years of contemplation before reentering the world. Although he never became a priest, he was ordained as a deacon, entitling him to preach. His messages were typical of a practical mysticism. To achieve true spiritual communion with God, people must imitate Jesus and lead lives dedicated to serving the needs of their fellow human beings. Groote emphasized a simple piety and morality based on Scripture and an avoidance of the complexities of theology.

Eventually, Groote attracted a group of followers who came to be known as the Brothers of the Common Life. From this small beginning, a movement developed that spread through the Netherlands and back into Germany. Houses of the Brothers, as well as separate houses for women (Sisters of the Common Life), were founded in one city after another. The Sisters and Brothers of the Common Life did not constitute regular religious orders. They were laypeople who took no formal monastic vows, but were nevertheless regulated by quasi-monastic rules that they imposed on their own communities. They also established schools throughout Germany and the Netherlands in which they stressed their message of imitating the life of Jesus by serving others. The Brothers and Sisters of the Common Life attest to the vitality of spiritual life among lay Christians in the fourteenth century. It is interesting to note, however, that popes feared the movement since it was not closely controlled by the ecclesiastical establishment.

A number of female mystics had their own unique spiritual experiences. For them, fasting and receiving the Eucharist (the communion wafer that supposedly contains the body of Jesus) became the mainstay of their religious practices. Catherine of Siena, for example, gave up eating any solid food at the age of twenty-three and thereafter lived only on cold water and herbs that she sucked and then spat out. Her primary nourishment, however, came from the Eucharist. She wrote: "The immaculate lamb [Christ] is food, table, and servant. . . . And we who eat at that table become like the food [that is, Christ], acting not for our own utility but for the honor of God and the salvation of neighbor."[14] For Catherine and a number of other female mystics, reception of the Eucharist was their primary instrument in achieving a mystical union with God.

Changes in Theology

The fourteenth century presented challenges not only to the institutional church but also to its theological framework, especially evidenced in the questioning of the grand synthesis attempted by Thomas Aquinas. In the thirteenth century, Thomas Aquinas's grand synthesis of faith and reason was not widely accepted outside his own Dominican order. At the same time, differences with Aquinas were kept within a framework of commonly accepted scholastic thought. In the fourteenth century, however, the philosopher William of Occam (1285–1329) posed a severe challenge to the scholastic achievements of the High Middle Ages.

Occam posited a radical interpretation of nominalism. He asserted that all universals or general concepts were simply names and that only individual objects perceived by the senses were real. Although the mind was capable of analyzing individual objects or observable phenomena, it could not establish any truths about the nature of external, higher reality. Reason could not be used to substantiate spiritual truths. It could not, for example, prove the statement that "God exists." For William of Occam as a Christian believer, this did not mean that God did not exist, however. It simply indicated that the truths of religion were not demonstrable by reason, but could only be known by an act of faith. The acceptance of Occam's nominalist philosophy at the University of Paris brought an element of uncertainty to late medieval theology by seriously weakening the synthesis of faith and reason that had characterized the theological thought of the High Middle Ages. Nevertheless, Occam's emphasis on using reason to analyze the observable phenomena of the world had an important impact on the development of physical science by creating support for rational and scientific analysis. Some late medieval theologians came to accept the compatibility of rational analysis of the material world with mystical acceptance of spiritual truths.

◆ The Cultural World of the Fourteenth Century

The cultural life of the fourteenth century was also characterized by ferment. In literature, several writers used their vernacular languages to produce notable works. In art, the Black Death and other problems of the century left their mark as many artists turned to morbid themes, but the period also produced Giotto, whose paintings expressed a new realism that would be developed further by the artists of the next century.

The Development of Vernacular Literature

Although Latin remained the language of the church liturgy and the official documents of both church and state, the fourteenth century witnessed the rapid growth of vernacular literature, especially in Italy. Spoken vernacular tongues had been used in Europe for centuries, and some notable literature in French and German had appeared during the High Middle Ages, but in Italy a vernacular literature had been largely lacking until the second half of the thirteenth century.

The development of an Italian vernacular literature was mostly the result of the efforts of three writers in the fourteenth century, Dante, Petrarch, and Boccaccio. Their use of the Tuscan dialect common in Florence and its surrounding countryside ensured that it would become the basis of the modern Italian language.

Dante (1265–1321) came from an old Florentine noble family that had fallen upon hard times. Although he had held high political office in republican Florence, factional conflict led to his exile from the city in 1302. Until the end of his life, Dante hoped to return to his beloved Florence, but his wish remained unfulfilled.

Dante's masterpiece in the Italian vernacular was his *Divine Comedy,* written between 1313 and 1321. Cast in a typical medieval framework, the *Divine Comedy* is basically the story of the soul's progression to salvation, a fundamental medieval preoccupation. The lengthy poem was divided into three major sections corresponding to the realms of the afterworld: hell, purgatory, and heaven or paradise. In the "Inferno" (see the box on p. 318), Dante is led by his guide, the classical author Virgil, who is a symbol of human reason. But Virgil (or reason) can only lead the poet so far on his journey. At the end of "Purgatory," Beatrice (the true love of Dante's life), who represents revelation—which alone can explain the mysteries of heaven—becomes his guide into "Paradise." Here, Beatrice presents Dante to Saint Bernard, a symbol of mystical contemplation. The saint turns Dante over to the Virgin Mary since grace is necessary to achieve the final step of entering the presence of God, where one beholds "The love that moves the sun and the other stars."[15] Symbolically, the "Inferno" represents despair, while "Purgatory," the

Dante's Vision of Hell

The Divine Comedy *of Dante Alighieri is regarded as one of the greatest literary works of all time. Many consider it the supreme summary of medieval thought. It combines allegory with a remarkable amount of contemporary history. Indeed, forty-three of the seventy-nine people consigned to hell in the "Inferno" were Florentines. This excerpt is taken from Canto XVIII of the "Inferno," in which Dante and Virgil visit the eighth circle of hell, which is divided into ten trenches containing those who had committed malicious frauds upon their fellow human beings.*

Dante, *"Inferno," The Divine Comedy*

We had already come to where the walk
crosses the second bank, from which it lifts
another arch, spanning from rock to rock.

Here we heard people whine in the next chasm,
and knock and thump themselves with open palms,
and blubber through their snouts as if in a spasm.

Steaming from that pit, a vapor rose
over the banks, crusting them with a slime
that sickened my eyes and hammered at my nose.

That chasm sinks so deep we could not sight
its bottom anywhere until we climbed
along the rock arch to its greatest height.

Once there, I peered down; and I saw long lines
of people in a river of excrement
that seemed the overflow of the world's latrines.

I saw among the felons of that pit
one wraith who might or might not have been
tonsured—
one could not tell, he was so smeared with shit.

He bellowed: "You there, why do you stare at me
more than at all the others in this stew?"
And I to him: "Because if memory

serves me, I knew you when your hair was dry.
You are Alessio Interminelli da Lucca.
That's why I pick you from this filthy fry."

And he then, beating himself on his clown's head:
"Down to this have the flatteries I sold
the living sunk me here among the dead."

And my Guide prompted then: "Lean forward a bit
and look beyond him, there—do you see that one
scratching herself with dungy nails, the strumpet

who fidgets to her feet, then to a crouch?
It is the whore Thäis who told her lover
when he sent to ask her, 'Do you thank me much?'

'Much? Nay, past all believing!' And with this
Let us turn from the sight of this abyss."

second stage of the journey, represents hope. "Paradise" represents perfection or salvation.

Some scholars have considered the *Divine Comedy* a synthesis of medieval Christian thought. Like the Gothic cathedrals and the *Summa Theologica,* it reminds us that Christian faith was, after all, the basic foundation of medieval culture. The theology of the *Divine Comedy* is that of Saint Thomas Aquinas; its science is that of Aristotle; and its politics centers on the Holy Roman Emperor as the savior of Italy.

Like Dante, Petrarch was a Florentine who spent much of his life outside his native city. Petrarch's role in the revival of the classics made him a seminal figure in the literary Italian Renaissance (see Chapter 12). His primary contribution to the development of the Italian vernacular was made in his sonnets. He is considered to be one of the greatest European lyric poets. His sonnets were inspired by his love for a married lady named Laura, whom he had met in 1327. While honoring an idealized female figure was a longstanding medieval tradition, Laura was very human and not just an ideal. She was a real woman with whom Petrarch was involved for a long time. He poured forth his lamentations in sonnet after sonnet:

I am as tired of thinking as my thought
Is never tired to find itself in you,
And of not yet leaving this life that brought
Me the too heavy weight of signs and rue;

And because to describe your hair and face
And the fair eyes of which I always speak,
Language and sound have not become too weak
And day and night your name they still embrace.

And tired because my feet do not yet fail
After following you in every part,
Wasting so many steps without avail,

From whence derive the paper and the ink
That I have filled with you; if I should sink,
It is the fault of Love, not of my art.[16]

Petrarch's lamentations over his inability to gain his lady's love were in the medieval tradition. Yet in analyzing every aspect of the unrequited lover's feelings, he appeared less concerned to sing his lady's praise than to immortalize his own thoughts. This interest in his own personality reveals a sense of individuality stronger than in any previous medieval literature.

Although he too wrote poetry, Boccaccio (1313–1375) is primarily known for his contributions to the development of Italian prose. Another Florentine, he also used the Tuscan dialect. While working for the Bardi banking

THE VISION OF CHRISTINE DE PIZAN. Christine de Pizan is one of the extraordinary vernacular writers of the late fourteenth and early fifteenth centuries. She is pictured here in a cover illustration from her *Book of the City of Ladies*. Reason, Righteousness, and Justice are shown appearing to Christine in a dream.

house in Naples, he fell in love with a noble lady whom he called his Fiammetta, his Little Flame. Under her inspiration, Boccaccio began to write prose romances. His best-known work, *The Decameron,* however, was not written until after he had returned to Florence. *The Decameron* is set at the time of the Black Death. Ten young people flee to a villa outside Florence to escape the plague and decide to while away the time by telling stories. Although the stories are not new and still reflect the acceptance of basic Christian values, Boccaccio does present the society of his time from a secular point of view. Boccaccio stresses cleverness and wit rather than piety and devotion. It is the seducer of women, not the knight or philosopher or pious monk, who is the real hero. Perhaps, as some historians have argued, *The Decameron* reflects the immediate easy-going, cynical postplague values. Boccaccio's later work certainly became gloomier and more pessimistic; as he grew older, he even rejected his earlier work as irrelevant. He commented in a 1373 letter that "I am certainly not pleased that you have allowed the illustrious women in your house to read my trifles. . . . You know how much in them is less than decent and opposed to modesty, how much stimulation to wanton lust, how many things that drive to lust even those most fortified against it."[17]

Another leading vernacular author was Geoffrey Chaucer (c. 1340–1400), who brought a new level of sophistication to the English vernacular language in his famous work *The Canterbury Tales.* His beauty of expression and clear, forceful language were important in transforming his East Midland dialect into the chief ancestor of the modern English language. *The Canterbury Tales* constitute a group of stories told by twenty-nine pilgrims journeying from the London suburb of Southwark to the tomb of Saint Thomas Becket at Canterbury. This format gave Chaucer the chance to portray an entire range of English society, both high and low born. Among others, he presented the Knight, the Yeoman, the Prioress, the Monk, the Merchant, the Student, the Lawyer, the Carpenter, the Cook, the Doctor, the Plowman, and, of course, "A Good Wife was there from beside the city of Bath—a little deaf, which was a pity." The stories these pilgrims told to while away the time on the journey were just as varied as the storytellers themselves: knightly romances, fairy tales, saints' lives, sophisticated satires, and crude anecdotes.

Chaucer also used some of his characters to criticize the corruption of the church in the late medieval period. His portrayal of the Friar leaves no doubt of Chaucer's disdain for the corrupt practices of clerics. Of the Friar, he says:

He knew the taverns well in every town.
The barmaids and innkeepers pleased his mind
Better than beggars and lepers and their kind.

And yet, Chaucer was still a pious Christian, never doubting basic Christian doctrines and remaining optimistic that the church could be reformed. The Parson was his model for what others should imitate:

I doubt there was a priest in any place
His better. He did not stand on dignity
Nor affect in conscience too much nicety,
But Christ's and his disciples' word he sought
To teach, and first he followed what he taught.[18]

One of the extraordinary vernacular writers of the age was Christine de Pizan (c. 1364–1430). Because of her father's position at the court of Charles V of France, she received a good education. Her husband died when she was only twenty-five (they had been married for ten years), leaving her with little income and three small children and her mother to support. Christine took the unusual step of becoming a writer in order to earn her living. Her poems were soon in demand, and by 1400 she had achieved financial security.

Christine de Pizan is best known, however, for her French prose works written in defense of women. In *The Book of the City of Ladies,* written in 1404, she denounced the many male writers who had argued that women needed to be controlled by men because women by their very nature were prone to evil, unable to learn, and easily swayed. With the help of Reason, Righteousness, and

GIOTTO, *PIETÀ*. The work of Giotto marked the first clear innovation in fourteenth-century painting, making him a forerunner of the early Renaissance. In this fresco, which was part of an elaborate series in the Arena chapel in Padua begun in 1305, the solidity of Giotto's human figures gives them a three-dimensional sense.

Justice, who appear to her in a vision, Christine refutes these antifeminist attacks. Women, she argues, are not evil by nature, and they, too, could learn as well as men if they could attend the same schools: "Should I also tell you whether a woman's nature is clever and quick enough to learn speculative sciences as well as to discover them, and likewise the manual arts. I assure you that women are equally well-suited and skilled to carry them out and to put them to sophisticated use once they have learned them."[19] Much of the book includes a detailed discussion of women from the past and present who have distinguished themselves as leaders, warriors, wives, mothers, and martyrs for their religious faith. She ends by encouraging women to defend themselves against the attacks of men who are unable to understand them.

Art and the Black Death

The fourteenth century produced an artistic outburst in new directions as well as a large body of morbid work influenced by the Black Death and the recurrence of the plague. The city of Florence witnessed the first dramatic break with medieval tradition in the work of Giotto (1266–1337), often considered a forerunner of Italian Renaissance painting. Born into a peasant family, Giotto acquired his painting skills in a workshop in Florence. Although he worked throughout Italy, his most famous works were done in Padua and Florence. Coming out of the formal Byzantine school, Giotto transcended it with a new kind of realism, a desire to imitate nature that Renaissance artists later identified as the basic component of classical art. Giotto's figures were solid and rounded and, placed realistically in relationship to each other and their background, provided a sense of three-dimensional depth. The expressive faces and physically realistic bodies gave his sacred figures human qualities with which spectators could identify. Although Giotto had no immediate successors, Florentine painting in the early fifteenth century pursued even more dramatically the new direction his work represents.

The Black Death made a visible impact on art. For one thing, it wiped out entire guilds of artists. At the same time, survivors, including the newly rich who patronized artists, were no longer so optimistic. Some were more guilty about enjoying life and more concerned about gaining salvation. Postplague art began to concentrate on pain and death. A fairly large number of artistic works came to exhibit a morbid concern with death, depicting coffins, decomposing bodies, and grim figures of Death, sometimes in the form of a witch flying through the air swinging a large scythe.

◆ Society in an Age of Adversity

In the midst of disaster, the fourteenth century proved creative in its own way. New inventions made an impact on daily life at the same time that the effects of plague were felt in many areas of medieval urban life.

Changes in Urban Life

One immediate by-product of the Black Death was a greater regulation of urban activities. Authorities tried to keep cities cleaner by enacting new sanitary ordinances. Viewed as unhealthy places, bathhouses were closed down, leading to a noticeable decline in cleanliness. Efforts at regulation also affected the practice of female prostitution.

Medieval society had tolerated prostitution as a lesser evil; it was better for males to frequent prostitutes than to seduce virgins or have sex with married women. Since many males in medieval towns married late, the demand for prostitutes was high and was met by a regular supply, derived no doubt from the need of many poor girls and women to survive. The recession of the fourteenth century probably increased the supply of prostitutes while the new hedonism prevalent after the Black Death also increased demand. As a result, in the later fourteenth century, cities intensified their regulation of prostitution.

By organizing brothels, city authorities could supervise as well as tax prostitutes. Officials granted charters to citizens who were allowed to set up brothels, provided they were located only in certain areas of town. Prostitutes were also expected to wear special items of clothing—such as red hats—to distinguish them from other women. In some towns, church officials forced prostitutes to sit in special areas if they wished to attend church services.

The Legal Rights of Women

During the High and Late Middle Ages, as women were increasingly viewed as weak beings who were unable to play independent roles, legal systems also began to limit the rights of women. These excerpts are taken from a variety of legal opinions in France, England, and a number of Italian cities.

Excerpts from Legal Opinions

France, 1270: No married woman can go to court . . . unless someone has abused or beaten her, in which case she may go to court without her husband. If she is a tradeswoman, she can sue and defend herself in matters connected with her business, but not otherwise.

England [probably fifteenth century]: Every Feme Covert [married woman] is a sort of infant. . . . It is seldom, almost never that a married woman can have any action to use her wit only in her own name: her husband is her stern, her prime mover, without whom she cannot do much at home, and less abroad. . . . It is a miracle that a wife should commit any suit without her husband.

England [probably fifteenth century]: The very goods which a man gives to his wife, are still his own, her chain, her bracelets, her apparel, are all the goodman's goods. . . . A wife however gallant she be, glitters but in the riches of her husband, as the moon has no light but it is the sun's. . . . For thus it is, if before marriage the woman was possessed of horses . . . sheep, corn, wool, money, plate and jewels, all manner of movable substance is presently . . . the husband's to sell, keep or bequeath if she die.

Pesaro, Italy [exact date unknown]: No wife can make a contract without the consent of her husband.

Florence, Italy, 1415: A married woman with children cannot draw up a last will in her own right, nor dispose of her dowry among the living to the detriment of husband and children.

Lucca, Italy [exact date unknown]: No married woman . . . can seal or give away [anything] unless she has the agreement of her husband and nearest [male] relative.

FAMILY LIFE AND GENDER ROLES IN LATE MEDIEVAL CITIES

The basic unit of the late medieval town was the nuclear family of husband, wife, and children. Especially in wealthier families, there might also be servants, apprentices, and other relatives, including widowed mothers and the husband's illegitimate children.

Before the Black Death, late marriages were common for urban couples. It was not unusual for husbands to be in their late thirties or forties and wives in their early twenties. The expense of setting up a household probably necessitated the delay in marriage. But the situation changed dramatically after the plague, reflecting new economic opportunities for the survivors and a new reluctance to postpone living in the presence of so much death.

The economic difficulties of the fourteenth century also had a tendency to strengthen the development of gender roles created by thirteenth-century scholastic theologians and to set new limits on employment opportunities for women. Thomas Aquinas and others had offered rigid conceptions of men and women that were unthinkable in earlier centuries when some women had played important roles. Based on the authority of Aristotle, Aquinas had advanced the belief that according to the natural order, men were active and domineering while women were passive and submissive. As more and more lawyers, doctors, and priests, who had been trained in universities where these notions were taught, entered society, these ideas about the different natures of men and women became widely accepted. This was evident in legal systems, many of which limited the legal capacity of women (see the box above). Increasingly, women were expected to give up any active functions in society and remain subject to direction from males. A fourteenth-century Parisian provost commented that among glass cutters "no master's widow who keeps working at his craft after her husband's death may take on apprentices, for the men of the craft do not believe that a woman can master it well enough to teach a child to master it, for the craft is a very delicate one."[20] Although this statement suggests that some women were, in fact, running businesses, it also reveals that they were viewed as incapable of undertaking all of men's activities. Based on a pattern of gender, Europeans created a division of labor roles between men and women that continued until the Industrial Revolution of the eighteenth and nineteenth centuries.

MEDIEVAL CHILDREN

Medieval parents of both the High and Later Middle Ages invested considerable resources and affection in rearing their children. The dramatic increase in specialized roles that accompanied the spread of commerce and the growth of cities demanded a commitment to educating children in the marketable skills needed for the new occupations. Philip of Navarre noted in the twelfth century that boys ought to be taught a trade "as soon as possible. Those who early become and long remain apprentices ought to be the best masters."[21] Some cities provided schools to educate the young. A Florentine chronicler related that between 8,000 and 10,000 boys and girls between the ages of six and

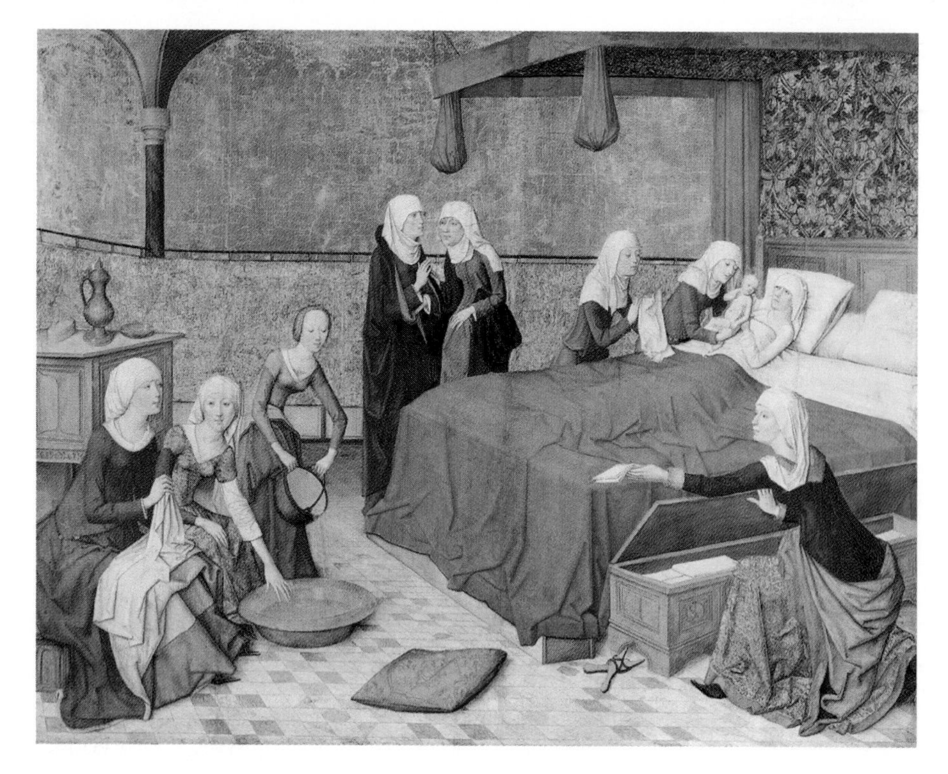

BIRTH OF A CHILD. This scene from the *Birth of the Virgin* by an unknown German artist is actually a painting of a wealthy fourteenth-century mother who has just given birth to a child. Female attendants prepare the water for the child's first bath while the mother holds her newborn in her canopied bed.

twelve attended the city's grammar schools, a figure that probably represented half of school-aged children. Although grammar school completed education for girls, around 1,100 boys went on to six secondary schools that prepared them for business careers while another 600 studied Latin and logic in four other schools that readied them for university training and a career in medicine, law, or the church. In the High Middle Ages, then, urban communities demonstrated a commitment to the training of the young.

As a result of the devastating effects of the plague and its recurrences, these same communities became concerned about investing in the survival and health of children. Although a number of hospitals existed in both Florence and Rome in the fourteenth century, it was not until the 1420s and 1430s that hospitals were established that catered only to the needs of foundlings, supporting them until boys could be taught a trade and girls could marry.

New Directions in Medicine

The medical community comprised a number of different functionaries. At the top of the medical hierarchy were the physicians, usually clergymen, who received their education in the medieval universities where they studied ancient authorities, such as Hippocrates and Galen. As a result, physicians were highly trained in theory, but had little or no clinical practice. By the fourteenth century, they were educated in six chief medical schools—Salerno, Montpellier, Bologna, Oxford, Padua, and Paris. The latter was regarded as the most prestigious by the time of the Black Death.

The preplague medicine of university-trained physicians was theoretically grounded in the classical Greek theory of the "four humors," each connected to a particular organ: blood (from the heart), phlegm (from the brain), yellow bile (from the liver), and black bile (from the spleen). The four humors, in turn, corresponded to the four elemental qualities of the universe, earth (black bile), air (blood), fire (yellow bile), and water (phlegm), making a human being a microcosm of the cosmos. Good health resulted from a perfect balance of the four humors; sickness meant that the humors were out of balance. The task of the medieval physician was to restore proper order by a number of cures, such as rest, diet, herbal medicines, or bloodletting.

Beneath the physicians in the hierarchy of the medical profession stood the surgeons, whose activities included performing operations, setting broken bones, and bleeding patients. Their knowledge was largely based on practical experience. Below surgeons were midwives and the barber-surgeons, who were less trained and performed menial tasks such as bloodletting and setting simple bone fractures. Barber-surgeons supplemented their incomes by shaving and cutting hair and pulling teeth. Apothecaries also constituted part of the medical establishment. They filled herbal prescriptions recommended by physicians and also prescribed drugs on their own authority.

All of these medical practitioners proved unable to deal with the plague. When King Philip VI of France requested the opinion of the medical faculty of the University of Paris on the plague, their advice proved worthless. This failure to understand the Black Death, however,

A MEDICAL TEXTBOOK. This illustration is taken from a fourteenth-century surgical textbook that stressed a "how-to" approach to surgical problems. *Top left,* a surgeon shows how to remove an arrow from a patient; *top right,* how to open a patient's chest; *bottom left,* how to deal with an injury to the intestines; *bottom right,* how to diagnose an abscess.

produced a crisis in medieval medicine that resulted in some new approaches to health care.

One result was the rise of surgeons to greater prominence because of their practical knowledge. Surgeons were now recruited by universities, which placed them on an equal level with physicians and introduced a greater emphasis on practical anatomy into the university curriculum. Connected to this was a rise in medical textbooks, often written in the vernacular and stressing practical, "how to" approaches to medical and surgical problems.

Finally, as a result of the plague, cities, especially in Italy, gave increased attention to public health and sanitation. Public health laws were instituted, and municipal boards of health came into being. The primary concern of the latter was to prevent plague, but gradually they came to control almost every aspect of health and sanitation. Boards of public health, consisting of medical practitioners and public officials, were empowered to enforce sanitary conditions, report on and attempt to isolate epidemics by quarantine (rarely successful), and regulate the activities of doctors. Some communities even began to hire "plague doctors," or municipal physicians and surgeons who were paid to treat victims.

Inventions and New Patterns

Despite its problems, the fourteenth century witnessed a continuation of the technological innovations that had characterized the High Middle Ages. The most extraordinary of these inventions, and one that made a visible impact on European cities, was the clock. There had been earlier experiments with waterpowered clocks, but they had obvious limitations, particularly in northern Europe where they froze in winter. The mechanical clock was invented at the end of the thirteenth century, but not perfected until the fourteenth. The time-telling clock was actually a by-product of a larger astronomical clock. The best-designed one was constructed by Giovanni di Dondi in the mid-fourteenth century. Dondi's clock contained the signs of the zodiac, but also struck on the hour. Since clocks were expensive, they were usually installed only in the towers of churches or municipal buildings. The first clock striking equal hours was in a church in Milan; in 1335, a chronicler described it as "a wonderful clock, with a very large clapper which strikes a bell twenty-four times according to the twenty-four hours of the day and night and thus at the first hour of the night gives one sound, at the second two strikes . . . and so distinguishes one hour from another, which is of greatest use to men of every degree."[22]

Clocks introduced a wholly new conception of time into the lives of Europeans; they revolutionized how people thought about and used time. Throughout most of the Middle Ages, time was determined by natural rhythms (daybreak and nightfall) or church bells that were rung at more or less regular three-hour intervals, corresponding to the ecclesiastical offices of the church. Clocks made it possible to plan one's day and organize one's activities around the regular striking of bells. This brought a new regularity into the life of workers and merchants, defining urban existence and enabling merchants and bankers to see the value of time in a new way. Indeed, it was a conception that ultimately led them to believe that "time is money."

Like clocks, eyeglasses were introduced in the thirteenth century, but not refined until the fourteenth. Even then they were not overly effective by modern standards and were still extremely expensive. The high cost of parchment forced people to write in extremely small script; doubtlessly, eyeglasses made it more readable. At the same time, a significant change in writing materials occurred in the fourteenth century when parchment was supplemented by much cheaper paper made from cotton rags. Although it was more subject to insect and water damage than parchment, medieval paper was actually superior to modern papers made of high-acid wood pulp.

Invented earlier by the Chinese, gunpowder also made its appearance in the west in the fourteenth century. The use of gunpowder eventually brought drastic changes to European warfare. Its primary use was in cannons, although early cannons were prone to blow up, making them as dangerous to those firing them as to the enemy.

Even as late as 1460, an attack on a castle using the "Lion," an enormous Flemish cannon, proved disastrous for the Scottish king James II when the "Lion" blew up, killing the king and a number of his retainers. Continued improvement in the construction of cannons, however, soon made them extremely valuable in reducing both castles and city walls. Gunpowder made castles, city walls, and armored knights obsolete.

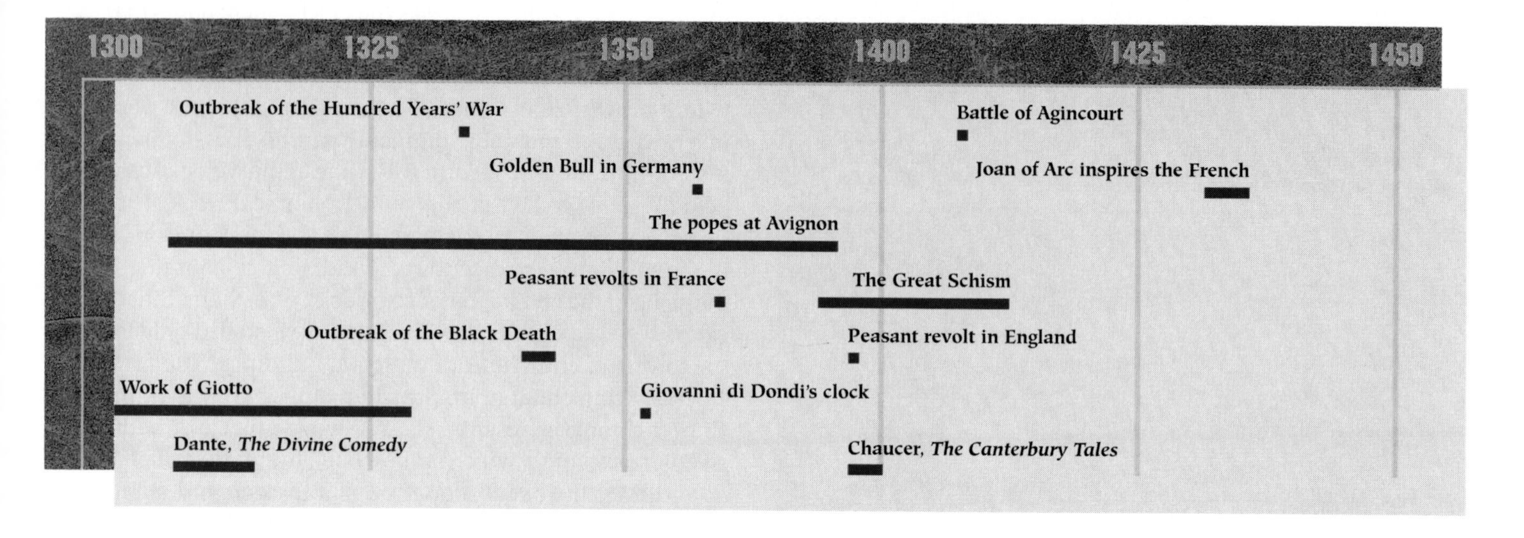

CONCLUSION

In the eleventh, twelfth, and thirteenth centuries, European civilization developed many of its fundamental features. Territorial states, parliaments, capitalist trade and industry, banks, cities, and vernacular literatures were all products of that fertile period. During the same time, the Catholic church under the direction of the papacy reached its apogee. Fourteenth-century European society, however, was challenged by an overwhelming number of crises. Devastating plague, decline in trade and industry, bank failures, peasant revolts pitting lower classes against the upper classes, seemingly constant warfare, aristocratic factional conflict that undermined political stability, the absence of the popes from Rome, and even the spectacle of two popes condemning each other as the Antichrist all seemed to overpower Europeans in this "calamitous century." Not surprisingly, much of the art of the period depicted the Four Horsemen of the Apocalypse described in the New Testament book of Revelation: Death, Famine, Pestilence, and War. No doubt, to some people the last days of the world appeared to be at hand.

The new European society, however, proved remarkably resilient. Periods of crisis are usually paralleled by the emergence of new ideas and new practices. Intellectuals of the period saw themselves as standing on the threshold of a new age or rebirth of the best features of classical civilization. It is their perspective that led historians to speak of a Renaissance in the fifteenth century.

NOTES

1. Quoted in H. S. Lucas, "The Great European Famine of 1315, 1316, and 1317," *Speculum* 5 (1930): 359.
2. Quoted in David Herlihy, *The Black Death and the Transformation of the West*, ed. Samuel K. Cohn, Jr. (Cambridge, Mass., 1997), p. 9.
3. Giovanni Boccaccio, *The Decameron*, trans. Frances Winwar (New York, 1955), p. xxv.
4. Ibid., p. xxvi.
5. Jean Froissart, *Chronicles*, ed. and trans. Geoffrey Brereton (Harmondsworth, 1968), p. 111.
6. Quoted in James B. Ross and Mary M. McLaughlin, *The Portable Medieval Reader* (New York, 1949), pp. 218–219.
7. Quoted in Barbara W. Tuchman, *A Distant Mirror* (New York, 1978), p. 175.
8. Froissart, Chronicles, p. 212.
9. Ibid., p. 89.
10. Oliver J. Thatcher and Edgar H. McNeal, eds., *A Source Book for Medieval History* (New York, 1905), p. 288.
11. Quoted in D. S. Chambers, *The Imperial Age of Venice, 1380–1580* (London, 1970), p. 30.
12. Quoted in Robert Coogan, *Babylon on the Rhône: A Translation of Letters by Dante, Petrarch, and Catherine of Siena* (Washington, D.C., 1983), p. 115.
13. Marsiglio of Padua, *The Defender of the Peace*, trans. Alan Gewirth (New York, 1956), 2:426.
14. Quoted in Caroline Walker Bynum, *Holy Feast and Holy Fast: The Religious Significance of Food to Medieval Women* (Berkeley, 1987), p. 180.
15. Dante Alighieri, *The Divine Comedy*, trans. Dorothy Sayers (New York, 1962), "Paradise," Canto XXXIII, line 145.
16. Petrarch, *Sonnets and Songs*, trans. Anna Maria Armi (New York, 1968), No. LXXIV, p. 127.

17. Quoted in Millard Meiss, *Painting in Florence and Siena after the Black Death* (Princeton, N.J., 1951), p. 161.
18. Geoffrey Chaucer, *The Canterbury Tales*, in *The Portable Chaucer*, ed. Theodore Morrisoon (New York, 1949), pp. 67, 75.
19. Christine de Pizan, *The Book of the City of Ladies*, trans. E. Jeffrey Richards (New York, 1982), pp. 83–84.
20. Quoted in Susan Mosher Stuard, "The Dominion of Gender or How Women Fared in the High Middle Ages," in Renate Bridenthal, Claudia Koonz, and Susan Stuard, eds., *Becoming Visible: Women in European History*, 3d ed. (Boston, 1998), p. 147.
21. Quoted in David Herlihy, "Medieval Children," in Bede K. Lackner and Kenneth R. Philp, eds., *Essays on Medieval Civilization* (Austin, 1978), p. 121.
22. Quoted in Jean Gimpel, *The Medieval Machine* (New York, 1976), p. 168.

SUGGESTIONS FOR FURTHER READING

For a general introduction to the fourteenth century, see D. P. Waley, *Later Medieval Europe*, 2d ed. (London, 1985); G. Holmes, *Europe: Hierarchy and Revolt, 1320–1450* (New York, 1975); and the well-written popular history by B. Tuchman, *A Distant Mirror* (New York, 1978).

On famine in the early fourteenth century, see W. C. Jordan, *The Great Famine: Northern Europe in the Early Fourteenth Century* (Princeton, N.J., 1996). On the Black Death, see P. Ziegler, *The Black Death* (New York, 1969); W. H. McNeill, *Plagues and People* (New York, 1976); and D. Herlihy, *The Black Death and the Transformation of the West*, ed. S. K. Cohn, Jr. (Cambridge, Mass., 1997). There is a good collection of sources in R. Horrox, ed., *The Black Death* (New York, 1994). On the peasant and urban revolts of the fourteenth century, see M. Mollat and P. Wolff, *The Popular Revolutions of the Late Middle Ages* (Winchester, Mass., 1973).

Recent accounts of the Hundred Years' War include A. Curry, *The Hundred Years War* (New York, 1993); and R. H. Neillands, *The Hundred Years War* (New York, 1990). On Joan of Arc, see M. Warner, *Joan of Arc: The Image of Female Heroism* (New York, 1981). On the political history of the period, see B. Guenée, *States and Rulers in Later Medieval Europe*, trans. J. Vale (Oxford, 1985). Works on individual countries include P. S. Lewis, *Later Medieval France: The Polity* (London, 1968); A. R. Myers, *England in the Late Middle Ages* (Harmondsworth, 1952); and F. R. H. Du Boulay, *Germany in the Later Middle Ages* (London, 1983). On the Italian political scene, see D. P. Waley, *The Italian City-Republics* (London, 1978); and J. Larner, *Italy in the Age of Dante and Petrarch, 1216–1380* (London, 1980).

A good general study of the church in the fourteenth century can be found in F. P. Oakley, *The Western Church in the Later Middle Ages* (Ithaca, N.Y., 1980). A good, readable biography is T. S. R. Boase, *Boniface VIII* (London, 1933). On the Avignonese papacy, see Y. Renouard, *The Avignon Papacy, 1305–1403* (London, 1970); and G. Mollat, *The Popes at Avignon* (New York, 1965). Other facets of the religious scene are examined in L. E. Boyle, *Pastoral Care, Clerical Education and Canon Law, 1200–1400* (London, 1981); and A. Hyma, *The Christian Renaissance: A History of the Devotio Moderna* (Hamden, Conn., 1965). On the role of food in the spiritual practices of medieval women, see C. W. Bynum, *Holy Feast and Holy Fast: The Religious Significance of Food to Medieval Women* (Berkeley, 1987).

A classic work on the life and thought of the Later Middle Ages is J. Huizinga, *The Autumn of the Middle Ages*, trans. R. J. Payton and U. Mammitzsch (Chicago, 1996). On the impact of the plague on culture, see the brilliant study by M. Meiss, *Painting in Florence and Siena after the Black Death* (New York, 1964). On Dante, see J. Freccero, *Dante and the Poetics of Conversion* (Cambridge, Mass., 1986). On Chaucer, see G. Kane, *Chaucer* (New York, 1984). The best work on Christine de Pizan is by C. C. Willard, *Christine de Pizan: Her Life and Works* (New York, 1984).

A wealth of material on everyday life is provided in the second volume of *A History of Private Life* edited by G. Duby, *Revelations of the Medieval World* (Cambridge, Mass., 1988). On women in the Late Middle Ages, see S. Shahar, *The Fourth Estate: A History of Women in the Middle Ages*, trans. C. Galai (London, 1983); and D. Herlihy, *Women, Family and Society: Historical Essays, 1978–1991* (Providence, R.I., 1995). On childhood, see the article by D. Herlihy cited in the notes; and B. Hanawalt, *Growing Up in Medieval London* (New York, 1993). The subject of medieval prostitution is examined in L. L. Otis, *Prostitution in Medieval Society* (Chicago, 1984). For late medieval townspeople, see J. F. C. Harrison, *The Common People of Great Britain* (Bloomington, Ind., 1985). Poor people are discussed in M. Mollat, *The Poor in the Middle Ages* (New Haven, Conn., 1986). For a general introduction to the changes in medicine, see T. McKeown, *The Role of Medicine* (Princeton, N.J., 1979). The importance of inventions is discussed in J. Gimpel, *The Medieval Machine* (New York, 1976). Another valuable discussion of medieval technology can be found in J. Le Goff, *Time, Work and Culture in the Middle Ages* (Chicago, 1980).

For additional reading, go to InfoTrac College Edition, your online research library at http://web1.infotrac-college.com

Enter the search terms *Middle Ages* using the Subject Guide.

Enter the search terms *Black Death* using Key Terms.

Enter the search terms *Edward III* using Key Terms.

Enter the search terms *Hundred Years War* using Key Terms.

CHAPTER 12
Recovery and Rebirth: The Age of the Renaissance

CHAPTER OUTLINE

- Meaning and Characteristics of the Italian Renaissance
- The Making of Renaissance Society
- The Italian States in the Renaissance
- The Intellectual Renaissance in Italy
- The Artistic Renaissance
- The European State in the Renaissance
- The Church in the Renaissance
- Conclusion

FOCUS QUESTIONS

- What characteristics distinguish the Renaissance from the Middle Ages?
- How did Machiavelli's works reflect the political realities of Renaissance Italy?
- What was humanism, and what effect did it have on philosophy, education, attitudes toward politics, and the writing of history?
- What were the chief characteristics of Renaissance art, and how did it differ in Italy and northern Europe?
- Why do historians sometimes refer to the monarchies of the late fifteenth century as "new monarchies" or "Renaissance states"?

MEDIEVAL AND RENAISSANCE HISTORIANS have argued interminably over the significance of the fourteenth and fifteenth centuries. Did they witness a continuation of the Middle Ages or the beginning of a new era? Obviously, both positions contain a modicum of truth. Although the disintegrative patterns of the fourteenth century continued into the fifteenth, at the same time there were elements of recovery that made the fifteenth century a period of significant political, economic, artistic, and intellectual change. The humanists or intellectuals of the age called their period (from the mid-fourteenth to the mid-sixteenth century) an age of rebirth, believing that they had restored arts and letters to new glory after they had been "neglected" or "dead" for centuries. The humanists also saw their age as one of great individuals who dominated the landscape of their time. Michelangelo, the great Italian artist of the early sixteenth century, and Pope Julius II, the "warrior pope," were two such titans. The artist's temperament and the pope's temper led to many lengthy and often loud quarrels between the two. Among other commissions, the pope had hired Michelangelo to paint the ceiling of the Sistine Chapel in Rome, a difficult task for a man long accustomed to being a sculptor. Michelangelo undertook the project but refused for a long time to allow anyone, including the pope, to see his work. Julius grew anxious, pestering Michelangelo on a regular basis about when the ceiling would be finished. Exasperated by the pope's requests, Michelangelo once replied, according to Giorgio Vasari, his contemporary biographer, that the ceiling would be completed "when it satisfies me as an artist." The pope responded, "and we want you to satisfy us and finish it soon," and then threatened that if Michelangelo did not "finish the ceiling quickly he would have him thrown down from the scaffolding." Fearing the pope's anger, Michelangelo "lost no time in doing all that was wanted" and quickly completed the ceiling, one of the great masterpieces in the history of Western art.

The humanists' view of their age as a rebirth of the classical civilization of the Greeks and Romans ultimately led historians to use the word Renaissance *to identify this age. Although recent historians have emphasized the many elements of continuity between the Middle Ages and the Renaissance, the latter age was also distinguished by its own unique characteristics.*

◆ Meaning and Characteristics of the Italian Renaissance

The word *Renaissance* means "rebirth." A number of people who lived in Italy between c. 1350 and c. 1550 believed that they had witnessed a rebirth of antiquity or Greco-Roman civilization, which marked a new age. To them, the approximately 1,000 years between the end of the Roman Empire and their own era was a middle period (hence the "Middle Ages"), characterized by darkness because of its lack of classical culture. Historians of the nineteenth century later used similar terminology to describe this period in Italy. The Swiss historian and art critic Jacob Burckhardt created the modern concept of the Renaissance in his celebrated work, *Civilization of the Renaissance in Italy,* published in 1860. He portrayed Italy in the fourteenth and fifteenth centuries as the birthplace of the modern world (the Italians were "the firstborn among the sons of modern Europe") and saw the revival of antiquity, the "perfecting of the individual," and secularism ("worldliness of the Italians") as its distinguishing features. No doubt, Burckhardt exaggerated the individuality and secularism of the Renaissance and failed to recognize the depths of its religious sentiment. Nevertheless, he established the framework for all modern interpretations of the Renaissance. Although contemporary scholars do not believe that the Renaissance represents a sudden or dramatic cultural break with the Middle Ages (as Burckhardt argued)—there was after all much continuity in economic, political, and social life between the two periods—the Renaissance can still be viewed as a distinct period of European history that manifested itself first in Italy and then spread to the rest of Europe. What, then, are the characteristics of the Italian Renaissance?

Renaissance Italy was largely an urban society. As a result of its commercial preeminence and political evolution, northern Italy by the mid-fourteenth century was mostly a land of independent cities that dominated the country districts around them. These city-states became the centers of Italian political, economic, and social life. Within this new urban society, a secular spirit emerged as increasing wealth created new possibilities for the enjoyment of worldly things.

Above all, the Renaissance was an age of recovery from the "calamitous fourteenth century." Italy and Europe began a slow process of recuperation from the effects of the Black Death, political disorder, and economic recession. By the end of the fourteenth and beginning of the fifteenth centuries, Italians were using the words *recovery* and *revival* and were actively involved in a rebuilding process.

Recovery was accompanied by rebirth, specifically, a rebirth of the culture of classical antiquity. Increasingly aware of their own historical past, Italian intellectuals became intensely interested in the Greco-Roman culture of the ancient Mediterranean world. This new revival of classical antiquity (the Middle Ages, after all, had preserved much of ancient Latin culture) affected activities as diverse as politics and art and led to new attempts to reconcile the pagan philosophy of the Greco-Roman world with Christian thought, as well as new ways of viewing human beings.

Though not entirely new, a revived emphasis on individual ability became characteristic of the Italian Renaissance. As the fifteenth-century Florentine architect Leon Battista Alberti expressed it: "Men can do all things if they will."[1] A high regard for human dignity and worth and a realization of individual potentiality created a new social ideal of the well-rounded personality or universal person (*l'uomo universale*) who was capable of achievements in many areas of life.

These general features of the Italian Renaissance were not characteristic of all Italians, but were primarily the preserve of the wealthy upper classes who constituted a small percentage of the total population. The achievements of the Italian Renaissance were the product of an elite, rather than a mass, movement. Nevertheless, indirectly it did have some impact on ordinary people, especially in the cities where so many of the intellectual and artistic accomplishments of the period were most apparent and visible.

◆ The Making of Renaissance Society

The cultural flowering that we associate with the Italian Renaissance actually began in an era of severe economic difficulties. The commercial revolution of the twelfth, thirteenth, and early fourteenth centuries had produced great wealth and given rise to a money economy and the development of a capitalist system. Under this system, the capital or liquid wealth accumulated by private entrepreneurs was used to make further profits in trade, industry, and banking. After three centuries of economic expansion, in the second half of the fourteenth century, Europeans experienced severe economic reversals and social upheavals (see Chapter 11). By the middle of the fifteenth century, a gradual economic recovery had begun with an increase in the volume of manufacturing and trade. Economic growth varied from area to area, however, and despite the recovery Europe did not experience the economic boom of the High Middle Ages.

Economic Recovery

By the fourteenth century, Italian merchants were carrying on a flourishing commerce throughout the Mediterranean and had also expanded their lines of trade north along the Atlantic seaboard. The great galleys of the Venetian Flanders Fleet maintained a direct sea route from Venice to England and the Netherlands, where Italian merchants came into contact with the increasingly powerful Hanseatic League of merchants. Hard hit by the plague, the Italians lost their commercial preeminence while the Hanseatic League continued to prosper.

The Hanseatic League or Hansa had been formed as early as the thirteenth century, when some north German coastal towns, such as Lübeck, Hamburg, and Bremen, began to cooperate to gain favorable trading rights in Flemish cities. To protect themselves from pirates and competition from Scandinavian merchants, these and other northern towns formed a commercial and military league. By 1500, more than eighty cities belonged to the league, which had established settlements and commercial bases in many cities in England and northern Europe, including the chief towns of Denmark, Norway, and Sweden. For almost 200 years, the Hansa had a monopoly on northern European trade in timber, fish, grain, metals, honey, and wines. Its southern outlet in Flanders, the city of Bruges, became the economic crossroads of Europe in the fourteenth century since it served as the meeting place between Hanseatic merchants and the Flanders Fleet of Venice. In the fifteenth century, however, Bruges slowly began to decline. So, too, did the Hanseatic League as it proved increasingly unable to compete with the developing larger territorial states.

Overall, trade recovered dramatically from the economic contraction of the fourteenth century. The Italians and especially the Venetians, despite new restrictive pressures on their eastern Mediterranean trade from the Ottoman Turks (see The Ottoman Turks and the End of Byzantium later in this chapter), continued to maintain a wealthy commercial empire. Not until the sixteenth century, when the overseas discoveries gave new importance to the states facing the Atlantic, did the petty Italian city-states begin to suffer from the competitive advantages of the ever-growing and more powerful national territorial states.

The economic depression of the fourteenth century also affected patterns of manufacturing. The woolen industries of Flanders and the northern Italian cities had been particularly devastated. By the beginning of the fifteenth century, however, the Florentine woolen industry was experiencing a recovery. At the same time, the Italian cities began to develop and expand luxury industries, especially silk, glassware, and handworked items in metal and precious stones. Unfortunately, these luxury industries employed fewer people than the woolen industry and contributed less to overall prosperity.

Other new industries, especially printing, mining, and metallurgy, began to rival the textile industry in importance in the fifteenth century. New machinery and techniques for digging deeper mines and for separating metals from ore and purifying them were put into operation. When rulers began to transfer their rights to underground minerals to financiers as collateral for loans, these entrepreneurs quickly developed large mining operations to produce copper, iron, and silver. Especially valuable were the rich mineral deposits in central Europe, Hungary, the Tyrol, Bohemia, and Saxony. Expanding iron production and new skills in metalworking, in turn, contributed to the development of firearms that were more effective than the crude weapons of the fourteenth century.

The city of Florence regained its preeminence in banking in the fifteenth century, primarily due to the Medici family (see the box on p. 329). The Medici had expanded from cloth production into commerce, real estate, and banking. In its best days (in the fifteenth century), the House of Medici was the greatest banking house in Europe, with branches in Venice, Milan, Rome, Avignon, Bruges, London, and Lyons. Moreover, the family had controlling interests in industrial enterprises for wool, silk, and the mining of alum, used in the dyeing of textiles. Except for a brief interruption, the Medici were also the principal bankers for the papacy, a position that produced big profits and influence at the papal court. Despite its great success in the early and middle part of the fifteenth century, the Medici bank suffered a rather sudden decline at the end of the century due to poor leadership and a series of bad loans, especially uncollectible loans to rulers. In 1494, when the French expelled the Medici from Florence and confiscated their property, the Medicean financial edifice collapsed.

Social Changes in the Renaissance

The Renaissance inherited a tripartite division of society from the Middle Ages. Society was fundamentally divided into three estates: the clergy, whose preeminence was grounded in the belief that people should be guided to spir-

Florence: "Queen City of the Renaissance"

Florence has long been regarded by many historians as the "queen city of the Renaissance." It was the intellectual and cultural center of Italy in the fifteenth century. In a letter written to a Venetian in 1472, Benedetto Dei, a Florentine merchant, gave a proud and boastful description of Florence's economy under the guidance of Lorenzo de' Medici.

❋ *Benedetto Dei, Florence*

Florence is more beautiful and five hundred years older than your Venice. We spring from triply noble blood. We are one-third Roman, one-third Frankish, and one-third Fiesolan [an ancient Etruscan town three miles northeast of Florence]. . . . We have round about us thirty thousand estates, owned by noblemen and merchants, citizens and craftsmen, yielding us yearly bread and meat, wine and oil, vegetables and cheese, hay and wood, to the value of nine hundred thousand ducats in cash, as you Venetians, Genoese, Chians, and Rhoadians who come to buy them know well enough. We have two trades greater than any four of yours in Venice put together—the trades of wool and silk. . . .

Our beautiful Florence contains within the city in this present year two hundred seventy shops belonging to the wool merchants' guild, from whence their wares are sent to Rome and the Marches, Naples and Sicily, Constantinople and Pera, Adrianople, . . . and the whole of Turkey. It contains also eighty-three rich and splendid warehouses of the silk merchants' guild, and furnishes gold and silver stuffs, velvet, brocade, damask, taffeta, and satin to Rome, Naples, Catalonia, and the whole of Spain, especially Seville, and to Turkey and Barbary. The principal fairs to which these wares go are those of Genoa, the Marches, Ferrara, Mantua, and the whole of Italy; Lyons, Avignon, Montpellier, Antwerp, and London. The number of banks amount to thirty-three; the shops of the cabinetmakers, whose business is carving and inlaid work, to eighty-four; and the workshops of the stonecutters and marble workers in the city and its immediate neighborhood, to fifty-four. There are forty-four goldsmiths' and jewelers' shops, thirty gold-beaters, silver wire-drawers, and a wax-figure maker [wax images were used in all churches]. . . . Go through all the cities of the world, nowhere will you ever be able to find artists in wax equal to those we now have in Florence. . . . Another flourishing industry is the making of light and elegant gold and silver wreaths and garlands, which are worn by young maidens of high degree, and which have given their names to the artist family of Ghirlandaio. Sixty-six is the number of the apothecaries' and grocer shops; seventy that of the butchers, besides eight large shops in which are sold fowls of all kinds, as well as game and also the native wine called Trebbiano, from San Giovanni in the upper Arno Valley; it would awaken the dead in its praise.

itual ends; the nobility, whose privileges were based on the principle that the nobles provided security and justice for society; and the third estate, which consisted of the peasants and inhabitants of the towns and cities. This social order experienced certain adaptations in the Renaissance, which we can see by examining the second and third estates (the clergy will be examined in Chapter 13).

THE SOCIAL CLASSES: THE NOBILITY

Throughout much of Europe, the landholding nobles were faced with declining real incomes during the greater part of the fourteenth and fifteenth centuries, while the expense of maintaining noble status was rising. Nevertheless, members of the old nobility survived and new blood infused its ranks. A reconstruction of the aristocracy was well under way by 1500.

As a result of this reconstruction, the nobles, old and new, who constituted between 2 and 3 percent of the population in most countries, managed to dominate society as they had done in the Middle Ages, serving as military officers and holding important political posts as well as advising the king. Increasingly in the sixteenth century, members of the aristocracy pursued education as the means to maintain their role in government. One noble in the Low Countries, in a letter outlining how his son should be formally educated, stated that, due to his own lack of learning, he dared not express his opinions in the king's council and often "felt deep shame and humiliation" at his ignorance.

In northern Europe, the fifteenth century also saw the final flourishing of chivalry. Nobles played at being great warriors, but their tournaments were now characterized less by bloodshed than by flamboyance and a display of brilliant costumes that showed off an individual's social status.

THE DEVELOPMENT OF A COURTLY SOCIETY IN ITALY

One of the more interesting social developments during the Renaissance was the change that occurred in Italian society. In the Early Renaissance, old noble families had moved into the cities and generally merged with the merchant middle classes to form the upper classes in these new urban societies. Consequently, Italy seemed to lose the notion of nobility or aristocracy. In the fifteenth century, this began to change as the tenor of Italian upper-class urban society became more aristocratic. Although this was especially evident in the princely states, such as

A Renaissance Banquet

As in Greek and Roman society, the Renaissance banquet was an occasion for good food, interesting conversation, music, and dancing. In Renaissance society, it was also a symbol of status and an opportunity to impress people with the power and wealth of one's family. Banquets were held to celebrate public and religious festivals, official visits, anniversaries, and weddings. The following menu lists the foods served at a grand banquet given by Pope Pius V in the sixteenth century.

A Sixteenth-Century Banquet

First Course: Cold Delicacies from the Sideboard

Pieces of marzipan and marzipan balls
Neapolitan spice cakes
Malaga wine and Pisan biscuits
Fresh grapes
Prosciutto cooked in wine, served with capers and grape pulp
Salted pork tongues cooked in wine, sliced
Spit-roasted songbirds, cold, with their tongues sliced over them
Sweet mustard

Second Course: Hot Foods from the Kitchen, Roasts

Fried veal sweetbreads and liver
Spit-roasted skylarks with lemon sauce
Spit-roasted quails with sliced eggplants
Stuffed spit-roasted pigeons with capers sprinkled over them
Spit-roasted rabbits, with sauce and crushed pine nuts
Partridges larded and spit-roasted, served with lemon
Heavily seasoned poultry with lemon slices
Slices of veal, spit-roasted, with a sauce made from the juices
Leg of goat, spit-roasted with a sauce made from the juices
Soup of almond paste, with the flesh of three pigeons to each serving

Third Course: Hot Foods from the Kitchen, Boiled Meats and Stews

Stuffed fat geese, boiled Lombard style and covered with sliced almonds
Stuffed breast of veal, boiled, garnished with flowers
Very young calf, boiled, garnished with parsley
Almonds in garlic sauce
Turkish-style rice with milk, sprinkled with cinnamon
Stewed pigeons with mortadella sausage and whole onions
Cabbage soup with sausages
Poultry pie, two chickens to each pie
Fricasseed breast of goat dressed with fried onions
Pies filled with custard cream
Boiled calves' feet with cheese and egg

Fourth Course: Delicacies from the Sideboard

Bean tarts
Quince pastries
Pear tarts, the pears wrapped in marzipan
Parmesan cheese and Riviera cheese
Fresh almonds on vine leaves
Chestnuts roasted over the coals and served with salt and pepper
Milk curds
Ring-shaped cakes
Wafers made from ground grain

the duchy of Milan where a courtly society emerged around the duke, even in the Italian republics the behavior of the upper class took on an aristocratic appearance (see the box above).

By 1500, certain ideals came to be expected of the noble or aristocrat. These were best expressed in *The Book of the Courtier* by the Italian Baldassare Castiglione (1478–1529). First published in 1528, Castiglione's work soon was popular throughout Europe and became a fundamental handbook for European aristocrats.

In *The Book of the Courtier,* Castiglione described the three basic attributes of the perfect courtier. First, nobles should possess fundamental native endowments, such as impeccable character, grace, talents, and noble birth. The perfect courtier must also cultivate certain achievements. Primarily, he should participate in military and bodily exercises since the principal profession of a courtier was arms. But unlike the medieval knight who had only been required to have military skill, the Renaissance courtier was also expected to have a classical education and to adorn his life with the arts by playing a musical instrument, drawing, and painting. In Castiglione's hands, the Renaissance ideal of the well-developed personality became a social ideal of the aristocracy. Finally, the aristocrat was expected to follow a certain standard of conduct. Nobles were expected to make good impressions; while being modest, they should not hide their accomplishments, but show them with grace.

But what was the purpose of these courtly standards? Castiglione said:

> Therefore, I think that the aim of the perfect Courtier, which we have not spoken of up to now, is so to win for himself, by means of the accomplishments ascribed to him by these gentlemen, the favor and mind of the prince whom he serves that he may be able to tell him, and always will tell him, the truth about everything he needs to know, without fear or risk of displeasing him; and that when he sees the mind of his prince inclined to a wrong action, he may dare to oppose him . . . so as to dissuade him of every evil intent and bring him to the path of virtue.[2]

This ideal of service to the prince reflected the secular ethic of the active life espoused by the earlier civic humanists (see Italian Renaissance Humanism later in this chapter). Castiglione put the new moral values of the Renaissance into a courtly, aristocratic form that was now acceptable to the nobility throughout Europe. Nobles would adhere to his principles for hundreds of years as they continued to dominate European life socially and politically.

THE SOCIAL CLASSES: THE THIRD ESTATE OF PEASANTS AND TOWNSPEOPLE

Traditionally, peasants made up the overwhelming mass of the third estate and indeed continued to constitute as much as 85 to 90 percent of the total European population, except in the highly urbanized areas of northern Italy and Flanders. The most noticeable trend produced by the economic crisis of the fourteenth century was the decline of the manorial system and the continuing elimination of serfdom. This process had already begun in the twelfth century when the introduction of a money economy made possible the conversion of servile labor dues into rents paid in money, although they also continued to be paid in kind or labor. The contraction of the peasantry after the Black Death simply accelerated this process since lords found it convenient to deal with the peasants by granting freedom and accepting rents. The lord's lands were then tilled by hired workers or rented out. By the end of the fifteenth century, serfdom was declining, and more and more peasants were becoming legally free, although in many places lords were able to retain many of the fees they charged their peasants. Lords, then, became rentiers, and the old manorial system was replaced by a new arrangement based on cash. It is interesting to note that while serfdom was declining in western Europe, eastern Europe experienced a reverse trend. The weakness of eastern rulers enabled nobles to tie their peasants to the land and use servile labor in the large-scale production of grain for an ever-growing export market.

The remainder of the third estate centered around the inhabitants of towns and cities, originally the merchants and artisans who formed the burghers. The Renaissance town or city of the fifteenth century actually possessed a multitude of townspeople widely separated socially and economically.

At the top of urban society were the patricians, whose wealth from capitalistic enterprises in trade, industry, and banking enabled them to dominate their urban communities economically, socially, and politically. Below them were the petty burghers, the shopkeepers, artisans, guildmasters, and guild members who were largely concerned with providing goods and services for local consumption. Below these two groups were the propertyless workers earning pitiful wages and the unemployed, living squalid and miserable lives. These people constituted as much as 30 or 40 percent of the urban population. In many places in Europe in the late fourteenth and fifteenth centuries, urban poverty had increased dramatically. One rich merchant of Florence wrote:

> Those that are lazy and indolent in a way that does harm to the city, and who can offer no just reason for their condition, should either be forced to work or expelled from the Commune. The city would thus rid itself of that most harmful part of the poorest class. . . . If the lowest order of society earn enough food to keep them going from day to day, then they have enough.[3]

But even this large group was not at the bottom of the social scale; beneath them were the slaves, especially in the Italian cities.

SLAVERY IN THE RENAISSANCE

Agricultural slavery had continued to exist in the Early Middle Ages, but had declined for economic reasons and been replaced by serfdom by the ninth century. Although some domestic slaves remained, slavery in European society had largely disappeared by the eleventh century. It reappeared first in Spain, where both Christians and Muslims used captured prisoners as slaves during the lengthy *reconquista*. In the second half of the fourteenth century, the shortage of workers after the Black Death led Italians to introduce slavery on a fairly large scale. In 1363, for example, the government of Florence authorized the unlimited importation of foreign slaves.

In the Italian cities, slaves were used as skilled workers, making handcrafted goods for their masters, or as household workers. Girls served as nursemaids and boys as playmates. Fiammetta Adimari wrote to her husband in 1469: "I must remind you that when Alfonso is weaned we ought to get a little slave-girl to look after him, or else one of the black boys to keep him company."[4] In Florence, wealthy merchants might possess two or three slaves. Often, men of the household took slaves as concubines, which sometimes led to the birth of illegitimate children. In 1392, the wealthy merchant Francesco Datini fathered an illegitimate daughter by Lucia, his twenty-year-old slave. His wife Margherita, who was unable to bear any children, reluctantly agreed to raise the girl as their own daughter. Many illegitimate children were not as fortunate.

Slaves for the Italian market were obtained primarily from the eastern Mediterranean and the Black Sea region and included Tartars, Russians, Albanians, and Dalmatians. There were also slaves from Africa, either Moors or Ethiopians, and Muslims from Spain. Because of the lucrative nature of the slave trade, Italian merchants became

WEDDING BANQUET. Parents arranged marriages in Renaissance Italy to strengthen business or family ties. A legally binding marriage contract was considered a necessary part of the marital arrangements. So, too, was a wedding feast. This painting by Botticelli shows the wedding banquet in Florence that celebrated the marriage of Nastagio degli Onesti and the daughter of Paulo Traversaro.

involved in the transportation of slaves. Between 1414 and 1423, 10,000 slaves were sold on the Venetian market. Most slaves were females, many of them young girls.

By the end of the fifteenth century, slavery had declined dramatically in the Italian cities. Many slaves had been freed by their owners for humanitarian reasons, and the major source of slaves dried up as the Black Sea slave markets were closed to Italian traders after the Turks conquered the Byzantine Empire. Although some other sources remained, prices rose dramatically, further cutting demand. Moreover, a general feeling had arisen that slaves—the "domestic enemy" as they were called—were dangerous and not worth the effort. By the sixteenth century, slaves were in evidence only at princely courts where they were kept as curiosities; this was especially true of black slaves.

In the fifteenth century, the Portuguese had imported increasing numbers of African slaves for southern European markets. It has been estimated that between 1444 and 1505, 140,000 slaves were shipped from Africa. The presence of blacks in European society was not entirely new. Saint Maurice, a Christian martyr of the fourth century, was portrayed by medieval artists as a black knight and became the center of a popular cult in the twelfth and thirteenth centuries. The number of blacks in Europe was small, however, until their importation as slaves.

THE FAMILY IN RENAISSANCE ITALY

The family played an important role in Renaissance Italy. Family meant, first of all, the extended household of parents, children, and servants (if the family was wealthy) and could also include grandparents, widowed mothers, and even unmarried sisters. Families that were related and bore the same surname often lived near each other and might dominate an entire urban district. Old family names, such as the Strozzi, Rucellai, and Medici, conferred great status and prestige. The family bond was a source of great security in a dangerous and violent world, and its importance helps explain the vendetta in the Italian Renaissance. A crime committed by one family member fell on the entire family, ensuring that retaliation by the offended family would be a bloody affair involving large numbers of people.

To maintain the family, careful attention was given to marriages, which were arranged by parents, often to strengthen business or family ties. Details were worked out well in advance, sometimes when children were only two or three, and reinforced by a legally binding marriage contract (see the box on p. 333). The important aspect of the contract was the size of the dowry, a sum of money presented by the wife's family to the husband upon marriage. The dowry could involve large sums of money and was expected of all families. The size of the dowry was an indication of whether the bride was moving upward or downward in society. With a large dowry, a daughter could marry a man of higher social status, thereby enabling her family to move up in society; if the daughter married a man of lower social status, however, then her dowry would be smaller since the reputation of her family would raise the status of the husband's family. Since poor families often had difficulty providing a dowry, wealthy families established societies to provide dowries for poor girls.

The father-husband was the center of the Italian family. He gave it his name, was responsible for it in all legal matters, managed all finances (his wife had no share in his wealth), and made the crucial decisions that determined his children's lives. A father's authority over his children was absolute until he died or formally freed his children. In Renaissance Italy, children did not become adults on reaching a certain age; instead adulthood came only when the father went before a judge and formally emancipated them. The age of emancipation varied from early teens to late twenties.

The wife managed the household, a position that gave women a certain degree of autonomy in their daily lives. Most wives, however, also knew that their primary function was to bear children. Upper-class wives were frequently pregnant; Alessandra Strozzi of Florence, for example, who had been married at the age of sixteen, bore eight children in ten years. Poor women did not conceive at the same rate because they nursed their own babies.

Marriage Negotiations

Marriages were so important in maintaining families in Renaissance Italy that much energy was put into arranging them. Parents made the choices for their children, most often for considerations that had little to do with the modern notion of love. This selection is taken from the letters of a Florentine matron of the illustrious Strozzi family to her son Filippo in Naples. The family's considerations were complicated by the fact that the son was in exile.

Alessandra Strozzi to Her Son Filippo in Naples

[April 20, 1464] . . . Concerning the matter of a wife [for Filippo], it appears to me that if Francesco di Messer Tanagli wishes to give his daughter, that it would be a fine marriage. . . . Now I will speak with Marco [Parenti, Alessandra's son-in-law], to see if there are other prospects that would be better, and if there are none, then we will learn if he wishes to give her [in marriage]. . . . Francesco Tanagli has a good reputation, and he has held office, not the highest, but still he has been in office. You may ask: "Why should he give her to someone in exile?" There are three reasons. First, there aren't many young men of good family who have both virtue and property. Secondly, she has only a small dowry, 1,000 florins, which is the dowry of an artisan [although not a small sum, either—senior officials in the government bureaucracy earned 300 florins a year]. . . . Third, I believe that he will give her away, because he has a large family and he will need help to settle them. . . .

[July 26, 1465] . . . Francesco is a good friend of Marco and he trusts him. On S. Jacopo's day, he spoke to him discreetly and persuasively, saying that for several months he had heard that we were interested in the girl and . . . that when we had made up our minds, she will come to us willingly. [He said that] you were a worthy man, and that his family had always made good marriages, but that he had only a small dowry to give her, and so he would prefer to send her out of Florence to someone of worth, rather than to give her to someone here, from among those who were available, with little money. . . . We have information that she is affable and competent. She is responsible for a large family (there are twelve children, six boys and six girls), and the mother is always pregnant and isn't very competent. . . .

[August 31, 1465] . . . I have recently received some very favorable information [about the Tanagli girl] from two individuals. . . . They are in agreement that whoever gets her will be content. . . . Concerning her beauty, they told me what I had already seen, that she is attractive and well-proportioned. Her face is long, but I couldn't look directly into her face, since she appeared to be aware that I was examining her . . . and so she turned away from me like the wind. . . . She reads quite well . . . and she can dance and sing. . . .

So yesterday I sent for Marco and told him what I had learned. And we talked about the matter for a while, and decided that he should say something to the father and give him a little hope, but not so much that we couldn't withdraw, and find out from him the amount of the dowry. . . . May God help us to choose what will contribute to our tranquility and to the consolation of us all.

[September 13, 1465] . . . Marco came to me and said that he had met with Francesco Tanagli, who had spoken very coldly, so that I understand that he had changed his mind. . . .

[Filippo Strozzi eventually married Fiametta di Donato Adimari in 1466.]

Wealthy women gave their infants out to wet nurses, which enabled them to become pregnant more quickly after the birth of a child.

For women in the Renaissance, childbirth was a fearful occasion. Not only was it painful, but it could be deadly; as many as 10 percent of mothers died in childbirth. In his memoirs, the Florentine merchant Gregorio Dati recalled that three of his four wives had died in childbirth. His third wife, after bearing eleven children in fifteen years, "died in childbirth after lengthy suffering, which she bore with remarkable strength and patience."[5] Nor did the tragedies end with childbirth. Surviving mothers often faced the death of their children as well. In Florence in the fifteenth century, for example, almost 50 percent of the children born to merchant families died before the age of twenty. Given these mortality rates, many upper-class families sought to have as many children as possible to ensure that there would be a surviving male heir to the family fortune. This concern is evident in the Florentine humanist Leon Battista Alberti's treatise *On the Family*, where one of the characters remarks, "How many families do we see today in decadence and ruin! . . . Of all these families not only the magnificence and greatness but the very men, not only the men but the very names are shrunk away and gone. Their memory . . . is wiped out and obliterated."[6]

Considering that marriages had been arranged, marital relationships ran the gamut from deep emotional attachments to purely formal ties. The lack of emotional attachment from arranged marriages did encourage extramarital relationships, especially for those groups whose lifestyle offered special temptations. Although sexual license for males was the norm for princes and their courts, women were supposed to follow different guidelines. The first wife of Duke Filippo Maria Visconti of Milan had an affair with the court musician and was executed for it.

The great age difference between husbands and wives that was noticeable in Italian Renaissance marriage patterns also heightened the need for sexual outlets outside marriage. In Florence in 1427–1428, the average difference was thirteen years. Though females married between the ages of sixteen and eighteen, factors of environment, wealth, and demographic trends favored relatively late ages for the first marriages of males, who were usually in their thirties or even early forties. The existence of large numbers of young, unmarried males encouraged extramarital sex as well as prostitution. Prostitution was viewed as a necessary vice; since it could not be eliminated, it should be regulated. In Florence in 1415, the city fathers established communal brothels:

> Desiring to eliminate a worse evil by means of a lesser one, the lord priors . . . have decreed that the priors . . . may authorize the establishment of two public brothels in the city of Florence, in addition to the one which already exists. . . . [They are to be located] in suitable places or in places where the exercise of such scandalous activity can best be concealed, for the honor of the city and of those who live in the neighborhood in which these prostitutes must stay to hire their bodies for lucre.[7]

A prostitute in Florence was required to wear a traditional garb of "gloves on her hands and a bell on her head."

CHRONOLOGY

The Italian States in the Renaissance

Duchy of Milan	
Viscontis	1311–1447
Sforzas	1450–1494
Florence	
Cosimo de' Medici	1434–1464
Lorenzo de' Medici	1469–1492
Peace of Lodi	1454
Beginning of Italian wars—French invasion of Italy	1494
Sack of Rome	1527

◆ The Italian States in the Renaissance

By the fifteenth century, five major powers dominated the Italian peninsula—the duchy of Milan, Venice, Florence, the Papal States, and the kingdom of Naples. Northern Italy was divided between the duchy of Milan and Venice. After the death of the last Visconti ruler of Milan in 1447, Francesco Sforza, one of the leading *condottieri* (see Chapter 11) of the time, turned on his Milanese employers, conquered the city, and became its new duke. Both the Visconti and the Sforza rulers worked to create a highly centralized territorial state. They were especially successful in devising systems of taxation that generated enormous revenues for the government. The maritime republic of Venice remained an extremely stable political entity governed by a small oligarchy of merchant-aristocrats. Its commercial empire brought in enormous revenues and gave it the status of an international power. At the end of the fourteenth century, Venice embarked upon the conquest of a territorial state in northern Italy to protect its food supply and its overland trade routes. Although expansion on the mainland made sense to the Venetians, it frightened Milan and Florence, which worked to curb what they perceived as the expansionary designs of the Venetians.

The republic of Florence dominated the region of Tuscany. By the beginning of the fifteenth century, Florence was governed by a small merchant oligarchy that manipulated the apparently republican government. In 1434, Cosimo de' Medici took control of this oligarchy. Although the wealthy Medici family maintained republican forms of government for appearance' sake, it ran the government from behind the scenes. Through their lavish patronage and careful courting of political allies, Cosimo (1434–1464), and later his grandson Lorenzo the Magnificent (1469–1492), were successful in dominating the city at a time when Florence was the center of the cultural Renaissance.

The Papal States lay in central Italy. Nominally under the political control of the popes, papal residence in Avignon and the Great Schism had enabled individual cities and territories, such as Urbino, Bologna, and Ferrara, to become independent of papal authority. The Renaissance popes of the fifteenth century directed much of their energy toward reestablishing their control over the Papal States (see The Renaissance Papacy later in this chapter).

The kingdom of Naples, which encompassed most of southern Italy and usually the island of Sicily, was fought over by the French and the Aragonese until the latter established their domination in the mid-fifteenth century. Throughout the Renaissance, the kingdom of Naples remained a largely feudal monarchy with a population consisting largely of poverty-stricken peasants dominated by unruly barons. It shared little in the cultural glories of the Renaissance.

Besides the five major states, there were a number of independent city-states under the control of powerful ruling families that became brilliant centers of Renaissance culture in the fifteenth century. These included Mantua under the enlightened rule of the Gonzaga lords, Ferrara governed by the flamboyant d'Este family, and perhaps the most famous, Urbino, ruled by the Montefeltro dynasty.

Federigo da Montefeltro, who ruled Urbino from 1444 to 1482, received a classical education typical of the famous humanist school in Mantua run by Vittorino da Feltre. He had also learned the skills of fighting, since the

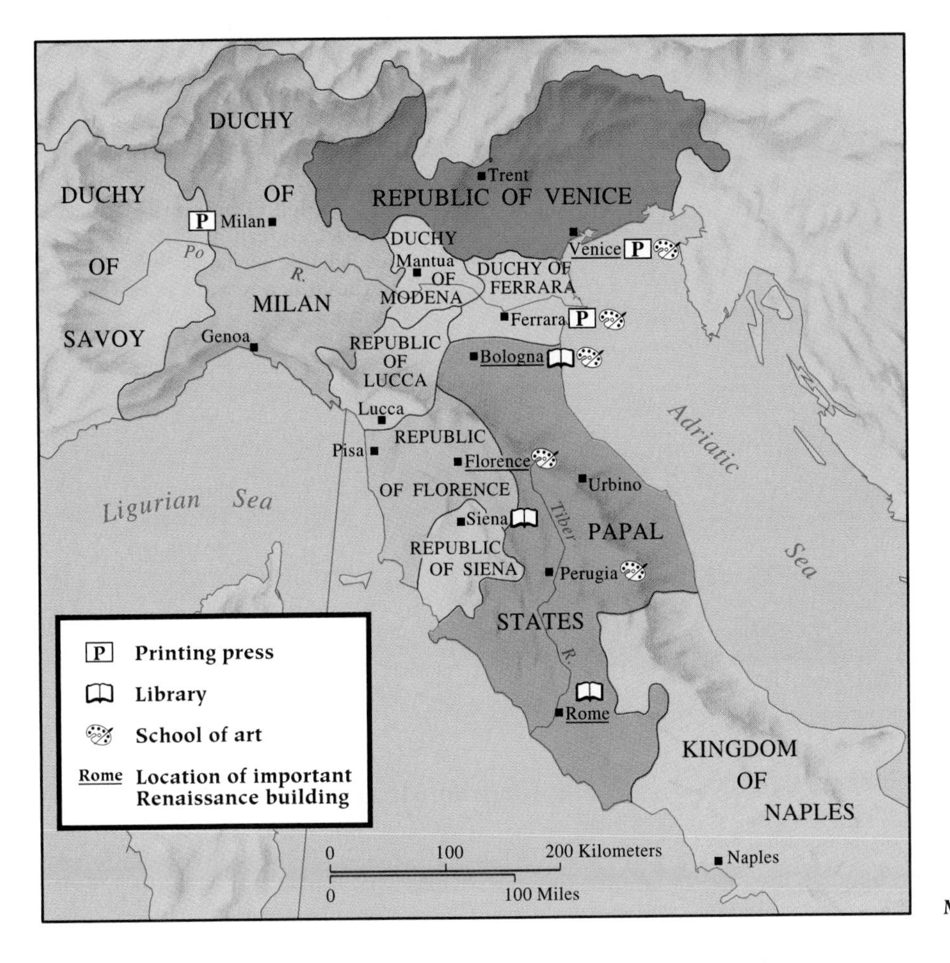

MAP 12.1 Renaissance Italy.

Montefeltro family compensated for the poverty of Urbino by hiring themselves out as *condottiere*. Federigo was not only a good ruler, but a rather unusual *condottiere* by fifteenth-century standards. Although not a brilliant general, he was reliable and honest. He did not break his promises, even when urged to do so by a papal legate. His employers included two kings of Naples, three popes, and two dukes of Milan. At the same time, Duke Federigo was one of the greatest patrons of Renaissance culture. Under his direction, Urbino became a well-known cultural and intellectual center. Though a despot, he was also benevolent. It was said of him that he could walk safely through the streets of Urbino unaccompanied by a bodyguard, a feat few Renaissance rulers dared to emulate.

A noticeable feature of these smaller Renaissance courts was the important role played by women. Battista Sforza, niece of the ruler of Milan, was the wife of Federigo da Montefeltro. The duke called his wife "the delight of both my public and my private hours." An intelligent woman, she was well versed in both Greek and Latin and did much to foster art and letters in Urbino. As a prominent *condottiere*, Federigo was frequently absent, and like earlier feudal wives, Battista Sforza was respected for governing the state "with firmness and good sense."

Perhaps the most famous of the Renaissance ruling women was Isabella d'Este (1474–1539), daughter of the duke of Ferrara, who married Francesco Gonzaga, marquis of Mantua. Their court was another important center of art and learning in the Renaissance. Educated at the brilliant court of Ferrara, Isabella was known for her intelligence and political wisdom. Called the "first lady of the world," she attracted artists and intellectuals to the Mantuan court and was responsible for amassing one of the finest libraries in all of Italy. Her numerous letters to friends, family, princes, and artists all over Europe disclose her political acumen as well as a good sense of humor (see the box on p. 337). Both before and after the death of her husband Francesco, she effectively ruled Mantua and won a reputation as a clever negotiator.

The frenzied world of the Italian territorial states gave rise to a political practice that was later used on a larger scale by competing European states. This was the concept of a balance of power, designed to prevent the aggrandizement of any one state at the expense of the others. This system was especially evident after 1454 when the Italian states signed the Peace of Lodi, which ended almost a half-century of war and inaugurated a relatively peaceful era in Italy until 1494. An alliance system (Milan, Florence, and Naples versus Venice and the papacy) was then created that led to a workable balance of power within Italy. It failed, however, to establish lasting cooperation among the major powers or a common foreign policy.

PIERO DELLA FRANCESCA, *DUKE AND DUCHESS OF URBINO*. Federigo da Montefeltro and his wife, Battista Sforza, ruled the small central Italian principality of Urbino. These profile portraits by Piero della Francesca gave a realistic rendering of the two figures. Visible in the background are the hills and valleys of Urbino.

The growth of powerful monarchical states (see The "New Monarchies" later in this chapter) led to trouble for the Italians. Italy soon became a battlefield for the great power struggle between the French and Spanish monarchies. Italian wealth and splendor would probably have been inviting to its northern neighbors under any circumstances, but it was actually the breakdown of the Italian balance of power that encouraged the invasions and began the Italian wars. Feeling isolated, Ludovico Sforza, the duke of Milan, foolishly invited the French to intervene in Italian politics. The French king Charles VIII (1483–1498) was eager to do so and in 1494, with an army of 30,000 men, advanced through Italy and occupied the kingdom of Naples. Other Italian states turned to the Spanish for help, and Ferdinand of Aragon indicated his willingness to intervene. For the next fifteen years, the French and Spanish competed to dominate Italy. Beginning in the decade of the 1510s, the war was continued by a new generation of rulers, Francis I of France and Charles I of Spain (see Chapter 13). This war was part of a long struggle for power throughout Europe between the Valois and Habsburg dynasties. Italy was only a pawn for the two great powers, a convenient arena for fighting battles. The terrible sack of Rome in 1527 by the armies of the Spanish king Charles I brought a temporary end to the Italian wars. Hereafter, the Spaniards dominated Italy.

Although some Italians had developed a sense of national consciousness and differentiated between Italians and "barbarians" (all foreigners), few Italians conceived of creating an alliance or confederation of states that could repel foreign invaders. Italians remained fiercely loyal to their own petty states, making invasion a fact of life in Italian history for all too long. Italy would not achieve unification and nationhood until 1870.

The Birth of Modern Diplomacy

The modern diplomatic system was a product of the Italian Renaissance. There were ambassadors in the Middle Ages, but they were used only on a temporary basis. Moreover, an ambassador, regardless of whose subject he was, regarded himself as the servant of all Christendom, not just of his particular employer. As a treatise on diplomacy stated: "An ambassador is sacred because he acts for the general welfare." Since he was the servant of all Christendom, "the business of an ambassador is peace."[8]

This concept of an ambassador changed during the Italian Renaissance because of the political situation in Italy. A large number of states existed, many so small that their security was easily threatened by their neighbors. To survive, the Italian states began to send resident diplomatic agents to each other to ferret out useful information. During the Italian wars, the practice of resident diplomats spread to the rest of Europe, and in the course of the sixteenth and seventeenth centuries, Europeans developed the diplomatic machinery still in use today, such as the rights of ambassadors in host countries and the proper procedures for conducting diplomatic business.

With the use of permanent resident agents or ambassadors, the conception of the purpose of the ambassador also changed. A Venetian diplomat attempted to define the function of an ambassador in a treatise written at the end of the fifteenth century. He wrote: "The first duty of an ambassador is exactly the same as that of any other servant of a government, that is, to do, say, advise, and think whatever may best serve the preservation and aggrandizement of his own state."[9] An ambassador was now simply an agent of the territorial state that sent him, not the larger body of Christendom. He could

The Letters of Isabella d'Este

Many Italian and European rulers at the beginning of the sixteenth century regarded Isabella d'Este as an important political figure. These excerpts from her letters reveal Isabella's political skills and her fierce determination. After her husband was taken prisoner by the Venetians in 1509, she refused to accept the condition for his release—namely, that her son Federico be kept as a hostage by the Venetians or the Holy Roman Emperor. She wrote to both the emperor and her husband, refusing to do as they asked.

Letter of Isabella d'Este to the Imperial Envoy

As to the demand for our dearest first-born son Federico, besides being a cruel and almost inhuman thing for any one who knows the meaning of a mother's love, there are many reasons which render it difficult and impossible. Although we are quite sure that his person would be well cared for and protected by His Majesty [the Holy Roman Emperor], how could we wish him to run the risk of this long and difficult journey, considering the child's tender and delicate age? And you must know what comfort and solace, in his father's present unhappy condition, we find in the presence of this dear son, the hope and joy of all our people and subjects. To deprive us of him, would be to deprive us of life itself, and of all we count good and precious. If you take Federico away you might as well take away our life and state. . . . Once for all, we will suffer any loss rather than part from our son, and this you may take to be our deliberate and unchanging resolution.

Letter of Isabella d'Este to her Husband [who had ordered her to send the boy to Venice]

If in this matter Your Excellency were to despise me and deprive me of your love and grace, I would rather endure such harsh treatment, I would rather lose our State, than deprive us of our children. I am hoping that in time your own prudence and kindness will make you understand that I have acted more lovingly toward you than you have to yourself.

Have patience! You can be sure that I think continuously of your liberation and when the time comes I will not fail you, as I have not relaxed my efforts. As witness I cite the Pope, the Emperor, the King of France, and all the other reigning heads and potentates of Christendom. Yes, and the infidels as well [she had written to the Turkish sultan for help]. If it were *really* the only means of setting you free, I would not only send Federico but all the other children as well. I will do everything imaginable. Some day I hope I can make you understand. . . .

Pardon me if this letter is badly written and worse composed, but I do not know if I am dead or alive.

Isabella, who desires the best for Your Excellency, written with her own hand

[Isabella's husband was not pleased with her response and exclaimed angrily: "That whore of my wife is the cause of it all. Send me into battle alone, do what you like with me. I have lost in one blow my state, my honor and my freedom. If she does not obey, I'll cut her vocal cords."]

use any methods that were beneficial to the political interests of his own state. We are at the beginning of modern politics when the interests of the state supersede all other considerations.

Machiavelli and the New Statecraft

No one gave better expression to the Renaissance preoccupation with political power than Niccolò Machiavelli (1469–1527). He entered the service of the Florentine republic in 1498, four years after the Medici family had been expelled from the city. As a secretary to the Florentine Council of Ten, he made numerous diplomatic missions, including trips to France and Germany, and saw the workings of statecraft firsthand. Since Italy had been invaded in 1494, Machiavelli was active during a period of Italian tribulation and devastation. In 1512, French defeat and Spanish victory led to the reestablishment of Medici power in Florence. Staunch republicans, including Machiavelli, were sent into exile. Forced to give up politics, the great love of his life, Machiavelli now reflected on political power and wrote books, including *The Prince* (1513), one of the most famous treatises on political power in the Western world.

Machiavelli's ideas on politics stemmed from two major sources, his preoccupation with Italy's political problems and his knowledge of ancient Rome. His major concerns in *The Prince* were the acquisition and expansion of political power as the means to restore and maintain order in his time. Machiavelli was aware that his own approach to political power was different from previous political theorists. Late medieval political theorists believed that a ruler was justified in exercising political power only if it contributed to the common good of the people he served. The ethical side of a prince's activity—how a ruler ought to behave based on Christian moral principles—was the focus of many late medieval treatises on politics. Machiavelli bluntly contradicted this approach:

> But my hope is to write a book that will be useful, at least to those who read it intelligently, and so I thought it sensible

MACHIAVELLI. In *The Prince*, Machiavelli gave concrete expression to the Renaissance preoccupation with political power. This slender volume remains one of the most famous Western treatises on politics. Machiavelli is seen here in a portrait by Santi di Tito.

> to go straight to a discussion of how things are in real life and not waste time with a discussion of an imaginary world. . . . for the gap between how people actually behave and how they ought to behave is so great that anyone who ignores everyday reality in order to live up to an ideal will soon discover he had been taught how to destroy himself, not how to preserve himself.[10]

Machiavelli considered his approach far more realistic than that of his medieval forebears.

From Machiavelli's point of view, a prince's attitude toward power must be based on an understanding of human nature, which he perceived as basically self-centered: "For of men one can, in general, say this: They are ungrateful, fickle, deceptive and deceiving, avoiders of danger, eager to gain." Political activity, therefore, could not be restricted by moral considerations. The prince acts on behalf of the state and for the sake of the state must be willing to let his conscience sleep. As Machiavelli put it:

> You need to understand this: A ruler, and particularly a ruler who is new to power, cannot conform to all those rules that men who are thought good are expected to respect, for he is often obliged, in order to hold on to power, to break his word, to be uncharitable, inhumane, and irreligious. So he must be mentally prepared to act as circumstances and changes in fortune require. As I have said, he should do what is right if he can; but he must be prepared to do wrong if necessary.[11]

Machiavelli found a good example of the new Italian ruler in Cesare Borgia, the son of Pope Alexander VI, who used ruthless measures to achieve his goal of carving out a new state in central Italy. As Machiavelli said: "So anyone who decides that the policy to follow when one has newly acquired power is to destroy one's enemies, to secure some allies, to win wars, whether by force or by fraud, to make oneself both loved and feared by one's subjects, . . . cannot hope to find, in the recent past, a better model to imitate than Cesare Borgia." Machiavelli was among the first to abandon morality as the basis for the analysis of political activity (see the box on p. 339).

Because of the ideas in *The Prince,* Machiavelli is often considered the founder of modern, secular power politics, but we should note that Machiavelli himself was primarily concerned with Italy's tragic political condition. If it hoped to free itself from the "barbarous cruelties and outrages" perpetrated by the monarchical territorial states to the north, Italy needed "someone who could bind her wounds and . . . heal her sores which long ago became infected." If any person undertook the task, "What Italian would refuse to pledge him allegiance?"[12] If he followed the principles enunciated in *The Prince,* he would succeed. Machiavelli's own sympathies for a republican form of government were clearly evident in *The Discourses*, a political treatise written a few years after *The Prince.* In this work, Machiavelli reflected on the many lessons people of his age could learn from examining the institutions of the Roman Republic. And yet, Machiavelli doubted whether it was possible, in the turbulent politics of his age, to establish a republic. He said in *The Discourses:* "If any one wanted to establish a republic at the present time, he would find it much easier with the simple mountaineers, who are almost without any civilization, than with such as are accustomed to live in cities, where civilization is already corrupt."[13]

◆ The Intellectual Renaissance in Italy

The emergence and growth of individualism and secularism as characteristics of the Italian Renaissance are most noticeable in the intellectual and artistic realms. Italian culture had matured by the fourteenth century. For the next two centuries, Italy was the cultural leader of Europe. This new Italian culture was primarily the product of a relatively wealthy, urban lay society. The most important literary movement we associate with the Renaissance is humanism.

Italian Renaissance Humanism

Renaissance humanism was a form of education and culture based on the study of the classics. Humanism was not so much a philosophy of life as an educational program

Machiavelli: "Is it Better to be Loved than Feared?"

In 1513, Niccolò Machiavelli wrote a short treatise on political power that, justly or unjustly, has given him a reputation as a political opportunist. In this passage from Chapter 17 of The Prince, *Machiavelli analyzes whether it is better for a ruler to be loved than feared.*

Machiavelli, *The Prince*

This leads us to a question that is in dispute: Is it better to be loved than feared, or vice versa? My reply is one ought to be both loved and feared; but, since it is difficult to accomplish both at the same time, I maintain it is much safer to be feared than loved, if you have to do without one of the two. For of men one can, in general, say this: They are ungrateful, fickle, deceptive and deceiving, avoiders of danger, eager to gain. As long as you serve their interests, they are devoted to you. They promise you their blood, their possessions, their lives, and their children, as I said before, so long as you seem to have no need of them. But as soon as you need help, they turn against you. Any ruler who relies simply on their promises and makes no other preparations, will be destroyed. For you will find that those whose support you buy, who do not rally to you because they admire your strength of character and nobility of soul, these are people you pay for, but they are never yours, and in the end you cannot get the benefit of your investment. Men are less nervous of offending someone who makes himself lovable, than someone who makes himself frightening. For love attaches men by ties of obligation, which, since men are wicked, they break whenever their interests are at stake. But fear restrains men because they are afraid of punishment, and this fear never leaves them. Still, a ruler should make himself feared in such a way that, if he does not inspire love, at least he does not provoke hatred. For it is perfectly possible to be feared and not hated. You will only be hated if you seize the property or the women of your subjects and citizens. Whenever you have to kill someone, make sure that you have a suitable excuse and an obvious reason; but, above all else, keep your hands off other people's property; for men are quicker to forget the death of their father than the loss of their inheritance. Moreover, there are always reasons why you might want to seize people's property; and he who begins to live by plundering others will always find an excuse for seizing other people's possessions; but there are fewer reasons for killing people, and one killing need not lead to another.

When a ruler is at the head of his army and has a vast number of soldiers under his command, then it is absolutely essential to be prepared to be thought cruel; for it is impossible to keep an army united and ready for action without acquiring a reputation for cruelty.

that revolved around a clearly defined group of intellectual disciplines or "liberal arts"—grammar, rhetoric, poetry, moral philosophy or ethics, and history—all based on an examination of classical authors.

The central importance of literary preoccupations in Renaissance humanism is evident in the professional status or occupations of the humanists. Some of them were teachers of the humanities in secondary schools and universities, where they either gave occasional lectures or held permanent positions, often as professors of rhetoric. Others served as secretaries in the chancelleries of Italian city-states or at the courts of princes or popes. All of these occupations were largely secular, and most humanists were laymen rather than members of the clergy.

THE EMERGENCE OF HUMANISM

Petrarch (1304–1374) has often been called the father of Italian Renaissance humanism (see Chapter 11 on Petrarch's use of the Italian vernacular). Petrarch had rejected his father's desire that he become a lawyer and took up a literary career instead. Although he lived in Avignon for a time, most of his last decades were spent in Italy as the guest of various princes and city governments. With his usual lack of modesty, Petrarch once exclaimed, "Some of the greatest kings of our time have loved me and cultivated my friendship. . . . When I was their guest it was more as if they were mine."[14]

Petrarch did more than any other individual in the fourteenth century to foster the development of Renaissance humanism. He was the first intellectual to characterize the Middle Ages as a period of darkness, promoting the mistaken belief that medieval culture was ignorant of classical antiquity. Petrarch condemned the scholastic philosophy of the Middle Ages for its "barbarous" Latin and use of logic, rather than rhetoric, to harmonize faith and reason. Philosophy, he argued, should be the "art of virtuous living," not a science of logic chopping. Petrarch's interest in the classics led him on a quest for forgotten Latin manuscripts and set in motion a ransacking of monastic libraries throughout Europe. In his preoccupation with the classics and their secular content, Petrarch worried at times whether he was sufficiently attentive to spiritual ideals (see the box on p. 340). His qualms, however, did not prevent him from inaugurating the humanist emphasis on the use of pure classical Latin, making it fashionable for humanists to use Cicero as a model for prose and Virgil for poetry.

Petrarch: Mountain Climbing and the Search for Spiritual Contentment

Petrarch has long been regarded as the father of Italian Renaissance humanism. One of his literary masterpieces was The Ascent of Mt. Ventoux. *Its colorful description of an attempt to climb a mountain in Provence in southern France and survey the world from its top has unwisely led some to see it as a vivid example of the humanists' rediscovery of nature after the medieval period's concentration on the afterlife. Of course, medieval people had been aware of the natural world. Moreover, Petrarch's primary interest is in presenting an allegory of his own soul's struggle to achieve a higher spiritual state. The work is addressed to a professor of theology in Paris who had initially led Petrarch to read Augustine. The latter had experienced a vivid conversion to Christianity almost 1,000 years earlier.*

Petrarch, *The Ascent of Mt. Ventoux*

Today I ascended the highest mountain in this region, which, not without cause, they call the Windy Peak. Nothing but the desire to see its conspicuous height was the reason for this undertaking. For many years I have been intending to make this expedition. You know that since my early childhood, as fate tossed around human affairs, I have been tossed around in these parts, and this mountain, visible far and wide from everywhere, is always in your view. So I was at last seized by the impulse to accomplish what I had always wanted to do. . . .

[After some false starts, Petrarch finally achieves his goal and arrives at the top of Mt. Ventoux.]

I was glad of the progress I had made, but I wept over my imperfection and was grieved by the fickleness of all that men do. In this manner I seemed to have somehow forgotten the place I had come to and why, until I was warned to throw off such sorrows, for which another place would be more appropriate. I had better look around and see what I had intended to see in coming here. The time to leave was approaching, they said. . . . Like a man aroused from sleep, I turned back and looked toward the west. . . . one could see most distinctly the mountains of the province of Lyons to the right and, to the left, the sea near Marseilles as well as the waves that break against Aigues Mortes. . . . The Rhône River was directly under our eyes.

I admired every detail, now relishing earthly enjoyment, now lifting up my mind to higher spheres after the example of my body, and I thought it fit to look in the volume of Augustine's *Confessions* which I owe to your loving kindness and preserve carefully, keeping it always in my hands, in remembrance of the author as well as the donor. It is a little book of smallest size but full of infinite sweetness. I opened it with the intention of reading whatever might occur to me first: nothing, indeed, but pious and devout sentences could come to hand. I happened to hit upon the tenth book of the work. . . . Where I fixed my eyes first, it was written: "And men go to admire the high mountains, the vast floods of the sea, the huge streams of the rivers, the circumference of the ocean, and the revolutions of the stars—and desert themselves." I was stunned, I confess. I bade my brother [who had accompanied him], who wanted to hear more, not to molest me, and closed the book, angry with myself that I still admired earthly things. Long since I ought to have learned, even from pagan philosophers, that "nothing is admirable besides the soul; compared to its greatness nothing is great."

I was completely satisfied with what I had seen of the mountain and turned my inner eye toward myself. From this hour nobody heard me say a word until we arrived at the bottom. These words occupied me sufficiently. I could not imagine that this had happened to me by chance: I was convinced that whatever I had read there was said to me and to nobody else. I remembered that Augustine once suspected the same regarding himself, when, while he was reading the Apostolic Epistles, the first passage that occurred to him was, as he himself relates: "Not in banqueting and drunkenness, not in chambering and wantonness, not in strife and envying; but put you on the Lord Jesus Christ, and make no provision for the flesh to fulfill your lusts."

As Petrarch said, "Christ is my God; Cicero is the prince of the language."

HUMANISM IN FIFTEENTH-CENTURY ITALY

In Florence, the humanist movement took a new direction at the beginning of the fifteenth century when it became closely tied to Florentine civic spirit and pride, giving rise to what one modern scholar has labeled "civic humanism." Fourteenth-century humanists such as Petrarch had described the intellectual life as one of solitude. They rejected family and a life of action in the community. In the busy civic world of Florence, however, intellectuals began to take a new view of their role as intellectuals. The classical Roman Cicero, who was both a statesman and an intellectual, became their model. Leonardo Bruni (1370–1444), a humanist, Florentine patriot, and chancellor of the city, wrote a biography of Cicero entitled the *New Cicero*, in which he waxed enthusiastically about the fusion of political action and literary creation in Cicero's life. From Bruni's time on, Cicero

A Humanist's Enthusiasm for Greek

One of the first humanists to have a thorough knowledge of both Latin and Greek was the Florentine chancellor Leonardo Bruni. Bruni was fortunate to be instructed by the Greek scholar Manuel Chrysoloras, who was persuaded by the Florentines to come to Florence to teach Greek. As this selection illustrates, Bruni seized the opportunity to pursue his passion for Greek letters.

Leonardo Bruni, *History of His Own Times in Italy*

Then first came the knowledge of Greek letters, which for 700 years had been lost among us. It was the Byzantine, Chrysoloras, a nobleman in his own country and most skilled in literature, who brought Greek learning back to us. Because his country was invaded by the Turks, he came by sea to Venice; but as soon as his fame went abroad, he was cordially invited and eagerly besought to come to Florence on a public salary to spread his abundant riches before the youth of the city [1396]. At that time I was studying Civil Law. But my nature was afire with the love of learning and I had already given no little time to dialectic and rhetoric. Therefore at the coming of Chrysoloras I was divided in my mind, feeling that it was a shame to desert the Law and no less wrong to let slip such an occasion for learning Greek. And often with youthful impulsiveness I addressed myself thus: "When you are privileged to gaze upon and have converse with Homer, Plato, and Demosthenes as well as the other poets, philosophers, and orators of whom such wonderful things are reported, and when you might saturate yourself with their admirable teachings, will you turn your back and flee? Will you permit this opportunity, divinely offered you, to slip by? For 700 years now no one in Italy has been in possession of Greek and yet we agree that all knowledge comes from that source. What great advancement of knowledge, enlargement of fame, and increase of pleasure will come to you from an acquaintance with this tongue! There are everywhere quantities of doctors of the Civil Law and the opportunity of completing your study in this field will not fail you. However, should the one and only doctor of Greek letters disappear, there will be no one from whom to acquire them."

Overcome at last by these arguments, I gave myself to Chrysoloras and developed such ardor that whatever I learned by day, I revolved with myself in the night while asleep.

served as the inspiration for the Renaissance ideal that it was the duty of an intellectual to live an active life for one's state. An individual only "grows to maturity—both intellectually and morally—through participation" in the life of the state. Civic humanism reflected the values of the urban society of the Italian Renaissance. Humanists came to believe that their study of the humanities should be put to the service of the state. It is no accident that humanists served the state as chancellors, councillors, and advisers.

Also evident in the humanism of the first half of the fifteenth century was a growing interest in Greek. One of the first Italian humanists to gain a thorough knowledge of Greek was Leonardo Bruni, who became an enthusiastic pupil of the Byzantine scholar Manuel Chrysoloras, who taught in Florence from 1396 to 1400 (see the box above). Humanists eagerly perused the works of Plato as well as Greek poets, dramatists, historians, and orators, such as Thucydides, Euripides, and Sophocles, all of whom had been ignored by the scholastics of the High Middle Ages as irrelevant to the theological questions they were examining.

By the fifteenth century, a consciousness of being humanists had emerged. This was especially evident in the career of Lorenzo Valla (1407–1457). Valla was brought up in Rome and educated in both Latin and Greek. Eventually, during the pontificate of Nicholas V (1447–1455), he achieved his chief ambition of becoming a papal secretary. It was Valla, above all others, who turned his attention to the literary criticism of ancient texts. His most famous work was his demonstration that the Donation of Constantine, a document used by the popes, especially in the ninth and tenth centuries (see Chapter 8), to claim temporal sovereignty over all the west, was a forgery written in the eighth century. Valla's other major work, *The Elegances of the Latin Language,* was an effort to purify medieval Latin and restore Latin to its proper position over the vernacular. The treatise examined the proper use of classical Latin and created a new literary standard. Early humanists had tended to take as classical models any author (including Christians) who had written before the seventh century A.D. Valla identified different stages in the growth of the Latin language and accepted only the Latin of the last century of the Roman Republic and the first century of the empire.

Another significant humanist of this period was Poggio Bracciolini (1380–1459), who reflected the cult of humanism at its best. Born and educated in Florence, he went on to serve as a papal secretary for fifty years, a position that enabled him to become an avid collector of classical manuscripts. He was responsible for finding all of the writings of fifteen different authors. Poggio's best-known literary work was the *Facetiae,* a lighthearted collection of jokes, which included a rather cynical criticism of the clergy:

> A friar of Tivoli, who was not very considerate of the people, was once thundering away with many words about the detestability of adultery. Among other things, he declared that this sin was so grave that he would prefer to lie with ten virgins than with one married woman. And many of those present shared his opinion.[15]

Poggio and other Italian humanists were very critical of the Catholic church at times, but fundamentally they accepted the church and above all wished only to restore a simpler, purer, and more ethical Christianity. To the humanists, the study of the classics was perfectly compatible with Christianity.

HUMANISM AND PHILOSOPHY

In the second half of the fifteenth century, a dramatic upsurge of interest in the works of Plato occurred, especially evident among the members of the Florentine Platonic Academy. This academy was not a formal school, but rather an informal discussion group. Cosimo de' Medici, the de facto ruler of Florence, became its patron and commissioned a translation of Plato's dialogues by Marsilio Ficino (1433–1499), one of the academy's leaders. Ficino dedicated his life to the translation of Plato and the exposition of the Platonic philosophy known as Neoplatonism.

In two major works, Ficino undertook the synthesis of Christianity and Platonism into a single system. His Neoplatonism was based upon two primary ideas, the Neoplatonic hierarchy of substances and a theory of spiritual love. Drawing upon the Neoplatonists of the ancient world, Ficino restated the idea of a hierarchy of substances, or great chain of being, from the lowest form of physical matter (plants) to the purest spirit (God), in which humans occupied a central or middle position. They were the link between the material world (through the body) and the spiritual world (through the soul), and their highest duty was to ascend toward that union with God that was the true end of human existence. Ficino's theory of spiritual or Platonic love maintained that just as all people are bound together in their common humanity by love, so too are all parts of the universe held together by bonds of sympathetic love.

Renaissance Hermeticism was another product of the Florentine intellectual environment of the late fifteenth century. Upon the request of Cosimo de' Medici, Ficino translated into Latin a Greek work entitled the *Corpus Hermeticum.* The Hermetic manuscripts contained two kinds of writings. One type stressed the occult sciences with emphasis on astrology, alchemy, and magic. The other focused on theological and philosophical beliefs and speculations. Some parts of the Hermetic writings were distinctly pantheistic, seeing divinity embodied in all aspects of nature, in the heavenly bodies as well as in earthly objects. As Giordano Bruno, one of the most prominent of the sixteenth-century Hermeticists stated: "God as a whole is in all things."[16] For Renaissance intellectuals, the Hermetic revival offered a new view of humankind. They believed that human beings had been created as divine beings endowed with divine creative power, but had freely chosen to enter the material world (nature). Humans could recover their divinity, however, through a regenerative experience or purification of the soul. Thus regenerated, they became true sages or magi, as the Renaissance called them, who had knowledge of God and of truth. In regaining their original divinity, they reacquired an intimate knowledge of nature and the ability to employ the powers of nature for beneficial purposes.

In Italy, the most prominent magi in the late fifteenth century were Ficino and his friend and pupil, Giovanni Pico della Mirandola (1463–1494). Pico produced one of the most famous writings of the Renaissance, the *Oration on the Dignity of Man,* a preface to his *900 Conclusions,* which were meant to be a summation of all learning and were offered as theses for a public debate. Pico combed diligently through the writings of many philosophers of different backgrounds for the common "nuggets of universal truth" that he believed were all part of God's revelation to humanity. In the *Oration* (see the box on p. 343), Pico offered a ringing statement of unlimited human potential: "To him it is granted to have whatever he chooses, to be whatever he wills."[17] Like Ficino, Pico took an avid interest in Hermetic philosophy, accepting it as the "science of the Divine," which "embraces the deepest contemplation of the most secret things, and at last the knowledge of all nature."[18]

Education in the Renaissance

The humanist movement had a profound effect on education. Renaissance humanists believed that human beings could be dramatically changed by education. They wrote books on education and developed secondary schools based on their ideas. Most famous was the one founded in 1423 by Vittorino da Feltre (1378–1446) at Mantua, where the ruler of that small Italian state, Gian Francesco I Gonzaga, wished to provide a humanist school for his children. Vittorino based much of his educational system on the ideas of classical authors, particularly Cicero and Quintilian.

At the core of the academic training Vittorino offered were the "liberal studies." The Renaissance view of the value of the liberal arts was most strongly influenced by a treatise on education called *Concerning Character* by Pietro Paolo Vergerio (1370–1444). This work stressed the importance of the liberal arts as the key to true freedom, enabling individuals to reach their full potential. According to Vergerio, "we call those studies liberal which are worthy of a free man; those studies by which we attain and practice virtue and wisdom; that education which calls forth, trains, and develops those highest gifts of body and mind which ennoble men, and which are rightly judged to

Pico della Mirandola and the Dignity of Man

Giovanni Pico della Mirandola was one of the foremost intellects of the Italian Renaissance. Pico boasted that he had studied all schools of philosophy, whch he tried to demonstrate by drawing up 900 theses for public disputation at the age of twenty-four. As a preface to his theses, he wrote his famous oration, On the Dignity of Man, *in which he proclaimed the unlimited potentiality of human beings.*

Pico della Mirandola, *Oration on the Dignity of Man*

At last the best of artisans [God] ordained that that creature to whom He had been able to give nothing proper to himself should have joint possession of whatever had been peculiar to each of the different kinds of being. He therefore took man as a creature of indeterminate nature, and assigning him a place in the middle of the world, addressed him thus: "Neither a fixed abode nor a form that is yours alone nor any function peculiar to yourself have we given you, Adam, to the end that according to your longing and according to your judgment you may have and possess what abode, what form, and what functions you yourself desire. The nature of all other beings is limited and constrained within the bounds of laws prescribed by Us. You, constrained by no limits, in accordance with your own free will, in whose hand We have placed you, shall ordain for yourself the limits of your nature. We have set you at the world's center that you may from there more easily observe whatever is in the world. We have made you neither of heaven nor of earth, neither mortal nor immortal, so that with freedom of choice and with honor, as though the maker and molder of yourself, you may fashion yourself in whatever shape you shall prefer. You shall have the power to degenerate into the lower forms of life, which are brutish. You shalt have the power, out of your soul's judgment, to be reborn into the higher forms, which are divine."

O supreme generosity of God the Father, O highest and most marvelous felicity of man! To him it is granted to have whatever he chooses, to be whatever he wills. Beasts as soon as they are born bring with them from their mother's womb all they will ever possess. Spiritual beings, either from the beginning or soon thereafter, become what they are to be for ever and ever. On man when he came into life the Father conferred the seeds of all kinds and the germs of every way of life. Whatever seeds each man cultivates will grow to maturity and bear in him their own fruit. If they be vegetative, he will be like a plant. If sensitive, he will become brutish. If rational, he will grow into a heavenly being. If intellectual, he will be an angel and the son of God.

rank next in dignity to virtue only."[19] What, then, are the "liberal studies"?

> Amongst these I accord the first place to History, on grounds both of its attractiveness and of its utility, qualities which appeal equally to the scholar and to the statesman. Next in importance ranks Moral Philosophy, which indeed is, in a peculiar sense, a "Liberal Art," in that its purpose is to teach men the secret of true freedom. History, then, gives us the concrete examples of the precepts inculcated by Philosophy. The one shows what men should do, the other what men have said and done in the past, and what practical lessons we may draw therefrom for the present day. I would indicate as the third main branch of study, Eloquence. . . . By philosophy we learn the essential truth of things, which by eloquence we so exhibit in orderly adornment as to bring conviction to differing minds.[20]

The remaining liberal studies included letters (grammar and logic), poetry, mathematics, astronomy, and music ("as to Music," said Vergerio, "the Greeks refused the title of 'Educated' to anyone who could not sing or play"). Crucial to all liberal studies was the mastery of Greek and Latin since it enabled students to read the great classical authors who were the foundation stones of the liberal arts. In short, the purpose of a liberal education was to produce individuals who followed a path of virtue and wisdom and possessed the rhetorical skills to persuade others to take it.

Following the Greek precept of a sound mind in a sound body, Vittorino's school at Mantua stressed the need for physical education. Pupils were taught the arts of javelin throwing, archery, and dancing and encouraged to run, wrestle, hunt, and swim frequently. Nor was Christianity excluded from Vittorino's school. His students were taught the Scriptures and the works of the church fathers, especially Augustine. A devout Christian, Vittorino required his pupils to attend mass daily and be reverent in word and deed.

Although a small number of children from the lower classes were provided free educations, humanist schools such as Vittorino's were primarily geared for the education of an elite, the ruling classes of their communities. Also largely absent from such schools were females. Vittorino's only female pupils were the two daughters of the Gonzaga ruler of Mantua. Though these few female students studied the classics and were encouraged to know some history and to ride, dance, sing, play the lute, and appreciate poetry, they were discouraged from learning mathematics and rhetoric. In the educational treatises of the time, religion and morals were thought to "hold the first place in the education of a Christian lady."

Nevertheless, some women in Italy who were educated in the humanist fashion went on to establish their own literary careers. Isotta Nogarola, born to a noble family in Verona, mastered Latin and wrote numerous letters and treatises that brought her praise from male Italian intellectuals. Cassandra Fedele of Venice, who learned both Latin and Greek from humanist tutors hired by her family, became prominent in Venice for her public recitations of orations. In one of her writings, Cassandra defended the unusual practice of women studying the liberal arts.

The humanist schools of the Renaissance aimed to develop the human personality to the fullest extent and underscored the new social ideal of the Renaissance, the creation of the universal being known to us as the "Renaissance man." We should also note that Vittorino and other humanist educators considered a humanist education to be a practical preparation for life. The aim of humanist education was not to create great scholars but rather to produce complete citizens who could participate in the civic life of their communities. As Vittorino said: "Not everyone is obliged to excel in philosophy, medicine, or the law, nor are all equally favored by nature; but all are destined to live in society and to practice virtue."[21] Humanist schools, combining the classics and Christianity, provided the model for the basic education of the European ruling classes until the twentieth century.

Humanism and History

Humanism had a strong impact on the writing of history. Influenced by Roman and Greek historians, the humanists approached the writing of history differently from the chroniclers of the Middle Ages. The humanists' belief that classical civilization had been followed by an age of barbarism (the Middle Ages), which, in turn, had been succeeded by their own age with its rebirth of the study of the classics, enabled them to think in terms of the passage of time, of the past as past. Their division of the past into ancient world, dark ages, and their own age provided a new sense of chronology or periodization in history.

The humanists were also responsible for secularizing the writing of history. Humanist historians reduced or eliminated the role of miracles in historical interpretation, not because they were anti-Christian, but because they took a new approach to sources. They wanted to use documents and exercised their newly developed critical skills in examining them. Greater attention was paid to the political events and forces that affected their city-states or larger territorial units. Thus, Leonardo Bruni wrote a *History of the Florentine People;* the German scholar Jacob Wimpheling penned *On the Excellence and Magnificence of the Germans.* The new emphasis on secularization was also evident in the humanists' conception of causation in history. In much medieval historical literature, historical events were often portrayed as being caused by God's active involvement in human affairs. Humanists deemphasized divine intervention in favor of human motives, stressing political forces or the role of individuals in history.

The high point of Renaissance historiography was achieved at the beginning of the sixteenth century in the works of Francesco Guicciardini (1483–1540). He has been called by some Renaissance scholars the greatest historian between Tacitus in the first century A.D. (see Chapter 6) and Voltaire and Gibbon in the eighteenth century (see Chapter 17). His *History of Italy* and *History of Florence* represent the beginning of "modern analytical historiography." To Guicciardini, the purpose of writing history was to teach lessons, but he was so impressed by the complexity of historical events that he felt those lessons were not always obvious. From his extensive background in government and diplomatic affairs, he developed the political skills that enabled him to analyze political situations precisely and critically. Emphasizing political and military history, his works relied heavily on personal examples and documentary sources.

The Impact of Printing

The period of the Renaissance witnessed the invention of printing, one of the most important technological innovations of Western civilization. The art of printing made an immediate impact on European intellectual life and thought.

Printing from hand-carved wooden blocks had been present in the west since the twelfth century. What was new in the fifteenth century was multiple printing with movable metal type. The development of printing from movable type was a gradual process that culminated some time between 1445 and 1450; Johannes Gutenberg of Mainz played an important role in bringing the process to completion. Gutenberg's Bible, completed in 1455 or 1456, was the first real book produced from movable type.

The new printing spread rapidly throughout Europe in the last half of the fifteenth century. Printing presses were established throughout the Holy Roman Empire in the 1460s and within ten years had spread to Italy, England, France, the Low Countries, Spain, and eastern Europe. Especially well known as a printing center was Venice, home by 1500 to almost 100 printers who had produced almost two million volumes.

By 1500, there were more than 1,000 printers in Europe who had published almost 40,000 titles (between 8 and 10 million copies). Probably 50 percent of these books were religious in character—Bibles and biblical commentaries, books of devotion, and sermons. Next in importance were the Latin and Greek classics, medieval grammars, legal handbooks, works on philosophy, and an ever-growing number of popular romances.

Printing became one of the largest industries in Europe, and its effects were soon felt in many areas of European life. Although some humanists condemned printing because they believed that it vulgarized learn-

MASACCIO, *TRIBUTE MONEY*. With the frescoes of Masaccio, regarded by many as the first great works of Early Renaissance art, a new realistic style of painting was born. The *Tribute Money* was one of a series of frescoes that Masaccio painted in the Brancacci Chapel in the Church of Santa Maria del Carmine in Florence. In illustrating a story from the Bible, Masaccio used a rational system of perspective to create a realistic relationship between the figures and their background.

ing, the printing of books actually encouraged the development of scholarly research and the desire to attain knowledge. Moreover, printing facilitated cooperation among scholars and helped produce standardized and definitive texts. Printing also stimulated the development of an ever-expanding lay reading public, a development that had an enormous impact on European society. Indeed, without the printing press, the new religious ideas of the Reformation would never have spread as rapidly as they did in the sixteenth century.

◆ The Artistic Renaissance

Leonardo da Vinci, one of the great Italian Renaissance artists, once explained: "Hence the painter will produce pictures of small merit if he takes for his standard the pictures of others, but if he will study from natural objects he will bear good fruit . . . those who take for their standard any one but nature . . . weary themselves in vain."[22] Renaissance artists considered the imitation of nature to be their primary goal. Their search for naturalism became an end in itself: to persuade onlookers of the reality of the object or event they were portraying. At the same time, the new artistic standards reflected a new attitude of mind as well, one in which human beings became the focus of attention, the "center and measure of all things," as one artist proclaimed.

Leonardo and other Italians maintained that it was Giotto in the fourteenth century (see Chapter 11) who began the imitation of nature. But what Giotto had begun was not taken up again until the work of Masaccio (1401–1428) in Florence. Masaccio's cycle of frescoes in the Brancacci Chapel has long been regarded as the first masterpiece of Early Renaissance art. With his use of monumental figures, demonstration of a more realistic relationship between figures and landscape, and visual representation of the laws of perspective, a new realistic style of painting was born. Onlookers become aware of a world of reality that appears to be a continuation of their own world. Masaccio's massive, three-dimensional human figures provided a model for later generations of Florentine artists.

This new or Renaissance style was absorbed and modified by other Florentine painters in the fifteenth century. Especially important was the development of an experimental trend that took two directions. One emphasized the mathematical side of painting, the working out of the laws of perspective and the organization of outdoor space and light by geometry and perspective. In the work of Paolo Uccello (1397–1475), figures became mere stage props to show off his mastery of the laws of perspective. The other aspect of the experimental trend involved the investigation of movement and anatomical structure. *The Martyrdom of St. Sebastian* by Antonio Pollaiuolo (c. 1432–1498) revels in classical motifs and attempts to portray the human body under stress. Indeed, the realistic portrayal of the human nude became one of the foremost preoccupations of Italian Renaissance art. The fifteenth century, then, was a period of experimentation and technical mastery.

During the last decades of the fifteenth century, a new sense of invention emerged in Florence, especially in the circle of artists and scholars who formed part of the court of the city's leading citizen, Lorenzo the Magnificent. One of this group's prominent members was Sandro Botticelli (1445–1510), whose interest in Greek and Roman mythology was well reflected in one of his most famous works, *Primavera* or *Spring*. The painting is set in the garden of Venus, a garden of eternal spring. Though Botticelli's figures are well defined, they also possess an otherworldly quality that is far removed from the realism that characterized the painting of the Early Renaissance.

The revolutionary achievements of Florentine painters in the fifteenth century were matched by equally

BOTTICELLI, *PRIMAVERA*. This work reflects Botticelli's strong interest in classical antiquity. At the center of the painting is Venus, the goddess of love. At the right stands Flora, a Roman goddess of flowers and fertility, while the Three Graces dance playfully at the left. Cupid, the son of Venus, aims his arrow at the Three Graces. At the far left of the picture is Mercury, the messenger of the gods. Later in his life, Botticelli experienced a profound religious crisis, leading him to reject his earlier preoccupation with pagan gods and goddesses. He burned many of his early paintings and then produced only religious works.

stunning advances in sculpture and architecture. Donato di Donatello (1386–1466) spent time in Rome, studying and copying the statues of antiquity. His subsequent work in Florence reveals how well he had mastered the essence of what he saw. Among his numerous works was a statue of David, which is the first known "lifesize freestanding bronze nude in European art since antiquity." With the severed head of the giant Goliath beneath David's feet, Donatello's statue celebrated Florentine heroism in the triumph of the Florentines over the Milanese in 1428. Like Donatello's other statues, *David* also radiated a simplicity and strength that reflected the dignity of humanity.

Filippo Brunelleschi (1377–1446) was a friend of Donatello and accompanied him to Rome. Brunelleschi drew much inspiration from the architectural monuments of Roman antiquity, and when he returned to Florence, he poured his new insights into the creation of a new architecture. When the Medici commissioned him to design the Church of San Lorenzo, Brunelleschi, inspired by Roman models, created a church interior very different from that of the great medieval cathedrals. San Lorenzo's classical columns, rounded arches, and coffered ceiling created an environment that did not overwhelm the worshiper

FILIPPO BRUNELLESCHI, INTERIOR OF SAN LORENZO. Cosimo de' Medici contributed massive amounts of money to the rebuilding of the Church of San Lorenzo. As seen in this view of the nave and choir of the church, Brunelleschi's architectural designs were based on the basilica plan borrowed by early Christians from pagan Rome. San Lorenzo's simplicity, evident in its rows of slender Corinthian columns, created a human-centered space.

DONATELLO, *DAVID*. Donatello's *David* first stood in the courtyard of the Medici Palace. On its base was an inscription praising Florentine heroism and virtue, leading art historians to assume that the statue was meant to commemorate the victory of Florence over Milan in 1428.

materially and psychologically as Gothic cathedrals did, but comforted as a space created to fit human, not divine, measurements. Like painters and sculptors, Renaissance architects sought to reflect a human-centered world.

The new assertion of human individuality, evident in Early Renaissance art, was also reflected in the new emphasis on portraiture. Patrons appeared in the corners of sacred pictures, and monumental tombs and portrait statues honored many of Florence's prominent citizens. By the mid-fifteenth century, artists were giving an accurate rendering of their subjects' facial features while revealing the inner qualities of their personalities. The portraits of the duke and duchess of Urbino by Piero della Francesca (c. 1410–1492) provide accurate representations as well as a sense of both the power and the wealth of the rulers of Urbino.

By the end of the fifteenth century, Italian painters, sculptors, and architects had created a new artistic environment. Many artists had mastered the new techniques for a scientific observation of the world around them and were now ready to move into individualistic forms of creative expression. This final stage of Renaissance art, which flourished between 1480 and 1520, is called the High Renaissance. The shift to the High Renaissance was marked by the increasing importance of Rome as a new cultural center of the Italian Renaissance.

The High Renaissance was dominated by the work of three artistic giants, Leonardo da Vinci (1452–1519), Raphael (1483–1520), and Michelangelo (1475–1564). Leonardo represents a transitional figure in the shift to High Renaissance principles. He carried on the fifteenth-century experimental tradition by studying everything and even dissecting human bodies to better see how nature worked. But Leonardo stressed the need to advance beyond such realism and initiated the High Renaissance's preoccupation with the idealization of nature, or the attempt to generalize from realistic portrayal to an ideal form. Leonardo's *Last Supper,* painted in Milan, is a brilliant summary of fifteenth-century trends in its organization of space and use of perspective to depict subjects three-dimensionally in a two-dimensional medium. But it is also more. The figure of Philip is idealized, and there are profound psychological dimensions to the work. The words of

LEONARDO DA VINCI, *THE LAST SUPPER*. Leonardo da Vinci was the impetus behind the High Renaissance concern for the idealization of nature, moving from a realistic portrayal of the human figure to an idealized form. Evident in Leonardo's *Last Supper* is his effort to depict a person's character and inner nature by the use of gesture and movement. Unfortunately, Leonardo used an experimental technique in this fresco, which soon led to its physical deterioration.

RAPHAEL, *SCHOOL OF ATHENS*. Raphael arrived in Rome in 1508 and began to paint a series of frescoes commissioned by Pope Julius II for the papal apartments at the Vatican. In the *School of Athens*, painted about 1510–1511, Raphael created an imaginary gathering of ancient philosophers. In the center stand Plato and Aristotle. At the left is Pythagoras, showing his system of proportions on a slate. At the right is Ptolemy, holding a celestial globe.

Jesus that "one of you shall betray me" are experienced directly as each of the apostles reveals his personality and his relationship to Jesus. Through gestures and movement, Leonardo hoped to reveal a person's inner life.

Raphael blossomed as a painter at an early age; at twenty-five, he was already regarded as one of Italy's best painters. Raphael was acclaimed for his numerous madonnas, in which he attempted to achieve an ideal of beauty far surpassing human standards. He is well known for his frescoes in the Vatican Palace; his *School of Athens* reveals a world of balance, harmony, and order—the underlying principles of the art of the classical world of Greece and Rome.

Michelangelo, an accomplished painter, sculptor, and architect, was another giant of the High Renaissance. Fiercely driven by his desire to create, he worked with great passion and energy on a remarkable number of projects. Michelangelo was influenced by Neoplatonism, especially evident in his figures on the ceiling of the Sistine Chapel in Rome. These muscular figures reveal an ideal type of human being with perfect proportions. In good Neoplatonic fashion, their beauty is meant to be a reflection of divine beauty; the more beautiful the body, the more Godlike the figure.

Another manifestation of Michelangelo's search for ideal beauty was his *David*, a colossal marble statue commissioned by the Florentine government in 1501 and completed in 1504. Michelangelo maintained that the form of a statue already resided in the uncarved piece of stone: "I only take away the surplus, the statue is already there."[23] Out of a piece of marble that had remained unused for fifty years, Michelangelo created a fourteen-foot-high figure, the largest piece of sculpture in Italy since the time of Rome. An awe-inspiring hero, Michelangelo's *David* proudly proclaims the beauty of the human body and the glory of human beings.

A High Renaissance in architecture was also evident, especially in the work of Donato Bramante (1444–1514). He came from Urbino but took up residence in Rome, where he designed a small temple on the supposed site of Saint Peter's martyrdom. The Tempietto—or little temple—with its Doric columns surrounding a sanctuary enclosed by a dome, summarized the architectural ideals of the

MICHELANGELO, *CREATION OF ADAM*. **In 1508, Pope Julius II recalled Michelangelo to Rome and commissioned him to decorate the ceiling of the Sistine Chapel. This colossal project was not completed until 1512. Michelangelo attempted to tell the story of the Fall of Man by depicting nine scenes from the biblical Book of Genesis. In this scene, the well-proportioned figure of Adam, meant by Michelangelo to be a reflection of divine beauty, awaits the divine spark.**

High Renaissance. Columns, dome, and sanctuary form a monumental and harmonious whole. Inspired by antiquity, Bramante had recaptured the grandeur of ancient Rome. His achievement led Pope Julius II to commission him to design a new basilica for Rome, which eventually became the great St. Peter's.

The Artist and Social Status

Early Renaissance artists began their careers as apprentices to masters in craft guilds. Apprentices with unusual talent might eventually become masters and run their own workshops. As in the Middle Ages, artists were still largely viewed as artisans. Since guilds depended on commissions for their projects, patrons played an important role in the art of the Early Renaissance. The wealthy upper classes determined both the content and purpose of the paintings and pieces of sculpture they commissioned.

By the end of the fifteenth century, a transformation in the position of the artist had occurred. Especially talented individuals, such as Leonardo, Raphael, and Michelangelo, were no longer seen as artisans, but as artistic geniuses with creative energies akin to the divine (see the box on p. 350). Artists were heroes, individuals who were praised more for their creativity than for their competence as craftspeople. Michelangelo, for example, was frequently addressed as "Il Divino"—the Divine One. As society excused their eccentricities and valued their creative genius, the artists of the High Renaissance became the first to embody the modern concept of the artist.

As respect for artists grew, so too did their ability to profit economically from their work and to rise on the social scale. Now welcomed as equals into the circles of the upper classes, they mingled with the political and intellectual elite of their society and became more aware of new intellectual theories, which they then embodied in their art. The Platonic Academy and Renaissance Neoplatonism had an especially important impact on Florentine painters.

MICHELANGELO, *DAVID*. **This statue of David, cut from an eighteen-foot-high piece of marble, exalts the beauty of the human body and is a fitting symbol of the Italian Renaissance's affirmation of human power. Completed in 1504, the *David* was moved by Florentine authorities to a special location in front of the Palazzo Vecchio, the seat of the Florentine government.**

The Genius of Leonardo da Vinci

During the Renaissance, artists came to be viewed as creative geniuses with almost divine qualities. One individual who helped to create this image of the Renaissance artist was himself a painter. Giorgio Vasari was an avid admirer of Italy's great artists and wrote a series of brief biographies of them. This excerpt is taken from his account of Leonardo da Vinci.

Giorgio Vasari, *Lives of the Artists*

In the normal course of events many men and women are born with various remarkable qualities and talents; but occasionally, in a way that transcends nature, a single person is marvelously endowed by heaven with beauty, grace, and talent in such abundance that he leaves other men far behind, all his actions seem inspired, and indeed everything he does clearly comes from God rather than from human art.

Everyone acknowledged that this was true of Leonardo da Vinci, an artist of outstanding physical beauty who displayed infinite grace in everything he did and who cultivated his genius so brilliantly that all problems he studied he solved with ease. He possessed great strength and dexterity; he was a man of regal spirit and tremendous breadth of mind; and his name became so famous that not only was he esteemed during his lifetime but his reputation endured and became even greater after his death. . . .

He was marvelously gifted, and he proved himself to be a first-class geometrician in his work as a sculptor and architect. In his youth Leonardo made in clay several heads of women, with smiling faces, of which plaster casts are still being made, as well as some children's heads executed as if by a mature artist. He also did many architectural drawings both of ground plans and of other elevations, and, while still young, he was the first to propose reducing the Arno River to a navigable canal between Pisa and Florence. He made designs for mills, fulling machines, and engines that could be driven by waterpower; and as he intended to be a painter by profession he carefully studied drawing from life. . . . Altogether, his genius was so wonderfully inspired by the grace of God, his powers of expression were so powerfully fed by a willing memory and intellect, and his writing conveyed his ideas so precisely, that his arguments and reasonings confounded the most formidable critics. In addition, he used to make models and plans showing how to excavate and tunnel through mountains without difficulty, so as to pass from one level to another; and he demonstrated how to lift and draw great weights by means of levers and hoists and ways of cleaning harbors and using pumps to suck up water from great depths.

The Northern Artistic Renaissance

In trying to provide an exact portrayal of their world, the artists of the north (especially the Low Countries) and Italy took different approaches. In Italy, the human form became the primary vehicle of expression as Italian artists sought to master the technical skills that allowed them to portray humans in realistic settings. The large wall spaces of Italian churches had given rise to the art of fresco painting, but in the north, the prevalence of Gothic cathedrals with their stained glass windows resulted in more emphasis on illuminated manuscripts and wooden panel painting for altarpieces. The space available in these works was limited, and great care was required to depict each object, leading northern painters to become masters at rendering details.

BRAMANTE, TEMPIETTO. Ferdinand and Isabella of Spain commissioned Donato Bramante to design a small building in Rome that would commemorate the place where Saint Peter supposedly was crucified. Completed in 1502, the temple reflected Bramante's increasing understanding of ancient Roman remains.

JAN VAN EYCK, *GIOVANNI ARNOLFINI AND HIS BRIDE.* **Northern painters took great care in depicting each object and became masters at rendering details. This emphasis on a realistic portrayal is clearly evident in this oil painting, supposedly a portrait of Giovanni Arnolfini, an Italian merchant who had settled in Bruges, and his wife, Giovanna Cenami.**

ALBRECHT DÜRER, *ADORATION OF THE MAGI.* **By the end of the fifteenth century, northern artists had begun to study in Italy and to adopt many of the techniques used by Italian painters. As is evident in this painting, which was the central panel for an altarpiece done for Frederick the Wise in 1504, Albrecht Dürer masterfully incorporated the laws of perspective and the ideals of proportion into his works. At the same time, he did not abandon the preoccupation with detail typical of northern artists.**

The most influential northern school of art in the fifteenth century was centered in Flanders. Jan van Eyck (1390?–1441) was among the first to use oil paint, a medium that enabled the artist to use a varied range of colors and make changes to create fine details. In the famous *Giovanni Arnolfini and His Bride,* van Eyck's attention to detail is staggering: precise portraits, a glittering chandelier, and a mirror reflecting the objects in the room. Although each detail was rendered as observed, it is evident that van Eyck's comprehension of perspective was still uncertain. His work is truly indicative of northern Renaissance painters, who, in their effort to imitate nature, did so not by mastery of the laws of perspective and proportion, but by empirical observation of visual reality and the accurate portrayal of details. Moreover, northern painters placed great emphasis on the emotional intensity of religious feeling and created great works of devotional art, especially in their altarpieces. Michelangelo summarized the difference between northern and Italian Renaissance painting in these words:

> In Flanders, they paint, before all things, to render exactly and deceptively the outward appearance of things. The painters choose, by preference, subjects provoking transports of piety, like the figures of saints or of prophets. But most of the time they paint what are called landscapes with plenty of figures. Though the eye is agreeably impressed, these pictures have neither choice of values nor grandeur. In short, this art is without power and without distinction; it aims at rendering minutely many things at the same time, of which a single one would have sufficed to call forth a man's whole application.[24]

By the end of the fifteenth century, however, artists from the north began to study in Italy and were visually influenced by what artists were doing there.

One northern artist of this later period who was greatly affected by the Italians was Albrecht Dürer (1471–1528) from Nuremberg. Dürer made two trips to

MAP 12.2 Europe in the Renaissance.

Italy and absorbed most of what the Italians could teach, as is evident in his mastery of the laws of perspective and Renaissance theories of proportion. He wrote detailed treatises on both subjects. At the same time, as in his famous *Adoration of the Magi,* Dürer did not reject the use of minute details characteristic of northern artists. He did try, however, to integrate those details more harmoniously into his works and, like the Italian artists of the High Renaissance, tried to achieve a standard of ideal beauty by a careful examination of the human form.

Music in the Renaissance

For much of the fifteenth century, an extraordinary cultural environment was fostered in the domains of the dukes of Burgundy in northern Europe. The court of the dukes attracted some of the best artists and musicians of the time. Among them was Guillaume Dufay (c. 1400–1474), perhaps the most important composer of his time. Born in northern France, Dufay lived for a few years in Italy and was thus well suited to combine the late medieval style of France with the early Renaissance style of Italy. One of Dufay's greatest contributions was a change in the composition of the mass. He was the first to use secular tunes to replace Gregorian chants as the fixed melody that served as the basis for the mass. Dufay also composed a number of secular songs, an important reminder that during the Renaissance music ceased to be used chiefly in the service of God and moved into the secular world of courts and cities. In Italy and France, the chief form of secular music was the madrigal.

The Renaissance madrigal was a poem set to music, and its origins were in the fourteenth-century Italian courts. The texts were usually twelve-line poems written in the vernacular, and their theme was emotional or erotic love. By the mid-sixteenth century, most madrigals were written for five or six voices and employed a technique called text painting, in which the music tried to portray the literal meaning of the text. Thus, the melody would rise for the word "heaven" or use a wavelike motion to represent the word "water." By the mid-sixteenth century, the madrigal had also spread to England, where the most popular form was characterized by the fa-la-la refrain like that found in the English carol "Deck the Halls."

◆ The European State in the Renaissance

The High Middle Ages had witnessed the emergence of territorial states that began to develop the administrative machinery of centralized government. Professional bureaucracies, royal courts, and parliamentary assemblies were all products of the twelfth and thirteenth centuries. Strong monarchy had provided the organizing power for the development of these states, but in the fourteenth century, the internal stability of European governments had been threatened by financial and dynastic problems as well as challenges from their nobilities. By the fifteenth century, rulers began to rebuild their states by checking the violent activities of their nobles and maintaining internal order. Some territorial units, such as the Holy Roman Empire and Italy, failed to develop strong national monarchies, but even in these areas, strong princes and city councils managed to centralize their authority within their smaller territorial states. In Italy, Milan, Venice, and Florence managed to become fairly well centralized territorial states. Some historians believe that the Italian Renaissance states, with their preoccupation with political power, were the first true examples of the modern secular state.

The "New Monarchies"

In the first half of the fifteenth century, European states continued the disintegrative patterns of the previous century. In the second half of the fifteenth century, however, recovery set in, and attempts were made to reestablish the centralized power of monarchical governments. To characterize the results, some historians have used the label "Renaissance states"; others have spoken of the "new monarchies," especially those of France, England, and Spain at the end of the fifteenth century. Although appropriate, the term "new monarch" can also be misleading. These Renaissance monarchs were new in their concentration of royal authority, their attempts to suppress the nobility, their efforts to control the church in their lands, and their insistence upon having the loyalty of people living within definite territorial boundaries. Like the rulers of fifteenth-century Italian states, the "new monarchs" were often crafty men obsessed with the acquisition and expansion of political power. Of course, none of these characteristics was entirely new in that a number of medieval monarchs, especially in the thirteenth century, had also exhibited them. Nevertheless, the Renaissance period does mark the further extension of centralized royal authority. Of course, the degree to which monarchs were successful in extending their political authority varied from area to area. In central and eastern Europe, decentralization rather than centralization of political authority remained a fact of life.

CHRONOLOGY

The "New Monarchies"

France	
Charles VII	1422–1461
Pragmatic Sanction of Bourges	1438
Louis XI the Spider	1461–1483
Charles VIII	1483–1498
Louis XII	1498–1515
England	
War of the Roses	1450s–1485
Richard III	1483–1485
Henry VII	1485–1509
Spain	
Isabella of Castile	1474–1504
Ferdinand of Aragon	1479–1516
Marriage of Ferdinand and Isabella	1469
Introduction of Inquisition	1478
Expulsion of the Jews	1492
Expulsion of the Muslims	1502
Holy Roman Empire	
Frederick III	1440–1493
Maximilian I	1493–1519
Eastern Europe	
Creation of Lithuanian-Polish state	1386
Hungary: Matthias Corvinus	1458–1490
Russia: Ivan III	1462–1505
Fall of Constantinople and Byzantine Empire	1453

THE GROWTH OF THE FRENCH MONARCHY

The Hundred Years' War had left France prostrate. Depopulation, desolate farmlands, ruined commerce, and independent and unruly nobles had made it difficult for the kings to assert their authority. But the war had also developed a strong degree of French national feeling toward a common enemy that the kings could use to reestablish monarchical power. The need to prosecute the war provided an excuse to strengthen the authority of the king, already evident in the policies of Charles VII (1422–1461) after he was crowned king at Reims. With the consent of the Estates-General, Charles established a royal army composed of cavalry and archers. He received from the Estates-General the right to levy the *taille*, an annual direct tax usually on land or property, without any need for further approval from the Estates-General. Losing control of the purse meant less power for this parliamentary body. Charles VII also secured the Pragmatic Sanction of Bourges (1438), an agreement with the papacy that strengthened the liberties of the French church administratively at the expense of the papacy and enabled the king to begin to assume control over the church in France.

The process of developing a French territorial state was greatly advanced by King Louis XI (1461–1483), known as the Spider because of his wily and devious ways. Some historians have called this "new monarch" the founder of the French national state. By retaining the *taille* as a permanent tax imposed by royal authority, Louis secured a sound, regular source of income. Louis was not, however, completely successful in repressing the French nobility whose independence posed a threat to his own state building. A major problem was his supposed vassal, Charles the Bold, duke of Burgundy (1467–1477). Charles attempted to create a middle kingdom between France and Germany, stretching from the Low Countries in the north to Switzerland. Louis opposed his action, and when Charles was killed in 1477 fighting the Swiss, Louis added part of Charles's possessions, the duchy of Burgundy, to his own lands. Three years later, the provinces of Anjou, Maine, Bar, and Provence were brought under royal control. Louis the Spider also encouraged the growth of industry and commerce in an attempt to bolster the French economy. For example, he introduced new industries, such as the silk industry to Lyons.

Many historians believe that Louis created a base for the later development of a strong French monarchy. In any case, the monarchy was at least well enough established to weather the policies of the next two monarchs, Charles VIII (1483–1498) and Louis XII (1498–1515), whose attempts to subdue parts of Italy initiated a series of Italian wars. Internally, France survived these wars without too much difficulty.

ENGLAND: CIVIL WAR AND A NEW MONARCHY

The Hundred Years' War had also strongly affected the other protagonist in that conflict. The cost of the war in its final years and the losses in manpower strained the English economy. Moreover, the end of the war brought even greater domestic turmoil to England when the War of the Roses broke out in the 1450s. This civil war pitted the ducal house of Lancaster, whose symbol was a red rose, against the ducal house of York, whose symbol was a white rose. Many aristocratic families of England were drawn into the conflict. Finally, in 1485, Henry Tudor, duke of Richmond, defeated the last Yorkist king, Richard III (1483–1485), at Bosworth Field and established the new Tudor dynasty.

As the first Tudor king, Henry VII (1485–1509) worked to reduce internal dissension and establish a strong monarchical government. The English aristocracy had been much weakened by the War of the Roses because many nobles had been killed. Henry eliminated the private wars of the nobility by abolishing "livery and maintenance," the practice by which wealthy aristocrats maintained private armies of followers dedicated to the service of their lord. Since England, unlike France and Spain, did not possess a standing army, the king relied on special commissions to trusted nobles to raise troops for a specific campaign, after which the troops were disbanded. Henry also controlled the irresponsible activity of the nobles by establishing the Court of Star Chamber, which did not use juries and allowed torture to be used to extract confessions.

Henry VII was particularly successful in extracting income from the traditional financial resources of the English monarch, such as the crown lands, judicial fees and fines, and customs duties. By using diplomacy to avoid wars, which are always expensive, the king avoided having to call Parliament on any regular basis to grant him funds. By not overburdening the landed gentry and middle class with taxes, Henry won their favor, and they provided much support for his monarchy.

Henry also encouraged commercial activity. By increasing wool exports, royal export taxes on wool rose. Henry's thriftiness as well as his domestic and foreign policies enabled him to leave England with a stable and prosperous government and an enhanced status for the monarchy itself.

THE UNIFICATION OF SPAIN

During the Middle Ages, several independent Christian kingdoms had emerged in the course of the long reconquest of the Iberian peninsula from the Muslims. Aragon and Castile were the strongest Spanish kingdoms; in the west was the independent monarchy of Portugal; in the north, the small kingdom of Navarre, oriented toward France; and in the south, the Muslim kingdom of Granada. Few people at the beginning of the fifteenth century could have predicted the unification of the Iberian kingdoms.

A major step in that direction was taken with the marriage of Isabella of Castile (1474–1504) and Ferdinand of Aragon (1479–1516) in 1469. This marriage was a dynastic union of two rulers, not a political union. Both kingdoms maintained their own parliaments (Cortes), courts, laws, coinage, speech, customs, and political organs. Nevertheless, the two rulers worked to strengthen royal control of government, especially in Castile. The royal council, which was supposed to supervise local administration and oversee the implementation of government policies, was stripped of aristocrats and filled primarily with middle-class lawyers. Trained in the principles of Roman law, these officials operated on the belief that the monarchy embodied the power of the state.

The towns were also enlisted in the policy of state building. Medieval town organizations known as *hermandades* ("brotherhoods"), which had been organized to maintain law and order, were revived. Ferdinand and Isabella transformed them into a kind of national militia whose primary goal was to stop the wealthy landed aristocrats from disturbing the peace, a goal also favored by the middle class. The *hermandades* were disbanded by 1498 when the royal administration became strong enough to deal with lawlessness. The appointment of *corregidores* by the crown to replace corrupt municipal officials enabled the monarchs to extend the central authority of royal government into the towns.

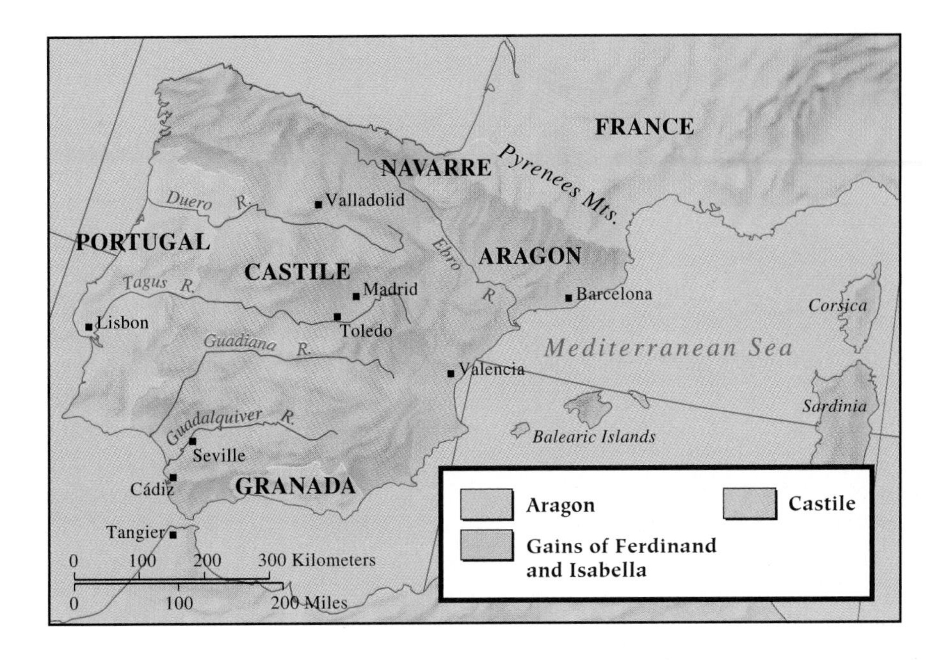

MAP 12.3 **The Iberian Peninsula.**

Seeking to replace the undisciplined feudal levies they had inherited with a more professional royal army, Ferdinand and Isabella reorganized the military forces of Spain. The development of a strong infantry force as the heart of the new Spanish army made it the best in Europe by the sixteenth century.

Ferdinand and Isabella recognized the importance of controlling the Catholic church with its vast power and wealth. They secured from the pope the right to select the most important church officials in Spain, virtually guaranteeing the foundation of a Spanish Catholic church in which the clergy became an instrument for the extension of royal power. The monarchs, who were sincere Catholics, also used their authority over the church to institute reform. Isabella's chief minister, the able and astute Cardinal Ximenes, restored discipline and eliminated immorality among the monks and secular clergy.

The religious zeal exhibited in Cardinal Ximenes's reform program was also evident in the policy of strict religious uniformity pursued by Ferdinand and Isabella. Of course, it served a political purpose as well: to create unity and further bolster royal power. Spain possessed two large religious minorities, the Jews and Muslims, both of whom had been largely tolerated in medieval Spain. In some areas of Spain, Jews exercised much influence in economic and intellectual affairs. Increased persecution in the fourteenth century, however, led the majority of Spanish Jews to convert to Christianity. Although many of these *conversos* came to play important roles in Spanish society, complaints that they were secretly reverting to Judaism prompted Ferdinand and Isabella to ask the pope to introduce the Inquisition into Spain in 1478. Under royal control, the Inquisition worked with cruel efficiency to guarantee the orthodoxy of the *conversos*, but had no authority over practicing Jews. Consequently, in 1492, flush with the success of the conquest of Muslim Granada, Ferdinand and Isabella took the drastic step of expelling all professed Jews from Spain. It is estimated that 150,000 out of possibly 200,000 Jews fled.

Muslims, too, were "encouraged" to convert to Christianity after the conquest of Granada. In 1502, Isabella issued a decree expelling all professed Muslims from her kingdom. To a very large degree, the "Most Catholic" monarchs had achieved their goal of absolute religious orthodoxy as a basic ingredient of the Spanish state. To be Spanish was to be Catholic, a policy of uniformity enforced by the Inquisition.

During the reigns of Ferdinand and Isabella, Spain (or the union of Castile and Aragon) began to emerge as an important power in European affairs. Both Granada and Navarre had been conquered and incorporated into the royal realms. Nevertheless, Spain remained divided in many ways. Only the royal dynasty provided the centralizing force, and when a single individual, the grandson of Ferdinand and Isabella, succeeded both rulers as Charles I in 1516, he inherited lands that made him the most powerful monarch of his age.

THE HOLY ROMAN EMPIRE: THE SUCCESS OF THE HABSBURGS

Unlike France, England, and Spain, the Holy Roman Empire failed to develop a strong monarchical authority. After 1438, the position of Holy Roman Emperor remained in the hands of the Habsburg dynasty. Having gradually acquired a number of possessions along the Danube, known collectively as Austria, the house of Habsburg had become one of the wealthiest landholders in the empire and by the mid-fifteenth century began to play an important role in European affairs.

Much of the Habsburg success in the fifteenth century was due not to military success, but to a well-executed

EMPEROR MAXIMILIAN I. Although the Holy Roman Emperor possessed little power in Germany, the Habsburg dynasty, which held the position of emperor after 1438, steadily increased its wealth and landholdings through dynastic marriages. This portrait of Emperor Maximilian I reflects well the description by a Venetian ambassador: "He is not very fair of face, but well proportioned, exceedingly robust, of sanguine and choleric complexion and very healthy for his age."

policy of dynastic marriages. As the old Habsburg motto said: "Leave the waging of wars to others! But you, happy Austria, marry; for the realms which Mars [god of war] awards to others, Venus [goddess of love] transfers to you." Although Frederick III (1440–1493) lost the traditional Habsburg possessions of Bohemia and Hungary, he gained Franche-Comté in east-central France, Luxembourg, and a large part of the Low Countries by marrying his son Maximilian to Mary, the daughter of Duke Charles the Bold of Burgundy. The addition of these territories made the Habsburg dynasty an international power and brought them the undying opposition of the French monarchy because the rulers of France feared they would be surrounded by the Habsburgs.

Much was expected of the flamboyant Maximilian I (1493–1519) when he became emperor. Through the Reichstag, the imperial diet or parliament, Maximilian attempted to centralize the administration by creating new institutions common to the entire empire. Opposition from the German princes doomed these efforts, however. Maximilian's only real success lay in his marriage alliances. Philip of Burgundy, the son of Maximilian's marriage to Mary, was married to Joanna, the daughter of Ferdinand and Isabella. Philip and Joanna produced a son, Charles, who, through a series of unexpected deaths, became heir to all three lines, the Habsburg, Burgundian, and Spanish, making him the leading monarch of his age (see Chapter 13).

Although the Holy Roman Empire did not develop along the lines of a centralized monarchical state, within the empire the power of the independent princes and electors increased steadily. In numerous German states, such as Bavaria, Hesse, Brandenburg, and the Palatinate, princes built up bureaucracies, developed standing armies, created fiscal systems, and introduced Roman law, just like the national monarchs of France, England, and Spain. They posed a real threat to the church, the emperor, and other smaller independent bodies in the Holy Roman Empire, especially the free imperial cities.

THE STRUGGLE FOR STRONG MONARCHY IN EASTERN EUROPE

In eastern Europe, rulers struggled to achieve the centralization of their territorial states but faced serious obstacles. Although the population was mostly Slavic, there were islands of other ethnic groups that caused untold difficulties. Religious differences also troubled the area, as Roman Catholics, Greek Orthodox Christians, and pagans confronted each other.

Much of Polish history revolved around the bitter struggle between the crown and the landed nobility. The dynastic union of Jagiello, grand prince of Lithuania, with the Polish queen Jadwiga resulted in a large Lithuanian-Polish state in 1386. Jagiello and his immediate successors were able to control the landed magnates, but by the end of the fifteenth century, the preoccupation of Poland's rulers with problems in Bohemia and Hungary as well as war with the Russians and Turks enabled the aristocrats to reestablish their power. Through their control of the *Sejm* or national diet, the magnates reduced the peasantry to serfdom by 1511 and established the right to elect their kings. The Polish kings proved unable to establish a strong royal authority.

Bohemia, Poland's neighbor, was part of the Holy Roman Empire, but distrust of the Germans and close ethnic ties to the Poles and Slovaks encouraged the Czechs to associate with their northeastern Slavic neighbors. The Hussite wars (see The Problems of Heresy and Reform later in this chapter) led to further dissension and civil war. Because of a weak monarchy, the Bohemian nobles increased their authority and wealth at the expense of both crown and church.

The history of Hungary had been closely tied to that of central and western Europe by its conversion to Roman Catholicism by German missionaries. The church became a large and prosperous institution. Wealthy bishops, along with the great territorial lords, became powerful, independent political figures. For a brief while, Hungary developed into an important European state, the dominant power in eastern Europe. King Matthias Corvinus (1458–1490) broke the power of the wealthy lords and created a well-organized bureaucracy. Like a typical Renais-

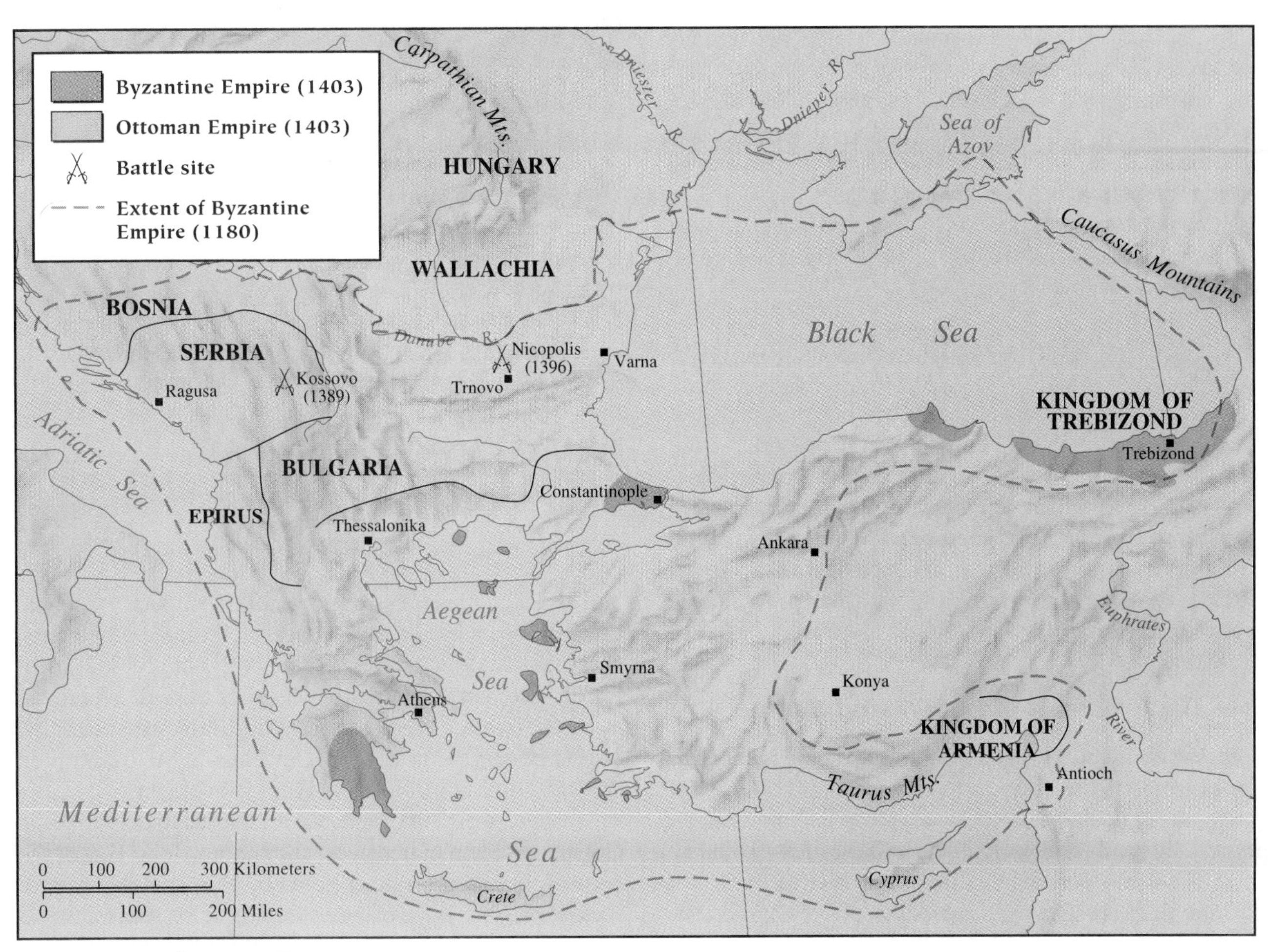

MAP 12.4 **Southeastern Europe.**

sance prince, he patronized the new humanist culture, brought Italian scholars and artists to his capital at Buda, and made his court one of the most brilliant outside Italy. After his death, Hungary returned to weak rule, and the work of Corvinus was largely undone.

Since the thirteenth century, Russia had been under the domination of the Mongols. Gradually, the princes of Moscow rose to prominence by using their close relationship to the Mongol khans to increase their wealth and expand their possessions. In the reign of the great prince Ivan III (1462–1505), a new Russian state was born. Ivan III annexed other Russian principalities and took advantage of dissension among the Mongols to throw off their yoke by 1480. He invaded the lands of the Lithuanian-Polish dynasty and added the territories around Kiev, Smolensk, and Chernigov to his new Muscovite state.

THE OTTOMAN TURKS AND THE END OF BYZANTIUM

Eastern Europe was increasingly threatened by the steadily advancing Ottoman Turks. The Byzantine Empire had, of course, served as a buffer between the Muslim Middle East and the Latin West for centuries. It was severely weakened by the sack of Constantinople in 1204 and its occupation by the west. Although the Palaeologus dynasty (1260–1453) had tried to reestablish Byzantine power in the Balkans after the overthrow of the Latin Empire, the threat from the Turks finally doomed the long-lasting empire.

Beginning in northeastern Asia Minor in the thirteenth century, the Ottoman Turks spread rapidly, seizing the lands of the Seljuk Turks and the Byzantine Empire. In 1345, they bypassed Constantinople and moved into the Balkans, which they conquered by the end of the century. Finally, in 1453, the great city of Constantinople fell to the Turks after a siege of several months. After consolidating their power, the Turks prepared to exert renewed pressure on the west, both in the Mediterranean and up the Danube valley toward Vienna. By the end of the fifteenth century, they were threatening Hungary, Austria, Bohemia, and Poland. The Holy Roman Emperor, Charles V, became their bitter enemy in the sixteenth century.

Our survey of European political developments makes it clear that, although individual German or especially Italian princes had developed culturally brilliant states, the future belonged to territorial states organized by national monarchies. They possessed superior resources and were developing institutions that represented the interests of much of the population. Nevertheless, the Renaissance states were still only dynastic states, not nation-states. The interests of a state were the interests of its ruling dynasty. Loyalty was owed to the ruler, not the state. Residents of France considered themselves subjects of the French king, not citizens of France. Moreover, although Renaissance monarchs were strong rulers centralizing their authority, they were by no means absolute monarchs. Some chance of representative government still remained in the form of Parliament, Estates-General, Cortes, or Reichstag. Monarchs were strongest in the west and, with the exception of the Russian rulers, weakest in the east.

◆ The Church in the Renaissance

As a result of the efforts of the Council of Constance, the Great Schism had finally been brought to an end in 1417 (see Chapter 11). The council had had three major objectives: to end the schism, to eradicate heresy, and to reform the church in "head and members." The ending of the schism proved to be the council's easiest task; it was much less successful in dealing with the problems of heresy and reform.

The Problems of Heresy and Reform

Heresy was, of course, not a new problem, and in the thirteenth century, the church had developed inquisitorial machinery to deal with it. But two widespread movements in the fourteenth and early fifteenth centuries—Lollardy and Hussitism—posed new threats to the church.

English Lollardy was a product of the Oxford theologian John Wyclif (c. 1328–1384), whose disgust with clerical corruption led him to a far-ranging attack on papal authority and medieval Christian beliefs and practices. Wyclif alleged that there was no basis in Scripture for papal claims of temporal authority and advocated that the popes be stripped of both their authority and property. At one point, he even denounced the pope as the Antichrist. Believing that the Bible should be a Christian's sole authority, Wyclif urged that it be made available in the vernacular languages so that every Christian could read it. Rejecting all practices not mentioned in Scripture, Wyclif condemned pilgrimages, the veneration of saints, and a whole series of rituals and rites that had developed in the medieval church.

Wyclif has sometimes been viewed as a forerunner of the Reformation of the sixteenth century because his arguments attacked the foundations of the medieval Catholic church's organization and practices. His attacks on church property were especially popular, and he attracted a number of followers who came to be known as Lollards. Persecution by royal and church authorities who feared the socioeconomic consequences of Wyclif's ideas forced the Lollards to go underground after 1400.

A marriage between the royal families of England and Bohemia enabled Lollard ideas to spread to Bohemia, where they reinforced the ideas of a group of Czech reformers led by the chancellor of the university at Prague, John Hus (1374–1415). In his call for reform, Hus urged the elimination of the worldliness and corruption of the clergy and attacked the excessive power of the papacy within the Catholic church. Hus's objections fell on receptive ears, since the Catholic church as one of the largest landowners in Bohemia was already widely criticized. Moreover, many clergymen were German, and the native Czechs' strong resentment of the Germans who dominated Bohemia also contributed to Hus's movement.

The Council of Constance attempted to deal with the growing problem of heresy by summoning John Hus to the council. Granted a safe conduct by Emperor Sigismund, Hus went in the hope of a free hearing of his ideas. Instead he was arrested, condemned as a heretic (by a narrow vote), and burned at the stake in 1415. This action turned the unrest in Bohemia into revolutionary upheaval. The resulting Hussite wars combined religious, social, and national issues and wracked the Holy Roman Empire until a truce was arranged in 1436.

The reform of the church in "head and members" was even less successful than the attempt to eradicate heresy. Two reform decrees were passed by the Council of Constance. *Sacrosancta* stated that a general council of the church received its authority from God; hence, every Christian, including the pope, was subject to its authority. The decree *Frequens* provided for the regular holding of general councils to ensure that church reform would continue. Taken together, *Sacrosancta* and *Frequens* provided for an ecclesiastical legislative system within the church superior to the popes.

Decrees alone, however, proved insufficient to reform the church. Councils could issue decrees, but popes had to execute them and popes would not cooperate with councils that diminished their authority. Beginning as early as Martin V in 1417, successive popes worked steadfastly for the next thirty years to defeat the conciliar movement. The victory of the popes and the final blow to the conciliar movement came in 1460, when Pope Pius II issued the papal bull *Execrabilis*, condemning appeals to a council over the head of a pope as heretical.

By the mid-fifteenth century, the popes had reasserted their supremacy over the Catholic church. No

CHRONOLOGY

The Church in the Renaissance

Council of Constance	1414–1418
Burning of John Hus	1415
End of the Great Schism	1417
Pius II issues the papal bull *Execrabilis*	1460
The Renaissance papacy	
Sixtus IV	1471–1484
Alexander VI	1492–1503
Julius II	1503–1513
Leo X	1513–1521

longer, however, did they have any possibility of asserting supremacy over temporal governments as the medieval papacy had. Although the papal monarchy had been maintained, it had lost much moral prestige. In the fifteenth century, the Renaissance papacy contributed to an even further decline in the moral leadership of the popes.

The Renaissance Papacy

Historians use the phrase "Renaissance papacy" to refer to the line of popes from the end of the Great Schism (1417) to the beginnings of the Reformation in the early sixteenth century. The primary concern of the papacy is governing the Catholic church as its spiritual leader. But as heads of the church, popes had temporal preoccupations as well, and the story of the Renaissance papacy is really an account of how the latter came to overshadow the popes' spiritual functions. In the process, the Renaissance papacy and the Catholic church became noticeably secularized.

The preoccupation of the popes with the territory of the Papal States and Italian politics was not new to the Renaissance. Popes had been temporal as well as spiritual rulers for centuries. The manner in which Renaissance popes pursued their temporal interests, however, especially their use of intrigue, deceit, and open bloodshed, was shocking. Of all the Renaissance popes, Julius II (1503–1513) was most involved in war and politics. The fiery "warrior-pope" personally led armies against his enemies, much to the disgust of pious Christians who viewed the pope as a spiritual leader. The great humanist Erasmus (see Chapter 13) witnessed the triumphant entry of Julius II into Bologna at the head of his troops and later wrote scathing indictments of the papal proclivity for warfare. With Julius II in mind, he proclaimed in *The Complaint of Peace:* "How, O bishop standing in the room of the Apostles, dare you teach the people the things that pertain to war?"

To further their territorial aims in the Papal States, the popes needed financial resources and loyal servants. Preoccupation with finances was not new, but its grossness received considerable comment: "Whenever I entered the chambers of the ecclesiastics of the Papal court, I found brokers and clergy engaged and reckoning money which lay in heaps before them."[25] Since they were not hereditary monarchs, popes could not build dynasties over several generations and came to rely on the practice of nepotism to promote their families' interests. Pope Sixtus IV (1471–1484), for example, made five of his nephews cardinals and gave them an abundance of church offices to build up their finances (the word *nepotism* is, in fact, derived from *nepos,* meaning nephew). Alexander VI (1492–1503), a member of the Borgia family who was known for his debauchery and sensuality, raised one son, one nephew, and the brother of one mistress to the cardinalate. A Venetian envoy stated that Alexander, "joyous by nature, thought of nothing but the aggrandizement of his children." Alexander scandalized the church by encouraging his son Cesare to carve a territorial state in central Italy out of the territories of the Papal States.

A RENAISSANCE POPE: SIXTUS IV. The Renaissance popes allowed secular concerns to overshadow their spiritual duties. They became concerned with territorial expansion, finances, and Renaissance culture. Pope Sixtus IV built the Sistine Chapel and later had it decorated by some of the leading artists of his day. This fresco by Melozzo da Forlì shows the pope on his throne receiving the humanist Platina (kneeling), who was keeper of the Vatican Library.

The Renaissance popes were great patrons of Renaissance culture, and their efforts made Rome the focal point of the High Renaissance at the beginning of the sixteenth century. For the warrior-pope Julius II, the patronage of Renaissance culture was mostly a matter of policy as he endeavored to add to the splendor of his pontificate by tearing down the Basilica of Saint Peter, which had been built by the emperor Constantine, and beginning construction of the greatest building in Christendom, the present Saint Peter's Basilica. Julius's successor, Leo X (1513–1521), was also a patron of Renaissance culture, not as a matter of policy, but as a deeply involved participant. Such might be expected of the son of Lorenzo de' Medici. Made an archbishop at the age of eight and a cardinal at thirteen, he acquired a refined taste in art, manners, and social life among the Florentine Renaissance elite. He became pope at the age of thirty-seven, supposedly remarking to the Venetian ambassador, "Let us enjoy the papacy, since God has given it to us." Humanists were made papal secretaries, Raphael was commissioned to do paintings, and the construction of Saint Peter's was accelerated as Rome became the literary and artistic center of the Renaissance.

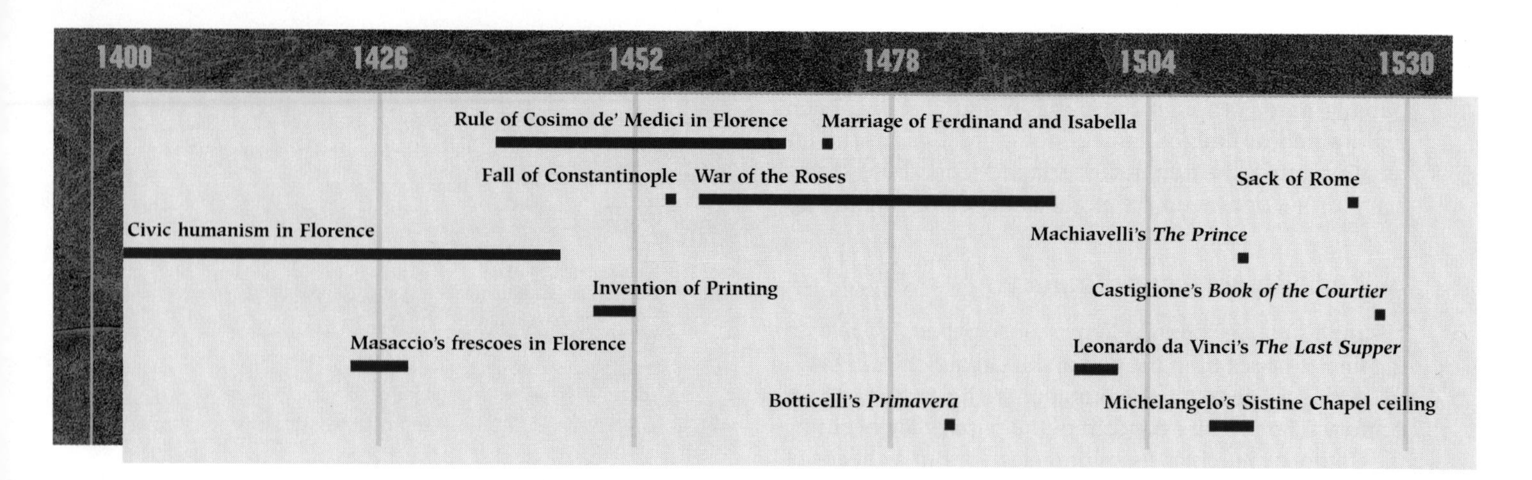

CONCLUSION

Whether the Renaissance represents the end of the Middle Ages or the beginning of a new era, a frequently debated topic among medieval and Renaissance historians, is perhaps an irrelevant question. The Renaissance was a period of transition that witnessed a continuation of the economic, political, and social trends that had begun in the High Middle Ages. It was also a movement in which intellectuals and artists proclaimed a new vision of humankind and raised fundamental questions about the value and importance of the individual. Of course, intellectuals and artists wrote and painted for the upper classes, and the brilliant intellectual, cultural, and artistic accomplishments of the Renaissance were products of and for the elite. The ideas of the Renaissance did not have a broad base among the masses of the people. As Lorenzo the Magnificent, ruler of Florence, once commented: "Only men of noble birth can obtain perfection. The poor, who work with their hands and have no time to cultivate their minds, are incapable of it."

The Renaissance did, however, raise new questions about medieval traditions. In advocating a return to the early sources of Christianity and criticizing current religious practices, the humanists raised fundamental issues about the Catholic church, which was still an important institution. In the sixteenth century, the intellectual revolution of the fifteenth century gave way to a religious renaissance that touched the lives of people, including the masses, in new and profound ways. After the Reformation, Europe would never again be the unified Christian commonwealth it once believed it was.

NOTES

1. Quoted in Jacob Burckhardt, *The Civilization of the Renaissance in Italy,* trans. S. G. C. Middlemore (London, 1960), p. 81.
2. Baldassare Castiglione, *The Book of the Courtier,* trans. Charles S. Singleton (Garden City, N.Y., 1959), pp. 288–289.
3. Quoted in De Lamar Jensen, *Renaissance Europe* (Lexington, Mass., 1981), p. 94.
4. Quoted in Iris Origo, "The Domestic Enemy: The Eastern Slaves in Tuscany in the Fourteenth and Fifteenth Centuries," *Speculum* 30 (1955): 333.
5. Gene Brucker, ed., *Two Memoirs of Renaissance Florence* (New York, 1967), p. 132.
6. Quoted in Margaret L. King, *Women of the Renaissance* (Chicago, 1991), p. 3.
7. Gene Brucker, ed., *The Society of Renaissance Florence* (New York, 1971), p. 190.
8. Quoted in Garrett Mattingly, *Renaissance Diplomacy* (Baltimore, 1964), p. 42.
9. Ibid., p. 95.
10. Niccolò Machiavelli, *The Prince,* trans. David Wootton (Indianapolis, 1995), p. 48.
11. Ibid., p. 55.
12. Ibid., pp. 27, 77, 80.
13. Niccolò Machiavelli, *The Discourses,* trans. Christian Detmold (New York, 1950), p. 148.
14. Petrarch, "Epistle to Posterity," *Letters from Petrarch,* trans. Morris Bishop (Bloomington, Ind., 1966), pp. 6–7.
15. Bernhardt J. Hurwood, trans., *The Facetiae of Giovanni Francesco Poggio Bracciolini* (New York, 1968), p. 57.
16. Quoted in Frances Yates, *Giordano Bruno and the Hermetic Tradition* (Chicago, 1964), p. 211.
17. Giovanni Pico della Mirandola, *Oration on the Dignity of Man,* in E. Cassirer, P. O. Kristeller, J. H. Randall, Jr., eds., *The Renaissance Philosophy of Man* (Chicago, 1948), p. 225.
18. Ibid., pp. 247–249.
19. W. H. Woodward, *Vittorino da Feltre and Other Humanist Educators* (Cambridge, 1897), p. 102.
20. Ibid., pp. 106–107.
21. Quoted in Iris Origo, "The Education of Renaissance Man," *The Light of the Past* (New York, 1959), p. 136.
22. Quoted in Elizabeth G. Holt, ed., *A Documentary History of Art* (Garden City, N.Y., 1957), 1:286.
23. Quoted in Rosa M. Letts, *The Cambridge Introduction to Art: The Renaissance* (Cambridge, 1981), p. 86.
24. Quoted in Johan Huizinga, *The Waning of the Middle Ages* (Garden City, N.Y., 1956), p. 265.
25. Quoted in Alexander C. Flick, *The Decline of the Medieval Church* (London, 1930), 1:180.

SUGGESTIONS FOR FURTHER READING

The classic study of the Italian Renaissance is J. Burckhardt, *The Civilization of the Renaissance in Italy*, trans. S. G. C. Middlemore (London, 1960), first published in 1860. General works on the Renaissance in Europe include D. L. Jensen, *Renaissance Europe* (Lexington, Mass., 1981); P. Burke, *The European Renaissance: Centres and Peripheries* (Oxford, 1998); E. Breisach, *Renaissance Europe, 1300–1517* (New York, 1973); J. Hale, *The Civilization of Europe in the Renaissance* (New York, 1994); and the classic work by M. P. Gilmore, *The World of Humanism, 1453–1517* (New York, 1962). Although many of its interpretations are outdated, W. Ferguson's *Europe in Transition, 1300–1520* (Boston, 1962), contains a wealth of information. The brief study by P. Burke, *The Renaissance*, 2d ed. (New York, 1997), is a good summary of recent literature on the Renaissance. For beautifully illustrated introductions to the Renaissance, see G. Holmes, *Renaissance* (New York, 1996); and M. Aston, ed., *The Panorama of the Renaissance* (New York, 1996).

Brief, but basic works on Renaissance economic matters are H. A. Miskimin, *The Economy of Early Renaissance Europe, 1300–1460* (New York, 1975) and *The Economy of Later Renaissance Europe, 1460–1600* (New York, 1978). For a new interpretation of economic matters, see L. Jardine, *Worldly Goods* (New York, 1996). Numerous facets of social life in the Renaissance are examined in J. R. Hale, *Renaissance Europe: The Individual and Society* (London, 1971); B. Pullan, *Rich and Poor in Renaissance Venice* (Cambridge, Mass., 1971); J. H. Langbein, *Prosecuting Crime in the Renaissance* (Cambridge, Mass., 1974); and G. Ruggiero, *The Boundaries of Eros: Sex Crime and Sexuality in Renaissance Venice* (Oxford, 1985). On family and marriage, see D. Herlihy, *The Family in Renaissance Italy* (St. Louis, 1974); C. Klapisch-Zuber, *Women, Family, and Ritual in Renaissance Italy* (Chicago, 1985); and the well-told story by G. Brucker, *Giovanni and Lusanna: Love and Marriage in Renaissance Florence* (Berkeley, 1986). On women, see M. L. King, *Women of the Renaissance* (Chicago, 1991); and N. Z. Davis and A. Farge, eds., *A History of Women: Renaissance and Enlightenment Paradoxes* (Cambridge, Mass., 1993).

The best overall study of the Italian city-states is L. Martines, *Power and Imagination: City-States in Renaissance Italy* (New York, 1979), although D. Hay and J. Law, *Italy in the Age of the Renaissance* (London, 1989), is also a good survey. There is an enormous literature on Renaissance Florence. The best introduction is G. A. Brucker, *Renaissance Florence*, rev. ed. (Berkeley and Los Angeles, 1983). A popular biography of Isabella d'Este is G. Marek, *The Bed and the Throne* (New York, 1976). On the *condottieri*, see M. Mallett, *Mercenaries and Their Masters: Warfare in Renaissance Italy* (Totowa, 1974). The work by G. Mattingly, *Renaissance Diplomacy* (Boston, 1955) remains the basic one on the subject. Machiavelli's life can be examined in Q. Skinner, *Machiavelli* (Oxford, 1981).

Brief introductions to Renaissance humanism can be found in D. R. Kelley, *Renaissance Humanism* (Boston, 1991); C. G. Nauert, Jr., *Humanism and the Culture of Renaissance Europe* (Cambridge, 1995); and F. B. Artz, *Renaissance Humanism, 1300–1550* (Oberlin, Ohio, 1966). For a good collection of essays, see J. Kraye, ed., *The Cambridge Companion to Renaissance Humanism* (Cambridge, 1996). The fundamental work on fifteenth-century civic humanism is H. Baron, *The Crisis of the Early Italian Renaissance*, 2d ed. (Princeton, N.J., 1966). The classic work on humanist education is W. H. Woodward, *Vittorino da Feltre and Other Humanist Educators* (New York, 1963), first published in 1897. A basic work on the writing of history in the Italian Renaissance is E. Cochrane, *Historians and Historiography in the Italian Renaissance* (Chicago, 1981). The impact of printing is exhaustively examined in E. Eisenstein, *The Printing Press as an Agent of Change*, 2 vols. (New York, 1978).

For brief introductions to Renaissance art, see R. M. Letts, *The Cambridge Introduction to Art: The Renaissance* (Cambridge, 1981); and B. Cole and A. Gealt, *Art of the Western World* (New York, 1989), Chapters 6–8. Good surveys of Renaissance art include F. Hartt, *History of Italian Renaissance Art*, 4th ed. (Englewood Cliffs, N.J., 1994); S. Elliott, *Italian Renaissance Painting*, 2d ed. (London, 1993); R. Turner, *Renaissance Florence: The Invention of a New Art* (New York, 1997); and L. Murray, *The High Renaissance* (New York, 1967). For studies of individual artists, see J. H. Beck, *Raphael* (New York, 1994); M. Kemp, *Leonardo da Vinci: The Marvellous Works of Nature and of Man* (London, 1981); and A. Hughes, *Michelangelo* (London, 1997). On music, see the specialized work by H. M. Brown, *Music in the Renaissance*, 2d ed. (Englewood Cliffs, N.J., 1999).

For a general work on the political development of Europe in the Renaissance, see J. H. Shennan, *The Origins of the Modern European State, 1450–1725* (London, 1974). On France, see D. Potter, *A History of France, 1460–1560* (London, 1995). Early Renaissance England is examined in J. R. Lander, *Crown and Nobility, 1450–1509* (London, 1976). On the first Tudor king, see S. B. Chrimes, *Henry VII* (Berkeley, 1972). Good coverage of Renaissance Spain can be found in J. N. Hillgarth, *The Spanish Kingdoms, 1250–1516*, vol. 2, *Castilian Hegemony, 1410–1516* (New York, 1978). Some good works on eastern Europe include P. W. Knoll, *The Rise of the Polish Monarchy* (Chicago, 1972); and C. A. Macartney, *Hungary: A Short History* (Edinburgh, 1962). On the Ottomans and their expansion, see H. Inalcik, *The Ottoman Empire: The Classical Age, 1300–1600* (London, 1973); and the classic work by S. Runciman, *The Fall of Constantinople, 1453* (Cambridge, 1965).

On problems of heresy and reform, see C. Crowder, *Unity, Heresy and Reform, 1378–1460* (London, 1977). Aspects of the Renaissance papacy can be examined in E. Lee, *Sixtus IV and Men of Letters* (Rome, 1978); and M. Mallett, *The Borgias* (New York, 1969). On Rome, see especially P. Partner, *Renaissance Rome, 1500–1559: A Portrait of a Society* (Berkeley, 1976).

For additional reading, go to InfoTrac College Edition, your online research library at http://web1.infotrac-college.com

Enter the search term *Renaissance* using the Subject Guide.

Enter the search term *Machiavelli* using Key Terms.

Enter the search term *humanism* using Subject Guide.

Enter the search terms *Leonardo da Vinci* using Key Terms.

C H A P T E R

13 The Age of Reformation

CHAPTER OUTLINE

- Prelude to Reformation: The Northern Renaissance
- Prelude to Reformation: Church and Religion on the Eve of the Reformation
- Martin Luther and the Reformation in Germany
- Germany and the Reformation: Religion and Politics
- The Spread of the Protestant Reformation
- The Social Impact of the Protestant Reformation
- The Catholic Reformation
- Conclusion

FOCUS QUESTIONS

- Who were the Christian humanists, and how did they differ from the Protestant reformers?
- What were Martin Luther's main disagreements with the Roman Catholic church, and why did the movement he began spread so quickly across Europe?
- What were the main tenets of Lutheranism, Zwinglianism, Calvinism, and Anabaptism, and how did they differ from each other and from Catholicism?
- What impact did the Protestant Reformation have on the society of the sixteenth century?
- What measures did the Roman Catholic church take to reform itself and to combat Protestantism in the sixteenth century?

ON APRIL 18, 1520, a lowly monk stood before the emperor and princes of Germany in the city of Worms. He had been called before this august gathering to answer charges of heresy, charges that could threaten his very life. The monk was confronted with a pile of his books and asked if he wished to defend them all or reject a part. Courageously, Martin Luther defended them all and asked to be shown where any part was in error on the basis of "Scripture and plain reason." The emperor was outraged by Luther's response and made his own position clear the next day: "Not only I, but you of this noble German nation, would be forever disgraced if by our negligence not only heresy but the very suspicion of heresy were to survive. After having heard yesterday the obstinate defense of Luther, I regret that I have so long delayed in proceeding against him and his false teaching. I will have no more to do with him." Luther's appearance at Worms set the stage for a serious challenge to the authority of the Catholic church. This was by no means the first crisis in the church's 1,500-year history, but its consequences were more far-reaching than anyone at Worms in 1520 could have imagined.

Throughout the Middle Ages, the Catholic church continued to assert its primacy of position. It had overcome defiance of its temporal authority by emperors, and challenges to its doctrines had been crushed by the Inquisition and combated by new religious orders that carried its message of salvation to all the towns and villages of medieval Europe. The growth of the papacy had paralleled the growth of the church, but by the end of the Middle Ages challenges to papal authority from the rising power of monarchical states had resulted in a loss of papal temporal authority. An even greater threat to papal authority and church unity arose in the sixteenth century when the unity of Christendom was shattered by the Reformation.

The movement begun by Martin Luther when he made his dramatic stand quickly spread across Europe, a clear indication of dissatisfaction with Catholic practices. Within a short time, new forms of religious practices, doctrines, and organizations, including Zwinglianism, Calvinism, Anabaptism, and Anglicanism, were attracting adherents all over Europe. Although seemingly helpless to stop the new Protestant churches, the Catholic church also underwent a religious renaissance and managed by the mid-sixteenth century to revive its fortunes. Those historians who speak of the Reformation as the beginning of the modern world exaggerate its importance, but there is no doubt that the splintering of Christendom had consequences that ushered in new ways of thinking and at least prepared the ground for modern avenues of growth.

◆ Prelude to Reformation: The Northern Renaissance

Martin Luther's reform movement was not the first in sixteenth-century Europe. Christian or northern Renaissance humanism, which evolved as Italian Renaissance humanism spread to northern Europe, had as one of its major goals the reform of Christendom. The new classical learning of the Italian Renaissance did not spread to the European countries north of the Alps until the second half of the fifteenth century. Northern Europe had fewer ties to the classical past than Italy and was initially less interested in recovering Greco-Roman culture. Gradually, however, a number of intellectuals and artists from the cities north of the Alps went to Italy and returned home enthusiastic about the new education and the recovery of ancient thought and literature that we associate with Italian Renaissance humanism. In this manner, Italian humanism spread to the north, but with some noticeable differences. What, then, are the distinguishing characteristics of northern Renaissance humanism, a movement that flourished from the late fifteenth century until it was overwhelmed by the Reformation in the 1520s?

Christian or Northern Renaissance Humanism

Like their Italian counterparts, northern humanists cultivated a knowledge of the classics, the one common bond that united all humanists into a kind of international fellowship. The northern humanists brought out translations or scholarly editions of the classics for the printing press and sought to reconcile the ethical content of those works with Christian ethics. In the classics, northern humanists felt they had found a morality more humane than the theological arguments of the medieval scholastics.

In returning to the writings of antiquity, northern humanists (who have been called Christian humanists by historians because of their profound preoccupation with religion) also focused on the sources of early Christianity, the Holy Scriptures and the writings of such church fathers as Augustine, Ambrose, and Jerome. In these early Christian writings, they discovered a simple religion that they came to feel had been distorted by the complicated theological arguments of the Middle Ages. Their interest in Christian writings also led them to master Greek for the express purpose of reading the Greek New Testament and such early Greek church fathers as John Chrysostom. Some northern humanists even mastered Hebrew to study the Old Testament in its original language.

Although Christian humanists sought positions as teachers and scholars, the influence of scholastic theologians in the universities often made it difficult for them to do so. So long as they stuck to the classics, Christian humanists coexisted amicably with the scholastic theologians, but when they began to call for radical change in the methods and aims of theological study, they ran into bitter opposition. On the other hand, northern Renaissance humanists had opportunities to serve as secretaries to kings, princes, and cities, where their ability to write good prose and deliver orations made them useful. Support for humanism came from other directions as well, notably from patricians, lawyers, and civic officials, especially in the south German cities.

The most important characteristic of northern humanism was its reform program. With their belief in the ability of human beings to reason and improve themselves, the northern humanists felt that through education in the sources of classical, and especially Christian, antiquity, they could instill a true inner piety or an inward religious feeling that would bring about a reform of the church and society. For this reason, Christian humanists supported schools, brought out new editions of the classics, and prepared new editions of the Bible and writings of the church fathers. In the preface to his edition of the Greek New Testament, the famous humanist Erasmus wrote:

> Indeed, I disagree very much with those who are unwilling that Holy Scripture, translated into the vulgar tongue, be read by the uneducated, as if Christ taught such intricate doctrines that they could scarcely be understood by very few theologians, or as if the strength of the Christian religion consisted in men's ignorance of it . . . I would that even the lowliest women read the Gospels and the Pauline Epistles. And I would that they were translated into all languages so that they could be read and understood not only by Scots and Irish but also by Turks and Saracens. . . . Would that, as a result, the farmer sing some portion of them at the plow, the weaver hum some parts of them to the movement of his shuttle, the traveler lighten the weariness of the journey with stories of this kind![1]

ERASMUS. Desiderius Erasmus was the most influential of the northern Renaissance humanists. He sought to restore Christianity to the early simplicity found in the teachings of Jesus. This portrait of Erasmus was painted in 1523 by Hans Holbein the Younger, who had formed a friendship with the great humanist while they were both in Basel.

This belief in the power of education would remain an important characteristic of European civilization. Like later intellectuals, Christian humanists believed that to change society they must first change the human beings who compose it. Although some have viewed the Christian humanists as naive, they themselves were very optimistic. Erasmus proclaimed in a letter to Pope Leo X: "I congratulate this our age—which bids fair to be an age of gold, if ever such there was—wherein I see . . . three of the chief blessings of humanity are about to be restored to her. I mean, first, that truly Christian piety, . . . secondly, learning of the best sort, . . . and thirdly, the public and lasting concord of Christendom."[2] This belief that a golden age could be achieved by applying the new learning to the reform of church and society proved to be a common bond among the Christian humanists. The turmoil of the Reformation shattered much of this intellectual optimism, as the lives and careers of two of the most prominent Christian humanists, Desiderius Erasmus and Thomas More, illustrate.

ERASMUS

The most influential of all the Christian humanists, and in a way the symbol of the movement itself, was Desiderius Erasmus (1466–1536), who formulated and popularized the reform program of Christian humanism. Born in Holland, Erasmus was educated at one of the schools of the Brothers of the Common Life. He wandered to France, England, Italy, Germany, and Switzerland, conversing everywhere in the classical Latin that might be called his mother tongue. By 1500, he had turned seriously toward religious studies where he concentrated on reconciling the classics and Christianity through their common ethical focus.

In 1500, Erasmus published the *Adages,* an anthology of proverbs from ancient authors that showed his ability in the classics. The *Handbook of the Christian Knight,* printed in 1503, reflected his preoccupation with religion. He called his conception of religion "the philosophy of Christ," by which he meant that Christianity should be a guiding philosophy for the direction of daily life rather than the system of dogmatic beliefs and practices that the medieval church seemed to stress. In other words, he emphasized inner piety and deemphasized the external forms of religion (such as the sacraments, pilgrimages, fasts, veneration of saints, and relics). To return to the simplicity of the early church, people needed to understand the original meaning of the Scriptures and early church fathers. Believing that the standard Latin edition of the Bible, known as the Vulgate, contained errors, Erasmus edited the Greek text of the New Testament from the earliest available manuscripts and published it, along with a new Latin translation, in 1516.

Erasmus: In Praise of Folly

The Praise of Folly is one of the most famous pieces of literature of the sixteenth century. Erasmus, who wrote it in a short period of time during a visit to the home of Thomas More, considered it a "little diversion" from his "serious work." Yet both contemporaries and later generations have appreciated "this laughing parody of every form and rank of human life." In this selection, Erasmus belittles one of his favorite objects of scorn—the monks.

Erasmus, *The Praise of Folly*

Those who are the closest to these [the theologians] in happiness are generally called "the religious" or "monks," both of which are deceiving names, since for the most part they stay as far away from religion as possible and frequent every sort of place. I cannot, however, see how any life could be more gloomy than the life of these monks if I [Folly] did not assist them in many ways. Though most people detest these men so much that accidentally meeting one is considered to be bad luck, the monks themselves believe that they are magnificent creatures. One of their chief beliefs is that to be illiterate is to be of a high state of sanctity, and so they make sure that they are not able to read. Another is that when braying out their gospels in church they are making themselves very pleasing and satisfying to God, when in fact they are uttering these psalms as a matter of repetition rather than from their hearts. . . .

Moreover, it is amusing to find that they insist that everything be done in fastidious detail, as if employing the orderliness of mathematics, a small mistake in which would be a great crime. Just so many knots must be on each shoe and the shoelace may be of only one specified color; just so much lace is allowed on each habit; the girdle must be of just the right material and width; the hood of a certain shape and capacity; their hair of just so many fingers' length; and finally they can sleep only the specified number of hours per day. Can they not understand that, because of a variety of bodies and temperaments, all this equality of restrictions is in fact very unequal? Nevertheless, because of all this detail that they employ they think that they are superior to all other people. And what is more, amid all their pretense of Apostolic charity, the members of one order will denounce the members of another order clamorously because of the way in which the habit has been belted or the slightly darker color of it. . . .

Many of them work so hard at protocol and at traditional fastidiousness that they think one heaven hardly a suitable reward for their labors; never recalling, however, that the time will come when Christ will demand a reckoning of that which he had prescribed, namely charity, and that he will hold their deeds of little account. One monk will then exhibit his belly filled with every kind of fish; another will profess a knowledge of over a hundred hymns. Still another will reveal a countless number of fasts that he has made, and will account for his large belly by explaining that his fasts have always been broken by a single large meal. Another will show a list of church ceremonies over which he has officiated so large that it would fill seven ships.

To Erasmus, the reform of the church meant spreading an understanding of the philosophy of Jesus, providing enlightened education in the sources of early Christianity, and making commonsense criticism of the abuses in the church. The latter is especially evident in his work, *The Praise of Folly,* written in 1509. It is a satirical view of his contemporary society in which folly, personified as a woman, shows how she dominates the affairs of humankind. Through this scheme, Erasmus was able to engage in a humorous, yet effective criticism of the most corrupt practices of his own society. He was especially harsh on the abuses within the ranks of the clergy (see the box above).

Erasmus's reform program was not destined to effect the reform of the church that he so desired. His moderation and his emphasis on education were quickly overwhelmed by the violence unleashed by the passions of the Reformation. Undoubtedly, though, his work helped to prepare the way for the Reformation; as contemporaries proclaimed, "Erasmus laid the egg that Luther hatched." Yet Erasmus eventually disapproved of Luther and the Protestant reformers. He had no intention of destroying the unity of the medieval Christian church, for his whole program was based on reform within the church.

THOMAS MORE

Born the son of a London lawyer, Thomas More (1478–1535) received the benefits of a good education. Although trained in the law, he took an avid interest in the new classical learning and became proficient in both Latin and Greek. Like the Italian humanists who believed in putting their learning at the service of the state, More embarked on a public career that ultimately took him to the highest reaches of power as lord chancellor of England.

His career in government service, however, did not keep More from the intellectual and spiritual interests that were so dear to him. He was well acquainted with other English humanists and became an intimate friend of Erasmus. He made translations from Greek authors and wrote both prose and poetry in Latin. A deeply devout man, he spent many hours in prayer and private devotions. Many praised his household as a shining model of Christian family life.

More's most famous work, and one of the most controversial of his age, was *Utopia*, written in 1516. This literary masterpiece is an account of the idealistic life and institutions of the community of Utopia (literally "nowhere"), an imaginary island in the vicinity of the New World. It reflects More's own concerns with the economic, social, and political problems of his day. He presented a new social system in which cooperation and reason replaced power and fame as the proper motivating agents for human society. Utopian society, therefore, is based on communal ownership rather than private property. All persons work but six hours a day, regardless of occupation, and are rewarded according to their needs. Possessing abundant leisure time and relieved of competition and greed, Utopians were free to do wholesome and enriching things. As More stated in Book II: "All the rest of the twenty-four [hours] they're free to do what they like—not to waste their time in idleness or self-indulgence, but to make good use of it in some congenial activity."[3] More envisioned Utopia as an orderly world where social relations, recreation, and even travel were carefully controlled for the moral welfare of society and its members.

In serving King Henry VIII, More came face to face with the abuses and corruption he had criticized in *Utopia*. But he did not allow the idealism of Utopia to outweigh his own ultimate realism, and in *Utopia* itself he justified his service to the king:

> If you can't completely eradicate wrong ideas, or deal with inveterate vices as effectively as you could wish, that's no reason for turning your back on public life altogether. You wouldn't abandon ship in a storm just because you couldn't control the winds. On the other hand, it's no use attempting to put across entirely new ideas, which will obviously carry no weight with people who are prejudiced against them. You must go to work indirectly. You must handle everything as tactfully as you can, and what you can't put right you must try to make as little wrong as possible. For things will never be perfect, until human beings are perfect—which I don't expect them to be for quite a number of years.[4]

More's religious devotion and belief in the universal Catholic church proved even more important than his service to the king, however. Always the man of conscience, More willingly gave up his life opposing England's break with the Roman Catholic church over the divorce of King Henry VIII.

◆ Prelude to Reformation: Church and Religion on the Eve of the Reformation

The institutional problems of the Catholic church in the fourteenth and fifteenth centuries, especially the failure of the Renaissance popes to provide spiritual leadership, were bound to affect the spiritual life of all Christendom. The general impression of the tenor of religious life on the eve of the Reformation is one of much deterioration, coupled with evidence of a continuing desire for meaningful religious experience from millions of devout laypeople.

The Clergy

The economic changes of the Late Middle Ages and Renaissance and the continuing preoccupation of the papal court with finances had an especially strong impact upon the clergy. One need only read the names of the cardinals in the fifteenth century to realize that the highest positions of the clergy were increasingly held by either the nobility or the wealthier members of the bourgeoisie. At the same time, to enhance their revenues, high church officials accumulated church offices in ever-larger numbers. This practice of pluralism (the holding of many church offices) led, in turn, to the problem of absenteeism, as church officeholders neglected their episcopal duties and delegated the entire administration of their dioceses to priests, who were often underpaid and little interested in performing their duties.

At the same time, these same economic forces led to a growing division between the higher and lower clergy. While cardinals, archbishops, bishops, and abbots vied for church offices and accumulated great wealth, many members of the lower clergy—the parish priests—tended to exist at the same economic level as their parishioners. Social discontent grew, especially among those able and conscientious priests whose path to advancement was blocked by the nobles' domination of higher church offices. By the same token, pluralism on the lower levels left many parishes without episcopal direction of any kind. Such a lack of leadership often resulted in lower clergy of poor quality. The fifteenth century was rife with complaints about the ignorance and incapacity of parish priests, as well as their greed and sexual offenses.

Popular Religion

The atmosphere of the Late Middle Ages and Renaissance, with its uncertainty of life and immediacy of death, brought a craving for meaningful religious expression and certainty of salvation. This impulse, especially strong in Germany, expressed itself in two ways that often seemed contradictory.

One manifestation of religious piety in the fifteenth century was the almost mechanical view of the process of salvation. Collections of relics grew as more and more people sought certainty of salvation through their veneration. By 1509, Frederick the Wise, elector of Saxony and Luther's prince, had amassed over 5,000 relics to which were attached indulgences that could officially reduce one's time in purgatory by 1,443 years (an indulgence is a remission of all or part of the temporal punishment due to sin). Despite the physical dangers, increasing numbers of Christians made pilgrimages to such holy centers as Rome and Jerusalem to gain spiritual benefits.

Another form of religious piety, the quest for a tranquil spirituality, was evident in the popular mystical movement known as the Modern Devotion (see Chapter 11), which spawned the lay religious order, the Brothers and Sisters of the Common Life, and a reform of monastic life in Germany and the Low Countries. The best-known member of the Brothers of the Common Life in the fifteenth century was Thomas à Kempis (1380–1471), to whom most scholars ascribe the writing of the great mystical classic of the Modern Devotion, *The Imitation of Christ*.

One notable feature of *The Imitation of Christ* was its de-emphasis of religious dogma. A life of inner piety, totally dedicated to the moral and ethical precepts of Jesus, was preferable to dogma and intellectual speculation. As Thomas à Kempis stated, "Truly, at the day of judgment we shall not be examined by what we have read, but what we have done; not how well we have spoken, but how religiously we have lived." This portrayal of formal theology as secondary to living a good life had deep roots in an emphasis on the Bible as a Christian's primary guide to the true Christian life. In the New Testament, one could find models for the imitation of Jesus that even the uneducated could understand. The copying and dissemination of the Bible, as well as its exposition, played an important role in the work of the Brothers of the Common Life.

Popular mysticism, then, as seen in the Modern Devotion, bears an important relationship to the Reformation. Although adherents of the Modern Devotion did not question the traditional beliefs or practices of the church, their de-emphasis of them in favor of the inner life of the spirit and direct communion with God minimized the importance of the formal church and undermined the position of the church and its clergy in Christians' lives. At the same time, the movement gained its strength through its appeal to laypeople, especially townspeople who liked its direct personal approach to religion.

What is striking about the revival of religious piety in the fifteenth century—whether expressed through such external forces as the veneration of relics and the buying of indulgences or the mystical path—was its adherence to the orthodox beliefs and practices of the Catholic church. The agitation for certainty of salvation and spiritual peace occurred within the framework of the "holy mother Church." But disillusionment grew as the devout experienced the clergy's inability to live up to their expectations. The deepening of religious life, especially in the second half of the fifteenth century, found little echo among the worldly-wise clergy, and it is this environment that helps to explain the tremendous and immediate impact of Luther's ideas.

◆ Martin Luther and the Reformation in Germany

The Protestant Reformation had its beginning in a typical medieval question—what must I do to be saved? Martin Luther, a deeply religious man, found an answer that did not fit within the traditional teachings of the late medieval church. Ultimately, he split with that church, destroying the religious unity of western Christendom. That other people were concerned with the same question is evident in the rapid spread of the Reformation. But religion was so entangled in the social, economic, and political forces of the period that the Protestant reformers' hope of transforming the church quickly proved illusory.

The Early Luther

Martin Luther was born on November 10, 1483, into a peasant family, although his father raised himself into the ranks of the lower bourgeoisie by going into mining. His father wanted him to become a lawyer, so Luther enrolled at the University of Erfurt where he received his bachelor's degree in 1502. In 1505, after becoming a master in the liberal arts, the young Martin began to study law. Luther was not content with the study of law and all along had shown religious inclinations. In the summer of 1505, en route back to Erfurt after a brief visit home, he was caught in a ferocious thunderstorm and vowed that, if he were spared, he would become a monk. He then entered the monastic order of the Augustinian Hermits in Erfurt, much to his father's disgust. While in the monastery, Luther focused on his major concern, the assurance of salvation. The traditional beliefs and practices of the church seemed unable to relieve his obsession with this question, especially evident in his struggle with the sacrament of penance or confession. The sacraments were a Catholic's chief means of receiving God's grace; that of confession offered the opportunity to have one's sins forgiven. Luther spent hours confessing his sins, but he was always doubtful. Had he remembered all of his sins? Even more, how could a hopeless sinner be acceptable to a totally just and all-powerful God? Luther threw himself into his monastic routine with a vengeance:

> I was indeed a good monk and kept my order so strictly that I could say that if ever a monk could get to heaven through monastic discipline, I was that monk. . . . And yet my conscience would not give me certainty, but I always doubted and said, "You didn't do that right. You weren't contrite enough. You left that out of your confession." The more I tried to remedy an uncertain, weak and troubled conscience with human traditions, the more I daily found it more uncertain, weaker and more troubled.[5]

Despite his herculean efforts, Luther achieved no certainty and even came, as he once expressed it, to hate "this just God who punishes sinners."

To help overcome his difficulties, his superiors recommended that the intelligent, yet disturbed monk study theology. He received his doctorate in 1512 and then became a professor in the theological faculty at the University of Wittenberg, lecturing on the Bible. Probably sometime between 1513 and 1516, through his study of the Bible, he arrived at an answer to his problem.

Luther's dilemma had derived from his concept of the "justice of God," which he interpreted as a punitive justice in which God weighs the merits or good works

MARTIN LUTHER. **This painting by Lucas Cranach the Elder in 1533 shows Luther at the age of 50. By this time, Luther's reforms had taken hold in many parts of Germany, and Luther himself was a happily married man with five children.**

performed by humans as a necessary precondition for salvation. To Luther it appeared that the church was saying that one must earn salvation by good works. In Luther's eye, human beings, weak and powerless in the sight of an almighty God, could never do enough to justify salvation in these terms. Through his study of the Bible, especially his work on Paul's Epistle to the Romans, Luther rediscovered another way of viewing the justice of God:

> Night and day I pondered until I saw the connection between the justice of God and the statement that "the just shall live by his faith." Then I grasped that the justice of God is that righteousness by which through grace and sheer mercy God justifies us through faith. Thereupon I felt myself to be reborn and to have gone through open doors into paradise.[6]

To Luther, the "justice of God" was now not a punitive justice but the grace of God that bestows salvation freely to humans, not through their good works, but through the sacrifice of Jesus on the cross. Even faith or the power of belief is a product of divine grace or a gift of God. Humans do nothing to merit grace; it is purely God's decision. The doctrine of justification by grace through faith alone became the primary doctrine of the Protestant Reformation (justification is the act by which a person is made deserving of salvation). Since Luther had arrived at this doctrine from his study of Scripture, the Bible became for Luther as for all other Protestants the chief guide to religious truth. Justification by faith and the Bible as the sole authority in religious affairs were the twin pillars of the Protestant Reformation.

The event that propelled Luther into an open confrontation with church officials and forced him to see the theological implications of justification by faith alone was the indulgence controversy. In 1517, Pope Leo X had issued a special jubilee indulgence to finance the ongoing construction of the new Saint Peter's Basilica (see Chapter 12). This special indulgence was connected to political and ecclesiastical affairs in Germany through one Albrecht of Brandenburg. Though he was already both bishop of Halberstadt and archbishop of Magdeburg, Albrecht purchased a special dispensation from Pope Leo X to obtain yet another church office, the archbishopric of Mainz. To get the money, Albrecht borrowed from the Fugger banking firm in Augsburg, which paid the pope. Albrecht was then given the rights to sell the special jubilee indulgence in Germany for ten years, with half of the proceeds going to the Fuggers to pay off his debt and the other half to Rome to rebuild Saint Peter's. Johann Tetzel, a rambunctious Dominican, hawked the indulgences with the slogan, "As soon as the coin in the coffer rings, the soul from purgatory springs."

Luther was greatly distressed by the sale of indulgences, certain that people were simply guaranteeing their eternal damnation by relying on these pieces of paper to assure themselves of salvation. In response, he issued his Ninety-Five Theses, although scholars are unsure whether he nailed them to a church door in Wittenberg, as is traditionally alleged, or mailed them to his ecclesiastical superior. In either case, his theses were a stunning indictment of the abuses in the sale of indulgences (see the box on p. 369). If the pope had the power to grant indulgences, "Why does not the Pope empty purgatory for the sake of most holy love and the supreme need of souls?" It is doubtful that Luther intended any break with the church over the issue of indulgences. If the pope had clarified the use of indulgences, as Luther wished, then he would probably have been satisfied and the controversy closed. But the Renaissance pope Leo X did not take the issue seriously and is even reported to have said that Luther was simply "some drunken German who will amend his ways when he sobers up." But the development of printing prevented such a speedy resolution. A German translation of the Ninety-Five Theses was quickly printed in thousands of copies and received sympathetically in a Germany that had a long tradition of dissatisfaction with papal policies and power.

The controversy reached an important turning point with the Leipzig Debate in July 1519. There Luther's opponent, the capable Catholic theologian Johann Eck, forced Luther to move beyond indulgences and deny the authority of popes and councils. In effect, Luther was compelled to see the consequences of his new theology. At the beginning of 1520, he proclaimed: "Farewell, unhappy, hopeless, blasphemous Rome! The Wrath of God has come upon you, as you deserve. We have cared for Babylon, and

Luther and the Ninety-Five Theses

To most historians, the publication of Luther's Ninety-Five Theses marks the beginning of the Reformation. To Luther, they were simply a response to what he considered to be Johann Tetzel's blatant abuses in selling indulgences. Although written in Latin, the theses were soon translated into German and disseminated widely across Germany. They made an immense impression on Germans already dissatisfied with the ecclesiastical and financial policies of the papacy.

Martin Luther, Selections from the Ninety-Five Theses

5. The Pope has neither the will nor the power to remit any penalties beyond those he has imposed either at his own discretion or by canon law.
20. Therefore the Pope, by his plenary remission of all penalties, does not mean "all" in the absolute sense, but only those imposed by himself.
21. Hence those preachers of Indulgences are wrong when they say that a man is absolved and saved from every penalty by the Pope's Indulgences.
27. It is mere human talk to preach that the soul flies out [of purgatory] immediately the money clinks in the collection-box.
28. It is certainly possible that when the money clinks in the collection-box greed and avarice can increase; but the intercession of the Church depends on the will of God alone.
50. Christians should be taught that, if the Pope knew the exactions of the preachers of Indulgences, he would rather have the basilica of St. Peter reduced to ashes than built with the skin, flesh and bones of his sheep.
81. This wanton preaching of pardons makes it difficult even for learned men to redeem respect due to the Pope from the slanders or at least the shrewd questionings of the laity.
82. For example: "Why does not the Pope empty purgatory for the sake of most holy love and the supreme need of souls? This would be the most righteous of reasons, if he can redeem innumerable souls for sordid money with which to build a basilica, the most trivial of reasons."
86. Again: "Since the Pope's wealth is larger than that of the crassest Crassi of our time, why does he not build this one basilica of St. Peter with his own money, rather than with that of the faithful poor?"
90. To suppress these most conscientious questionings of the laity by authority only, instead of refuting them by reason, is to expose the Church and the Pope to the ridicule of their enemies, and to make Christian people unhappy.
94. Christians should be exhorted to seek earnestly to follow Christ, their Head, through penalties, deaths, and hells.
95. And let them thus be more confident of entering heaven through many tribulations rather than through a false assurance of peace.

she is not healed: let us then, leave her, that she may be the habitation of dragons, spectres, and witches."[7] At the same time, Luther was convinced that he was doing God's work and had to proceed regardless of the consequences. To a friend who had urged moderation, he exclaimed: "Let there be a new and great conflagration, who can resist the counsel of God? Who knows whether these insensate men are not predestined by Him as the means of revealing the truth? . . . God alone is in this business. We are carried away by Him. We are led rather than lead."[8]

In three pamphlets published in 1520, Luther moved toward a more definite break with the Catholic church. The *Address to the Nobility of the German Nation* was a political tract written in German. The papacy, Luther declared, had used three claims to prevent reform: that the church is superior to the state, that only the pope can interpret Scripture, and that only the pope can call a council. Luther believed that all three were false, and he called upon the German princes to overthrow the papacy in Germany and establish a reformed German church. *The Babylonian Captivity of the Church*, written in Latin for theologians, attacked the sacramental system as the means by which the pope and church had held the real meaning of the Gospel in captivity for 1,000 years. He called for the reform of monasticism and for the clergy to marry. Though virginity is good, Luther argued, marriage is better, and freedom of choice is best. *On the Freedom of a Christian Man* was a short treatise on the doctrine of salvation. It is faith alone, not good works, which justifies, frees, and brings salvation through Jesus. Being saved and freed by his faith in Jesus, however, does not free the Christian from doing good works. Rather, he performs good works out of gratitude to God. "Good works do not make a good man, but a good man does good works." From faith flows love and from love a free spirit that is disposed to serve one's neighbor voluntarily. Hence, "a Christian man is the most free lord of all, and subject to none; a Christian man is the most dutiful servant of all, and subject to everyone."[9]

Unable to countenance Luther's forcefully worded dissent from traditional Catholic teachings, the church excommunicated him in January 1521. He was also summoned to appear before the imperial diet or Reichstag of the Holy Roman Empire in Worms, convened by the newly elected emperor Charles V (1519–1556). Expected to

WOODCUT: LUTHER VERSUS THE POPE. **In the 1520s, after Luther's return to Wittenberg, his teachings began to spread rapidly, ending ultimately in a reform movement supported by state authorities. Pamphlets containing picturesque woodcuts were important in the spread of Luther's ideas. In the woodcut shown here, the crucified Jesus attends Luther's service on the left, while on the right the pope is at a table selling indulgences.**

recant the heretical doctrines he had espoused, Luther refused and made the famous reply that became the battle cry of the Reformation:

> Since then Your Majesty and your lordships desire a simple reply, I will answer without horns and without teeth. Unless I am convicted by Scripture and plain reason—I do not accept the authority of popes and councils, for they have contradicted each other—my conscience is captive to the Word of God. I cannot and I will not recant anything, for to go against conscience is neither right nor safe. Here I stand, I cannot do otherwise. God help me. Amen.[10]

Luther's heroic stand at Worms was once viewed as a step in the development of religious freedom, but that interpretation overlooked an important consideration. Though Luther clearly placed his conscience above the authority of the church, he also believed that he had arrived at the truth, from which others were not allowed to deviate. As Luther once expressed it: "I have neither the power nor the will to deny the Word of God. If any man has a different opinion concerning me, he does not think straight or understand what I have actually said."

The young emperor Charles was outraged at Luther's audacity and gave his opinion that "a single friar who goes counter to all Christianity for 1,000 years must be wrong." By the Edict of Worms, Martin Luther was made an outlaw within the empire. His works were to be burned and Luther himself captured and delivered to the emperor. Because of his religious conviction, Luther had been forced to defy both church and emperor and was now forced to depend on the German princes and people. As he did so, his religious movement became a revolution.

The Development of Lutheranism

After a brief period of hiding, Luther returned to Wittenberg at the beginning of 1522 and began to organize a reformed church. In the decade of the 1520s, Lutheranism had much appeal and spread rapidly. The University of Wittenberg served as a center for the diffusion of Luther's ideas. Between 1520 and 1560, 16,000 students from all over Germany matriculated at the university and returned home to spread Luther's teachings. The preaching of evangelical sermons, based on a return to the original message of the Bible, found favor throughout Germany. In city after city, the arrival of preachers presenting Luther's teachings was soon followed by a public debate in which the new preachers proved victorious. A reform of the church was then instituted by state authorities. Also useful to the spread of the Reformation were pamphlets illustrated with vivid woodcuts portraying the pope as a hideous Antichrist and titled with catchy phrases, such as "I Wonder Why There Is No Money in the Land" (which, of course, was an attack on papal greed). Luther also insisted on the use of music as a means to teach the Gospel, and his own "A Mighty Fortress Is Our God" became the battle hymn of the Reformation:

Standing alone are we undone, the Fiend would soon enslave us;
but for us fights a mighty One whom God has sent to save us.
Ask you who is this? Jesus Christ is He, Lord God of Hosts
There is no other God; He can and will uphold us.

Lutheranism spread to both princely and ecclesiastical states in northern and central Germany as well as to two-thirds of the free imperial cities, especially those of southern Germany, where prosperous burghers, for both religious and secular reasons, became committed to Luther's cause. Nuremberg, where an active city council led by the dynamic city secretary Lazarus Spengler brought a conversion as early as 1525, was the first imperial city to convert to Lutheranism. At its outset, the Reformation in Germany was largely an urban phenomenon.

A series of crises in the mid-1520s made it apparent, however, that spreading the word of God was not as easy as Luther had originally envisioned, the usual plight of most reformers. Luther experienced dissent within his own ranks in Wittenberg from people such as Andreas Carlstadt, who wished to initiate a more radical reform by abolishing all relics, images, and the mass. Luther had no sooner dealt with them when he was faced with defection from the Christian humanists. Many had initially supported Luther, believing that he shared their goal of reforming the abuses within the church. But after 1521, when it became apparent that Luther's movement threatened the unity of Christendom, the older generation of Christian humanists, including Erasmus, broke with the reformer. A younger generation of Christian humanists, however, played a significant role in Lutheranism. Philip Melanchthon (1497–1560) arrived in Wittenberg in 1518 (at the age of twenty-one) to teach Greek and Hebrew, was immediately attracted to Luther's ideas, and became his staunch supporter.

Luther's greatest challenge in the mid-1520s, however, came from the Peasants' War. Peasant dissatisfaction in Germany stemmed from several sources. Many peasants had not been touched by the gradual economic improvement of the early sixteenth century. In some areas, especially southwestern Germany, influential local lords continued to abuse their peasants, and new demands for taxes and other services caused them to wish for a return to "the good old days." Social discontent soon became entangled with religious revolt as peasants looked to Martin Luther for support. It was not Luther, however, but one of his ex-followers, the radical Thomas Müntzer, who inflamed the peasants against their rulers with his fiery language: "Strike while the iron is hot!" Revolt first erupted in southwestern Germany in June 1524 and spread northward and eastward.

Luther reacted quickly and vehemently against the peasants. In his pamphlet, *Against the Robbing and Murdering Hordes of Peasants,* he called upon the German princes to "stab, smite, and slay" the stupid and stubborn peasantry (see the box on p. 372). The issue was clear to Luther. Although convinced that he himself was compelled by the word of God to rebel against church authorities, he did not believe in social revolution. To Luther, the state and its rulers were ordained by God, who had given them the authority to maintain the peace and order necessary for the spread of the Gospel. It was the responsibility of subjects to obey these authorities, and it was the duty of princes to suppress all revolt. But Luther was no political thinker, and he certainly knew how much his reformation of the church depended upon the full support of the German princes and magistrates. Luther was fully prepared to lend religious dignity to the rulers in return for their ongoing support. In May 1525, the German princes ruthlessly massacred the remaining peasant hordes in a bloodbath at Frankenhausen. By this time, Luther found himself ever more dependent on state authorities for the growth and maintenance of his reformed church.

Church and State

Justification by faith alone was the starting point for most of Protestantism's major doctrines. Since Luther downplayed the role of good works in salvation, the sacraments also had to be redefined. No longer were they merit-earning works, but divinely established signs signifying the promise of salvation. Based on his interpretation of scriptural authority, Luther kept only two of the Catholic church's seven sacraments, baptism and the Lord's Supper. Baptism signified rebirth through grace. As to the sacrament of the Lord's Supper, Luther denied the Catholic doctrine of transubstantiation, which taught that the substance of the bread and wine is miraculously transformed into the body and blood of Jesus. Yet he continued to insist upon the real presence of Jesus' body and blood in the bread and wine given as a testament to God's forgiveness of sin.

Luther's emphasis on the importance of Scripture led him to reject the Catholic belief that the authority of Scripture must be supplemented by the traditions and decrees of the church. The word of God as revealed in the Bible was sufficient authority in religious affairs. A hierarchical priesthood was thus unnecessary since all Christians who followed the word of God were their own priests ("priesthood of all believers"). Though Luther thus considered the true church to be an invisible one, the difficulties of actually creating a reformed church led him to believe that a visible, organized church was needed. Since the Catholic ecclesiastical hierarchy had been scrapped, Luther came

Luther and the "Robbing and Murdering Hordes of Peasants"

The Peasants' War of 1524–1525 encompassed a series of risings by German peasants who were suffering from economic changes they did not comprehend. In a sense, it was part of a century of peasant discontent. Led by radical religious leaders, the revolts quickly became entangled with the religious revolt set in motion by Luther's defiance of the church. But it was soon clear that Luther himself did not believe in any way in social revolution. This excerpt is taken from Luther's pamphlet written in May 1525 at the height of the peasants' power, but not published until after their defeat.

Martin Luther, *Against the Robbing and Murdering Hordes of Peasants*

The peasants have taken on themselves the burden of three terrible sins against God and man, by which they have abundantly merited death in body and soul. In the first place they have sworn to be true and faithful, submissive and obedient, to their rulers, as Christ commands, when he says, "Render unto Caesar the things that are Caesar's," and in Romans XIII, "Let everyone be subject unto the higher powers." Because they are breaking this obedience, and are setting themselves against the higher powers, willfully and with violence, they have forfeited body and soul, as faithless, perjured, lying, disobedient knaves and scoundrels are wont to do. . . .

In the second place, they are starting a rebellion, and violently robbing and plundering monasteries and castles which are not theirs, by which they have a second time deserved death in body and soul, if only as highwaymen and murderers. . . . For rebellion is not simple murder, but is like a great fire, which attacks and lays waste a whole land. . . . Therefore, let everyone who can, smite, slay and stab, secretly or openly, remembering that nothing can be more poisonous, hurtful or devilish than a rebel. . . .

In the third place, they cloak this terrible and horrible sin with the Gospel, call themselves "Christian brothers," receive oaths and homage, and compel people to hold with them to these abominations. Thus they become the greatest of all blasphemers of God and slanderers of his holy Name, serving the devil, under the outward appearance of the Gospel, thus earning death in body and soul ten times over. . . . It does not help the peasants, when they pretend that, according to Genesis I and II, all things were created free and common, and that all of us alike have been baptized. . . . For baptism does not make men free in body and property, but in soul; and the Gospel does not make goods common. . . . Since the peasants, then, have brought both God and man down upon them and are already so many times guilty of death in body and soul, . . . I must instruct the worldly governors how they are to act in the matter with a clear conscience.

First, I will not oppose a ruler who, even though he does not tolerate the Gospel, will smite and punish these peasants without offering to submit the case to judgment. For he is within his rights, since the peasants are not contending any longer for the Gospel, but have become faithless, perjured, disobedient, rebellious murderers, robbers and blasphemers, whom even heathen rulers have the right and power to punish; nay, it is their duty to punish them, for it is just for this purpose that they bear the sword, and are "the ministers of God upon him that doeth evil."

to rely increasingly on the princes or state authorities to organize and guide the new Lutheran reformed churches. He had little choice. By the sixteenth century, secular authorities in Germany as elsewhere were already playing an important role in church affairs. By 1530, in the German states that had converted to Lutheranism, both princes and city councils appointed officials who visited churches in their territories and regulated matters of worship. The Lutheran churches in Germany (and later in Scandinavia) quickly became territorial or state churches in which the state supervised and disciplined church members.

As part of the development of these state-dominated churches, Luther also instituted new religious services to replace the mass. These featured a worship service consisting of a German liturgy that focused on Bible reading, preaching the word of God, and song. Following his own denunciation of clerical celibacy, Luther married a former nun, Katherina von Bora, in 1525. His union provided a model of married and family life for the new Protestant minister.

◆ Germany and the Reformation: Religion and Politics

From its very beginning, the fate of Luther's movement was closely tied to political affairs. In 1519, Charles I, king of Spain and the grandson of the Emperor Maximilian, was elected Holy Roman Emperor as Charles V (1519–1556). Charles V ruled over an immense empire, consisting of Spain and its overseas possessions, the traditional Austrian Habsburg lands, Bohemia, Hungary, the Low Coun-

FRANCIS I. The conflict between Francis I of France and Emperor Charles V prevented Charles from effectively dealing with the Lutheran problem in Germany. Feeling surrounded by Charles's possessions, Francis initiated a series of Habsburg-Valois Wars, which were fought over a period of twenty-four years. Pictured here is a portrait of Francis I attributed to Jean Clouet.

tries, and the kingdom of Naples in southern Italy. The extent of his possessions was reflected in the languages he used: "I speak Spanish to God, Italian to women, French to men, and German to my horse." Politically, Charles wanted to maintain his dynasty's control over his enormous empire; religiously, he hoped to preserve the unity of the Catholic faith throughout his empire. Despite his strengths, Charles spent a lifetime in futile pursuit of his goals. Four major problems—the French, the Turks, the papacy, and Germany's internal situation—cost him both his dream and his health. At the same time, the emperor's problems gave Luther's movement time to grow and organize before facing the concerted onslaught of the Catholic forces.

The chief political concern of Charles V was his rivalry with the king of France. Francis I (1515–1547), the benevolent despot of the Valois dynasty, proved a worthy adversary. Encircled by the possessions of the Habsburg empire, Francis became embroiled in conflict with Charles over disputed territories in southern France, the Netherlands, the Rhineland, northern Spain, and Italy. These conflicts, known as the Habsburg-Valois Wars, were fought intermittently over twenty-four years (1521–1544), preventing Charles from concentrating his attention on the Lutheran problem in Germany.

Meanwhile, Charles was faced with two other enemies. The Habsburg emperor expected papal cooperation in dealing with the Lutheran heresy. Papal policy, however, was guided by political considerations, not religious ones. Fearful of Charles's power in Italy, Pope Clement VII (1523–1534) joined the side of Francis I in the second Habsburg-Valois War (1527–1529), but with catastrophic results. In April 1527, the Spanish-imperial army of Charles V went berserk while attacking Rome and subjected the capital of Catholicism to a fearful and bloody sack. Sobered by the experience, Clement came to terms with the emperor, and by 1530 Charles V stood supreme over much of Italy.

In the meantime, a new threat to the emperor's power had erupted in the eastern part of his empire. The Ottoman Turks, under the competent Suleiman the Magnificent (1520–1566), had defeated and killed King Louis of Hungary, Charles's brother-in-law, at the Battle of Mohács in 1526. Subsequently, the Turks overran most of Hungary, moved into Austria, and advanced as far as Vienna, where they were finally repulsed in 1529.

By the end of 1529, Charles was ready to deal with Germany. The second Habsburg-Valois War had ended, the Turks had been defeated temporarily, and the pope subdued. The internal political situation in the Holy Roman Empire was not in his favor, however. Germany was a land of several hundred territorial states: princely states, ecclesiastical principalities, and free imperial cities (see Chapter 12). Though all owed loyalty to the emperor, Germany's medieval development had enabled these states to become quite independent of imperial authority. They had no desire to have a strong emperor. Although those states that had become Lutheran were most concerned about that possibility, even Catholic authorities that might approve of the emperor's anti-Lutheran policies had no real desire to strengthen the emperor's hand politically.

Charles's attempt to settle the Lutheran problem at the Diet of Augsburg in 1530 proved completely inadequate, and the emperor wound up demanding that the Lutherans return to the Catholic church by April 15, 1531. In February 1531, fearful of Charles's intentions, eight

CHRONOLOGY

Politics and the German Reformation

First Habsburg-Valois War	1521–1525
Battle of Mohács	1526
Second Habsburg-Valois War	1527–1529
Defeat of the Turks at Vienna	1529
Diet of Augsburg	1530
Formation of Schmalkaldic League	1531
Third Habsburg-Valois War	1535–1538
Fourth Habsburg-Valois War	1542–1544
Schmalkaldic Wars	1546–1555
Peace of Augsburg	1555

princes and eleven imperial cities—all Lutheran—formed a defensive alliance known as the Schmalkaldic League. These Protestant German states vowed to assist each other "whenever any one of us is attacked on account of the Word of God and the doctrine of the Gospel." Religion was dividing the empire into two armed camps.

The renewed threat of the Turks against Vienna forced Charles once again to seek compromise instead of war with the Protestant authorities. From 1532 to 1535, Charles was forced to fight off a Turkish, Arab, and Barbary attack on the Mediterranean coasts of Italy and Spain. Two additional Habsburg-Valois Wars (1535–1538 and 1542–1544) soon followed and kept Charles preoccupied with military campaigns in southern France and the Low Countries. Finally, Charles made peace with Francis in 1544 and the Turks in 1545. Fifteen years after the Diet of Augsburg, Charles was finally free to resolve his problem in Germany.

By the time of Luther's death in February 1546, all hopes of a peaceful compromise had faded. Charles brought a sizable imperial army of German, Dutch, Italian, and Spanish troops to do battle with the Protestants. In the first phase of the Schmalkaldic Wars (1546–1547), the emperor's forces decisively defeated the Lutherans at the Battle of Mühlberg. Charles V was at the zenith of his power, and the Protestant cause seemed doomed.

Appearances proved misleading, however. The Schmalkaldic League was soon reestablished, and the German Protestant princes allied themselves with the new French king, Henry II (1547–1559)—a Catholic—to revive the war in 1552. This time, Charles was less fortunate and was forced to negotiate a truce. Exhausted by his efforts to maintain religious orthodoxy and the unity of his empire, Charles abandoned German affairs to his brother Ferdinand, abdicated all of his titles in 1556, and retired to his country estate in Spain to spend the remaining two years of his life in solitude.

An end to religious warfare in Germany came in 1555 with the Peace of Augsburg, which marks an important turning point in the history of the Reformation. The division of Christianity was formally acknowledged, with Lutheranism being granted the same legal rights as Catholicism. Although the German states were now free to choose between Catholicism and Lutheranism, the peace settlement did not recognize the principle of religious toleration for individuals; the right of each German ruler to determine the religion of his subjects was accepted, but not the right of the subjects to choose their religion.

CHARLES V. Charles V sought to create religious unity throughout his vast empire by keeping all his subjects within the bounds of the Catholic church. Due to his conflict with Francis I in addition to his difficulties with the Turks, the papacy, and the German princes, Charles was never able to check the spread of Lutheranism. This is a portrait of Charles V by the Venetian painter Titian.

The Peace of Augsburg was a victory for the German princes. The independence of the numerous German territorial states guaranteed the weakness of the Holy Roman Empire and the continued decentralization of Germany. Charles's hope for a united empire had been completely dashed. At the same time, what had at first been merely feared was now confirmed: the ideal of medieval Christian unity was irretrievably lost. The rapid proliferation of new Protestant groups served to underscore the new reality.

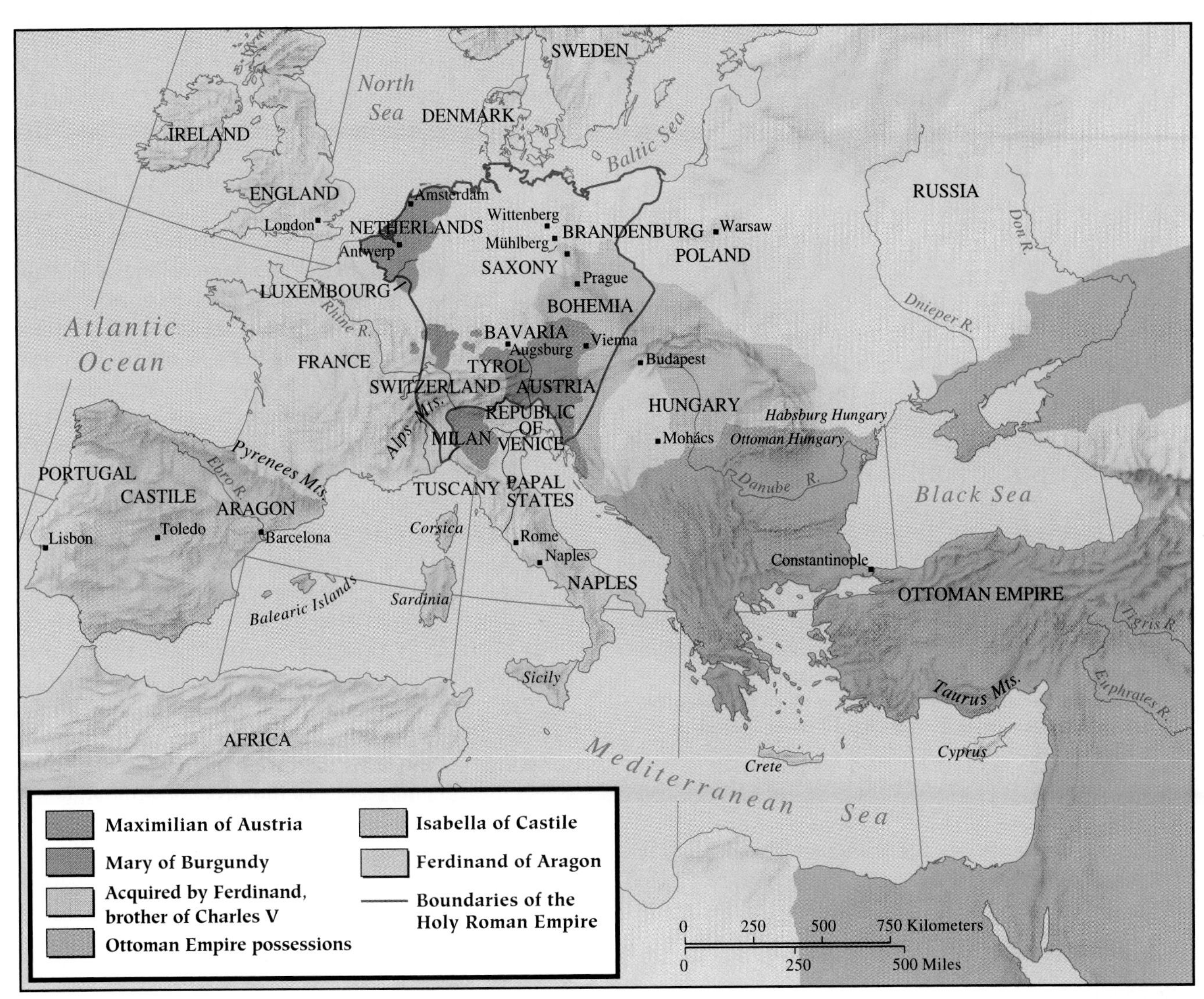

MAP 13.1 The Empire of Charles V.

◆ The Spread of the Protestant Reformation

To Catholic critics, Luther's heresy had opened the door to more extreme forms of religious and social upheaval. For both Catholics and Protestant reformers, it also raised the question of how to determine what constituted the correct interpretation of the Bible. The inability to agree on this issue led not only to theological confrontations but also to bloody warfare as each Christian group was unwilling to admit that it could be wrong.

Lutheranism in Scandinavia

In 1397, the Union of Kalmar had brought about the unification of Denmark, Norway, and Sweden under the rule of one monarch, the king of Denmark. This union, however, failed to achieve any real social or political unification of the three states, particularly since the independent-minded, landed nobles worked to frustrate any increase in monarchical centralization. By the beginning of the sixteenth century, the union was on the brink of disintegration. In 1520, Christian II (1513–1523) of Denmark, ruler of the three Scandinavian kingdoms, was overthrown by Swedish barons led by Gustavus Vasa. Three years later, Vasa became king of an independent Sweden (1523–1560) and took the lead in establishing a Lutheran Reformation in his country. Swedish nobles supported his efforts, while Olavus Petri, who had studied at Wittenberg, wrote treatises based on Luther's writings and published the first Swedish New Testament in 1526. By the 1530s, a Swedish Lutheran National Church had been created.

Meanwhile, Christian II had also been deposed as the king of Denmark by the Danish nobility; he was succeeded by his uncle, who became Frederick I (1523–1533). Frederick encouraged Lutheran preachers to spread their evangelical doctrines and to introduce a Lutheran liturgy into the Danish church service. In the 1530s, under Frederick's successor, Christian III (1534–1559), a Lutheran state church was installed with the king as the supreme authority in all ecclesiastical affairs. Christian was also instrumental in spreading Lutheranism to Norway. By the 1540s, Scandinavia had become a Lutheran stronghold.

ZWINGLI. Ulrich Zwingli began the Reformation in Switzerland through his preaching in Zürich. Zwingli's theology was accepted in Zürich and soon spread to other Swiss cities. This portrait of Zwingli was done by Hans Asper, probably in 1531.

Like the German princes, the Scandinavian monarchs had been the dominant force in establishing state-run churches.

The Zwinglian Reformation

Switzerland, which has played little role in our history to date, was home to two major Reformation movements, Zwinglianism and Calvinism. In the sixteenth century, the Swiss Confederation was a loose association of thirteen self-governing states called cantons. Theoretically part of the Holy Roman Empire, they had become virtually independent after the Swiss defeated the forces of Emperor Maximilian in 1499. The six forest cantons were democratic republics; the seven urban cantons, which included Zürich, Bern, and Basel, were mostly governed by city councils controlled by narrow oligarchies of wealthy citizens. Perennially troubled by a weak economy, the Swiss had grown accustomed to selling their warriors as mercenary soldiers and had become the principal exporters of mercenaries in the sixteenth century. All in all, the Swiss Confederation was a loose conglomeration of states that possessed no common institutions and worked together only for survival and gain.

Ulrich Zwingli (1484–1531) was a product of the Swiss rural cantons. The precocious son of a relatively prosperous peasant, the young Zwingli eventually obtained both the bachelor of arts and master of arts degrees. During his university education at Vienna and Basel, Zwingli was strongly influenced by Christian humanism. Ordained a priest in 1506, he accepted a parish post in rural Switzerland until his appointment as a cathedral priest in the Great Minster of Zürich in 1518. Through his preaching there, Zwingli began the Reformation in Switzerland.

Zwingli always maintained that he came to his evangelical theology independently of Luther: "I began to preach the Gospel of Christ in 1516, long before anyone in our region had ever heard of Luther. . . . Why don't you call me a Paulinian since I am preaching as St. Paul preached. . . . If Luther preaches Christ, he does just what I do." Modern scholars doubt Zwingli's protestation, believing that he was influenced by Luther's writings, beginning at least in 1519. In any case, Zwingli's evangelical preaching caused such unrest that in 1523 the city council held a public disputation or debate in the town hall. The disputation became a standard method of spreading the Reformation to many cities. It gave an advantage to reformers since they had the power of new ideas and Catholics were not used to defending their teachings. Zwingli's party was accorded the victory, and the council declared that "Mayor, Council and Great Council of Zürich, in order to do away with disturbance and discord, have upon due deliberation and consultation decided and resolved that Master Zwingli should continue as heretofore to proclaim the Gospel and the pure sacred Scripture."[11] City magistrates were not always motivated solely by religious considerations. By removing the Catholic church—a rival for authority in their town—the secular authorities enhanced their own power.

Over the next two years, evangelical reforms were promulgated in Zürich by a city council strongly influenced by Zwingli. Zwingli looked to the state to supervise the church. "A church without the magistrate is mutilated and incomplete," he declared. Relics and images were abolished; all paintings and decorations were removed from the churches and replaced by whitewashed walls. The mass was replaced by a new liturgy consisting of Scripture reading, prayer, and sermons. Music was eliminated from the service as a distraction from the pure word of God. Monasticism, pilgrimages, the veneration of saints, clerical celibacy, and the pope's authority were all abolished as remnants of papal Christianity. Zwingli's movement soon spread to other cities in Switzerland, including Bern in 1528 and Basel in 1529.

By 1528, Zwingli's reform movement faced a serious political problem as the forest cantons remained staunchly Catholic. Zürich feared an alliance between them and the Habsburgs. To counteract this danger, Zwingli attempted to build a league of evangelical cities by seeking an agreement with Luther and the German reformers. An alliance between them seemed possible, since the Reformation had spread to the south German cities, especially Strasbourg, where a moderate reform movement containing characteristics of both Luther's and Zwingli's movements had been instituted by Martin Bucer (1491–1551). Both the German and the Swiss reformers realized the need for unity to defend against imperial and conservative opposition. Protestant political leaders, especially Landgrave

A Reformation Debate: The Marburg Colloquy

Debates played a crucial role in the Reformation period. They were a primary instrument in introducing the Reformation into innumerable cities as well as a means of resolving differences among like-minded Protestant groups. This selection contains an excerpt from the vivacious and often brutal debate between Luther and Zwingli over the sacrament of the Lord's Supper at Marburg in 1529. The two protagonists failed to reach agreement.

❁ *The Marburg Colloquy, 1529*

THE HESSIAN CHANCELLOR FEIGE: My gracious prince and lord [Landgrave Philip of Hesse] has summoned you for the express and urgent purpose of settling the dispute over the sacrament of the Lord's Supper. . . . And let everyone on both sides present his arguments in a spirit of moderation, as becomes such matters. . . . Now then, Doctor Luther, you may proceed.

LUTHER: Noble prince, gracious lord! Undoubtedly the colloquy is well intentioned. . . . Although I have no intention of changing my mind, which is firmly made up, I will nevertheless present the grounds of my belief and show where the others are in error. . . . Your basic contentions are these: In the last analysis you wish to prove that a body cannot be in two places at once, and you produce arguments about the unlimited body which are based on natural reason. I do not question how Christ can be God and man and how the two natures can be joined. For God is more powerful than all our ideas, and we must submit to his word.

Prove that Christ's body is not there where the Scripture says, "This is my body!" Rational proofs I will not listen to. . . . God is beyond all mathematics and the words of God are to be revered and carried out in awe. It is God who commands, "Take, eat, this is my body." I request, therefore, valid scriptural proof to the contrary.

Luther writes on the table in chalk, "This is my body," and covers the words with a velvet cloth.

OECOLAMPADIUS [leader of the reform movement in Basel and a Zwinglian partisan]: The sixth chapter of John clarifies the other scriptural passages. Christ is not speaking there about a local presence. "The flesh is of no avail," he says [John 6:63]. It is not my intention to employ rational, or geometrical, arguments—neither am I denying the power of God—but as long as I have the complete faith I will speak from that. For Christ is risen; he sits at the right hand of God; and so he cannot be present in the bread. Our view is neither new nor sacrilegious, but is based on faith and Scripture. . . .

ZWINGLI: I insist that the words of the Lord's Supper must be figurative. This is ever apparent, and even required by the article of faith: "taken up into heaven, seated at the right hand of the Father." Otherwise, it would be absurd to look for him in the Lord's Supper at the same time that Christ is telling us that he is in heaven. One and the same body cannot possibly be in different places. . . .

LUTHER: I call upon you as before: your basic contentions are shaky. Give way, and give glory to God!

ZWINGLI: And we call upon you to give glory to God and to quit begging the question! The issue at stake is this: Where is the proof of your position? I am willing to consider your words carefully—no harm meant! You're trying to outwit me. I stand by this passage in the sixth chapter of John, verse 63 and shall not be shaken from it. You'll have to sing another tune.

LUTHER: You're being obnoxious.

ZWINGLI: (*excitedly*) Don't you believe that Christ was attempting in John 6 to help those who did not understand?

LUTHER: You're trying to dominate things! You insist on passing judgment! Leave that to someone else! . . . It is your point that must be proved, not mine. But let us stop this sort of thing. It serves no purpose.

ZWINGLI: It certainly does! It is for you to prove that the passage in John 6 speaks of a physical repast.

LUTHER: You express yourself poorly and make about as much progress as a cane standing in a corner. You're going nowhere.

ZWINGLI: No, no, no! This is the passage that will break your neck!

LUTHER: Don't be so sure of yourself. Necks don't break this way. You're in Hesse, not Switzerland.

Philip of Hesse, fearful of Charles V's ability to take advantage of the division between the reformers, attempted to promote an alliance of the Swiss and German reformed churches by persuading the leaders of both groups to attend a colloquy (or conference) at Marburg to resolve their differences. Able to agree on virtually everything else, the gathering splintered over the interpretation of the Lord's Supper (see the box above). Zwingli believed that the scriptural words "This is my Body, This is my blood" should be taken figuratively, not literally, and refused to accept Luther's insistence on the real presence of the body and blood of Jesus "in, with, and under the bread and wine." The Marburg Colloquy of 1529 produced no agreement and no evangelical alliance. Although this failure to reach an accord was a setback for Lutheranism and Philip of Hesse, it proved even more harmful to Zwingli.

In October 1531, war erupted between the Swiss Protestant and Catholic cantons. Zürich's army was

AN ANABAPTIST EXECUTION IN THE NETHERLANDS. The Anabaptists were the radicals of the Reformation. They advocated adult baptism and believed that the true Christian should not actively participate in or be governed by the secular state. Due to their radical ideas, the Anabaptists were persecuted and put to death by Catholics and Protestants alike. This sixteenth-century woodcut depicts the execution of Anabaptist reformers.

routed, and Zwingli was found wounded on the battlefield. His enemies killed him, cut up his body, and burned the pieces, scattering the ashes. Although Zwingli was succeeded by the able Heinrich Büllinger, the momentum of the Zwinglian reform movement was slowed. This Swiss civil war of 1531 provided an early indication of what religious passions would lead to in the sixteenth century. Unable to find peaceful ways to agree on the meaning of the Gospel, the disciples of Christianity resorted to violence and decision by force. When he heard of Zwingli's death, Martin Luther, who had not forgotten the confrontation at Marburg, is supposed to have remarked that Zwingli got what he deserved.

The Radical Reformation: The Anabaptists

Since the Reformation had broken down traditional standards and relationships, reformers such as Luther sought a new authority by allowing the state to play an important, if not dominant, role in church affairs. But some people favored a far more radical approach. Collectively called the Anabaptists, these radicals actually formed a large variety of different groups who, nevertheless, shared some common characteristics. Although some middle-class intellectuals participated in this movement, Anabaptism was especially attractive to those peasants, weavers, miners, and artisans who had been adversely affected by the economic changes of the age. The upper classes were aware of the obvious link between social dissatisfaction and religious radicalism, which was particularly evident in commercial and industrial cities like Zürich, Strasbourg, Nuremberg, and Augsburg. All of these cities initiated a Lutheran or Zwinglian Reformation early on but, thanks to their relatively large lower classes affected by economic upheavals, also became centers for radical religious groups.

Anabaptists everywhere shared some common ideas. To them, the true Christian church was a voluntary association of believers who had undergone spiritual rebirth and had then been baptized into the church. Anabaptists advocated adult rather than infant baptism. They also tried to return literally to the practices and spirit of early Christianity. Adhering to the accounts of early Christian communities in the New Testament, they followed a strict sort of democracy in which all believers were considered equal. Each church chose its own minister, who might be any member of the community since all Christians were considered priests (though women were often excluded). Those chosen as ministers had the duty to lead services, which were very simple and contained nothing not found in the early church. Anabaptists rejected theological speculation in favor of simple Christian living according to what they believed was the pure word of God. The Lord's Supper was interpreted as a remembrance, a meal of fellowship celebrated in the evening in private houses according to Jesus' example. Finally, unlike the Catholics and other Protestants, most Anabaptists believed in the complete separation of church and state. Not only was government to be excluded from the realm of religion, it was not even supposed to exercise political jurisdiction over real Christians. Anabaptists refused to hold political office or bear arms because many took literally the commandment "Thou shall not kill," although some Anabaptist groups did become quite violent. Their political beliefs as much as their religious beliefs caused the Anabaptists to be regarded as dangerous radicals who threatened the very fabric of sixteenth-century society. Indeed, the chief thing Protestants and Catholics could agree on was the need to persecute Anabaptists.

One early group of Anabaptists known as the Swiss Brethren arose in Zürich. Their ideas frightened Zwingli, and they were soon expelled from the city. As their teachings spread through southern Germany, the Austrian Habsburg lands, and Switzerland, Anabaptists suffered ruthless persecution, especially after the Peasants' War of 1524–1525, when the upper classes resorted to repression. To Catholics and Lutherans alike, the Anabaptists threatened not only religious peace but also secular authority

The Trial of Michael Sattler

Michael Sattler had been prior of a Benedictine monastery before abandoning Catholicism for Lutheranism and then Anabaptism. He was responsible for drawing up a set of seven articles (the Schleitheim Articles) in 1527, which constituted the "first formal Anabaptist confession of faith." Both Catholics and other Protestant sects viewed Anabaptists as dangerous radicals, subversive of both church and state. This excerpt, taken from a contemporary account of Sattler's trial for heresy by Austrian authorities, begins after Sattler has given a speech detailing his beliefs. As his sentence indicates, Anabaptists were subjected to cruel and unusual punishments.

❋ *The Trial of Michael Sattler*

Upon this speech the judges laughed and put their heads together, and the town clerk of Ensisheim said, "Yes, you infamous, desperate rascal of a monk, should we dispute with you? The hangman will dispute with you, I assure you!"

Michael said: "God's will be done."

The town clerk said: "It were well if you had never been born."

Michael replied: "God knows what is good."

The town clerk: "You archheretic, you have seduced pious people. If they would only now forsake their error and commit themselves to grace!"

Michael: "Grace is with God alone."

The town clerk: "Yes, you desperate villain, you archheretic, I say, if there were no hangman here, I would hang you myself and be doing God a good service thereby."

Michael: "God will judge aright."

The town clerk then admonished the judges and said: "He will not cease from this chatter anyway. Therefore, my Lord Judge, you may proceed with the sentence. I call for a decision of the court."

The judge asked Michael Sattler whether he too committed it to the court. He replied: "Ministers of God, I am not sent to judge the Word of God. We are sent to testify and hence cannot consent to any adjudication, since we have no command from God concerning it. But we are not for that reason removed from being judged and we are ready to suffer and to await what God is planning to do with us. We will continue in our faith in Christ so long as we have breath in us, unless we be dissuaded from it by the Scriptures."

The town clerk, said: "The hangman will instruct you, he will dispute with you, archheretic."

Michael: "I appeal to the Scriptures."

Then the judges arose and went into another room where they . . . determined on the sentence. . . .

The judges having returned to the room, the sentence was read. It was as follows: "In the case of the attorney of His Imperial Majesty [Holy Roman Emperor] vs. Michael Sattler, judgment is passed that Michael Sattler shall be delivered to the executioner, who shall lead him to the place of execution and cut out his tongue, then forge him fast to a wagon and thereon with red-hot tongs twice tear pieces from his body; and after he has been brought outside the gate, he shall be plied five times more in the same manner."

because of their political ideas (see the box above). After the movement was virtually stamped out in Germany, Anabaptist survivors emerged in Moravia, Poland, and the Netherlands. In the latter, Anabaptism took on a strange form.

In the 1530s, the city of Münster in Westphalia in northwestern Germany near the Dutch border was the site of an Anabaptist uprising that determined the fate of Dutch Anabaptism. Seat of a powerful Catholic prince-bishop, Münster had experienced severe economic disasters, including crop failure and plague. Although converted to Lutheranism in 1532, Münster experienced a more radical mass religious hysteria that led to legal recognition for the Anabaptists. Soon Münster became a haven for Anabaptists from the surrounding neighborhood, especially the more wild-eyed variety known as Melchiorites who adhered to a vivid millenarianism. They believed that the end of the world was at hand and that they would usher in the Kingdom of God with Münster as the New Jerusalem. By the end of February 1534, these millenarian Anabaptists had taken control of the city, driven out those they considered godless or unbelievers, burned all books except the Bible, and proclaimed communal ownership of all property. Eventually, the leadership of this New Jerusalem fell into the hands of one man, John of Leiden, who proclaimed himself king of the New Jerusalem. As king, he would lead out the elect from Münster to cover the entire world and purify it of evil by the sword in preparation for Jesus' Second Coming and the creation of a New Age. In this new kingdom, John of Leiden believed, all goods would be held in common and the saints would live without suffering.

But it was not to be. As the Catholic prince-bishop of Münster gathered a large force and laid siege to the city, the new king repeatedly had to postpone the ushering forth from Münster. Finally, after many inhabitants had starved, a joint army of Catholics and Lutherans recaptured the city in June 1535 and executed the radical Anabaptist leaders in a gruesome fashion. The New Jerusalem had ceased to exist.

Purged of its fantasies and more extreme elements, Dutch Anabaptism reverted to its pacifist tendencies, especially evident in the work of Menno Simons (1496–1561), the man most responsible for rejuvenating Dutch Anabaptism. A popular leader, Menno dedicated his life to the spread of a peaceful, evangelical Anabaptism that stressed separation from the world in order to truly emulate the life of Jesus. Simons imposed strict discipline on his followers and banned those who refused to conform to the rules. The Mennonites, as his followers were called, spread from the Netherlands into northwestern Germany and eventually into Poland and Lithuania as well as the New World. Both the Mennonites and the Amish, who are also descended from the Anabaptists, can be found in the United States today.

The Reformation in England

At one time, a Reformation in England would have been unthinkable. Had not Henry VIII penned an attack against Martin Luther in 1521, the *Defense of the Seven Sacraments,* and been rewarded for it by the pope with the title "Defender of the Faith"? Nevertheless, there were elements of discontent in England. Antipapal feeling ran high as many of the English resented papal influence in English affairs, especially in matters of taxation and justice. There was also criticism of the activities of the clergy as people denounced greedy clerics who flaunted their great wealth. One layman charged that "These [the clergy] are not the shepherds, but the ravenous wolves going in shepherds' clothing, devouring the flock."

Anticlericalism and antipapal feelings were not the only manifestations of religious sentiment in early sixteenth-century England. A craving for spiritual expression fostered the spread of Lutheran ideas, encouraged in part by two different traditions of dissent. Heretical Lollardy, stressing the use of the Bible in the vernacular and the rejection of papal supremacy, continued to exert influence among the lower classes, while Christian humanism, with its calls for reform, influenced the English middle and upper classes. People influenced by Lollardy and Christian humanism were among the first to embrace Lutheran writings when they began to arrive in England in the 1520s.

Despite these factors, there might not have been a Reformation in England had it not been for the king's desire to divorce his first wife, Catherine of Aragon. Henry VIII's reasons were twofold. Catherine had produced no male heir, an absolute essential if his Tudor dynasty were to flourish. At the same time, Henry had fallen in love with Anne Boleyn, a lady-in-waiting to Queen Catherine. Her unwillingness to be only the king's mistress, as well as the king's desire to have a legitimate male heir, made a new marriage imperative. The king's first marriage stood in the way, however.

Henry relied upon Cardinal Wolsey, the highest ranking English church official and lord chancellor to the king, to obtain an annulment of his marriage from Pope Clement VII. Normally, the pope might have been willing to oblige, but the sack of Rome in 1527 had made the pope dependent upon the Holy Roman Emperor Charles V, who happened to be the nephew of Queen Catherine. Discretion dictated delay in granting the English king's

HENRY VIII, HIS WIFE, AND CHILDREN. The desire of Henry VIII for a male heir played a significant role in his break with the Catholic church. Pictured here in the central panel of this 1545 portrait by an unknown artist are Henry VIII, Jane Seymour, his third wife, and Prince Edward, who became King Edward VI in 1547. On the far left is Princess Mary and on the far right is Princess Elizabeth.

request. Impatient with the process, Henry dismissed Wolsey in 1529.

Two new advisers now became the king's agents in fulfilling his wishes. These were Thomas Cranmer (1489–1556), who became archbishop of Canterbury in 1532, and Thomas Cromwell (1485–1540), the king's principal secretary after the fall of Wolsey. They advised the king to obtain an annulment of his marriage in England's own ecclesiastical courts. The most important step toward this goal was the promulgation by Parliament of an act cutting off all appeals from English church courts to Rome, a piece of legislation that essentially abolished papal authority in England. Henry no longer needed the pope to attain his annulment. He was now in a hurry because Anne Boleyn had become pregnant and he had secretly married her in January 1533 to legitimize the expected heir. In May, as archbishop of Canterbury and head of the highest ecclesiastical court in England, Thomas Cranmer ruled that the king's marriage to Catherine was "null and absolutely void," and then validated Henry's marriage to Anne. At the beginning of June, Anne was crowned queen. Three months later a child was born. Much to the king's disappointment, the baby was a girl, the future Queen Elizabeth I.

In 1534, Parliament completed the break of the Church of England with Rome by passing the Act of Supremacy, which declared that the king was "taken, accepted, and reputed the only supreme head on earth of the Church of England." This meant that the English monarch now controlled the church in all matters of doctrine, clerical appointments, and discipline. In addition, Parliament passed a Treason Act making it punishable by death to deny that the king was the supreme head of the church. The Act of Supremacy and the Treason Act went beyond religious issues in their implications, for they asserted that there could be no higher authority over England than laws made by the king and Parliament.

Few challenged the new order. One who did was Thomas More, the humanist and former lord chancellor, who saw clearly to the heart of the issue: loyalty to the pope in Rome was now treason in England. More refused to publicly support the new laws and was duly tried for treason. At his trial, he asked, rhetorically, what the effect of the actions of the king and Parliament would be: "Therefore am I not bound . . . to conform my conscience to the Council of one realm [England] against the general Council of Christendom?"[12] Because his conscience could not accept the victory of the national state over the church, nor would he, as a Christian, bow his head to a secular ruler in matters of faith, More was beheaded in London on July 6, 1535.

Thomas Cromwell worked out the details of the Tudor government's new role in church affairs based on the centralized power exercised by the king and Parliament. Cromwell also came to his extravagant king's financial rescue with a daring plan for the dissolution of the monasteries. About 400 religious houses were closed in 1536, and their land and possessions confiscated by the king. Many were sold to nobles, gentry, and some merchants. The king received a great boost to his treasury, as well as creating a group of supporters who now had a stake in the new Tudor order.

Although Henry VIII had broken with the papacy, little change occurred in matters of doctrine, theology, and ceremony. Some of his supporters, such as Archbishop Thomas Cranmer, wished to have a religious reformation as well as an administrative one, but Henry was unyielding. To counteract a growing Protestant sentiment, the king had Parliament pass the Six Articles Act of 1539, which reaffirmed transubstantiation, clerical celibacy, and other aspects of Catholic doctrine. No doubt, Henry's conservatism helped the English accept the basic changes he had made; since religious doctrine and worship had changed very little, most people were indifferent to the transformation that had occurred. Popular acceptance was also furthered by Henry's strategy of involving Parliament in all the changes.

The last decade of Henry's reign was preoccupied with foreign affairs, factional intrigue, and a continued effort to find the perfect wife. Henry soon tired of Anne Boleyn and had her beheaded in 1536 on a charge of adultery. His third wife, Jane Seymour, produced the long-awaited male heir but died during childbirth. His fourth marriage to Anne of Cleves, a German princess, was arranged for political reasons and on the basis of a painted portrait. Henry was shocked at her physical appearance when he first saw her in person and soon divorced her. His fifth wife, Catherine Howard, was more attractive but less moral. When she committed adultery, Henry had her beheaded. His last wife was Catherine Parr, who married the king in 1543 and outlived him. Henry was succeeded by the underage and sickly Edward VI (1547–1553), the son of his third wife.

Since the new king was only nine years old at the time of his accession to the throne, real control of England passed to a council of regency. During Edward's reign, Archbishop Cranmer and others inclined toward Protestant doctrines were able to move the Church of England in a more Protestant direction. New acts of Parliament instituted the right of the clergy to marry, the elimination of images, and the creation of a revised Protestant liturgy that was elaborated in a new prayer book and liturgical guide known as the Book of Common Prayer. These rapid changes in doctrine and liturgy aroused much opposition and prepared the way for the reaction that occurred when Mary, Henry's first daughter by Catherine of Aragon, came to the throne.

There was no doubt that Mary (1553–1558) was a Catholic who intended to restore England to Roman Catholicism. But she understood little about the practical nature of politics and even less about the changes that had swept over England in the past thirty years.

Mary's restoration of Catholicism, achieved by joint action of the monarch and Parliament, aroused much opposition. Although the new owners of monastic lands were assured otherwise, many feared that the lands confiscated by Henry would be restored to the church. Moreover, there was widespread antipathy to Mary's unfortunate marriage to Philip II, the son of Charles V and the future king of Spain. Philip was strongly disliked in England, and Mary's foreign policy of alliance with Spain aroused further hostility, especially when her forces lost Calais, the last English possession from the Hundred Years' War. The burning of more than 300 Protestant heretics roused further ire against "bloody Mary." As a result of her policies, Mary managed to achieve the opposite of what she had intended: England was more Protestant by the end of her reign than it had been at the beginning. When she came to power, Protestantism had become identified with church destruction and religious anarchy. Now people identified it with English resistance to Spanish interference. The death of Mary in 1558 ended the restoration of Catholicism in England.

John Calvin and the Development of Calvinism

Of the second generation of Protestant reformers, one stands out as the systematic theologian and organizer of the Protestant movement—John Calvin (1509–1564). Born a generation later than Luther, Calvin reached manhood when Christian unity had for all intents and purposes already disappeared.

John Calvin began his academic training in humanistic studies in 1523 at the University of Paris, but switched to the study of law at Orléans and Bourges from 1528 to 1531, while simultaneously studying Greek. In 1531, he returned to Paris to concentrate on his humanistic pursuits. In his early development, Calvin was also influenced by Luther's writings, which were being circulated and read by French intellectuals as early as 1523. By 1533, Calvin had received a remarkably diverse education. In that same year, he experienced a religious crisis that determined the rest of his life's work. He described it in these words:

> God, by a sudden conversion, subdued and brought my mind to a teachable frame, which was more hardened in such matters than might have been expected from one at my early period of life. Having thus received some taste and knowledge of true godliness, I was immediately inflamed with so intense a desire to make progress therein, although I did not leave off other studies, I yet pursued them with less ardor.[13]

Calvin's conversion was solemn and straightforward. He was so convinced of the inner guidance of God that he became the most determined of all the Protestant reformers.

After his conversion and newfound conviction, Calvin was no longer safe in Paris, since King Francis I periodically persecuted Protestants. Eventually, Calvin made his way to Basel, where in 1536 he published the first edition of the *Institutes of the Christian Religion*, a masterful synthesis of Protestant thought, a manual for ecclesiastical organization, and a work that immediately secured his reputation as one of the new leaders of Protestantism. Although the *Institutes* were originally written in Latin, Calvin published a French edition in 1541, facilitating the spread of his ideas in French-speaking lands.

JOHN CALVIN. After a conversion experience, John Calvin abandoned his life as a humanist and became a reformer. In 1536, Calvin began working to reform the city of Geneva, where he remained until his death in 1564. This sixteenth-century portrait of Calvin pictures him near the end of his life.

On most important doctrines, Calvin stood very close to Luther. He adhered to the doctrine of justification by faith alone to explain how humans achieved salvation. But Calvin also placed much emphasis on the absolute sovereignty of God or the "power, grace, and glory of God." Thus, "God asserts his possession of omnipotence, and claims our acknowledgment of this attribute; not such as is imagined by sophists, vain, idle, and almost asleep, but vigilant, efficacious, operative and engaged in continual action."[14]

One of the ideas derived from his emphasis on the absolute sovereignty of God—predestination—gave a unique cast to Calvin's teachings. Although it was but one aspect of his doctrine of salvation, predestination became the central focus of succeeding generations of Calvinists. This "eternal decree," as Calvin called it, meant that God had predestined some people to be saved (the elect) and others to be damned (the reprobate). According to Calvin, "He has once for all determined, both whom he would admit to salvation, and whom he would condemn to

The Role of Discipline in the "Most Perfect School of Christ on Earth"

To John Calvin's followers, the church that the French reformer had created in Geneva was, in the words of John Knox, "the most perfect school of Christ on earth." Calvin had emphasized in his reform movement that the church should have the ability to enforce proper behavior. Consequently, the Ecclesiastical Ordinances of 1541, the constitution of the church in Geneva, provided for an order of elders whose function was to cooperate with the pastors in maintaining discipline, "to have oversight of the life of everyone," as Calvin expressed it. These selections from the official records of the Consistory show the nature of its work.

Reports of the Genevan Consistory

Donna Jane Peterman is questioned concerning her faith and why she does not receive communion and attend worship. She confesses her faith and believes in one God and wants to come to God and the holy Church and has no other faith. She recited the Lord's Prayer in the vernacular. She said that she believes what the Church believes. Is questioned why she never participates in communion when it is celebrated in this town, but goes to other places. She answers that she goes where it seems good to her. Is placed outside the faith.

The sister of Sr. Curtet, Lucresse, to whom remonstrances have been made on account of her going with certain monies to have masses said at Nessy by the monks of St. Claire. Questioned whether she has no scruples as to what she says. Replied that her father and mother have brought her up to obey a different law from the one now in force here. However, she does not desire the present law. Asked as to when was the festival of St. Felix, she replied that it was yesterday. Asked if she had not fasted, she replied that she fasted when it pleased her. Asked if she did not desire to pray to a single God; said that she did. Asked if she did not pray to St. Felix; said that she prayed to St. Felix and other saints who interceded for her. She is very obstinate. Decision that she be sent to some minister of her choice every sermon day and that the Lord's Supper be withheld from her.

At about this time, by resolution of the Consistory . . . the marriage contracted between the widow of Jean Archard, aged more than 70, and a servant of hers, aged about 27 or 28, was dissolved because of the too great inequality of age. The Consistory resolved further that Messieurs should be requested to make a ruling on this matter for the future.

destruction."[15] Calvin identified three tests that might indicate possible salvation: an open profession of faith, a "decent and godly life," and participation in the sacraments of baptism and communion. In no instance did Calvin ever suggest that worldly success or material wealth was a sign of election. Most importantly, although Calvin stressed that there could be no absolute certainty of salvation, some of his followers did not always make this distinction. The practical psychological effect of predestination was to give some later Calvinists an unshakable conviction that they were doing God's work on earth. Thus, Calvinism became a dynamic and activist faith. It is no accident that Calvinism became the militant international form of Protestantism.

To Calvin, the church was a divine institution responsible for preaching the word of God and administering the sacraments. Calvin kept only two sacraments, baptism and the Lord's Supper. Baptism was a sign of the remission of sins. Calvin believed in the real presence of Jesus in the sacrament of the Lord's Supper, but only in a spiritual sense. Jesus' body is at the right hand of God and thus cannot be in the sacrament, but to the believer, Jesus is spiritually present in the Lord's Supper. Finally, Calvin agreed with other reformers that the church had the power to discipline its members. This element of his thought was apparent when Calvin finally had the opportunity to establish his church in Geneva.

Up to 1536, John Calvin had essentially been a scholar. But in that year, he took up a ministry in Geneva that lasted until his death in 1564. Calvin achieved a major success in 1541 when the city council accepted his new church constitution known as the Ecclesiastical Ordinances. This document established four orders or offices: pastors, teachers (or doctors), elders, and deacons. The duties of the pastors or ministers were to preach the Gospel, administer the sacraments, and correct un-Christian behavior. To the teachers was given the responsibility to "instruct the faithful in sound doctrine, in order that the purity of the Gospel may not be corrupted." The elders or presbyters were laymen, chosen from and by the city magistrates; their function was to maintain discipline: "to have oversight of the life of everyone, to admonish amicably those whom they see to be erring or to be living a disordered life, and . . . to enjoin fraternal corrections." The deacons were also laymen who were responsible for the care of the poor, widows, and orphans and the administration of the city's hospitals.

The Ecclesiastical Ordinances created a special body for enforcing moral discipline. Consisting of five pastors and twelve elders, the Consistory functioned as a court to oversee the moral life, daily behavior, and doctrinal orthodoxy of Genevans and to admonish and correct deviants (see the box above). As its power increased, the Consistory went from "fraternal corrections" to the use of public penance and excommunication. More serious cases could be turned over to the city council for punishments greater than excommunication. During Calvin's last years, stricter laws against blasphemy were enacted and enforced with banishment and public whippings. Although Calvin's detractors felt that Geneva was an example of religious fanaticism, to visitors of similar inclination, it presented a glorious sight. John Knox, the Calvinist reformer of Scotland, called it "the most perfect school of Christ on earth."

Calvin's success in Geneva enabled the city to become a vibrant center of Protestantism. Following Calvin's lead, missionaries trained in Geneva were sent to all parts of Europe. Calvinism became established in France, the Netherlands, Scotland, and central and eastern Europe. By the mid-sixteenth century, Calvinism had replaced Lutheranism as the international form of Protestantism while Calvin's Geneva stood as the fortress of the Reformation.

◆ The Social Impact of the Protestant Reformation

Christianity was such an integral part of European life that it was inevitable that the Reformation would have an impact on the family, education, and popular religious practices.

The Family

For centuries, Catholicism had praised the family and sanctified its existence by making marriage a sacrament. But the Catholic church's high regard for abstinence from sex as the surest way to holiness made the celibate state of the clergy preferable to marriage. Nevertheless, since not all men could remain chaste, marriage offered the best means to control sexual intercourse and give it a purpose, the procreation of children. To some extent, this attitude persisted among the Protestant reformers; Luther, for example, argued that sex in marriage allowed one to "make use of this sex in order to avoid sin," and Calvin advised that every man should "abstain from marriage only so long as he is fit to observe celibacy." If "his power to tame lust fails him," then he must marry.

But the Reformation did bring some change to the conception of the family. Both Catholic and Protestant clergy preached sermons advocating a positive view of family relationships. The Protestants were especially important in developing this new idea of the family. Since Protestantism had eliminated any idea of special holiness for celibacy, abolishing both monasticism and a celibate clergy, the family could be placed at the center of human life, and a new stress on "mutual love between man and wife" could be extolled. But were doctrine and reality the same? For more radical religious groups, at times they were (see the box on p. 385). One Anabaptist wrote to his wife before his execution: "My faithful helper, my loyal friend. I praise God that he gave you to me, you who have sustained me in all my trial."[16] But more often reality reflected the traditional roles of husband as the ruler and wife as the obedient servant whose chief duty was to please her husband. Luther stated it clearly:

> The rule remains with the husband, and the wife is compelled to obey him by God's command. He rules the home and the state, wages war, defends his possessions, tills the soil, builds, plants, etc. The woman on the other hand is like a nail driven into the wall . . . so the wife should stay at home and look after the affairs of the household, as one who has been deprived of the ability of administering those affairs that are outside and that concern the state. She does not go beyond her most personal duties.[17]

But obedience to her husband was not a wife's only role; her other important duty was to bear children. To Calvin and Luther, this function of women was part of the divine plan. God punishes women for the sins of Eve by the burdens of procreation and feeding and nurturing their children, but, said Luther, "it is a gladsome punishment if you consider the hope of eternal life and the honor of motherhood which had been left to her."[18] Although the Protestant reformers sanctified this role of woman as mother and wife, viewing it as a holy vocation, Protestantism also left few alternatives for women. Since monasticism had been destroyed, that career avenue was no longer available; for most Protestant women, family life was their only destiny. At the same time, by emphasizing the father as "ruler" and hence the center of household religion, Protestantism even removed the woman from her traditional role as controller of religion in the home.

Protestant reformers called upon men and women to read the Bible and participate in religious services together. In this way, the reformers provided a stimulus for the education of girls so they could read the Bible and other religious literature. The city council of Zwickau, for example, established a girls' school in 1525. But these schools were designed to encourage proper moral values rather than intellectual development and really did little to improve the position of women in society. Likewise, when women attempted to take more active roles in religious life, reformers—Lutheran and Calvinist alike—shrank back in horror. To them, the equality of the Gospel did not mean overthrowing the inequality of social classes or the sexes. Overall, the Protestant Reformation did not noticeably transform women's subordinate place in society.

Education in the Reformation

The Reformation had an important effect upon the development of education in Europe. Renaissance humanism had significantly altered the content of education (see Chapter 12), and Protestant educators were very successful in implementing and using humanist methods in Protestant secondary schools and universities. Unlike the humanist schools, however, which had been mostly for an elite, the sons and a few daughters of the nobility and wealthier bourgeoisie, Protestant schools were aimed at a much wider audience. Protestantism created an increased

A Protestant Woman

In the initial zeal of the Protestant Reformation, women were frequently allowed to play unusual roles. Katherine Zell of Germany (c. 1497–1562) first preached beside her husband in 1527. After the death of her two children, she devoted the rest of her life to helping her husband and their Anabaptist faith. This selection is taken from one of her letters to a young Lutheran minister who had criticized her activities.

❊ *Katherine Zell to Ludwig Rabus of Memmingen*

I, Katherine Zell, wife of the late lamented Mathew Zell, who served in Strasbourg, where I was born and reared and still live, wish you peace and enhancement in God's grace. . . .

From my earliest years I turned to the Lord, who taught and guided me, and I have at all times, in accordance with my understanding and His grace, embraced the interests of His church and earnestly sought Jesus. Even in youth this brought me the regard and affection of clergymen and others much concerned with the church, which is why the pious Mathew Zell wanted me as a companion in marriage; and I, in turn, to serve the glory of Christ, gave devotion and help to my husband, both in his ministry and in keeping his house. . . . Ever since I was ten years old I have been a student and a sort of church mother, much given to attending sermons. I have loved and frequented the company of learned men, and I conversed much with them, not about dancing, masquerades, and worldly pleasures but about the kingdom of God. . . .

Consider the poor Anabaptists, who are so furiously and ferociously persecuted. Must the authorities everywhere be incited against them, as the hunter drives his dog against wild animals? Against those who acknowledge Christ the Lord in very much the same way we do and over which we broke with the papacy? Just because they cannot agree with us on lesser things, is this any reason to persecute them and in them Christ, in whom they fervently believe and have often professed in misery, in prison, and under the torments of fire and water?

Governments may punish criminals, but they should not force and govern belief, which is a matter for the heart and conscience not for temporal authorities. . . . When the authorities pursue one, they soon bring forth tears, and towns and villages are emptied.

need for at least a semiliterate body of believers who could read the Bible for themselves.

While adopting the classical emphasis of humanist schools, Protestant reformers broadened the base of those being educated. Convinced of the need to provide the church with good Christians and good pastors as well as the state with good administrators and citizens, Martin Luther advocated that all children should have the opportunity of an education provided by the state. To that end, he urged the cities and villages of Saxony to establish schools paid for by the public. Luther's ideas were shared by his Wittenberg co-worker, Philip Melanchthon, whose educational efforts earned him the title of *Praecepter Germaniae*, the Teacher of Germany. In his scheme for education in Saxony, Melanchthon divided students into three classes or divisions based on their age or capabilities.

Following Melanchthon's example, the Protestants in Germany were responsible for introducing the gymnasium,

A SIXTEENTH-CENTURY CLASSROOM. Protestants in Germany developed secondary schools that combined instruction in the liberal arts with religious education. This scene from a painting by Hans Holbein shows a schoolmaster instructing a pupil in the alphabet while his wife helps a little girl.

or secondary school, where the humanist emphasis on the liberal arts based on instruction in Greek and Latin was combined with religious instruction. Most famous was the school in Strasbourg founded by Johannes Sturm in 1538, which served as a model for other Protestant schools. John Calvin's Genevan Academy, founded in 1559, was organized in two distinct parts. The "private school" or gymnasium was divided into seven classes for young people who were taught Latin and Greek grammar and literature as well as logic. In the "public school," students were taught philosophy, Hebrew, Greek, and, most importantly, theology. The Genevan Academy, which eventually became a university, came to concentrate on preparing ministers to spread the Calvinist view of the Gospel.

Catholics also perceived the importance of secondary schools and universities in educating people to Catholic perspectives. The Jesuits (see The Society of Jesus later in the next section) were especially proficient in combining humanist educational methods with religious instruction. Although both Catholic and Protestant secondary schools and universities were influenced by humanism, some humanists attacked them for misusing humanist methods. No doubt, as the Reformation progressed, confessional struggles made education increasingly serve the religious goal of producing zealous Protestants or Catholics. Virtually everywhere, teachers and professors were expected to follow the creeds of their ruling authorities.

Religious Practices and Popular Culture

Although Protestant reformers were conservative in their political and social attitudes, their attacks on the Catholic church led to radical changes in religious practices. The Protestant Reformation abolished or severely curtailed such customary practices as indulgences, the veneration of relics and saints, pilgrimages, monasticism, and clerical celibacy. In Protestant cities, attacks on the veneration of saints brought an end to popular religious processions that had been an important focus of religious devotion and often served as rituals to placate nature. The elimination of saints put an end to the numerous celebrations of religious holy days and changed a community's sense of time. Thus, in Protestant communities, religious ceremonies and imagery, such as processions and statues, tended to be replaced with individual private prayer, family worship, and collective prayer and worship at the same time each week on Sunday.

Many religious practices that had played an important role in popular culture were criticized by Protestant reformers as superstitious or remnants of pagan culture. Smarting under pressure from these Protestant attacks, even Catholic leaders sought to eliminate the more frivolous aspects of popular practices, although they never went as far as the Protestants. In addition to abolishing saints' days and religious carnivals, some Protestant reformers even tried to eliminate customary forms of entertainment. English Puritans (as English Calvinists were called), for example, attempted to ban drinking in taverns, dramatic performances, and dancing. Dutch Calvinists denounced the tradition of giving small presents to children on the feast of Saint Nicholas, near Christmas. Many of these Protestant attacks on popular culture were unsuccessful, however. The importance of taverns in English social life made it impossible to eradicate them, and celebrating at Christmas time persisted in the Dutch Netherlands.

◆ The Catholic Reformation

By the mid-sixteenth century, Lutheranism had become established in parts of Germany and Scandinavia, and Calvinism in parts of Switzerland, France, the Netherlands, and eastern Europe. In England, the split from Rome had resulted in the creation of a national church. The situation in Europe did not look particularly favorable for the Roman Catholic church. But even at the beginning of the sixteenth century, constructive, positive forces were at work for reform within the Catholic church, and by the mid-sixteenth century, they came to be directed by a revived and reformed papacy, giving the Catholic church new strength. By the second half of the sixteenth century, Catholicism had regained much that it had lost, especially in Germany and eastern Europe, and was able to make new conversions as well, particularly in the New World. We call the story of the revival of Roman Catholicism the Catholic Reformation, although some historians prefer to use the term Counter-Reformation, especially for those elements of the Catholic Reformation that were directly aimed at stopping the spread of the Protestant Reformation.

The Catholic Reformation was a mixture of old and new elements. The best features of medieval Catholicism were revived and then adjusted to meet new conditions, a situation most apparent in the revival of mysticism and monasticism. The emergence of a new mysticism, closely tied to the traditions of Catholic piety, was especially evident in the life of the Spanish mystic, Saint Teresa of Avila (1515–1582). A nun of the Carmelite order, Teresa experienced a variety of mystical visions that she claimed resulted in the ecstatic union of her soul with God. But Teresa also believed that mystical experience should lead to an active life of service on behalf of her Catholic faith. Consequently, she founded a new order of barefoot Carmelite nuns and worked to foster their mystical experiences.

The regeneration of religious orders also proved invaluable to the reform of Catholicism. Old orders, such as the Benedictines and Dominicans, were reformed and renewed. The Capuchins emerged when a group of Franciscans decided to return to the simplicity and poverty of Saint Francis of Assisi, the medieval founder of the Franciscan order. In addition to caring for the sick and the poor, the Capuchins focused on preaching the Gospel directly to the people and emerged as an effective force against Protestantism.

New religious orders and brotherhoods were also created. The Theatines, founded in 1524, placed their emphasis on reforming the secular clergy and encouraging those

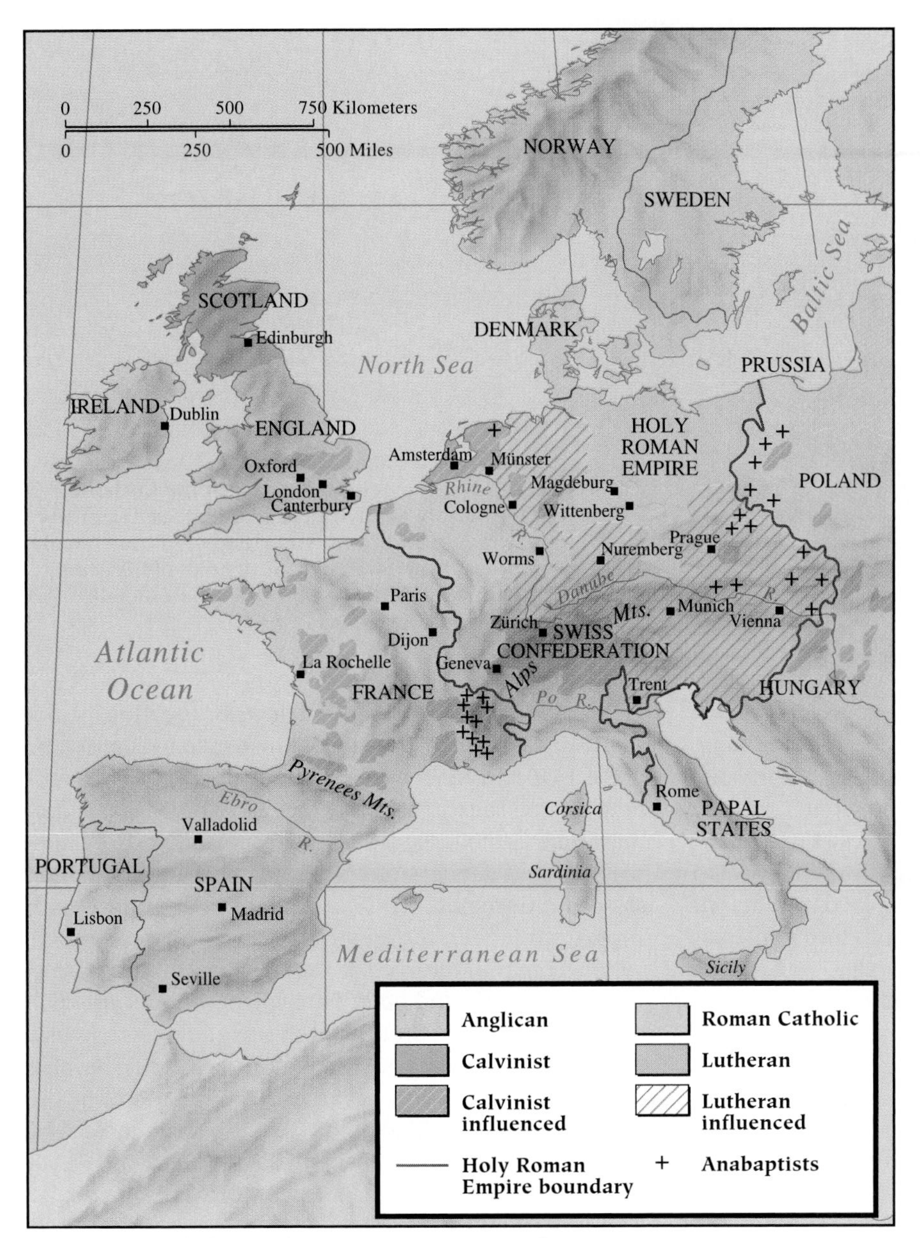

MAP 13.2 Catholics and Protestants in Europe by 1560.

clerics to fulfill their duties among the laity. The Theatines also founded orphanages and hospitals to care for the victims of war and plague. The Ursulines, a new order of nuns founded in Italy in 1535, focused their attention on establishing schools for the education of girls.

The Oratory of Divine Love, first organized in Italy in 1497, was not a new religious order but an informal group of clergy and laymen who worked to foster reform by emphasizing personal spiritual development and outward acts of charity. The "philosophy of Christ," advocated by the Christian humanist Erasmus, was especially appealing to many of them. The Oratory's members included a number of cardinals who favored the reform of the Catholic church.

The Society of Jesus

Of all the new religious orders, the most important was the Society of Jesus, known as the Jesuits, who became the chief instrument of the Catholic Reformation. The Society of Jesus was founded by a Spanish nobleman, Ignatius of Loyola (1491–1556), whose injuries in battle cut short his military career. Loyola experienced a spiritual torment similar to Luther's but, unlike Luther, resolved his problems not by a new doctrine, but by a decision to submit his will to the will of the church. Unable to be a real soldier, he vowed to be a soldier of God. Over a period of twelve years, Loyola prepared for his lifework by mortification, prayer, pilgrimages, going to school, and working out a spiritual program in his brief, but powerful book, *The Spiritual Exercises*. This was a training manual for spiritual development emphasizing exercises by which the human will could be strengthened and made to follow the will of God as manifested through his instrument, the Catholic church (see the box on p. 389).

Gradually, Loyola gathered together a small group of individuals who shared his single-minded devotion and were eventually recognized as a religious order, the Society of Jesus, by a papal bull in 1540. The new order was grounded on the principles of absolute obedience to the papacy, a strict hierarchical order for the society, the use of education to achieve its goals, and a dedication to engage in "conflict for God." Jesuit organization came to resemble the structure of a military command. A two-year novitiate weeded out all but the most dedicated. Executive leadership was put in the hands of a general, who nominated all important positions in the order and was to be revered as the absolute head of the order. Loyola served as the first general of the order until his death in 1556. A special vow of absolute obedience to the pope made the Jesuits an important instrument for papal policy.

The Jesuits pursued three major activities. They established highly disciplined schools, borrowing freely from humanist schools for their educational methods. To the Jesuits, the thorough education of young people was crucial to combat the advance of Protestantism. In the course of the sixteenth century, the Jesuits took over the premier academic posts in Catholic universities, and by 1600, they were the most famous educators in Europe. Another prominent Jesuit activity was the propagation of the Catholic faith among non-Christians. Francis Xavier (1506–1552), one of the original members of the Society of Jesus, carried the message of Catholic Christianity to the East, ministering to

IGNATIUS LOYOLA. The Jesuits became the most important new religious order of the Catholic Reformation. Shown here in a sixteenth-century painting by an unknown artist is Ignatius Loyola, founder of the Society of Jesus. Loyola is seen kneeling before Pope Paul III, who officially recognized the Jesuits in 1540.

India and Japan before dying of fever. Although conversion efforts in Japan proved short-lived, Jesuit activity in China, especially that of the Italian Matteo Ricci, was more long lasting. Finally, the Jesuits were determined to carry the Catholic banner and fight Protestantism. Jesuit missionaries proved singularly successful in restoring Catholicism to parts of Germany and eastern Europe. Poland was, in fact, largely won back for the Catholic church through Jesuit efforts. As the "shock troops of the papacy," the Jesuits proved invaluable allies of papal policies.

A Revived Papacy

The involvement of the Renaissance papacy in dubious finances and Italian political and military affairs had created numerous sources of corruption. The meager steps taken to control corruption left the papacy still in need of serious reform, and it took the jolt of the Protestant Reformation to bring it about. Indeed, the change in the papacy in the course of the sixteenth century was one of the more remarkable aspects of the Catholic Reformation.

The pontificate of Pope Paul III (1534–1549) proved to be a turning point in the reform of the papacy. Raised in the lap of Renaissance luxury, Paul III continued Renaissance papal practices by appointing his nephews as cardinals, involving himself in politics, and patronizing arts and letters on a lavish scale. Nevertheless, he perceived the need for change and expressed it decisively. Advocates of reform, such as Gasparo Contarini and Gian Pietro Caraffa, were made cardinals. In 1535, Paul took the audacious step of appointing a Reform Commission to study the church's condition. The commission's report in 1537, which blamed the church's problems on the corrupt policies of popes and cardinals, was used even by Protestants to demonstrate that their criticisms of Catholic corruption had been justified. Paul III also formally recognized the Jesuits and summoned the Council of Trent.

A decisive turning point in the direction of the Catholic Reformation and the nature of papal reform came in the 1540s. In 1541, a colloquy had been held at Regensburg in a final attempt to settle the religious division peacefully. Here Catholic moderates, such as Cardinal Contarini, who favored concessions to Protestants in the hope of restoring Christian unity, reached a compromise with Protestant moderates on a number of doctrinal issues. When Contarini returned to Rome with these proposals, Cardinal Caraffa and other hard-liners, who regarded all compromise with Protestant innovations as heresy, accused him of selling out to the heretics. It soon became apparent that the conservative reformers were in the ascendancy when Caraffa was able to persuade Paul III to establish a Roman Inquisition or Holy Office in 1542 to ferret out doctrinal errors. There was to be no compromise with Protestantism.

When Cardinal Caraffa was chosen pope as Paul IV (1555–1559), he so increased the power of the Inquisition that even liberal cardinals were silenced. This "first true pope of the Catholic Counter-Reformation," as he has been called, also created an Index of Forbidden Books, a list of books that Catholics were not allowed to read. It included all the works of Protestant theologians as well as authors considered "unwholesome," a category general enough to include the works of Erasmus. Rome, the capital of Catholic Christianity, was rapidly becoming fortress Rome; any hope of restoring Christian unity by compromise was fast fading. The activities of the Council of Trent made compromise virtually impossible.

The Council of Trent

In 1542, Pope Paul III took the decisive step of calling for a general council of Christendom to resolve the religious differences created by the Protestant revolt. It was not until March 1545, however, that a group of cardinals,

Loyola and Obedience to "Our Holy Mother, the Hierarchical Church"

In his Spiritual Exercises, *Ignatius Loyola developed a systematic program for "the conquest of self and the regulation of one's life" for service to the hierarchical Catholic church. Ignatius's supreme goal was the commitment of the Christian to active service under Jesus' banner in the Church of Christ (the Catholic church). In the final section of the* Spiritual Exercises, *Loyola explained the nature of that commitment in a series of "Rules for Thinking with the Church."*

Ignatius Loyola, "Rules for Thinking with the Church"

The following rules should be observed to foster the true attitude of mind we ought to have in the Church militant.

1. We must put aside all judgment of our own, and keep the mind ever ready and prompt to obey in all things the true Spouse of Jesus Christ, our holy Mother, the hierarchical Church.
2. We should praise sacramental confession, the yearly reception of the Most Blessed Sacrament [the Lord's Supper], and praise more highly monthly reception, and still more weekly Communion. . . .
3. We ought to praise the frequent hearing of Mass, the singing of hymns, psalmody, and long prayers whether in the church or outside. . . .
4. We must praise highly religious life, virginity, and continency; and matrimony ought not be praised as much as any of these.
5. We should praise vows of religion, obedience, poverty, chastity, and vows to perform other works of supererogation conducive to perfection. . . .
6. We should show our esteem for the relics of the saints by venerating them and praying to the saints. We should praise visits to the Station Churches, pilgrimages, indulgences, jubilees, the lighting of candles in churches.
7. We must praise the regulations of the Church, with regard to fast and abstinence, for example, in Lent, on Ember Days, Vigils, Fridays, and Saturdays.
8. We ought to praise not only the building and adornment of churches, but also images and veneration of them according to the subject they represent.
9. Finally, we must praise all the commandments of the Church, and be on the alert to find reasons to defend them, and by no means in order to criticize them.
10. We should be more ready to approve and praise the orders, recommendations, and way of acting of our superiors than to find fault with them. Though some of the orders, etc., may not have been praiseworthy, yet to speak against them, either when preaching in public or in speaking before the people, would rather be the cause of murmuring and scandal than of profit. As a consequence, the people would become angry with their superiors, whether secular or spiritual. But while it does harm in the absence of our superiors to speak evil of them before the people, it may be profitable to discuss their bad conduct with those who can apply a remedy.

13. If we wish to proceed securely in all things, we must hold fast to the following principle: What seems to me white, I will believe black if the hierarchical Church so defines. For I must be convinced that in Christ our Lord, the bridegroom, and in His spouse the Church, only one Spirit holds sway, which governs and rules for the salvation of souls.

archbishops, bishops, abbots, and theologians met in the city of Trent on the border between Germany and Italy. This Council of Trent met intermittently from 1545 to 1563 in three major sessions. Two fundamental struggles determined its outcome. Whereas the pope hoped to focus on doctrinal issues, the Holy Roman Emperor Charles V wanted church reform to be the chief order of business, since he realized that defining doctrine first would only make the split in the church permanent. A second conflict focused on the division between Catholic moderates and conservatives. The former believed that compromises would have to be made in formulating doctrinal definitions, whereas the latter favored an uncompromising restatement of Catholic doctrines in strict opposition to Protestant positions. The latter group won, although not without a struggle. The Protestants were invited to attend the council, but since they were not permitted to participate, they refused the meaningless invitation. By and large, the popes controlled the council.

The final doctrinal decrees of the Council of Trent reaffirmed traditional Catholic teachings in opposition to Protestant beliefs. Scripture and tradition were affirmed as equal authorities in religious matters; only the church could interpret Scripture. Both faith and good works were declared necessary for salvation. The seven sacraments, the Catholic doctrine of transubstantiation, and clerical celibacy were all upheld. Belief in purgatory and in the efficacy of indulgences was affirmed, although the hawking of indulgences was prohibited. Of the reforming decrees that were passed, the most important established theological seminaries in every diocese for the training of priests.

After the Council of Trent, the Roman Catholic church possessed a clear body of doctrine and a unified church under the acknowledged supremacy of the popes who had triumphed over bishops and councils. The Roman Catholic church had become one Christian denomination among many with an organizational framework and doctrinal pattern that would not be significantly altered until Vatican Council II 400 years later. With a new spirit of confidence, the Catholic church entered a militant phase, as well prepared as the Calvinists to do battle for the Lord. An era of religious warfare was about to unfold.

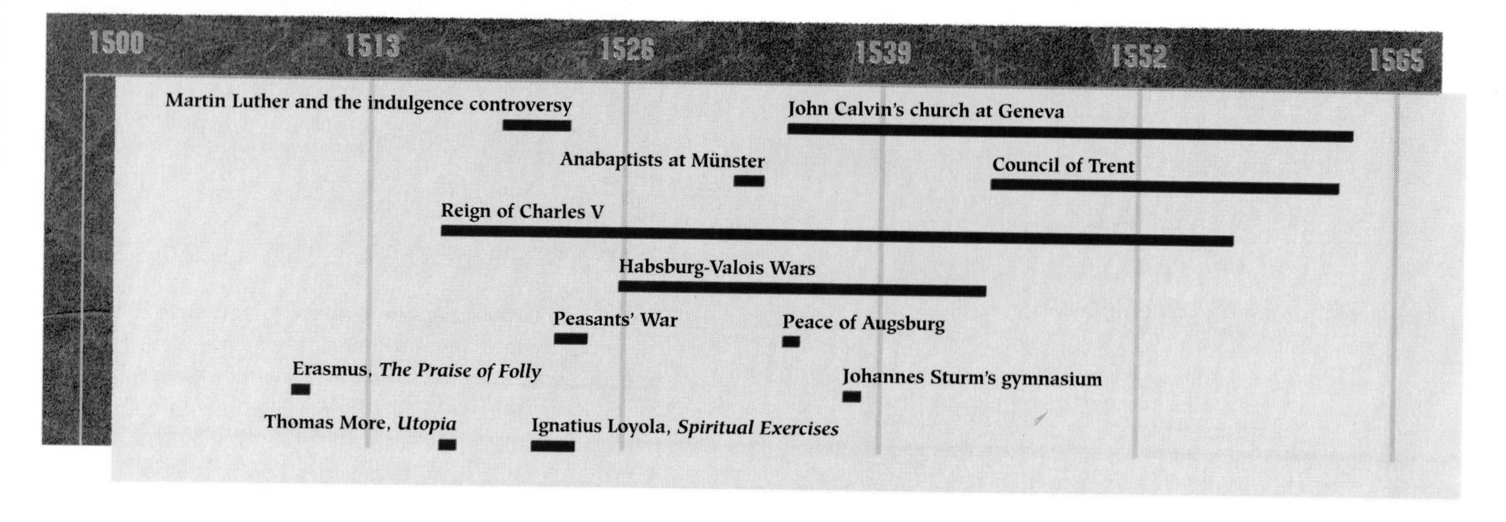

CONCLUSION

When the Augustinian monk Martin Luther entered the public scene with a series of theses on indulgences, few people in Europe, or Germany for that matter, suspected that these theses would eventually produce a division of Europe along religious lines. But the yearning for reform of the church and meaningful religious experience caused a seemingly simple dispute to escalate into a powerful movement. Clearly, the papacy and other elements in the Catholic church underestimated the strength of Martin Luther and the desire for religious change.

Although Luther felt that his revival of Christianity based on his interpretation of the Bible should be acceptable to all, others soon appeared who also read the Bible but interpreted it in different ways. Protestantism split into different sects, which, though united in their dislike of Catholicism, were themselves divided over the interpretation of the sacraments and religious practices. As reform ideas spread, religion and politics became ever more intertwined. Political support played a crucial role in the spread of the Reformation.

Although Lutheranism was legally acknowledged in the Holy Roman Empire by the Peace of Augsburg in 1555, it had lost much of its momentum and apart from Scandinavia had scant ability to attract new supporters. Its energy was largely replaced by the new Protestant form of Calvinism, which had a clarity of doctrine and a fervor that made it attractive to a whole new generation of Europeans. Although Calvinism's militancy enabled it to expand across Europe, Catholicism was also experiencing its own revival and emerged as a militant faith, prepared to do combat for the souls of the faithful. An age of religious passion would tragically be followed by an age of religious warfare.

NOTES

1. Erasmus, *The Paraclesis,* in John Olin, ed., *Christian Humanism and the Reformation: Selected Writings of Erasmus,* 3d ed. (New York, 1987), p. 101.
2. Quoted in James B. Ross and Mary M. McLaughlin, eds., *The Portable Renaissance Reader* (New York, 1953), p. 83.
3. Thomas More, *Utopia,* trans. Paul Turner (Harmondsworth, 1965), p. 76.
4. Ibid., pp. 63–64.
5. Quoted in Alister E. McGrath, *Reformation Thought: An Introduction* (Oxford, 1988), p. 72.
6. Quoted in Roland Bainton, *Here I Stand: A Life of Martin Luther* (New York, 1950), pp. 49–50.
7. Quoted in Gordon Rupp, *Luther's Progress to the Diet of Worms* (New York, 1964), p. 82.
8. Quoted in ibid., p. 81.
9. *On the Freedom of a Christian Man,* quoted in E. G. Rupp and Benjamin Drewery, eds., *Martin Luther* (New York, 1970), p. 50.
10. Quoted in Bainton, *Here I Stand,* p. 144.
11. Quoted in De Lamar Jensen, *Reformation Europe* (Lexington, Mass., 1981), p. 83.
12. Quoted in A. G. Dickens and Dorothy Carr, eds., *The Reformation in England to the Accession of Elizabeth I* (New York, 1968), p. 72.
13. Quoted in Lewis W. Spitz, *The Renaissance and Reformation Movements* (Chicago, 1971), p. 414.
14. John Calvin, *Institutes of the Christian Religion,* trans. John Allen (Philadelphia, 1936), 1:220.
15. Ibid., 1:228; 2:181.
16. Quoted in Roland Bainton, *Women of the Reformation in Germany and Italy* (Minneapolis, 1971), p. 154.

17. Quoted in Bonnie S. Anderson and Judith P. Zinsser, *A History of Their Own: Women in Europe from Prehistory to the Present* (New York, 1988), 1:259.
18. Quoted in John A. Phillips, *Eve: The History of an Idea* (New York, 1984), p. 105.

SUGGESTIONS FOR FURTHER READING

Basic surveys of the Reformation period include H. J. Grimm, *The Reformation Era, 1500–1650,* 2d ed. (New York, 1973); C. Lindberg, *The European Reformations* (Cambridge, Mass., 1996); D. L. Jensen, *Reformation Europe* (Lexington, Mass., 1981); G. R. Elton, *Reformation Europe, 1517–1559* (Cleveland, 1963); and E. Cameron, *The European Reformation* (New York, 1991). L. W. Spitz, *The Protestant Reformation, 1517–1559* (New York, 1985), is a sound and up-to-date history. The significance of the Protestant Reformation is examined in S. Ozment, *Protestants: The Birth of a Revolution* (New York, 1992). A brief but very useful introduction to the theology of the Reformation can be found in A. McGrath, *Reformation Thought: An Introduction,* 2d ed. (Oxford, 1993). For an overview of how European religious life in the Late Middle Ages affected the Reformation, see J. Bossy, *Christianity in the West: 1400–1700* (Oxford, 1987). There are good collections of essays in A. Pettegree, *The Early Reformation in Europe* (Cambridge, 1992); and B. Scribner, R. Porter, and M. Teich, eds., *The Reformation in National Context* (Cambridge, 1994).

The development of humanism outside Italy is examined in C. G. Nauert, Jr., *Humanism and the Culture of Renaissance Europe* (Cambridge, 1995). On Thomas More, see R. Marius, *Thomas More: A Biography* (New York, 1984). The best general biography of Erasmus is still R. Bainton, *Erasmus of Christendom* (New York, 1969), although the shorter works by J. K. Sowards, *Desiderius Erasmus* (Boston, 1975), and J. McConica, *Erasmus* (Oxford, 1991), are also good.

The Reformation in Germany can be examined in H. Holborn, *A History of Modern Germany: The Reformation* (New York, 1959), still an outstanding survey of the entire Reformation period in Germany; and J. Lortz, *The Reformation in Germany,* trans. R. Walls, 2 vols. (New York, 1968), a detailed Catholic account. The classic account of Martin Luther's life is R. Bainton, *Here I Stand: A Life of Martin Luther* (New York and Nashville, 1950). More recent works include H. A. Oberman, *Luther* (New York, 1992); W. von Loewenich, *Martin Luther: The Man and His Work* (Minneapolis, 1986); and J. M. Kittelson, *Luther the Reformer: The Story of the Man and His Career* (Minneapolis, 1986). Luther's relations with early Protestant dissenters from his ideas can be examined in M. Edwards, Jr., *Luther and the False Brethren* (Stanford, 1975). On the Peasants' War, see especially P. Blickle, *The Revolution of 1525: The German Peasants' War from a New Perspective* (Baltimore, 1981). The spread of Luther's ideas in Germany can be examined in M. Hannemann, *The Diffusion of the Reformation in Southwestern Germany, 1518–1534* (Chicago, 1975); B. Moeller, *Imperial Cities and the Reformation* (Durham, N.C., 1982); S. Ozment, *The Reformation in the Cities* (New Haven, Conn., 1975); and R. Po-Chia Hsia, ed., *The German People and the Reformation* (Ithaca, N.Y., 1988).

The best account of Ulrich Zwingli is G. R. Potter, *Zwingli* (Cambridge, 1976), although W. P. Stephens, *Zwingli* (Oxford, 1994) is an important study of Zwingli's ideas. One aspect of the spread of the Reformation in Switzerland is examined in J. M. Kittelson, *Wolfgang Capito: From Humanist to Reformer* (Leiden, 1975).

The most comprehensive account of the various groups and individuals who are called Anabaptists is G. H. Williams, *The Radical Reformation,* 2d ed. (Kirsville, M.O., 1992). Other valuable studies include C.-P. Clasen, *Anabaptism: A Social History, 1525–1618* (Ithaca, N.Y., 1972); and M. Mullett, *Radical Religious Movements in Early Modern Europe* (London, 1980). Also see R. Po-Chia Hsia, *Society and Reformation in Münster, 1535–1618* (New Haven, Conn., 1984).

Two worthwhile surveys of the English Reformation are A. G. Dickens, *The English Reformation,* 2d ed. (New York, 1989); and G. R. Elton, *Reform and Reformation: England, 1509–1558* (Cambridge, Mass., 1977). Good biographies of the leading personalities of the age include J. J. Scarisbrick, *Henry VIII* (Berkeley, 1968); B. W. Beckensgale, *Thomas Cromwell, Tudor Minister* (Totowa, N.J., 1978); J. Ridley, *Thomas Cranmer* (Oxford, 1962); and D. M. Loades, *The Reign of Mary Tudor* (London, 1979). Other specialized works on the period include the controversial classic by G. R. Elton, *The Tudor Revolution in Government,* 2d ed. (Cambridge, 1973); and D. Knowles, *Bare Ruined Choirs: The Dissolution of the English Monasteries* (New York, 1976).

On John Calvin, see A. McGrath, *A Life of John Calvin: A Study in the Shaping of Western Culture* (Cambridge, Mass., 1990); and W. J. Bouwsma, *John Calvin* (New York, 1988). The best account of Calvin's work in the city of Geneva is W. Monter, *Calvin's Geneva* (New York, 1967).

On the impact of the Reformation on the family, see J. F. Harrington, *Reordering Marriage and Society in Reformation Germany* (New York, 1995). M. E. Wiesner's *Working Women in Renaissance Germany* (New Brunswick, N.J., 1986), covers primarily the sixteenth century. There is also a good collection of essays in S. Marshall, ed., *Women in Reformation and Counter-Reformation Europe: Public and Private Worlds* (Bloomington, Ind., 1989). On education, see G. Strauss, *Luther's House of Learning* (Baltimore, 1978). R. W. Scribner's *For the Sake of Simple Folk* (Cambridge, 1981) deals with a number of issues on the popular culture of the German Reformation.

A good introduction to the Catholic Reformation can be found in the beautifully illustrated brief study by A. G. Dickens, *The Counter Reformation* (New York, 1969). Also valuable is M. R. O'Connell, *The Counter Reformation, 1559–1610* (New York, 1974). On Loyola, see P. Caravan, *Ignatius Loyola, A Biography of the Founder of the Jesuits* (San Francisco, 1990); and W. W. Meissner, *Ignatius of Loyola: The Psychology of a Saint* (New Haven, Conn., 1994). The work by J. O'Malley, *The First Jesuits* (Cambridge, Mass., 1995), offers a clear discussion of the founding of the Jesuits. On the new religious orders, see R. L. Demolen, ed., *Religious Orders of the Catholic Reformation* (New York, 1996).

CHAPTER

14 Discovery and Crisis in the Sixteenth and Seventeenth Centuries

CHAPTER OUTLINE

FOCUS QUESTIONS

- Why did Europeans begin to amass overseas empires during the sixteenth century, and what effects did this experience have on both the Europeans and conquered peoples?
- What role did religion play in the European wars of the sixteenth century and the Thirty Years' War of the seventeenth century?
- How did the religious policy, the foreign policy, and the governments of Philip II of Spain and Elizabeth I of England differ?
- What economic and social crises did Europe experience between 1560 and 1650?
- How did the turmoil in Europe between 1560 and 1650 contribute to the witchcraft craze and to the artistic and intellectual developments of the period?

BY THE MIDDLE of the sixteenth century, it was apparent that the religious passions of the Reformation era had brought an end to the religious unity of medieval Europe. The religious division (Catholics versus Protestants) was instrumental in beginning a series of wars that dominated much of European history between 1560 and 1650. The struggles fought in Germany at the beginning of the seventeenth century (known as the Thirty Years' War) were especially brutal and devastating. When the Catholic general Johann Tilly captured Neubrandenburg, his forces massacred the 3,000 defenders. A month later, the army of the Protestant leader Gustavus Adolphus retaliated by slaughtering the entire garrison of 2,000 men at Frankfurt-an-der-Oder. Noncombatants suffered as well, as is evident from the contemporary description by Otto von Guericke of the sack of Magdeburg. Once the city had been captured, Tilly's forces were let loose: "Then there was nothing but beating and burning, plundering, torture, and murder." All the buildings were looted of anything valuable, and then the city was "given over to the flames, and thousands of innocent men, women, and children, in the midst of a horrible noise of heartrending shrieks and cries, were tortured and put to death in so cruel and shameful a manner that no words would suffice to describe." Thus, "in a single day this noble and famous city, the pride of the whole country, went up in fire and smoke, and the remnant of its citizens, with their wives and children, were taken prisoners and driven away by the enemy."

The wars, in turn, worsened the economic and social crises that were besetting Europe. Wars, rebellions and constitutional crises, economic depression, social disintegration, a witchcraft craze, and a demographic crisis all afflicted Europe and have led some historians to speak of the ninety years between 1560 and 1650 as an age of crisis in European life.

Periods of crisis, however, are frequently ages of opportunities, nowhere more apparent than in the geographical discoveries that made this an era of European expansion into new worlds. Although the discovery of new territories began before the sixteenth century, it was not until the sixteenth and seventeenth centuries that Europeans began to comprehend the significance of their discoveries and to exploit them for their material gain.

◆ An Age of Discovery and Expansion

Nowhere has the dynamic and even ruthless energy of Western civilization been more apparent than in its expansion into the rest of the world. By the sixteenth century, the Atlantic seaboard had become the center of a commercial activity that raised Portugal and Spain and later the Dutch Republic, England, and France to prominence. The age of expansion was a crucial factor in the European transition from the agrarian economy of the Middle Ages to a commercial and industrial capitalistic system. Expansion also led Europeans into new and lasting contacts with non-European peoples that inaugurated a new age of world history in the sixteenth century.

The Motives

For almost a millennium, Catholic Europe had been confined to one geographical area. Its one major attempt to expand beyond those frontiers, the crusades, had largely failed. Of course, Europe had never completely lost touch with the outside world: the goods of Asia and Africa made their way into medieval castles; the works of Muslim philosophers were read in medieval universities; and in the ninth and tenth centuries the Vikings had even made their way to the eastern fringes of North America. But in all cases, contacts with non-European civilizations remained limited until the end of the fifteenth century, when Europeans embarked upon a remarkable series of overseas journeys. What caused Europeans to undertake such dangerous voyages to the ends of the earth?

Europeans had long been attracted to lands outside Europe. Indeed, a large body of fantasy literature about "other worlds" blossomed in the Middle Ages. In the fourteenth century, the author of *The Travels of John Mandeville* spoke of realms (which he had never seen) filled with precious stones and gold. Other lands were more frightening. In one country, "the folk be great giants of twenty-eight foot long, or thirty foot long. . . . And they eat more gladly man's flesh than any other flesh." Further north was a land inhabited by "full cruel and evil women. And they have precious stones in their eyes. And they be of that kind that if they behold any man with wrath they slay him at once with the beholding."[1] Other writers spoke of mysterious Christian kingdoms: the magical kingdom of Prester John in Africa and a Christian community in southern India that was supposedly founded by Thomas, the apostle of Jesus.

Although Muslim control of central Asia cut Europe off from the countries further east, the Mongol conquests in the thirteenth century had reopened the doors. The most famous medieval travelers to the East were the Polos of Venice. Niccolò and Maffeo, merchants from Venice, accompanied by Niccolò's son Marco, undertook the lengthy journey to the court of the great Mongol ruler Khubilai Khan (1259–1294) in 1271. As one of the Great Khan's ambassadors, Marco went on missions as well and did not return to Italy until 1295. An account of his experiences, the *Travels*, proved to be the most informative of all the descriptions of Asia by medieval European travelers. Others followed the Polos, but in the fourteenth century, the conquests of the Ottoman Turks and then the breakup of the Mongol Empire reduced Western traffic to the East. With the closing of the overland routes, a number of people in Europe became interested in the possibility of reaching Asia by sea to gain access to the spices and other precious items of the region. Christopher Columbus had a copy of Marco Polo's *Travels* in his possession when he began to envision his epoch-making voyage across the Atlantic Ocean.

An economic motive thus looms large in Renaissance European expansion. Merchants, adventurers, and government officials had high hopes of finding precious metals and new areas of trade, in particular, more direct sources for the spices of the East. The latter continued to come to Europe via Arab intermediaries but were outrageously expensive. Many European explorers and conquerors did not hesitate to express their desire for material gain. One Spanish conquistador explained that he and his kind went to the New World to "serve God and His

Majesty, to give light to those who were in darkness, and to grow rich, as all men desire to do."[2]

This statement expresses another major reason for the overseas voyages—religious zeal. A crusading mentality was particularly strong in Portugal and Spain where the Muslims had largely been driven out in the Middle Ages. Contemporaries of Prince Henry the Navigator of Portugal (see the next section) said that he was motivated by "his great desire to make increase in the faith of our Lord Jesus Christ and to bring him all the souls that should be saved." Although most scholars believe that the religious motive was secondary to economic considerations, it would be foolish to overlook the genuine desire on the part of both explorers and conquistadors, let alone missionaries, to convert the heathen to Christianity. Hernán Cortés, the conqueror of Mexico, asked his Spanish rulers if it was not their duty to ensure that the native Mexicans "are introduced into and instructed in the holy Catholic faith," and predicted that if "the devotion, trust and hope which they now have in their idols turned so as to repose with the divine power of the true God . . . they would work many miracles."[3] Spiritual and secular affairs were closely intertwined in the sixteenth century. No doubt, grandeur and glory as well as plain intellectual curiosity and spirit of adventure also played some role in European expansion.

If "God, glory, and gold" were the primary motives, what made the voyages possible? First of all, the expansion of Europe was connected to the growth of centralized monarchies during the Renaissance. Although historians still debate the degree of that centralization, the reality is that Renaissance expansion was a state enterprise. By the second half of the fifteenth century, European monarchies had increased both their authority and their resources and were in a position to turn their energies beyond their borders. For France, that meant the invasion of Italy, but for Portugal, a state not strong enough to pursue power in Europe, it meant going abroad. The Spanish scene was more complex because the Spanish monarchy was strong enough by the sixteenth century to pursue power both in Europe and beyond.

At the same time, by the end of the fifteenth century, Europeans had achieved a level of wealth and technology that enabled them to make a regular series of voyages beyond Europe. Although the highly schematic and symbolic medieval maps were of little help to sailors, the *portolani,* or detailed charts made by medieval navigators and mathematicians in the thirteenth and fourteenth centuries, were more useful. With details on coastal contours, distances between ports, and compass readings, they proved of great value for voyages in European waters. But because the *portolani* were drawn on a flat scale and took no account of the curvature of the earth, they were of little use for longer overseas voyages. Only when seafarers began to venture beyond the coast of Europe did they begin to accumulate information about the actual shape of the earth. By the end of the fifteenth century, cartography had developed to the point that Europeans possessed fairly accurate maps of the known world.

In addition, Europeans had developed remarkably seaworthy ships as well as new navigational techniques. European shipmakers had mastered the use of the axial rudder (an import from China) and had learned to combine the use of lateen sails with a square rig. With these innovations, they could construct ships mobile enough to sail against the wind and engage in naval warfare and also large enough to mount heavy cannon and carry a substantial amount of goods over long distances. Previously, sailors had used a quadrant and their knowledge of the position of the Pole Star to ascertain their latitude. Below the equator, however, this technique was useless. Only

THE CARAVEL, WORKHORSE OF THE AGE OF EXPLORATION. Prior to the fifteenth century, most European ships were either small craft with lateen sails used in the Mediterranean or slow, unwieldly square-rigged vessels operating in the North Atlantic. By the sixteenth century, European naval architects began to build ships that combined the maneuverability and speed offered by lateen sails with the carrying capacity and seaworthiness of the square-riggers. Shown here is a representation of Christopher Columbus's flagship *Santa Maria,* which took part in the first Spanish voyage across the Atlantic Ocean.

with the assistance of new navigational aids such as the compass and the astrolabe were they able to explore the high seas with confidence.

A final spur to exploration was the growing knowledge of the wind patterns in the Atlantic Ocean. The first European fleets sailing southward along the coast of West Africa had found their efforts to return hindered by the strong winds that blew steadily from the north along the coast. By the late fifteenth century, however, sailors had learned to tack out into the ocean, where they were able to catch westerly winds in the vicinity of the Azores islands that brought them back to the coast of western Europe. Christopher Columbus used this technique in his voyages to the Americas, and others relied on their new knowledge of the winds to round the continent of Africa in search of the Spice Islands.

The Development of a Portuguese Maritime Empire

Portugal took the lead in exploring the coast of Africa under the sponsorship of Prince Henry the "Navigator" (1394–1460), whose motives were a blend of seeking a Christian kingdom as an ally against the Muslims, acquiring trade opportunities for Portugal, and extending Christianity. In 1419, Prince Henry founded a school for navigators on the southwestern coast of Portugal. Shortly thereafter, Portuguese fleets began probing southward along the western coast of Africa in search of gold, which had been carried northward from south of the Atlas Mountain in central Morocco for centuries. In 1441, Portuguese ships reached the Senegal River, just north of Cape Verde, and brought home a cargo of black Africans, most of whom were then sold as slaves to wealthy buyers elsewhere in Europe. Within a few years, an estimated 1,000 slaves were shipped annually from the area back to Lisbon.

Through regular expeditions, the Portuguese gradually crept down the African coast, and in 1471, they discovered a new source of gold along the southern coast of the hump of West Africa (an area that would henceforth be known to Europeans as the Gold Coast). A few years later, they established contact with the state of Bakongo, near the mouth of the Zaire (Congo) River in central Africa. To facilitate trade in gold, ivory, and slaves (some of the latter were brought back to Lisbon while others were bartered to local merchants for gold), the Portuguese leased land from local rulers and built stone forts along the coast.

Hearing reports of a route to India around the southern tip of Africa, Portuguese sea captains continued their probing. In 1488, Bartholomeu Dias (c. 1450–1500) took advantage of westerly winds in the South Atlantic to round the Cape of Good Hope, but he feared a mutiny from his crew and returned home without continuing onward. Ten years later, a fleet under the command of Vasco da Gama (c. 1460–1524) rounded the cape and stopped at several ports controlled by Muslim merchants along the coast of East Africa. Then, da Gama's fleet crossed the Arabian Sea and reached the port of Calicut, on the southwestern coast of India, on May 18, 1498. On arriving in Calicut, da Gama announced to his surprised hosts that he had arrived in search of "Christians and spices." He found no Christians, but he did find the spices he sought. Although he lost two ships en route, da Gama's remaining vessels returned to Europe with their holds filled with ginger and cinnamon, a cargo that earned the investors a profit of several thousand percent.

For the next several years, Portuguese fleets returned annually to the area, seeking to destroy Arabic shipping and establish a monopoly in the spice trade. In 1509, a Portuguese armada defeated a combined fleet of Turkish and Indian ships off the coast of India and began to impose a blockade on the entrance to the Red Sea to cut off the flow of spices to Muslim rulers in Egypt and the Ottoman Empire. The following year, seeing the need for a land base in the area, Admiral Alfonso de Albuquerque (c. 1462–1515) set up port facilities at Goa, on the western coast of India south of present-day Bombay. Goa henceforth became the headquarters for Portuguese operations throughout the entire region. Although Indian merchants were permitted to continue their trading activities, the Portuguese conducted raids against Arab shippers, provoking the following brief report from an Arab source: "In this year the vessels of the Portuguese appeared at sea en route for India and those parts. They took about seven vessels, killing those on board and making some prisoner. This was their first action, may God curse them."[4]

The Portuguese now began to range more widely in search of the source of the spice trade. In 1511, Albuquerque sailed into the harbor of Malacca on the Malay peninsula. Malacca had been transformed by its Muslim rulers into a thriving port and a major stopping point for the spice trade. For Albuquerque, control of Malacca would serve two purposes. It could help to destroy the Arab spice trade and also provide the Portuguese with a way station on the route to the Moluccas, then known as the Spice Islands. After a short but bloody battle, the Portuguese seized the city and massacred the local Arab population. This slaughter initiated a fierce and brutal struggle between the Portuguese and the Arabs. According to one account, "to enhance the terror of his name he [Albuquerque] always separated Arabs from the other inhabitants of a captured city, and cut off the right hand of the men, and the noses and ears of the women."[5]

From Malacca, the Portuguese launched expeditions further east, to China and the Spice Islands. There they signed a treaty with a local ruler for the purchase and export of cloves to the European market. The Portuguese trading empire was now complete. Within a few years, they had managed to seize control of the spice trade from Muslim traders and had garnered substantial profits for the Portuguese monarchy. Nevertheless, the Portuguese Empire remained limited, consisting only of trading posts on the coasts of India and China. The Portuguese lacked the power, the population, and the desire to colonize the Asian regions.

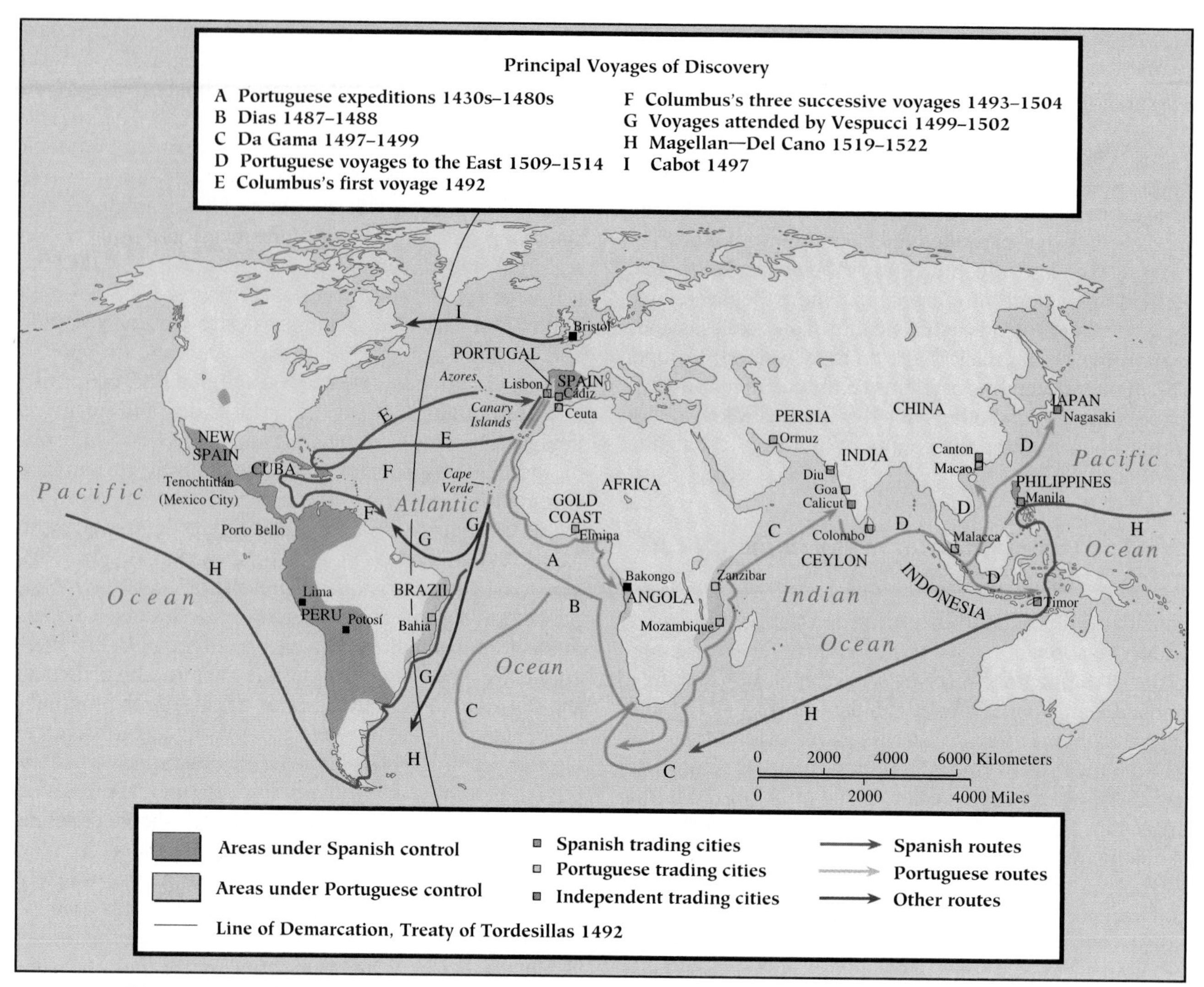

MAP 14.1 Discoveries and Possessions in the Fifteenth and Sixteenth Centuries.

Why were the Portuguese so successful? Basically, their success was a matter of guns and seamanship. The first Portuguese fleet to arrive in Indian waters was relatively modest in size, consisting of three ships and twenty guns, a force sufficient for self-defense and intimidation, but not for serious military operations. Later Portuguese fleets, which began to arrive with regularity early in the sixteenth century, were more heavily armed and were able not only to intimidate but also to inflict severe defeats if necessary on local naval and land forces. The Portuguese by no means possessed a monopoly on the use of firearms and explosives, but their effective use of naval technology, their heavy guns that could be mounted in the hulls of their sturdy vessels, and their tactics gave them a military superiority over lightly armed rivals that they were able to exploit until the arrival of other European forces several decades later.

Voyages to the New World

While the Portuguese were seeking access to the spice trade of the Indies by sailing eastward through the Indian Ocean, the Spanish were attempting to reach the same destination by sailing westward across the Atlantic. Although the Spanish came to overseas discovery and exploration after the initial efforts of Henry the Navigator, their greater resources enabled them to establish a far grander overseas empire of a quite different nature than the Portuguese Empire.

An important figure in the history of Spanish exploration was an Italian known as Christopher Columbus (1451–1506). Knowledgeable Europeans were aware that the world was round, but had little understanding of its circumference or the extent of the continent of Asia. Convinced that the circumference of the earth was less than contemporaries believed and that Asia was larger than people thought, Columbus felt that Asia could be reached by sailing west instead of around Africa. After being rejected by the Portuguese, he persuaded Queen Isabella of Spain to finance his exploratory expedition.

With three ships, the *Santa María*, *Niña*, and *Pinta*, manned by ninety men, Columbus set sail on August 3, 1492. On October 12, he reached the Bahamas and then went on to explore the coastline of Cuba and the northern

CHRISTOPHER COLUMBUS. Columbus was an Italian explorer who worked for the queen of Spain. He has become a symbol for two entirely different perspectives. To some, he was a great and heroic explorer who discovered the New World; to others, especially in Latin America, he was responsible for beginning a process of invasion that led to the destruction of an entire way of life. This painting by the Italian Sebastiano del Piombo in 1519 is the earliest known portrait of Columbus, but it was done thirteen years after his death and reveals as much about the painter's conception of Columbus as it does about the explorer himself.

shores of Hispaniola (present-day Haiti and the Dominican Republic). Columbus believed that he had reached Asia, and in his reports to Queen Isabella and King Ferdinand, he assured them not only that he would eventually find gold but that they had a golden opportunity to convert the natives to Christianity:

> These islands are very green and fertile and the breezes are very soft, and it is possible that there are in them many things, of which I do not know, because I did not wish to delay in finding gold, by discovering and going about many islands. And since these men give these signs that they wear it on their arms and legs, and it is gold because I showed them some pieces of gold which I have, I cannot fail, with the aid of Our Lord, to find the place whence it comes.
>
> . . . So your Highnesses should resolve to make them Christians, for I believe that, if you begin, in a little while you will achieve the conversion of a great number of peoples to our holy faith, with the acquisition of great lordships and riches and all their inhabitants for Spain. For without a doubt there is a very great amount of gold in these lands.[6]

In three subsequent voyages (1493, 1498, 1502), Columbus sought in vain to find a route through the outer lands to the Asian mainland. In his four voyages, Columbus reached all the major islands of the Caribbean and the mainland of Central America.

Although Columbus clung to his belief until his death, other explorers soon realized that he had discovered a new frontier altogether. State-sponsored explorers joined the race to the New World. A Venetian seaman, John Cabot, explored the New England coastline of the Americas under a license from King Henry VII of England. The continent of South America was discovered accidentally by the Portuguese sea captain Pedro Cabral in 1500. Amerigo Vespucci, a Florentine, accompanied several voyages and wrote a series of letters describing the geography of the New World. The publication of these letters led to the use of the name "America" (after Amerigo) for the new lands.

The first two decades of the sixteenth century witnessed numerous overseas voyages that explored the eastern coasts of both North and South America. Vasco Nuñez de Balboa, a Spanish explorer, led an expedition across the Isthmus of Panama and reached the Pacific Ocean in 1513. Perhaps the most dramatic of all these expeditions was the journey of Ferdinand Magellan (1480–1521) in 1519. After passing through the straits named after him at the southern tip of South America, he sailed across the Pacific Ocean and reached the Philippines (named after King Philip of Spain by Magellan's crew) where he met his death at the hands of the natives. Although only one of his original fleet of five ships survived and returned to Spain, Magellan's name is still associated with the first known circumnavigation of the earth.

The newly discovered territories were called the New World, although they possessed flourishing civilizations populated by millions of people when the Europeans arrived. The Americas were, of course, new to the Europeans who quickly saw opportunities for conquest and exploitation. The Spanish, in particular, were interested because in 1494 the Treaty of Tordesillas had divided up the newly discovered world into separate Portuguese and Spanish spheres of influence. Hereafter the route east around the Cape of Good Hope was to be reserved for the Portuguese while the route across the Atlantic (except for the eastern hump of South America) was assigned to Spain.

The Spanish Empire in the New World

The Spanish conquistadors were hardy individuals motivated by a typical sixteenth-century blend of glory, greed, and religious crusading zeal. Although sanctioned by the Castilian crown, these groups were financed and outfitted privately, not by the government. Their superior weapons, organizational skills, and determination brought the conquistadors incredible success. They also benefited from rivalries among the native peoples.

In 1519, a Spanish expedition under the command of Hernán Cortés (1485–1547) landed at Veracruz, on the Gulf of Mexico. He marched to the city of Tenochtitlán (see

The Spanish Conquistador: Cortés and the Conquest of Mexico

Hernán Cortés was a minor Spanish nobleman who came to the New World in 1504 to seek his fortune. Contrary to his superior's orders, Cortés waged an independent campaign of conquest and overthrew the Aztec Empire in Mexico (1519–1521). Cortés wrote a series of five reports to Emperor Charles V to justify his action. The second report includes a description of Tenochtitlán, the capital of the Aztec Empire. The Spanish conquistador and his men were obviously impressed by this city, awesome in its architecture yet built by people who lacked European technology, such as wheeled vehicles and tools of hard metal.

Cortés's Description of an Aztec City

The great city Tenochtitlán is built in the midst of this salt lake, and it is two leagues from the heart of the city to any point on the mainland. Four causeways lead to it, all made by hand and some twelve feet wide. The city itself is as large as Seville or Córdoba. The principal streets are very broad and straight, the majority of them being of beaten earth, but a few and at least half of the smaller thoroughfares are waterways along which they pass in their canoes. Moreover, even the principal streets have openings at regular distances so that the water can freely pass from one to another, and these openings which are very broad are spanned by great bridges of huge beams, very stoutly put together, so firm indeed that over many of them ten horsemen can ride at once. Seeing that if the natives intended any treachery against us they would have every opportunity from the way in which the city is built, for by removing the bridges from the entrances and exits they could leave us to die of hunger with no possibility of getting to the mainland, I immediately set to work as soon as we entered the city on the building of four brigs, and in a short space of time had them finished so that we could ship 300 men and the horses to the mainland whenever we so desired.

The city has many open squares in which markets are continuously held and the general business of buying and selling proceeds. One square in particular is twice as big as that of Salamanca and completely surrounded by arcades where there are daily more than 60,000 folk buying and selling. Every kind of merchandise such as may be met with in every land is for sale there, whether of food and victuals, or ornaments of gold and silver, or lead, brass, copper, tin, precious stones, bones, shells, snails and feathers; limestone for building is likewise sold there, stone both rough and polished, bricks burnt and unburnt, wood of all kinds and in all stages of preparation. . . . There is a street of herb-sellers where there are all manner of roots and medicinal plants that are found in the land. There are houses as it were of apothecaries where they sell medicines made from these herbs, both for drinking and for use as ointments and salves. There are barbers' shops where you may have your hair washed and cut. There are other shops where you may obtain food and drink. . . .

Finally, to avoid being wordy in telling all the wonders of this city, I will simply say that the manner of living among the people is very similar to that in Spain, and considering that this is a barbarous nation shut off from a knowledge of the true God or communication with enlightened nations, one may well marvel at the orderliness and good government which is everywhere maintained.

The actual service of Moctezuma and those things which call for admiration by their greatness and state would take so long to describe that I assure your Majesty I do not know where to begin with any hope of ending. For as I have already said, what could there be more astonishing than that a barbarous monarch such as he should have reproductions made in gold, silver, precious stones, and feathers of all things to be found in his land, and so perfectly reproduced that there is no goldsmith or silversmith in the world who could better them, nor can one understand what instrument could have been used for fashioning the jewels; as for the featherwork its like is not to be seen in either wax or embroidery; it is so marvelously delicate.

the box above) at the head of a small contingent of troops (550 soldiers and 16 horses); as he went, he made alliances with city-states that had tired of the oppressive rule of the Aztecs. Especially important was Tlaxcala, a state that the Aztecs had not been able to conquer. In November Cortés arrived at Tenochtitlán, where he received a friendly welcome from the Aztec monarch Moctezuma (often called Montezuma). At first, Moctezuma believed that his visitor was a representative of Quetzalcoatl, the god who had departed from his homeland centuries before and had promised that he would return. Riddled with fears, Moctezuma offered gifts of gold to the foreigners and gave them a palace to use while they were in the city.

But trouble eventually erupted between the Spaniards and the Aztecs. The Spaniards took Moctezuma hostage and began to pillage the city. In the fall of 1520, one year after Cortés had first arrived, the local population revolted and drove the invaders from the city. Many of the Spaniards were killed, but the Aztecs soon experienced new disasters. As one Aztec related: "But at about the time that the Spaniards had fled from Mexico, there came a great sickness, a pestilence, the smallpox." With no natural immunity to the diseases of Europeans, many Aztecs fell sick and died. Meanwhile, Cortés received fresh soldiers from his new allies; the state of Tlaxcala alone provided 50,000 warriors. After four months, the city capitu-

THE SLAUGHTER OF THE AZTECS. Fearful of growing Aztec resistance, the Spaniards responded by slaughtering many Aztecs. This sixteenth-century watercolor shows the massacre of Aztecs at Cholula, carried out on the orders of Cortés.

lated. And then the destruction began. The pyramids, temples, and palaces were leveled, and the stones used to build Spanish government buildings and churches. The rivers and canals were filled in. The mighty Aztec Empire on mainland Mexico was no more. Between 1531 and 1550, the Spanish gained control of northern Mexico.

The Inca Empire high in the Peruvian Andes was still flourishing when the first Spanish expeditions arrived in the area. In December 1530, Francisco Pizarro (c. 1475–1541) landed on the Pacific coast of South America with only a small band of about 180 men, but like Cortés, he had steel weapons, gunpowder, and horses, none of which were familiar to his hosts. Pizarro was also lucky because the Inca Empire had already succumbed to an epidemic of smallpox. Like the Aztecs, the Inca had no immunities to European diseases, and all too soon, smallpox was devastating entire villages. In another stroke of good fortune for Pizarro, even the Inca emperor was a victim. Upon the emperor's death, two sons claimed the throne, leading to a civil war. Pizarro took advantage of the situation by seizing Atahualpa, whose forces had just defeated his brother's. Armed only with stones, arrows, and light spears, Incan soldiers provided little challenge to the charging horses of the Spanish, let alone their guns and cannons. After executing Atahualpa, Pizarro and his soldiers, aided by their Incan allies, marched on Cuzco and captured the Incan capital. By 1535, Pizarro had established a capital at Lima for a new colony of the Spanish Empire.

ADMINISTRATION OF THE SPANISH EMPIRE

Spanish policy toward the Indians of the New World was a combination of confusion, misguided paternalism, and cruel exploitation. Whereas the conquistadors made decisions based on expediency and their own interests, Queen Isabella declared the natives to be subjects of Castile and instituted the Spanish *encomienda,* a system that permitted the conquering Spaniards to collect tribute from the natives and use them as laborers. In return, the holders of an *encomienda* were supposed to protect the Indians, pay them wages, and supervise their spiritual needs. In practice, this meant that the settlers were free to implement the paternalistic system of the government as they pleased. Three thousand miles from Spain, Spanish settlers largely ignored their government and brutally used the Indians to pursue their own economic interests. Indians were put to work on plantations and in the lucrative gold and silver mines. Forced labor, starvation, and especially disease took a fearful toll of Indian lives. With little or no natural resistance to European diseases, the Indians of America were ravaged by the smallpox, measles, and typhus that came with the explorers and the conquistadors. Although

Las Casas and the Spanish Treatment of the American Natives

Bartolomé de Las Casas (1474–1566) participated in the conquest of Cuba and received land and Indians in return for his efforts. But in 1514 he underwent a radical transformation and came to believe that the Indians had been cruelly mistreated by his fellow Spaniards. He became a Dominican friar and spent the remaining years of his life (he lived to the age of ninety-two) fighting for the Indians. This selection is taken from his most influential work, which is known to English readers as The Tears of the Indians. *This work was largely responsible for the "black legend" of the Spanish as inherently "cruel and murderous fanatics." Most scholars feel that Las Casas may have exaggerated his account in order to shock his contemporaries into action.*

Bartolomé de Las Casas, *The Tears of the Indians*

There is nothing more detestable or more cruel, than the tyranny which the Spaniards use toward the Indians for the getting of pearl. Surely the infernal torments cannot much exceed the anguish that they endure, by reason of that way of cruelty; for they put them under water some four or five ells [fifteen to eighteen feet] deep, where they are forced without any liberty of respiration, to gather up the shells wherein the pearls are; sometimes they come up again with nets full of shells to take breath, but if they stay any while to rest themselves, immediately comes a hangman row'd in a little boat, who as soon as he has well beaten them, drags them again to their labor. Their food is nothing but filth, and the very same that contains the pearl, with a small portion of that bread which that country affords; in the first whereof there is little nourishment; and as for the latter, it is made with great difficulty, besides that they have not enough of that neither for sustenance; they lie upon the ground in fetters, lest they should run away; and many times they are drown'd in this labor, and are never seen again till they swim upon the top of the waves: oftentimes they also are devoured by certain sea monsters, that are frequent in those seas. Consider whether this hard usage of the poor creatures be consistent with the precepts which God commands concerning charity to our neighbor, by those that cast them so undeservedly into the dangers of a cruel death, causing them to perish without any remorse or pity, or allowing them the benefit of the sacraments, or the knowledge of religion; it being impossible for them to live any time under the water; and this death is so much the more painful, by reason that by the constricting of the breast, while the lungs strive to do their office, the vital parts are so afflicted that they die vomiting the blood out of their mouths. Their hair also, which is by nature black, is hereby changed and made of the same color with that of the sea wolves; their bodies are also so besprinkled with the froth of the sea, that they appear rather like monsters than men.

scholarly estimates of native populations vary drastically, a reasonable guess is that 30 to 40 percent of the natives died. On Hispaniola alone, out of an initial population of 100,000 natives when Columbus arrived in 1493, only 300 Indians survived by 1570. In 1542, largely in response to the publications of Bartolomé de Las Casas, a Dominican friar who championed the Indians (see the box above), the government abolished the *encomienda* system and provided more protection for the natives.

In the New World, the Spanish developed an administrative system based on viceroys. Spanish possessions were initially divided into two major administrative units: New Spain (Mexico, Central America, and the Caribbean islands) with its center in Mexico City, and Peru (western South America), governed by a viceroy in Lima. Each viceroy served as the king's chief civil and military officer and was aided by advisory groups called *audiencias,* which also functioned as supreme judicial bodies.

By papal agreement, the Catholic monarchs of Spain were given extensive rights over ecclesiastical affairs in the New World. They could appoint all bishops and clergy, build churches, collect fees, and supervise the affairs of the various religious orders that sought to Christianize the heathen. Catholic missionaries—especially the Dominicans, Franciscans, and Jesuits—fanned out across the Spanish Empire where they converted and baptized hundreds of thousands of Indians in the early years of the conquest. To facilitate their efforts, the missionaries brought Indians together into villages where they could be converted, taught trades, and encouraged to grow crops. Removing the Indians from their homes to these villages helped the missionaries not only to gain control over the Indians' lives but also to ensure that they would be docile subjects of the empire.

The mass conversion of the Indians brought the organizational and institutional structures of Catholicism to the New World. Dioceses, parishes, cathedrals, schools, and hospitals—all the trappings of civilized European society—soon appeared in the Spanish Empire. So, too, did the Spanish Inquisition, established first in Peru in 1570 and then in Mexico in 1571.

The Impact of Expansion

European expansion made an enormous impact on both the conquerors and the conquered. The native American civilizations, which had their own unique qualities and a degree of sophistication not much appreciated by Europeans, were virtually destroyed. Ancient social and political structures were ripped up and replaced by European institutions, religion, language, and culture. The Portuguese trading posts in the East, on the other hand, had much less impact on native Asian civilizations.

For some Europeans, expansion abroad in the sixteenth century also brought hopes for land, riches, and social advancement. One Spaniard commented in 1572 that many "poor young men" left Spain for Mexico, where they might hope to acquire landed estates and call themselves "gentlemen." Although some wives accompanied their husbands abroad, many ordinary European women found new opportunities for marriage in the New World because of the lack of white women. Indeed, as one commentator bluntly put it, even "a whore, if handsome, [can] make a wife for some rich planter."[7] In the violence-prone world of early Spanish America, a number of women also found themselves rich after their husbands were killed unexpectedly. In one area of Central America, women owned about 25 percent of the landed estates by 1700.

European expansion also had other economic effects on the conquerors. Wherever they went in the New World, Europeans sought to find sources of gold and silver. One Aztec commented that the Spanish conquerors "longed and lusted for gold. Their bodies swelled with greed, and their hunger was ravenous; they hungered like pigs for that gold."[8] Rich silver deposits were found and exploited in Mexico and southern Peru (modern Bolivia). When the mines at Potosí in Peru were opened in 1545, the value of precious metals imported into Europe quadrupled. Between 1503 and 1650, an estimated 16 million kilograms (over 35 million pounds) of silver and 185,000 kilograms (407,000 pounds) of gold entered the port of Seville and helped to create a price revolution that affected the Spanish economy.

But gold and silver were only two of the products that became part of the exchange between the New World and the Old. Europeans brought horses and sheep to the New World and also introduced the cultivation of wheat. Back to Seville flowed sugar, dyes, cotton, vanilla, and hides from livestock raised on the grass-covered plains of South America. New agricultural products such as potatoes, coffee, corn, and tobacco were also imported. Because of its trading posts in Asia, Portugal soon challenged the Italian states as the chief entry point of the eastern trade in spices, jewels, silk, carpets, ivory, leather, and perfumes, although the Venetians clung tenaciously to the spice trade until they lost out to the Dutch in the seventeenth century. Economic historians believe that the increase in the volume and area of European trade and the rise in fluid capital due to this expansion were crucial factors in producing a new era of commercial capitalism that represented the first step toward the world economy that has characterized the modern historical era.

European expansion, which was in part a product of European rivalries, also deepened those rivalries and increased the tensions among European states. Bitter conflicts arose over the cargoes coming from the New World and Asia. Although the Spanish and Portuguese were the first to enter the competition, the Dutch, French, and English soon became involved on a large scale and by the seventeenth century were challenging the Portuguese and Spanish monopolies.

Finally, how does one evaluate the psychological impact of colonization on the colonizers? The relatively easy European success in dominating native peoples reinforced Christian Europe's belief in the inherent superiority of European civilization. The Scientific Revolution of the seventeenth century (see Chapter 16), the Enlightenment of the eighteenth (see Chapter 17), and the imperialism of the nineteenth (see Chapter 24) would all strengthen this Eurocentric perspective that has pervaded Western civilization's relationship with the rest of the world.

◆ Politics and the Wars of Religion in the Sixteenth Century

The so-called wars of religion were a product of Reformation ideologies that allowed little room for compromise or toleration of differing opinions. By the middle of the sixteenth century, Calvinism and Catholicism had become highly militant religions dedicated to spreading the word of God as they interpreted it. Although their struggle for the minds and hearts of Europeans is at the heart of the religious wars of the sixteenth century, economic, social, and political forces also played an important role in these conflicts. Of the sixteenth-century religious wars, none were more momentous or shattering than the French civil wars known as the French Wars of Religion.

The French Wars of Religion (1562–1598)

France seemed an unlikely place for a religious war. The Valois monarchs Francis I (1515–1547) and Henry II (1547–1559) had been strong rulers aided by royal officials, a permanent mercenary army, the power to tax, and the ability to control the French church by nominating bishops. But when Henry II was killed accidentally in a tournament in 1559 and was succeeded by a series of weak, feeble, and neurotic sons, two of whom were dominated by their mother, Catherine de' Medici (1519–1589), as regent, the forces held in check by the strong monarchy broke loose, beginning a series of intermittent and confused civil wars. Religious, political, economic, and social forces all contributed to these wars.

The religious forces were the most important. Concerned by the growth of Calvinism, the French kings tried to stop its spread by persecuting Calvinists but had little success. Huguenots (as the French Calvinists were called) came from all levels of society: artisans and shopkeepers hurt by rising prices and a rigid guild system; merchants and lawyers in provincial towns whose local privileges were tenuous; and members of the nobility. Possibly 40 to 50 percent of the French nobility became Huguenots, including the house of Bourbon, which stood next to the Valois in the royal line of succession and ruled the southern French kingdom of Navarre. The conversion of so many nobles made the Huguenots a potentially dangerous political threat to monarchical power. Though the Calvinists constituted only about 7 percent of the population, they were a strong-willed and well-organized minority.

The Catholic majority greatly outnumbered the Calvinist minority. The Valois monarchy was staunchly Catholic, and its control of the Catholic church gave it little incentive to look favorably upon Protestantism. As regent for her sons, the moderate Catholic Catherine de' Medici looked to religious compromise as a way to defuse the political tensions, but found to her consternation that both sides possessed their share of religious fanatics unwilling to make concessions. The extreme Catholic party—known as the ultra-Catholics—favored strict opposition to the Huguenots and was led by the Guise family. Possessing the loyalty of Paris and large sections of northern and northwestern France through their client-patronage system, they could recruit and pay for large armies and received support abroad from the papacy and Jesuits who favored the Guises' uncompromising Catholic position. Ironically, the allegiance of the Catholic Guises to their own dynasty and international Catholicism posed a strong threat to the Catholic Valois monarchy.

The religious issue was not the only factor that contributed to the French civil wars. Towns and provinces, which had long resisted the growing power of monarchical centralization, were only too willing to join a revolt against the monarchy. This was also true of the nobility, and because so many of them were Calvinists, they formed an important base of opposition to the crown. The French Wars of Religion, then, constituted a major constitutional crisis for France and temporarily halted the development of the French centralized territorial state. The claim of the state's ruling dynasty to a person's loyalties was temporarily superseded by loyalty to one's religious belief. For some people, the unity of France was less important than religious truth. But there also emerged in France a group of politiques who placed politics before religion and believed that no religious truth was worth the ravages of civil war. The politiques ultimately prevailed, but not until both sides were exhausted by bloodshed.

The wars erupted in 1562 when the powerful duke of Guise massacred a peaceful congregation of Huguenots at Vassy. In the decade of the 1560s, the Huguenots held their own. Too small a group to conquer France, their armies were so good at defensive campaigns that they could not be defeated either, even with the infamous Saint Bartholomew's Day massacre.

This massacre of Huguenots in August 1572 occurred at a time when the Catholic and Calvinist parties had apparently been reconciled through the marriage of the sister of the reigning Valois king Charles IX (1560–1574) and Henry of Navarre, the Bourbon ruler of

CHRONOLOGY

The French Wars of Religion (1562–1598)

Francis I	1515–1547
Henry II	1547–1559
Charles IX	1560–1574
Duke of Guise massacres Huguenot congregation at Vassy	1562
Saint Bartholomew's Day massacre	1572
Henry III	1574–1589
Formation of the Holy League	1576
War of the Three Henries	1588–1589
Assassination of Henry III	1589
Coronation of Henry IV	1594
Edict of Nantes	1598

THE SAINT BARTHOLOMEW'S DAY MASSACRE. Although the outbreak of religious war seemed unlikely in France, the collapse of the strong monarchy with the death of Henry II unleashed forces that led to a series of civil wars. Pictured here is the Saint Bartholomew's Day massacre of 1572. This contemporary painting by the Huguenot artist François Dubois depicts a number of the incidents of that day when approximately 3,000 Huguenots were murdered in Paris.

Navarre. Henry was the son of Jeanne d'Albret, queen of Navarre, who had been responsible for introducing Calvinist ideas into her kingdom. Henry was also the acknowledged political leader of the Huguenots, and many Huguenots traveled to Paris for the wedding.

But the Guise family persuaded the king and his mother, Catherine de' Medici, that this gathering of Huguenots posed a threat to them. Charles and his advisers decided to eliminate the Huguenot leaders with one swift blow. According to one French military leader, Charles and his advisers believed that civil war would soon break out anyway and that "it was better to win a battle in Paris, where all the leaders were, than to risk it in the field and fall into a dangerous and uncertain war."[9]

The massacre began early in the day on August 24 when the king's guards sought out and killed some prominent Huguenot leaders. These murders soon unleashed a wave of violence that gripped the city of Paris. For three days, frenzied Catholic mobs roamed the streets of Paris, killing Huguenots in an often cruel and bloodthirsty manner. According to one eyewitness account: "Then they took her [Françoise Lussault] and dragged her by the hair a long way through the streets, and spying the gold bracelets on her arms, without having the patience to unfasten them, cut off her wrists."[10] Three days of killing left 3,000 Huguenots dead, although not Henry of Navarre who saved his life by promising to turn Catholic. Thousands more were killed in provincial towns. The massacre boomeranged, however, because it discredited the Valois dynasty without ending the conflict.

The fighting continued. The Huguenots rebuilt their strength, and in 1576 the ultra-Catholics formed a Holy League, vowing to exterminate heresy and seat a true Catholic champion—Henry, duke of Guise—on the French throne in place of the ruling king, Henry III (1574–1589), who had succeeded his brother Charles IX in 1574. The turning point in the conflict came in the War of the Three Henries in 1588–1589. Henry, duke of Guise, in the pay of Philip II of Spain, seized Paris and forced King Henry III to make him his chief minister. To rid himself of Guise influence, Henry III assassinated the duke of Guise and then joined with Henry of Navarre (who meanwhile had returned to Calvinism), who was next in line to the throne, to crush the Catholic Holy League and retake the city of Paris. Although successful, Henry III in turn was assassinated in 1589 by a monk who was repelled by the spectacle of a Catholic king cooperating with a Protestant. Henry of Navarre now claimed the throne. Realizing, however, that he would never be accepted by Catholic France, Henry took the logical way out and converted once again to Catholicism. With his coronation in 1594, the French Wars of Religion finally came to an end.

Nevertheless, the religious problem persisted until the Edict of Nantes was issued in 1598. The edict acknowledged Catholicism as the official religion of France, but guaranteed the Huguenots the right to worship in selected places in every district and allowed them to retain a number of fortified towns for their protection. In addition, Huguenots were allowed to enjoy all political privileges, including the holding of public offices. Although the Edict of Nantes recognized the rights of the Protestant minority and ostensibly the principle of religious toleration, it did so only out of political necessity, not out of conviction. The French Wars of Religion also demonstrated once again to many French people the necessity for strong government, laying a foundation for the growth of monarchy in the seventeenth century.

Philip II and the Cause of Militant Catholicism

The greatest advocate of militant Catholicism and the most important political figure in the second half of the sixteenth century was King Philip II of Spain (1556–1598), the son and heir of Charles V (see the box on p. 404). Philip's reign ushered in an age of Spanish greatness, both politically and culturally. A tremendous price was paid, however, for the political and military commitments that Philip made, and we can see in retrospect that the golden age of Spain was also the period in which Spain's decline began.

The first major goal of Philip II was to consolidate and secure the lands he had inherited from his father, Charles V. These included Spain, the Netherlands, and the possessions in Italy and the New World. For Philip this meant a strict conformity to Catholicism, enforced by aggressive use of the Spanish Inquisition, and the establishment of strong, monarchical authority. The latter was not an easy task because Philip had inherited a governmental structure in which each of the various states and territories of his empire stood in an individual relationship to the king. Philip did manage, however, to expand royal power in Spain by making the monarchy less dependent on the traditional landed aristocracy, especially in the higher echelons of government. He enlarged the system of administrative councils first developed by Ferdinand and Isabella and broadened by his father. Although Philip found that his ability to enforce his will was restricted by local legal traditions, lack of rapid communication, and an inadequate bureaucracy, he tried to be the center of the whole system and supervised the work of all departments, even down to the smallest details. His meticulousness was tragic for both Philip and Spain. Unwilling to delegate authority, he failed to distinguish between important and trivial matters and fell weeks behind on state correspondence, where he was inclined to make marginal notes and even correct spelling. One Spanish official said, "If God used the Escorial [the royal palace where Philip worked] to deliver my death sentence, I would be immortal." Philip's administrative machinery enabled him to do little more than maintain the status quo.

One of Philip's aims was to make Spain a dominant power in Europe. To a great extent, Spain's preeminence depended upon a prosperous economy fueled by its importation of gold and silver from its New World possessions, its agriculture, its commerce, and its industry, especially in textiles, silk, and leather goods. The importation of silver

Philip II, the Most Catholic King of Spain

After the abdication of Charles V in 1556, his son Philip II became king of Spain at the age of twenty-nine. Modern historical opinions of Phillip II have varied widely. Some Protestant historians have viewed him as a moral monster, but Catholic apologists have commended him for his sincerity and sense of responsibility. These selections include an assessment of Philip II by a contemporary, the Venetian ambassador to Spain, and a section from a letter by Philip II to his daughters, revealing the more loving side of the king.

Suriano, An Estimate of Philip II

The Catholic king was born in Spain, in the month of May, 1527, and spent a great part of his youth in that kingdom. Here, in accordance with the customs of the country and the wishes of his father and mother, . . . he was treated with all the deference and respect which seemed due to the son of the greatest emperor whom Christendom had ever had, and to the heir to such a number of realms and to such grandeur. As a result of this education, when the king left Spain for the first time and visited Flanders, passing on his way through Italy and Germany, he everywhere made an impression of haughtiness and severity, so that the Italians liked him but little, the Flemings were quite disgusted with him, and the Germans hated him heartily. But when he had been warned by the cardinal of Trent and his aunt, and above all by his father, that this haughtiness was not in place in a prince destined to rule over a number of nations so different in manners and sentiment, he altered his manner so completely that on his second journey, when we went to England, he everywhere exhibited such distinguished mildness and affability that no prince has ever surpassed him in these traits. . . .

In the king's eyes no nation is superior to the Spaniards. It is among them that he lives, it is they that he consults, and it is they that direct his policy; in all this he is acting quite contrary to the habit of his father. He thinks little of the Italians and Flemish and still less of the Germans. Although he may employ the chief men of all the countries over which he rules, he admits none of them to his secret counsels, but utilizes their services only in military affairs, and then perhaps not so much because he really esteems them, as in the hope that he will in this way prevent his enemies from making use of them.

A Letter of Philip II to His Daughters

It is good news for me to learn that you are so well. It seems to me that your little sister is getting her eye teeth pretty early. Perhaps they are in place of the two which I am on the point of losing and which I shall probably no longer have when I get back. But if I had nothing worse to trouble me, that might pass. . . .

I am sending you also some roses and an orange flower, just to let you see that we have them here [Lisbon]. Calabrés brings me bunches of both these flowers every day, and we have had violets for a long time. . . . After this rainy time I imagine that you will be having flowers, too, by the time my sister arrives, or soon after. God keep you as I would have him!

had detrimental effects as well, however, as it helped set off a spiraling inflation that disrupted the Spanish economy, eventually hurting both textile production and agriculture. Moreover, the expenses of war, especially after 1580, proved devastating to the Spanish economy. American gold and silver never constituted more than 20 percent of the royal revenue, leading the government to impose a crushing burden of direct and indirect taxes, especially on the people of Castile. Even then the government was forced to borrow. Philip repudiated his debts seven times; still two-thirds of state income went to pay interest on the debt by the end of his reign. The attempt to make Spain a great power led to the decline of Spain after Philip's reign.

Crucial to an understanding of Philip II is the importance of Catholicism to the Spanish people and their ruler. Driven by a heritage of crusading fervor, the Spanish had little difficulty seeing themselves as a nation of people divinely chosen to save Catholic Christianity from the Protestant heretics. Philip II, the "Most Catholic King," became the champion of Catholicism throughout Europe, a role that led to spectacular victories and equally spectacular defeats for the Spanish king. Spain's leadership of a Holy League against Turkish encroachments in the Mediterranean, especially the Muslim attack on the island of Cyprus, resulted in a stunning victory over the Turkish fleet in the Battle of Lepanto in 1571. But Philip was to experience few other such successes. His intervention in France on behalf of the ultra-Catholics at the end of the 1580s and the beginning of the 1590s was an utter failure. But the major thrust of his foreign policy was aimed at the Netherlands and England. Philip's attempt to crush the revolt in the Netherlands and his tortured relations with the English queen Elizabeth led to his greatest misfortunes.

The Revolt of the Netherlands

One of the richest parts of Philip's empire, the Spanish Netherlands was of great importance to the "Most Catholic King." The Netherlands consisted of seventeen provinces (modern Netherlands, Belgium, and Luxembourg). The

CHRONOLOGY

Philip II and Militant Catholicism

Philip II	1556–1598
Outbreak of revolt in the Netherlands	1566
Battle of Lepanto	1571
Recall of the Duke of Alva	1573
Pacification of Ghent	1576
Union of Arras	1579
The Spanish Armada	1588
Twelve-year truce (Spain and Netherlands)	1609
Independence of the United Provinces	1648

seven northern provinces were largely Germanic in culture and Dutch speaking, while the French- and Flemish-speaking southern provinces were closely tied to France. Situated at the commercial crossroads of northwestern Europe, the Netherlands had become prosperous through commerce and a flourishing textile industry. Because of its location, the Netherlands was open to the religious influences of the age. Though some inhabitants had adopted Lutheranism or Anabaptism, by the time of Philip II, Calvinism was also making inroads. These provinces had no real political bond holding them together except their common ruler, and that ruler was Philip II, a foreigner who was out of touch with the situation in the Netherlands.

Philip II hoped to strengthen his control in the Netherlands, regardless of the traditional privileges of the separate provinces. This was strongly opposed by the nobles, towns, and provincial states, which stood to lose politically if their jealously guarded privileges and freedoms were weakened. Resentment against Philip was also aroused when the residents of the Netherlands realized that the taxes they paid were being used for Spanish interests. Finally, religion became a major catalyst for rebellion when Philip attempted both to reorganize the ecclesiastical structure of the Dutch Catholic church and to crush heresy. Calvinism continued to spread, especially among the nobility and artisans in the towns. Philip's policy of repression alienated the Calvinists without halting the spread of the movement. Resistance against the king's policies increased, especially from the aristocrats led by William of Nassau, the prince of Orange, also known as William the Silent. Violence erupted in 1566 when Calvinists—especially nobles—began to destroy statues and stained glass windows in Catholic churches. Philip responded by sending the duke of Alva with 10,000 veteran Spanish and Italian troops to crush the rebellion.

The repressive policies of the duke proved counterproductive. The levying of a permanent sales tax alienated many merchants and commoners who now joined the nobles and Calvinists in the struggle against Spanish rule. A special tribunal, known as the Council of Troubles (nicknamed by the Dutch the Council of Blood), inaugurated a reign of terror in which even powerful aristocrats were executed. As a result, the revolt now became organized, especially in the northern provinces where William of Orange and Dutch pirates known as the "Sea Beggars" mounted growing resistance. In 1573, Philip removed the duke of Alva and shifted to a more conciliatory policy to bring an end to the costly revolt.

William of Orange wished to unify all seventeen provinces, a goal seemingly realized in 1576 with the Pacification of Ghent. This agreement stipulated that all the provinces would stand together under William's leadership, respect religious differences, and demand that Spanish troops be withdrawn. But religious

PHILIP II OF SPAIN. This portrait depicts Philip II of Spain at the age of fifty-two. The king's attempts to make Spain a great power led to large debts and crushing taxes, and his military actions in defense of Catholicism ended in failure and misfortune in both France and the Netherlands.

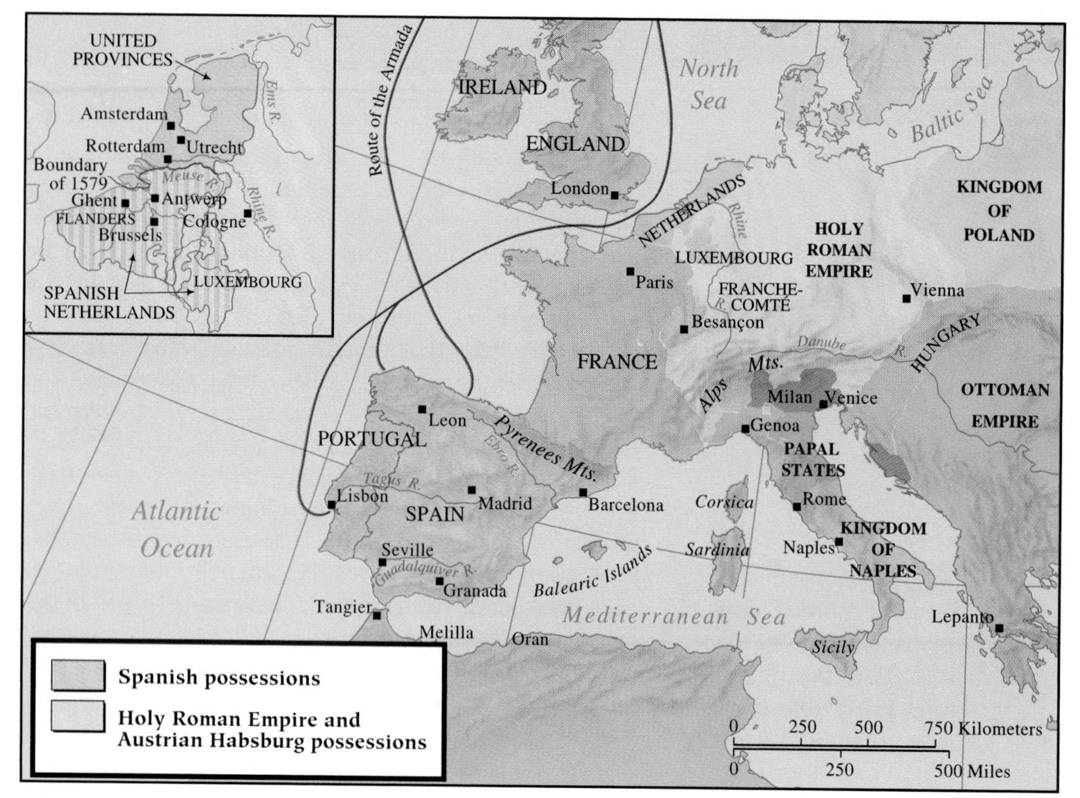

MAP 14.2 **Philip II and the Height of Spanish Power.**

differences proved too strong for any lasting union. When the duke of Parma, the next Spanish leader, arrived in the Netherlands, he astutely played upon the religious differences of the provinces and split their united front. The southern provinces formed a Catholic union—the Union of Arras—in 1579 and accepted Spanish control. To counter this, William of Orange organized the northern, Dutch-speaking states into a Protestant union—the Union of Utrecht—determined to oppose Spanish rule. The Netherlands was now divided along religious, geographical, and political lines into two hostile camps. Unwilling to rule themselves, the northern provinces sought to place themselves under the French king and then the English queen Elizabeth. Both refused, although Elizabeth further antagonized Philip II by continuing military assistance. The struggle went on for several years after both Philip and Elizabeth had died; finally, in 1609, the war ended with a twelve-year truce that virtually recognized the independence of the northern provinces. These "United Provinces" soon emerged as the Dutch Republic, although the Spanish did not formally recognize them as independent until 1648. The southern provinces remained a Spanish possession.

The England of Elizabeth

After the death of Queen Mary in 1558, her half-sister Elizabeth ascended the throne of England. During Elizabeth's reign, England rose to prominence as the relatively small island kingdom became the leader of the Protestant nations of Europe, laid the foundations for a world empire, and experienced a cultural renaissance.

The daughter of King Henry VIII and Anne Boleyn, Elizabeth had had a difficult early life. During Mary's reign, she had even been imprisoned for a while and had learned early to hide her true feelings from both private and public sight. Though appearing irresolute in avoiding confrontation as long as possible, she was capable of decisive action when it was finally forced upon her. Intelligent and self-confident, she moved quickly to solve the difficult religious problem she had inherited from Mary, who had become extremely unpopular when she tried to return England to the Catholic fold.

Elizabeth's religious policy was based on moderation and compromise. Although she had some deep religious feelings, the changes she had experienced had taught her caution and tolerance. As a ruler, she wished to prevent England from being torn apart over matters of religion. Interests of state and personal choice combined to favor a temperate approach to religious affairs. As the Scottish Calvinist reformer John Knox remarked, "Elizabeth was neither a good Protestant nor yet a resolute Papist." Nor did she care what her subjects believed privately as long as they did not threaten the state's power.

Parliament cooperated with the queen in initiating the Elizabethan religious settlement in 1559. The Catholic legislation of Mary's reign was repealed, and a new Act of Supremacy designated Elizabeth as "the only supreme governor of this realm, as well in all spiritual or ecclesiastical things or causes, as temporal." An Act of Unifor-

PROCESSION OF QUEEN ELIZABETH I. Intelligent and learned, Elizabeth Tudor was familiar with Latin and Greek and spoke several European languages. Served by able administrators, Elizabeth ruled for nearly forty-five years and generally avoided open military action against any major power. Her participation in the revolt of the Netherlands, however, brought England into conflict with Spain. This picture painted near the end of her reign shows the queen on a ceremonial procession.

mity restored the church service of the Book of Common Prayer from the reign of Edward VI with some revisions to make it more acceptable to Catholics. Elizabeth's religious settlement was basically Protestant, but it was a moderate Protestantism that avoided overly subtle distinctions and extremes.

The new religious settlement worked, at least to the extent that it smothered religious differences in England in the second half of the sixteenth century. Two groups, however, the Catholics and Puritans, continued to oppose the new religious settlement. By the end of Elizabeth's reign, the Catholics had dwindled to a tiny minority, a process aided by the identification of Catholicism in English minds with the Spanish King Philip II, but earlier they appeared to pose a significant threat. One of Elizabeth's greatest challenges came from her Catholic cousin, Mary, queen of Scots, who was next in line to the English throne. Mary was ousted from Scotland by rebellious Calvinist nobles in 1568 and fled for her life to England. There Elizabeth placed her under house arrest and for fourteen years tolerated her involvement in a number of ill-planned Catholic plots designed to kill Elizabeth and replace her on the throne with the Catholic Mary. Finally, in 1587, after Mary became embroiled in a far more serious plot, Elizabeth had her cousin beheaded to end the threats to her regime.

Potentially more dangerous to Anglicanism in the long run were the Puritans. The word *Puritanism* first appeared in 1564 when it was used to refer to those Protestants within the Anglican church who, inspired by Calvinist theology, wanted to remove any trace of Catholicism from the Church of England. Elizabeth managed to contain the Puritans during her reign, but the indefatigable Puritans would dominate the English scene in the middle part of the seventeenth century.

Elizabeth proved as adept in government and foreign policy as in religious affairs. She was well served administratively by the principal secretary of state, an office created by Thomas Cromwell during the reign of Henry VIII. The talents of Sir William Cecil and Sir Francis Walsingham, who together held the office for thirty-two years, ensured much of Elizabeth's success in foreign and domestic affairs. Elizabeth also handled Parliament with much skill; it met only thirteen times during her entire reign (see the box on p. 408).

Caution, moderation, and expediency also dictated Elizabeth's foreign policy. Fearful of other countries' motives, Elizabeth realized that war could be disastrous for her island kingdom and her own rule. Unofficially, however, she encouraged English seamen to raid Spanish ships and colonies. Francis Drake was especially adept at plundering Spanish fleets loaded with gold and silver from Spain's New World empire. While encouraging English piracy and providing clandestine aid to French Huguenots and Dutch Calvinists to weaken France and Spain, Elizabeth pretended complete aloofness and avoided alliances that would force her into war with any major power.

Gradually, however, Elizabeth was drawn into more active involvement in the Netherlands and by 1585 had reluctantly settled upon a policy of active military intervention there. This move accelerated the already mounting friction between Spain and England. After years of resisting the idea of invading England as too impractical, Philip II of Spain was finally persuaded to do so by advisers who assured him that the people of England would rise against their queen when the Spaniards arrived. Moreover, Philip was easily convinced that the revolt in the Netherlands would never be crushed as long as England provided support for it. In any case, a successful invasion of England would mean the overthrow of heresy and the return of England to Catholicism, surely an act in accordance with the will of God. The execution of Mary, queen of Scots, in 1587 reinforced the king's decision, especially when the pope, angered by Mary's beheading, offered to provide financial support for the undertaking. Accordingly, Philip ordered preparations for an Armada that would rendezvous with the army of the duke of Parma in Flanders and escort his troops across the English Channel for the invasion.

Queen Elizabeth Addresses Parliament (1601)

Queen Elizabeth I ruled England from 1558 to 1603 with a consummate skill that contemporaries considered unusual in a woman. Though shrewd and paternalistic, Elizabeth, like other sixteenth-century monarchs, depended for her power upon the favor of her people. This selection is taken from her speech to Parliament in 1601, when she had been forced to retreat on the issue of monopolies after vehement protests by members of Parliament. Although the speech was designed to make peace with Parliament, some historians also feel that it was a sincere expression of the rapport that existed between the queen and her subjects.

❋ *Queen Elizabeth I, "The Golden Speech"*

I do assure you there is no prince that loves his subjects better, or whose love can countervail our love. There is no jewel, be it of never so rich a price, which I set before this jewel: I mean your love. For I do esteem it more than any treasure or riches. . . . And, though God has raised me high, yet this I count the glory of my crown, that I have reigned with your loves. This makes me that I do not so much rejoice that God has made me to be a Queen, as to be a Queen over so thankful a people. . . .

Of myself I must say this: I never was any greedy, scraping grasper, nor a strait, fast-holding Prince, nor yet a waster. My heart was never set on any worldly goods, but only for my subjects' good. What you bestow on me, I will not hoard it up, but receive it to bestow on you again. Yea, mine own properties I account yours, to be expended for your good. . . .

I have ever used to set the Last-Judgement Day before mine eyes, and so to rule as I shall be judged to answer before a higher Judge, to whose judgement seat I do appeal, that never thought was cherished in my heart that tended not unto my people's good. And now, if my kingly bounties have been abused, and my grants turned to the hurt of my people, contrary to my will and meaning, and if any in authority under me neglected or perverted what I have committed to them, I hope God will not lay their culps [crimes] and offenses to my charge; who, though there were danger in repealing our grants, yet what danger would I not rather incur for your good, than I would suffer them still to continue?

There will never Queen sit in my seat with more zeal to my country, care for my subjects, and that will sooner with willingness venture her life for your good and safety, than myself. For it is my desire to live nor reign no longer than my life and reign shall be for your good. And though you have had and may have many princes more mighty and wise sitting in this seat, yet you never had nor shall have any that will be more careful and loving.

The Armada proved to be a disaster. The Spanish fleet that finally set sail had neither the ships nor the manpower that Philip had planned to send. A conversation between a papal emissary and an officer of the Spanish fleet before the Armada departed reveals the fundamental flaw:

> "And if you meet the English armada in the Channel, do you expect to win the battle?" "Of course," replied the Spaniard.
>
> "How can you be sure?" [asked the emissary]
>
> "It's very simple. It is well known that we fight in God's cause. So, when we meet the English, God will surely arrange matters so that we can grapple and board them, either by sending some strange freak of weather or, more likely, just by depriving the English of their wits. If we can come to close quarters, Spanish valor and Spanish steel (and the great masses of soldiers we shall have on board) will make our victory certain. But unless God helps us by a miracle the English, who have faster and handier ships than ours, and many more long-range guns, and who know their advantage just as well as we do, will never close with us at all, but stand aloof and knock us to pieces with their culverins, without our being able to do them any serious hurt. So," concluded the captain, and one fancies a grim smile, "we are sailing against England in the confident hope of a miracle."[11]

The hoped-for miracle never materialized. The Spanish fleet, battered by a number of encounters with the English, sailed back to Spain by a northward route around Scotland and Ireland where it was further battered by storms. Although the English and Spanish would continue their war for another sixteen years, the defeat of the Armada guaranteed for the time being that England would remain a Protestant country. Although Spain made up for its losses within a year and a half, the defeat was a psychological blow to the Spaniards.

◆ Economic and Social Crises

The period of European history from 1560 to 1650 witnessed severe economic and social crises as well as political upheaval. Economic uncertainties, intensified by wildly fluctuating boom and bust cycles, were accompanied by social uncertainties and stark contrasts between the living standards of the rich and the poor. Although historians commonly refer to a sixteenth-century price revolution and a seventeenth-century economic crisis, the lack of concrete data has made it difficult to be precise in these areas, leading to numerous historical controversies.

Inflation and Economic Stagnation

Inflation was a major economic problem in the sixteenth and early seventeenth centuries. This so-called price revolution was a Europeanwide phenomenon, although different areas were affected at different times. Though the inflation rate was probably a relatively low 2 to 3 percent a year, it was noticeable in a Europe accustomed to stable prices. Foodstuffs were most subject to price increases, especially evident in the price of wheat. An upward surge in wheat prices was first noticed in the Mediterranean area—in Spain, southern France, and Italy—and reached its peak there in the 1590s. By the 1620s and 1630s, wheat prices in northern Europe had undergone similar increases.

Although precise data are lacking, economic historians believe that as a result of the price revolution, wages failed to keep up with price increases. Wage earners, especially agricultural laborers and salaried workers in urban areas, began to experience a lower standard of living. At the same time, landed aristocrats who could raise rents managed to prosper. Commercial and industrial entrepreneurs also benefited from the price revolution because of rising prices, expanding markets, and relatively cheaper labor costs. Some historians regard this profit inflation as a valuable stimulus to investment and the growth of capitalism, helping to explain the economic expansion and prosperity of the sixteenth century. Governments were likewise affected by inflation. They borrowed heavily from bankers and imposed new tax burdens on their subjects, often creating additional discontent.

The causes of the price revolution are a subject of much historical debate. Already in the 1560s European intellectuals had associated the rise in prices with the great influx of precious metals from the New World. Although this view was accepted for a long time, many economic historians now believe that the increase in population in the sixteenth century played an important role in creating inflationary pressures. A growing population increased the demand for land and food and drove up prices for both.

But the inflation-fueled prosperity of the sixteenth century showed signs of slackening by the beginning of the seventeenth century. Economic contraction began to be evident in some parts of Europe by the 1620s. In the 1630s and 1640s, as imports of silver declined, economic recession intensified, especially in the Mediterranean area. The industrial and financial center of Europe in the age of the Renaissance, Italy was now becoming an economic backwater. Spain's economy was also seriously failing by the decade of the 1640s.

Trade, Industry, Banking, and Agriculture

The flourishing European trade of the sixteenth century revolved around three major areas: the Mediterranean in the south, the Low Countries and the Baltic region in the north, and central Europe, whose inland trade depended on the Rhine and Danube Rivers. As overseas trade expanded, however, the Atlantic seaboard began to play a more important role, linking the Mediterranean, Baltic, and central European trading areas together and making the whole of Europe into a more integrated market that was all the more vulnerable to price shifts. With their cheaper and faster ships, the Dutch came to monopolize both European and world trade, although they were increasingly challenged by the English and French in the seventeenth century.

The commercial expansion of the sixteenth and seventeenth centuries was made easier by new forms of commercial organization, especially the joint-stock trading company. Individuals bought shares in a company and received dividends on their investment while a board of directors ran the company and made the important business decisions. The return on investments could be spectacular. During its first ten years, investors received 30 percent on their money from the Dutch East India Company, which opened the Spice Islands and Southeast Asia to Dutch activity. The joint-stock company made it easier to raise large amounts of capital for world trading ventures.

Enormous profits were also being made in shipbuilding and in mining and metallurgy, where technological innovations, such as the use of pumps and new methods of extracting metals from ores, proved highly successful. The mining industry was closely tied to sixteenth-century family banking firms. In exchange for arranging large loans to Charles V, Jacob Fugger was given a monopoly over silver, copper, and mercury mines in the Habsburg possessions of central Europe that produced profits in excess of 50 percent per year. Though these close relationships between governments and entrepreneurs could lead to stunning successes, they could also be precarious. The House of Fugger went bankrupt at the end of the sixteenth century when the Habsburgs defaulted on their loans.

By the seventeenth century, the traditional family banking firms were no longer able to supply the numerous services needed for the commercial capitalism of the seventeenth century. New institutions arose to take their place. The city of Amsterdam created the Bank of Amsterdam in 1609 as both a deposit and a transfer institution and the Amsterdam Bourse or Exchange where the trading of stocks replaced the exchange of goods. By the first half of the seventeenth century, the Amsterdam Exchange had emerged as the hub of the European business world, just as Amsterdam itself had replaced Antwerp as the greatest commercial and banking center of Europe.

Despite the growth of commercial capitalism, most of the European economy still depended on an agricultural system that had experienced few changes since the thirteenth century. At least 80 to 90 percent of Europeans till worked on the land. Almost all of the peasants of western Europe were free of serfdom, although many still owed a variety of feudal dues to the nobility. Despite the

JACOB FUGGER THE RICH. Jacob Fugger, head of one of the wealthiest banking firms of the sixteenth century, is pictured here with his faithful secretary, Matthaus Schwartz, who painted this scene in 1516. The cabinet in the background lists the names of the cities where Fugger's firm had branch offices, including Milan, Innsbruck, Nuremberg, and Lisbon.

expanding markets and rising prices, European peasants saw little or no improvement in their lot as they faced increased rents and fees and higher taxes imposed by the state. In eastern Europe, the peasants' position even worsened as they were increasingly tied to the land in a new serfdom enforced by powerful landowners (see Chapter 15).

Population and the Growth of Cities

The sixteenth century was a period of expanding population, possibly related to a warmer climate and increased food supplies. It has been estimated that the population of Europe increased from 60 million in 1500 to 85 million by 1600, the first major recovery of the European population since the devastation of the Black Death in the mid-fourteenth century. However, records also indicate that the population had leveled off by 1620 and even begun to decline by 1650, especially in central and southern Europe. Only the Dutch, English, and, to a lesser degree, the French grew in number in the first half of the seventeenth century. Europe's longtime adversaries, war, famine, and plague, continued to affect population levels. In 1630, for example, northern Italy was hit by a devastating recurrence of bubonic plague; Verona and Mantua lost 60 to 70 percent of their populations. Europe's entry into another "little ice age" after the middle of the sixteenth century, when average temperatures fell and glaciers even engulfed small Alpine villages, affected harvests and gave rise to famines. Historians have noted the parallels between population increase and economic prosperity in the sixteenth century and population decline and economic recession in the seventeenth century.

The rise in population was reflected in the growth of cities. In 1500, Paris, Constantinople, and four cities in Italy (Naples, Venice, Milan, Genoa) had populations above 100,000 people. By 1600, Naples had grown to 300,000, while Rome, Palermo, and Messina reached 100,000. Cities along coasts and well-traveled trade routes grew the most, reflecting the close ties between commerce and urban growth. Naples became the largest port in Italy while Seville in Spain, the port of entry for the wealth of the New World, and Lisbon in Portugal had populations over 100,000 by 1600. Across the English Channel, London's domination of the commercial and financial life of England pushed its population to 250,000 by 1600. By that year, Europe's greatest and most populous city was Paris with its 500,000 people.

Seventeenth-century cities visibly reflected the remarkable disparity in wealth during the seventeenth century. The beautiful houses and palaces of rich nobles and wealthy merchants contrasted sharply with the crowded tenements and dirty hovels of the lower classes. Crime, pollution, filth, and lack of sanitation, fresh water, and food were accompanied by social tensions between landed nobles who moved into the cities and the wealthy merchants who resented their presence.

◆ Seventeenth-Century Crises: War and Rebellions

Although many Europeans responded to the upheavals of the second half of the sixteenth century with a desire for peace and order, the first fifty years of the seventeenth century continued to be a period of crisis. A devastating war that affected much of Europe and rebellions seemingly everywhere protracted an atmosphere of disorder and violence.

The Thirty Years' War

Religion, especially the struggle between a militant Catholicism and a militant Calvinism, certainly played an important role in the outbreak of the Thirty Years' War, often called the "last of the religious wars." As the war progressed, however, it became increasingly clear that secular, dynastic-nationalist considerations were far more important.

Although much of the fighting in the Thirty Years' War (1618–1648) took place in the Germanic lands of the Holy Roman Empire, the war became a Europeanwide struggle. In fact, some historians view it as part of a larger conflict between the Bourbon dynasty of France and the Habsburg dynasties of Spain and the Holy Roman Empire for European leadership and date it from 1609 to 1659. A brief look at the motives of the European states and the situation in the Holy Roman Empire provides the background necessary to understand the war.

Since the beginning of the sixteenth century, France had worked to break out of what it perceived as its encirclement by the house of Habsburg. The situation had eased in 1556 when Charles V abdicated and divided his empire. His son Philip inherited Spain, the Netherlands, Italy, and the New World while his brother Ferdinand became Holy Roman Emperor and received the Habsburg possessions in Austria and eastern Europe. France felt threatened by the Spanish Habsburgs and feared the consolidation of the Holy Roman Empire by the Habsburg emperor.

Spain, which viewed the twelve-year truce negotiated with the Dutch in 1609 as only temporary, was determined to regain control of the Netherlands, specifically, the northern Dutch provinces. English and Dutch control of the seas, however, forced the Spanish to seek an alternative route for shipping supplies and men to the Dutch provinces by way of Italy and western Germany.

The Austrian Habsburgs wished to consolidate their holdings in Austria and Bohemia by eliminating Protestantism and establishing stronger central authority. At the same time, as Holy Roman Emperors, they remained frustrated by their lack of real authority over the lands of Germany where hundreds of individual states still provided the real basis of political power. It was among these German states that the Thirty Years' War had its immediate beginnings.

The Peace of Augsburg in 1555 had brought an end to the religious warfare between German Catholics and Lutherans. Religion, however, continued to play a divisive role in German life as Lutherans and Catholics persisted in vying for control of various principalities. In addition,

MAP 14.3 The Thirty Years' War.

although the treaty had not recognized the rights of Calvinists, a number of German states had adopted Calvinism as their state church. At the beginning of the seventeenth century, the Calvinist ruler of the Palatinate, the Elector Palatine Frederick IV, assumed the leadership in forming a league of German Protestant states called the Protestant Union. To counteract it, a Catholic League of German states was organized by Duke Maximilian of the south German state of Bavaria. This division of Germany into two armed camps was made even more dangerous by the involvement of foreign states. The Protestant Union gained the support of the Dutch, English, and French, while Spain and the Holy Roman Emperor aided the Catholic League. By 1609, then, Germany was dividing into two armed camps in anticipation of religious war.

The religious division was exacerbated by a constitutional issue. The desire of the Habsburg emperors to consolidate their authority in the Holy Roman Empire was resisted by the princes who fought for their "German liberties," their constitutional rights and prerogatives as individual rulers. To pursue their policies, the Habsburg emperors looked to Spain for assistance while the princes turned to the enemies of Spain, especially France, for help against the emperor. The divisions in the Holy Roman Empire and Europe made it almost inevitable that if war did erupt, it would be widespread and difficult to stop. Events in Bohemia in 1617 and 1618 finally brought the outbreak of the war everyone dreaded.

CHRONOLOGY

The Thirty Years' War

The Protestant Union	1608
The Catholic League	1609
Election of Habsburg Archduke Ferdinand as king of Bohemia	1617
Bohemian revolt against Ferdinand	1618
The Bohemian Phase	1618–1625
Battle of White Mountain	1620
Spanish conquest of Palatinate	1622
The Danish phase	1625–1629
Edict of Restitution	1629
The Swedish phase	1630–1635
Battle of Lützen	1632
Battle of Nördlingen	1634
The Franco-Swedish phase	1635–1648
Battle of Rocroi	1643
Peace of Westphalia	1648
Peace of the Pyrenees	1659

Historians have traditionally divided the Thirty Years' War into four major phases. The Bohemian phase (1618–1625) began in one of the Habsburgs' own territories. In 1617, the Bohemian Estates (primarily the nobles) accepted the Habsburg Archduke Ferdinand as their king but soon found themselves unhappy with their choice. Though many of the nobles were Calvinists, Ferdinand was a devout Catholic who began a process of re-Catholicizing Bohemia and strengthening royal power. The Protestant nobles rebelled against Ferdinand in May 1618 and proclaimed their resistance by throwing two of the Habsburg governors and a secretary out of the window of the royal castle in Prague, the seat of Bohemian government. The Catholic side claimed that their seemingly miraculous escape from death in the seventy-foot fall from the castle was due to the intercession of the Virgin Mary, while Protestants pointed out that they fell into a manure pile. The Bohemian rebels now seized control of Bohemia, deposed Ferdinand, and elected as his replacement the Protestant ruler of the Palatinate, Elector Frederick V, who was also head of the Protestant Union.

Ferdinand, who in the meantime had been elected as Holy Roman Emperor, refused to accept his deposition. Aided by the imposing forces of Maximilian of Bavaria and the Catholic League, the imperial forces defeated Frederick and the Bohemian nobles at the Battle of White Mountain outside Prague on November 8, 1620. Spanish troops meanwhile took advantage of Frederick's predicament by invading the Palatinate and conquering it by the end of 1622. The unfortunate Frederick who had lost two crowns—Bohemia and the Palatinate—fled into exile in Holland. The Spanish took control of the western part of the Palatinate (to gain the access route from Italy to the Netherlands that they had wanted), and Duke Maximilian of Bavaria took the rest of the territory. Reestablished as king of Bohemia, Emperor Ferdinand declared Bohemia a hereditary Habsburg possession, confiscated the land of the Protestant nobles, and established Catholicism as the sole religion. Some 30,000 Protestant families emigrated to Saxony and Hungary. The Spanish renewed their attack on the Dutch, and the forces of Catholicism seemed on the road to victory. But the war was far from over.

The second phase of the war, the Danish phase (1625–1629), began when King Christian IV of Denmark (1588–1648), a Lutheran, intervened on behalf of the Protestant cause by leading an army into northern Germany. Most likely, he also wished to annex territories in northern Germany that would give him control of the southern Baltic. His campaign turned out to be a complete fiasco.

The imperial forces were now led by a brilliant and enigmatic commander, Albrecht von Wallenstein, a Bohemian nobleman who had taken advantage of Ferdinand's victory to become the country's wealthiest landowner. Wallenstein marched the imperial army north, utterly defeated the Danes, and occupied parts of northern Germany, including the Baltic ports of Hamburg, Lübeck, and Bremen. Christian IV's total defeat ended Danish involvement in the Thirty Years' War and even meant the end of Danish supremacy in the Baltic.

After the success of the imperial armies, the emperor Ferdinand II was at the height of his power and took this opportunity to issue the Edict of Restitution in March 1629. His proclamation prohibited Calvinist worship and

SOLDIERS PILLAGING A FARM. This painting shows a group of soldiers running amok on a French peasant's farm. This scene was typical of many that occurred during the Thirty Years' War, especially in Germany where the war caused enormous destruction.

restored to the Catholic church all property taken by Protestant princes or cities during the past seventy-five years. But this sudden growth in the power of the Habsburg emperor frightened many German princes who feared for their independent status and reacted by forcing the emperor to dismiss Wallenstein. At the same time, Ferdinand was faced with another intervention by foreign powers as the war entered its third phase.

The Swedish phase (1630–1635) marked the entry of Gustavus Adolphus, king of Sweden (1611–1635), into the war. Gustavus Adolphus was responsible for reviving Sweden and making it into a great Baltic power. The French, disturbed by the Habsburg consolidation of power, provided financial support to Gustavus, a military genius who brought a disciplined and well-equipped Swedish army to northern Germany. Gustavus had no desire to see the Habsburgs in northern Germany since he wanted the Baltic Sea to be a Swedish lake. At the same time, Gustavus Adolphus was a devout Lutheran who felt compelled to aid his coreligionists in Germany.

Gustavus's army swept the imperial forces out of the north and moved into the heart of Germany. In desperation, the imperial side recalled Wallenstein, who was given command of the imperial army that met Gustavus Adolphus's troops near Leipzig. At the Battle of Lützen (1632), the Swedish forces prevailed but paid a high price for the victory when the Swedish king was killed in the battle. Although the Swedish forces remained in Germany, they proved much less effective. Despite the loss of Wallenstein, who was assassinated in 1634 by one of his own captains, the imperial army decisively defeated the Swedes at the Battle of Nördlingen at the end of 1634 and drove them out of southern Germany. This imperial victory guaranteed that southern Germany would remain Catholic. The emperor used this opportunity to make peace with the German princes by agreeing to annul the Edict of Restitution of 1629. But peace failed to come to war-weary Germany. The Swedes wished to continue while the French, under the direction of Cardinal Richelieu, the chief minister of King Louis XIII (see Chapter 15), entered the war directly, beginning the fourth and final phase of the war, the Franco-Swedish phase (1635–1648).

By this time, religious issues were losing their significance as dynastic power politics came to the fore. The Catholic French, after all, were now supporting the Protestant Swedes against the Catholic Habsburgs of Germany and Spain. This phase of the war was fought by Sweden in northern Germany and by France in the Netherlands and along the Rhine in western Germany. The Battle of Rocroi in 1643 proved decisive as the French beat the Spanish and brought an end to Spanish military greatness. The French then moved on to victories over the imperialist-Bavarian armies in southern Germany. By this time all parties were ready for peace, and after five years of protracted negotiations, the war in Germany was officially ended by the Peace of Westphalia in 1648. The war between France and Spain, however, continued until the Peace of the Pyrenees in 1659. By that time, Spain had become a second-class power, and France had emerged as the dominant nation in Europe.

What were the results of this "basically meaningless conflict," as one historian has called it? The Peace of Westphalia ensured that all German states, including the Calvinist ones, were free to determine their own religion. Territorially, France gained parts of western Germany, part of Alsace and the three cities of Metz, Toul, and Verdun, giving the French control of the Franco-German border area and excellent bases for future military operations in Germany. While Sweden and the German states of Brandenburg and Bavaria gained some territory in Germany, the Austrian Habsburgs did not really lose any, but did see their authority as rulers of Germany further diminished. The more than 300 states that made up the Holy Roman Empire were virtually recognized as independent states, since each received the power to conduct its own foreign

The Face of War in the Seventeenth Century

The Thirty Years' War was the most devastating war Europeans had experienced since the Hundred Years' War. Destruction was especially severe in Germany. We have a firsthand account of the face of war in Germany from a picaresque novel called Simplicius Simplicissimus, *written by Jakob von Grimmelshausen. The author's experiences as a soldier in the Thirty Years' War give his descriptions of the effect of the war on ordinary people a certain vividness and reality. This selection describes the fate of a peasant farm, an experience all too familiar to thousands of German peasants between 1618 and 1648.*

Jakob von Grimmelshausen, *Simplicius Simplicissimus*

The first thing these horsemen did in the nice back rooms of the house was to put in their horses. Then everyone took up a special job, one having to do with death and destruction. Although some began butchering, heating water, and rendering lard, as if to prepare for a banquet, others raced through the house, ransacking upstairs and down; not even the privy chamber was safe, as if the golden fleece of Jason might be hidden there. Still others bundled up big packs of cloth, household goods, and clothes, as if they wanted to hold a rummage sale somewhere. What they did not intend to take along they broke and spoiled. Some ran their swords into the hay and straw, as if there hadn't been hogs enough to stick. Some shook the feathers out of beds and put bacon slabs, hams, and other stuff in the ticking, as if they might sleep better on these. Others knocked down the hearth and broke the windows, as if announcing an everlasting summer. They flattened out copper and pewter dishes and baled the ruined goods. They burned up bedsteads, tables, chairs, and benches, though there were yards and yards of dry firewood outside the kitchen. Jars and crocks, pots and casseroles all were broken, either because they preferred their meat broiled or because they thought they'd eat only one meal with us. In the barn, the hired girl was handled so roughly that she was unable to walk away, I am ashamed to report. They stretched the hired man out flat on the ground, stuck a wooden wedge in his mouth to keep it open, and emptied a milk bucket full of stinking manure drippings down his throat; they called it a Swedish cocktail. He didn't relish it and made a very wry face. By this means they forced him to take a raiding party to some other place where they carried off men and cattle and brought them to our farm. Among those were my father, mother, and Ursula [sister].

Then they used thumbscrews, which they cleverly made out of their pistols, to torture the peasants, as if they wanted to burn witches. Though he had confessed to nothing as yet, they put one of the captured hayseeds in the bake-oven and lighted a fire in it. They put a rope around someone else's head and tightened it like a tourniquet until blood came out of his mouth, nose, and ears. In short, every soldier had his favorite method of making life miserable for peasants, and every peasant had his own misery. My father was, as I thought, particularly lucky because he confessed with a laugh what others were forced to say in pain and martyrdom. No doubt because he was the head of the household, he was shown special consideration; they put him close to a fire, tied him by his hands and legs, and rubbed damp salt on the bottoms of his feet. Our old nanny goat had to lick it off and this so tickled my father that he could have burst laughing. This seemed so clever and entertaining to me—I had never seen or heard my father laugh so long—that I joined him in laughter, to keep him company or perhaps to cover up my ignorance. In the midst of such glee he told them the whereabouts of hidden treasure much richer in gold, pearls, and jewelry than might have been expected on a farm.

I can't say much about the captured wives, hired girls, and daughters because the soldiers didn't let me watch their doings. But I do remember hearing pitiful screams from various dark corners and I guess that my mother and our Ursula had it no better than the rest.

policy; this brought an end to the Holy Roman Empire as a political entity and ensured German disunity for another 200 years. The Peace of Westphalia also made it clear that religion and politics were now separate worlds. The pope was completely ignored in all decisions at Westphalia, and political motives became the guiding forces in public affairs as religion moved closer to becoming primarily a matter of personal conviction and individual choice.

The economic and social effects of the Thirty Years' War on Germany are still debated. The most recent work pictures a ruined German economy and a decline in German population from 21 to 16 million between 1618 and 1650. Some areas of Germany were completely devastated, but others remained relatively untouched and even experienced economic growth. In any case, the Thirty Years' War was undoubtedly the most destructive conflict Europeans had yet experienced (see the box above). Unfortunately, it was not the last.

A Military Revolution?

By the seventeenth century, war played an increasingly important role in European affairs. One historian has calculated that between 1562 and 1721 there were only four years in which all Europe was at peace. Military power was considered essential to a ruler's reputation and power;

thus, the pressure to build an effective military machine was intense. Although some would disagree, some historians believe that the changes that occurred in the science of warfare between 1560 and 1650 warrant the title of military revolution.

Medieval warfare, with its mounted knights and supplementary archers, had been transformed in the Renaissance by the employment of infantry armed with pikes and halberds and arranged in massed rectangles, known as squadrons or battalions. The squadron of pikemen became a crucial element in sixteenth-century armies and helps to explain the success of the Spanish who perfected its use. The utilization of firearms required adjustments to the size and shape of the massed infantry and made the cavalry less effective.

It was Gustavus Adolphus, the king of Sweden, who developed the first standing army of conscripts, notable for the flexibility of its tactics. The infantry brigades of Gustavus's army were composed of equal numbers of musketeers and pikemen, standing six men deep. They employed the salvo in which all rows of the infantry fired at once instead of row by row. These salvos of fire, which cut up the massed ranks of the opposing infantry squadrons, were followed by a pike charge, giving the infantry a primarily offensive deployment. Gustavus also used the cavalry in a more mobile fashion. After shooting a pistol volley, they charged the enemy with their swords. Additional flexibility was obtained by utilizing lighter artillery pieces that were more easily moved during battle. All of these changes required coordination, careful training, and better discipline, forcing rulers to move away from undisciplined mercenary forces. Naturally, the success of Gustavus Adolphus led to imitation. Perhaps the best example was the New Model Army of Oliver Cromwell (see Chapter 15). His army consisted of infantry (two-thirds musketeers and one-third pikemen), cavalry, mounted infantry known as dragoons, and artillery units. A well-integrated and disciplined army, it was known for its mobility and flexibility.

The military changes between 1560 and 1650 included an increased use of firearms and cannon, greater flexibility and mobility in tactics, and better disciplined and trained armies. These innovations necessitated standing armies, based partly on conscription, which grew ever larger and more expensive as the seventeenth century progressed. Such armies could only be maintained by levying heavier taxes, making war an economic burden and an ever more important part of the early modern European state. To some historians, the creation of large bureaucracies to supervise the military resources of the state was the real reason for the rise of royal absolutism in the seventeenth century (see Chapter 15).

Rebellions

Before, during, and after the Thirty Years' War, a series of rebellions and civil wars stemming from the discontent of both nobles and commoners rocked the domestic stability of many European governments. To strengthen their power, monarchs attempted to extend their authority at the expense of traditional powerful elements who resisted the rulers' efforts. At the same time, to fight their battles, governments increased taxes and created such hardships that common people also rose in opposition.

Between 1590 and 1640, peasant and lower-class revolts erupted in central and southern France, Austria, and Hungary. In the decades of the 1640s and 1650s, even greater unrest occurred. Portugal and Catalonia rebelled against the Spanish government in 1640. The common people in Naples and Sicily revolted against both the government and the landed nobility in 1647. Russia, too, was rocked by urban uprisings in 1641, 1645, and 1648. Nobles rebelled in France from 1648 to 1652 to halt the growth of royal power (see Chapter 15). The northern states of Sweden, Denmark, and Holland were also not immune from upheavals involving clergy, nobles, and mercantile groups. Even relatively stable Switzerland had a peasant rebellion in 1656. By far the most famous and wide-ranging struggle, however, was the civil war and rebellion in England, commonly known as the English Revolution (see Chapter 15).

◆ The Witchcraft Craze

In the midst of the turmoil created by wars, rebellions, and economic and social uncertainties, yet another source of disorder arose as hysteria over witchcraft came to affect the lives of many Europeans in the sixteenth and seventeenth centuries. Witchcraft trials were prevalent in England, Scotland, Switzerland, Germany, some parts of France and the Low Countries, and even New England in America. As is evident from this list, the witchcraft craze affected both Catholic and Protestant countries.

Witchcraft was not a new phenomenon in the sixteenth and seventeenth centuries. Its practice had been part of traditional village culture for centuries, but it came to be viewed as both sinister and dangerous when the medieval church began to connect witches to the activities of the devil, thereby transforming witchcraft into a heresy that had to be wiped out. After the creation of the Inquisition in the thirteenth century, some people were accused of a variety of witchcraft practices and, following the biblical injunction, "Thou shalt not suffer a witch to live," were turned over to secular authorities for burning at the stake or hanging (in England).

The search for scapegoats to explain the disaster of the Black Death in the fourteenth century led to a rise in the persecution of people accused of sorcery. In a papal bull of 1484, Pope Innocent VIII made official the belief of the Catholic church in such pernicious practices:

> It has recently come to our ears, not without great pain to us, that in some parts of upper Germany, . . . many persons of both sexes, heedless of their own salvation and forsaking the catholic faith, give themselves over to devils male and

THE ACTIVITIES OF WITCHES. **Hysteria over witchcraft affected the daily lives of many Europeans in the sixteenth and seventeenth centuries. This picture by Frans Francken the Young, painted in 1607, shows a number of activities commonly attributed to witches. In the center, several witches are casting spells with their magic books and instruments, and at the top, a witch on a post prepares to fly off on her broomstick.**

> female, and by their incantations, charms, and conjurings, . . . ruin and cause to perish the offspring of women, the foal of animals, the products of the earth, the grapes of vines, and the fruits of trees, as well as men and women, cattle and flocks and herds and animals of every kind . . . ; that they afflict and torture with dire pains and anguish, both internal and external, these men, women, cattle, flocks, herds, and animals, and hinder men from begetting and women from conceiving, and prevent all consummation of marriage; . . . that, moreover, at the instigation of the enemy of mankind [Satan], they do not fear to commit and perpetrate many other abominable offenses and crimes.[12]

To combat these dangers, Innocent sent two Dominican friars, Jacob Sprenger and Heinrich Krämer, to Germany to investigate and root out the witches. In 1486, based on their findings, they wrote the *Malleus Maleficarum (The Hammer of the Witches),* which until the eighteenth century remained one of the standard handbooks on the practices of witchcraft and the methods that could be used to discover and try witches.

What distinguished witchcraft in the sixteenth and seventeenth centuries from these previous developments was the increased number of trials and executions of presumed witches. Although estimates have varied widely, the most recent figures indicate that more than 100,000 people were prosecuted throughout Europe on charges of witchcraft. As more and more people were brought to trial, the fear of witches as well as the fear of being accused of witchcraft escalated to frightening proportions. Approximately 25 percent of the villages in the English county of Essex, for example, had at least one witchcraft trial in the sixteenth and seventeenth centuries. Although larger cities were affected first, the trials also spread to smaller towns and rural areas as the hysteria persisted well into the seventeenth century (see the box on p. 417).

From an account of witch persecution in the German city of Trier, we get some glimpse of who the accused were: "Scarcely any of those who were accused escaped punishment. Nor were there spared even the leading men in the city of Trier." Although this statement makes it clear that the witchcraft trials had gone so far that even city officeholders were not immune from persecution, it also implies what is borne out in most witchcraft trials—that women of the lower classes were more likely to be accused of witchcraft. Indeed, where lists are given, those mentioned most often are milkmaids, peasant women, and servant girls. In the witchcraft trials of the sixteenth and seventeenth centuries, 80 percent of those accused were women, most of them single or widowed and many over fifty years old. Moreover, almost all victims belonged to the lower classes, the poor and propertyless.

The accused witches usually confessed to a number of practices. Many of their confessions were extracted by torture, greatly adding to the number and intensity of activities mentioned. But even when people confessed voluntarily, certain practices stand out. Many said that they had sworn allegiance to the devil and attended sabbats or nocturnal gatherings where they feasted, danced, and even copulated with the devil in sexual orgies. More common, however, were admissions of using evil incantations and special ointments and powders to wreak havoc on neigh-

A Witchcraft Trial in France

Persecutions for witchcraft reached their high point in the sixteenth and seventeenth centuries when tens of thousands of people were brought to trial. In this excerpt from the minutes of a trial in France in 1652, we can see why the accused witch stood little chance of exonerating herself.

The Trial of Suzanne Gaudry

28 May, 1652. . . . Interrogation of Suzanne Gaudry, prisoner at the court of Rieux. . . . [During interrogations on May 28 and May 29, the prisoner confessed to a number of activities involving the devil.]

Deliberation of the Court—June 3, 1652

The undersigned advocates of the Court have seen these interrogations and answers. They say that the aforementioned Suzanne Gaudry confesses that she is a witch, that she had given herself to the devil, that she had renounced God, Lent, and baptism, that she has been marked on the shoulder, that she has cohabited with the devil and that she has been to the dances, confessing only to have cast a spell upon and caused to die a beast of Philippe Cornié. . . .

Third Interrogation—June 27

This prisoner being led into the chamber, she was examined to know if things were not as she had said and confessed at the beginning of her imprisonment.

—Answers no, and that what she has said was done so by force.

Pressed to say the truth, that otherwise she would be subjected to torture, having pointed out to her that her aunt was burned for this same subject.

—Answers that she is not a witch. . . .

She was placed in the hands of the officer in charge of torture, throwing herself on her knees, struggling to cry, uttering several exclamations, without being able, nevertheless to shed a tear. Saying at every moment that she is not a witch.

The Torture

On this same day, being at the place of torture.

This prisoner, before being strapped down, was admonished to maintain herself in her first confessions and to renounce her lover.

—Says that she denies everything she has said, and that she has no lover. Feeling herself being strapped down, says that she is not a witch, while struggling to cry. . . . and upon being asked why she confessed to being one, said that she was forced to say it.

Told that she was not forced, that on the contrary she declared herself to be a witch without any threat.

—Says that she confessed it and that she is not a witch, and being a little stretched [on the rack] screams ceaselessly that she is not a witch. . . .

Asked if she did not confess that she had been a witch for twenty-six years.

—Says that she said it, that she retracts it, crying that she is not a witch.

Asked if she did not make Philippe Cornié's horse die, as she confessed.

—Answers no, crying Jesus-Maria, that she is not a witch.

The mark having been probed by the officer, in the presence of Doctor Bouchain, it was adjudged by the aforesaid doctor and officer truly to be the mark of the devil.

Being more tightly stretched upon the torture-rack, urged to maintain her confessions.

—Said that it was true that she is a witch and that she would maintain what she had said.

Asked how long she has been in subjugation to the devil.

—Answers that it was twenty years ago that the devil appeared to her, being in her lodgings in the form of a man dressed in a little cow-hide and black breeches. . . .

Verdict

July 9, 1652. In the light of the interrogations, answers and investigations made into the charge against Suzanne Gaudry, . . . seeing by her own confessions that she is said to have made a pact with the devil, received the mark from him, . . . and that following this, she had renounced God, Lent, and baptism and had let herself be known carnally by him, in which she received satisfaction. Also, seeing that she is said to have been a part of nocturnal carols and dances.

For expiation of which the advice of the undersigned is that the office of Rieux can legitimately condemn the aforesaid Suzanne Gaudry to death, tying her to a gallows, and strangling her to death, then burning her body and burying it here in the environs of the woods.

bors by killing their livestock, injuring their children, or raising storms to destroy their crops.

A number of contributing factors have been suggested to explain why the witchcraft craze became so widespread in the sixteenth and seventeenth centuries. Religious uncertainties clearly played some part. Many witchcraft trials occurred in areas where Protestantism had been recently victorious or in regions, such as southwestern Germany, where Protestant-Catholic controversies still raged. As religious passions became inflamed, accusations of being in league with the devil became common on both sides.

Recently, however, historians have emphasized the importance of social conditions, especially the problems of a society in turmoil, in explaining the witchcraft hysteria. At a time when the old communal values that stressed working together for the good of the community were disintegrating before the onslaught of a new economic ethic that emphasized that each person should look out for himself or herself, property owners became more fearful of the growing numbers of poor in their midst and transformed them psychologically into agents of the devil. Old women were particularly susceptible to suspicion. Many of them, no longer the recipients of the local charity available in traditional society, may even have tried to survive by selling herbs, potions, or secret remedies for healing. When problems arose—and there were many in this crisis-laden period—these same women were the most likely scapegoats at hand.

That women should be the chief victims of witchcraft trials was hardly accidental. Indeed, the authors of the *Malleus Maleficarum* had argued that there was a direct link between witchcraft and women. According to them, women were inferior to men both mentally and morally. Women's moral weaknesses made them especially open to temptation and hence especially vulnerable to the allures of Satan. The strong beliefs of the authors of the *Malleus Maleficarum* were repeated in virtually all of the new witchcraft treatises written in the sixteenth and seventeenth centuries. Nicholas Rémy, a witchcraft judge in France in the 1590s, found it "not unreasonable that this scum of humanity (i.e., witches) should be drawn chiefly from the feminine sex." To another judge, it came as no surprise that witches would confess to sexual experiences with Satan: "The Devil uses them so, because he knows that women love carnal pleasures, and he means to bind them to his allegiance by such agreeable provocations."[13] Of course, not only witch hunters held such low estimates of women. Most theologians, lawyers, and philosophers in early modern Europe believed in the natural inferiority of women and thus would have found it plausible that women would be more susceptible to witchcraft.

By the mid-seventeenth century, the witchcraft hysteria began to subside. The destruction of the religious wars had at least forced people to accept a grudging toleration, causing religious passions to subside. Moreover, as governments began to stabilize after the period of crisis, fewer magistrates were willing to accept the unsettling and divisive conditions generated by the trials of witches. Finally, by the end of the seventeenth and beginning of the eighteenth centuries, more and more educated people were questioning altogether their old attitudes toward religion and finding it especially contrary to reason to believe in the old view of a world haunted by evil spirits.

◆ Culture in a Turbulent World

Art and literature passed through two major stylistic stages between the Renaissance and 1650. These changes were closely linked to the religious, political, and intellectual developments of the period.

Art: Mannerism and the Baroque

The artistic Renaissance came to an end when a new movement called Mannerism emerged in Italy in the decades of the 1520s and 1530s. The age of the Reformation had brought a revival of religious values accompanied by much political turmoil. Especially in Italy, the worldly enthusiasm of the Renaissance gave way to anxiety, uncertainty, suffering, and a yearning for spiritual experience. Mannerism reflected this environment in its deliberate attempt to break down the High Renaissance principles of balance, harmony, and moderation (the term *Mannerism* derives from critics who considered their contemporary artists to be second-rate imitators, painting in the "manner" of Michelangelo's late style). Italian Mannerist painters deliberately distorted the rules of proportion by portraying elongated figures that conveyed a sense of suffering and a strong emotional atmosphere filled with anxiety and confusion.

Mannerism spread from Italy to other parts of Europe and perhaps reached its apogee in the work of El Greco (1541–1614). Doménikos Theotocópoulos (called "the Greek"—El Greco) was from Crete, but after studying in Venice and Rome, he moved to Spain in the 1570s where he became a church painter in Toledo. El Greco's elongated and contorted figures, portrayed in unusual shades of yellow and green against an eerie background of turbulent grays, reflect well the artist's desire to create a world of intense emotion.

Mannerism was eventually replaced by a new movement—the Baroque—that dominated the artistic world for another century and a half. The Baroque began in Italy in the last quarter of the sixteenth century and spread to the rest of Europe. Baroque artists sought to harmonize the classical traditions of Renaissance art with the intense religious feelings fostered by the revival of religion in the Reformation. The Baroque first appeared in Rome in the Jesuit church of Il Gesù, whose facade was completed in 1575. Although Protestants were also affected, the Baroque was most wholeheartedly embraced by the Catholic reform movement, as is evident at the Catholic courts, especially those of the Habsburgs in Madrid, Prague, Vienna, and Brussels. Although it was resisted in France, England, and Holland, eventually the Baroque style spread to all of Europe and to Latin America.

In large part, Baroque art and architecture reflected the search for power that was characteristic of much of the seventeenth century. Baroque churches and palaces featured richly ornamented facades, sweeping staircases, and an overall splendor that were meant to impress people. Kings and princes wanted other kings and princes as well

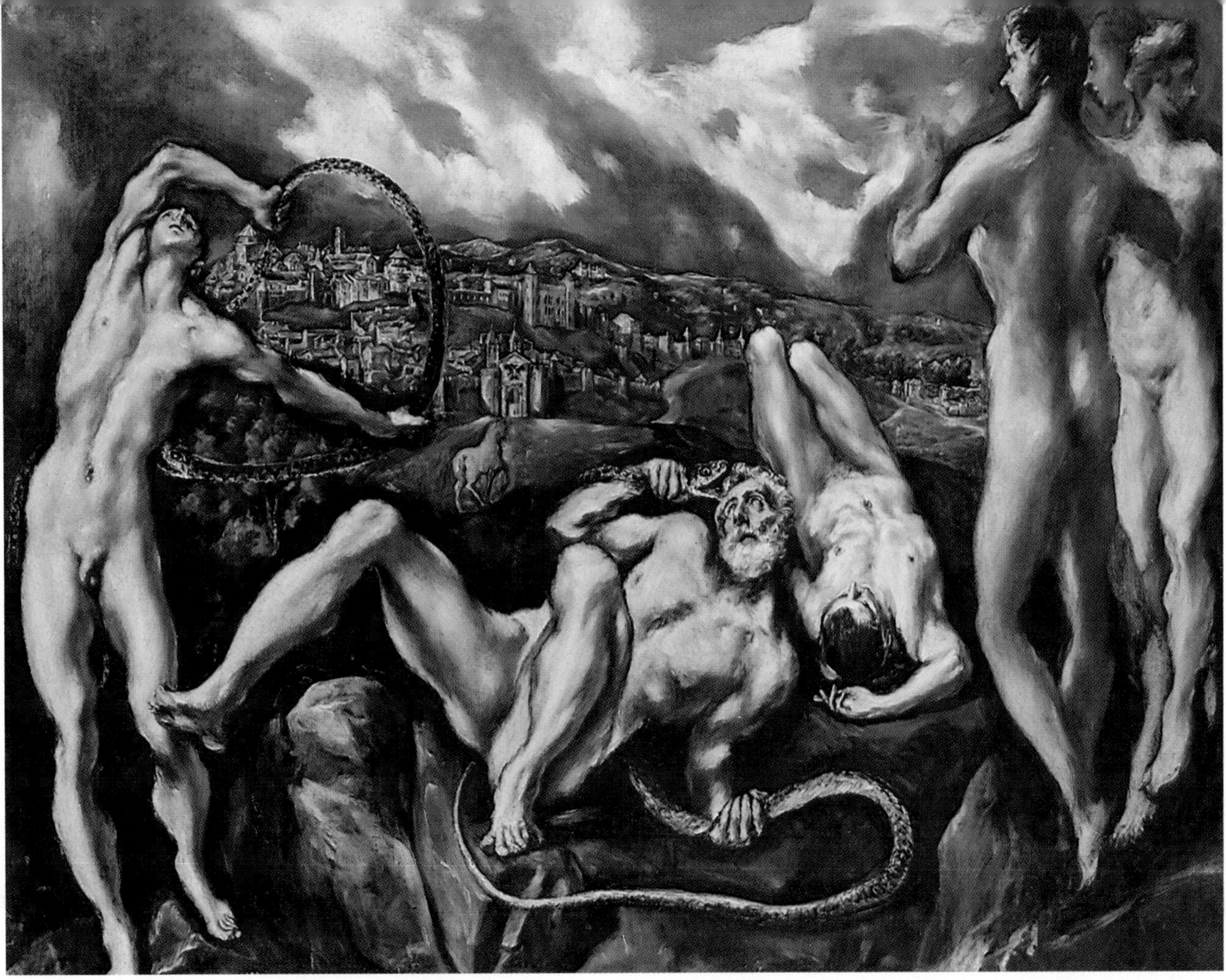

EL GRECO, *LAOCÖON*. Mannerism reached one of its highest expressions in the work of El Greco. Born in Crete, trained in Venice and Rome, and settling finally in Spain, El Greco worked as a church painter in Toledo. Pictured here is his version of the *Laocöon*, a famous piece of Hellenistic sculpture that had been discovered in Rome in 1506. The elongated, contorted bodies project a world of suffering while the somber background scene of the city of Toledo adds a sense of terror and doom.

as their subjects to be in awe of their power. The Catholic church, which commissioned many new churches, wanted people to see clearly the triumphant power of the Catholic faith.

Baroque painting was known for its use of dramatic effects to heighten emotional intensity. This style was especially evident in the works of Peter Paul Rubens (1577–1640), a prolific artist and an important figure in the spread of the Baroque from Italy to other parts of Europe. In his artistic masterpieces, bodies in violent motion, heavily fleshed nudes, a dramatic use of light and shadow, and rich sensuous pigments converge to show intense emotions. The restless forms and constant movement blend together into a dynamic unity.

IL GESÙ. The Jesuit church of Il Gesù in Rome was the first example of Baroque. Its facade, seen here, was completed in 1575. With its use of classical columns, entablatures, and pediments, it served as a model for later church designs done in the Baroque style.

Perhaps the greatest figure of the Baroque was the Italian architect and sculptor Gian Lorenzo Bernini (1598–1680), who completed Saint Peter's Basilica and designed the vast colonnade enclosing the piazza in front of it. Action, exuberance, profusion, and dramatic effects mark the work of Bernini in the interior of Saint Peter's, where his *Throne of Saint Peter* hovers in mid-air, held by the hands of the four great doctors of the Catholic church. Above the chair, rays of golden light drive a mass of clouds and angels toward the spectator. In his most

PETER PAUL RUBENS, *THE LANDING OF MARIE DE' MEDICI AT MARSEILLES*. Peter Paul Rubens played a key role in spreading the Baroque style from Italy to other parts of Europe. In *The Landing of Marie de' Medici at Marseilles*, Rubens made a dramatic use of light and color, bodies in motion, and luxurious nudes to heighten the emotional intensity of the scene. This was one of a cycle of twenty-one paintings dedicated to the queen mother of France.

striking sculptural work, the *Ecstasy of Saint Theresa*, Bernini depicts a moment of mystical experience in the life of the sixteenth-century Spanish saint. The elegant draperies and the expression on her face create a sensuously real portrayal of physical ecstasy.

Less well-known than the male artists who dominated the art world of seventeenth-century Italy but prominent in her own right was Artemisia Gentileschi (1593–1653). Born in Rome, she studied painting under her father's direction. In 1616, she moved to Florence and began a successful career as a painter. At the age of twenty-three, she became the first woman to be elected to the Florentine Academy of Design. Although she was known internationally in her day as a portrait painter, her fame now rests on a series of pictures of heroines from the Old Testament, including Judith, Esther, and Bathsheba. Most famous is her *Judith Beheading Holofernes*, a dramatic rendering of the biblical scene in which Judith slays the Assyrian general Holofernes to save her besieged town from the Assyrian army.

Thought: The World of Montaigne

The crises between 1550 and 1650 produced challenges to the optimistic moral and intellectual premises of the Renaissance. The humanist emphasis on the dignity of man and the role of education in producing moral virtue seemed questionable in view of the often violent passions of dynastic and religious warfare. Intellectuals and writers began to adopt new approaches in criticizing tradition and authority. The concept of a positive skepticism is closely associated with the work of Michel de Montaigne (1533–1592).

Son of a prosperous French merchant, Montaigne received the kind of classical education advocated by Renaissance humanists. Montaigne served as a lawyer and magistrate in the Parlement of Bordeaux, but the religious wars so disgusted him that he withdrew to his country estate to think and write his *Essays*, the first two books of which were published in 1580. His aim was to "disclose himself," or to use self-knowledge as an instrument to understand the world. Montaigne questioned tradition and authority and attacked moral absolutists. He was especially critical of the Huguenot and ultra-Catholic fanatics of the French Wars of Religion who deluded themselves and took the easy way out of life's complexities by trying to kill each other: "instead of transforming themselves into angels, they transform themselves into beasts."

To counteract fanaticism, Montaigne preached moderation and toleration or the "middle way." In his *Essay on Experience*, he wrote: "It is much easier to go along the sides, where the outer edge serves as a limit and a guide, than by the middle way, wide and open, and to go by art than by nature; but it is also much less noble and less commendable. Greatness of soul is not so much pressing upward and forward as knowing how to set oneself in order."[14] Montaigne also brought his middle way and skep-

GIAN LORENZO BERNINI, *ECSTASY OF SAINT THERESA*. **One of the greatest figures of the Baroque period was the Italian sculptor and architect Gian Lorenzo Bernini. *The Ecstasy of Saint Theresa,* created for the Cornaro Chapel in the Church of Santa Maria della Vittoria in Rome, was one of Bernini's most famous pieces of sculpture. Bernini sought to convey visually Theresa's own description of her mystical experience when an angel supposedly pierced her heart repeatedly with a golden arrow.**

ARTEMISIA GENTILESCHI, *JUDITH BEHEADING HOLOFERNES*. **Artemisia Gentileschi painted a series of pictures portraying scenes from the lives of courageous Old Testament women. In this painting, a determined Judith, armed with her victim's sword, struggles to saw off the head of Holofernes. Gentileschi realistically and dramatically shows the bloody nature of Judith's act.**

tical mind to bear on other subjects of the day. He wondered, for example, whether "civilized" Europeans were superior to the "savages" of the New World.

Montaigne was secular minded and discussed moral issues without reference to Christian truths. He was, in many ways, out of step with his own age of passionate religious truths and hatreds, but his ideas would be welcomed by many Europeans once Europe passed through this stage of intense intolerance. His maturity, experience, gentleness, and openness all made Montaigne one of the timeless writers of Western civilization.

A Golden Age of Literature: England and Spain

Periods of crisis often produce great writing, and so it was of this age, which was characterized by epic poetry, experimental verse, the first great chivalric novel, and, above all, a golden age of theater. In both England and Spain, writing for the stage reached new heights between 1580 and 1640. All of this impressive literature was written in the vernacular. Except for academic fields, such as theology, philosophy, jurisprudence, and the sciences, Latin was no longer a universal literary language.

The golden age of English literature is often called the Elizabethan era because much of the English cultural flowering of the late sixteenth and early seventeenth centuries occurred during her reign. Elizabethan literature exhibits the exuberance and pride associated with English exploits under Queen Elizabeth (see the box on p. 423). Of all the forms of Elizabethan literature, none expressed the energy and intellectual versatility of the era better than drama. Of all the dramatists, none is more famous than William Shakespeare (1564–1616).

Shakespeare was the son of a prosperous glovemaker from Stratford-upon-Avon. When he appeared in London in 1592, Elizabethans were already addicted to the stage. By 1576, two professional theaters run by actors' companies were in existence. Elizabethan theater became a tremendously successful business. In or near London, at least four to six theaters were open six afternoons a week. London theaters ranged from the Globe, which was a

WILLIAM SHAKESPEARE. The golden age of English literature is identified with the Elizabethan era. Drama flourished during the period, and the greatest dramatist of the age was William Shakespeare. An actor and shareholder in a theatrical company as well as a playwright, Shakespeare wrote a number of tragedies, comedies, romances, and histories.

circular unroofed structure holding 3,000, to the Blackfriars, which was roofed and held only 500. In the former, an admission charge of one or two pennies enabled even the lower classes to attend; the higher prices in the latter ensured an audience of the well-to-do. Elizabethan audiences varied greatly, putting pressure on playwrights to write works that pleased nobles, lawyers, merchants, and even vagabonds.

William Shakespeare was a "complete man of the theater." Although best known for writing plays, he was also an actor and shareholder in the chief company of the time, the Lord Chamberlain's Company, which played in theaters as diverse as the Globe and the Blackfriars. Shakespeare has long been recognized as a universal genius. A master of the English language, he was instrumental in transforming a language that was still in a period of transition. His technical proficiency, however, was matched by an incredible insight into human psychology. Whether in his tragedies or comedies, Shakespeare exhibited a remarkable understanding of the human condition.

The theater was also one of the most creative forms of expression during Spain's golden century. The first professional theaters established in Seville and Madrid in the 1570s were run by actors' companies as in England. Soon a public playhouse could be found in every large town, including Mexico City in the New World. Touring companies brought the latest Spanish plays to all parts of the Spanish Empire.

Beginning in the 1580s, the agenda for playwrights was set by Lope de Vega (1562–1635). Like Shakespeare, he was from a middle-class background. He was an incredibly prolific writer; almost 500 of his 1,500 plays survive. They have been characterized as witty, charming, action-packed, and realistic. Lope de Vega made no apologies for the fact that he wrote his plays to please his audiences. In a treatise on drama written in 1609, he stated that the foremost duty of the playwright was to satisfy public demand. Shakespeare undoubtedly believed the same thing since his livelihood depended on public approval, but Lope de Vega was considerably more cynical about it: he remarked that if anyone thought he had written his plays for fame, "undeceive him and tell him that I wrote them for money."

One of the crowning achievements of the golden age of Spanish literature was the work of Miguel de Cervantes (1547–1616), whose *Don Quixote* has been acclaimed as one of the greatest literary works of all time. While satirizing medieval chivalric literature, Cervantes also perfected the chivalric novel and reconciled it with literary realism. The two main figures of his famous work represented the dual nature of the Spanish character. The knight Don Quixote from La Mancha is the visionary who is so involved in his lofty ideals that he is oblivious to the hard realities around him. To him, for example, windmills appear as four-armed giants. In contrast, the knight's fat and earthy squire, Sancho Panza, is the realist who cannot get his master to see the realities in front of him. But after adventures that took them to all parts of Spain, each came to see the value of the other's perspective. We are left with Cervantes's conviction that idealism and realism, visionary dreams and the hard work of reality, are both necessary to the human condition.

William Shakespeare: In Praise of England

William Shakespeare is one of the most famous playwrights of the Western world. He was a universal genius, outclassing all others in his psychological insights, depth of characterization, imaginative skills, and versatility. His historical plays reflected the patriotic enthusiasm of the English in the Elizabethan era, as this excerpt from Richard II *illustrates.*

❊ William Shakespeare, *Richard II*

This royal throne of kings, this sceptered isle,
This earth of majesty, this seat of Mars,
This other Eden, demi-Paradise,
This fortress built by Nature for herself
Against infection and the hand of war,
This happy breed of men, this little world,
This precious stone set in the silver sea,
Which serves it in the office of a wall
Or as a moat defensive to a house
Against the envy of less happier lands—
This blessed plot, this earth, this realm, this England,
This nurse, this teeming womb of royal kings,
Feared by their breed and famous by their birth,
Renowned for their deeds as far from home,
For Christian service and true chivalry,
As is the sepulcher in stubborn Jewry [the Holy Sepulcher in Jerusalem]
Of the world's ransom, blessed Mary's Son—
This land of such dear souls, this dear dear land,
Dear for her reputation through the world,
Is now leased out, I die pronouncing it,
Like a tenement or pelting farm.
England, bound in with the triumphant sea,
Whose rocky shore beats back the envious siege
Of watery Neptune, is now bound in with shame,
With inky blots and rotten parchment bonds.
That England, what was wont to conquer others,
Hath made a shamful conquest of itself.
Ah, would the scandal vanish with my life,
How happy then were my ensuing death!

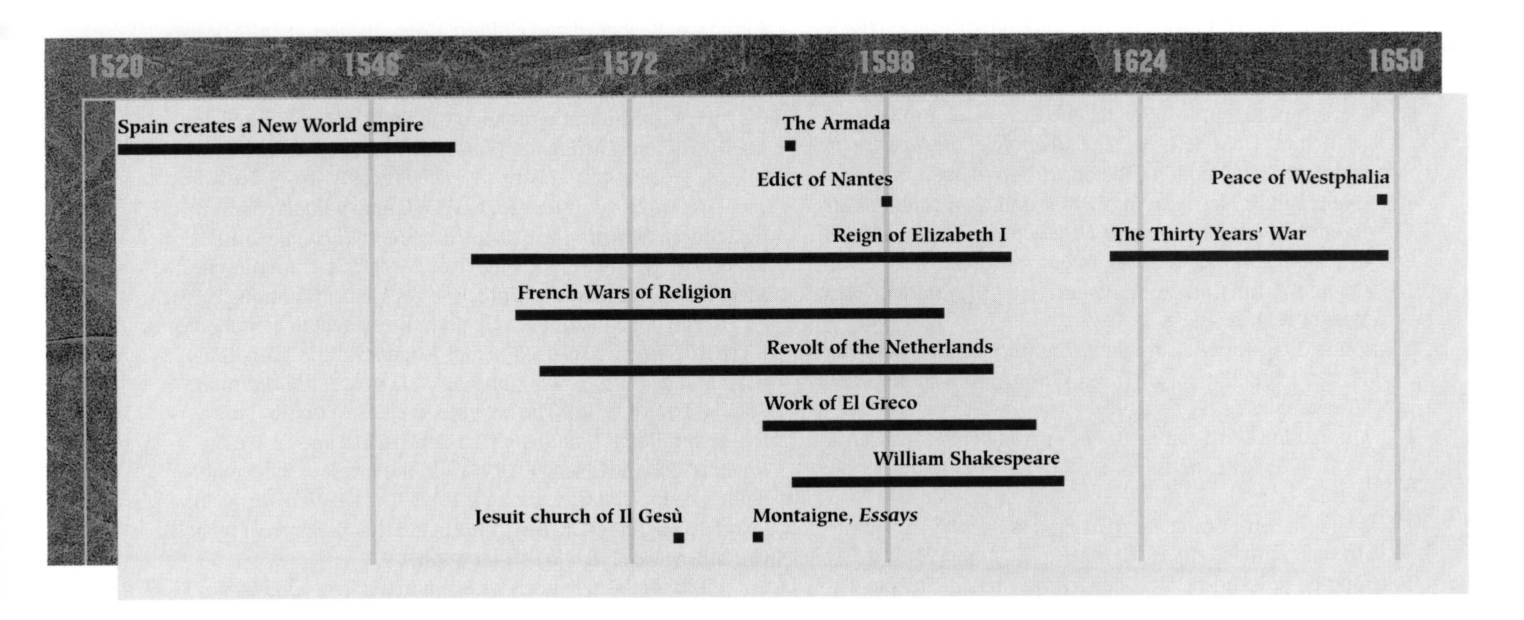

CONCLUSION

The period from 1560 to 1650 witnessed Europe's attempt to adjust to a whole range of change-laden forces. Population contracted as economic expansion gave way to economic recession. The discovery of new trade routes to the East and the "accidental" discovery of the Americas led Europeans to plunge outside the medieval world in which they had been enclosed for virtually 1,000 years. The conquest of the Americas brought out the worst and some of the best of European civilization. The greedy plundering of resources and the brutal repression, enslavement, and virtual annihilation of millions of Indians were hardly balanced by attempts to create new institutions, convert the natives to Christianity, and foster the rights of the indigenous peoples.

In the sixteenth century, the discoveries made little impact on Europeans preoccupied with the problems of dynastic expansion and, above all, religious division. It took 100 years of religious warfare complicated by serious political, economic and social issues—the worst series of wars and civil wars since the collapse of the Roman Empire in the west—before Europeans finally admitted that they would have to tolerate different ways of worshiping God. That men who were disciples of the Apostle of Peace would kill each other—often in brutal and painful fashion—aroused skepticism about Christianity itself. As one German writer put it in 1650: "Lutheran, popish, and Calvinistic, we've got all these beliefs here; but there is some doubt about where Christianity has got to."[15] *It is surely no accident that the search for a stable, secular order of politics and for order in the universe through natural laws played such important roles in the seventeenth century. The religious wars of the sixteenth and seventeenth centuries opened the door to the secular perspectives that have characterized modern Western civilization.*

NOTES

1. Quoted in J. R. Hale, *Renaissance Exploration* (New York, 1968), p. 32.
2. Quoted in J. H. Parry, *The Age of Reconnaissance: Discovery, Exploration and Settlement, 1450 to 1650* (New York, 1963), p. 33.
3. Quoted in Richard B. Reed, "The Expansion of Europe," in Richard DeMolen, ed., *The Meaning of the Renaissance and Reformation* (Boston, 1974), p. 308.
4. Quoted in K. N. Chaudhuri, *Trade and Civilization in the Indian Ocean: An Economic History from the Rise of Islam to 1750* (Cambridge, 1985), p. 65.
5. Quoted in Ian Cameron, *Explorers and Exploration* (New York, 1991), p. 42.
6. Quoted in Mary B. Campbell, *The Witness and the Other World: Exotic European Travel Writing, 400–1600* (Ithaca, N.Y., 1991), p. 197.
7. Quoted in G. V. Scammell, *The First Imperial Age: European Overseas Expansion, c. 1400–1715* (London, 1989), p. 62.
8. Miguel Leon-Portilla, ed., *The Broken Spears: The Aztec Account of the Conquest of Mexico* (Boston, 1969), p. 51.
9. Quoted in R. J. Knecht, *The French Wars of Religion, 1559–1598,* 2d ed. (New York, 1996), p. 47.
10. Quoted in Mack P. Holt, *The French Wars of Religion, 1562–1629* (Cambridge, 1995), p. 86.
11. Quoted in Garrett Mattingly, *The Armada* (Boston, 1959), pp. 216–217.
12. Quoted in Alan Kors and Edward Peters, eds., *Witchcraft in Europe, 1100–1700* (Philadelphia, 1972), p. 112.
13. Quoted in Joseph Klaits, *Servants of Satan: The Age of the Witch Hunts* (Bloomington, Ind., 1985), p. 68.
14. *The Complete Essays of Montaigne,* trans. Donald Frame (Stanford, 1958), p. 852.
15. Quoted in Theodore Schieder, *Handbuch der Europäischen Geschichte* (Stuttgart, 1979), 3:579.

SUGGESTIONS FOR FURTHER READING

General works on the period from 1560 to 1650 include C. Wilson, *The Transformation of Europe, 1558–1648* (Berkeley, 1976); and R. Bonney, *The European Dynastic States, 1494–1660* (Oxford, 1991). For an extremely detailed account of all aspects of life in the Mediterranean basin in the second half of the sixteenth century, see F. Braudel, *The Mediterranean and the Mediterranean World in the Age of Philip II,* trans. S. Reynolds, 2 vols. (New York, 1972–73).

The best general accounts of European discovery and expansion are G. V. Scammell, *The First Imperial Age: European Overseas Expansion, c. 1400–1715* (London, 1989); J. H. Parry, *The Age of Reconnaissance: Discovery, Exploration and Settlement, 1450 to 1650* (New York, 1963); and B. Penrose, *Travel and Discovery in the Renaissance, 1420–1620* (New York, 1962). On the medieval background to European expansion, see J. R. S. Phillips, *The Medieval Expansion of Europe* (New York, 1988). On European perceptions of the world outside Europe, see M. Campbell, *The Witness and the Other World: Exotic European Travel Writing, 400–1600* (Ithaca, N.Y., 1991). On Columbus, see the brief biography by J. S. Collis, *Christopher Columbus* (London, 1976); and F. Fernandez-Armesto, *Columbus* (New York, 1991). The impact of expansion on European consciousness is explored in J. H. Elliott, *The Old World and the New, 1492–1650* (Cambridge, 1970). The human and ecological effects of the interaction of New World and Old World cultures are examined thoughtfully in A. W. Crosby, *The Columbian Exchange, Biological and Cultural Consequences of 1492* (Westport, Conn., 1972); and *Ecological Imperialism: The Biological Expansion of Europe* (New York, 1986).

For good introductions to the French Wars of Religion, see M. P. Holt, *The French Wars of Religion, 1562–1629* (Cambridge, 1995); and R. J. Knecht, *The French Wars of Religion, 1559–1598,* 2d ed. (New York, 1996). Also valuable is B. B. Diefendorf, *Beneath the Cross: Catholics and Huguenots in Sixteenth-Century Paris* (New York, 1991). On Catherine de' Medici, see R. J. Knecht, *Catherine de' Medici* (London, 1998).

Two good histories of Spain in the sixteenth century are J. Lynch, *Spain, 1516–1598: From Nation-State to World Empire* (Cambridge, Mass., 1994); and A. W. Lovett, *Early Habsburg Spain* (Oxford, 1986). The best biographies of Philip II are P. Pierson, *Philip II of Spain* (London, 1975); and G. Parker, *Philip II,* 3d ed. (Chicago, 1995). On the revolt of the Netherlands, see the classic work by P. Geyl, *The Revolt of the Netherlands, 1555–1609* (London, 1962); and the more recent work of G. Parker, *The Dutch Revolt* (London, 1977).

Elizabeth's reign can be examined in two good biographies, C. Haigh, *Elizabeth I,* 2d ed. (New York, 1998); and W. T. MacCaffrey, *Elizabeth I* (London, 1993). The classic work on the Armada is the beautifully written *The Armada* by G. Mattingly (Boston, 1959).

The classic study on the Thirty Years' War is C. V. Wedgwood, *The Thirty Years' War* (Garden City, N.Y., 1961), but it needs to be supplemented by the more recent works by G. Parker, ed, *The Thirty Years' War,* 2d ed. (London, 1997); R. G. Asch, *The Thirty Years' War: The Holy Roman Empire and Europe, 1618–1648* (New York, 1997); and the brief study by S. J. Lee, *The Thirty Years' War* (London, 1991). On Gustavus Adolphus, see M. Roberts, *Gustavus Adolphus and the Rise of Sweden* (London, 1973).

The story of the witchcraft craze can be examined in three recent works, J. Klaits, *Servants of Satan: The Age of the Witch Hunts* (Bloomington, Ind., 1985); J. B. Russell, *A History of Witchcraft* (London, 1980); and B. P. Levack, *The Witch-Hunt in Early Modern Europe* (London, 1987).

For a brief, readable guide to Mannerism, see L. Murray, *The Late Renaissance and Mannerism* (New York, 1967). For a general survey of Baroque culture, see M. and L. Mainstone, *The Cambridge Introduction to Art: The Seventeenth Century* (Cambridge, 1981); and J. S. Held, *Seventeenth and Eighteenth Century Art: Baroque Painting, Sculpture, Architecture* (New York, 1971). The best biography of Montaigne remains D. M. Frame, *Montaigne: A Biography* (New York, 1965). On the Spanish golden century of literature, see R. O. Jones, *The Golden Age: Prose and Poetry,* which is volume 2 of *The Literary History of Spain* (London, 1971). The literature on Shakespeare is enormous. For a biography, see A. L. Rowse, *The Life of Shakespeare* (New York, 1963).

For additional reading, go to InfoTrac College Edition, your online research library at http://web1.infotrac-college.com

Enter the search terms *Vasco da Gama* using Key Terms.

Enter the search terms *Christopher Columbus* using the Subject Guide.

Enter the search terms *Thirty Years' War* using Key Terms.

Enter the search terms *Elizabeth I* using Key Terms.

CHAPTER

15

Response to Crisis: State Building and the Search for Order in the Seventeenth Century

CHAPTER OUTLINE

FOCUS QUESTIONS

- What theories of government were proposed by Jacques Bossuet, Thomas Hobbes, and John Locke, and how did their respective theories reflect concerns and problems of the seventeenth century?
- What was absolutism in theory, and how did its actual practice in France reflect or differ from the theory?
- What developments enabled Brandenburg-Prussia, Austria, and Russia to emerge as major powers in the seventeenth century?
- What were the main issues in the struggle between king and Parliament in seventeenth-century England, and how were they resolved?
- What role did the Netherlands play in the political, economic, and artistic life of the seventeenth century?

THE AGE OF CRISIS from 1560 to 1650 was accompanied by a decline in religious orientation and a growing secularization that affected both the political and the intellectual worlds of Europe (on the intellectual effect, see the Scientific Revolution in Chapter 16). Some historians like to speak of the seventeenth century as a turning point in the evolution of a modern state system in Europe. The idea of a united Christian Europe (the practice of a united Christendom had actually been moribund for some time) gave way to the practical realities of a system of secular states in which reason of state took precedence over the salvation of subjects' souls. Of course, these states had emerged and begun their development during the Middle Ages, but medieval ideas about statehood had still been couched in religious terms. By the seventeenth century, the credibility of Christianity had been so weakened in the religious wars that more and more Europeans could think of politics in secular terms.

One of the responses to the crises of the seventeenth century was a search for order. As the internal social and political rebellions and revolts died down, it became apparent that the privileged classes of society—the aristocrats—remained in control, although the various states exhibited important differences in political forms. The most general trend saw an extension of monarchical power as a stabilizing force. This development, which historians have called absolutism or absolute monarchy, was most evident in France during the flamboyant reign of Louis XIV, regarded by some as the perfect embodiment of an absolute monarch. In his memoirs, the duc de Saint-Simon, who had firsthand experience of French court life, said that Louis was "the very figure of a hero, so imbued with a natural but most imposing majesty that it appeared even in his most insignificant gestures and movements." The king's natural grace gave him a special charm as well: "He was as dignified and majestic in his dressing gown as when dressed in robes of state, or on horseback at the head of his troops." He spoke well and learned quickly. He was naturally kind and "he loved truth, justice, order, and reason." His life was orderly: "Nothing could be regulated with greater exactitude than were his days and hours." His self-control was impeccable: "He did not lose control of himself ten times in his whole life, and then only with inferior persons." But even absolute monarchs had imperfections, and Saint-Simon had the courage to point them out: "Louis XIV's vanity was without limit or restraint," which led to his "distaste for all merit, intelligence, education, and, most of all, for all independence of character and sentiment in others," as well as "to mistakes of judgment in matters of importance."

But absolutism was not the only response to crisis in the seventeenth century. Other states, such as England, reacted differently to domestic crisis, and another very different system emerged where monarchs were limited by the power of their representative assemblies. Absolute and limited monarchy were the two poles of seventeenth-century state building.

◆ The Theory of Absolutism

Absolute monarchy or absolutism meant that the sovereign power or ultimate authority in the state rested in the hands of a king who claimed to rule by divine right. But what did sovereignty mean? The late sixteenth-century political theorist Jean Bodin believed that sovereign power consisted of the authority to make laws, tax, administer justice, control the state's administrative system, and determine foreign policy. These powers made a ruler sovereign.

One of the chief theorists of divine-right monarchy in the seventeenth century was the French theologian and court preacher Bishop Jacques Bossuet (1627–1704), who expressed his ideas in a book entitled *Politics Drawn from the Very Words of Holy Scripture*. Bossuet argued first that government was divinely ordained so that humans could live in an organized society. God established kings and through them reigned over all the peoples of the world. Since kings received their power from God, their authority was absolute. They were responsible to no one (including parliaments) except God. Nevertheless, Bossuet cautioned, although a king's authority was absolute, his power was not since he was limited by the law of God. Bossuet believed there was a difference between absolute monarchy and arbitrary monarchy. The latter contradicted the rule of law and the sanctity of property and was simply lawless tyranny. Bossuet's distinction between absolute and arbitrary government was not always easy to maintain. There was also a large gulf between the theory of absolutism as expressed by Bossuet and the practice of absolutism. As we shall see in our survey of seventeenth-century states, a monarch's absolute power was often limited greatly by practical realities.

◆ Absolutism in Western Europe

An examination of seventeenth-century absolutism must begin with western Europe since France during the reign of Louis XIV (1643–1715) has traditionally been regarded as the best example of the practice of absolute monarchy in the seventeenth century.

France and Absolute Monarchy

By the end of the seventeenth century, France had come to play a dominant role in European affairs. French culture, language, and manners influenced all levels of European society. French diplomacy and wars shaped the political affairs of western and central Europe. The court of Louis XIV seemed to be imitated everywhere in Europe. Of course, the stability of Louis's reign was magnified by the instability that had preceded it.

FOUNDATIONS OF FRENCH ABSOLUTISM

The history of France before the reign of Louis XIV was hardly the story of steady, unbroken progress toward the ideal of absolute monarchy that many historians have tended to portray. During the fifty years or so before Louis, royal and ministerial governments had to struggle to avoid the breakdown of the state. The line between order and anarchy was often a narrow one. The situation was especially complicated by the fact that both Louis XIII (1610–1643) and Louis XIV were only boys when they succeeded to the throne in 1610 and 1643, respectively,

CARDINAL RICHELIEU. A key figure in the emergence of a strong monarchy in France was Cardinal Richelieu, pictured here in a portrait by Philippe de Champagne. Chief minister to Louis XIII, Richelieu strengthened royal authority by eliminating the private armies and fortified cities of the Huguenots and by crushing aristocratic conspiracies.

leaving the government dependent on royal ministers. Two especially competent ministers played crucial roles in maintaining monarchical authority.

Cardinal Richelieu, Louis XIII's chief minister from 1624 to 1642, initiated policies that eventually strengthened the power of the monarchy. By eliminating the political and military rights of the Huguenots while preserving their religious ones, Richelieu transformed the Huguenots into more reliable subjects. Richelieu acted more cautiously in "humbling the pride of the great men," the important French nobility. He understood the influential role played by the nobles in the French state. The dangerous ones were those who asserted their territorial independence when they were excluded from participating in the central government. Proceeding slowly but determinedly, Richelieu developed an efficient network of spies to uncover noble plots and then crushed the conspiracies and executed the conspirators, thereby eliminating a major threat to royal authority.

To reform and strengthen the central administration, initially for financial reasons, Richelieu sent out royal officials called intendants to the provinces to execute the orders of the central government. As the functions of the intendants grew, they came into conflict with provincial governors. Since the intendants were victorious in most of these disputes, they further strengthened the power of the crown. Richelieu proved less capable in financial matters, however. Not only was the basic system of state finances corrupt, but so many people benefited from the system's inefficiency and injustice that the government faced strong resistance when it tried to reform it. The *taille* (an annual direct tax usually levied on land or property) was increased—in 1643 it was two and a half times what it had been in 1610—and crown lands were mortgaged again. Expenditures, especially the cost of war preparations, soon outstripped the additional revenues, however, and French debt continued its upward spiral under Richelieu.

The general success of Richelieu's domestic policy in strengthening the central role of the monarchy was mirrored by a successful foreign policy. That policy was dictated, first of all, by opposition to Spain, which led in turn to further anti-Habsburg activity in the Holy Roman Empire to France's east. Eventually, the Catholic cardinal of France came to subsidize Protestant Sweden and then in 1635 to intervene directly with French troops to support the Protestant cause against the Habsburgs (see Chapter 14). Although both Richelieu and Louis XIII died before the Thirty Years' War ended, French policy had proved successful at one level as France emerged as Europe's leading power by 1648.

Richelieu died in 1642, followed five months later by King Louis XIII, who was succeeded by his son Louis XIV, then but four years old. This necessitated a regency under Anne of Austria, wife of the dead king. But she allowed Cardinal Mazarin, Richelieu's trained successor, to dominate the government. An Italian who had come to France as a papal legate and then become naturalized, Mazarin attempted to carry on Richelieu's policies until his death in 1661.

The most important event during Mazarin's rule was a revolt known as the Fronde, which can be viewed as the last serious attempt to limit the growing power of the crown until the French Revolution. As a foreigner, Mazarin was greatly disliked by all elements of the French population. The nobles, who particularly resented the centralized administrative power being built up at the expense of the provincial nobility, temporarily allied with the members of the Parlement of Paris, who opposed the new taxes levied by the government to pay the costs of the Thirty Years' War, and with the masses of Paris, who were also angry at the additional taxes. The Parlement of Paris was the most important court in France with jurisdiction over half of the kingdom, and its members formed the nobles of the robe, the service nobility of lawyers and administrators. These nobles of the robe led the first Fronde (1648–1649), which broke out in Paris and was ended by compromise. The second Fronde, begun in 1650, was led by the nobles of the sword, whose ancestors were medieval nobles. They were interested in overthrowing Mazarin for their own purposes: to secure their positions and increase their own

Louis XIV: Kingly Advice

Throughout his reign, Louis XIV was always on stage, acting the role of the wise "Grand Monarch." In 1661, after he became a father, Louis began his Memoirs for the Dauphin, *a frank collection of precepts for the education of his oldest son and heir to the throne. He continued to add to these* Memoirs *over the next twenty years.*

Louis XIV, *Memoirs for the Dauphin*

Kings are often obliged to do things which go against their inclinations and offend their natural goodness. They should love to give pleasure and yet they must often punish and destroy persons on whom by nature they wish to confer benefits. The interest of the state must come first. One must constrain one's inclinations and not put oneself in the position of berating oneself because one could have done better in some important affair but did not because of some private interest, because one was distracted from the attention one should have for the greatness, the good and the power of the state. Often there are troublesome places where it is difficult to make out what one should do. One's ideas are confused. As long as this lasts, one can refrain from making a decision. But as soon as one has fixed one's mind upon something which seems best to do, it must be acted upon. This is what enabled me to succeed so often in what I have done. The mistakes which I made, and which gave me infinite trouble, were the result of the desire to please or of allowing myself to accept too carelessly the opinions of others. Nothing is more dangerous than weakness of any kind whatsoever. In order to command others, one must raise oneself above them and once one has heard the reports from every side one must come to a decision upon the basis of one's own judgment, without anxiety but always with the concern not to command anything which is of itself unworthy either of one's place in the world or of the greatness of the state. Princes with good intentions and some knowledge of their affairs, either from experience or from study and great diligence in making themselves capable, find numerous cases which instruct them that they must give special care and total application to everything. One must be on guard against oneself, resist one's own tendencies, and always be on guard against one's own natural bent. The craft of a king is great, noble and delightful when one feels worthy of doing well whatever one promises to do. But it is not exempt from troubles, weariness and worries. Sometimes uncertainty causes despair, and when one has spent a reasonable time in examining an affair, one must make a decision and take the step which one believes to be best. When one has the state in view, one works for one's self. The good of the one constitutes the glory of the other. When the former is fortunate, eminent and powerful, he who is the cause thereof becomes glorious and consequently should find more enjoyment than his subjects in all the pleasant things of life for himself and for them. When one has made a mistake, it must be corrected as soon as possible, and no other consideration must stand in the way, not even kindness.

power. The second Fronde was crushed by 1652, a task made easier when the nobles began fighting each other instead of Mazarin. With the end of the Fronde, the vast majority of the French concluded that the best hope for stability in France lay in the crown. When Mazarin died in 1661, the greatest of the seventeenth-century monarchs, Louis XIV, took over supreme power.

THE REIGN OF LOUIS XIV (1643–1715)

The day after Cardinal Mazarin's death, Louis XIV, at the age of twenty-three, expressed his determination to be a real king and the sole ruler of France:

> Up to this moment I have been pleased to entrust the government of my affairs to the late Cardinal. It is now time that I govern them myself. You [secretaries and ministers of state] will assist me with your counsels when I ask for them. I request and order you to seal no orders except by my command, . . . I order you not to sign anything, not even a passport . . . without my command; to render account to me personally each day and to favor no one.[1]

His mother, who was well aware of Louis's proclivity for fun and games and getting into the beds of the maids in the royal palace, laughed aloud at these words. But Louis was quite serious.

Louis proved willing to pay the price of being a strong ruler (see the box above). He established a conscientious routine from which he seldom deviated, but he did not look upon his duties as drudgery since he judged his royal profession to be "grand, noble, and delightful." Eager for glory (in the French sense of achieving what was expected of one in an important position), Louis created a grand and majestic spectacle at the court of Versailles (see Daily Life at the Court of Versailles later in this chapter). Consequently, Louis and his court came to set the standard for monarchies and aristocracies all over Europe. Less than fifty years after his death, the great French writer Voltaire selected the title "Age of Louis XIV" for his history of Europe from 1661 to 1715. Historians have tended to use it ever since.

Although Louis may have believed in the theory of absolute monarchy and consciously fostered the myth of himself as the Sun King, the source of light for all of his people, historians are quick to point out that the realities fell far short of the aspirations. Despite the centralizing

LOUIS XIV. Louis XIV was determined to be the sole ruler of France. Louis eliminated the threat of the high nobility by removing them from the royal council and replacing them with relatively new aristocrats whom he could dominate. This portrait by Hyacinth Rigaud captures the king's sense of royal dignity and grandeur.

efforts of Cardinals Richelieu and Mazarin, seventeenth-century France still possessed a bewildering system of overlapping authorities. Provinces had their own regional parlements, their own local Estates, their own sets of laws. Members of the high nobility with their huge estates and clients among the lesser nobility still exercised much authority. Both towns and provinces possessed privileges and powers seemingly from time immemorial that they would not easily relinquish. Much of Louis's success rested less on the modernization of administrative machinery, as is frequently claimed, than on his clever and adroit manipulation of the traditional priorities and values of French society.

One of the keys to Louis's power was that he was able to restructure the central policy-making machinery of government because it was part of his own court and household. The royal court was an elaborate structure that served three purposes simultaneously: it was the personal household of the king, the location of central governmental machinery, and the place where powerful subjects came to find favors and offices for themselves and their clients as well as the main arena where rival aristocratic factions jostled for power. The greatest danger to Louis's personal rule came from the very high nobles and princes of the blood (the royal princes) who considered it their natural function to assert the policy-making role of royal ministers. Louis eliminated this threat by removing them from the royal council, the chief administrative body of the king and overseer of the central machinery of government, and enticing them to his court where he could keep them preoccupied with court life and out of politics.

Instead of the high nobility and royal princes, Louis relied for his ministers on nobles who came from relatively new aristocratic families. Such were François Michel Le Tellier, secretary of state for war; Hugues de Lionne, secretary for foreign affairs; and Nicholas Fouquet, superintendent of finances. His ministers were expected to be subservient; said Louis, "I had no intention of sharing my authority with them." When Fouquet began to flaunt the enormous wealth and power he had amassed in the king's service, Louis ordered his arrest and imprisoned him for life. Fouquet was replaced in the king's council by Jean-Baptiste Colbert (1619–1683), another noble of bourgeois origin. Louis's domination of his ministers and secretaries gave him control of the central policy-making machinery of government and thus authority over the traditional areas of monarchical power: the formulation of foreign policy, the making of war and peace, the assertion of the secular power of crown against any religious authority, and the ability to levy taxes to fulfill these functions.

Louis had considerably less success with the internal administration of the kingdom. The traditional groups and institutions of French society—the nobles, officials, town councils, guilds, and representative Estates in some provinces—were simply too powerful for the king to have direct control over the lives of his subjects. Louis had three ways of ruling the provinces. Officially, he worked through hereditary officeholders, usually aristocrats, who were untrustworthy since they were always inclined to balance the king's wishes against their own interests. The king also had his intendants as direct royal agents, but they, too, proved unreliable and their actions often provoked disturbances in the provinces. The intendants were not so much the instruments by which the central government carried out decisions, but simply the "eyes and ears of the ministers" in the provinces. Finally, the king had an informal system of royal patronage, which Louis used successfully. The king and his ministers enlisted the aid of nobles and senior churchmen and their clients by granting them offices and pensions. Thus, the central government exercised its control over the provinces and the people by carefully bribing the important people to ensure that the king's policies were executed. Nevertheless, local officials could still obstruct the execution of policies they disliked, indicating clearly that a so-called absolute monarch was not always that absolute.

The maintenance of religious harmony had long been considered an area of monarchical power. The desire to keep it led Louis into conflict with the French Huguenots. Louis XIV did not want to allow Protestants

PALACE OF VERSAILLES. Louis XIV spent untold sums of money in the construction of a new royal residence at Versailles. The enormous palace of Versailles also housed the members of the king's government and served as home for thousands of French nobles. As the largest royal residence in Europe, Versailles impressed foreigners and became a source of envy for other rulers.

to practice their faith in largely Catholic France. Perhaps he was motivated by religion, but it is more likely that Louis, who believed in the motto, "one king, one law, one faith," felt that the existence of this minority undermined his own political authority. His anti-Protestant policy, aimed at converting the Huguenots to Catholicism, began mildly by offering rewards, but escalated by 1681 to a policy of forced conversions. The most favored method was to quarter French soldiers in Huguenot communities and homes with the freedom to misbehave so that their hosts would "see the light quickly." This approach did produce thousands of immediate conversions. In October 1685, Louis issued the Edict of Fontainebleau. In addition to revoking the Edict of Nantes, the new edict provided for the destruction of Huguenot churches and the closing of their schools. Although they were forbidden to leave France, it is estimated that 200,000 Huguenots left for shelter in England, the United Provinces, and the German states. Through their exodus, France lost people who had commercial and industrial skills, although some modern scholars have argued that their departure had only a minor impact on the French economy.

The cost of building Versailles and other palaces, maintaining his court, and pursuing his wars made finances a crucial issue for Louis XIV. He was most fortunate in having the services of Colbert as controller-general of finances. Colbert sought to increase the wealth and power of France through general adherence to that loose collection of economic policies called mercantilism, which stressed government regulation of economic activities to benefit the state (see Mercantilism later in this chapter). To decrease the need for imports and increase exports, Colbert attempted to expand the quantity and improve the quality of French manufactured goods. He founded new luxury industries, such as the royal tapestry works at Beauvais; invited Venetian glassmakers and Flemish clothmakers to France; drew up instructions regulating the quality of goods produced; oversaw the training of workers; and granted special privileges, including tax exemptions, loans, and subsidies, to those who established new industries. To improve communications and the transportation of goods internally, he built roads and canals. To decrease imports directly, he raised tariffs on foreign manufactured goods, especially English and Dutch cloth, and created a merchant marine to facilitate the conveyance of French goods.

Although Colbert's policies are given much credit for fostering the development of manufacturing, some historians are dubious about the usefulness of many of his mercantilistic policies. Regulations were often evaded, and the imposition of high tariffs brought foreign retaliation. French trading companies entered the scene too late to be really competitive with the English and the Dutch. And above all, Colbert's economic policies, which were geared to making his king more powerful, were ultimately self-defeating. The more revenue Colbert collected to enable the king to make war, the faster Louis depleted the treasury. At the same time, the burden of taxes fell increasingly upon the peasants who still constituted the overwhelming majority of the French population.

DAILY LIFE AT THE COURT OF VERSAILLES

The court of Louis XIV at Versailles set a standard that was soon followed by other European rulers. In 1660, Louis, who disliked Paris as a result of his humiliating experiences at the hands of Parisian mobs during the Fronde, decided to convert a hunting lodge at Versailles, located near Paris, into a chateau. Not until 1688, after untold sums of money had been spent and tens of thousands of workers had labored incessantly, was most of the construction completed on the enormous palace that housed thousands of people.

Versailles served many purposes. It was the residence of the king, a reception hall for state affairs, an office building for the members of the king's government, and the home of thousands of royal officials and aristocratic courtiers. Versailles became a symbol for the French absolutist state and the power of the Sun King, Louis XIV. As a visible manifestation of France's superiority and wealth, this lavish court was intended to overawe subjects and impress foreign powers. If an age's largest buildings reflect its values, then Versailles is a reminder of the seventeenth-century preoccupation with monarchical authority and magnificence.

Travels with the King

The duc de Saint-Simon was one of many noble courtiers who lived at Versailles and had firsthand experience of court life there. In this Memoirs, *he left a controversial and critical account of Louis XIV and his court. In this selection, Saint-Simon describes the price court ladies paid for the "privilege" of riding with the great king.*

Duc de Saint-Simon, *Memoirs*

The King always traveled with his carriage full of women: His mistresses, his bastard daughters, his daughters-in-law, sometimes Madame [the wife of the king's brother], and the other ladies of the court when there was room. This was the case for hunts, and trips to Fontainebleau, Chantilly, Compiégne, and the like. . . . In his carriage during these trips there was always an abundance and variety of things to eat: meats, pastries, and fruit. Before the carriage had gone a quarter league the King would ask who was hungry. He never ate between meals, not even a fruit, but he enjoyed watching others stuff themselves. It was mandatory to eat, with appetite and good grace, and to be gay; otherwise; he showed his displeasure by telling the guilty party she was putting on airs and trying to be coy. The same ladies or princesses who had eaten that day at the King's table were obliged to eat again as though they were weak from hunger. What is more, the women were forbidden to mention their personal needs, which in any case they could not have relieved without embarrassment, since there were guards and members of the King's household in front and in back of the carriage, and officers and equerries riding alongside the doors. The dust they kicked up choked everyone in the carriage, but the King, who loved fresh air, insisted that all the windows remain open. He would have been extremely displeased if one of the ladies had pulled a curtain to protect herself from the sun, the wind, or the cold.

He pretended not to notice his passengers' discomfort, and always traveled very fast, with the usual number of relays. Sickness in the carriage was a demerit which ruled out further invitations. . . . When the king had to relieve himself he did not hesitate to stop the carriage and get out; but the ladies were not allowed to budge.

Versailles also served a practical political purpose. It became home to the high nobility and princes of the blood (the royal princes), those powerful figures who had aspired to hold the policy-making role of royal ministers. By keeping them involved in the myriad activities that made up daily life at the court of Versailles, Louis excluded them from real power while allowing them to share in the mystique of power as companions of the king.

Life at Versailles became a court ceremony with Louis XIV at the center of it all. The king had little privacy; only when he visited his wife or mother or mistress or met with ministers was he free of the noble courtiers who swarmed about the palace. Most daily ceremonies were carefully staged, such as those attending Louis's rising from bed, dining, praying, attending mass, and going to bed. A mob of nobles aspired to assist the king in carrying out these solemn activities. It was considered a great honor for a noble to be chosen to hand the king his shirt while dressing. But why did nobles participate in so many ceremonies, some of which were so obviously demeaning? Active involvement in the activities at Versailles was the king's prerequisite for obtaining the offices, titles, and pensions that only he could grant. This policy reduced great nobles and ecclesiastics, the "people of quality," to a plane of equality, allowing Louis to exercise control over them and prevent them from interfering in the real lines of power. To maintain their social prestige, the "people of quality" were expected to adhere to rigid standards of court etiquette appropriate to their rank.

Indeed, court etiquette became a complex matter. Nobles and royal princes were arranged in an elaborate order of seniority and expected to follow certain rules of precedence. Who could sit down and on what kind of chair was a subject of much debate. When Philip of Orleans, the king's brother, and his wife Charlotte sought to visit their daughter, the duchess of Lorraine, they encountered problems with Louis. Charlotte told why in one of her letters:

> The difficulty is that the Duke of Lorraine claims that he is entitled to sit in an armchair in the presence of Philip and myself because the Emperor gives him an armchair. To this the King [Louis] replied that the Emperor's ceremonial is one thing and the King's another, and that, for example, the Emperor gives the cardinals armchairs, whereas here they may never sit at all in the King's presence.[2]

Louis refused to compromise; the Duke of Lorraine was only entitled to a stool. The duke refused, and Philip and Charlotte canceled their visit.

Who could sit where at meals with the king was also carefully regulated. On one occasion, when the wife of a minister sat closer to the king than a duchess at dinner, Louis XIV became so angry that he did not eat for the rest of the evening. Another time, Louis reproached his talkative brother for the sin of helping himself to a dish before Louis had touched it with the biting words: "I perceive that you are no better able to control your hands than your tongue."[3]

Besides the daily and occasional ceremonies that made up the regular side of court life at Versailles and the many hours a day Louis spent with his ministers on affairs of state, daily life at Versailles included numerous forms of entertainment. While he was healthy, Louis and his courtiers hunted at least once a week; members of the royal family nearly every day. Walks through the Versailles gardens, boating trips, performances of tragedies and comedies, ballets, and concerts all provided sources of pleasure (see the box on p. 432). Three evenings a week, from seven to ten, Louis also held an *appartement* where he was at "home" to his court. The *appartement* was characterized by a formal informality. Relaxed rules of etiquette even allowed people to sit down in the presence of their superiors. The evening's entertainment began with a concert, followed by games of billiards or cards, and ended with a sumptuous buffet.

One form of entertainment—gambling—became an obsession at Versailles. Although a few of the courtiers made a living by their gambling skill, many others were simply amateurs. This did not stop them from playing regularly and losing enormous sums of money. One princess described the scene: "Here in France as soon as people get together they do nothing but play [cards]; they play for frightful sums, and the players seem bereft of their senses. . . . One shouts at the top of his voice, another strikes the table with his fist, a third blasphemes. . . . it is horrible to watch them."[4] Louis did not share the princess's sensibilities; he was not horrified by an activity that kept the Versailles nobles busy and out of mischief.

INTERIOR OF VERSAILLES: HALL OF MIRRORS. Pictured here is the exquisite Hall of Mirrors at Versailles. A number of daily and occasional ceremonies dominated the lives of the residents of Versailles. Rules of etiquette became so complex that they guided virtually every aspect of behavior.

THE WARS OF LOUIS XIV

The increase in royal power that Louis pursued as well as his desire for military glory led the king to develop a standing army subject to the monarch's command. In itself, the standing army was neither new nor a product of absolute monarchy—the first real standing armies had been organized earlier by Venice and the United Provinces. But French resources enabled Louis to develop the largest standing army that Europe had yet seen.

Under the secretary of war, François Michel Le Tellier, the marquis of Louvois, France developed a professional army numbering 100,000 men in peacetime and 400,000 in time of war. Unable to fill the ranks with volunteers, the French resorted to conscription, a practice that led to other problems as unwilling soldiers were eager to desert. But the new standing armies did not exist to be admired. Louis and other monarchs used them to make war an almost incessant activity of the seventeenth and eighteenth centuries.

Louis XIV had a great proclivity for war. Historians have debated the assertion that Louis pursued war to expand his kingdom to its "natural frontiers"—the Alps, Pyrenees, and Rhine River. But few doubt his desire to achieve the prestige and military glory befitting a Sun King as well as his dynastic ambition, his desire to ensure the domination of his Bourbon dynasty over European affairs. His ends soon outstripped his means, however, as his ambitions roused much of Europe to form coalitions that even he could not overcome.

In 1667, Louis began his first war by invading the Spanish Netherlands to his north and Franche-Comté to the east. But a Triple Alliance of the Dutch, English, and Swedes forced Louis to sue for peace in 1668 and accept a few towns in the Spanish Netherlands for his efforts. He never forgave the Dutch for arranging the Triple Alliance, and in 1672, after isolating the Dutch, France invaded the United Provinces with some initial success. But the French victories led Brandenburg, Spain, and the Holy Roman Emperor to form a new coalition that forced Louis to end the Dutch War by making peace at Nimwegen in 1678. While Dutch territory remained intact, France received Franche-Comté from Spain, which served merely to stimulate Louis's appetite for even more land.

This time, Louis moved eastward against the Holy Roman Empire, which he perceived from his previous war as feeble and unable to resist. The gradual annexation of the provinces of Alsace and Lorraine was followed by the occupation of the city of Strasbourg, a move that led to widespread protest and the formation of a new coalition. The creation of this League of Augsburg, consisting of Spain, the Holy Roman Emperor, the United Provinces, Sweden, and England, led to Louis's third war, the War of the League of Augsburg (1689–1697). This bitterly contested eight-year struggle brought economic depression and famine to France. The Treaty of Ryswick ending the war forced Louis to give up most of his conquests in the empire, although he was allowed to keep Strasbourg and part of Alsace. The gains were hardly worth the bloodshed and misery he had caused the French people.

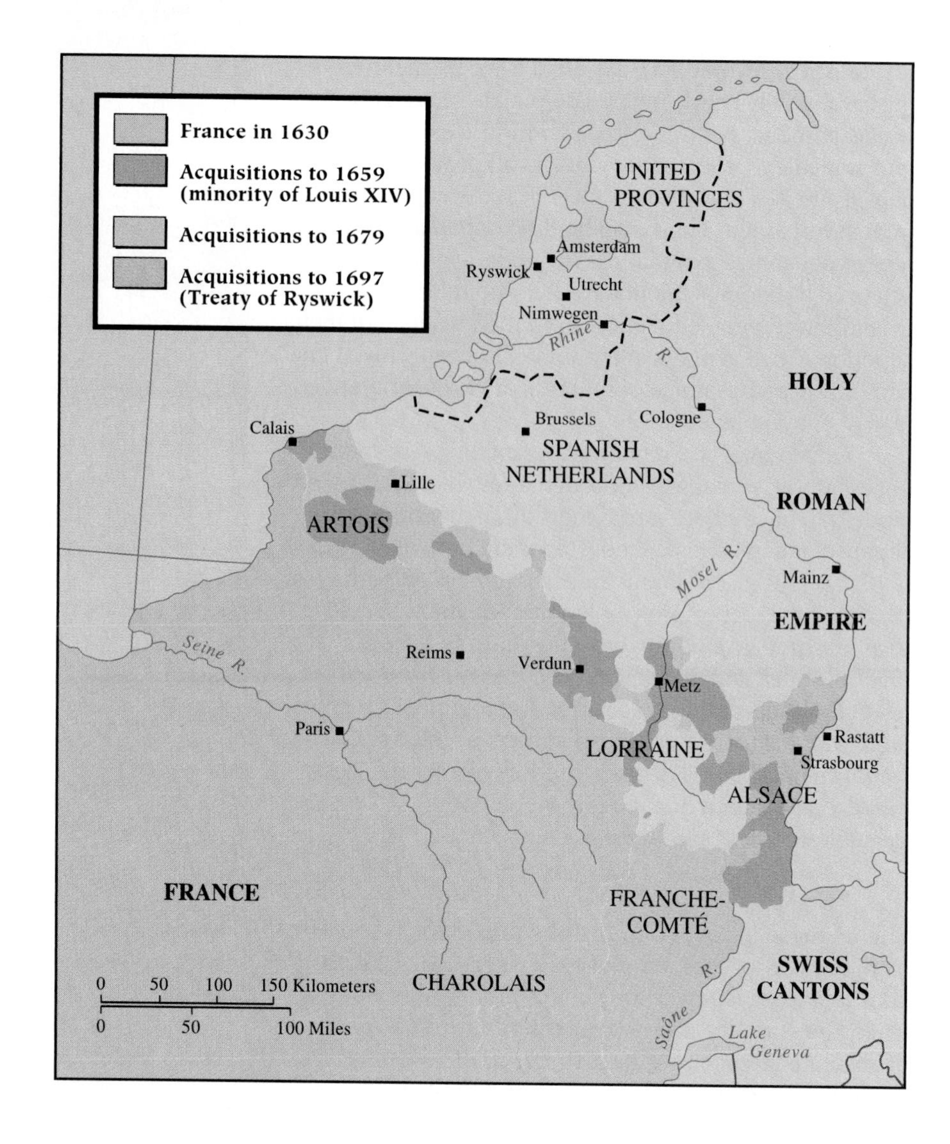

MAP 15.1 The Wars of Louis XIV.

Louis's fourth war, the War of the Spanish Succession (1702–1713), was over bigger stakes, the succession to the Spanish throne. Charles II, the sickly and childless Habsburg ruler, left the throne of Spain in his will to a grandson of Louis XIV. When the latter became King Philip V of Spain after Charles's death, the suspicion that Spain and France would eventually be united in the same dynastic family caused the formation of a new coalition, determined to prevent a Bourbon hegemony that would mean the certain destruction of the European balance of power. This coalition of England, Holland, Habsburg Austria, and German states opposed France and Spain in a war that dragged on in Europe and the colonial empires in North America from 1702 to 1713. In a number of battles, including the memorable defeat of the French forces at Blenheim in 1704 by allied troops led by the English commander, John Churchill, duke of Marlborough, the coalition wore down Louis's forces. An end to the war finally came with the Peaces of Utrecht in 1713 and Rastatt in 1714. Although these peace treaties confirmed Philip V as the Spanish ruler, initiating a Spanish Bourbon dynasty that would last into the twentieth century, they also affirmed that the thrones of Spain and France were to remain separated. The Spanish Netherlands, Milan, and Naples were given to Austria, and the newly emerging Brandenburg-Prussia gained additional territories. The real winner at Utrecht, however, was England, which received Gibraltar as well as the French possessions in America of Newfoundland, Hudson's Bay Territory, and Nova Scotia. Though France, by its sheer size and position, remained a great power, England had emerged as a formidable naval power.

Only two years after the treaty, the Sun King was dead, leaving France impoverished and surrounded by enemies. On his deathbed, the seventy-six-year-old monarch seemed remorseful when he told his successor:

> Soon you will be King of a great kingdom. I urge you not to forget your duty to God; remember that you owe everything to Him. Try to remain at peace with your neighbors. I loved war too much. Do not follow me in that or in overspending. Take advice in everything; try to find the best course and follow it. Lighten your people's burden as soon as possible, and do what I have had the misfortune not to do myself.[5]

Did Louis mean it? Did Louis ever realize how tarnished the glory he had sought had become? One of his subjects wrote ten years before the end of his reign: "Even the people . . . who have so much loved you, and have placed such trust in you, begin to lose their love, their trust, and even their respect. . . . They believe you have no pity for their sorrows, that you are devoted only to your power and your glory."[6] In any event, the advice to his successor was probably not remembered; his great-grandson was only five years old.

The Decline of Spain

At the beginning of the seventeenth century, Spain possessed the most populous empire in the world, controlling almost all of South America and a number of settlements in Asia and Africa. To most Europeans, Spain still seemed the greatest power of the age, but the reality was quite different. The rich provinces of the Netherlands were lost. The treasury was empty; Philip II went bankrupt in 1596 from excessive expenditures on the Armada while his successor Philip III did the same in 1607 by spending a fortune on his court. The armed forces were out-of-date; the government inefficient; and the commercial class weak in the midst of a suppressed peasantry, a luxury-loving class of nobles, and an oversupply of priests and monks. Spain continued to play the role of a great power, but appearances were deceiving.

During the reign of Philip III (1598–1621), many of Spain's weaknesses became only too apparent. Interested only in court luxury or miracle-working relics, Philip III allowed his first minister, the greedy duke of Lerma, to run the country. The aristocratic Lerma's primary interest was accumulating power and wealth for himself and his family. While important offices were filled with his relatives, crucial problems went unsolved. His most drastic decision was to expel all remaining Moriscos (see Chapter 12) from Spain, a spectacular blunder in view of their importance to Spain's economy. During Lerma's misrule, the gap between privileged and unprivileged grew wider. Notably absent was a prosperous urban middle class, as an astute public official observed in 1600. Spain, he said, had come "to be an extreme contrast of rich and poor, . . . we have rich who loll at ease, or poor who beg, and we lack people of the middling sort, whom neither wealth nor poverty prevents from pursuing the rightful kind of business enjoined by natural law."[7] An apparent factor in this imbalance was the dominant role played by the Catholic church. While maintaining strict orthodoxy by efficient inquisitorial courts, the church prospered and attracted ever-larger numbers of clerics to its ranks. The Castilian Cortes (parliament) was informed in 1626 that Castile alone possessed 9,000 monasteries for men. The existence of so many official celibates offered little help to Spain's declining economy or its declining population.

At first, the reign of Philip IV (1621–1665) seemed to offer hope for a revival of Spain's energies, especially in the capable hands of his chief minister, Gaspar de Guzman, the count of Olivares. This clever, hard-working, and power-hungry statesman dominated the king's every move and worked to revive the interests of the monarchy. A flurry of domestic reform decrees, aimed at curtailing the power of the church and the landed aristocracy, was soon followed by a political reform program whose purpose was to further centralize the government of all Spain and its possessions in monarchical hands. All of these efforts met with little real success, however, since both the number (estimated at one-fifth of the population) and power of the Spanish aristocrats made them too strong to curtail in any significant fashion. At the same time, most of the efforts of Olivares and Philip were undermined by their desire to pursue Spain's imperial glory and by a series of internal revolts.

During the 1620s, 1630s, and 1640s, Spain's involvement in the Thirty Years' War led to a series of frightfully expensive military campaigns that intensified the economic misery of the overtaxed Spanish subjects. Unfortunately for Spain, the campaigns also failed to produce victory. As Olivares wrote to King Philip IV, "God wants us to make peace; for He is depriving us visibly and absolutely of all the means of war."[8] At the same time, increasingly heavy financial exactions to fight the wars led to internal revolts, first in Catalonia, the northeastern province, in 1640, then in the same year in Portugal, which had been joined to Spain in 1580 by Philip II, and finally in the Italian dependency of Naples in 1647. After years of civil war, the Spanish government regained control of all these territories except for Portugal, which successfully reestablished the monarchy of the old ruling house of Braganza when Duke John was made King John IV in 1640.

The defeats in Europe and the internal revolts of the 1640s ended any illusions about Spain's greatness. The actual extent of Spain's economic difficulties is still a much

CHRONOLOGY

Absolutism in Western Europe

France	
Henry IV	1589–1610
Louis XIII	1610–1643
Cardinal Richelieu as chief minister	1624–1642
Ministry of Cardinal Mazarin	1642–1661
First Fronde	1648–1649
Second Fronde	1650–1652
Louis XIV	1643–1715
First war (vs. Triple Alliance)	1667–1668
Dutch War	1672–1678
Edict of Fontainebleau	1685
War of the League of Augsburg	1689–1697
War of the Spanish Succession	1702–1713
Spain	
Philip III	1598–1621
Philip IV	1621–1665
Revolts in Catalonia and Portugal	1640
Revolt in Naples	1647
Charles II	1665–1700

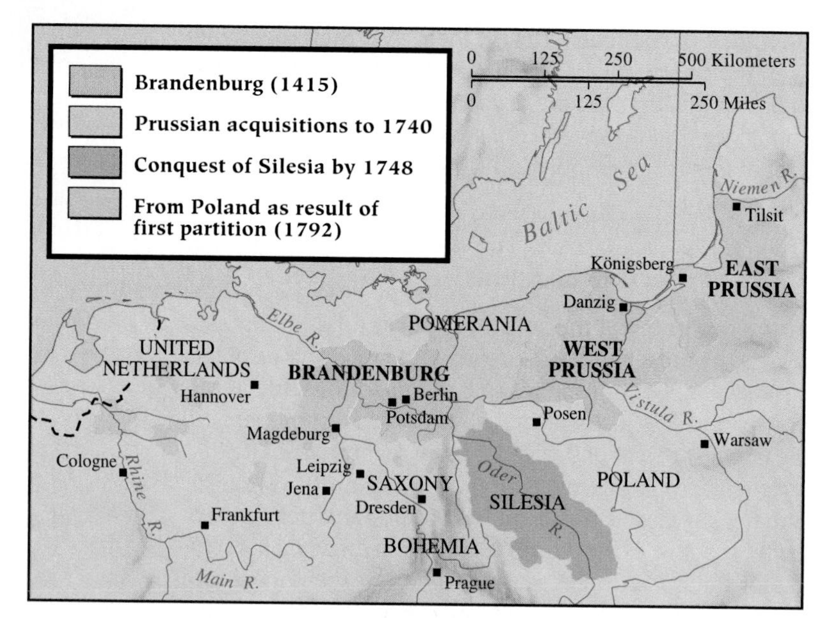

MAP 15.2 The Growth of Brandenburg-Prussia.

debated historical topic, but there is no question about Spain's foreign losses. Dutch independence was formally recognized by the Peace of Westphalia in 1648, and the Peace of the Pyrenees with France in 1659 meant the surrender of Artois and the outlying defenses of the Spanish Netherlands as well as certain border regions that went to France. It did not augur well for the future of Spain that the king who followed Philip IV, Charles II (1665–1700), perhaps unfairly characterized by historians as a "moribund half-wit," was only of interest to the rest of Europe because he had no heirs. The French and Austrians anxiously awaited his death in the hope of placing a member of their royal houses on the Spanish throne. When he died in 1700, the War of the Spanish Succession soon followed.

◆ Absolutism in Central, Eastern, and Northern Europe

During the seventeenth century, a development of great importance for the modern Western world took place in central and eastern Europe, the appearance of three new powers: Prussia, Austria, and Russia.

The German States

The Peace of Westphalia, which officially ended the Thirty Years' War in 1648, left each of the 300 or more German states comprising the Holy Roman Empire virtually autonomous and sovereign. After 1648, the Holy Roman Empire was largely a diplomatic fiction; as the French intellectual Voltaire said in the eighteenth century, the Holy Roman Empire was neither holy, nor Roman, nor an empire. Properly speaking, there was no German state, but more than 300 "Germanies." Of these states, two emerged as great European powers in the seventeenth and eighteenth centuries.

THE RISE OF BRANDENBURG-PRUSSIA

The development of Brandenburg as a state was largely the story of the Hohenzollern dynasty, which in 1415 had come to rule the rather insignificant principality in northeastern Germany. In 1609, the Hohenzollerns inherited some lands in the Rhine valley in western Germany; nine years later, they received the duchy of Prussia (or East Prussia). By the seventeenth century, then, the dominions of the house of Hohenzollern, now called Brandenburg-Prussia, consisted of three disconnected masses in western, central, and eastern Germany. Each had its own privileges, customs, and loyalties; only the person of the Hohenzollern ruler connected them. Unlike France, an old kingdom possessing a reasonably common culture based on almost 1,000 years of history, Brandenburg-Prussia was an artificial creation, highly vulnerable and dependent upon its ruling dynasty to create a state where none existed.

The first important Hohenzollern ruler and the one who laid the foundation for the Prussian state was Frederick William the Great Elector (1640–1688), who came to power in the midst of the Thirty Years' War. Realizing that Brandenburg-Prussia was a small, open territory with no natural frontiers for defense, Frederick William built a competent and efficient standing army. By 1678, he possessed a force of 40,000 men that absorbed more than 50 percent of the state's revenues. To sustain the army and his own power, Frederick William established the General War Commissariat to levy taxes for the army and oversee its growth and training. The Commissariat soon evolved into an agency for civil government as well, collecting the new excise tax in the towns and overseeing the foundation of new industrial and commercial enterprises. Directly responsible to the elector, the new bureaucratic machine became his chief instrument for governing the state. Many of its officials were members of the Prussian landed aristocracy, the Junkers, who also served as officers in the all-important army.

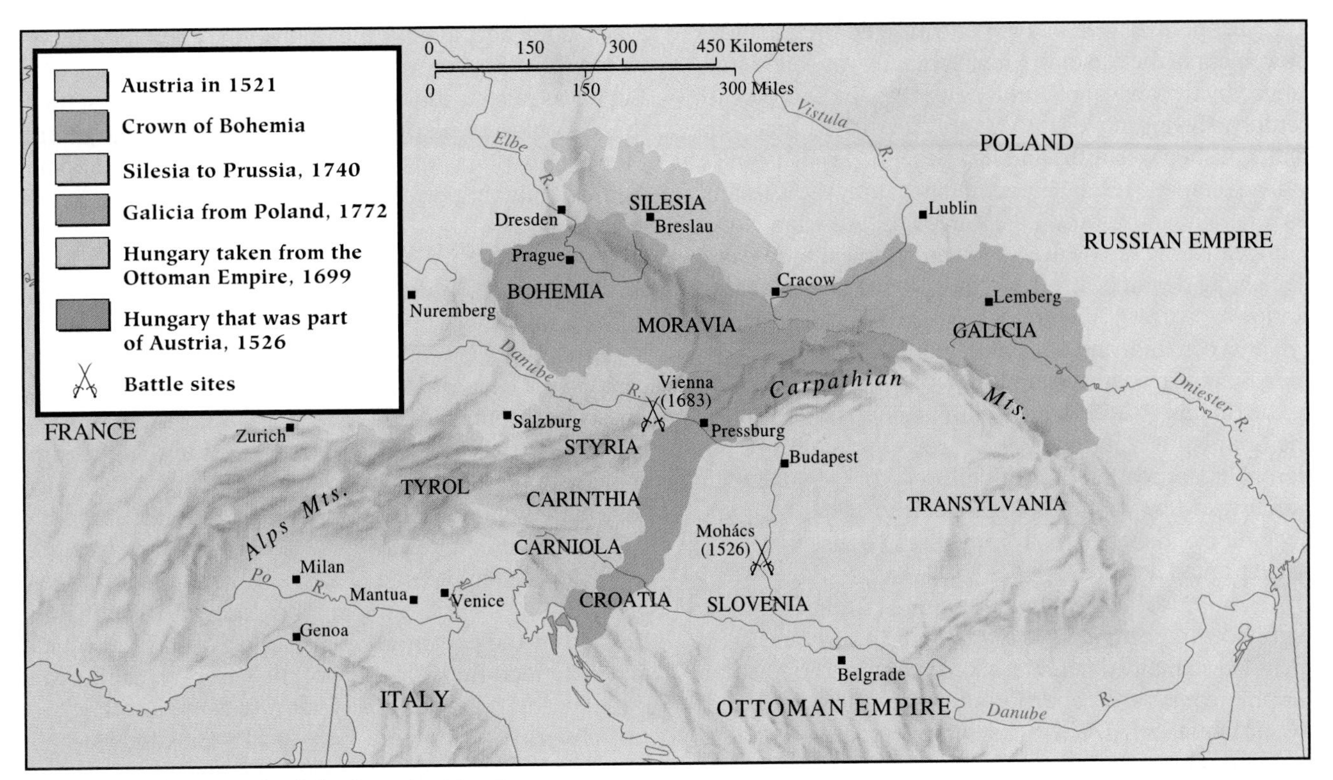

MAP 15.3 **The Growth of the Austrian Empire.**

The nobles' support for Frederick William's policies derived from the tacit agreement that he made with them. In order to eliminate the power that the members of the nobility could exercise in their provincial Estates-General, Frederick William made a deal with the nobles. In return for a free hand in running the government (in other words, for depriving the provincial Estates of their power), he gave the nobles almost unlimited power over their peasants, exempted them from taxation, and awarded them the highest ranks in the army and the Commissariat with the understanding that they would not challenge his political control. As for the peasants, the nobles were allowed to appropriate their land and bind them to the soil as serfs.

To build Brandenburg-Prussia's economy, Frederick William followed the fashionable mercantilist policies, using high tariffs, subsidies, and monopolies for manufacturers to stimulate domestic industry and the construction of roads and canals. Wisely, Frederick William invited people from other countries to settle in Brandenburg-Prussia and, in 1685, issued an edict encouraging the dispossessed Huguenots from Louis XIV's France to come to Prussia. Almost 20,000 did. At the same time, however, Frederick William continued to favor the interests of the nobility at the expense of the commercial and industrial middle classes in the towns.

In these ways, Frederick William the Great Elector laid the foundations for the Prussian state, although it would be misleading to think that he had a modern conception of that state. He thought nothing of amending his will to give pieces of his supposedly unified state as independent principalities to his younger sons. He was succeeded by his son Frederick III (1688–1713), who, less rigid and militaristic than his father, spent much of the treasury building palaces, establishing a university, and imitating the splendors of the court of Louis XIV. He did make one significant contribution to the development of Prussia. In return for aiding the Holy Roman Emperor in the War of the Spanish Succession, he received officially the title of king in Prussia. Elector Frederick III was transformed into King Frederick I, and Brandenburg-Prussia became simply Prussia. In the eighteenth century, Prussia emerged as a great power on the European stage.

THE EMERGENCE OF AUSTRIA

The Austrian Habsburgs had long played a significant role in European politics as Holy Roman Emperors, but by the end of the Thirty Years' War, the Habsburg hopes of creating an empire in Germany had been dashed. In the seventeenth century, then, the house of Austria made an important transition; the German empire was lost, but a new empire was created in eastern and southeastern Europe.

The nucleus of the new Austrian Empire remained the traditional Austrian hereditary possessions: Lower and Upper Austria, Carinthia, Carniola, Styria, and Tyrol. To these had been added the kingdom of Bohemia, which had been reclaimed by the Habsburgs during the Thirty Years' War. Since 1526, the Habsburg ruler had also been king of Hungary, although he exercised little real power except in northwestern Hungary. The eastern Hungarian principality of Transylvania remained independent while the central parts of Hungary were controlled by the Ottoman Turks.

Leopold I (1658–1705) encouraged the eastward movement of the Austrian Empire, but he was sorely challenged by the revival of Turkish power in the seventeenth century. Having moved into Transylvania, the Turks eventually pushed westward and laid siege to Vienna in 1683. Only a dramatic rescue by a combined army of Austrians, Saxons, Bavarians, and Poles saved the Austrian city. A European army, led by the Austrians, counterattacked and decisively defeated the Turks in 1687. By the Treaty of Karlowitz in 1699, Austria took control of Hungary, Transylvania, Croatia, and Slovenia, thus establishing an Austrian Empire in southeastern Europe. At the end of the War of the Spanish Succession, Austria gained possession of the Spanish Netherlands and received formal recognition of its occupation of the Spanish possessions in Italy, namely, Milan, Mantua, Sardinia, and Naples. By the beginning of the eighteenth century, the house of Austria had acquired a new empire of considerable size.

The Austrian monarchy, however, never became a highly centralized, absolutist state, primarily because it included so many different national groups. The Austrian Empire remained a collection of territories held together by a personal union. The Habsburg emperor was archduke of Austria, king of Bohemia, and king of Hungary. Each of these areas had its own laws, Estates-General, and political life. The landed aristocrats throughout the empire were connected by a common bond of service to the house of Habsburg, whether as military officers or government bureaucrats, but no other common sentiment tied the regions together. The nobles in the Austrian Empire remained quite strong and were also allowed to impose serfdom on their peasants. By the beginning of the eighteenth century, Austria was a populous empire in central Europe of great potential military strength.

Italy: From Spanish to Austrian Rule

By 1530, Emperor Charles V had managed to defeat the French armies in Italy and become the arbiter of Italy (see Chapter 13). Initially, he was content to establish close ties with many native Italian rulers and allow them to rule, provided that they recognize his dominant role. But in 1540, he gave the duchy of Milan to his son Philip II and transferred all imperial rights over Italy to the Spanish monarchy.

From the beginning of Philip II's reign in 1559 to 1713, the Spanish presence was felt everywhere in Italy. Only the major states of Florence, the Papal States, and Venice managed to maintain relatively independent policies. At the same time, the influence of the papacy became oppressive in Italy as the machinery of the Catholic Counter-Reformation—the Inquisition, Index, and the Jesuits—was used to stifle any resistance to the Catholic orthodoxy created by the Council of Trent (see Chapter 13). Though artistic and intellectual activity continued in post-Renaissance Italy, it often exacted a grievous cost. Some intellectuals, such as Galilei Galileo and Giordano Bruno (see Chapter 16), found themselves imprisoned or executed by the Inquisition.

At the beginning of the eighteenth century, Italy suffered further from the struggles between France and Spain. But it was Austria, not France, that benefited the most from the War of the Spanish Succession. By gaining Milan, Mantua, Sardinia, and Naples, Austria supplanted Spain as the dominant power in Italy.

From Muscovy to Russia

Since its origins in the Middle Ages, Russia had existed only on the fringes of European society, remote and isolated from the Western mainstream. But in the seventeenth century, the energetic Peter the Great (1689–1725) pushed Russia westward and raised it to the status of a great power.

A new Russian state had emerged in the fifteenth century under the leadership of the principality of Muscovy and its grand dukes (see Chapter 12). In the sixteenth century, Ivan IV the Terrible (1533–1584), who was the first ruler to take the title of tsar, expanded the territories of Russia eastward, after finding westward expansion blocked by the powerful Swedish and Polish states. Ivan also extended the autocracy of the tsar by crushing the power of the Russian nobility, known as the boyars.

Ivan's dynasty came to an end in 1598 and was followed by a resurgence of aristocratic power in a period of anarchy known as the Time of Troubles. It did not end until the Zemsky Sobor, or national assembly, chose Michael Romanov (1613–1645) as the new tsar, beginning a dynasty that lasted until 1917.

In the seventeenth century, Muscovite society was highly stratified. At the top was the tsar, who claimed to be a divinely ordained autocratic ruler, assisted by two consultative bodies, a Duma, or council of boyars, and the Zemsky Sobor, a landed assembly begun in 1550 by Ivan IV to facilitate support for his programs. Russian society was dominated by an upper class of landed aristocrats who, in the course of the seventeenth century, managed to bind their peasants to the land. An abundance of land and a shortage of peasants made serfdom desirable to the landowners. Under a law of 1625, the penalty for killing another's serf was merely to provide a replacement. Townspeople were also stratified and controlled. Artisans were sharply separated from merchants, and many of the latter were not allowed to move from their cities without government permission or to sell their businesses to anyone outside their class. In the seventeenth century, merchant and peasant revolts as well as a schism in the Russian Orthodox church created very unsettled conditions. In the midst of these political and religious upheavals, seventeenth-century Muscovy was experiencing more frequent contacts with the West while Western ideas also began to penetrate a few Russian circles. At the end of the seventeenth century, Peter the Great noticeably accelerated this westernizing process.

THE REIGN OF PETER THE GREAT (1689–1725)

Peter the Great was an unusual character. A strong man, towering six feet, nine inches tall, Peter was coarse in his tastes and rude in his behavior. He enjoyed a low kind

Peter the Great Deals with a Rebellion

During his first visit to the West in 1697–1698, Peter received word that the streltsy, an elite military unit stationed in Moscow, had revolted against his authority. Peter hurried home and crushed the revolt in a very savage fashion. This selection is taken from an Austrian account of how Peter dealt with the rebels.

Peter and the Streltsy

How sharp was the pain, how great the indignation, to which the tsar's Majesty was mightily moved, when he knew of the rebellion of the Streltsy, betraying openly a mind panting for vengeance! He was still tarrying at Vienna, quite full of the desire of setting out for Italy; but, fervid as was his curiosity of rambling abroad, it was, nevertheless, speedily extinguished on the announcement of the troubles that had broken out in the bowels of his realm. Going immediately to Lefort . . . , he thus indignantly broke out: "Tell me, Francis, how I can reach Moscow by the shortest way, in a brief space, so that I may wreak vengeance on this great perfidy of my people, with punishments worthy of their abominable crime. Not one of them shall escape with impunity. Around my royal city, which, with their impious efforts, they planned to destroy, I will have gibbets and gallows set upon the walls and ramparts, and each and every one of them will I put to a direful death." Nor did he long delay the plan for his justly excited wrath; he took the quick post, as his ambassador suggested, and in four weeks' time he had got over about 300 miles without accident, and arrived the 4th of September, 1698—a monarch for the well deposed, but an avenger for the wicked.

His first anxiety after his arrival was about the rebellion—in what it consisted, what the insurgents meant, who dared to instigate such a crime. And as nobody could answer accurately upon all points, and some pleaded their own ignorance, others the obstinacy of the Streltsy, he began to have suspicions of everybody's loyalty. . . . No day, holy or profane, were the inquisitors idle; every day was deemed fit and lawful for torturing. There was as many scourges as there were accused, and every inquisitor was a butcher. . . . The whole month of October was spent in lacerating the backs of culprits with the knout and with flames; no day were those that were left alive exempt from scourging or scorching; or else they were broken upon the wheel, or driven to the gibbet, or slain with the ax. . . .

To prove to all people how holy and inviolable are those walls of the city which the Streltsy rashly meditated scaling in a sudden assault, beams were run out from all the embrasures in the walls near the gates, in each of which two rebels were hanged. This day beheld about two hundred and fifty die that death. There are few cities fortified with as many palisades as Moscow has given gibbets to her guardian Streltsy.

of humor—belching contests, crude jokes, comical funerals—and vicious punishments including floggings, impalings, roastings, and beard burnings (see the box above). Peter gained a firsthand view of the West when he made a trip there in 1697–1698 and returned home with a firm determination to westernize or Europeanize Russia. Perhaps too much has been made of Peter's desire to westernize a "backward country." Peter's policy of Europeanization was largely technical. He admired European technology and gadgets and desired to transplant these to Russia. Only this kind of modernization could give him the army and navy he needed to make Russia a great power. His only consistent purpose was to win military victories.

As could be expected, one of his first priorities was the reorganization of the army and the creation of a navy. Employing both Russians and Europeans as officers, he conscripted peasants for twenty-five-year stints of service to build a standing army of 210,000 men. Peter has also been given credit for forming the first Russian navy.

Peter reorganized the central government, partly along Western lines. What remained of the consultative bodies disappeared; neither the Duma of boyars nor the Zemsky Sobor was ever summoned. In 1711, Peter created a Senate to supervise the administrative machinery of the state while he was away on military campaigns. In time the Senate became something like a ruling council, but its ineffectiveness caused Peter to borrow the Western institution of "colleges," or boards of administrators entrusted with specific functions, such as foreign affairs, war, and justice. To impose the rule of the central government more effectively throughout the land, Peter divided Russia into eight provinces and later, in 1719, into fifty. Although he hoped to create a "police state," by which he meant a well-ordered community governed in accordance with law, few of his bureaucrats shared his concept of honest service and duty to the state. One of his highest officials even stated: "Would your Majesty like to be a ruler without any subjects? We all steal, only some do it on a bigger scale, and in a more conspicuous way, than others."[9] Peter hoped for a sense of civic duty, but his own forceful personality created an atmosphere of fear that prevented it. He wrote to one administrator, "According to these orders act, act, act. I won't write more, but you will pay with your head if you interpret orders again." But when others were understandably cautious in interpreting his written instructions, he stated: "This is as if a servant, seeing his master drowning, would not save him until he had

PETER THE GREAT. Peter the Great wished to westernize Russia, especially in the realm of technical skills. His foremost goal was the creation of a strong army and navy in order to make Russia a great power. A Dutch painter created this portrait of the armored tsar during his visit to the West in 1697.

satisfied himself as to whether it was written down in his contract that he should pull him out of the water."[10] Peter wanted his administrators to be slaves and free men at the same time, and it did not occur to him that he was asking the impossible.

To further his administrative aims, Peter demanded that all members of the landholding class serve in either military or civil offices. Moreover, in 1722, Peter instituted a Table of Ranks to create opportunities for nonnobles to serve the state and join the ranks of the nobility. All civil offices were ranked according to fourteen levels; a parallel list of fourteen grades was also created for all military offices. Every official was then required to begin at level one and work his way up the ranks. When a nonnoble reached the eighth rank, he acquired the status of nobility. This attempt by Peter to create a new nobility based on merit was not carried on by his successors.

To obtain the enormous amount of money needed for an army and navy that absorbed as much as four-fifths of the state revenue, Peter adopted Western mercantilistic policies to stimulate economic growth. He tried to increase exports and develop new industries while exploiting domestic resources like the iron mines in the Urals. But his military needs were endless, and he came to rely on the old expedient of simply raising taxes, imposing additional burdens upon the hapless peasants who were becoming ever more oppressed in Peter's Russia.

Peter also sought to gain state control of the Russian Orthodox church. In 1721, he abolished the position of patriarch and created a body called the Holy Synod to make decisions for the church. At its head stood a procurator, a layman who represented the interests of the tsar and assured Peter of effective domination of the church.

Already after his first trip to the West in 1697–1698, Peter began to introduce Western customs, practices, and manners into Russia. He ordered the preparation of the first Russian book of etiquette to teach Western manners. Among other things, it pointed out that it was not polite to spit on the floor or scratch oneself at dinner. Since westerners did not wear beards or the traditional long-skirted coat, Russian beards had to be shaved and coats shortened, a reform Peter personally enforced at court by shaving off his nobles' beards and cutting their coats at the knees with his own hands. Outside the court, barbers and tailors planted at town gates enforced the edicts by cutting the beards and cloaks of those who entered or left. Anyone who failed to conform was to be "beaten without mercy." For the nobles, who were already partly westernized, these changes were hardly earth-shattering. But to many others who believed that shaving the beard was a "defacement of the image of God," the attack was actually blasphemous.

One group of Russians benefited greatly from Peter's cultural reforms—women. Having watched women mixing freely with men in Western courts, Peter shattered the seclusion of upper-class Russian women and demanded that they remove the traditional veils that covered their faces. Peter also decreed that social gatherings be held three times a week in the large houses of St. Petersburg where men and women could mix for conversation, card games, and dancing, which Peter had learned in the West. The tsar also now insisted that women could marry of their own free will.

The object of Peter's domestic reforms was to make Russia into a great state and military power. His primary goal was to "open a window to the west," meaning an ice-free port easily accessible to Europe. This could only be achieved on the Baltic, but at that time the Baltic coast was controlled by Sweden, the most important power in northern Europe. Desirous of these lands, Peter, with the support of Poland and Denmark, attacked Sweden in the summer of 1700, believing that the young king of Sweden, Charles XII, could easily be defeated. Charles, however, proved to be a brilliant general. He smashed the Danes, flattened the Poles, and, with a well-disciplined force of only 8,000 men, routed the Russian army of 40,000 at the Battle of Narva (1700). The Great Northern War (1701–1721) had begun.

But Peter fought back. He reorganized his army along Western lines and in 1702 overran the Swedish Baltic provinces while Charles was preoccupied elsewhere. When the Swedish king turned his attention to Peter again in 1708, he decided to invade Russia and capture Moscow, the cap-

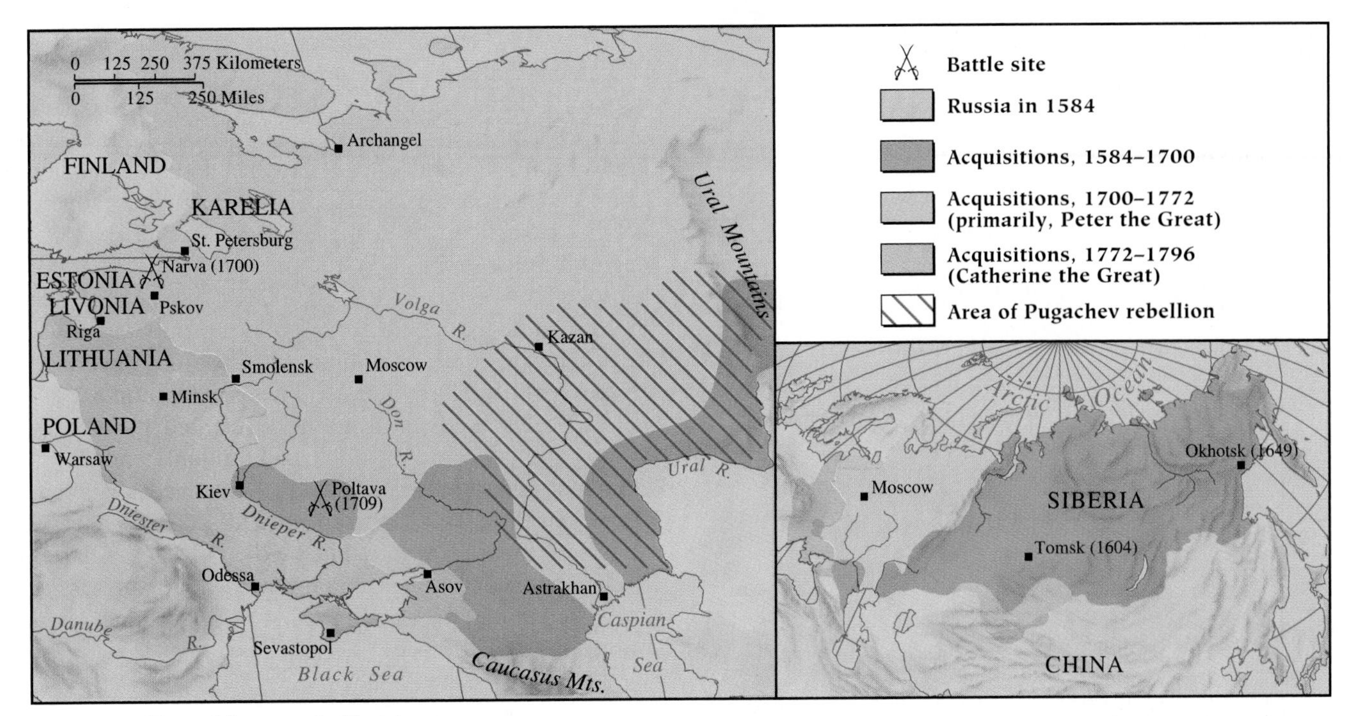

MAP 15.4 From Muscovy to Russia.

ital, but Russian weather and scorched-earth tactics devastated his army. In July 1709, at the Battle of Poltava, Peter's forces defeated Charles's army decisively. Although the war dragged on for another twelve years, the Peace of Nystadt in 1721 gave formal recognition to what Peter had already achieved: the acquisition of Estonia, Livonia, and Karelia. Sweden became a second-rate power while Russia was now the great European state Peter had wanted.

Already in 1703, in the northern marshlands along the Baltic, Peter had begun to construct a new city, St. Petersburg, his window on the west and a symbol that Russia was looking westward to Europe. Though its construction cost the lives of thousands of peasants, St. Petersburg was finished during Peter's lifetime. It remained the Russian capital until 1917.

It is difficult to assess the work of Peter the Great. He modernized and westernized Russia to the extent that it became a great military power and, by his death in 1725, an important member of the European state system. But his policies were also detrimental to Russia. Westernization was a bit of a sham, since Western culture reached only the upper classes and the real object of the reforms, the creation of a strong military, only added more burdens to the masses of the Russian people. The forceful way in which Peter the Great imposed westernization led to a distrust of Europe and Western civilization. Russia was so strained by Peter the Great that after his death an aristocratic reaction undid much of his work.

The Growth of Monarchy in Scandinavia

As the economic link between the products of eastern Europe and the West, the Baltic Sea bestowed special importance on the lands surrounding it. In the sixteenth century, Sweden had broken its ties with Denmark and emerged as an independent state (see Chapter 13). Despite their common Lutheran religion, Denmark's and Sweden's territorial ambitions in northern Europe kept them in rather constant rivalry in the seventeenth century.

Under Christian IV (1588–1648), Denmark seemed the likely candidate for expansion, but it met with little success. The system of electing monarchs forced the kings to share their power with the Danish nobility who exercised strict control over the peasants who worked their lands. Danish ambitions for ruling the Baltic were severely curtailed by the losses they sustained in the Thirty Years' War and later in the so-called Northern War (1655–1660) with Sweden. Danish military losses led to a constitutional crisis in which a meeting of Denmark's Estates brought to pass a bloodless revolution in 1660. The power of the nobility was curtailed, a hereditary monarchy reestablished, and a new, absolutist constitution proclaimed in 1665. Under Christian V (1670–1699), a centralized administration was instituted with the nobility as the chief officeholders.

Compared to Denmark, Sweden seemed a relatively poor country, and historians have had difficulty explaining why it played such a large role in European affairs in the seventeenth century. Sweden's economy was weak, and the monarchy was still locked in conflict with the powerful Swedish nobility. During the reign of Gustavus Adolphus (1611–1632), his wise and dedicated chief minister, Axel Oxenstierna, persuaded the king to adopt a new policy in which the nobility formed a "first estate" occupying the bureaucratic positions of an expanded central government. This created a stable monarchy and freed the king to raise a formidable army and participate in the Thirty Years' War, only to be killed in battle in 1632.

CHRONOLOGY

Absolutism in Central, Eastern, and Northern Europe

Brandenburg-Prussia	
Hohenzollerns established in Brandenburg	1415
Hohenzollerns acquire lands along the Rhine	1609
Hohenzollerns acquire East Prussia	1618
Frederick William the Great Elector	1640–1688
Elector Frederick III (King Frederick I)	1688–1713
The Austrian Empire	
Leopold I	1658–1705
Turkish siege of Vienna	1683
Treaty of Karlowitz	1699
Russia	
Ivan IV the Terrible	1533–1584
Time of Troubles	1598–1613
Michael Romanov	1613–1645
Peter the Great	1689–1725
First trip to the West	1697–1698
Great Northern War	1701–1721
Construction of St. Petersburg begins	1703
Battle of Poltava	1709
Holy Synod	1721
Denmark	
Christian IV	1588–1648
"Bloodless Revolution"	1660
Christian V	1670–1699
Sweden	
Gustavus Adolphus	1611–1632
Christina	1633–1654
Charles X	1654–1660
Charles XI	1660–1697
Charles XII	1697–1718
The Ottoman Empire	
Suleiman I the Magnificent	1520–1566
Battle of Lepanto	1571
Turkish defeat at Vienna	1683

Sweden experienced a severe political crisis after the death of Gustavus Adolphus. His daughter Christina (1633–1654) proved to be far more interested in philosophy and religion than ruling. Her tendency to favor the interests of the nobility led the other estates of the Riksdag, Sweden's parliament—the burghers, clergy, and peasants—to protest. In 1654, tired of ruling and wishing to become a Catholic, which was forbidden in Sweden, Christina abdicated in favor of her cousin, who became King Charles X (1654–1660). His accession to the throne defused a potentially explosive peasant revolt against the nobility.

Charles X reestablished domestic order, but it was his successor, Charles XI (1660–1697), who did the painstaking work of building the Swedish monarchy along the lines of an absolute monarchy. By resuming control of the crown lands and the revenues attached to them from the nobility, Charles managed to weaken the independent power of the nobility. He built up a bureaucracy, subdued both the Riksdag and the church, improved the army and navy, and left to his son, Charles XII (1697–1718), a well-organized Swedish state that dominated northern Europe. In 1693, he and his heirs were acclaimed as "absolute, sovereign kings, responsible for their actions to no man on earth."

Charles XII was primarily interested in military affairs. Energetic and regarded as a brilliant general, his grandiose plans and strategies, which involved Sweden in conflicts with Poland, Denmark, and Russia, proved to be Sweden's undoing. By the time he died in 1718, Charles XII had lost much of Sweden's northern empire to Russia, and Sweden's status as a first-class northern power had proved to be short-lived.

The Ottoman Empire

After their conquest of Constantinople in 1453, the Ottoman Turks tried to complete their conquest of the Balkans, where they had been established since the fourteenth century. Although they were successful in taking the Romanian territory of Wallachia in 1476, the resistance of the Hungarians kept them from advancing up the Danube valley. From 1480 to 1520, internal problems and the need to consolidate their eastern frontiers kept the Turks from any further attacks on Europe.

The reign of Sultan Suleiman I the Magnificent (1520–1566), however, brought the Turks back to Europe's attention. Advancing up the Danube, the Turks seized Belgrade in 1521 and Hungary by 1526, although their attempts to conquer Vienna in 1529 were repulsed. At the same time, the Turks extended their power into the western Mediterranean, threatening to turn it into a Turkish lake until a large Turkish fleet was destroyed by the Spanish at Lepanto in 1571. Despite the defeat, the Turks continued to hold nominal control over the southern shores of the Mediterranean.

Although Europeans frequently spoke of new Christian crusades against the infidel Turks, by the beginning of the seventeenth century the Ottoman Empire was being treated like another European power by European rulers seeking alliances and trade concessions. The Ottoman Empire possessed a highly effective governmental system, especially when it was led by strong sultans or powerful grand viziers (prime ministers). The splendid capital Constantinople possessed a population far larger than any European city. Nevertheless, Ottoman politics periodically degenerated into bloody intrigues as factions fought each other for influence and the throne. In one particularly gruesome practice, a ruling sultan would murder his brothers to avoid challenges to his rule. Despite the periodic bouts

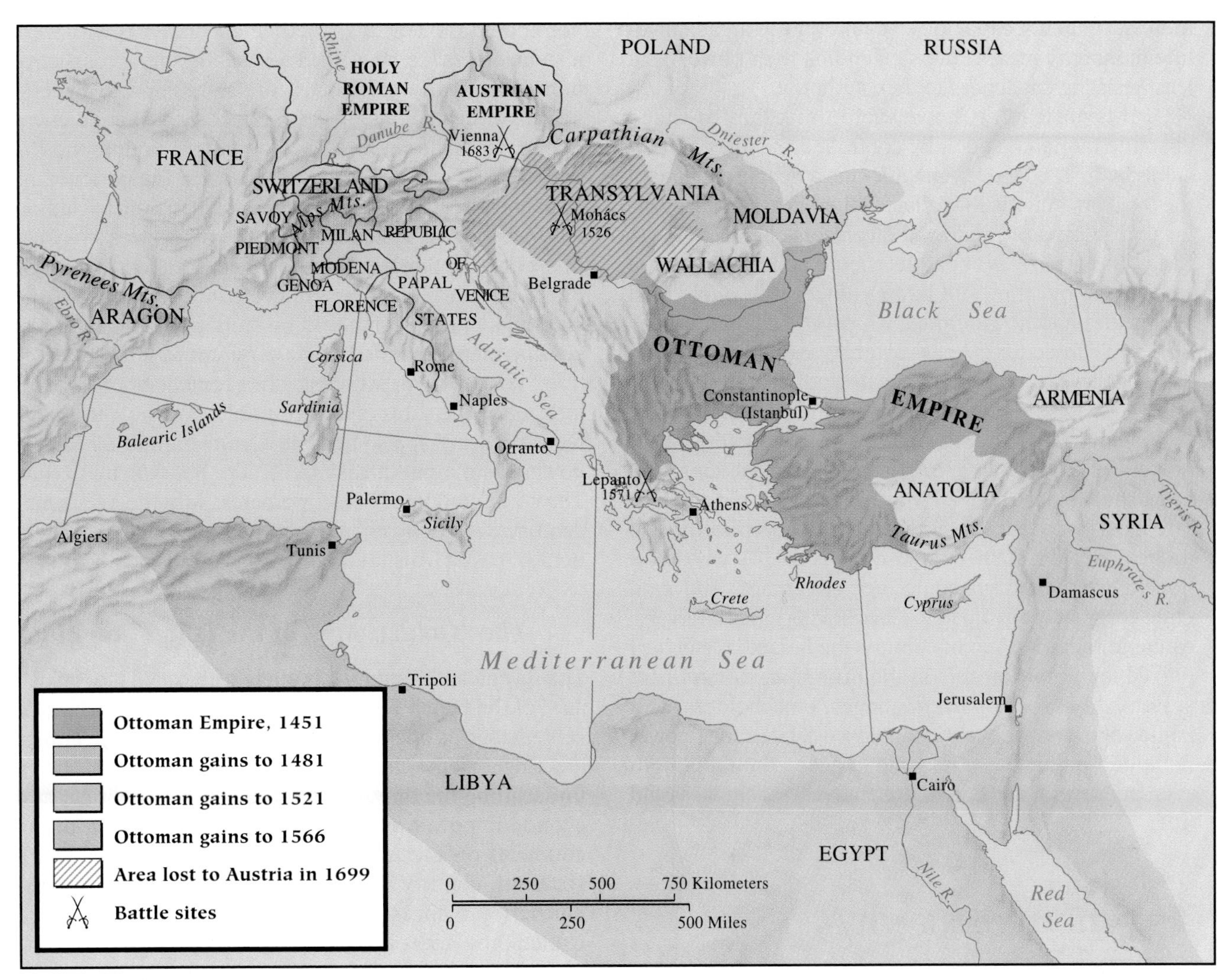

MAP 15.5 The Ottoman Empire.

of civil chaos, a well-trained bureaucracy of civil servants continued to administer state affairs efficiently.

A well-organized military system also added to the strength of the Ottoman Empire. Especially outstanding were the Janissaries, composed of Christian boys who had been taken from their parents, converted to the Muslim faith, and subjected to rigid military discipline to form an elite core of 8,000 troops personally loyal to the sultan. Like other praetorian guards, however, the Janissaries came to play an important role in making and unmaking sultans.

In the first half of the seventeenth century, the Ottoman Empire was a "sleeping giant." Occupied by domestic bloodletting and severely threatened by a challenge from Persia, the Ottomans were content with the status quo in eastern Europe. But under a new line of grand viziers in the second half of the seventeenth century, the Ottoman Empire again took the offensive. By mid-1683, the Ottomans had marched through the Hungarian plain and laid siege to Vienna. Repulsed by a mixed army of Austrians, Poles, Bavarians, and Saxons, the Turks retreated and were pushed out of Hungary by a new European coalition. Although they retained the core of their empire, the Ottoman Turks would never again be a threat to Europe. Although the Ottoman Empire held together for the rest of the seventeenth and eighteenth centuries, it would be faced with new challenges from the ever-growing Austrian Empire in southeastern Europe and the new Russian giant to the north.

The Limits of Absolutism

In recent decades, historical studies of local institutions have challenged the traditional picture of absolute monarchs. Control of the administrative machinery of state did not enable rulers to dominate the everyday lives of their subjects, as was once thought. The centralization of power was an important element in the growth of the seventeenth-century state, however, and the most successful monarchs were those who managed to restructure the central policy-making machinery of government to give them a certain amount of control over the traditional areas of monarchical power: formulation of foreign policy, making of war and peace, the church, and taxation. Seventeenth-century governments also intervened in economic affairs to strengthen their war-making capacities. In all of these areas, absolute monarchy meant rulers extending their power or at least resisting challenges to their authority.

It is misleading, however, to think that so-called absolute monarchs actually controlled the lives of their subjects. In 1700, government for most people still meant the local institutions that affected their lives: local courts, local tax collectors, and local organizers of armed forces. Kings and ministers might determine policies and issue guidelines, but they still had to function through local agents and had no guarantee whatever that their wishes would be carried out. A mass of urban and provincial privileges, liberties, and exemptions (including from taxation) and a whole host of corporate bodies and interest groups—provincial and national Estates, clerical officials, officeholders who had bought or inherited their positions, and provincial nobles—limited what monarchs could achieve. The most successful rulers were not those who tried to destroy the old system, but those like Louis XIV who knew how to use the old system to their advantage. Above all other considerations stood the landholding nobility. Everywhere in the seventeenth century, the landed aristocracy played an important role in the European monarchical system. As military officers, judges, officeholders, and landowners in control of vast, untaxed estates, their power remained immense. In some places, their strength even put severe limits on how effectively monarchs could rule.

◆ Limited Monarchy and Republics

Almost everywhere in Europe in the seventeenth century, kings and their ministers were in control of central governments. But not all European states followed the pattern of absolute monarchy. In eastern Europe, the Polish aristocracy controlled a virtually powerless king. In western Europe, two great states—the Dutch Republic and England—successfully resisted the power of hereditary monarchs.

The Weakness of the Polish Monarchy

Poland had played a major role in eastern Europe in the fifteenth century and had ruled over Lithuania and much of Ukraine by the end of the sixteenth. After the elective throne of Poland had been won by the Swede Sigismund III (1587–1631), Poland had a king who even thought seriously of creating a vast Polish empire that would include at least Russia and possibly Finland and Sweden. Poland not only failed to achieve this goal, but by the end of the seventeenth century, it had become a weak, decentralized state.

It was the elective nature of the Polish monarchy that reduced it to impotence. The *Sejm*, or Polish diet, was a two-chamber assembly in which landowners completely dominated the few townspeople and lawyers who were also members. To be elected to the kingship, prospective monarchs (who were mostly foreigners) had to agree to share power with the *Sejm* (in effect with the nobles) in matters of taxation, foreign and military policy, and the appointment of state officials and judges. The power of the *Sejm* had disastrous results for central monarchical authority since the real aim of most of its members was to ensure that central authority would not affect their local interests. The acceptance of the liberum veto in 1652, whereby the meetings of the *Sejm* could be stopped by a single dissenting member, reduced government to virtual chaos.

Poland, then, was basically a confederation of semi-independent estates of landed nobles. By the late seventeenth century, it also became a battleground for foreign powers who found it easy to invade, but difficult to rule. The continuation of Polish weakness into the eighteenth century eventually encouraged its more powerful neighbors—Prussia, Austria, and Russia—to dismember it.

The "Golden Age" of the Dutch Republic

The seventeenth century has often been called the "golden age" of the Dutch Republic as the United Provinces held center stage as one of Europe's great powers. Like France and England, the United Provinces was an Atlantic power, underlining the importance of the shift of political and economic power from the Mediterranean basin to the countries on the Atlantic seaboard. As a result of the sixteenth-century revolt of the Netherlands, the seven northern provinces, which began to call themselves the United Provinces of the Netherlands in 1581, became the core of the modern Dutch state. The new state was officially recognized by the Peace of Westphalia in 1648.

With independence came internal dissension. There were two chief centers of political power in the new state. Each province had an official known as a stadholder who was responsible for leading the army and maintaining order. Beginning with William of Orange and his heirs, the house of Orange occupied the stadholderate in most of the seven provinces and favored the development of a centralized government with themselves as hereditary monarchs. The States General, an assembly of representatives from every province, opposed the Orangist ambitions and advocated a decentralized or republican form of government.

The political rivalry between the monarchical and republican blocs was intensified by religious division within the Calvinist church, which remained the official church of the Dutch Republic. But other religious groups were tolerated as long as they worshiped in private. Catholics, other Protestants, and even Jewish communities felt relatively free in Holland, the richest and largest province, and especially in Amsterdam. In their religious toleration, the Dutch were truly unique in the seventeenth century.

For much of the seventeenth century, the republican forces were in control. But in 1672, burdened with war against both France and England, the United Provinces

DAM SQUARE. **This work by J. van der Ulft, done in 1659, shows Dam Square in Amsterdam. Merchants unloaded their cargoes here, making Dam Square one of the busiest centers of the city.**

turned once again to the house of Orange and restored it to the stadholderate in the person of William III (1672–1702). From that year on, William III worked consciously to build up his pseudo-royal power. When he succeeded to the throne of England in 1688 (see England and the Emergence of Constitutional Monarchy later in the chapter), his position in the Netherlands was strengthened as well. However, his death in 1702, without direct heirs, enabled the republican forces to gain control once more. The Dutch Republic would not be seriously threatened again by the monarchical forces.

Underlying Dutch prominence in the seventeenth century was its economic prosperity, fueled by the Dutch role as carriers of European trade. But war proved disastrous to the Dutch Republic. Wars with France and England placed heavy burdens on Dutch finances and manpower. English shipping began to challenge what had been Dutch commercial supremacy, and by 1715, the Dutch were experiencing a serious economic decline.

LIFE IN SEVENTEENTH-CENTURY AMSTERDAM

By the beginning of the seventeenth century, Amsterdam had replaced Antwerp as the financial and commercial capital of Europe. In 1570, Amsterdam had 30,000 inhabitants; by 1610, that number had doubled as refugees poured in, especially from the Spanish Netherlands. Intellectuals and Jews drawn by the city's reputation for toleration, as well as merchants and workers attracted by the city's prosperity, added to the number of new inhabitants. In 1613, this rapid growth caused the city government to approve an "urban expansion plan" that expanded the city's territory from 500 to 1,800 acres through the construction of three large, concentric canals. Builders prepared plots for the tall, narrow-fronted houses that were characteristic of the city by hammering wooden columns through the mud to the firm sand underneath. The canals in turn made it possible for merchants and artisans to utilize the upper stories of their houses as storerooms for their goods. Wares carried by small boats were hoisted to the top windows of these dwellings by block and tackle beams fastened to the gables of the roofs. Amsterdam's physical expansion was soon matched by its population as the city grew to 200,000 by 1660.

The exuberant expansion of Amsterdam in the seventeenth century was based upon the city's new role as the commercial and financial center of Europe (see the box on p. 446). But what had made this possible? For one thing, Amsterdam merchants possessed vast fleets of ships, many of which were used for the lucrative North Sea herring catch. Amsterdam ships were also important carriers for the products of other countries. The Dutch invention of the fluyt, a shallow-draft ship of large capacity, enabled them to transport enormous quantities of cereals, timber, and iron. The Dutch produced large ships for ocean voyages as well.

Amsterdam merchants unloaded their cargoes at Dam Square, where all goods above fifty pounds in weight were recorded and tested for quality. The quantity of goods brought to Amsterdam soon made the city a crossroads for many of Europe's chief products. Amsterdam was, of course, the chief port for the Dutch West and East Indian trading companies (see Overseas Trade and Colonies later

The Economic Superiority of the Dutch

Europeans were astonished by the apparent prosperity of the Dutch in the first half of the seventeenth century. This selection is taken from a treatise entitled Observations Touching Trade and Commerce with the Hollanders, and Other Nations. *It was written by an Englishman named John Keymer who believed that the Dutch economy could serve as a guide for the English.*

John Keymer, *Observations Touching Trade and Commerce with the Hollanders, and Other Nations*

I have diligently in my travels observed how the countries herein mentioned [mainly Holland] do grow potent with abundance of all things to serve themselves and other nations, where nothing grows; and that their never dried fountains of wealth, by which they raise their estate to such an admirable height, [so] that they are . . . [now] a wonder to the world, [come] from your Majesty's seas and lands.

I thus moved, began to delve into the depth of their policies and circumventing practices, whereby they drain, and still covet to exhaust, the wealth and coin of this kingdom, and so with our own commodities to weaken us, and finally beat us quite out of trading in other countries. I found that they more fully obtained these their purposes by their convenient privileges, and settled constitutions; than England with all the laws, and superabundance of home-bred commodities which God has vouchsafed your sea and land. . . .

To bring this to pass they have many advantages of us; the one is, by their fashioned ships . . . that are made to hold great bulk of merchandise, and to sail with a few men for profit. For example . . . [Dutch ships] do serve the merchant better cheap by one hundred pounds [English money] in his freight than we can, by reason he has but nine or ten mariners, and we near thirty; thus he saves twenty men's meat and wages in a voyage; and so in all other their ships according to their burden, by which means they are freighted wheresoever they come, to great profit, while our ships lie still and decay. . . .

Thus they and others glean this wealth and strength from us to themselves; and these reasons following procure them this advantage to us.

1. The merchants . . . which make all things in abundance, by reason of their store-houses continually replenished with all kind of commodities.
2. The liberty of free traffic for strangers to buy and sell in Holland, and other countries and states, as if they were free-born, makes great intercourse.
3. The small duties levied upon merchants, draws all nations to trade with them.
4. Their fashioned ships continually freighted before ours, by reason of their few mariners and great bulk, serving the merchant cheap.
5. Their forwardness to further all manner of trading.
6. Their wonderful employment of their busses [herring boats] for fishing, and the great returns they make.
7. Their giving free custom inward and outward, for any new-erected trade, by means whereof they have gotten already almost the sole trade into their hands.

in this chapter). Moreover, city industries turned imported raw materials into finished goods, making Amsterdam an important producer of woolen cloth, refined sugar and tobacco products, glass, beer, paper, books, jewelry, and leather goods. Some of the city's great wealth came from war profits: by 1700, Amsterdam was the principal supplier of military goods in Europe; its gun foundries had customers throughout the continent.

A third factor in Amsterdam's prosperity was its importance as a financial center. Trading profits provided large quantities of capital for investment. Its financial role was greatly facilitated by the foundation in 1609 of the Exchange Bank of Amsterdam, long the greatest public bank in northern Europe. As an English gentleman noted, the reputation of the bank was "another invitation for People to come, and lodge here what part of their Money they could transport, and knew no way of securing at home."[11] The city also founded the Amsterdam Stock Exchange for speculating in commodities.

Amsterdam's prosperity (it possessed the highest per capita income in Europe) did not prevent it from having enormous social differences. At the bottom of the social ladder were the beggars, unskilled day laborers, and poor immigrants attracted by Amsterdam's riches. Many of these poor people were forcefully recruited as ordinary sailors, especially for dangerous overseas voyages. Above this lower class stood the artisans and manual laborers, who belonged to the guilds or worked for guild members. Since widows were allowed to take their husbands' places in the craft guilds, Amsterdam was known for its high number of businesswomen. The artisans lived in a district called the Jordaan, built outside the three new canals. Its crowded quarters and small streets crisscrossed by canals created a quaint atmosphere and sense of fellowship that appealed to many of Amsterdam's artists.

Above the craftspeople stood a professional class of lawyers, teachers, bureaucrats, and wealthier guild members, but above them were the landed nobles who intermarried with the wealthier burghers and built more elaborate town houses. At the very top of Amsterdam's society stood a select number of very prosperous manufacturers, shipyard owners, and merchants, whose wealth enabled them to control the city government of Amsterdam as well as the Dutch Republic's States General.

In the first half of the seventeenth century, the Calvinist background of the wealthy Amsterdam burghers led them to adopt a simple lifestyle. They wore dark clothes and lived in substantial, but simply furnished houses, known for their steep, narrow stairways. The oft-quoted phrase that "cleanliness is next to Godliness" was literally true for these self-confident Dutch burghers. Their houses were clean and orderly; foreigners often commented that Dutch housewives always seemed to be scrubbing. But in the second half of the seventeenth century, the wealthy burghers began to reject their Calvinist heritage, a transformation that is especially evident in their more elaborate and colorful clothes.

England and the Emergence of Constitutional Monarchy

One of the most prominent examples of resistance to absolute monarchy came in seventeenth-century England where king and Parliament struggled to determine the role each should play in governing England. But the struggle over this political issue was complicated by a deep and profound religious controversy. With the victory of Parliament came the foundation for constitutional monarchy by the end of the seventeenth century.

REVOLUTION AND CIVIL WAR

With the death of Queen Elizabeth in 1603, the Tudor dynasty became extinct, and the Stuart line of rulers was inaugurated with the accession to the throne of Elizabeth's cousin, King James VI of Scotland (son of Mary, queen of Scots), who became James I (1603–1625) of England. Although used to royal power as king of Scotland, James understood little about the laws, institutions, and customs of the English. He espoused the divine right of kings, the belief that kings receive their power directly from God and are responsible to no one except God. This viewpoint alienated Parliament, which had grown accustomed under the Tudors to act on the premise that monarch and Parliament together ruled England as a "balanced polity." Parliament expressed its displeasure with James's claims by refusing his requests for additional monies needed by the king to meet the increased cost of government. Parliament's power of the purse proved to be its trump card in its relationship with the king.

Some members of Parliament were also alienated by James's religious policy. The Puritans—those Protestants within the Anglican church inspired by Calvinist theology—wanted James to eliminate the episcopal system of church organization used in the Church of England (in which the bishop or *episcopos* played the major administrative role) in favor of a Presbyterian model (used in Scotland and patterned after Calvin's church organization in Geneva, where ministers and elders—also called presbyters—played an important governing role). James refused because he realized that the Anglican church, with its bishops appointed by the crown, was a major support of monarchical authority. But the Puritans were not easily cowed and added to the rising chorus of opposition to the king. Many of England's gentry, mostly well-to-do landowners below the level of the nobility, had become Puritans, and these Puritan gentry not only formed an important and substantial part of the House of Commons, the lower house of Parliament, but also held important positions locally as justices of the peace and sheriffs. It was not wise to alienate them.

The conflict that had begun during the reign of James came to a head during the reign of his son Charles I (1625–1649). In 1628, Parliament passed a Petition of Right that the king was supposed to accept before being granted any taxes. This petition prohibited taxes without Parliament's consent, arbitrary imprisonment, the quartering of soldiers in private houses, and the declaration of martial law in peacetime. Although he initially accepted it, Charles later reneged on the agreement because of its limitations on royal power. In 1629, Charles decided that since he could not work with Parliament, he would not summon it to meet. From 1629 to 1640, Charles pursued a course of "personal rule," which forced him to find ways to collect taxes without the cooperation of Parliament. One expedient was a tax called Ship Money, a levy on seacoast towns to pay for coastal defense, which was now collected annually by the king's officials throughout England and used to finance other government operations besides defense. This use of Ship Money aroused opposition from middle-class merchants and landed gentry who believed the king was attempting to tax without Parliament's consent.

The king's religious policy also proved disastrous. His marriage to Henrietta Maria, the Catholic sister of King Louis XIII of France, aroused suspicions about the king's own religious inclinations. Even more important, however, the efforts of Charles and William Laud, the archbishop of Canterbury, to introduce more ritual into the Anglican church struck the Puritans as a return to Catholic popery. Grievances mounted, yet Charles might have survived unscathed if he could have avoided calling Parliament, which alone could provide a focus for the many cries of discontent throughout the land. But when the king and Archbishop Laud attempted to impose the Anglican Book of Common Prayer upon the Scottish Presbyterian church, the Scots rose up in rebellion against the king. Financially strapped and unable to raise troops to defend against the Scots, the king was forced to call Parliament into session. Eleven years of frustration welled up to create a Parliament determined to deal with the king.

In its first session from November 1640 to September 1641, the so-called Long Parliament (because it lasted in one form or another from 1640 to 1660) took a series of steps that placed severe limitations upon royal authority.

OLIVER CROMWELL. Oliver Cromwell was a dedicated Puritan who formed the New Model Army and defeated the forces supporting King Charles I. Unable to work with Parliament, he came to rely on military force to rule England. Cromwell is pictured here in 1649, on the eve of his ruthless military campaign in Ireland.

These included the abolition of arbitrary courts, the abolition of taxes that the king had collected without Parliament's consent, such as Ship Money, and the passage of the revolutionary Triennial Act, which specified that Parliament must meet at least once every three years, with or without the king's consent. By the end of 1641, one group within Parliament was prepared to go no further, but a group of more radical parliamentarians pushed for more change, including the elimination of bishops in the Anglican church. When the king tried to take advantage of the split by arresting some members of the more radical faction in Parliament, a large group in Parliament led by John Pym and his fellow Puritans decided that the king had gone too far. England now slipped into civil war (1642).

Parliament proved victorious in the first phase of the English Civil War (1642–1646). Most important to Parliament's success was the creation of the New Model Army by Oliver Cromwell. The New Model Army was composed primarily of more extreme Puritans known as the Independents, who believed they were doing battle for the Lord. It is striking to read in Cromwell's military reports such statements as "Sir, this is none other but the hand of God; and to Him alone belongs the glory." We might also attribute some of the credit to Cromwell himself since his crusaders were well disciplined and trained in the new continental military tactics. Supported by the New Model Army, Parliament ended the first phase of the civil war with the capture of King Charles I in 1646.

A split now occurred in the parliamentary forces. A Presbyterian majority wanted to disband the army and restore Charles I with a Presbyterian state church. The army, composed mostly of the more radical Independents, who opposed an established Presbyterian church, marched on London in 1647 and began negotiations with the king. Charles took advantage of this division to flee and seek help from the Scots. Enraged by the king's treachery, Cromwell and the army engaged in a second civil war (1648) that ended with Cromwell's victory and the capture of the king. This time Cromwell was determined to achieve a victory for the army's point of view. The Presbyterian members of Parliament were purged, leaving a Rump Parliament of fifty-three members of the House of Commons who then tried and condemned the king on a charge of treason and adjudged that "he, the said Charles Stuart, as a tyrant, traitor, murderer, and public enemy to the good people of this nation, shall be put to death by the severing of his head from his body." On January 30, 1649, Charles was beheaded, a most uncommon act in the seventeenth century. The revolution had triumphed, and the monarchy in England had been destroyed, at least for the moment.

After the death of the king, the Rump Parliament abolished the monarchy and the House of Lords and proclaimed England a republic or Commonwealth (1649–1653). This was not an easy period for Cromwell. As commander-in-chief of the army, he had to crush a Catholic uprising in Ireland, which he accomplished with a brutality that earned him the eternal enmity of the Irish people, as well as an uprising in Scotland on behalf of the son of Charles I. He also faced opposition at home, especially from more radically minded groups who took advantage of the upheaval in England to push their agendas. The Levellers, for example, advocated such advanced ideas as freedom of speech, religious toleration, and a democratic republic. Cromwell, a country gentleman and defender of property and the ruling classes, smashed the radicals by force. At the same time, Cromwell found it difficult to work with the Rump Parliament and finally dispersed it by force. As the members of Parliament departed (April 1653), he shouted after them: "It's you that have forced me to do this, for I have sought the Lord night and day that He would slay me rather than put upon me the doing of this work." With the certainty of one who is convinced he is right, Cromwell had destroyed both king and Parliament.

The army provided a new government when it drew up the Instrument of Government, England's first and last written constitution. Executive power was vested in the Lord Protector (a position held by Cromwell) and legislative power in a Parliament. But the new system also failed to work. Cromwell found it difficult to work with the Parliament, especially when its members debated his authority and advocated once again the creation of a Presbyterian state church. In 1655, Cromwell dissolved Parliament and divided the country into eleven regions, each ruled by a major general who served virtually as a military governor. To meet the cost of military government, Cromwell levied a 10 percent land tax on all former Royalists. Unable to establish a constitutional basis for a working government, Cromwell had resorted to military force to maintain the rule of the Independents, ironically using even more arbitrary policies than those of Charles I.

Oliver Cromwell died in 1658. After floundering for eighteen months, the military establishment decided that arbitrary rule by the army was no longer feasible and reestablished the monarchy in the person of Charles II, the son of Charles I. The restoration of the Stuart monarchy ended England's time of troubles, but it was not long before England experienced yet another constitutional crisis.

RESTORATION AND A GLORIOUS REVOLUTION

After eleven years of exile, Charles II (1660–1685) returned to England. As he entered London amid the acclaim of the people, he remarked sardonically, "I never knew that I was so popular in England." The restoration of the monarchy and the House of Lords did not mean, however, that the work of the English Revolution was undone. Parliament kept much of the power it had won: its role in government was acknowledged; the necessity for its consent to taxation was accepted; and arbitrary courts were still abolished. Yet Charles continued to push his own ideas, some of which were clearly out of step with many of the English people.

A serious religious problem disturbed the tranquillity of Charles II's reign. After the restoration of the monarchy, a new Parliament (the Cavalier Parliament) met in 1661 and restored the Anglican church as the official church of England. In addition, laws were passed to force everyone, particularly Catholics and Puritan Dissenters, to conform to the Anglican church. Charles, however, was sympathetic to and perhaps even inclined to Catholicism. Moreover, Charles's brother James, heir to the throne, did not hide the fact that he was a Catholic. Parliament's suspicions were therefore aroused in 1672 when Charles took the audacious step of issuing a Declaration of Indulgence that suspended the laws that Parliament had passed against Catholics and Puritans. Parliament would have none of it and induced the king to suspend the declaration. Propelled by a strong anti-Catholic sentiment, Parliament then passed a Test Act in 1673, specifying that only Anglicans could hold military and civil offices.

A supposed Catholic plot to assassinate King Charles and place his brother James on the throne, although shown to be imaginary, inflamed Parliament to attempt to pass an Exclusion Bill between 1678 and 1681 that would have barred James from the throne as a professed Catholic. Although these attempts failed, the debate over the bill created two political groupings: the Whigs, who wanted to exclude James and establish a Protestant king with toleration of Dissenters, and the Tories, who supported the king, despite their dislike of James as a Catholic, because they did not believe Parliament should tamper with the lawful succession to the throne. To foil these efforts, Charles dismissed Parliament in 1681, relying on French subsidies to rule alone. When he died in 1685, his Catholic brother came to the throne.

The accession of James II (1685–1688) to the crown virtually guaranteed a new constitutional crisis for England. An open and devout Catholic, his attempt to further Catholic interests made religion once more a primary cause of conflict between king and Parliament. Contrary to the Test Act, James named Catholics to high positions in the government, army, navy, and universities. In 1687, he issued a Declaration of Indulgence, which suspended all laws barring Catholics and Dissenters from office. Parliamentary outcries against James's policies stopped short of rebellion because members knew that he was an old man and his successors were his Protestant daughters Mary and Anne, born to his first wife. But on June 10, 1688, a son was born to James II's second wife, also a Catholic. Suddenly the specter of a Catholic hereditary monarchy loomed large. A group of seven prominent English noblemen invited William of Orange, husband of James's daughter Mary, to invade England. An inveterate foe of Louis XIV, William welcomed this opportunity to fight France with England's resources. William and Mary raised an army and invaded England while James, his wife, and infant son fled to France. With almost no

CHRONOLOGY

Limited Monarchy and Republics

Poland	
Sigismund III	1587–1631
Beginning of liberum veto	1652
The United Provinces	
Official recognition of United Provinces	1648
House of Orange	
William III	1672–1702
England	
James I	1603–1625
Charles I	1625–1649
Petition of Right	1628
First Civil War	1642–1646
Second Civil War	1648
Execution of Charles I	1649
Commonwealth	1649–1653
Death of Cromwell	1658
Restoration of monarchy—Charles II	1660
Charles II	1660–1685
Cavalier Parliament	1661
Declaration of Indulgence	1672
Test Act	1673
James II	1685–1688
Declaration of Indulgence	1687
Glorious Revolution	1688
Bill of Rights	1689

The Bill of Rights

In 1688, the English experienced yet another revolution, a rather bloodless one in which the Stuart king James II was replaced by Mary, James's daughter, and her husband, William of Orange. After William and Mary had assumed power, Parliament passed a Bill of Rights that specified the rights of Parliament and laid the foundation for a constitutional monarchy.

The Bill of Rights

Whereas the said late King James II having abdicated the government, and the throne being thereby vacant, his Highness the prince of Orange (whom it has pleased Almighty God to make the glorious instrument of delivering this kingdom from popery and arbitrary power) did (by the device of the lords spiritual and temporal, and diverse principal persons of the Commons) cause letters to be written to the lords spiritual and temporal, being Protestants, and other letters to the several counties, cities, universities, boroughs, and Cinque Ports, for the choosing of such persons to represent them, as were of right to be sent to parliament, to meet and sit at Westminster upon the two and twentieth day of January, in this year 1689, in order to such an establishment as that their religion, laws, and liberties might not again be in danger of being subverted; upon which letters elections have been accordingly made.

And thereupon the said lords spiritual and temporal and Commons, pursuant to their respective letters and elections, being now assembled in a full and free representation of this nation, taking into their most serious consideration the best means for attaining the ends aforesaid, do in the first place (as their ancestors in like case have usually done), for the vindication and assertion of their ancient rights and liberties, declare:

1. That the pretended power of suspending laws, or the execution of laws, by regal authority, without consent of parliament is illegal.
2. That the pretended power of dispensing with the laws, or the execution of law by regal authority, as it has been assumed and exercised of late, is illegal.
3. That the commission for erecting the late court of commissioners for ecclesiastical causes, and all other commissions and courts of like nature, are illegal and pernicious.
4. That levying money for or to the use of the crown by pretense of prerogative, without grant of parliament, for longer time or in other manner than the same is or shall be granted, is illegal.
5. That it is the right of the subjects to petition the king, and all commitments and prosecutions for such petitioning are illegal.
6. That the raising or keeping a standing army within the kingdom in time of peace, unless it be with consent of parliament, is against law.
7. That the subjects which are Protestants may have arms for their defense suitable to their conditions, and as allowed by law.
8. That election of members of parliament ought to be free.
9. That the freedom of speech, and debates or proceedings in parliament, ought not to be impeached or questioned in any court or place out of parliament.
10. That excessive bail ought not to be required, nor excessive fines imposed, nor cruel and unusual punishments inflicted.
11. That jurors ought to be duly impaneled and returned, and jurors which pass upon men in trials for high treason ought to be freeholders.
12. That all grants and promises of fines and forfeitures of particular persons before conviction are illegal and void.
13. And that for redress of all grievances, and for the amending, strengthening, and preserving of the laws, parliament ought to be held frequently.

bloodshed, England had undergone a "Glorious Revolution," not over the issue of whether there would be a monarchy, but rather over who would be monarch.

The events of late 1688 constituted only the initial stage of the Glorious Revolution. The second, and far more important part, was the Revolution Settlement that confirmed William and Mary as monarchs. In January 1689, a Convention Parliament asserted that James had tried to subvert the constitution "by breaking the original contract between king and people," and declared the throne of England vacant. It then offered the throne to William and Mary, who accepted it along with the provisions of a Declaration of Rights, later enacted into law as a Bill of Rights in 1689 (see the box above). The Bill of Rights affirmed Parliament's right to make laws and levy taxes and made it impossible for kings to oppose or do without Parliament by stipulating that standing armies could be raised only with the consent of Parliament. Both elections and debates of Parliament had to be free, meaning that the king could not interfere. The rights of citizens to petition the sovereign, keep arms, have a jury trial, and not be subject to excessive bail were also confirmed. The Bill of Rights helped to fashion a system of government based on the rule of law and a freely elected Parliament, thus laying the foundation for a constitutional monarchy.

The Bill of Rights did not settle the religious questions that had played such a large role in England's troubles in the seventeenth century. The Toleration Act of 1689

Hobbes and Locke: Two Views of Political Authority

The seventeenth-century obsession with order and power was well reflected in the political thought of the Englishmen Thomas Hobbes and John Locke. In his Leviathan, *Hobbes presented the case for the state's claim to absolute authority over its subjects. John Locke, on the other hand, argued for limiting government power in his* Two Treatises of Government.

Thomas Hobbes, *Leviathan*

The only way to erect a Common Power, as may be able to defend them from the invasion of foreigners and the injuries of one another, and thereby to secure them in such sort, as that by their own industry, and by the fruits of the Earth, they may nourish themselves and live contentedly; is, to confer all their power and strength upon one Man, or upon one Assembly of men, that may reduce all their Wills, by plurality of voices, unto one Will . . . and therein to submit their Wills, every one to his Will, and their Judgments, to his Judgment. This is more than Consent, or Concord; it is a real Unity of them all, in one and the same Person, made by Covenant of every man with every man. . . . This done, the Multitude so united in one Person, is called a COMMONWEALTH. . . .

They that have already instituted a Commonwealth, being thereby bound by Covenant cannot lawfully make a new Covenant, among themselves, to be obedience to any other, in any thing whatsoever, without his permission. And therefore, they that are subjects to a Monarch, cannot without his leave cast off Monarchy, and return to the confusion of a disunited Multitude; nor transfer their Person from him that bears it, to another Man, or other Assembly of men: for they . . . are bound, every man to every man, to acknowledge that he that already is their Sovereign, shall do, and judge fit to be done; so that those who do not obey break their Covenant made to that man, which is injustice. . . . Consequently, none of the sovereign's Subjects, by any pretense of forfeiture, can be free from his Subjection.

John Locke, *The Second Treatise of Government*

There is, therefore, another way whereby governments are dissolved, and that is when the legislative or the prince, either of them, act contrary to their trust. . . . Whenever the legislators endeavor to take away and destroy the property of the people, or to reduce them to slavery under arbitrary power, they put themselves into a state of war with the people who are thereupon absolved from any further obedience, and are left to the common refuge which God has provided for all men against force and violence. Whensoever, therefore, the legislative shall transgress this fundamental rule of society, and either by ambition, fear, folly, or corruption, endeavor to grasp themselves, or put into the hands of any other, an absolute power over the lives, liberties, and estates of the people, by this breach of trust they forfeit the power the people had put into their hands for quite contrary ends, and it devolves to the people, who have a right to resume their original liberty and, by the establishment of a new legislative, such as they shall think fit, provide for their own safety and security, which is the end for which they are in society. What I have said here concerning the legislative in general holds true also concerning the supreme executor, who having a double trust put in him—both to have a part in the legislative and the supreme execution of the law—acts against both when he goes about to set up his own arbitrary will as the law of the society.

granted Puritan Dissenters the right of free public worship (Catholics were still excluded), although they did not yet have full civil and political equality since the Test Act was not repealed. Although the Toleration Act did not mean complete religious freedom and equality, it marked a departure in English history: few people would ever again be persecuted for religious reasons.

Many historians have viewed the Glorious Revolution as the end of the seventeenth-century struggle between king and Parliament. By deposing one king and establishing another, Parliament had destroyed the divine-right theory of kingship (William was, after all, king by grace of Parliament, not God) and confirmed its right to participate in the government. Parliament did not have complete control of the government, but it now had an unquestioned right to participate in affairs of state. Over the next century, it would gradually prove to be the real authority in the English system of constitutional monarchy.

RESPONSES TO REVOLUTION

The English revolutions of the seventeenth century prompted very different responses from two English political thinkers—Thomas Hobbes and John Locke (see the box above). Thomas Hobbes (1588–1679), who lived during the English Civil War, was alarmed by the revolutionary upheavals in his contemporary England. Hobbes's name has since been associated with the state's claim to absolute authority over its subjects, a topic that he elaborated in his major treatise on political thought known as the *Leviathan*, published in 1651.

Hobbes claimed that in the state of nature, before society was organized, human life was "solitary, poor, nasty, brutish, and short." Humans were guided not by reason and moral ideals, but by animalistic instincts and a ruthless struggle for self-preservation. To save themselves from destroying each other (the "war of every man against every man"), people contracted to form a commonwealth, which Hobbes called "that great Leviathan (or rather, to speak more reverently, that mortal god) to which we owe our peace and defense." This commonwealth placed its collective power into the hands of a sovereign authority, preferably a single ruler, who served as executor, legislator, and judge. This absolute ruler possessed unlimited power. In Hobbes's view, subjects may not rebel; if they do, they must be suppressed.

John Locke (1632–1704) viewed the exercise of political power quite differently from Hobbes and argued against the absolute rule of one man. Locke's experience of English politics during the Glorious Revolution was incorporated into a political work called *Two Treatises of Government.* Like Hobbes, Locke began with the state of nature before human existence became organized socially. But, unlike Hobbes, Locke believed humans lived then in a state of equality and freedom rather than a state of war. In this state of nature, humans had certain inalienable natural rights—to life, liberty, and property. Like Hobbes, Locke did not believe all was well in the state of nature. Since there was no impartial judge in the state of nature, people found it difficult to protect these natural rights. So they mutually agreed to establish a government to ensure the protection of their rights. This agreement established mutual obligations: government would protect the rights of the people while the people would act reasonably toward government. But if a government broke this agreement—if a monarch, for example, failed to live up to his obligation to protect the natural rights or claimed absolute authority and made laws without the consent of the community—the people might form a new government. "The community perpetually retains a supreme power," Locke claimed. For Locke, however, the community of people was primarily the landholding aristocracy who were represented in Parliament, not the landless masses. Locke was hardly an advocate of political democracy, but his ideas proved important to both Americans and French in the eighteenth century and were used to support demands for constitutional government, the rule of law, and the protection of rights.

◆ Economic Trends: Mercantilism and European Colonies in the Seventeenth Century

The seventeenth century was marked by economic contraction, although variations existed depending on the country or region. Trade, industry, and agriculture all felt the pinch of a depression, which some historians believe bottomed out between 1640 and 1680, while others argue that the decade of the 1690s was still bad, especially in France. Translated into everyday life, for many people the economic contraction of the seventeenth century meant scarce food, uncertain employment, and high rates of taxation.

Climate, too, played a factor in this economic reversal as Europeans experienced worsening weather patterns. In this "little ice age," extending from the sixteenth well into the eighteenth century, average temperatures fell, winters were colder, summers were wetter, and devastating storms seemed more frequent. Although the exact impact of climatic changes is uncertain, there were numerous reports of crop failures, the worst in 1649, 1660–1661, and the 1690s.

Population was also affected. Based on the birthrate of the seventeenth century, demographers would expect the European population to have doubled every twenty-five years. In reality, the population either declined or increased only intermittently as a result of a variety of factors. Infant mortality rates were high, 30 percent in the first year of life and 50 percent before the age of ten. Epidemics and famines were again common experiences in European life. The last great epidemic of bubonic plague spread across Europe in the middle and late years of the seventeenth century. The Mediterranean region suffered from 1646 to 1657, when the plague killed off 130,000 persons in Naples alone. In 1665, it struck England and devastated London, killing 20 percent of its population.

Mercantilism

Mercantilism is the name historians use to identify a set of economic principles that dominated economic thought in the seventeenth century. Fundamental to mercantilism was the belief that the total volume of trade was unchangeable. Therefore, as Colbert, the French practitioner of mercantilism, stated: "Trade causes perpetual conflict, both in war and in peace, among the nations of Europe, as to who should carry off the greatest part. The Dutch, the English and the French are the actors in this conflict."[12] Since one nation could expand its trade and hence its prosperity only at the expense of others, to mercantilists, economic activity was war carried on by peaceful means.

According to the mercantilists, the prosperity of a nation depended upon a plentiful supply of bullion, or gold and silver. For this reason, it was desirable to achieve a favorable balance of trade in which goods exported were of greater value than those imported, promoting an influx of gold and silver payments that would increase the quantity of bullion. Furthermore, to encourage exports, governments should stimulate and protect export industries and trade by granting trade monopolies, encouraging investment in new industries through subsidies, importing foreign artisans, and improving transportation systems by building roads, bridges, and canals. By placing high tariffs on foreign goods, they could be kept out of the country and

THE DUTCH EAST INDIA COMPANY IN INDIA. Pictured here is the Dutch trading post known as Hugly, founded in Bengal in 1610. This 1665 painting shows warehouses laid out in precise patterns surrounded by protective walls. Hugly was an important link in the network of bases that constituted Holland's trading empire in the East.

prevented from competing with domestic industries. Colonies were also deemed valuable as sources of raw materials and markets for finished goods.

As a system of economic principles, mercantilism focused on the role of the state, believing that state intervention in some aspects of the economy was desirable for the sake of the national good. Government regulations to ensure the superiority of export goods, the construction of roads and canals, and the granting of subsidies to create trade companies were all predicated on government involvement in economic affairs.

Overseas Trade and Colonies

Mercantilist theory on the role of colonies was matched in practice by Europe's overseas expansion. With the development of colonies and trading posts in the Americas and the East, Europeans entered into an age of international commerce in the seventeenth century. Although some historians speak of a world economy, we should remember that local, regional, and intra-European trade still dominated the scene. At the end of the seventeenth century, for example, English imports totaled 360,000 tons, but only 5,000 tons came from the East Indies. About one-tenth of English and Dutch exports were shipped across the Atlantic; slightly more went to the East. What made the transoceanic trade rewarding, however, was not the volume, but the value of its goods. Dutch, English, and French merchants were bringing back products that were still consumed largely by the wealthy, but were beginning to make their way into the lives of artisans and merchants. Pepper and spices from the Indies, West Indian and Brazilian sugar, and Asian coffee and tea were becoming more readily available to European consumers. The first coffee and tea houses opened in London in the 1650s and spread rapidly to other parts of Europe.

In 1600, much overseas trade was still carried by the Spanish and Portuguese, who alone possessed colonies of any significant size. But war and steady pressure from their Dutch and English rivals eroded Portuguese trade in both the West and the East, although Portugal continued to profit from its large colonial empire in Brazil. The Spanish also maintained an enormous South American empire, but Spain's importance as a commercial power declined rapidly in the seventeenth century because of a drop in the output of the silver mines and the poverty of the Spanish monarchy.

Although the Dutch became the leading carriers of European products within Europe, they faced more severe competition when they moved into Asian and American markets. The Dutch East India Company was formed in 1602 to consolidate the gains made at the expense of the Portuguese and exploit the riches of the East. Since the wealthy oligarchy that controlled the company also dominated the Dutch government, this joint-stock company not only had a monopoly on all Asian trade but also possessed the right to make war, sign treaties, establish military and trading bases, and appoint governing officials. Gradually, the Dutch East India Company took control of most of the Portuguese bases in the East and opened trade with China and Japan. Its profits were spectacular in the first ten years.

The Dutch West India Company, created in 1621, was less successful. Its efforts were aimed against Portuguese and Spanish trade and possessions, and though it made some inroads in Portuguese Brazil and the Caribbean, they were not enough to compensate for the company's expenditures. Dutch settlements were also established on the North American continent. The mainland colony of New Netherlands stretched from the mouth of the Hudson as far north as Albany, New York. Present-day names such as Staten Island and Harlem remind us that it was the Dutch who initially settled the Hudson River valley. In the second half of the seventeenth century, competition from the English and French and years of warfare with those rivals led to the decline of the Dutch commercial empire. In 1664, the English seized the colony of

West Meets East: An Exchange of Royal Letters

Economic gain was not the only motivation of Western rulers who wished to establish a European presence in the East. In 1681, King Louis XIV of France wrote a letter to the king of Tonkin asking permission for Christian missionaries to proselytize in Vietnam. The king of Tonkin politely declined the request.

A Letter to the King of Tonkin

Most high, most excellent, most mighty and most magnanimous Prince, our very dear and good friend, may it please God to increase your greatness with a happy end!

We hear from our subjects who were in your Realm what protection you accorded them. We appreciate this all the more since we have for you all the esteem that one can have for a prince as illustrious through his military valor as he is commendable for the justice which he exercises in his Realm. . . . Since the war which we have had for several years, in which all of Europe had banded together against us, prevented our vessels from going to the Indies, at the present time, when we are at peace after having gained many victories and expanded our Realm through the conquest of several important places, we have immediately given orders to the Royal Company to establish itself in your kingdom as soon as possible. . . . We have given orders to have brought to you some presents which we believe might be agreeable to you. But the one thing in the world which we desire most, both for you and for your Realm, would be to obtain for your subjects who have already embraced the law of the only true God of heaven and earth, the freedom to profess it, since this law is the highest, the noblest, the most sacred and especially the most suitable to have kings reign absolutely over the people.

We are even quite convinced that, if you knew the truths and the maxims which it teaches, you would give first of all to your subjects the glorious example of embracing it. We wish you this incomparable blessing together with a long and happy reign, and we pray God that it may please Him to augment your greatness with the happiest of endings.

Your very dear and good friend,
Louis

Answers from the King of Tonkin to Louis XIV

The King of Tonkin sends to the King of France a letter to express to him his best sentiments. . . . Your communication, which comes from a country which is a thousand leagues away, and which proceeds from the heart as a testimony of your sincerity, merits repeated consideration and infinite praise. Politeness toward strangers is nothing unusual in our country. There is not a stranger who is not well received by us. How then could we refuse a man from France, which is the most celebrated among the kingdoms of the world and which for love of us wishes to frequent us and bring us merchandise? These feelings of fidelity and justice are truly worthy to be applauded. As regards your wish that we should cooperate in propagating your religion, we do not dare to permit it, for there is an ancient custom, introduced by edicts, which formally forbids it. Now, edicts are promulgated only to be carried out faithfully; without fidelity nothing is stable. How could we disdain a well-established custom to satisfy a private friendship? . . . This then is my letter. We send you herewith a modest gift which we offer you with a glad heart.

This letter was written at the beginning of winter and on a beautiful day.

New Netherlands and renamed it New York; soon afterward the Dutch West India Company went bankrupt. By the end of the seventeenth century, the Dutch golden age was beginning to tarnish.

The Dutch overseas trade and commercial empire faced two major rivals in the seventeenth century—the English and French. The English had founded their own East India Company in 1601 and proceeded to create a colonial empire in the New World along the Atlantic seaboard of North America. The failure of the Virginia Company made it evident that the colonizing of American lands was not necessarily conducive to quick profits. But the desire to practice one's own religion combined with economic interests could lead to successful colonization, as the Massachusetts Bay Company demonstrated. The Massachusetts colony had 4,000 settlers in its early years, but by 1660 had swelled to 40,000. Although the English had established control over most of the eastern seaboard by the end of the seventeenth century, the North American colonies were still of only minor significance to the English economy.

French commercial companies in the East experienced much difficulty. Though due in part to a late start, French problems also demonstrated the weakness of a commerce dependent on political rather than economic impetus (see the box above). The East India Companies set up by Henry IV and Richelieu all failed. In 1664, Colbert established a new East India Company that only barely managed to survive. The French had greater success in North America where in 1663 Canada was made the property of the crown and administered like a French province. But the French failed to provide adequate men or money, allowing their continental wars to take precedence over the conquest of the North American continent. Already in 1713, by the Treaty of Utrecht, the French began to cede some of their American possessions to their English rival.

◆ The World of Seventeenth-Century Culture

The seventeenth century was a remarkably talented one. In addition to the intellectuals responsible for the Scientific Revolution (see Chapter 16), the era was blessed with a number of prominent thinkers, artists, and writers. Some historians have even labeled it a century of genius.

Art: French Classicism and Dutch Realism

In the second half of the seventeenth century, France replaced Italy as the cultural leader of Europe. Rejecting the Baroque style as overly showy and passionate, the French remained committed to the classical values of the High Renaissance. French late Classicism with its emphasis on clarity, simplicity, balance, and harmony of design was, however, a rather austere version of the High Renaissance style. Its triumph reflected the shift in seventeenth-century French society from chaos to order. Though it rejected the emotionalism and high drama of the Baroque, French Classicism continued the Baroque's conception of grandeur in the portrayal of noble subjects, especially those from classical antiquity. Nicholas Poussin (1594–1665) exemplified these principles in his paintings. His choice of scenes from classical mythology, the orderliness of his landscapes, the postures of his figures copied from the sculptures of antiquity, and his use of brown tones all reflect French Classicism of the late seventeenth century.

The supremacy of Dutch commerce in the seventeenth century was paralleled by a brilliant flowering of Dutch painting. Wealthy patricians and burghers of Dutch urban society commissioned works of art for their guild halls, town halls, and private dwellings. The interests of this burgher society were reflected in the subject matter of many Dutch paintings: portraits of themselves, group portraits of their military companies and guilds, landscapes, seascapes, genre scenes, still lifes, and the interiors of their residences. Neither classical nor Baroque, Dutch painters were primarily interested in the realistic portrayal of secular, everyday life.

This interest in painting scenes of everyday life is evident in the work of Judith Leyster (c. 1609–1660), who established her own independent painting career, a remarkable occurrence in seventeenth-century Europe. Leyster became the first female member of the painting Guild of St. Luke in Haarlem, which enabled her to set up her own workshop and take on three male pupils. Musicians playing their instruments, women sewing, children laughing while playing games, and actors performing, all form the subject matter of Leyster's portrayals of everyday Dutch life. But she was also capable of introspection, as is evident in her *Self-Portrait*.

The finest example of the golden age of Dutch painting was Rembrandt van Rijn (1606–1669). Rembrandt's early career was reminiscent of Rubens in that he painted opulent portraits and grandiose scenes in often colorful fashion. Like Rubens, he was prolific and successful; unlike Rubens, he turned away from materialistic success and public approval to follow his own artistic path. In the process, he lost public support and died bankrupt.

NICHOLAS POUSSIN, *LANDSCAPE WITH THE BURIAL OF PHOCIAN*. France became the new cultural leader of Europe in the second half of the seventeenth century. French Classicism upheld the values of High Renaissance style, but in a more static version. In Nicholas Poussin's work, we see the emphasis of French Classicism on the use of scenes from classical sources and the creation of a sense of grandeur and noble strength in both human figures and landscape.

REMBRANDT VAN RIJN, *SYNDICS OF THE CLOTH GUILD*. **The Dutch experienced a golden age of painting during the seventeenth century. The burghers and patricians of Dutch urban society commissioned works of art, and these quite naturally reflected the burghers' interests, as this painting by Rembrandt illustrates.**

Although Rembrandt shared the Dutch predilection for realistic portraits, he became more introspective as he grew older. He refused to follow his contemporaries whose pictures were largely secular in subject matter; half of his paintings focused on scenes from biblical tales. Since the Protestant tradition of hostility to religious pictures had discouraged artistic expression, Rembrandt stands out as the one great Protestant painter of the seventeenth century. Rembrandt's religious pictures, however, avoided the monumental subjects, such as the Creation and Last Judgment, that were typical of Catholic artists. Instead, he favored pictures that focused on the individual's relationship with God and depicted people's inward suffering in quiet, evocative scenes.

JUDITH LEYSTER, *SELF-PORTRAIT*. **Although Judith Leyster was a well-known artist to her Dutch contemporaries, her fame diminished soon after her death. In the late nineteenth century, however, a Dutch art historian rediscovered her work. In her *Self-Portrait*, painted in 1635, she is seen pausing in her work in front of one of the scenes of daily life that made her such a popular artist in her own day.**

French Comedy: The Would-Be Gentleman

The comedy writer Jean-Baptiste Molière has long been regarded as one of the best playwrights of the age of Louis XIV. Molière's comedy, The Would-Be Gentleman, *focuses on Monsieur Jourdain, a vain and pretentious Parisian merchant who aspires to become a gentleman (at that time, a term for a member of the nobility who possessed, among other things, a title, fine clothes, and good taste). Jourdain foolishly believes that he can buy these things and hires a number of teachers to instruct him. In this scene from Act II, Jourdain learns from his philosophy teacher that he has been speaking prose all his life.*

Jean-Baptiste Molière, *The Would-Be Gentleman*

PHILOSOPHY MASTER: I will explain to you all these curiosities to the bottom.

M. JOURDAIN: Pray do. But now, I must commit a secret to you. I'm in love with a person of great quality, and I should be glad you would help me to write something to her in a short *billet-doux* [love letter], which I'll drop at her feet.

PHILOSOPHY MASTER: Very well.

M. JOURDAIN: That will be very gallant, won't it?

PHILOSOPHY MASTER: Without doubt. Is it verse that you would write to her?

M. JOURDAIN: No, no, none of your verse.

PHILOSOPHY MASTER: You would only have prose?

M. JOURDAIN: No, I would neither have verse nor prose.

PHILOSOPHY MASTER: It must be one or the other.

M. JOURDAIN: Why so?

PHILOSOPHY MASTER: Because, sir, there's nothing to express one's self by, but prose, or verse.

M. JOURDAIN: Is there nothing then but prose, or verse?

PHILOSOPHY MASTER: No, sir, whatever is not prose, is verse; and whatever is not verse, is prose.

M. JOURDAIN: And when one talks, what may that be then?

PHILOSOPHY MASTER: Prose.

M. JOURDAIN: How? When I say, Nicole, bring me my slippers, and give me my nightcap, is that prose?

PHILOSOPHY MASTER: Yes, sir.

M. JOURDAIN: On my conscience, I have spoken prose above these forty years without knowing anything of the matter; and I have all the obligations in the world to you for informing me of this. I would therefore put into a letter to her: Beautiful marchioness, your fair eyes make me die with love; but I would have this placed in a gallant manner; and have a gentle turn.

PHILOSOPHY MASTER: Why, add that the fire of her eyes has reduced your heart to ashes: that you suffer for her night and day all the torments—

M. JOURDAIN: No, no, no, I won't have all that—I'll have nothing but what I told you. Beautiful marchioness, your fair eyes make me die with love.

PHILOSOPHY MASTER: You must by all means lengthen the thing out a little.

M. JOURDAIN: No, I tell you, I'll have none but those very words in the letter: but turned in a modish way, ranged handsomely as they should be. I desire you'd show me a little, that I may see the different manners in which one may place them.

PHILOSOPHY MASTER: One may place them first of all as you said: Beautiful marchioness, your fair eyes make me die for love. Or suppose: For love die me make, beautiful marchioness, your fair eyes. Or perhaps: Your eyes fair, for love me make, beautiful marchioness, die. Or suppose: Die your fair eyes, beautiful marchioness, for love me make. Or however: Me make your eyes fair die, beautiful marchioness, for love.

M. JOURDAIN: But of all these ways, which is best?

PHILOSOPHY MASTER: That which you said: Beautiful marchioness, your fair eyes make me die for love.

M. JOURDAIN: Yet at the same time, I never studied it, and I made the whole of it at the first touch. I thank you with all my heart, and desire you would come in good time tomorrow.

PHILOSOPHY MASTER: I shall not fail.

The Theater: The Triumph of French Neoclassicism

As the great age of theater in England and Spain was drawing to a close around 1630, a new dramatic era began to dawn in France that lasted into the 1680s. Unlike Shakespeare in England and Lope de Vega in Spain, French playwrights wrote more for an elite audience and were forced to depend upon royal patronage. Louis XIV used theater as he did art and architecture—to attract attention to his monarchy.

French dramatists cultivated a classical style in which the Aristotelian rules of dramatic composition, observing the three unities of time, place, and action, were closely followed. French Neoclassicism emphasized the clever, polished, and correct over the emotional and imaginative. Many of the French works of the period derived both their themes and their plots from Greek and Roman sources, especially evident in the works of Jean-Baptiste Racine (1639–1699). In *Phédre,* which has been called his best play, Racine followed closely the plot of the Greek tragedian Euripides' *Hippolytus*. Like the ancient tragedians,

Racine, who perfected the French neoclassical tragic style, focused on conflicts, such as between love and honor or inclination and duty, that characterized and revealed the tragic dimensions of life.

Jean-Baptiste Molière (1622–1673) enjoyed the favor of the French court and benefited from the patronage of the Sun King. He wrote, produced, and acted in a series of comedies that often satirized the religious and social world of his time (see the box on p. 455). In *The Misanthrope,* he mocked the corruption of court society, while in *Tartuffe,* he ridiculed religious hypocrisy. Molière's satires, however, sometimes got him into trouble. The Paris clergy did not find *Tartuffe* funny and had it banned for five years. Only the protection of Louis XIV saved Molière from more severe harassment.

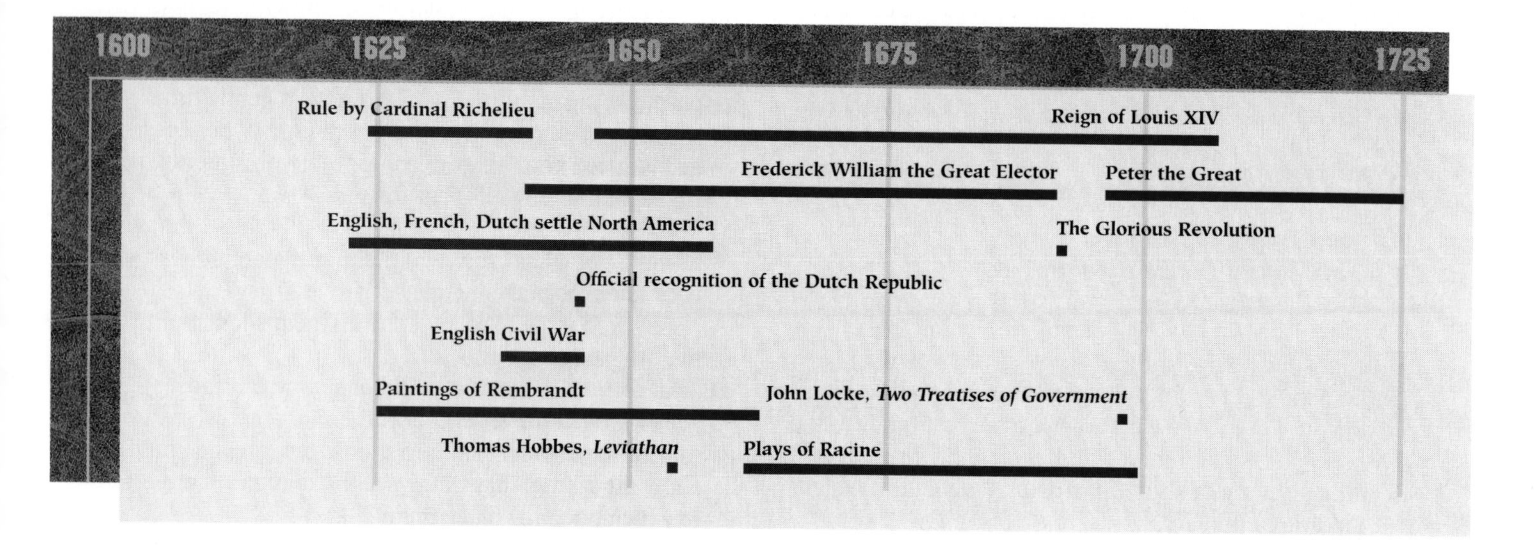

CONCLUSION

To many historians, the seventeenth century has assumed extraordinary proportions. The divisive effects of the Reformation had been assimilated and the concept of a united Christendom, held as an ideal since the Middle Ages, had been irrevocably destroyed by the religious wars, making possible the emergence of a system of nation-states in which power politics took on an increasing significance. The growth of political thought focusing on the secular origins of state power reflected the changes that were going on in seventeenth-century society.

Within those states, there slowly emerged some of the machinery that made possible a growing centralization of power. In those states called absolutist, strong monarchs with the assistance of their aristocracies took the lead in providing the leadership for greater centralization. But in England, where the landed aristocracy gained power at the expense of the monarchs, the foundations were laid for a constitutional government in which Parliament provided the focus for the institutions of centralized power. In all the major European states, a growing concern for power and dynastic expansion led to larger armies and greater conflict. War remained an endemic feature of Western civilization.

But the search for order and harmony continued, evident in art and literature. At the same time, though it would be misleading to state that Europe had become a secular world, we would have to say that religious preoccupations and values were losing ground to secular considerations. The seventeenth century was a transitional period to a more secular spirit that has characterized modern Western civilization until the present time. No stronger foundation for this spirit could be found than in the new view of the universe that was created by the Scientific Revolution of the seventeenth century, and it is to that story that we must now turn.

NOTES

1. Quoted in John B. Wolf, *Louis XIV* (New York, 1968), p. 134.
2. Quoted in James B. Collins, *The State in Early Modern France* (Cambridge, 1995), p. 130.
3. Quoted in W. H. Lewis, *The Splendid Century* (Garden City, N.Y., 1953), pp. 39–40.
4. Quoted in Wolf, *Louis XIV,* p. 284.
5. Quoted in ibid., p. 618.
6. Quoted in D. H. Pennington, *Europe in the Seventeenth Century,* 2d ed. (London and New York, 1989), p. 494.
7. Quoted in J. H. Elliott, *Imperial Spain, 1469–1716* (New York, 1963), p. 306.

8. Quoted in ibid., p. 338.
9. Quoted in Vasili Klyuchevsky, *Peter the Great,* trans. Liliana Archibald (New York, 1958), p. 244.
10. Quoted in B. H. Sumner, *Peter the Great and the Emergence of Russia* (New York, 1962), p. 122.
11. Quoted in Violet Barbour, *Capitalism in Amsterdam in the 17th Century* (Ann Arbor, Mich., 1963), p. 46.
12. Quoted in H. G. Koenigsberger, *Early Modern Europe: 1500–1798* (London, 1987), p. 172.

SUGGESTIONS FOR FURTHER READING

In addition to the general works listed in Chapter 14, see also D. H. Pennington, *Europe in the Seventeenth Century*, 2d ed. (London and New York, 1989); T. Munck, *Seventeenth Century Europe, 1598–1700* (London, 1990); and R. S. Dunn, *The Age of Religious Wars, 1559–1715*, 2d ed. (New York, 1979).

For brief accounts of seventeenth-century French history, see R. Briggs, *Early Modern France, 1560–1715* (Oxford, 1977); and J. B. Collins, *The State in Early Modern France* (Cambridge, 1995). More detailed studies on France during the periods of Cardinals Richelieu and Mazarin are R. Bonney, *Society and Government in France under Richelieu and Mazarin, 1624–1662* (London, 1985); and J. Bergin, *Cardinal Richelieu: Power and the Pursuit of Wealth* (London, 1985). A solid and very readable biography of Louis XIV is J. B. Wolf, *Louis XIV* (New York, 1968). For a brief study, see P. R. Campbell, *Louis XIV, 1661–1715* (London, 1993). Also of value are the works by O. Bernier, *Louis XIV* (New York, 1988); and P. Goubert, *Louis XIV and Twenty Million Frenchmen*, trans. A. Carter (New York, 1970). A now classic work on life in Louis XIV's France is W. H. Lewis, *The Splendid Century* (Garden City, N.Y., 1953). Well-presented summaries of revisionist views on Louis's monarchical power are R. Mettam, *Power and Faction in Louis XIV's France* (Oxford, 1988); and W. Beik, *Absolutism and Society in Seventeenth-Century France* (Cambridge, 1985). C. W. Cole, *Colbert and a Century of French Mercantilism*, 2 vols. (London, 1939), is still the fundamental study.

Good general works on seventeenth-century Spanish history include J. Lynch, *Spain under the Habsburgs*, 2d ed. (New York, 1981); and the relevant sections of J. H. Elliott, *Imperial Spain, 1469–1716* (New York, 1963; rev. ed. 1977). The important minister Olivares is examined in J. H. Elliott, *The Count-Duke of Olivares: The Statesman in an Age of Decline* (London, 1986).

An older, but still valuable survey of the German states in the seventeenth century can be found in H. Holborn, *A History of Modern Germany, 1648–1840* (London, 1965). An important recent work is M. Hughes, *Early Modern Germany, 1477–1806* (Philadelphia, 1992). On the creation of an Austrian state, see R. J. W. Evans, *The Making of the Habsburg Monarchy, 1550–1700* (Oxford, 1979); and C. Ingrao, *The Habsburg Monarchy, 1618–1815* (Cambridge, 1994). The older work by F. L. Carsten, *The Origins of Prussia* (Oxford, 1954), remains an outstanding study of early Prussian history. A good biography of the dynamic Charles XII is R. Hatton, *Charles XII of Sweden* (London, 1968). For an introduction to Polish history, see N. Davies, *God's Playground: A History of Poland,* vol. 1, *The Origins to 1795* (Oxford, 1981).

On Russian history before Peter the Great, see the classic work by V. O. Klyuchevsky, *A Course in Russian History: The Seventeenth Century* (Chicago, 1968). Works on Peter the Great include L. Hughes, *Russia in the Age of Peter the Great* (New Haven, Conn., 1998); M. S. Anderson, *Peter the Great,* 2d ed. (New York, 1995); and the massive popular biography by R. K. Massie, *Peter the Great* (New York, 1980).

Good general works on the period of the Revolution include M. A. Kishlansky, *A Monarchy Transformed* (London, 1996); G. E. Aylmer, *Rebellion or Revolution? England, 1640–1660* (New York, 1986); and A. Hughes, *The Causes of the English Civil War* (New York, 1991). On the war itself, see R. Ashton, *The English Civil War: Conservatism and Revolution, 1604–1649* (London, 1976). On Oliver Cromwell, see R. Howell, Jr., *Cromwell* (Boston, 1977); and P. Gaunt, *Oliver Cromwell* (Cambridge, Mass., 1996). For a general survey of the post-Cromwellian era, see J. R. Jones, *Country and Court: England, 1658–1714* (London, 1978). A more specialized study is W. A. Speck, *The Revolution of 1688* (Oxford, 1988). On Charles II, see the scholarly biography by R. Hutton, *Charles II* (Oxford, 1989). Locke's political ideas are examined in J. H. Franklin, *John Locke and the Theory of Sovereignty* (London, 1978). On Thomas Hobbes, see D. D. Raphael, *Hobbes* (London, 1977).

On the United Provinces, there is a valuable but very lengthy study by J. Israel, *The Dutch Republic: Its Rise, Greatness, and Fall* (New York, 1995). See also the short, but sound introduction by K. H. D. Haley, *The Dutch in the Seventeenth Century* (London, 1972). Of much value is S. Schama, *The Embarrassment of Riches: An Interpretation of Dutch Culture in the Golden Age* (New York, 1987).

On the economic side of the seventeenth century, there are the three volumes by F. Braudel, *Civilization and Capitalism in the 15th to 18th Century*, which obviously cover much more than just the seventeenth century: *The Structures of Everyday Life* (London, 1981); *The Wheels of Commerce* (London, 1982); and *The Perspective of the World* (London, 1984). Two single-volume comprehensive surveys are J. de Vries, *The Economy of Europe in an Age of Crisis* (Cambridge, 1976); and R. S. Duplessis, *Transitions to Capitalism in Early Modern Europe* (Cambridge, 1997). On overseas trade and colonial empires, see C. R. Boxer, *The Dutch Seaborne Empire, 1600–1800* (New York, 1965); and R. Davis, *English Overseas Trade, 1500–1700* (London, 1973). Although frequently criticized, the standard work on mercantilism remains E. Hecksher, *Mercantilism*, 2 vols. (London, 1935).

French theater and literature are examined in A. Adam, *Grandeur and Illusion: French Literature and Society, 1600–1715*, trans. J. Tint (New York, 1972). For an examination of French and Dutch art, see A. Merot, *French Painting in the Seventeenth Century* (New Haven, Conn., 1995); and S. Slive, *Dutch Painting, 1600–1800* (New Haven, Conn., 1993).

For additional reading, go to InfoTrac College Edition, your online research library at http://web1.infotrac-college.com

Enter the search terms *Louis XIV* using Key Terms.

Enter the search terms *Peter the Great* using Key Terms.

Enter the search terms *Oliver Cromwell* using Key Terms.

Enter the search term *mercantilism* using the Subject Guide.

CHAPTER

16

Toward a New Heaven and a New Earth: The Scientific Revolution and the Emergence of Modern Science

CHAPTER OUTLINE

- Background to the Scientific Revolution
- Toward a New Heaven: A Revolution in Astronomy
- Advances in Medicine
- Women in the Origins of Modern Science
- Toward a New Earth: Descartes, Rationalism, and a New View of Humankind
- The Scientific Method
- Science and Religion in the Seventeenth Century
- The Spread of Scientific Knowledge
- Conclusion

FOCUS QUESTIONS

- What developments during the Middle Ages and Renaissance contributed to the Scientific Revolution of the seventeenth century?
- What did Copernicus, Kepler, Galileo, and Newton contribute to a new vision of the universe, and how did it differ from the Ptolemaic conception of the universe?
- What role did women play in the Scientific Revolution?
- What problems did the Scientific Revolution present for organized religion, and how did both the church and the emerging scientists attempt to solve these problems?
- How were the ideas of the Scientific Revolution disseminated, and what impact did they have on society?

IN ADDITION to the political, economic, social, and international crises of the seventeenth century, we need to add an intellectual one. The Scientific Revolution questioned and ultimately challenged conceptions and beliefs about the nature of the external world and reality that had crystallized into a rather strict orthodoxy by the Late Middle Ages. Derived from the works of ancient Greeks and Romans and grounded in Christian thought, the medieval worldview had become a formidable one. No doubt, the breakdown of Christian unity during the Reformation and the subsequent religious wars had created an environment in which Europeans had become accustomed to challenging both the ecclesiastical and political realms. Should it surprise us that a challenge to intellectual authority soon followed?

The Scientific Revolution brought Europeans a new way of viewing the universe and their place in it. The shift from an earth-centered to a sun-centered cosmos had an emotional as well as an intellectual effect upon those who understood it. Thus, the Scientific Revolution, popularized in the eighteenth-century Enlightenment, stands as the major force in the transition to the largely secular, rational, and materialistic perspective that has defined the modern Western mentality since its full acceptance in the nineteenth and twentieth centuries.

The transition to a new worldview was not an easy one, however. In the seventeenth century, the Italian scientist Galileo, an outspoken advocate of the new worldview, found that his ideas were strongly opposed by the authorities of the Catholic church. Galileo's position was clear: "I hold the sun to be situated motionless in the center of the revolution of the celestial bodies, while the earth rotates on its axis and revolves about the sun." Moreover, "nothing physical that sense-experience sets before our eyes . . . ought to be called in question (much less condemned) upon the testimony of Biblical passages." But the church had a different view, and in 1633, Galileo, now sixty-eight and in ill health, was called before the dreaded Inquisition in Rome. He was kept waiting for two months before he was tried and found guilty of heresy and disobedience. Completely shattered by the experience, he denounced his errors: "With a sincere heart and unfeigned faith I curse and detest the said errors and heresies contrary to the Holy Church, and I swear that I will nevermore in future say or assert anything that may give rise to a similar suspicion of me." Legend holds that when he left the trial room, Galileo muttered to himself: "And yet it does move!" In any case, Galileo had been silenced, but his writings remained, and they began to spread through Europe. The Inquisition had failed to stop the spread of the new ideas of the Scientific Revolution.

In one sense, the Scientific Revolution was not a revolution. It was not characterized by the explosive change and rapid overthrow of traditional authority that we normally associate with the word revolution. *The Scientific Revolution did overturn centuries of authority, but only in a gradual and piecemeal fashion. Nevertheless, its results were truly revolutionary. The Scientific Revolution was a key factor in setting Western civilization along its modern secular and material path.*

◆ Background to the Scientific Revolution

To say that the Scientific Revolution brought about a dissolution of the medieval worldview is not to say that the Middle Ages was a period of scientific ignorance. Many educated Europeans took an intense interest in the world around them since it was, after all, "God's handiwork" and therefore an appropriate subject for study. Late medieval scholastic philosophers had advanced mathematical and physical thinking in many ways, but the subjection of these thinkers to a strict theological framework and their unquestioning reliance on a few ancient authorities, especially Aristotle and Galen, limited where they could go. Many "natural philosophers," as medieval scientists were called, preferred refined logical analysis to systematic observations of the natural world. A number of historians have argued, however, that some of the natural philosophers developed ideas that came to fruition in the seventeenth century. These historians have pointed out, for example, that Galileo's development of the science of mechanics was grounded upon the work of fourteenth-century scholastics. And yet, as other scholars have noted, there was still a great contrast between the "theoretical" approach of the scholastics and the "hands-on" experiments of Galileo that enabled him to make his case.

The historical debate over the issue of late medieval influence on the Scientific Revolution reminds us that historians have had a difficult time explaining the causes of the Scientific Revolution. They have pointed out, however, that a number of changes and advances in the fifteenth and sixteenth centuries may have played a major role in helping natural philosophers abandon their old views and develop new ones.

Whereas medieval scholars had made use of Aristotle, Galen, and Ptolemy in Latin translations to develop many of their positions in the fields of physics, medicine, and astronomy, the Renaissance humanists had mastered Greek as well as Latin and made available new works of Galen, Ptolemy, and Archimedes as well as Plato and the pre-Socratics. These writings made it apparent that even the unquestioned authorities of the Middle Ages, Aristotle and Galen, had been contradicted by other thinkers. The desire to discover which school of thought was correct stimulated new scientific work that sometimes led to a complete rejection of the classical authorities. We know that Copernicus, for example, founder of the heliocentric theory, had read in Plutarch (discovered by the Renaissance) that Philolaus and a number of other ancients had believed that it was the earth and not the sun that moved.

Renaissance artists have also been credited with making an impact on scientific study. Their desire to imitate nature led them to rely upon a close observation of nature. Their accurate renderings of rocks, plants, animals, and human anatomy established new standards for the study of natural phenomena. At the same time, the "scientific" study of the problems of perspective and correct anatomical proportions led to new insights. "No painter," one Renaissance artist declared, "can paint well without a thorough knowledge of geometry."[1] Renaissance artists were frequently called upon to be practicing mathematicians as well. Leonardo da Vinci devised "war machines" while Albrecht Dürer made designs for the fortifications of cities.

Although most of these artistic designs for technical innovations were not intended for actual use and remained on paper, mathematicians, military engineers, naval architects, and navigators were having to deal with such practical problems as how to navigate in unknown seas, how to compute the trajectories of cannonballs for more effective impact, and how to calculate the tonnage of ships accurately. These technical problems served to stimulate scientific activity because all of them required careful observation and accurate measurements. The fifteenth and sixteenth centuries witnessed a proliferation of books dedicated to machines and technology, all of which espoused the belief that innovation in techniques was necessary. The relationship between technology and the Scientific Revolution is not a simple one, however, for many technological experts did not believe in abstract or academic learning. Indeed, many of the technical innovations of the Middle Ages and Renaissance were accomplished outside the universities by people who emphasized practical rather than theoretical knowledge. In any case, the invention of new instruments and machines, such as the telescope and microscope, often made new scientific discoveries possible. Above all, the printing press had an indirect, but crucial role in spreading innovative ideas quickly and easily.

Mathematics, which played such a fundamental role in the scientific achievements of the sixteenth and seventeenth centuries, was promoted in the Renaissance by the rediscovery of the works of ancient mathematicians and the influence of Plato (see Chapter 12), who had emphasized the importance of mathematics in explaining the universe. While mathematics was applauded as the key to navigation, military science, and geography, the Renaissance also held the widespread belief that mathematics was the key to understanding the nature of things. According to Leonardo da Vinci, since God eternally geometrizes, nature is inherently mathematical: "Proportion is not only found in numbers and measurements but also in sounds, weights, times, positions, and in whatsoever power there may."[2] Moreover, mathematical reasoning was seen as promoting a degree of certainty that was otherwise impossible. In the words of Leonardo da Vinci: "There is no certainty where one can neither apply any of the mathematical sciences nor any of those which are based upon the mathematical sciences."[3] Copernicus, Kepler, Galileo, and Newton were all great mathematicians who believed that the secrets of nature were written in the language of mathematics.

A final factor in the origins of the Scientific Revolution, the role of magic, has been the object of heated scholarly debate. Renaissance magic (see Chapter 12) was the preserve of an intellectual elite from all of Europe (see the box on p. 463). By the end of the sixteenth century, Hermetic magic had become fused with alchemical thought into a single intellectual framework. According to this tradition, the world was a living embodiment of divinity. Humans, who it was believed also had that spark of divinity within, could use magic, especially mathematical magic, to understand and dominate the world of nature or employ the powers of nature for beneficial purposes. Was it Hermeticism, then, that inaugurated the shift in consciousness that made the Scientific Revolution possible, since the desire to control and dominate the natural world was a crucial motivating force in the Scientific Revolution? One scholar has argued:

> It is a movement of the will which really originates an intellectual movement. A new center of interest arises, surrounded by emotional excitement; the mind turns where the will has directed it and new attitudes, new discoveries follow. Behind the emergence of modern science there was a new direction of the will toward the world, its marvels, and mysterious workings, a new longing and determination to understand those workings and to operate with them.[4]

"This time," the author continues, "the return to the occult [Hermetic tradition] stimulates the genuine science."[5] Histories of the Scientific Revolution frequently overlook the fact that the great names we associate with the revolution in cosmology—Copernicus, Kepler, Galileo, and Newton—all had a serious interest in Hermetic ideas and the fields of astrology and alchemy. The mention of these names also reminds us of one final consideration in the origins of the Scientific Revolution: it largely resulted from the work of a handful of great intellectuals.

◆ Toward a New Heaven: A Revolution in Astronomy

The greatest achievements in the Scientific Revolution of the sixteenth and seventeenth centuries came in those fields most dominated by the ideas of the Greeks—astronomy, mechanics, and medicine. The cosmological views of the Late Middle Ages had been built upon a synthesis of the ideas of Aristotle, Claudius Ptolemy (the greatest astronomer of antiquity who lived in the second century A.D.), and Christian theology. In the resulting Ptolemaic or geocentric conception, the universe was seen as a series of concentric spheres with a fixed or motionless earth as its center. Composed of the material substances of earth, air, fire, and water, the earth was imperfect and constantly changing. The spheres that surrounded the earth were made of a crystalline, transparent substance and moved in circular orbits around the earth. Circular movement, according to Aristotle, was the most "perfect" kind of motion and hence appropriate for the "perfect" heavenly bodies thought to consist of a nonmaterial, incorruptible "quintessence." These heavenly bodies, pure orbs of light, were embedded in the moving, concentric spheres and in 1500 numbered ten. Working outward from the earth, eight spheres contained the moon, Mercury, Venus, the

Magic and Science: The Case of Girolamo Cardano

Girolamo Cardano or Jerome Cardan (1501–1576) was a very important figure in the history of mathematics. He also became a physician and professor of medicine at Pavia in 1547. Like many other intellectuals in the sixteenth century, Cardano was a student of magic and astrology. In this selection taken from his autobiography, The Book of My Life, *Cardano discusses the presence in his life of what we would call paranormal powers, including prescient dreams, extrasensory perception, and intuitive flashes of direct understanding.*

❊ Girolamo Cardano, *The Book of My Life*

I am conscious that some influence from without seems to bring a murmuring sound to my ear from precisely that direction or region where some one is discussing me. If this discussion be fair, the sound seems to come to rest on the right side; or, if perchance it approaches from the left, it penetrates to the right and becomes a steady hum. If, however, the talk be contentious, strangely conflicting sounds are heard; when evil is spoken, the noise rests in the left ear, and comes from the quarter exactly whence the voices of my detractors are making disturbance, and, accordingly, may approach from any side of my head. . . . Very often when the discussion about me has taken place in the same city, it has happened that the vibration has scarcely ceased before a messenger has appeared who addresses me in the name of my detractors. But if the conversation has taken place in another state and the messenger should appear, one has but to compute the space of time which had elapsed between the discussion and the beginning of the messenger's journey, and the moment I heard the voices and the time of the discussion itself will fall out the same. . . .

A few years later, eight perhaps, that is, about 1534, I began to see in my dreams the events shortly to come to pass. If these events were due to happen on the day following the dream, I used to have clear and defined visions of them just after sunrise, so that even on occasion I saw the motion for my admission to the College of Physicians straightway brought to vote, to a decision, and the motion lost. I dreamed, as well, that I was about to obtain my appointment to the professorship at Bologna. This manifestation by dreams ceased in the year just preceeding the cessation of the former manifestation, that is, about 1567. . . . And so it had lasted about thirty-three years.

A third peculiarity is an intuitive flash of direct knowledge. This I employed with gradually increasing advantage. It originated about the year 1529; its effectiveness was increased but it could never be rendered infallible, except toward the close of 1573. For a period between the end of August of that year and the beginning of September 1574, and particularly, as it seems to me, now in this year 1575, I have considered it infallible. It is, moreover, a gift which has not deserted me, and it replaces the power of those two latter faculties which did; it prepares me to meet my adversaries, and for any pressing necessity. Its component parts are an ingeniously exercised employment of the intuitive faculty, and an accompanying lucidity of understanding.

sun, Mars, Jupiter, Saturn, and the fixed stars. The ninth sphere imparted to the eighth sphere of the fixed stars its motion, and the tenth sphere was frequently described as the prime mover that moved itself and imparted motion to the other spheres. Beyond the tenth sphere was the Empyrean Heaven—the location of God and all the saved souls. This Christianized Ptolemaic universe, then, was a finite one. It had a fixed end in harmony with Christian thought and expectations.

This medieval, geocentric conception of the universe was one that accorded well with both Christianity and common sense at that time. God and the saved souls were at one end of the universe while humans were at the center. They had been given power over the earth, but their real purpose was to achieve salvation. To ordinary people, this conception of the universe also appeared sensible as they looked up at the night sky. The huge earth could easily be seen as motionless and surrounded by ethereal heavenly bodies circling around it.

This conception, however, did not satisfy professional astronomers who wished to ascertain the precise paths of the heavenly bodies across the sky. Finding that their observations did not always correspond to the accepted scheme, astronomers tried to "save appearances" by developing an elaborate system of devices. They proposed, for example, that the planetary bodies traveled on epicycles, concentric spheres within spheres, that would enable the paths of the planets to correspond more precisely to observations while adhering to Aristotle's ideas of circular planetary movement.

❊ Copernicus

Although Nicolaus Copernicus (1473–1543) received a doctorate in canon law and spent the last thirty years of his life as canon of a cathedral, mathematics and astronomy occupied most of his time. He had studied both subjects first at Cracow in his native Poland and later at the Italian universities of Bologna and Padua. Before he left Italy in 1506, he had become aware of ancient views that contradicted the Ptolemaic, earth-centered conception of the universe. Between 1506 and 1530, he completed the manuscript of his famous book, *On the Revolutions of the Heavenly Spheres*, but his own timidity and fear of ridicule from fellow astronomers kept him from publishing it until May 1543, shortly before his death.

Copernicus was not an accomplished observational astronomer and relied for his data on the records of his predecessors. But he was a mathematician who felt that Ptolemy's geocentric system was too complicated and failed to accord with the observed motions of the heavenly bodies (see the box on p. 466). Copernicus hoped that his heliocentric or sun-centered conception would offer a simpler, more accurate, and more elegant explanation for previously observed phenomena.

Using elaborate astronomical and mathematical calculations, Copernicus argued in his book that the universe consisted of eight spheres with the sun motionless at the center and the sphere of the fixed stars at rest in the eighth sphere. The planets revolved around the sun in the order of Mercury, Venus, the earth, Mars, Jupiter, and Saturn. The moon, however, revolved around the earth. Moreover, according to Copernicus, what appeared to be the movement of the sun and the fixed stars around the earth was really explained by the daily rotation of the earth on its axis and the journey of the earth around the sun each year.

Copernicus, however, was basically conservative. He did not reject Aristotle's principle of the existence of heavenly spheres moving in circular orbits. As a result, when he put forth the calculations to prove his new theory, he retained Ptolemy's epicycles and wound up with a system almost as complicated as that of the Alexandrian astronomer.

Nevertheless, the shift from an earth-centered to a sun-centered system was significant and raised serious questions about Aristotle's astronomy and physics despite Copernicus's own adherence to Aristotle. It also seemed to create uncertainty about the human role in the universe as well as God's location. Protestant reformers, adhering to a literal interpretation of Scripture, were the first to attack the new ideas. Martin Luther thundered against "the new astrologer who wants to prove that the earth moves and goes round. . . . The fool wants to turn the whole art of astronomy upside down. As Holy Scripture tells us, so did Joshua bid the sun stand still and not the earth." Luther's cohort at Wittenberg, Philip Melanchthon condemned Copernicus as well:

> The eyes are witness that the heavens revolve in the space of twenty-four hours. But certain men, either from the love of novelty, or to make a display of ingenuity, have concluded that the earth moves, and they maintain that neither the eighth sphere [of the fixed stars] nor the sun revolves. . . . Now it is a want of honesty and decency to assert such notions publicly, and the example is pernicious. It is the part of a good mind to accept the truth as revealed by God and to acquiesce in it.[6]

The Catholic church remained silent for the time being; it did not denounce Copernicus until the work of Galileo appeared. The denunciation came at a time when an increasing number of astronomers were being attracted to Copernicus's ideas.

MEDIEVAL CONCEPTION OF THE UNIVERSE. **As this sixteenth-century illustration shows, the medieval cosmological view placed the earth at the center of the universe, surrounded by a series of concentric spheres. The earth was imperfect and constantly changing, whereas the heavenly bodies that surrounded it were perfect and incorruptible. Beyond the tenth and final sphere was heaven where God and all the saved souls were located.**

Brahe and Kepler

Copernicus did not have a great impact immediately, however—no revolution occurred overnight. Nevertheless, although most people were not yet ready to accept the theory of Copernicus, doubts about the Ptolemaic system were growing. The next step in destroying the geocentric conception and supporting the Copernican system was taken by Johannes Kepler. It has been argued, however, that Kepler's work would not have occurred without the material provided by Tycho Brahe.

Although Tycho Brahe (1546–1601) advanced a new model of the solar system based on a compromise between Copernicus and Ptolemy—the sun and planets revolved around the earth while the other planets revolved around the sun—his real fame rests on a less spectacular contribution. A Danish nobleman, Brahe was granted possession of an island near Copenhagen by King Frederick II. Here Brahe built the elaborate Uraniborg castle, which he outfitted with a library, observatories, and instruments he had designed for more precise astronomical observations. For twenty years, Brahe patiently concentrated on compiling a detailed record of his observations of the positions and movements of the stars and planets, a series of observations that have been described as the most accurate up to that time. This body of data led him to reject the Aristotelian-Ptolemaic system, but at the same time he was unable to accept Copernicus's suggestion that the earth actually moved. Brahe's last years were spent in Prague as imperial mathematician to Emperor Rudolf II, who took a keen interest in astronomy, astrology, and the Hermetic tradition. While he was in Prague, Brahe took on an assistant by the name of Johannes Kepler.

Johannes Kepler (1571–1630) had been destined by his parents for a career as a Lutheran minister. While studying theology at the university at Tübingen, however, he fell under the influence of Michael Mästlin, Germany's best-known astronomer, and spent much time pursuing his real interests, mathematics and astronomy. He abandoned theology and became a teacher of mathematics and astronomy at Graz in Austria.

Kepler's work illustrates well the narrow line that often separated magic and science in the early Scientific Revolution. An avid astrologer, Kepler possessed a keen interest in Hermetic thought and Neoplatonic mathematical magic. In a book written in 1596, he elaborated upon his theory that the universe was constructed on the basis of geometric figures, such as the pyramid and the cube (see the box on p. 467). Believing that the harmony of the human soul (a divine attribute) was mirrored in the numerical relationships existing between the planets, he focused much of his attention upon discovering the "music of the spheres." Kepler was also a brilliant mathematician and astronomer and, after Brahe's death, succeeded him as imperial mathematician to Rudolf II. There he gained possession of Brahe's detailed astronomical data and, using them, arrived at his three laws of planetary motion. These laws may have confirmed Kepler's interest in the "music

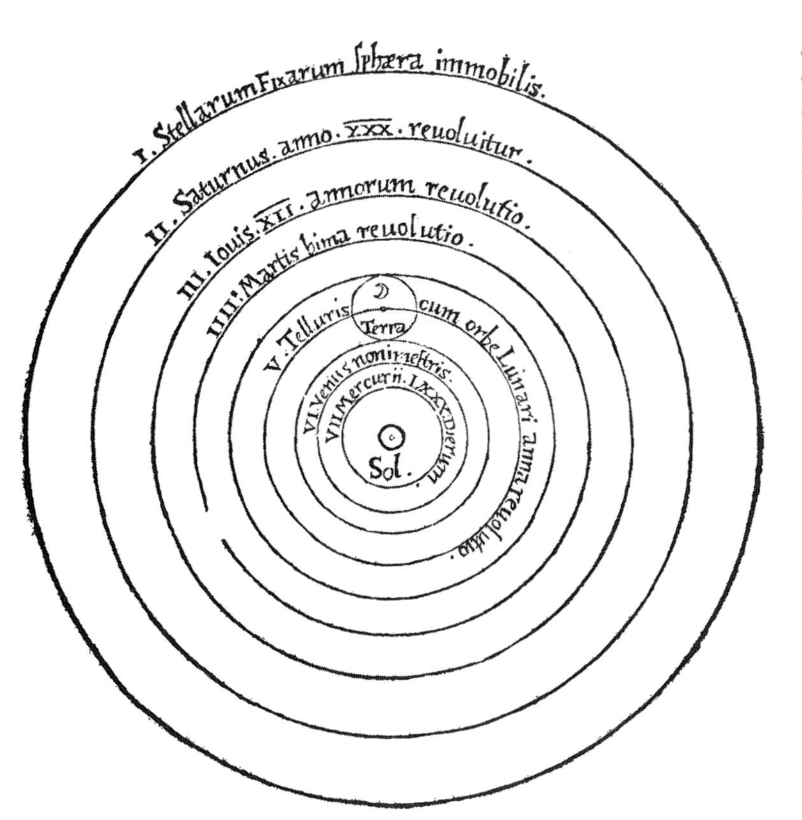

THE COPERNICAN SYSTEM. **The Copernican system was presented in *On the Revolutions of the Heavenly Spheres*, published shortly before Copernicus's death. As shown in this illustration from the first edition of the book, Copernicus maintained that the sun was the center of the universe and that the planets, including the earth, revolved around it. Moreover, the earth rotated daily on its axis.**

On the Revolutions of the Heavenly Spheres

Nicolaus Copernicus began a revolution in astronomy when he argued that it was the sun and not the earth that was at the center of the universe. Expecting controversy and scorn, Copernicus hesitated to publish the work in which he put forth his heliocentric theory. He finally relented, however, and managed to see a copy of it just before he died.

Nicolaus Copernicus, *On the Revolutions of the Heavenly Spheres*

For a long time, then, I reflected on this confusion in the astronomical traditions concerning the derivation of the motions of the universe's spheres. I began to be annoyed that the movements of the world machine, created for our sake by the best and most systematic Artisan of all, were not understood with greater certainty by the philosophers, who otherwise examined so precisely the most insignificant trifles of this world. For this reason I undertook the task of rereading the works of all the philosophers which I could obtain to learn whether anyone had ever proposed other motions of the universe's spheres than those expounded by the teachers of astronomy in the schools. And in fact first I found in Cicero that Hicetas supposed the earth to move. Later I also discovered in Plutarch that certain others were of this opinion. I have decided to set his words down here, so that they may be available to everybody:

> Some think that the earth remains at rest. But Philolaus the Pythagorean believes that, like the sun and moon, it revolves around the fire in an oblique circle. Heraclides of Pontus and Ecphantus the Pythagorean make the earth move, not in a progressive motion, but like a wheel in a rotation from the west to east about its own center.

Therefore, having obtained the opportunity from these sources, I too began to consider the mobility of the earth. And even though the idea seemed absurd, nevertheless I knew that others before me had been granted the freedom to imagine any circles whatever for the purpose of explaining the heavenly phenomena. Hence I thought that I too would be readily permitted to ascertain whether explanations sounder than those of my predecessors could be found for the revolution of the celestial spheres on the assumption of some motion of the earth.

Having thus assumed the motions which I ascribe to the earth later on in the volume, by long and intense study I finally found that if the motions of the other planets are correlated with the orbiting of the earth, and are computed for the revolution of each planet, not only do their phenomena follow therefrom but also the order and size of all the planets and spheres, and heaven itself is so linked together that in no portion of it can anything be shifted without disrupting the remaining parts and the universe as a whole. . . .

Hence I feel no shame in asserting that this whole region engirdled by the moon, and the center of the earth, traverse this grand circle amid the rest of the planets in an annual revolution around the sun. Near the sun is the center of the universe. Moreover, since the sun remains stationary, whatever appears as a motion of the sun is really due rather to the motion of the earth.

of the spheres," but more importantly, they confirmed Copernicus's heliocentric theory while modifying it in some ways. Above all, they drove another nail into the coffin of the Aristotelian-Ptolemaic system.

Kepler published his first two laws of planetary motion in 1609. Although at Tübingen he had accepted Copernicus's heliocentric ideas, in his first law he rejected Copernicus by showing that the orbits of the planets around the sun were not circular but elliptical in shape with the sun at one focus of the ellipse rather than at the center. In his second law, he demonstrated that the speed of a planet is greater when it is closer to the sun and decreases as its distance from the sun increases. This proposition destroyed a fundamental Aristotelian tenet that Copernicus had shared—that the motion of the planets was steady and unchanging. Published ten years later, Kepler's third law established that the square of a planet's period of revolution is proportional to the cube of its average distance from the sun. In other words, planets with larger orbits revolve at a slower average velocity than those with smaller orbits.

Kepler's three laws effectively eliminated the idea of uniform circular motion as well as the idea of crystalline spheres revolving in circular orbits. The basic structure of the traditional Ptolemaic system had been disproved, and people had been freed to think in new terms of the actual paths of planets revolving around the sun in elliptical orbits. By the end of Kepler's life, the Ptolemaic system was rapidly losing ground to the new ideas. Important questions remained unanswered, however: What were the planets made of? And how does one explain motion in the universe? It was an Italian scientist who achieved the next important breakthrough to a new cosmology by answering the first question and making important strides toward answering the second.

Galileo

Galileo Galilei (1564–1642) came from a lesser noble Pisan family. Knowing that his son was obviously gifted, his father encouraged him to study medicine, which at that time was a financially rewarding career. Before long Galileo abandoned medicine for his true love, mathe-

Kepler and the Emerging Scientific Community

The exchange of letters between intellectuals was an important avenue for scientific communication. Through letters, they could provide practical assistance to each other as well as offer encouragement when their innovative work was received negatively. After receiving a copy of Johannes Kepler's first major work, the Italian Galileo Galilei wrote to Kepler, inaugurating a correspondence between them. This selection contains samples of their letters to each other as well as Kepler's letter to his teacher at Tübingen.

Galileo to Kepler, Padua, August 4, 1597

Your book, highly learned gentleman, which you sent me through Paulus Amberger, reached me not days ago but only a few hours ago, and as this Paulus just informed me of his return to Germany, I should think myself indeed ungrateful if I should not express to you my thanks by this letter. I thank you especially for having deemed me worthy of such a proof of your friendship. . . . So far I have read only the introduction, but have learned from it in some measure your intentions and congratulate myself on the good fortune of having found such a man as a companion in the exploration of truth. For it is deplorable that there are so few who seek the truth and do not pursue a wrong method of philosophizing. But this is not the place to mourn about the misery of our century but to rejoice with you about such beautiful ideas proving the truth. . . . I would certainly dare to approach the public with my ways of thinking if there were more people of your mind. As this is not the case, I shall refrain from doing so. . . . I shall always be at your service. Farewell, and do not neglect to give me further good news of yourself.

Yours in sincere friendship,
Galilaeus Galilaeus
Mathematician at the Academy of Padua

Kepler to Michael Mästlin, Graz, September 1597

. . . Lately I have sent two copies of my little book to Italy. They were received with gladness by a mathematician named Galileo Galilei, as he signs himself. He has also been attached for many years to the Copernican heresy.

Kepler to Galileo, Graz, October 13, 1597

I received your letter of August 4 on September 1. It was a double pleasure to me. First because I became friends with you, the Italian, and second because of the agreement in which we find ourselves concerning Copernican cosmography. As you invite me kindly at the end of your letter to enter into correspondence with you, and I myself feel greatly tempted to do so, I will not let pass the occasion of sending you a letter with the present young nobleman. For I am sure, if your time has allowed it, you have meanwhile obtained a closer knowledge of my book. And so a great desire has taken hold of me, to learn your judgment. For this is my way, to urge all those to whom I have written to express their candid opinion. Believe me, the sharpest criticism of one single understanding man means much more to me than the thoughtless applause of the great masses.

I would, however, have wished that you who have such a keen insight into everything would choose another way to reach your practical aims. By the strength of your personal example you advise us, in a cleverly veiled manner, to go out of the way of general ignorance and warn us against exposing ourselves to the furious attacks of the scholarly crowd. (In this you are following the lead of Plato and Pythagoras, our true masters.) But after the beginning of a tremendous enterprise has been made in our time, and furthered by so many learned mathematicians, and after the statement that the earth moves can no longer be regarded as something new, would it not be better to pull the rolling wagon to its destination with united effort. . . . For it is not only you Italians who do not believe that they move unless they feel it, but we in Germany, too, in no way make ourselves popular with this idea. Yet there are ways in which we protect ourselves against these difficulties. . . . Be of good cheer, Galileo, and appear in public. If I am not mistaken there are only a few among the distinguished mathematicians of Europe who would dissociate themselves from us. So great is the power of truth. If Italy seems less suitable for your publication and if you have to expect difficulties there, perhaps Germany will offer us more freedom. But enough of this. Please let me know, at least privately if you do not want to do so publicly, what you have discovered in favor of Copernicus.

matics, and was soon teaching this subject, first at Pisa and later at Padua, one of the most prestigious universities in Europe.

Galileo was the first European to make systematic observations of the heavens by means of a telescope, thereby inaugurating a new age in astronomy. He had heard of a Flemish lens grinder who had created a "spyglass" that magnified objects seen at a distance and soon constructed his own after reading about it. Instead of peering at terrestrial objects, Galileo turned his telescope to the skies and made a remarkable series of discoveries: mountains and craters on the moon, four moons revolving around Jupiter, the phases of Venus, and sunspots. Galileo's observations seemed to destroy yet another

JOHANNES KEPLER. Abandoning theology in favor of mathematics and astrology, Kepler was a key figure in the rise of the new astronomy. Building upon Tycho Brahe's vast astronomical data, Kepler discovered the three laws of planetary motion that both confirmed and modified the Copernican theory. They also eliminated the Ptolemaic-Aristotelian ideas of uniform circular motion and crystalline spheres moving in circular orbits.

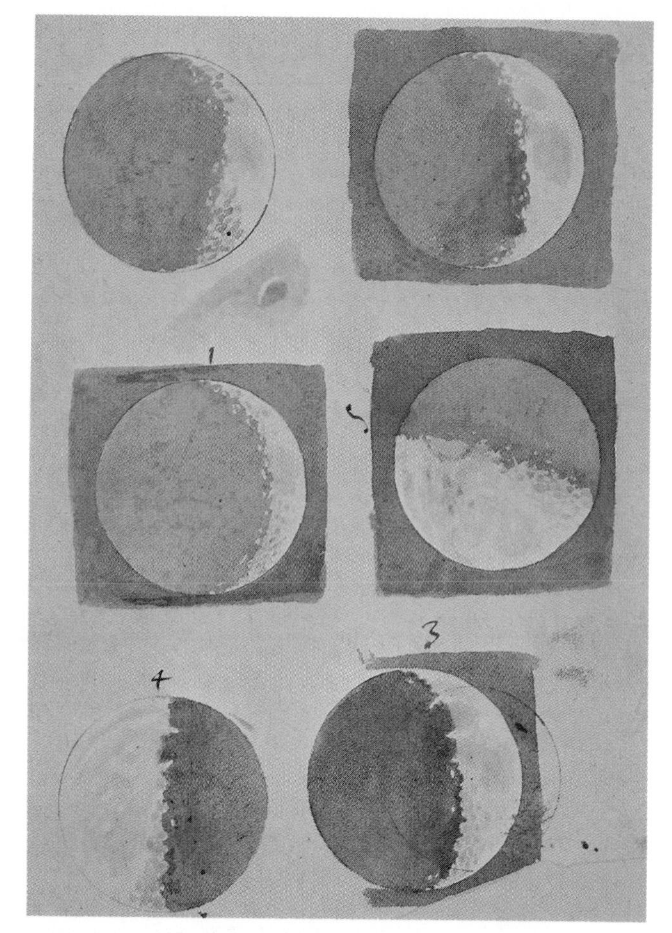

GALILEO'S SKETCH OF THE PHASES OF THE MOON. Galileo Galilei was the first European scientist to use a telescope in making systematic observations of the heavens. Galileo discovered mountains on the moon, sunspots, and the phases of Venus. Shown here are drawings of the moon from Galileo's notes for one of his books.

aspect of the traditional cosmology in that the universe seemed to be composed of material substance similar to that of the earth rather than ethereal or perfect and unchanging substance.

Galileo's revelations, published in *The Starry Messenger* in 1610, stunned his contemporaries and probably did more to make Europeans aware of the new picture of the universe than the mathematical theories of Copernicus and Kepler (see the box on p. 469). The English ambassador in Venice wrote to the chief minister of King James I in 1610:

> I send herewith unto His Majesty the strangest piece of news . . . that he has ever yet received from any part of the world; which is the annexed book of the Mathematical Professor at Padua [Galileo], who by the help of an optical instrument . . . has discovered four new planets rolling about the sphere of Jupiter. . . . So upon the whole subject he has first overthrown all former astronomy. . . . By the next ship your Lordship shall receive from me one of the above instruments [a telescope], as it is bettered by this man.[7]

During a trip to Rome, Galileo was received by cardinals and scholars as a conquering hero. Grand Duke Cosimo II of Florence offered him a new position as his court mathematician, which Galileo readily accepted. But even in the midst of his newfound acclaim, Galileo found himself increasingly suspect by the authorities of the Catholic church.

In *The Starry Messenger,* Galileo had revealed himself as a firm proponent of Copernicus's heliocentric system. Encouraged by the Dominicans, who held strongly to Aristotelian ideas, and the Jesuits, who feared that any dissension would weaken Catholicism in its struggle with Protestantism, the Roman Inquisition (or Holy Office) of the Catholic church condemned Copernicanism and ordered Galileo to reject the Copernican thesis. As one cardinal commented, "the intention of the Holy Spirit is to teach us not how the heavens go, but how to go to heaven." The report of the Inquisition ran: "That the doctrine that the sun was the center of the world and immovable was false and absurd, formally heretical and contrary

The Starry Messenger

The Italian Galileo Galilei was the first European to use a telescope to make systematic observations of the heavens. His observations, as reported in The Starry Messenger *in 1610, stunned European intellectuals by revealing that the celestial bodies were not perfect and immutable, as had been believed, but were apparently composed of material substance similar to the earth. In this selection, Galileo describes how he devised a telescope and what he saw with it.*

Galileo Galilei, *The Starry Messenger*

About ten months ago a report reached my ears that a certain Fleming had constructed a spyglass by means of which visible objects, though very distant from the eye of the observer, were distinctly seen as if nearby. Of this truly remarkable effect several experiences were related, to which some persons gave credence while others denied them. A few days later the report was confirmed to me in a letter from a noble Frenchman at Paris, Jacques Badovere, which caused me to apply myself wholeheartedly to inquire into the means by which I might arrive at the invention of a similar instrument. This I did shortly afterwards, my basis being the theory of refraction. First I prepared a tube of lead, at the ends of which I fitted two glass lenses, both plane on one side while on the other side one was spherically convex and the other concave. Then placing my eye near the concave lens I perceived objects satisfactorily large and near, for they appeared three times closer and nine times larger than when seen with the naked eye alone. Next I constructed another one, more accurate, which represented objects as enlarged more than sixty times. Finally, sparing neither labor nor expense, I succeeded in constructing for myself so excellent an instrument that objects seen by means of it appeared nearly one thousand times larger and over thirty times closer than when regarded without natural vision.

It would be superfluous to enumerate the number and importance of the advantages of such an instrument at sea as well as on land. But forsaking terrestrial observations, I turned to celestial ones, and first I saw the moon from as near at hand as if it were scarcely two terrestrial radii. After that I observed often with wondering delight both the planets and the fixed stars, and since I saw these latter to be very crowded, I began to seek (and eventually found) a method by which I might measure their distances apart. . . .

Now let us review the observations made during the past two months, once more inviting the attention of all who are eager for true philosophy to the first steps of such important contemplations. Let us speak first of that surface of the moon which faces us. For greater clarity I distinguish two parts of this surface, a lighter and a darker; the lighter part seems to surround and to pervade the whole hemisphere, while the darker part discolors the moon's surface like a kind of cloud, and makes it appear covered with spots. . . . From observation of these spots repeated many times I have been led to the opinion and conviction that the surface of the moon is not smooth, uniform, and precisely spherical as a great number of philosophers believe it (and the other heavenly bodies) to be, but is uneven, rough, and full of cavities and prominences, being not unlike the face of the earth, relieved by chains of mountains and deep valleys.

---

to Scripture, whereas the doctrine that the earth was not the center of the world but moved, and has further a daily motion, was philosophically false and absurd and theologically at least erroneous."[8] Galileo was told, however, that he could continue to discuss Copernicanism as long as he maintained that it was not a fact but a mathematical supposition. It is apparent from the Inquisition's response that the church attacked the Copernican system because it threatened not only Scripture, but also an entire conception of the universe. The heavens were no longer a spiritual world, but a world of matter. Humans were no longer at the center and God was no longer in a specific place. The new system raised such uncertainties that it seemed prudent simply to condemn it.

Galileo, however, never really accepted his condemnation. In 1632, he published his most famous work, *Dialogue on the Two Chief World Systems: Ptolemaic and Copernican.* Unlike most scholarly treatises, it was written in Italian rather than Latin, making it more widely available to the public, which no doubt alarmed the church authorities. The work took the form of a dialogue among Simplicio, a congenial but somewhat stupid supporter of Aristotle and Ptolemy; Sagredo, an open-minded layman; and Salviati, a proponent of Copernicus's ideas. There is no question who wins the argument, and the *Dialogue* was quickly perceived as a defense of the Copernican system. Galileo was dragged once more before the Inquisition in 1633, found guilty of teaching the condemned Copernican system, and forced to recant his errors. Placed under house arrest on his estate near Florence, he spent the remaining eight years of his life studying mechanics, a field in which he made significant contributions.

One of the problems that fell under the heading of mechanics was the principle of motion. The Aristotelian conception, which dominated the late medieval world, held that an object remained at rest unless a force was applied against it. If a force was constantly exerted, then the object moved at a constant rate, but if it was removed, then the object stopped. This conception encountered some difficulties, especially with a projectile thrown out of a cannon. Late medieval theorists had solved this problem by arguing that the rush of air behind the projectile kept it in motion. The Aristotelian principle of motion also raised problems in the new Copernican system. In the Ptolemaic system, the concentric spheres surrounding the earth were weightless, but in the Copernican system, if a constant force had to be applied to objects to cause movement, then what power or force kept the heavy earth and other planets in motion?

Galileo made two contributions to the problem of motion. First, he demonstrated by experiments that if a uniform force was applied to an object, it would move at an accelerated speed rather than a constant speed. Moreover, Galileo discovered the principle of inertia when he argued that a body in motion continues in motion forever unless deflected by an external force. Thus, a state of uniform motion is just as natural as a state of rest. Before Galileo, natural philosophers had tried to explain motion; now their task was to explain changes in motion. Historians agree that Galileo's work on inertia was important, but differ on whether his work was merely the culmination of the medieval tradition or pointed the way to Newton's law of dynamics.

The condemnation of Galileo by the Inquisition seriously hampered further scientific work in Italy, which had been at the forefront of scientific innovation. Leadership in science now passed to the northern countries, especially England, France, and the Dutch Netherlands. By the 1630s and 1640s, no reasonable astronomer could deny that Galileo's discoveries combined with Kepler's mathematical laws had made nonsense of the Ptolemaic-Aristotelian world system and clearly established the reasonableness of the Copernican model. Despite Galileo's theories of dynamics, the problem of explaining motion in the universe and tying together the ideas of Copernicus, Galileo, and Kepler had not yet been done. This would be the work of an Englishman who has long been considered the greatest genius of the Scientific Revolution.

ISAAC NEWTON. **Pictured here is a portrait of Isaac Newton by Sir Godfrey Kneller. With a single law, that of universal gravitation, Newton was able to explain all motion in the universe. His great synthesis of the work of his predecessors created a new picture of the universe, one in which the universe was viewed as a great machine operating according to natural laws.**

Newton

Born in the little English village of Woolsthorpe in 1642, the young Isaac Newton showed little brilliance until he attended Cambridge University and fell under the influence of the mathematician Isaac Barrow. Newton experienced his first great burst of creative energy in 1666 when the fear of plague closed Cambridge and forced him to return to Woolsthorpe for eighteen months. There Newton discovered his creative talents: "In those days I was in the prime of my life for invention and minded mathematics and philosophy more than at any time since."[9] During this period he invented the calculus, a mathematical means of calculating rates of change, began his investigations into the composition of light, and inaugurated his work on the law of universal gravitation. Two years after his return to Cambridge, in 1669, he accepted a chair of mathematics at the university. During a second intense period of creativity from 1684 to 1686, he wrote his famous *Principia* (see the box on p. 471). After a nervous breakdown in 1693, he sought and received an administrative post as warden of the royal mint and was advanced to master of the mint by 1699, a post he held until his death in 1727. Made president of the Royal Society (see The Scientific Societies later in this chapter) in 1703 and knighted in 1705 for his great achievements, Sir Isaac Newton wound up the only English scientist to be buried in Westminster Abbey.

Although Isaac Newton occupies a very special place in the history of modern science, we need to remember that he, too, remained extremely interested in aspects of the occult world. He left behind hundreds of manuscript pages of his studies of alchemy, and, in fact, his alchemical experiments were a major feature of his life until he moved to London in 1696 to become warden of the royal mint. The British economist John Maynard Keynes said of Newton after examining his manuscripts in 1936:

> Newton was not the first of the age of reason. He was the last of the magicians. . . . He looked on the whole universe and all that is in it as a riddle, as a secret which could be read by applying pure thought to certain evidence, certain mystic clues which God had laid about the world to allow a sort of philosopher's treasure hunt to the esoteric brotherhood. He believed that these clues were to be found partly in the evidence of the heavens and in the constitution of

Newton's Rules of Reasoning

In 1687, Isaac Newton published his masterpiece, the Mathematical Principles of Natural Philosophy. *In this work, Newton demonstrated the mathematical proofs for his universal law of gravitation and completed the new cosmology begun by Copernicus, Kepler, and Galileo. Newton's work demonstrated that the universe was one huge, regulated, and uniform machine operating according to natural laws. He also described the rules of reasoning by which he arrived at his universal law.*

Isaac Newton, *Rules of Reasoning in Philosophy*

Rule 1

We are to admit no more causes of natural things than such as are both true and sufficient to explain their appearances.

To this purpose the philosophers say that Nature does nothing in vain, and more is in vain when less will serve; for Nature is pleased with simplicity, and affects not the pomp of superfluous causes.

Rule 2

Therefore to the same natural effects we must, as far as possible, assign the same causes.

As to respiration in a man and in a beast; the descent of stones in Europe and in America; the light of our culinary fire and of the sun; the reflection of light in the earth, and in the planets.

Rule 3

The qualities of bodies, which admit neither intensification nor remission of degrees, and which are found to belong to all bodies within the reach of our experiments, are to be esteemed the universal qualities of all bodies whatsoever.

For since qualities of bodies are only known to us by experiments, we are to hold for universal all such as universally agree with experiments; and such as are not liable to diminution can never be quite taken away.

Rule 4

In experimental philosophy we are to look upon propositions inferred by general induction from phenomena as accurately or very nearly true, notwithstanding any contrary hypotheses that may be imagined, till such time as other phenomena occur, by which they may either be made more accurate, or liable to exceptions.

This rule we must follow, that the argument of induction may not be evaded by hypotheses.

> elements, . . . but also partly in certain papers and traditions handed down by the brethren in an unknown chain back to the original cryptic revelation in Babylonia.[10]

Although Newton may have considered himself a representative of the Hermetic tradition, he chose, it has been recently argued, for both political and psychological reasons to repress that part of his being, and it is as the "symbol of Western science" that Newton came to be viewed.

Newton's major work, the "hinge point of modern scientific thought," was his *Mathematical Principles of Natural Philosophy,* known simply as the *Principia* by the first word of its Latin title. In this work, the last, highly influential book in Europe to be written in Latin, Newton spelled out the mathematical proofs demonstrating his universal law of gravitation. Newton's work was the culmination of the theories of Copernicus, Kepler, and Galileo. Though each had undermined some part of the Ptolemaic-Aristotelian cosmology, until Newton no one had pieced together a coherent synthesis for a new cosmology.

In the first book of the *Principia,* Newton defined the basic concepts of mechanics by elaborating the three laws of motion: every object continues in a state of rest or uniform motion in a straight line unless deflected by a force; the rate of change of motion of an object is proportional to the force acting upon it; and to every action there is always an equal and opposite reaction. In Book Three, Newton applied his theories of mechanics to the problems of astronomy by demonstrating that these three laws of motion govern the planetary bodies as well as terrestrial objects. Integral to his whole argument was the universal law of gravitation, which explained why the planetary bodies did not go off in straight lines but continued in elliptical orbits about the sun. In mathematical terms, Newton explained that every object in the universe was attracted to every other object with a force (that is, gravity) that is directly proportional to the product of their masses and inversely proportional to the square of the distances between them.

The implications of Newton's universal law of gravitation were enormous, even though it took another century before they were widely recognized. Newton had demonstrated that one universal law mathematically proved could explain all motion in the universe, from the movements of the planets in the celestial world to an apple falling from a tree in the terrestrial world. The secrets of the natural world could be known by human investigations. At the same time, the Newtonian synthesis created a new cosmology in which the world was seen largely in mechanistic terms. The universe was one huge, regulated,

CHRONOLOGY

Important Works of the Scientific Revolution

Copernicus, *On the Revolutions of the Heavenly Spheres*	1543
Vesalius, *On the Fabric of the Human Body*	1543
Galileo, *The Starry Messenger*	1610
Harvey, *On the Motion of the Heart and Blood*	1628
Galileo, *Dialogue on the Two Chief World Systems*	1632
Cavendish, *Grounds of Natural Philosophy*	1668
Newton, *Principia*	1687

and uniform machine that operated according to natural laws in absolute time, space, and motion. Although Newton believed that God was "everywhere present" and acted as the force that moved all bodies on the basis of the laws he had discovered, later generations dropped his spiritual assumptions. Newton's world-machine, conceived as operating absolutely in time, space, and motion, dominated the Western worldview until the twentieth century, when the Einsteinian revolution based on a concept of relativity superseded the Newtonian mechanistic concept.

Newton's ideas were soon accepted in England, possibly out of national pride and conviction and, as has been argued recently, for political reasons (see Science and Society later in this chapter). Natural philosophers on the continent resisted Newton's ideas, and it took much of the eighteenth century before they were generally accepted everywhere in Europe. They were also reinforced by developments in other fields, especially medicine.

◆ Advances in Medicine

Although the Scientific Revolution of the sixteenth and seventeenth centuries is associated primarily with the dramatic changes in astronomy and mechanics that precipitated a new perception of the universe, a third field that had been dominated by Greek thought in the Late Middle Ages, that of medicine, also experienced a transformation. Late medieval medicine was dominated not by the teachings of Aristotle, but by those of the Greek physician Galen who had lived in the second century A.D.

Galen's influence on the medieval medical world was pervasive in anatomy, physiology, and disease. Galen had relied on animal, rather than human, dissection to arrive at a picture of human anatomy that was quite inaccurate in many instances. Even when Europeans began to practice human dissection in the Late Middle Ages, instruction in anatomy still relied on Galen. While a professor read a text of Galen, an assistant dissected a cadaver for illustrative purposes. Physiology, or the functioning of the body, was also dominated by Galenic hypotheses, including the belief that there were two separate blood systems. One controlled muscular activities and contained bright red blood moving upward and downward through the arteries; the other governed the digestive functions and contained dark red blood that ebbed and flowed in the veins.

Treatment of disease was highly influenced by Galen's doctrine of four bodily humors: blood, considered warm and moist; yellow bile, warm and dry; phlegm, cold and moist; and black bile, cold and dry. Since disease was supposedly the result of an imbalance of humors that could be discerned from the quantity and color of urine, the examination of a patient's urine became the chief diagnostic tool. Although purging and bleeding to remedy the imbalance were often harmful to patients, treatment with traditional herbal medicines sometimes proved beneficial.

Three figures are associated with the changes in medicine in the sixteenth and seventeenth centuries: Paracelsus, Andreas Vesalius, and William Harvey. Philippus Aureolus von Hohenheim (1493–1541), who renamed himself Paracelsus (or greater than Celsus, the ancient physician), was born in a small town near Zürich, the son of a country physician who dabbled in astrology. After leaving home at the age of fourteen, Paracelsus traveled widely and may have been awarded a medical degree from the University of Ferrara. He achieved a moment of glory when he was appointed city physician and professor of medicine at Basel in 1527. But this, like so many other appointments, proved short-lived due to his vanity, cantankerous nature, and quick temper. He could never disguise his contempt for universities and physicians who did not agree with his new ideas:

> I am *monarcha medicorum*, monarch of physicians, and I can prove to you what you cannot prove. . . . It was not the constellations that made me a physician: God made me . . . I need not don a coat of mail or a buckler against you, for you are not learned or experienced enough to refute even one word of mine. I wish I could protect my bald head against the flies as effectively as I can defend my monarchy. . . . Let me tell you this: every little hair on my neck knows more than you and all your scribes, and my shoebuckles are more learned than your Galen and Avicenna, and my beard has more experience than all your high colleges.[11]

Paracelsus was not easy to get along with, and he was forced to wander from one town to another until his death in 1541.

Paracelsus rejected the work of both Aristotle and Galen and attacked the universities as centers of their moribund philosophy. He and his followers hoped to replace the traditional system with a new chemical philosophy that was based upon a new understanding of nature derived from fresh observation and experiment. This chemical philosophy was, in turn, closely connected to a view of the universe based on the macrocosm-microcosm analogy. According to this view, a human being was a small replica (microcosm) of the larger world (macrocosm) about him. All parts of the universe were represented within each person. As Paracelsus said: "For the sun and the moon and all planets, as well as the stars and the whole chaos, are in man. . . . For what is outside is also inside; and what is not outside man is not inside. The outer and the inner are one thing."[12] In accordance with the macrocosmic-microcosmic principle, Paracelsus believed that the chemical reactions of the universe as a whole were reproduced in human beings on a smaller scale. Disease, then, was not caused by an imbalance of the four humors (as Galen had argued), but was due to chemical imbalances that were localized in specific organs and could be treated by chemical remedies.

Although others had used chemical remedies, Paracelsus and his followers differed from them in giving careful attention to the proper dosage of their chemically prepared metals and minerals. Gauging the proper amount was especially important because Paracelsus had turned against the Galenic principle that "contraries cure" in favor of the ancient Germanic folk principle that "like cures like." The poison that caused a disease would be its cure if used in proper form and quantity. This use of toxic substances to cure patients was, despite its apparent effectiveness (Paracelsus did have a strong reputation for actually curing his patients), viewed by Paracelsus's opponents as the practice of a "homicide Physician." Later generations came to view Paracelsus more favorably, and historians who have stressed Paracelsus's concept of disease and recognition of "new drugs" for medicine have viewed him as a father of modern medicine. Others have argued that his macrocosmic-microcosmic philosophy and use of "like cures like" drugs make him the forerunner of both homeopathy and the holistic medicine of the postmodern era.

Historians usually associate the name of Paracelsus with the diagnosis and treatment of disease. The new anatomy of the sixteenth century, however, was the work of Andreas Vesalius (1514–1564). His study of medicine at Paris involved him in the works of Galen, the great ancient authority. Especially important to him was a recently discovered text of Galen, *On Anatomical Procedures,* that led Vesalius to emphasize practical research as the principal avenue for understanding human anatomy. After receiving a doctorate in medicine at the University of Padua in 1536, he accepted a position there as professor of surgery. In 1543, he published his masterpiece, *On the Fabric of the Human Body.*

This book was based on his Paduan lectures, in which he deviated from traditional practice by personally dissecting a body to illustrate what he was discussing. Vesalius's anatomical treatise presented a careful examination of the individual organs and general structure of the human body. The book would not have been feasible without both the artistic advances of the Renaissance and technical developments in the art of printing. Together, they made possible the creation of illustrations superior to any hitherto produced.

Vesalius's "hands-on" approach to teaching anatomy enabled him to overthrow some of Galen's most glaring errors. He did not hesitate, for example, to correct Galen's assertion that the great blood vessels originated from the liver since his own observations made it apparent that they came from the heart. Nevertheless, Vesalius still clung to a number of Galen's erroneous assertions, including the Greek physician's ideas on the ebb and flow of two kinds of blood in the veins and arteries. It was not until William Harvey's work on the circulation of the blood that this Galenic misperception was corrected.

William Harvey (1578–1657) attended Cambridge University and later Padua where he received a doctorate of medicine in 1602. Appointed physician to St. Bartholomew's Hospital in 1609, he later became physician to King James I and Charles I. His reputation, however, rests upon his book, *On the Motion of the Heart and Blood,* published in 1628.

Although questions had been raised in the sixteenth century about Galen's physiological principles, no major break from his system had occurred. Harvey's work, which was based upon meticulous observations and experiments, led him to demolish the ancient Greek's work. Harvey demonstrated that the heart and not the liver was the beginning point of the circulation of blood in the body, that the same blood flows in both veins and arteries, and, most importantly, that the blood makes a complete circuit as it passes through the body. Although Harvey's work dealt a severe blow to Galen's theories, his ideas did not begin to achieve general recognition until the 1660s, when the capillaries, which explained how the body's blood passed from the arteries to the veins, were discovered. Harvey's theory of the circulation of the blood laid the foundation for modern physiology.

◆ Women in the Origins of Modern Science

During the Middle Ages, except for members of religious orders, women who sought a life of learning were severely hampered by the traditional attitude that a woman's proper role was as a daughter, wife, and mother. But in the late fourteenth and early fifteenth centuries, new opportunities for elite women emerged as enthusiasm for the new secular learning called humanism encouraged Europe's privileged and learned men to encourage women to read and study classical and Christian texts. The daughters and sisters of prominent Christian humanists, for example, were known for their learning. In northern Italy, a number of educated families allowed their young women to pursue a life of scholarship. The ideal of a humanist education for some of the daughters of Europe's elite persisted into the seventeenth century, but only for some privileged women.

In the same fashion as they were drawn to humanism, women were also attracted to the Scientific Revolution. Unlike females educated formally in humanist schools, women attracted to science had to obtain a largely informal education. Female contributions to science were

MARGARET CAVENDISH. Shown in this portrait is Margaret Cavendish, the duchess of Newcastle. Her husband, who was thirty years older, encouraged her to pursue her literary interests. In addition to scientific works, she wrote plays, an autobiography, and a biography of her husband entitled *The Life of the Thrice Noble, High and Puissant Prince William Cavendish, Duke, Marquess and Earl of Newcastle*. The autobiography and biography led one male literary critic to call her "a mad, conceited and ridiculous woman."

even more remarkable when we consider that women were largely excluded from universities and the new scientific societies. This was not quite the handicap that it would be today, however. Since science in the seventeenth century was not the preserve of universities, there was often no real dividing line between popular science and professional science, creating chances for women to enter scientific circles. Opportunities for women as well as alternatives to formal humanistic education could often be found in aristocratic and princely courts and in artisan workshops.

European nobles had the leisure and resources that gave them easy access to the world of learning. This door was also open to noblewomen who could participate in the informal scientific networks of their fathers and brothers. One of the most prominent female scientists of the seventeenth century, Margaret Cavendish (1623–1673), came from an aristocratic background. Cavendish was not a popularizer of science for women but a participant in the crucial scientific debates of her time. She also corresponded with important people on these issues. Despite her achievements, however, she was excluded from membership in the Royal Society (see The Scientific Societies later in this chapter), although she was once allowed to attend a meeting. She wrote a number of works on scientific matters including *Observations upon Experimental Philosophy* and *Grounds of Natural Philosophy*. In these works she did not hesitate to attack what she considered the defects of the rationalist and empiricist approaches to scientific knowledge and was especially critical of the growing belief that through science humans would be masters of nature: "We have no power at all over natural causes and effects. . . . for man is but a small part, . . . his powers are but particular actions of Nature, and he cannot have a supreme and absolute power."[13]

As an aristocrat, Margaret Cavendish was a good example of the women in France and England who worked in science. In Germany, women interested in science came from a different background. There the tradition of female participation in craft production enabled some women to become involved in observational science, especially entomology and astronomy. Between 1650 and 1710, 14 percent of all German astronomers were women.

A good example of female involvement in the Scientific Revolution stemming from the craft tradition was Maria Sibylla Merian (1647–1717), who had established a reputation as an important entomologist by the beginning of the eighteenth century. Merian's training came from working in her father's workshop where she learned the art of illustration, a training of great importance since her exact observation of insects and plants was only demonstrated through the superb illustrations she made. Her first work was the *Wonderful Metamorphosis and Special Nourishment of Caterpillars*, an illustrated study of caterpillars showing every stage in their development, which she had carefully observed and rendered in her drawings. In 1699, she undertook an expedition into the wilds of the Dutch colony of Surinam to collect and draw samples of plants and insect life. This led to her major scientific work, the *Metamorphosis of the Insects of Surinam*, in which she used sixty illustrations to show the reproductive and developmental cycles of Surinam's insect life.

The craft organization of astronomy also gave women opportunities to become involved in science. Those who did worked in family observatories; hence, daughters and wives received training as apprentices to fathers or husbands. The most famous of the female astronomers in Germany was Maria Winkelmann (1670–1720). She was educated by her father and uncle and received advanced training in astronomy from a nearby self-taught astronomer. Her opportunity to be a practicing astronomer came when she married Gottfried Kirch, Germany's foremost astronomer. She became his assistant at the astronomical observatory operated in Berlin by the Academy of Science. She made some original contributions, including a hitherto undiscovered comet, as her husband related:

> Early in the morning (about 2:00 A.M.) the sky was clear and starry. Some nights before, I had observed a variable star, and my wife (as I slept) wanted to find and see it for

> herself. In so doing, she found a comet in the sky. At which time she woke me, and I found that it was indeed a comet . . . I was surprised that I had not seen it the night before.[14]

Moreover, Winkelmann corresponded with the famous scientist Gottfried Leibniz (who invented the calculus independently of Newton), who praised her effusively as "a most learned woman who could pass as a rarity." When her husband died in 1710, she applied for a position as assistant astronomer for which she was highly qualified. As a woman—with no university degree—she was denied the post by the Berlin Academy, which feared that it would establish a precedent by hiring a woman ("mouths would gape"). Winkelmann managed, nevertheless, to continue her astronomical work a while longer at the private observatory of Baron Friederich von Krosigk in Berlin.

Winkelmann's difficulties with the Berlin Academy reflect the obstacles women faced in being accepted in scientific work, which was considered a male preserve. Although no formal statutes excluded women from membership in the new scientific societies, no woman was invited to join either the Royal Society of England or the French Academy of Sciences until the twentieth century. All of these women scientists were exceptional women since a life devoted to any kind of scholarship was still viewed as being at odds with the domestic duties women were expected to perform.

The nature and value of women had been the subject of an ongoing, centuries-long debate known as the *querelles des femmes*—arguments about women. Male opinions in the debate were largely a carryover from medieval times and were not favorable. Women were portrayed as inherently base, prone to vice, easily swayed, and "sexually insatiable." Hence, men needed to control them. Learned women were viewed as having overcome female liabilities to become like men. One man in praise of a woman scholar remarked that her writings were so good that you "would hardly believe they were done by a woman at all."

In the early modern era, women joined this debate by arguing against these male images of women. They argued that women also had rational minds and could grow from education. Further, since most women were pious, chaste, and temperate, there was no need for male authority over them. These female defenders of women in the *querelles des femmes* emphasized education as the key to women's ability to move into the world. How, then, did the era of the Scientific Revolution affect this debate over the nature of women? As an era of intellectual revolution in which traditional authorities were being overthrown, we might expect significant change in men's views of women. But by and large, instead of becoming an instrument for liberation, science was used to find new support for the old, traditional views about a woman's place in the scheme of things. This was done in a variety of ways.

One approach is evident in the work of William Harvey who was renowned for his work on the circulation of the blood. In his 1651 book on human reproduction, he argued that a woman provided "matter" but it was the man who gave it life and form from his semen. Harvey regarded semen as the active agent, and in his view it was so powerful that it was "vivifying, endowed with force and spirit and generative influence." By the end of the century, however, some scientists were arguing that males and females influenced the generative process equally. Likewise, new views on anatomy also appeared, but interestingly enough were used to perpetuate old stereotypes about women.

From the work of Galen until late in the sixteenth century, the male and female genitals had been portrayed as not significantly different. The uterus, for example, had been pictured as an internal and inadequate penis. According to Galen, "All parts that men have, women have too . . . the difference between them lies in only one thing . . . that in women the parts are within the body, whereas in men they are outside."[15] But this perspective was radically reevaluated in the seventeenth century, and the uterus was now presented as a perfect instrument for childbearing. It was not long before this view was used to reinforce the traditional argument that women were designed for their role as bearer of their husband's children.

An important project in the new anatomy of the sixteenth and seventeenth centuries was the attempt to illustrate the human body and skeleton. For Vesalius, the portrayal of physical differences between males and females was limited to external bodily form (the outlines of the body) and the sexual organs. Vesalius saw no difference in skeletons and portrayed them as the same for men and women. It was not until the eighteenth century, in fact, that a new anatomy finally prevailed. Drawings of female skeletons between 1730 and 1790 varied, but females tended to have a larger pelvic area, and, in some instances, female skulls were portrayed as smaller than those of males. Eighteenth-century studies on the anatomy and physiology of sexual differences provided "scientific evidence" to reaffirm the traditional inferiority of women. The larger pelvic area "proved" that women were meant to be childbearers whereas the larger skull "demonstrated" the superiority of the male mind. Male-dominated science had been used to "prove" male social dominance.

At the same time, during the seventeenth and eighteenth centuries, women even lost the traditional spheres of influence they had possessed, especially in the science-related art of midwifery. Women serving as midwives had traditionally been responsible for birthing. Similar to barber-surgeons or apothecaries (see Chapter 17), midwives had acquired their skills through apprenticeship. But the impact of the Scientific Revolution caused traditional crafts to be upgraded and then even professionalized as males took over. When medical men entered this arena, they also began to use devices and techniques derived from the study of anatomy. These were increasingly used to justify the male takeover of the traditional role of midwives. By the end of the eighteenth century, midwives were simply accessories to the art they had once controlled, except for the poor. Since little money was to be made in

The "Natural" Inferiority of Women

Despite the shattering of old views and the emergence of a new worldview in the Scientific Revolution of the seventeenth century, attitudes toward women remained tied to traditional perspectives. In this selection, the philosopher Benedict de Spinoza argues for the "natural" inferiority of women to men.

Benedict de Spinoza, *A Political Treatise*

But, perhaps, someone will ask, whether women are under men's authority by nature or institution? For if it has been by mere institution, then we had no reason compelling us to exclude women from government. But if we consult experience itself, we shall find that the origin of it is in their weakness. For there has never been a case of men and women reigning together, but wherever on the earth men are found, there we see that men rule, and women are ruled, and that on this plan, both sexes live in harmony. But on the other hand, the Amazons, who are reported to have held rule of old, did not suffer men to stop in their country, but reared only their female children, killing males to whom they gave birth. But if by nature women were equal to men, and were equally distinguished by force of character and ability, in which human power and therefore human right chiefly consist; surely among nations so many and different some would be found, where both sexes rule alike, and others, where men are ruled by women, and so brought up, that they can make less use of their abilities. And since this is nowhere the case, one may assert with perfect propriety, that women have not by nature equal right with men: but that they necessarily give way to men, and that thus it cannot happen, that both sexes should rule alike, much less that men should be ruled by women. But if we further reflect upon human passions, how men, in fact, generally love women merely from the passion of lust, and esteem their cleverness and wisdom in proportion to the excellence of their beauty, and also how very ill-disposed men are to suffer the women they love to show any sort of favor to others, and other facts of this kind, we shall easily see that men and women cannot rule alike without great hurt to peace.

serving them, midwives were allowed to continue to practice their traditional art for the lower classes.

Overall the Scientific Revolution reaffirmed traditional ideas about women's nature. Male scientists used the new science to spread the view that women were inferior by nature, subordinate to men, and suited by nature to play a domestic role as nurturing mothers. The widespread distribution of books ensured the continuation of these ideas (see the box above). Jean de La Bruyère, the seventeenth-century French moralist, was typical when he remarked that an educated woman was like a gun that was a collector's item "which one shows to the curious, but which has no use at all, any more than a carousel horse."[16]

◆ Toward a New Earth: Descartes, Rationalism, and a New View of Humankind

The fundamentally new conception of the universe contained in the cosmological revolution of the sixteenth and seventeenth centuries inevitably had an impact on the Western view of humankind. Nowhere is this more evident than in the work of René Descartes (1596–1650), an extremely important figure in Western history. Descartes began by reflecting the doubt and uncertainty that seemed pervasive in the confusion of the seventeenth century and ended with a philosophy that dominated Western thought until the twentieth century.

René Descartes was born into a family of the French lower nobility. After a Jesuit education, he studied law at Poitiers but traveled to Paris to study by himself. As far as can be deduced, he spent much of this period absorbed in the skeptical works of Montaigne. In 1618, at the beginning of the Thirty Years' War, Descartes volunteered for service in the army of Maurice of Nassau, but his motives seem to have been guided less by the desire for military action than for travel and leisure time to think. On the night of November 10, 1619, Descartes underwent what one historian has called an experience comparable to the "ecstatic illumination of the mystic." Having perceived in one night the outlines of a new rational-mathematical system, with a sense of divine approval he made a new commitment to mind, mathematics, and a mechanical universe. For the rest of his life, Descartes worked out the details of his vision.

The starting point for Descartes's new system was doubt, as he explained at the beginning of his most famous work, *Discourse on Method,* written in 1637:

> From my childhood I have been familiar with letters; and as I was given to believe that by their means a clear and assured knowledge can be acquired of all that is useful in life, I was extremely eager for instruction in them. As soon, however, as I had completed the course of study, at the close of which it is customary to be admitted into the order of the learned, I entirely changed my opinion. For I found myself entangled in so many doubts and errors that, as it seemed to me, the endeavor to instruct myself had served only to disclose to me more and more of my ignorance.[17]

DESCARTES WITH QUEEN CHRISTINA OF SWEDEN. René Descartes was one of the primary figures in the Scientific Revolution. Claiming to use reason as his sole guide to truth, Descartes posited a sharp distinction between mind and matter. He is shown here, standing to the right of Queen Christina of Sweden. The queen had a deep interest in philosophy and invited Descartes to her court.

Descartes decided to set aside all that he had learned and begin again. Having rejected the senses, because they are easily deceived, one fact seemed to Descartes beyond doubt—his own existence:

> But I immediately became aware that while I was thus disposed to think that all was false, it was absolutely necessary that I who thus thought should be something; and noting that this truth *I think, therefore I am,* was so steadfast and so assured that the suppositions of the skeptics, to whatever extreme they might all be carried, could not avail to shake it, I concluded that I might without scruple accept it as being the first principle of the philosophy I was seeking.[18]

With this emphasis on the mind, Descartes asserted that he would accept only those things that his reason said were true.

From his first postulate, Descartes deduced two additional principles, the existence of God and the separation of mind and matter. Since he—an imperfect being—had conceived of the idea of perfection, it could only have come from a perfect being, that is, God:

> And since it is no less contradictory that the more perfect should result from, and depend on, the less perfect than that something should proceed from nothing, it is equally impossible I should receive it from myself. Thus we are committed to the conclusion that it has been placed in me by a nature which is veritably more perfect than I am, and which has indeed within itself all the perfections of which I have any idea, that is to say, in a single word, that is God.[19]

Secondly, Descartes argued that since "the mind cannot be doubted but the body and material world can, the two must be radically different." From this came an absolute dualism between mind and body, or what has also been called Cartesian dualism.

According to Descartes, the universe contains two things, both of which God has created. One is thinking substance, what we call the mind. It is essentially spiritual and not composed of matter. Everything in the universe except the thinking substance or mind is extended substance, what we call matter. Using mind or human reason, the path to certain knowledge, and its best instrument, mathematics, humans can understand the material world because it is pure mechanism, a machine that is governed by its own physical laws because it was created by God—the great geometrician.

Descartes's conclusions about the nature of the universe and human beings had important implications. His separation of mind and matter allowed scientists to view matter as dead or inert, as something that was totally separate from themselves and could be investigated independently by reason. The split between mind and body led Westerners to equate their identity with mind and reason rather than with the whole organism. Descartes has rightly been called the father of modern rationalism (see the box on p. 478). His books were placed on the papal Index of Forbidden Books and condemned by many Protestant theologians. The radical Cartesian split between mind and matter, and between mind and body, had devastating implications not only for traditional religious views of the universe, but for how Westerners viewed themselves.

◆ The Scientific Method

In the course of the Scientific Revolution, attention was also paid to the problem of establishing the proper means to examine and understand the physical realm. This development of a scientific method was crucial to the evolution of science in the modern world.

Curiously enough, it was an Englishman with few scientific credentials who attempted to put forth a new method of acquiring knowledge that made an impact on the Royal Society in England in the seventeenth century and other European scientists in the eighteenth century. Francis Bacon (1561–1626), a lawyer and lord chancellor, rejected Copernicus and Kepler and misunderstood Galileo. And yet in his unfinished work, *The Great Instauration (The Great Restoration)*, he called for his contemporaries "to commence a total reconstruction of sciences, arts, and all human knowledge, raised upon the proper foundations." Bacon did not doubt humans' ability to

The Father of Modern Rationalism

René Descartes has long been viewed as the founder of modern rationalism and modern philosophy because he believed that human beings could understand the world—itself a mechanical system—by the same rational principles inherent in mathematical thinking. In his Discourse on Method, *he elaborated upon his approach to discovering truth.*

René Descartes, *Discourse on Method*

In place of the numerous precepts which have gone to constitute logic, I came to believe that the four following rules would be found sufficient, always provided I took the firm and unswerving resolve never in a single instance to fail in observing them.

The first was to accept nothing as true which I did not evidently know to be such, that is to say, scrupulously to avoid precipitance and prejudice, and in the judgments I passed to include nothing additional to what had presented itself to my mind so clearly and so distinctly that I could have no occasion for doubting it.

The second, to divide each of the difficulties I examined into as many parts as may be required for its adequate solution.

The third, to arrange my thoughts in order, beginning with things the simplest and easiest to know, so that I may then ascend little by little, as it were step by step, to the knowledge of the more complex, and in doing so, to assign an order of thought even to those objects which are not of themselves in any such order of precedence.

And the last, in all cases to make enumerations so complete, and reviews so general, that I should be assured of omitting nothing.

Those long chains of reasonings, each step simple and easy, which geometers are wont to employ in arriving even at the most difficult of their demonstrations, have led me to surmise that all the things we human beings are competent to know are interconnected in the same manner, and that none are so remote as to be beyond our reach or so hidden that we cannot discover them—that is, provided we abstain from accepting as true what is not thus related, i.e., keep always to the order required for their deduction one from another. And I had no great difficulty in determining what the objects are with which I should begin, for that I already knew, namely, that it was with the simplest and easiest. Bearing in mind, too, that of all those who in time past have sought for truth in the sciences, the mathematicians alone have been able to find any demonstrations, that is to say, any reasons which are certain and evident, I had no doubt that it must have been by a procedure of this kind that they had obtained them.

know the natural world, but he believed that they had proceeded incorrectly: "The entire fabric of human reason which we employ in the inquisition of nature is badly put together and built up, and like some magnificent structure without foundation."

Bacon's new foundation—a correct scientific method—was to be built upon inductive principles. Rather than beginning with assumed first principles from which logical conclusions could be deduced, he urged scientists to proceed from the particular to the general. From carefully organized experiments and thorough, systematic observations, correct generalizations could be developed.

Bacon was clear about what he believed his method could accomplish. His concern was more for practical than for pure science. He stated that "the true and lawful goal of the sciences is none other than this: that human life be endowed with new discoveries and power." He wanted science to contribute to the "mechanical arts" by creating devices that would benefit industry, agriculture, and trade. Bacon was prophetic when he said that "I am laboring to lay the foundation, not of any sect or doctrine, but of human utility and power." And how would this "human power" be used? To "conquer nature in action."[20] The control and domination of nature became a central proposition of modern science and the technology that accompanied it. Only in the twentieth century did some scientists begin to ask whether this assumption might not be at the heart of the earth's ecological crisis.

René Descartes proposed a different approach to scientific methodology by emphasizing deduction and mathematical logic. As Descartes explained in *Discourse on Method,* each step in an argument should be as sharp and well founded as a mathematical proof:

> These long chains of reasonings which geometers are accustomed to using to reach their most difficult demonstrations, had given me cause to imagine that everything which can be encompassed by man's knowledge is linked in the same way, and that provided only that one abstains from accepting any for true which is not true, and that one always keeps the right order for one thing to be deduced from that which precedes it, there can be nothing so distant that one does not reach it eventually, or so hidden that one cannot discover it.[21]

Descartes believed then that one could start with self-evident truths, comparable to geometrical axioms, and deduce more complex conclusions. His emphasis on deduction and mathematical order complemented Bacon's stress on experiment and induction. It was Sir Isaac Newton who synthesized them into a single scientific methodology by uniting Bacon's empiricism with Descartes's rationalism. This scientific method began with systematic observations and experiments, which were used to arrive at general concepts. New deductions derived from these general concepts could then be tested and verified by precise experiments.

The scientific method, of course, was valuable in answering the question "how" something works, and its success in doing this gave others much confidence in the method. It did not attempt to deal with the question of "why" something happens or the purpose and meaning behind the world of nature. This allowed religion still to be important in the seventeenth century.

◆ Science and Religion in the Seventeenth Century

In Galileo's struggle with the inquisitorial Holy Office of the Catholic church, we see the beginning of the conflict between science and religion that has marked the history of modern Western civilization. Since time immemorial, theology had seemed to be the queen of the sciences. It was natural that the churches would continue to believe that religion was the final measure of all things. To the emerging scientists, however, it often seemed that theologians knew not of what they spoke. These "natural philosophers" then tried to draw lines between the knowledge of religion and the knowledge of "natural philosophy" or nature. Galileo had clearly felt that it was unnecessary to pit science against religion:

> In discussions of physical problems we ought to begin not from the authority of scriptural passages, but from sense-experiences and necessary demonstrations; for the holy Bible and the phenomena of nature proceed alike from the divine word, the former as the dictate of the Holy Ghost and the latter as the observant executrix of God's commands. It is necessary for the Bible, in order to be accommodated to the understanding of every man, to speak many things which appear to differ from the absolute truth so far as the bare meaning of the words is concerned. But Nature, on the other hand, is inexorable and immutable; she never transgresses the laws imposed upon her, or cares a whit whether her abstruse reasons and methods of operation are understandable to men.[22]

To Galileo it made little sense for the church to determine the nature of physical reality on the basis of biblical texts that were subject to radically divergent interpretations. The church, however, decided otherwise in Galileo's case and lent its great authority to one scientific theory, the Ptolemaic-Aristotelian cosmology, no doubt because it fit so well with its own philosophical views of reality. But the church's decision had tremendous consequences, just as the rejection of Darwin's ideas did in the nineteenth century. For educated individuals, it established a dichotomy between scientific investigations and religious beliefs. As the scientific beliefs triumphed, it became almost inevitable that religious beliefs would suffer, leading to a growing secularization in European intellectual life, precisely what the church had hoped to combat by opposing Copernicanism. Many seventeenth-century intellectuals were both religious and scientific and believed that the implications of this split would be tragic. Some believed that the split was largely unnecessary while others felt the need to combine God, humans, and a mechanistic universe into a new philosophical synthesis. Two individuals—Spinoza and Pascal—illustrate some of the wide diversity in the response of European intellectuals to the implications of the cosmological revolution of the seventeenth century.

Benedict de Spinoza (1632–1677) was a philosopher who grew up in the relatively tolerant atmosphere of Amsterdam. He was excommunicated from the Amsterdam synagogue at the age of twenty-four for rejecting the tenets of Judaism. Ostracized by the local Jewish community and major Christian churches alike, Spinoza lived a quiet, independent life, earning a living by grinding optical lenses and refusing to accept an academic position in philosophy at the University of Heidelberg for fear of compromising his freedom of thought. Spinoza read a great deal of the new scientific literature and was influenced by Descartes.

Although he followed Descartes's rational approach to knowledge, Spinoza was unwilling to accept the implications of Descartes's ideas, especially the separation of mind and matter and the apparent separation of an infinite God from the finite world of matter. God was not simply creator of the universe, he was the universe. All that is is in God, and nothing can be apart from God. This philosophy of pantheism (others have labeled it panentheism or monism) was set out in Spinoza's book, *Ethics Demonstrated in the Geometrical Manner,* which was not published until after his death.

To Spinoza, human beings are not "situated in nature as a kingdom within a kingdom," but are as much a part of God or nature or the universal order as other natural objects. The failure to understand God had led to many misconceptions; for one, that nature exists only for one's use:

> As they find in themselves and outside themselves many means which assist them not a little in their search for what is useful, for instance, eyes for seeing, teeth for chewing, herbs and animals for yielding food, the sun for giving light, the sea for breeding fish, they come to look on the whole of nature as a means for obtaining such conveniences.[23]

Furthermore, unable to find any other cause for the existence of these things, they attributed them to a creator-God who must be worshiped to gain their ends: "Hence also it follows, that everyone thought out for himself, according to his abilities, a different way of worshiping God, so that God might love him more than his fellows, and direct the whole course of nature for the satisfaction of his blind cupidity and insatiable avarice." Then, when nature appeared unfriendly in the form of storms, earthquakes, and diseases, "they declared that such things happen, because the gods are angry at some wrong done them by men, or at some fault committed in their worship," rather than realizing "that good and evil fortunes fall to the lot of pious and impious alike."[24] Likewise, human beings made moral condemnations of others because they failed to understand that human emotions, "passions of hatred, anger, envy and so, considered in themselves, follow from the same necessity and efficacy of nature" and "nothing comes to pass in nature in contravention to her universal laws." To explain human emotions, like everything else, we need to analyze them as we would the movements of planets: "I shall, therefore, treat of the nature and strength of my emotions according to the same method as I employed heretofore in my investigations concerning God and the mind. I shall consider human actions and desires in exactly the same manner as though I were concerned with lines, planes, and solids."[25] Everything has a rational explanation and humans are capable of finding it. In using reason, people can find true happiness. Their real freedom comes when they understand the order and necessity of nature and achieve detachment from passing interests.

Spinoza's complex synthesis of God, humans, and the universe was not easily accepted by his contemporaries, and his pantheism was mistakenly condemned as "hideous atheism." Others were upset by his attitude toward morality because he viewed it as found in nature and known by reason, not revealed to people through the Bible. Even Spinoza declared that some would find strange his attempt to treat of human desires "in exactly the same manner as though I were concerned with lines, planes, and solids."

Blaise Pascal (1623–1662) was a French scientist who sought to keep science and religion united. He had a brief, but checkered career. For a short time, he was a reader of Montaigne and a companion of freethinkers. An accomplished scientist and brilliant mathematician, he excelled at both the practical, by inventing a calculating machine, and the abstract, by devising a theory of chance or probability and doing work on conic sections. After a profound mystical vision on the night of November 23, 1654, which assured him that God cared for the human soul, he devoted the rest of his life to religious matters. He planned to write an "Apology for the Christian Religion" but died before he could do so. He did leave a set of notes for the larger work, however, which in published form became known as *Pensées* or *The Thoughts.*

In *Pensées,* Pascal tried to convert rationalists to Christianity by appealing both to their reason and to their emotions. Humans were, he argued, frail creatures, often deceived by their senses, misled by reason, and battered by their emotions. And yet they were beings whose very nature involved thinking: "Man is but a reed, the weakest in nature; but he is a thinking reed. . . . Our whole dignity consists, therefore, in thought. By thought we must raise ourselves. . . . Let us endeavor, then, to think well; this is the beginning of morality."[26]

Pascal was determined to show that the Christian religion was not contrary to reason: "If we violate the principles of reason, our religion will be absurd, and it will be laughed at." Christianity, he felt, was the only religion that recognized people's true state of being as both vulnerable and great. To a Christian, a human being was both fallen and at the same time God's special creation. But it was not necessary to emphasize one at the expense of the other—to view humans as only rational or only hopeless. Thus,

PASCAL. Blaise Pascal was a brilliant scientist and mathematician who hoped to keep science and Christianity united. In the *Pensées,* he made a passionate argument on behalf of the Christian religion. He is pictured here in a posthumous portrait by Quesnel.

"knowledge of God without knowledge of man's wretchedness leads to pride. Knowledge of man's wretchedness without knowledge of God leads to despair. Knowledge of Jesus Christ is the middle course, because by it we discover both God and our wretched state." Pascal even had an answer for skeptics in his famous wager. God is a reasonable bet; it is worthwhile to assume that God exists. If he does, then we win all; if he does not, we lose nothing.

Despite his background as a scientist and mathematician, Pascal refused to rely on the scientist's world of order and rationality to attract people to God: "If we submit everything to reason, there will be no mystery and no supernatural element in our religion." In the new cosmology of the seventeenth century, "finite man," Pascal believed, was lost in the new infinite world, a realization that frightened him: "The eternal silence of those infinite spaces strikes me with terror" (see the box on p. 481). The world of nature, then, could never reveal God: "Because they have failed to contemplate these infinites, men have rashly plunged into the examination of nature, as though they bore some proportion to her. . . . Their assumption is as infinite as their object." A Christian could only rely on a God who through Jesus cared for human beings. In the final analysis, after providing reasonable arguments for Christianity, Pascal came to rest on faith. Reason, he believed, could take people only so far: "The heart has its reasons of which the reason knows nothing." As a Christian, faith was the final step: "The heart feels God, not the reason. This is what constitutes faith: God experienced by the heart, not by the reason."[27]

Pascal: "What Is a Man in the Infinite?"

Perhaps no intellectual in the seventeenth century gave greater expression to the uncertainties generated by the cosmological revolution than Blaise Pascal. Himself a scientist, Pascal's mystical vision of God's presence caused him to pursue religious truths with a passion. His work, the Pensées, *consisted of notes for a larger, unfinished work justifying the Christian religion. In this selection, Pascal presents his musings on the human place in an infinite world.*

Blaise Pascal, *Pensées*

Let man then contemplate the whole of nature in her full and exalted majesty. Let him turn his eyes from the lowly objects which surround him. Let him gaze on that brilliant light set like an eternal lamp to illumine the Universe; let the earth seem to him a dot compared with the vast orbit described by the sun, and let him wonder at the fact that this vast orbit itself is no more than a very small dot compared with that described by the stars in their revolutions around the firmament. But if our vision stops here, let the imagination pass on; it will exhaust its powers of thinking long before nature ceases to supply it with material for thought. All this visible world is no more than an imperceptible speck in nature's ample bosom. No idea approaches it. We may extend our conceptions beyond all imaginable space; yet produce only atoms in comparison with the reality of things. It is an infinite sphere, the center of which is everywhere, the circumference nowhere. In short, it is the greatest perceptible mark of God's almighty power that our imagination should lose itself in that thought.

Returning to himself, let man consider what he is compared with all existence; let him think of himself as lost in his remote corner of nature; and from this little dungeon in which he finds himself lodged—I mean the Universe—let him learn to set a true value on the earth, its kingdoms, and cities, and upon himself. What is a man in the infinite? . . .

For, after all, what is a man in nature? A nothing in comparison with the infinite, an absolute in comparison with nothing, a central point between nothing and all. Infinitely far from understanding these extremes, the end of things and their beginning are hopelessly hidden from him in an impenetrable secret. He is equally incapable of seeing the nothingness from which he came, and the infinite in which he is engulfed. What else then will he perceive but some appearance of the middle of things, in an eternal despair of knowing either their principle or their purpose? All things emerge from nothing and are borne onward to infinity. Who can follow this marvelous process? The Author of these wonders understands them. None but He can.

In retrospect, it is obvious that Pascal failed to achieve his goal of uniting Christianity and science. Increasingly, the gap between science and traditional religion grew wider as Europe continued along its path of secularization. Of course, traditional religions were not eliminated, nor is there any evidence that churches had yet lost their numbers. That would happen later. Nevertheless, more and more of the intellectual, social, and political elites began to act on the basis of secular rather than religious assumptions.

The Spread of Scientific Knowledge

In the course of the seventeenth century, scientific learning and investigation began to increase dramatically. Major universities in Europe established new chairs of science, especially in medicine. Royal and princely patronage of individual scientists became an international phenomenon. The king of Denmark constructed an astronomical observatory for Tycho Brahe; Emperor Rudolf II hired Tycho Brahe and Johannes Kepler as imperial mathematicians; the grand duke of Tuscany appointed Galileo to a similar post. Of greater importance to the work of science, however, was the emergence of new learned societies and journals that enabled the new scientists to communicate their ideas to each other and to disseminate them to a wider, literate public.

The Scientific Societies

The first of these scientific societies appeared in Italy, but those of England and France were ultimately of more significance. The English Royal Society evolved out of informal gatherings of scientists at London and Oxford in the 1640s, although it did not receive a formal charter from King Charles II until 1662. The French Royal Academy of Sciences also arose out of informal scientific meetings in Paris during the 1650s. In 1666, urged on by his minister Colbert, Louis XIV formally recognized the group. The French Academy received abundant state support and remained under government control; its members were appointed and paid salaries by the state. In contrast, the Royal Society of England received little government encouragement, and its fellows simply co-opted new members.

Early on, both the English and French scientific societies formally emphasized the practical value of scientific research. The Royal Society established a committee to investigate technological improvements for industry while

LOUIS XIV AND COLBERT VISIT THE ACADEMY OF SCIENCES. In the seventeenth century, individual scientists received royal and princely patronage, and a number of learned societies were established. In France, Louis XIV, urged on by his minister Colbert, gave formal recognition to the French Academy in 1666. In this painting by Henri Testelin, Louis XIV is shown seated, surrounded by Colbert and members of the French Royal Academy of Sciences.

the French Academy collected tools and machines. This concern with the practical benefits of science proved short-lived, however, as both societies came to focus their primary interest on theoretical work in mechanics and astronomy. The construction of observatories at Paris in 1667 and at Greenwich, England, in 1675 greatly facilitated research in astronomy by both groups. The French Academy, however, since it was controlled by the state, was forced by the war minister of France, the marquis de Louvois, to continue its practical work to benefit both the "king and the state." The French example was especially important as a model for the scientific societies established in neighboring Germany. German princes and city governments encouraged the foundation of small-scale scientific societies of their own. Most of them, such as the Scientific Academy created in 1700 by the elector of Brandenburg, as well as the scientific academies established in most European countries in the eighteenth century, were sponsored by governments and were mainly devoted to the betterment of the state. Although both the English and French societies made useful contributions to scientific knowledge in the second half of the seventeenth century, their true significance arose from their example that science should proceed as a cooperative venture.

Scientific journals furthered this concept of cooperation. The French *Journal des Savants*, published weekly beginning in 1665, printed results of experiments as well as general scientific knowledge. Its format appealed to both scientists and the educated public interested in the new science. The *Philosophical Transactions* of the Royal Society, however, also initiated in 1665, published papers of its members and learned correspondence and was aimed at practicing scientists. It became a prototype for the scholarly journals of later learned and academic societies and a crucial instrument for circulating news of scientific and academic activities.

THE ROYAL OBSERVATORY AT GREENWICH. To facilitate their astronomical investigations, both the English and the French constructed observatories, such as the one pictured here, which was built at Greenwich, England, in 1675. Here the royal astronomer works at the table while his two assistants make observations.

Science and Society

The importance of science in the history of modern Western civilization is usually taken for granted. No doubt the Industrial Revolution of the nineteenth century provided tangible proof of the effectiveness of science and ensured its victory over Western minds. But how did science become such an integral part of Western culture in the seventeenth and eighteenth centuries? Recent research has stressed that one cannot simply assert that people perceived that science was a rationally superior system. Two important social factors, however, might help to explain the relatively rapid acceptance of the new science.

It has been argued that the literate mercantile and propertied elites of Europe were attracted to the new science because it offered new ways to exploit resources for profit. Some of the early scientists made it easier for these groups to accept the new ideas by showing how they could be applied directly to specific industrial and technological needs. Galileo, for example, consciously sought an alliance between science and the material interests of the educated elite when he assured his listeners that the science of mechanics would be quite useful "when it becomes necessary to build bridges or other structures over water, something occurring mainly in affairs of great importance." At the same time, Galileo stressed that science was fit for the "minds of the wise" and not for "the shallow minds of the common people." This made science part of the high culture of Europe's wealthy elites at a time when that culture was being increasingly separated from the popular culture of the lower classes (see Chapter 17).

It has also been argued that political interests used the new scientific conception of the natural world to bolster social stability. One scholar has recently argued that "no single event in the history of early modern Europe more profoundly shaped the integration of the new science into Western culture than did the English Revolution (1640–1660)."[28] Fed by their millenarian expectations that the end of the world would come and usher in a 1,000-year reign of the saints, Puritan reformers felt it was important to reform and renew their society. They seized on the new science as a socially useful instrument to accomplish this goal. The Puritan Revolution's role in the acceptance of science, however, stemmed even more from the reaction to the radicalism spawned by the revolutionary ferment. The upheavals of the Puritan Revolution gave rise to groups, such as the Levellers, Diggers, and Ranters, who advocated not only radical political ideas, but also a new radical science based on Paracelsus and the natural magic associated with the Hermetic tradition. The chaplain of the New Model Army said that the radicals wanted "the philosophy of Hermes, revived by the Paracelsian schools." The propertied and educated elites responded vigorously to these challenges to the established order by supporting the new mechanistic science and appealing to the material benefits of science. Hence, the founders of the Royal Society were men who wanted to pursue an experimental science that would remain detached from radical reforms of church and state. Although willing to make changes, they now viewed those changes in terms of an increase in food production and commerce. By the eighteenth century, the Newtonian world-machine had been readily accepted, and Newtonian science would soon be applied to trade and industry by a mercantile and landed elite that believed that they "could retain a social order that primarily rewarded and enriched themselves while still improving the human condition."

CHRONOLOGY

The Impact of the Scientific Revolution: Important Works

Bacon, *The Great Instauration*	1620
Descartes, *Discourse on Method*	1637
Pascal, *Pensées*	1669
Spinoza, *Ethics Demonstrated in the Geometrical Manner*	1677

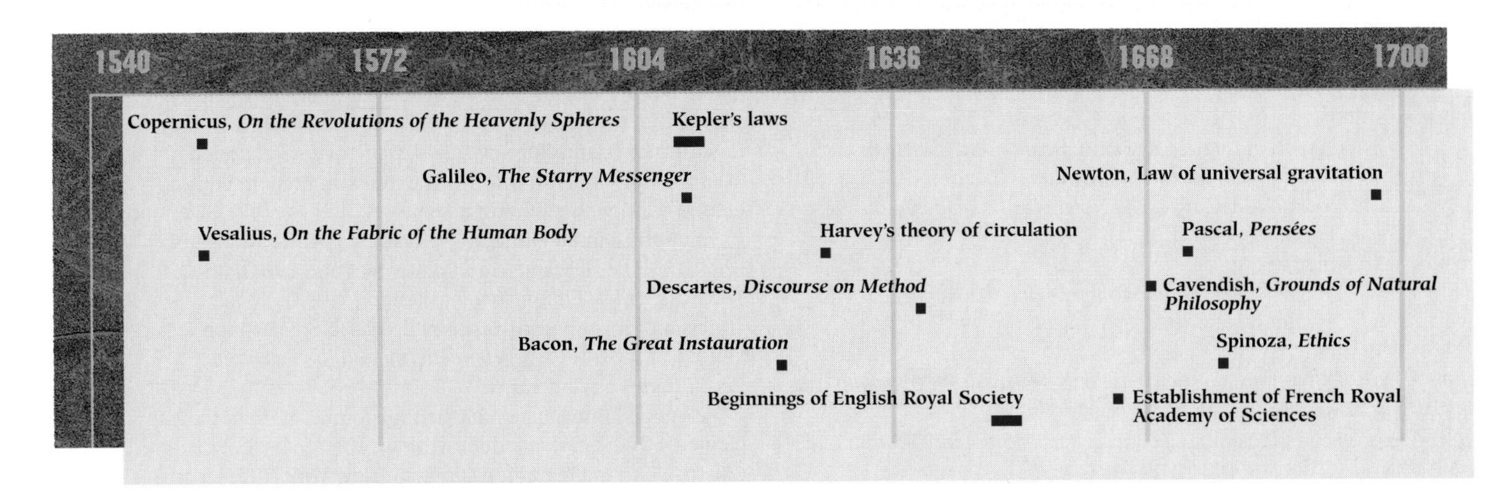

CONCLUSION

The Scientific Revolution represents a major turning point in modern Western civilization. In the Scientific Revolution, the Western world overthrew the medieval, Ptolemaic-Aristotelian worldview and arrived at a new conception of the universe: the sun at the center, the planets as material bodies revolving around the sun in elliptical orbits, and an infinite rather than finite world. With the changes in the conception of "heaven" came changes in the conception of "earth." The work of Bacon and Descartes left Europeans with the separation of mind and matter and the belief that by using only reason they could, in fact, understand and dominate the world of nature. The development of a scientific method furthered the work of scientists while the creation of scientific societies and learned journals spread its results. Although traditional churches stubbornly resisted the new ideas and a few intellectuals pointed to some inherent flaws, nothing was able to halt the replacement of the traditional ways of thinking by new ways of thinking that created a more fundamental break with the past than that represented by the breakup of Christian unity in the Reformation.

The Scientific Revolution forced Europeans to change their conception of themselves. At first, some were appalled and even frightened by its implications. Formerly, humans on earth had been at the center of the universe. Now the earth was only a tiny planet revolving around a sun that was itself only a speck in a boundless universe. Most people remained optimistic despite the apparent blow to human dignity. After all, had Newton not demonstrated that the universe was a great machine governed by natural laws? Newton had found one—the universal law of gravitation. Could others not find other laws? Were there not natural laws governing every aspect of human endeavor that could be found by the new scientific method? Thus, the Scientific Revolution leads us logically to the age of the Enlightenment of the eighteenth century.

NOTES

1. Quoted in Alan G. R. Smith, *Science and Society in the Sixteenth and Seventeenth Centuries* (London, 1972), p. 59.
2. Edward MacCurdy, *The Notebooks of Leonardo da Vinci* (London, 1948), 1:634.
3. Ibid., p. 636.
4. Frances Yates, *Giordano Bruno and the Hermetic Tradition* (New York, 1964), p. 448.
5. Ibid., p. 450.
6. Quoted in Smith, *Science and Society in the Sixteenth and Seventeenth Centuries*, p. 97.
7. Logan P. Smith, *Life and Letters of Sir Henry Wotton* (Oxford, 1907), 1:486–487.
8. Quoted in John H. Randall, *The Making of the Modern Mind* (Boston, 1926), p. 234.
9. Quoted in Smith, *Science and Society in the Sixteenth and Seventeenth Centuries*, p. 124.
10. Quoted in Betty J. Dobbs, *The Foundations of Newton's Alchemy* (Cambridge, 1975), pp. 13–14.
11. Jolande Jacobi, ed., *Paracelsus: Selected Writings* (New York, 1965), pp. 5–6.
12. Ibid., p. 21.
13. Quoted in Londa Schiebinger, *The Mind Has No Sex? Women in the Origins of Modern Science* (Cambridge, Mass., 1989), pp. 52–53.
14. Ibid., p. 85.
15. Galen, *On the Usefulness of the Parts of the Body*, trans. Margaret May (Ithaca, N.Y., 1968), 2:628–629.
16. Quoted in Phyllis Stock, *Better Than Rubies: A History of Women's Education* (New York, 1978), p. 16.
17. René Descartes, *Philosophical Writings*, ed. and trans. Norman K. Smith (New York, 1958), p. 95.
18. Ibid., pp. 118–119.
19. Ibid., p. 120.
20. Francis Bacon, *The Great Instauration*, trans. Jerry Weinberger (Arlington Heights, Ill., 1989), pp. (in order of quotations) 2, 8, 2, 16, 21.
21. Descartes, *Discourse on Method*, in *Philosophical Writings*, p. 75.
22. Stillman Drake, ed. and trans., *Discoveries and Opinions of Galileo* (New York, 1957), p. 182.
23. Benedict de Spinoza, *Ethics*, trans. R. H. M. Elwes (New York, 1955), pp. 75–76.
24. Ibid., p. 76.
25. Benedict de Spinoza, *Letters*, quoted in Randall, *The Making of the Modern Mind*, p. 247.
26. Blaise Pascal, *The Pensées*, trans. J. M. Cohen (Harmondsworth, 1961), p. 100.
27. Ibid., pp. (in order of quotations) 31, 45, 31, 52–53, 164, 165.
28. Margaret C. Jacob, *The Cultural Meaning of the Scientific Revolution* (New York, 1988), p. 73.

SUGGESTIONS FOR FURTHER READING

Four general surveys of the entire Scientific Revolution are A. G. R. Smith, *Science and Society in the Sixteenth and Seventeenth Centuries* (London, 1972); J. R. Jacob, *The Scientific Revolution: Aspirations and Achievements, 1500–1700* (Atlantic Highlands, N.J., 1998); S. Shapin, *The Scientific Revolution* (Chicago, 1996); and J. Henry, *The Scientific Revolution and the Origins of Modern Science* (New York, 1997). Also of much value is A. G. Debus, *Man and Nature in the Renaissance* (Cambridge, 1978), which covers the period from the mid-fifteenth through the mid-seventeenth century. On the relationship of magic to the beginnings of the Scientific Revolution, see the pioneering works by F. Yates, *Giordano Bruno and the Hermetic Tradition* (New York, 1964), and *The Rosicrucian Enlightenment* (London, 1975). Some criticism of this approach is provided in R. S. Westman and J. E. McGuire, eds., *Hermeticism and the Scientific Revolution* (Los Angeles, 1977).

A good introduction to the transformation from the late medieval to the early modern worldview is A. Koyré, *From the Closed World to the Infinite Universe* (New York, 1958). Also still of value is A. Koestler, *The Sleepwalkers: A History of Man's Changing Vision of the Universe* (New York, 1959). On the important figures of the revolution in astronomy, see E. Rosen, *Copernicus and the Scientific Revolution* (New York, 1984); M. Sharratt, *Galileo: Decisive Innovator* (Oxford, 1994); S. Drake, *Galileo, Pioneer Scientist* (Toronto, 1990); M. Casper, *Johannes Kepler,* trans. C. D. Hellman (London, 1959), the standard biography; and R. S. Westfall, *The Life of Isaac Newton* (New York, 1993). On Newton's relationship to alchemy, see the invaluable study by B. J. Dobbs, *The Foundations of Newton's Alchemy* (Cambridge, 1975); and M. White, *Isaac Newton: The Last Sorcerer* (Reading, Mass., 1997).

The worldview of Paracelsus and his followers can be examined in A. G. Debus, *The Chemical Philosophy: Paracelsian Science and Medicine in the Sixteenth and Seventeenth Centuries,* 2 vols. (New York, 1977). The standard biography of Vesalius is C. D. O'Malley, *Andreas Vesalius of Brussels, 1514–1564* (Berkeley, 1964). The work of Harvey is discussed in G. Whitteridge, *William Harvey and the Circulation of the Blood* (London, 1971). A good general account of the development of medicine can be found in W. P. D. Wightman, *The Emergence of Scientific Medicine* (Edinburgh, 1971).

The importance of Francis Bacon in the early development of science is underscored in P. Zagorin, *Francis Bacon* (Princeton, N.J., 1998). A good introduction to the work of Descartes can be found in G. Radis-Lewis, *Descartes: A Biography* (Ithaca, N.Y., 1998). The standard biography of Spinoza in English is S. Hampshire, *Spinoza* (New York, 1961).

For histories of the scientific academies, see R. Hahn, *The Anatomy of a Scientific Institution: The Paris Academy of Sciences, 1666–1803* (Berkeley, 1971); and M. Purver, *The Royal Society, Concept and Creation* (London, 1967).

On the subject of women and early modern science, see the comprehensive and highly informative work by L. Schiebinger, *The Mind Has No Sex? Women in the Origins of Modern Science* (Cambridge, Mass., 1989). See also C. Merchant, *The Death of Nature: Women, Ecology, and the Scientific Revolution* (San Francisco, 1980). There is a chapter on Maria Sibylla Merian in N. Davis, *Women on the Margins* (Cambridge, Mass., 1995). The social and political context for the triumph of science in the seventeenth and eighteenth centuries is examined in M. Jacobs, *The Cultural Meaning of the Scientific Revolution* (New York, 1988), and *The Newtonians and the English Revolution, 1689–1720* (Ithaca, N.Y., 1976).

For additional reading, go to InfoTrac College Edition, your online research library at http://web1.infotrac-college.com

Enter the search term *Copernicus* using Key Terms.

Enter the search terms *Galileo not Jupiter* using Key Terms.

Enter the search terms *Isaac Newton* using Key Terms.

Enter the search terms *Rene Descartes* using Key Terms.

CHAPTER 17 The Eighteenth Century: An Age of Enlightenment

CHAPTER OUTLINE

- The Enlightenment
- Culture and Society in an Age of Enlightenment
- Religion and the Churches
- Conclusion

FOCUS QUESTIONS

- What intellectual developments led to the emergence of the Enlightenment?
- Who were the leading figures of the Enlightenment, and what were their main contributions?
- In what type of social environment did the philosophes thrive, and what role did women play in that environment?
- What innovations in art, music, and literature occurred in the eighteenth century?
- How did popular culture and popular religion differ from high culture and institutional religion in the eighteenth century?

THE EARTH-SHATTERING WORK of the "natural philosophers" in the Scientific Revolution had affected only a relatively small number of Europe's educated elite. In the eighteenth century, this changed dramatically as a group of intellectuals known as the philosophes popularized the ideas of the Scientific Revolution and used them to undertake a dramatic reexamination of all aspects of life. In Paris, the cultural capital of Europe, women took the lead in bringing together groups of men and women to discuss the new ideas of the philosophes. At her fashionable home in the Rue St.-Honoré, Marie-Thérèse de Geoffrin, wife of a wealthy merchant, held sway over gatherings that became the talk of France and even Europe. Distinguished foreigners, including a future king of Sweden and a future king of Poland, competed to receive invitations. When Madame Geoffrin made a visit to Vienna, she was so well received that she exclaimed, "I am better known here than a couple of yards from my own house." Madame Geoffrin was an amiable but firm hostess who allowed wide-ranging discussions as long as they remained in good taste. When she found that artists and philosophers did not mix particularly well (the artists were high-strung and the philosophers talked too much), she set up separate meetings. Artists were invited only on Mondays; philosophers on Wednesdays. These gatherings were but one of many avenues for the spread of the ideas of the philosophes. And those ideas had such a widespread impact on their society that historians ever since have called the eighteenth century an age of Enlightenment.

For most of the philosophes, "enlightenment" included the rejection of traditional Christianity. The religious wars and intolerance of the sixteenth and seventeenth centuries had created an environment in which intellectuals had become so disgusted with religious fanaticism that they were open to the new ideas of the Scientific Revolution. Though the great scientists of the seventeenth century believed that their work exalted God, the intellectuals of the eighteenth century read their conclusions a different way and increasingly turned their backs on Christian orthodoxy. Consequently, European intellectual life in the eighteenth century was marked by the emergence of the secularization that has characterized the modern Western mentality. Although some historians have argued that this secularism first arose in the Renaissance, it never developed then to the same extent that it did in the eighteenth century. Ironically, at the same time that reason and materialism were beginning to replace faith and worship, a great outburst of religious sensibility manifested itself in music and art. Merely to mention the name of Johann Sebastian Bach is to remind us that the growing secularization of the eighteenth century had not yet captured the hearts and minds of all European intellectuals and artists.

◆ The Enlightenment

In 1784, the German philosopher Immanuel Kant defined the Enlightenment as "man's leaving his self-caused immaturity." Whereas earlier periods had been handicapped by the inability to "use one's intelligence without the guidance of another," Kant proclaimed as the motto of the Enlightenment: "Dare to Know!: Have the courage to use your own intelligence!" The eighteenth-century Enlightenment was a movement of intellectuals who dared to know. They were greatly impressed with the accomplishments of the Scientific Revolution, and when they used the word *reason*—one of their favorite words—they were advocating the application of the scientific method to the understanding of all life. All institutions and all systems of thought were subject to the rational, scientific way of thinking if only people would free themselves from the shackles of past, worthless traditions, especially religious ones. If Isaac Newton could discover the natural laws regulating the world of nature, they too by using reason could find the laws that governed human society. This belief in turn led them to hope that they could make progress toward a better society than the one they had inherited. Reason, natural law, hope, progress—these were common words in the heady atmosphere of the eighteenth century. But the philosophes were not naive optimists. Many of them realized that the ignorance and suffering of their society were not easily overcome and that progress would be slow and would exact a price.

The Paths to Enlightenment

Many philosophes saw themselves as the heirs of the pagan philosophers of antiquity and the Italian humanists of the Renaissance who had revived the world of classical antiquity. To the philosophes, the Middle Ages had been a period of intellectual darkness, when a society dominated by the dogmatic Catholic church allowed faith to obscure and diminish human reason. Closer to their own period, however, the philosophes were especially influenced by the revolutionary thinkers of the seventeenth century. What were the major intellectual changes, then, that culminated in the intellectual movement of the Enlightenment?

THE POPULARIZATION OF SCIENCE

Although the philosophes of the eighteenth century were much influenced by the scientific ideas of the seventeenth century, they did not always acquire this knowledge directly from the original sources. After all, Newton's *Principia* was not an easy book to read or comprehend. Scientific ideas were spread to ever-widening circles of educated Europeans not so much by scientists themselves as by popularizers. Especially important as the direct link between the Scientific Revolution of the seventeenth century and the philosophes of the eighteenth was Bernard de Fontenelle (1657–1757), secretary of the French Royal Academy of Science from 1691 to 1741.

Although Fontenelle neither performed any scientific experiments nor made any scientific discoveries, he possessed a deep knowledge of all the scientific work of earlier centuries and his own time. Moreover, he was able to communicate that body of scientific knowledge in a clear and even witty fashion that appealed to his upper-class audiences in a meaningful way. One of his most successful books, the *Plurality of Worlds,* was actually presented in the form of an intimate conversation between a lady aristocrat and her lover who are engaged in conversation under the stars. What are they discussing? "Tell me," she exclaims, "about these stars of yours." Her lover proceeds to tell her of the tremendous advances in cosmology after the foolish errors of their forebears:

> There came on the scene a certain German, one Copernicus, who made short work of all those various circles, all those solid skies, which the ancients had pictured to

THE POPULARIZATION OF SCIENCE: FONTENELLE AND THE *PLURALITY OF WORLDS*. The most important popularizer of the ideas of the Scientific Revolution was Bernard de Fontenelle who, though not a scientist himself, had much knowledge of scientific matters. In this frontispiece illustration to his *Plurality of Worlds*, an aristocratic lady listens while her astronomer-friend explains the details of the new cosmology.

> themselves. The former he abolished; the latter, he broke in pieces. Fired with the noble zeal of a true astronomer, he took the earth and spun it very far away from the center of the universe, where it had been installed, and in that center he put the sun, which had a far better title to the honor.[1]

In the course of two evenings under the stars, the lady learned the basic fundamentals of the new mechanistic universe. So too did scores of the educated elite of Europe. What bliss it was to learn the "truth" in such lighthearted fashion.

Thanks to Fontenelle, science was no longer the monopoly of experts, but part of literature. He was especially fond of downplaying the religious backgrounds of the seventeenth-century scientists. Himself a skeptic, Fontenelle contributed to the growing skepticism toward religion at the end of the seventeenth century by portraying the churches as enemies of scientific progress.

A NEW SKEPTICISM

The great scientists of the seventeenth century, such as Kepler, Galileo, and Newton, had pursued their work in a spirit of exalting God, not undermining Christianity. But as scientific knowledge spread, more and more educated men and women began to question religious truths and values. Skepticism about religion and a growing secularization of thought were especially evident in the work of Pierre Bayle (1647–1706), who remained a Protestant while becoming a leading critic of traditional religious attitudes. Bayle attacked superstition, religious intolerance, and dogmatism. In his view, compelling people to believe a particular set of religious ideas (as Louis XIV was doing in Bayle's contemporary France) was wrong. It simply created hypocrites and in itself was contrary to what religion should be about. Individual conscience should determine one's actions. Bayle argued for complete religious toleration, maintaining that the existence of many religions would benefit rather than harm the state.

Bayle was one of a number of intellectuals who believed that the new rational principles of textual criticism should be applied to the Bible as well as secular documents. In his most famous work, *Historical and Critical Dictionary,* Bayle demonstrated the results of his own efforts with a famous article on the Israelite King David. Undermining the traditional picture of the heroic David, he portrayed the king as a sensual, treacherous, cruel, and basically evil man. Bayle's *Dictionary,* which attacked traditional religious practices and heroes, was well known to eighteenth-century philosophes. One critic regarded it as the "Bible of the eighteenth century."

THE IMPACT OF TRAVEL LITERATURE

Skepticism about both Christianity and European culture itself was nourished by travel reports. In the course of the seventeenth century, traders, missionaries, medical practitioners, and navigators began to publish an increasing number of travel books that gave accounts of many different cultures. By the end of the seventeenth century, this travel literature began to make an impact on the minds of educated Europeans. The realization that there were highly developed civilizations with different customs in other parts of the world forced Europeans to evaluate their own civilization relative to others. What had seemed to be practices grounded in reason now appeared to be matters of custom. Certainties about European practices gave way to cultural relativism.

Cultural relativism was accompanied by religious skepticism. As these travel accounts made clear, the Christian perception of God was merely one of many. Some people were devastated by this revelation: "Some complete their demoralization by extensive travel, and lose whatever shreds of religion remained to them. Every day they see a new religion, new customs, new rites."[2]

THE LEGACY OF LOCKE AND NEWTON

The intellectual inspiration for the Enlightenment came primarily from two Englishmen, Isaac Newton and John Locke, acknowledged by the philosophes as two great minds. Newton was frequently singled out for praise as the "greatest and rarest genius that ever rose for the ornament and instruction of the species." One English poet declared: "Nature and Nature's Laws lay hid in Night; God said, 'Let Newton be,' and all was Light." Enchanted by the grand design of the Newtonian world-machine, the intellectuals of the Enlightenment were convinced that by following Newton's rules of reasoning they could discover the natural laws that governed politics, economics, justice, religion, and the arts. The world and everything in it were like a giant machine.

In the eyes of the philosophes, only the philosopher John Locke came close to Newton's genius. Although Locke's political ideas had an enormous impact on the Western world in the eighteenth century, it was his theory of knowledge that especially influenced the philosophes. In his *Essay Concerning Human Understanding*, written in 1690, Locke denied Descartes's belief in innate ideas. Instead, argued Locke, every person was born with a *tabula rasa*, a blank mind:

> Let us then suppose the mind to be, as we say, white paper, void of all characters, without any ideas. How comes it to be furnished? Whence comes it by that vast store which the busy and boundless fancy of man has painted on it with an almost endless variety? Whence has it all the materials of reason and knowledge? To this I answer, in one word, from experience. . . . Our observation, employed either about external sensible objects or about the internal operations of our minds perceived and reflected on by ourselves, is that which supplies our understanding with all the materials of thinking.[3]

Our knowledge, then, is derived from our environment, not from heredity; from reason, not from faith. Locke's philosophy implied that people were molded by their environment, by the experiences that they received through their senses from their surrounding world. By changing the environment and subjecting people to proper influences, they could be changed and a new society created. Evil was not innate in human beings, but a product of bad education, rotten institutions, and inherited prejudices. And how should the environment be changed? Newton had already paved the way by showing how reason enabled enlightened people to discover the natural laws to which all institutions should conform. No wonder the philosophes were enamored of Newton and Locke. Taken together, their ideas seemed to offer the hope of a "brave new world" built on reason.

The Philosophes and Their Ideas

The intellectuals of the Enlightenment were known by the French name of philosophes although not all of them were French and few were philosophers in the literal sense of the term. They were literary people, professors, journalists, statesmen, economists, political scientists, and, above all, social reformers. They came from both the nobility and the middle class, and a few even stemmed from lower-middle-class origins. Although it was a truly international and cosmopolitan movement, the Enlightenment also enhanced the dominant role being played by French culture. Paris was the recognized capital of the Enlightenment, and most of its leaders were French. The French philosophes, in turn, affected intellectuals elsewhere and created a movement that touched the entire Western world, including the British and Spanish colonies in America.

Although the philosophes faced different political circumstances depending upon the country in which they lived, they shared common bonds as part of a truly international movement. Although they were called philosophers, what did philosophy mean to them? The role of philosophy was to change the world, not just discuss it. As one writer said, the philosophe is one who "applies himself to the study of society with the purpose of making his kind better and happier." To the philosophes, rationalism did not mean the creation of a grandiose system of thought to explain all things. Reason was scientific method, and it meant an appeal to facts and experience. A spirit of rational criticism was to be applied to everything, including religion and politics. The philosophes aggressively pursued a secular view of life since their focus was not on an afterlife, but on this world and how it could be improved and enjoyed.

The philosophes' call for freedom of expression is a reminder that their work was done in an atmosphere of censorship. The philosophes were not free to write whatever they chose. Although standards fluctuated wildly at times, state censors decided what could be published, and protests from any number of government bodies could result in the seizure of books and the imprisonment of their authors, publishers, and sellers.

The philosophes found ways to get around state censorship. Some published under pseudonyms or anonymously or abroad, especially in Holland. The use of double meanings, such as talking about the Persians when they meant the French, became standard procedure for many. Books were also published and circulated secretly or in manuscript form to avoid the censors. As frequently happens with attempted censorship, the government's announcement that a book had been burned often made the book more desirable and more popular.

Although the philosophes constituted a kind of "family circle" bound together by common intellectual bonds, they often disagreed as well. Spanning almost an entire century, the Enlightenment evolved over time with each succeeding generation becoming more radical as it built upon the contributions of the previous one. A few people, however, dominated the landscape completely, and we might best begin our survey of the ideas of the philosophes by looking at three French giants—Montesquieu, Voltaire, and Diderot.

The Separation of Powers

The Enlightenment affected the "new world" of America as much as it did the "old world" of Europe. American philosophes, such as Benjamin Franklin, James Madison, and Thomas Jefferson, were well aware of the ideas of European Enlightenment thinkers. This selection from Montesquieu's The Spirit of the Laws *enunciates the "separation of powers" doctrine.*

Montesquieu, *The Spirit of the Laws*

Of the Constitution of England

In every government there are three sorts of power: the legislative; the executive in respect to things dependent on the law of nations; and the executive in regard to matters that depend on the civil law.

By virtue of the first, the prince or magistrate enacts temporary or perpetual laws, and amends or abrogates those that have been already enacted. By the second, he makes peace or war, sends or receives embassies, establishes the public security, and provides against invasions. By the third, he punishes criminals, or determines the disputes that arise between individuals. The latter we shall call the judiciary power, and the other simply the executive power of the state.

The political liberty of the subject is a tranquillity of mind arising from the opinion each person has of his safety. In order to have this liberty, it is requisite the government be so constituted as one man need not be afraid of another.

When the legislative and executive powers are united in the same person, or in the same body of magistrates, there can be no liberty; because apprehensions may arise, lest the same monarch or senate should enact tyrannical laws, to execute them in a tyrannical manner.

Again, there is no liberty, if the judiciary power be not separated from the legislative and executive. Were it joined with the legislative, the life and liberty of the subject would be exposed to arbitrary control; for the judge would be then the legislator. Were it joined to the executive power, the judge might behave with violence and oppression.

There would be an end of everything, were the same man or the same body, whether of the nobles or of the people, to exercise those three powers, that of enacting laws, that of executing the public resolutions, and of trying the causes of individuals.

MONTESQUIEU AND POLITICAL THOUGHT

Charles de Secondat, the baron de Montesquieu (1689–1755), came from the French nobility. He received a classical education and then studied law. His own estate, as well as his marriage to a wealthy Protestant heiress, enabled him to live a life dedicated to travel, study, and writing. In his first work, the *Persian Letters*, published in 1721, he used the format of two Persians supposedly traveling in Western Europe and sending their impressions back home, to enable him to criticize French institutions, especially the Catholic church and the French monarchy. Much of the program of the French Enlightenment is contained in this work: the attack on traditional religion, the advocacy of religious toleration, the denunciation of slavery, and the use of reason to liberate human beings from their prejudices.

Montesquieu's most famous work, *The Spirit of the Laws*, was published in 1748. This treatise was a comparative study of governments in which Montesquieu attempted to apply the scientific method to the social and political arena to ascertain the "natural laws" governing the social relationships of human beings. Montesquieu distinguished three basic kinds of governments: republics, suitable for small states and based on citizen involvement; monarchy, appropriate for middle-sized states and grounded in the ruling class's adherence to law; and despotism, apt for large empires and dependent on fear to inspire obedience. Montesquieu used England as an example of the second category, and it was his praise and analysis of England's constitution that led to his most far-reaching and lasting contribution to political thought—the importance of checks and balances created by means of a separation of powers (see the box above). He believed that England's system, with its separate executive, legislative, and judicial powers that served to limit and control each other, provided the greatest freedom and security for a state. In large part, Montesquieu misread the English situation and insisted on a separation of powers because he wanted the nobility of France (of which he was a member) to play an active role in the running of the French government. The translation of his work into English two years after publication ensured that it would be read by American philosophes, such as Benjamin Franklin, James Madison, John Adams, Alexander Hamilton, and Thomas Jefferson, who incorporated its principles into the U.S. Constitution (see Chapter 19).

VOLTAIRE AND THE ENLIGHTENMENT

The greatest figure of the Enlightenment was Francois-Marie Arouet, known simply as Voltaire (1694–1778). Son of a prosperous middle-class family from Paris, Voltaire received a classical education typical of Jesuit schools. Although he studied law, he wished to be a writer and achieved his first success as a playwright. By his mid-twenties, Voltaire had been hailed as the successor to Racine (see Chapter 15) for his tragedy *Oedipe* and his epic *Henriade* on his favorite king, Henry IV. His wit made him a darling of the Parisian intellectuals but also involved him in a quarrel with a dissolute nobleman that forced him to flee France and live in England for almost two years.

Well received in English literary and social circles, the young playwright was much impressed by England. His *Philosophic Letters on the English*, written in 1733, expressed a deep admiration of English life, especially its respect for merchants, scientists, and literary figures, its freedom of the press, its political freedom, and its religious toleration. In judging the English religious situation, he made the famous remark that "if there were just one religion in England, despotism would threaten, if there were two religions, they would cut each other's throats, but there are thirty religions, and they live together peacefully and happily." Although he clearly exaggerated the freedoms England possessed, in a roundabout way Voltaire had managed to criticize many of the ills oppressing France, especially royal absolutism and the lack of religious toleration and freedom of thought. He had left France a playwright; he came back a philosophe.

Upon his return to France, Voltaire's reputation as the author of the *Philosophic Letters* made it necessary for him to retire to Cirey, near France's eastern border, where he lived in semiseclusion on the estate of his mistress, Madame de Châtelet. He eventually settled on a magnificent estate at Ferney. Located in France near the Swiss border, Ferney gave Voltaire the freedom to write what he wished. By this time, through his writings, inheritance, and clever investments, Voltaire had become wealthy and now had the leisure to write an almost endless stream of pamphlets, novels, plays, letters, and histories.

Although he touched on all of the themes of importance to the philosophes, Voltaire was especially well known for his criticism of traditional religion and his strong attachment to the ideal of religious toleration (see the box on p. 492). He lent his prestige and skills as a polemicist to fight cases of intolerance in France. The most famous incident was the Calas affair. Jean Calas was a Protestant from Toulouse who was accused of murdering his own son to stop him from becoming a Catholic. Tortured to confess his guilt, Calas died shortly thereafter. An angry and indignant Voltaire published devastating broadsides that aroused public opinion and forced a retrial in which Calas was exonerated when it was proved that his son had actually committed suicide. The family was paid an indemnity, and Voltaire's appeals for toleration appeared all the more reasonable. In 1763, he penned his *Treatise on Toleration* in which he argued that religious toleration had created no problems for England and Holland and reminded governments that "all men are brothers under God." As he grew older, Voltaire became ever more strident in his denunciations. "Crush the infamous thing," he thundered repeatedly—the infamous thing being religious fanaticism, intolerance, and superstition.

Throughout his life, Voltaire championed not only religious tolerance, but also deism, a religious outlook shared by most other philosophes. Deism was built upon the Newtonian world-machine, which implied the existence of a mechanic (God) who had created the universe. Voltaire said: "In the opinion that there is a God, there are difficulties, but in the contrary opinion there are absurdities." To Voltaire and most other philosophes, God had no direct involvement in the world he had created and allowed to run according to its own natural laws. God did not extend grace or answer prayers as Christians liked to believe. Jesus might be a "good fellow," as Voltaire called him, but he was not divine as Christianity claimed.

VOLTAIRE. François-Marie Arouet, better known as Voltaire, achieved his first success as a playwright. A philosophe, Voltaire was well known for his criticism of traditional religion and his support of religious toleration.

DIDEROT AND THE *ENCYCLOPEDIA*

Denis Diderot (1713–1784) was the son of a skilled craftsman from eastern France. He received a Jesuit education and went on to the University of Paris to fulfill his father's hopes that he would be a lawyer or pursue a career in the church. Diderot did neither. Instead he became a freelance writer so that he could be free to study and read in many subjects and languages. For the rest of his life, Diderot remained dedicated to his independence and was always in love with new ideas.

Diderot's numerous writings reflected typical Enlightened interests. One of his favorite topics was Christianity, which he condemned as fanatical and unreasonable. As he grew older, his literary attacks on Christianity grew more vicious. Of all religions, he maintained, Christianity was the worst, "the most absurd and the most atrocious

The Attack on Religious Intolerance

Although Voltaire's attacks on religion were in no way original, his lucid prose, biting satire, and clever wit caused his works to be widely read and all the more influential. These two selections present different sides of Voltaire's attack on religious intolerance. The first is from his straightforward treatise, The Ignorant Philosopher, *and the second is from his only real literary masterpiece, the novel* Candide, *where he uses humor to make the same fundamental point about religious intolerance.*

Voltaire, *The Ignorant Philosopher*

The contagion of fanaticism then still subsists. . . . The author of the Treatise upon Toleration has not mentioned the shocking executions wherein so many unhappy victims perished in the valleys of Piedmont. He has passed over in silence the massacre of six hundred inhabitants of Valtelina, men, women, and children, who were murdered by the Catholics in the month of September, 1620. I will not say it was with the consent and assistance of the archbishop of Milan, Charles Borome, who was made a saint. Some passionate writers have averred this fact, which I am very far from believing; but I say, there is scarce any city or borough in Europe, where blood has not been spilt for religious quarrels; I say, that the human species has been perceptibly diminished, because women and girls were massacred as well as men; I say, that Europe would have had a third larger population, if there had been no theological disputes. In fine, I say, that so far from forgetting these abominable times, we should frequently take a view of them, to inspire an eternal horror for them; and that it is for our age to make reparation by toleration, for this long collection of crimes, which has taken place through the want of toleration, during sixteen barbarous centuries.

Let it not then be said, that there are no traces left of that shocking fanaticism, of the want of toleration; they are still everywhere to be met with, even in those countries that are esteemed the most humane. The Lutheran and Calvinist preachers, were they masters, would, perhaps, be as little inclined to pity, as obdurate, as insolent as they upbraid their antagonists with being.

Voltaire, *Candide*

At last he [Candide] approached a man who had just been addressing a big audience for a whole hour on the subject of charity. The orator peered at him and said:

"What is your business here? Do you support the Good Old Cause?"

"There is not effect without a cause," replied Candide modestly. "All things are necessarily connected and arranged for the best. It was my fate to be driven from Lady Cunégonde's presence and made to run the gauntlet, and now I have to beg my bread until I can earn it. Things should not have happened otherwise."

"Do you believe that the Pope is Antichrist, my friend?" said the minister.

"I have never heard anyone say so," replied Candide; "but whether he is or he isn't, I want some food."

"You don't deserve to eat," said the other. "Be off with you, you villain, you wretch! Don't come near me again or you'll suffer for it."

The minister's wife looked out of the window at that moment, and seeing a man who was not sure that the Pope was Antichrist, emptied over his head a chamber pot, which shows to what lengths ladies are driven by religious zeal.

in its dogma" (see the box on p. 494). Near the end of his life, he argued for an essentially materialistic conception of life: "This world is only a mass of molecules. There is a law of necessity that works without design, without effort, without intelligence, and without progress."

Diderot's most famous contribution to the Enlightenment was the twenty-eight–volume *Encyclopedia, or Classified Dictionary of the Sciences, Arts, and Trades,* that he edited and called the "great work of his life." Its purpose, according to Diderot, was to "change the general way of thinking." It did precisely that in becoming a major weapon of the philosophes' crusade against the old French society. The contributors included many philosophes who expressed their major concerns. They attacked religious superstition and advocated toleration as well as a program for social, legal, and political improvements that would lead to a society that was more cosmopolitan, more tolerant, more humane, and more reasonable. In later editions, the price of the *Encyclopedia* was drastically reduced, dramatically increasing its sales and making it available to doctors, clergy, teachers, lawyers, and even military officers. The ideas of the Enlightenment were spread even further as a result.

TOWARD A NEW "SCIENCE OF MAN"

The Enlightenment belief that Newton's scientific methods could be used to discover the natural laws underlying all areas of human life led to the emergence in the eighteenth century of what the philosophes called a "science of man" or what we would call the social sciences. In a number of areas, philosophes arrived at natural laws that they believed governed human actions. If these "natural laws" seem less than universal to us, it reminds us how much the philosophes were people of their times reacting to the conditions they faced. Nevertheless, their efforts did at least lay the foundations for the modern social sciences.

That a "science of man" was possible was a strong belief of the Scottish philosopher David Hume (1711–1776). An important figure in the history of philosophy, Hume has also been called "a pioneering social scientist." In his *Treatise on Human Nature,* which he subtitled "An Attempt to Introduce the Experimental Method of Reasoning into Moral Subjects," Hume argued that observation and reflection, grounded in "systematized common sense," made conceivable a "science of man." Careful examination of the experiences that constituted human life would lead to the knowledge of human nature that would make possible "a science, which will not be inferior in certainty, and will be much superior in utility, to any other of human comprehension."

The Physiocrats and Adam Smith have been viewed as founders of the modern discipline of economics. The leader of the Physiocrats was François Quesnay (1694–1774), a highly successful French court physician. Quesnay and the Physiocrats claimed they would discover the natural economic laws that governed human society because they were "susceptible of demonstration as severe and incontestable as those of geometry and algebra." Their first principle was that land constituted the only source of wealth and that wealth itself could be increased only by agriculture because all other economic activities were unproductive and sterile. To the Physiocrats, agriculture included the exploitation of natural resources, especially mining. Even the state's revenues should come from a single tax on the land rather than the hodgepodge of inequitable taxes and privileges currently in place. In stressing the economic primacy of agricultural production, the Physiocrats were rejecting the mercantilist emphasis on the significance of money—that is, gold and silver—as the primary determinants of wealth (see Chapter 15).

Their second major "natural law" of economics also represented a repudiation of mercantilism, specifically, its emphasis on a controlled economy for the benefit of the state. Instead the Physiocrats stressed that the existence of the natural economic forces of supply and demand made it imperative that individuals should be left free to pursue their own economic self-interest. In doing so, all of society would ultimately benefit. Consequently, they argued that the state should in no way interrupt the free play of natural economic forces by government regulation of the economy, but leave it alone, a doctrine that subsequently became known by its French name, *laissez-faire* (to let alone).

The best statement of laissez-faire was made in 1776 by a Scottish philosopher, Adam Smith (1723–1790), when he published his famous work, *Inquiry into the Nature and Causes of the Wealth of Nations,* known simply as *The Wealth of Nations.* In the process of enunciating three of his basic principles of economics, Smith presented a strong attack on mercantilism. First, he condemned the mercantilist use of protective tariffs to protect home industries. A tailor, he argued, does not try to make his own shoes, nor does a shoemaker try to make his own clothes. Following this line of reasoning, if one country can supply another country with a product cheaper than the latter can make it, it is better to purchase than to produce it. Each nation, then, should produce what it did best without the artificial barriers of tariffs. To Adam Smith, free trade was a fundamental economic principle. Smith's second principle was his labor theory of value. Like the Physiocrats, he claimed that gold and silver were not the source of a nation's true wealth, but, unlike the Physiocrats, he did not believe that soil was either. Rather labor—the labor of individual farmers, artisans, and merchants—constituted the true wealth of a nation. Finally, like the Physiocrats, Smith believed that the state should not interfere in economic matters; indeed, he gave to government only three basic functions: it should protect society from invasion (army); defend individuals from injustice and oppression (police); and keep up certain public works, such as roads and canals, that private individuals could not afford. Thus, in Smith's view the state should be a kind of "passive policeman" that stays out of the lives of individuals. In emphasizing the economic liberty of the individual, the Physiocrats and Adam Smith laid the foundation for what became known in the nineteenth century as economic liberalism.

DENIS DIDEROT. Editor of the *Encyclopedia,* Diderot was a major figure in propagating the ideas of the French philosophes. He had diverse interests and penned an incredible variety of literary works. He is shown here in a portrait by Jean Honoré Fragonard.

THE LATER ENLIGHTENMENT

By the late 1760s, a new generation of philosophes who had grown up with the worldview of the Enlightenment began to move beyond their predecessors' beliefs. Baron Paul d'Holbach (1723–1789), a wealthy German aristocrat who settled in Paris, preached a doctrine of strict

Diderot Questions Christian Sexual Standards

Denis Diderot was one of the bolder thinkers of the Enlightenment. Although best remembered for the Encyclopedia, *he was the author of many works that he considered too advanced and withheld from publication. In his* Supplement to the Voyage of Bouganville, *he constructed a dialogue between Orou, a Tahitian who symbolizes the wisdom of a philosophe, and a chaplain who defends Christian sexual mores. The dialogue gave Diderot the opportunity to criticize the practice of sexual chastity and monogamy.*

Denis Diderot, *Supplement to the Voyage of Bouganville*

[Orou] "You are young and healthy [speaking to the chaplain] and you have just had a good supper. He who sleeps alone sleeps badly; at night a man needs a woman at his side. Here is my wife and here are my daughters. Choose whichever one pleases you most, but if you would like to do me a favor, you will give your preference to my youngest girl, who has not yet had any children. . . ."

The chaplain replied that his religion, his holy orders, his moral standards and his sense of decency all prevented him from accepting Orou's invitation.

Orou answered: "I don't know what this thing is that you call religion, but I can only have a low opinion of it because it forbids you to partake of an innocent pleasure to which Nature, the sovereign mistress of us all, invites everybody. It seems to prevent you from bringing one of your fellow creatures into the world, from doing a favor asked of by a father, a mother and their children, from repaying the kindness of a host, and from enriching a nation by giving it an additional citizen. . . . Look at the distress you have caused to appear on the faces of these four women—they are afraid you have noticed some defect in them that arouses your distaste. . . ."

The Chaplain: "You don't understand—it's not that. They are all four of them equally beautiful. But there is my religion! My holy orders! . . . [God] spoke to our ancestors and gave them laws; he prescribed to them the way in which he wishes to be honored; he ordained that certain actions are good and others he forbade them to do as being evil."

Orou: "I see. And one of these evil actions which he has forbidden is that of a man who goes to bed with a woman or girl. But in that case, why did he make two sexes?"

The Chaplain: "In order that they might come together—but only when certain conditions are satisfied and only after certain initial ceremonies one man belongs to one woman and only to her; one woman belongs to one man and only to him." Orou: "For their whole lives?"

The Chaplain: "For their whole lives. . . ."

Orou: "I find these strange precepts contrary to nature, and contrary to reason. . . . Furthermore, your laws seem to me to be contrary to the general order of things. For in truth is there anything so senseless as a precept that forbids us to heed the changing impulses that are inherent in our being, or commands that require a degree of constancy which is not possible, that violate the liberty of both male and female by chaining them perpetually to one another? . . . I don't know what your great workman [God] is, but I am very happy that he never spoke to our forefathers, and I hope that he never speaks to our children, for if he does, he may tell them the same foolishness, and they may be foolish enough to believe it."

atheism and materialism. In his *System of Nature,* written in 1770, he argued that everything in the universe consisted of matter in motion. Human beings were simply machines; God was a product of the human mind and was unnecessary for leading a moral life. People needed only reason to live in this world: "Let us persuade men to be just, beneficent, moderate, sociable; not because the gods demand it, but because they must please men. Let us advise them to abstain from vice and crimes; not because they will be punished in the other world, but because they will suffer for it in this."[4] Holbach shocked almost all of his fellow philosophes with his uncompromising atheism. Most intellectuals remained more comfortable with deism and feared the effect of atheism on society.

Marie-Jean de Condorcet (1743–1794), another French philosophe, made an exaggerated claim for optimism that appears utopian in comparison with his predecessors' cautious hopes for gradual progress. Condorcet was a victim of the turmoil of the French Revolution and wrote his chief work, *The Progress of the Human Mind,* while in hiding during the Reign of Terror (see Chapter 19). His survey of human history convinced him that humans had progressed through nine stages of history. Now, with the spread of science and reason, humans were about to enter the tenth stage, one of perfection, in which they will see that "there is no limit to the perfecting of the powers of man; that human perfectibility is in reality indefinite, that the progress of this perfectibility . . . has no other limit than the duration of the globe upon which nature has placed us." Shortly after composing this work, the prophet of humankind's perfection died in a French revolutionary prison.

ROUSSEAU AND THE SOCIAL CONTRACT

No one was more critical of the work of his predecessors than Jean-Jacques Rousseau (1712–1778). Born in the city of Geneva, he was abandoned by his family at an early age and spent his youth wandering about France and Italy holding various jobs. He went back to school for a while to study music and the classics (he could afford to do so after becoming the paid lover of an older woman). Eventually, he made his way to Paris where he became a friend of Diderot and was introduced into the circles of the philosophes. He never really liked the social life of the cities, however, and frequently withdrew into long periods of solitude.

Rousseau's political beliefs were presented in two major works. In his *Discourse on the Origins of the Inequality of Mankind,* Rousseau began with humans in their primitive condition (or state of nature—see Chapter 15) where they were happy. There were no laws, no judges; all people were equal. But what had gone wrong?

> The first man who, having enclosed a piece of ground, thought of saying, This is mine, and found people simple enough to believe him, was the true founder of civil society. How many crimes, wars, murders; how much misery and horror the human race would have been spared if someone had pulled up the stakes and filled in the ditch, and cried to his fellow men: "Beware of listening to this impostor. You are lost if you forget that the fruits of the earth belong to everyone and that the earth itself belongs to no one!"[5]

In order to preserve their private property, people adopted laws and governors. In so doing, they rushed headlong not to liberty, but into chains. "What then is to be done? Must societies be totally abolished? . . . Must we return again to the forest to live among bears?" No, civilized humans could "no longer subsist on plants or acorns or live without laws and magistrates." Government was an evil, but a necessary one.

In his celebrated treatise *The Social Contract,* published in 1762, Rousseau tried to harmonize individual liberty with governmental authority (see the box on p. 496). The social contract was basically an agreement on the part of an entire society to be governed by its general will. If any individual wished to follow his own self-interest, then he should be compelled to abide by the general will. "This means nothing less than that he will be forced to be free," said Rousseau, because the general will represented a community's highest aspirations, that which was best for the entire community. Thus, liberty was achieved through being forced to follow what was best for all people because, he believed, what was best for all was best for each individual. True freedom is adherence to laws that one has imposed on one's self. To Rousseau, because everybody was responsible for framing the general will, the creation of laws could never be delegated to a parliamentary institution:

> Thus the people's deputies are not and could not be its representatives; they are merely its agents; and they cannot decide anything finally. Any law which the people has not ratified in person is void; it is not law at all. The English people believes itself to be free; it is gravely mistaken; it is free only during the election of Members of Parliament; as soon as the Members are elected, the people is enslaved; it is nothing.[6]

This is an extreme, idealistic statement, but it is the ultimate statement of participatory democracy. Perhaps Rousseau was thinking of his native city of Geneva, a

CHRONOLOGY

Works of the Philosophes

Work	Date
Montesquieu, *Persian Letters*	1721
Voltaire, *Philosophic Letters on the English*	1733
Hume, *Treatise on Human Nature*	1739–1740
Montesquieu, *The Spirit of the Laws*	1748
Voltaire, *The Age of Louis XIV*	1751
Diderot, *The Encyclopedia*	1751–1765
Rousseau, *The Social Contract, Emile*	1762
Voltaire, *Treatise on Toleration*	1763
Beccaria, *On Crimes and Punishments*	1764
Holbach, *System of Nature*	1770
Smith, *The Wealth of Nations*	1776
Gibbon, *The Decline and Fall of the Roman Empire*	1776–1788
Wollstonecraft, *Vindication of the Rights of Woman*	1792
Condorcet, *The Progress of the Human Mind*	1794

JEAN-JACQUES ROUSSEAU. By the late 1760s, a new generation of philosophes arose who began to move beyond and even to question the beliefs of their predecessors. Of the philosophes of the late Enlightenment, Jean-Jacques Rousseau was perhaps the most critical of his predecessors.

A Social Contract

Although Jean-Jacques Rousseau was one of the French philosophes, he has also been called "the father of Romanticism." His political ideas have proved extremely controversial. Though some have hailed him as the prophet of democracy, others have labeled him an apologist for totalitarianism. This selection is taken from one of his most famous books, The Social Contract.

Jean-Jacques Rousseau,
The Social Contract

Book 1, Chapter 6: The Social Pact

"How to find a form of association which will defend the person and goods of each member with the collective force of all, and under which each individual, while uniting himself with the others, obeys no one but himself, and remains as free as before." This is the fundamental problem to which the social contract holds the solution. . . .

Chapter 7: The Sovereign

Despite their common interest, subjects will not be bound by their commitment unless means are found to guarantee their fidelity.

For every individual as a man may have a private will contrary to, or different from, the general will that he has as a citizen. His private interest may he speak with a very different voice from that of the public interest; his absolute and naturally independent existence may make him regard what he owes to the common cause as a gratuitous contribution, the loss of which would be less painful for others than the payment is onerous for him; and fancying that the artificial person which constitutes the state is a mere rational entity, he might seek to enjoy the rights of a citizen without doing the duties of a subject. The growth of this kind of injustice would bring about the ruin of the body politic.

Hence, in order that the social pact shall not be an empty formula, it is tacitly implied in that commitment—which alone can give force to all others—that whoever refused to obey the general will shall be constrained to do so by the whole body, which means nothing other than that he shall be forced to be free; for this is the condition which, by giving each citizen to the nation, secures him against all personal dependence, it is the condition which shapes both the design and the working of the political machine, and which alone bestows justice on civil contracts—without it, such contracts would be absurd, tyrannical and liable to the grossest abuse.

community small enough that it could conform to these strict rules of absolute democracy. But we do not really know. *The Social Contract* has evoked contradictory interpretations ever since the outbreak of the French Revolution. The more radical revolutionaries used it during the second stage of the French Revolution to justify democratic politics, but others have viewed Rousseau's emphasis on a coercive general will ("forced to be free") as leading to a totalitarian system. Rousseau himself said, "Those who boast that they understand the whole of it are cleverer than I am."

Another influential treatise by Rousseau also appeared in 1762. Entitled *Emile,* it is one of the Enlightenment's most important works on education. Written in the form of a novel, the work was really a general treatise "on the education of the natural man." During the years from five to twelve, the boy Emile was allowed to encounter nature directly and learn by experience. From twelve to sixteen, he was open to more abstract thoughts; this was the time when education in ethics would take hold. Seventeen to nineteen was the proper time for encouraging the use of reason. Rousseau's fundamental concern was that education should foster rather than restrict children's natural instincts. Life's experiences had shown Rousseau the importance of the promptings of the heart, and what he sought was a balance between heart and mind, between sentiment and reason. This emphasis on heart and sentiment made him a precursor of the intellectual movement called Romanticism that dominated Europe at the beginning of the nineteenth century.

But Rousseau did not necessarily practice what he preached. His own children were sent to foundling homes, where many children died at a young age. Rousseau also viewed women as "naturally" different from men: "To fulfill [a woman's] functions, an appropriate physical constitution is necessary to her . . . she needs a soft sedentary life to suckle her babies. How much care and tenderness does she need to hold her family together." In Rousseau's *Emile,* Sophie, who was Emile's intended wife, was educated for her role as wife and mother by learning obedience and the nurturing skills that would enable her to provide loving care for her husband and children. Not everyone in the eighteenth century agreed with Rousseau, however, making ideas of gender an important issue in the Enlightenment.

THE "WOMAN'S QUESTION" IN THE ENLIGHTENMENT

For centuries, men had dominated the debate about the nature and value of women. In general, many male intellectuals had argued that the base nature of women made them inferior to men and made male domination of women

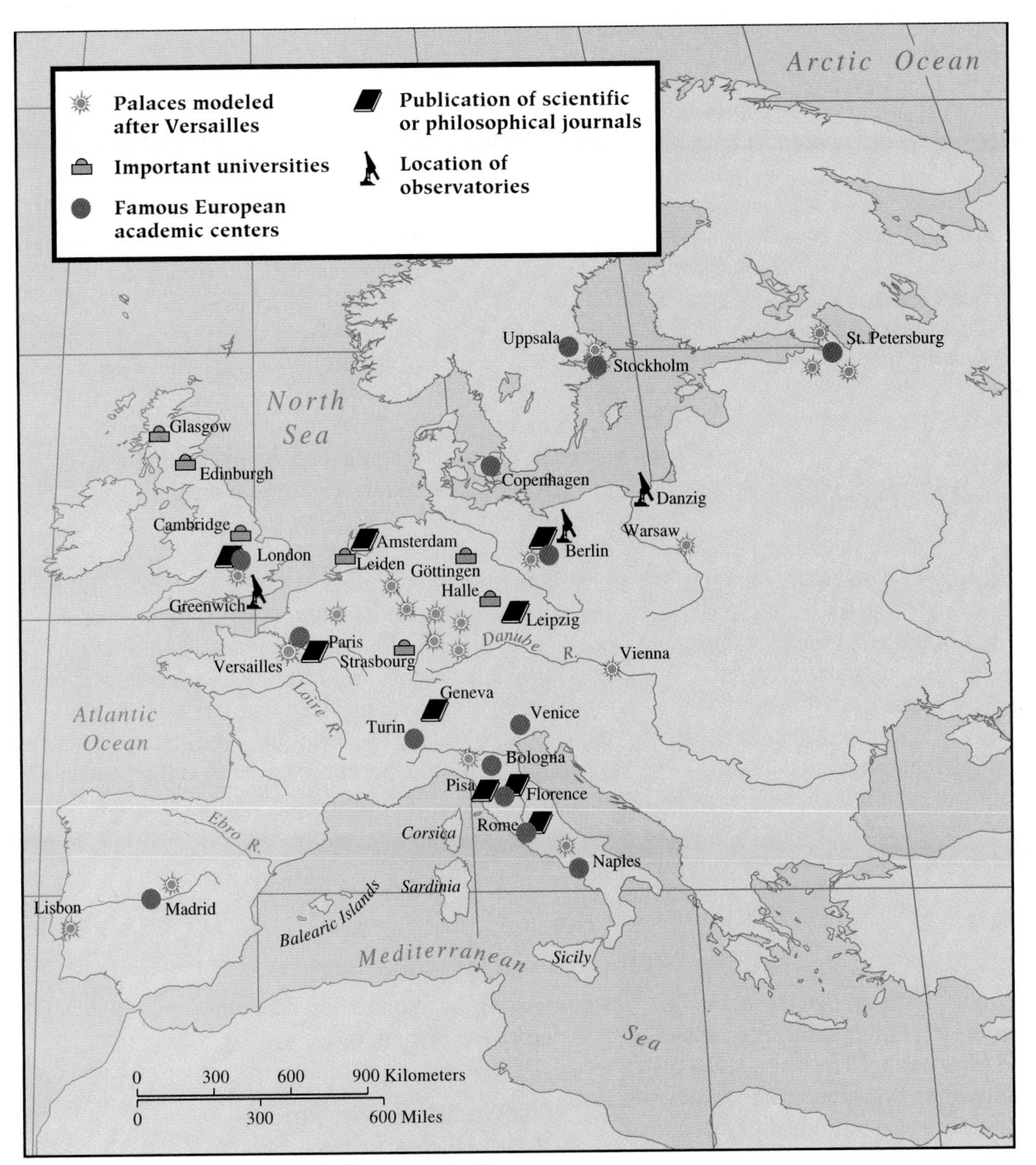

MAP 17.1 The Age of the Enlightenment in Europe.

necessary (see Chapter 16). In the seventeenth and eighteenth centuries, many male thinkers reinforced this view by arguing that it was based on "natural" biological differences between men and women. Like Rousseau, they argued that the female constitution made women mothers. Male writers, in particular, were critical of the attempts of some women in the Enlightenment to write on intellectual issues, arguing that women by nature were intellectually inferior to men. Nevertheless, some Enlightenment thinkers offered more positive views of women. Diderot, for example, maintained that men and women were not all that different, and Voltaire asserted that "women are capable of all that men are" in intellectual affairs.

It was women thinkers, however, who added new perspectives to the "woman's question" by making specific suggestions for improving the condition of women. Mary Astell (1666–1731), daughter of a wealthy English coal merchant, argued in 1697 in *A Serious Proposal to the Ladies* that women needed to become better educated. Men, she believed, would resent her proposal, "but they must excuse me, if I be as partial to my own sex as they are to theirs, and think women as capable of learning as men are, and that it becomes them as well."[7] In a later work entitled *Some Reflections upon Marriage,* Astell argued for the equality of the sexes in marriage: "If absolute sovereignty be not necessary in a state, how comes it to be so in a family. . . . For if arbitrary power is evil in itself, and an improper method of governing rational and free agents, it ought not be practiced anywhere. . . . If all men are born free, how is it that all women are born slaves?"[8]

The strongest statement for the rights of women in the eighteenth century was advanced by the English writer Mary Wollstonecraft (1759–1797), viewed by many as the founder of modern European feminism. In *Vindication of the Rights of Woman,* written in 1792, Wollstonecraft pointed out two contradictions in the views of women held by such Enlightenment thinkers as Rousseau. To argue that women must obey men, she said, was contrary to the

The Rights of Women

Mary Wollstonecraft responded to an unhappy childhood in a large family by seeking to lead an independent life. Few occupations were available for middle-class women in her day, but she survived by working as a teacher, chaperone, and governess to aristocratic children. All the while, she wrote and developed her ideas on the rights of women. This excerpt is taken from her Vindication of the Rights of Woman, *written in 1792. This work led to her reputation as the foremost British feminist thinker of the eighteenth century.*

Mary Wollstonecraft, *Vindication of the Rights of Woman*

It is a melancholy truth—yet such is the blessed effect of civilization—the most respectable women are the most oppressed; and, unless they have understandings far superior to the common run of understandings, taking in both sexes, they must, from being treated like contemptible beings, become contemptible. How many women thus waste life away the prey of discontent, who might have practiced as physicians, regulated a farm, managed a shop, and stood erect, supported by their own industry, instead of hanging their heads surcharged with the dew of sensibility, that consumes the beauty to which it at first gave luster. . . .

Proud of their weakness, however, [women] must always be protected, guarded from care, and all the rough toils that dignify the mind. If this be the fiat of fate, if they will make themselves insignificant and contemptible, sweetly to waste "life away," let them not expect to be valued when their beauty fades, for it is the fate of the fairest flowers to be admired and pulled to pieces by the careless hand that plucked them. In how many ways do I wish, from the purest benevolence, to impress this truth on my sex; yet I fear that they will not listen to a truth that dear-bought experience has brought home to many an agitated bosom, nor willingly resign the privileges of rank and sex for the privileges of humanity, to which those have no claim who do not discharge its duties. . . .

Would men but generously snap our chains, and be content with the rational fellowship instead of slavish obedience, they would find us more observant daughters, more affectionate sisters, more faithful wives, and more reasonable mothers—in a word, better citizens. We should then love them with true affection, because we should learn to respect ourselves; and the peace of mind of a worthy man would not be interrupted by the idle vanity of his wife.

beliefs of the same individuals that a system based on the arbitrary power of monarchs over their subjects or slave owners over their slaves was wrong. The subjection of women to men was equally wrong. In addition, she argued that the Enlightenment was based on an ideal of reason innate in all human beings. If women have reason, then they too are entitled to the same rights that men have. Women, Wollstonecraft declared, should have equal rights with men in education and in economic and political life as well (see the box above).

The Social Environment of the Philosophes

The social background of the philosophes varied considerably, from the aristocratic Montesquieu to the lower-

THE SALON OF MADAME GEOFFRIN. An important factor in the development of the Enlightenment was the spread of new ideas to the literate elites of European society. Salons were an important part of this process. Madame Geoffrin, who presided over one of the best-known Parisian salons, is shown here, the third figure from the right in the front row.

The Salon: Can Men and Women Be Friends without Sex?

The salon was established in the seventeenth century by aristocratic women who sought conversation with men as intellectual equals without the demands of sexual love. These "precious women," who sought to gain moral prestige over their male suitors by their chastity, dominated the French salon in the early seventeenth century. But in the late seventeenth and eighteenth centuries, the females who organized the salons were well known for their sexual affairs and marriages with the great men invited to their salons. It was now taken for granted "that relations between women and men, however intellectual or artistic they might appear, could not remain platonic." The first two selections are from the novel The Great Cyrus *by Mlle. de Scudéry, who maintained one of the most famous literary salons. She applauded platonic love and scorned marriage. The third selection is from a nostalgic letter of Abbé Galiani to his former salon hostess, Mme. Necker, and describes an eighteenth-century salon.*

Mlle. de Scudéry, *The Great Cyrus*

Among us, love is not a simple passion as it is elsewhere; it is one of the requirements for good breeding. Every man must be in love. Every lady must be loved. No one among us is indifferent. Anyone capable of such hardness of heart would be reproached as for a crime; such liberty is so shameful that those who are not in love at least pretend to be. Custom does not oblige ladies to love but merely to allow themselves to be loved, and they put their pride in making illustrious conquests and in never losing those whom they have brought under their rule; yet they are severe, for the honor of our beauties consists in keeping the slaves they have made by the sheer power of their attractions and not by according favors; so that, by this custom, to be a lover is almost necessarily to be unhappy. . . . Yet it is not forbidden to reward a lover's perseverance by a totally pure affection . . . whatever can render them more lovable and loving is allowed, provided it does not shock that purity or modesty which, despite their gallantry, is these ladies' supreme virtue.

Mlle. de Scudéry, *The Great Cyrus*

"Then, said Tisandre [to Sapho—the name under which Mlle. de Scudéry portrayed herself] "you can hardly regard marriage as desirable." "It is true," replied Sapho, "that I consider it a lengthy slavery." "So you think all men are tyrants" "I think they may all become so . . . I know of course that there are some very worthy men who deserve all my esteem and could even acquire some friendship from me; but again, as soon as I think of them as husbands, I see them as masters so likely to turn into tyrants that I cannot help hating them there and then and thank the gods for giving me an inclination totally opposed to marriage."

Abbé Galiani, Letter to Mme. Necker

Not a Friday passes but I visit you in spirit. I arrive. I find you putting the finishing touches to your clothes. I sit at your feet. . . . Dinner is announced. We come out. The others eat meat. I abstain. I eat a lot of that green Scotch cod which I love. I give myself indigestion while admiring Abbé Morellet's skill at carving a young turkey. We get up from table. Coffee is served. Everyone talks at once. The Abbé Raynal agrees with me that Boston has severed its links with England forever and the same time Creutz and Marmontel agree that Grétry is the Pergolese of France. M. Necker thinks everything is perfect, bows his head, and goes away. That is how I spend my Fridays.

middle-class Diderot and Rousseau. The Enlightenment was not the preserve of any one class, although obviously its greatest appeal was to the aristocracy and upper middle classes of the major cities. The common people, especially the peasants, were little affected by the Enlightenment.

Of great importance to the Enlightenment was the spread of its ideas to the literate elite of European society. Although the publication and sale of books and treatises were crucial to this process, the salon was also a factor. Salons came into being in the seventeenth century but rose to new heights in the eighteenth. The salons were the elegant drawing rooms in the great urban houses of the wealthy where invited philosophes and guests gathered together and engaged in witty, sparkling conversations often centered on the new ideas of the philosophes. In France's rigid hierarchical society, the salons were important in bringing together writers and artists with aristocrats, government officials, and wealthy bourgeoisie.

As hostesses of the salons, women found themselves in a position to affect the decisions of kings, sway political opinion, and influence literary and artistic taste. Salons provided havens for people and views unwelcome in the royal court. When the *Encyclopedia* was suppressed by the French authorities, Marie-Thérèse de Geoffrin (1699–1777), a wealthy bourgeois widow whose father had been a valet, welcomed the encyclopedists to her salon and offered financial assistance to complete the work in secret.

Mme. Geoffrin was not without rivals, however. The marquise du Deffand (1697–1780) had abandoned her husband in the provinces and established herself in Paris where her ornate drawing room attracted many of the Enlightenment's great figures, including Montesquieu, Hume, and

Voltaire. In 1754, after she began to go blind, she was joined as a hostess by her illegitimate niece, Julie de Lespinasse (1733–1776). For the next ten years, their salon was the most brilliant in Europe until they quarreled and separated.

Although the salons were run by women, the reputation of a salon depended upon the stature of the males a hostess was able to attract (see the box on p. 499). Despite this male domination, however, both French and foreign observers complained that females exerted undue influence in French political affairs. Though exaggerated, this perception led to the decline of salons during the French Revolution.

The salon served an important role in promoting conversation and sociability between upper-class men and women as well as spreading the ideas of the Enlightenment. But other means of spreading Enlightenment ideas were also available. Coffeehouses, cafés, reading clubs, and public lending libraries established by the state were gathering places to exchange ideas. Learned societies were formed in cities throughout Europe and America. At such gatherings as the Select Society of Edinburgh, Scotland, and the American Philosophical Society in Philadelphia, lawyers, doctors, and local officials gathered to discuss Enlightened ideas. Secret societies also developed. The most famous was the Freemasons, established in London in 1717, France and Italy in 1726, and Prussia in 1744, where Frederick II himself was a grand master. It was no secret that the Freemasons were sympathetic to the ideas of the philosophes.

◆ Culture and Society in an Age of Enlightenment

The intellectual adventure fostered by the philosophes was accompanied by both traditional practices and important changes in the eighteenth-century world of culture and society.

Innovations in Art, Music, and Literature

Although the Baroque and Neoclassical styles that had dominated the seventeenth century continued into the eighteenth century, by the 1730s a new style known as Rococo had begun to affect decoration and architecture all over Europe. Though a French invention and enormously popular in Germany, Rococo became a truly international style.

Unlike the Baroque, which stressed majesty, power, and movement, Rococo emphasized grace and gentle action. Rococo rejected strict geometrical patterns and had a fondness for curves; it liked to follow the wandering lines of natural objects, such as seashells and flowers. It made much use of interlaced designs colored in gold with delicate contours and graceful curves. Highly secular, its lightness and charm spoke of the pursuit of pleasure, happiness, and love.

Some of Rococo's appeal is evident already in the work of Antoine Watteau (1684–1721), whose lyrical views of aristocratic life—refined, sensual, civilized, with gentlemen and ladies in elegant dress—revealed a world of upper-class pleasure and joy. Underneath that exterior, however, was an element of sadness as the artist revealed the fragility and transitory nature of pleasure, love, and life.

Another aspect of Rococo was the sense of enchantment and exuberance, especially evident in the work of Giovanni Battista Tiepolo (1696–1770). Much of Tiepolo's painting came to adorn the walls and ceilings of churches and palaces. His masterpiece is the ceiling of the Bishop's Palace at Würzburg, a massive scene representing the four continents. Tiepolo's work reminds us that Rococo decorative work could easily be used with Baroque architecture.

The palace of Versailles had made an enormous impact on Europe. "Keeping up with the Bourbons" became important as the Austrian emperor, the Swedish king, German princes and prince-bishops, Italian princes,

ANTOINE WATTEAU, *THE PILGRIMAGE TO CYTHERA*. Antoine Watteau was one of the most gifted painters in eighteenth-century France. His portrayal of aristocratic life reveals a world of elegance, wealth, and pleasure. In this painting, Watteau depicts a group of aristocratic pilgrims about to depart the island of Cythera, where they have paid homage to Venus, the goddess of love.

VIERZEHNHEILIGEN, INTERIOR VIEW. Pictured here is the interior of the Vierzehnheiligen, the pilgrimage church designed by Balthasar Neumann. As this illustration shows, the Baroque-Rococo style of architecture created lavish buildings in which secular and spiritual elements became easily interchangeable. Elaborate detail, blazing light, rich colors, and opulent decoration were blended together to create a work of stunning beauty.

and even a Russian tsar built grandiose palaces. While emulating Versailles's size, they were modeled less after the French classical style of Versailles than after the seventeenth-century Italian Baroque, as modified by a series of brilliant German and Austrian sculptor-architects. This Baroque-Rococo architectural style of the eighteenth century was conceived as a total work of art in which building, sculptural figures, and wall and ceiling paintings were blended into a harmonious whole. This style was used in both palaces and churches, and often the same architects did both. This is evident in the work of one of the greatest architects of the eighteenth century, Balthasar Neumann (1687–1753).

Neumann's two masterpieces are the pilgrimage church of the Vierzehnheiligen (The Fourteen Saints) in southern Germany and the Bishop's Palace known as the Residenz, the residential palace of the Schönborn prince-bishop of Würzburg. Secular and spiritual become easily interchangeable as lavish and fanciful ornament, light, bright colors, and elaborate and rich detail greet us in both buildings. An even more stunning example of Rococo is evident in the pilgrimage church of the Wies in southern Bavaria, designed by Domenikus Zimmermann

VIERZEHNHEILIGEN, EXTERIOR VIEW. Balthasar Neumann, one of the most prominent architects of the eighteenth century, used the Baroque-Rococo style of architecture to design some of the most beautiful buildings of the century. Pictured here is the exterior of his pilgrimage church of the Vierzehnheiligen (The Fourteen Saints), located in southern Germany.

JACQUES-LOUIS DAVID, *OATH OF THE HORATII*. The Frenchman David was one of the most famous Neoclassical artists of the late eighteenth century. In order to immerse himself in the world of classical antiquity, he painted the *Oath of the Horatii* in Rome. With its emphasis on patriotic duty, the work became an instant success in both Paris and Rome.

(1685–1766). The pilgrim in search of holiness is struck by an incredible richness of detail. Persuaded by joy rather than fear, the believer is lifted toward heaven on a cloud of rapture.

Despite the popularity of the Rococo style, Neoclassicism continued to maintain a strong appeal and in the late eighteenth century emerged in France as an established movement. Neoclassical artists wanted to recapture the dignity and simplicity of the classical style of ancient Greece and Rome. Some were especially influenced by the recent excavations of the ancient Roman cities of Herculaneum and Pompeii. Classical elements are evident in the work of Jacques-Louis David (1748–1825). In the *Oath of the Horatii,* he re-created a scene from Roman history in which the three Horatii brothers swore an oath before their father, proclaiming their willingness to sacrifice their lives for their country. David's Neoclassical style, with its moral seriousness and its emphasis on honor and patriotism, made him extremely popular during the French Revolution.

THE DEVELOPMENT OF MUSIC

The seventeenth and eighteenth centuries were the formative years of classical music and saw the rise of the opera and oratorio, the sonata, the concerto, and the symphony. The Italians were the first to develop these genres, but were soon followed by the Germans, Austrians, and English. As in previous centuries, most musicians depended on a patron—a prince, a well-endowed ecclesiastic, or an aristocrat. The many individual princes, archbishops, and bishops, each with his own court, provided the patronage that made Italy and Germany the musical leaders of Europe.

Many of the techniques of the Baroque musical style, which dominated Europe between 1600 and 1750, were perfected by two composers—Bach and Handel—who stand out as musical geniuses. Johann Sebastian Bach (1685–1750) came from a family of musicians. Bach held the post of organist and music director at a number of small German courts before becoming director of church music at the Church of St. Thomas in Leipzig in 1723. There Bach composed his Mass in B Minor, his St. Matthew's Passion, and the cantatas and motets that have established his reputation as one of the greatest composers of all time. Like the architect Balthasar Neumann, Bach could move with ease from the religious to the secular. In fact, his secular music reflects a boisterous spirit; his Coffee Cantata was a dialogue between father and daughter over the daughter's desire to drink the new beverage. Bach had no problem adding religious texts to the secular music he had composed in princely courts to make it church music. Above all for Bach, music was a means to worship God; in his own words, his task in life was to make "well-ordered music in the honor of God."

The other great musical giant of the early eighteenth century, George Frederick Handel (1685–1759) was, like Bach, born in Saxony in Germany and in the same year. In contrast to Bach's quiet provincial life, however, Handel experienced a stormy international career and was profoundly secular in temperament. After studying in Italy, where he began his career by writing operas in the Italian manner, in 1712 he moved to England where he spent most of his adult life attempting to run an opera company. Although patronized by the English royal court, Handel wrote music for large public audiences and was not averse to writing huge, unusual-sounding pieces. The band for his Fireworks Music, for example, was supposed

MOZART AS CHILD PRODIGY. This painting, done in Paris between 1763 and 1764, shows the seven-year-old Mozart playing at the harpsichord while his composer-father Leopold plays the violin and his sister Nannerl sings. Crowds greeted the young Mozart enthusiastically throughout the family's three-year tour of northern Europe.

to be accompanied by 101 cannon. Although he wrote more than forty operas and much other secular music, ironically the worldly Handel is probably best known for his religious music. He had no problem moving from Italian opera to religious oratorios when they proved to be more popular with his English public. An oratorio was an extended musical composition on a religious subject, usually taken from a biblical story. Only one of Handel's great oratorios, the *Messiah,* is well known today. It has been called "one of those rare works that appeal immediately to everyone, and yet is indisputably a masterpiece of the highest order."[9]

Although Bach and Handel composed many instrumental suites and concerti, orchestral music did not come to the fore until the second half of the eighteenth century, when new instruments such as the piano appeared. A new musical period, the classical era (1750–1830), also emerged, represented by two great innovators—Haydn and Mozart. Their renown caused the musical center of Europe to shift from Italy and Germany to the Austrian Empire.

Franz Joseph Haydn (1732–1809) spent most of his adult life as musical director for the wealthy Hungarian princes, the Esterhazy brothers. Haydn was incredibly prolific, composing 104 symphonies in addition to string quartets, concerti, songs, oratorios, and masses. In particular, Haydn developed new forms of instrumental music. His visits to England in 1790 and 1794 introduced him to another world where musicians wrote for public concerts rather than princely patrons. This "liberty," as he called it, induced him to write his two great oratorios, *The Creation* and *The Seasons,* both of which were dedicated to the common people.

The concerto, symphony, and opera all witnessed a climax in the works of Wolfgang Amadeus Mozart (1756–1791), a child prodigy who gave his first harpsichord concert at six and wrote his first opera at twelve. He, too, sought a patron, but his discontent with the overly demanding archbishop of Salzburg forced him to move to Vienna where his failure to find a permanent patron made his life miserable. Nevertheless, he wrote music prolifically and passionately until he died at thirty-five, a debt-ridden pauper. Mozart carried the tradition of Italian comic opera to new heights with *The Marriage of Figaro,* based on a Parisian play of the 1780s in which a valet outwits and outsings his noble employers, and *Don Giovanni,* a "black comedy" about the havoc Don Giovanni wrought on earth before he descended into hell. *The Marriage of Figaro, The Magic Flute,* and *Don Giovanni* are three of the world's greatest operas. Mozart composed with an ease of melody and a blend of grace, precision, and emotion that arguably no one has ever excelled. Haydn remarked to Mozart's father that "your son is the greatest composer known to me either in person or by reputation."

THE DEVELOPMENT OF THE NOVEL

Literary historians credit the eighteenth century with the decisive steps in the development of the novel. The novel was not a completely new literary genre but grew out of the medieval romances and the picaresque stories of the sixteenth century, such as Cervantes's *Don Quixote.* The English are credited with establishing the "modern novel as the chief vehicle" for fiction writing. With no established rules, the novel was open to much experimentation. It also proved especially attractive to women readers and women writers.

Samuel Richardson (1689–1761) was a printer by trade who did not turn to writing until his fifties. His first novel, *Pamela: or, Virtue Rewarded,* focused on a servant girl's resistance to numerous seduction attempts by her master. Finally, by reading the girl's letters describing her feelings about his efforts, the master realizes that she has a good mind as well as body and marries her. Virtue is rewarded. *Pamela* won Richardson a large audience as he appealed to the growing cult of sensibility in the eighteenth century—the taste for the sentimental and emotional. Samuel Johnson, another great English writer of the century and an even greater wit, remarked, "If you were to read Richardson for the story . . . you would hang yourself. But you must read him for the sentiment."

Reacting against the moral seriousness of Richardson, Henry Fielding (1707–1754) wrote novels about people without scruples who survived by their wits. His best work was *The History of Tom Jones, A Foundling,* a lengthy novel about the numerous adventures of a young scoundrel. Fielding presented scenes of English life from the hovels of London to the country houses of the aristocracy. In a number of hilarious episodes, he described characters akin to real types in English society. Although he emphasized action rather than inner feeling, Fielding did his own moralizing by attacking the hypocrisy of his age.

THE WRITING OF HISTORY

The philosophes were responsible for creating a "revolution" in the writing of history. Their secular orientation caused them to eliminate the role of God in history and freed them to concentrate on events themselves and search for causal relationships within a natural world. Earlier, the humanist historians of the Renaissance had also placed their histories in purely secular settings, but not with the same intensity and complete removal of God. Whereas the humanists had de-emphasized Christian presuppositions in favor of humans, Voltaire and other philosophe-historians eliminated those presuppositions altogether.

The philosophe-historians also broadened the scope of history from the humanists' preoccupation with politics. Politics still predominated in the work of Enlightenment historians, but they also paid attention to economic, social, intellectual, and cultural developments. As Voltaire explained in his masterpiece, *The Age of Louis XIV:* "It is not merely the life of Louis XIV that we propose to write; we have a wider aim in view. We shall endeavor to depict for posterity, not the actions of a single man, but the spirit of men in the most enlightened age the world has ever seen."[10] In seeking to describe the "totality of past human experience," Voltaire initiated the modern ideal of social history. He was also one of the first historians to include art history in his work.

The weaknesses of these philosophe-historians stemmed from their preoccupations as philosophes. Following the ideals of the classics that dominated their minds, the philosophes sought to instruct as well as entertain. Their goal was to help civilize their age, and history could play a role by revealing its lessons according to their vision. Their emphasis on science and reason and their dislike of Christianity made them less than sympathetic to the period we call the Middle Ages. This is particularly noticeable in the other great masterpiece of eighteenth-century historiography, the six-volume *Decline and Fall of the Roman Empire* by Edward Gibbon (see the box on p. 505). Although Gibbon thought that the decline of Rome had many causes, he portrayed the growth of Christianity as a major reason for Rome's eventual collapse.

The High Culture of the Eighteenth Century

Historians and cultural anthropologists have grown accustomed to distinguishing between a civilization's high culture and its popular culture. By high culture is usually meant the literary and artistic culture of the educated and wealthy ruling classes; by popular culture is meant the written and unwritten culture of the masses, most of which is passed down orally. By the eighteenth century, European high culture consisted of a learned world of theologians, scientists, philosophers, intellectuals, poets, and dramatists, for whom Latin remained a truly international language. Their work was supported by a wealthy and literate lay group, the most important of whom were the landed aristocracy and the wealthier upper classes in the cities. European high culture was noticeably cosmopolitan. In addition to Latin, French had become an international language of the cultural elites. This high culture of Europe's elite was institutionally expressed in the salons, the universities, and the academies.

Especially noticeable in the eighteenth century was an expansion of both the reading public and publishing. One study of French publishing, for example, reveals that French publishers were issuing about 1,600 titles yearly in the 1780s, up from 300 titles in 1750. Though many of these titles were still aimed at small groups of the educated elite, many were also directed to the new reading public of the middle classes, which included women and even urban artisans. The growth of publishing houses made it possible for authors to make money from their works and be less dependent on wealthy patrons. Of course, the increase in quantity does not necessarily mean that people were reading books of greater significance and quality, as the best-seller in eighteenth-century England, Bishop Sherlock's *Letter from the Lord Bishop of London to the Clergy and People of London on the Occasion of the Late Earthquakes,* would indicate.

Gibbon and the Idea of Progress

Edward Gibbon's The Decline and Fall of the Roman Empire *was one of the great historical masterpieces of the eighteenth century. Like some of the philosophes, Gibbon believed in the idea of progress and, in reflecting on the decline and fall of Rome, expressed his optimism about the future of European civilization and the ability of Europeans to avoid the fate of the Romans.*

Edward Gibbon, *The Decline and Fall of the Roman Empire*

It is the duty of a patriot to prefer and promote the exclusive interest and glory of his native county; but a philosopher may be permitted to enlarge his views, and to consider Europe as one great republic, whose various inhabitants have attained almost the same level of politeness and cultivation. The balance of power will continue to fluctuate, and the prosperity of our own, or the neighboring kingdoms, may be alternately exalted or depressed; but these partial events cannot essentially injure our general state of happiness, the system of arts, and laws, and manners, which so advantageously distinguish, above the rest of mankind, the Europeans and their colonies. The savage nations of the globe are the common enemies of civilized society; and we may inquire, with anxious curiosity, whether Europe is still threatened with a repetition of those calamities, which formerly oppressed the arms and institutions of Rome. Perhaps the same reflections will illustrate the fall of the mighty empire, and explain the probable causes of our actual security. . . .

Should these speculations be found doubtful or fallacious, there still remains a more humble source of comfort and hope. The discoveries of ancient and modern navigators, and the domestic history, or tradition, of the most enlightened nations, represent the *human* savage, naked both in mind and body, and destitute of laws, of arts, of ideas, and almost of language. From this abject condition, perhaps the primitive and universal state of man, he has gradually arisen to command the animals, to fertilize the earth, to traverse the oceans, and to measure the heavens. His progress in the improvement and exercise of his mental and corporeal faculties has been irregular and various; infinitely slow in the beginning, and increasing by degree with redoubled velocity: ages of laborious ascent have been followed by a moment of rapid downfall; and the several climates of the globe have felt the vicissitudes of light and darkness. Yet the experience of four thousand years should enlarge our hopes, and diminish our apprehensions: we cannot determine to what height the human species may aspire in their advances toward perfection; but it may safely be presumed, that no people, unless the face of nature is changed, will relapse into their original barbarism. . . . Fortunately for mankind, the more useful, or, at least, more necessary arts, can be performed without superior talents, or national subordination. . . . Each village, each family, each individual must always possess both ability and inclination, to perpetuate the use of fire and of metals; the propagation and service of domestic animals; the methods of hunting and fishing; the rudiments of navigation; the imperfect cultivation of corn, or other nutritive grain; and the simple practice of the mechanic trades. Private genius and public industry may be extirpated; but these hardy plants survive the tempest, and strike an everlasting root into the most unfavorable soil. The splendid days of Augustus and Trajan were eclipsed by a cloud of ignorance: and the Barbarians subverted the laws and palaces of Rome. But the scythe . . . still continued annually to mow the harvests of Italy. . . .

Since the first discovery of the arts, war, commerce, and religious zeal have diffused, among the savages of the Old and New World, these inestimable gifts: they have been successively propagated; they can never be lost. We may therefore acquiesce in the pleasing conclusion, that every age of the world has increased, and still increases, the real wealth, the happiness, the knowledge, and perhaps the virtue of the human race.

An important aspect of the growth of publishing and reading in the eighteenth century was the development of magazines for the general public. Great Britain, an important center for the new magazines, saw 25 periodicals published in 1700, 103 in 1760, and 158 in 1780. Although short-lived, the best known was Joseph Addison's and Richard Steele's *Spectator,* begun in 1711. Its goal was "to enliven Morality with wit, and to temper Wit with Morality. . . . To bring Philosophy out of the closets and libraries, schools and colleges, to dwell in clubs and assemblies, at tea-tables and coffeehouses." In keeping with one of the chief intellectual goals of the philosophes, the *Spectator* wished to instruct and entertain at the same time. With its praise of family, marriage, and courtesy, the *Spectator* also had a strong appeal to women. Some of the new magazines were aimed specifically at women, such as *The Female Spectator* in England, which was also edited by a woman, Eliza Haywood, and featured articles by female writers.

Along with magazines came daily newspapers. The first was printed in London in 1702, but by 1780 thirty-seven other English towns had their own newspapers. Filled with news and special features, they were relatively cheap and were provided free in coffeehouses. Books, too, received wider circulation through the development of public libraries in the cities as well as private circulating libraries, which offered books for rental.

A LONDON COFFEEHOUSE. Coffeehouses first appeared in Venice and Constantinople but quickly spread throughout Europe by the beginning of the eighteenth century. In addition to drinking coffee, patrons of coffeehouses could read magazines and newspapers, exchange ideas, play chess, smoke, and even engage in business transactions. In this scene from a London coffeehouse of 1705, well-attired gentlemen make bids on commodities. Bidding went on until pins, which had been placed in lit candles, fell to the table. Thus, bidding stopped when patrons could "hear a pin drop."

EDUCATION AND UNIVERSITIES

By the eighteenth century, Europe was home to a large number of privately endowed secondary schools, such as the grammar and public school in England, the gymnasium in German-speaking lands, and the collège in France and Spain. In many countries these secondary schools were often dominated by religious orders, especially by the Jesuits who had made education an important part of their philosophy.

These schools tended to be elitist, designed to meet the needs of the children of the upper classes of society. Some scholarships were provided for poor children if they were sponsored by local clerics or nobles. But their lot was not easy, and poor students who completed their studies usually went into the ranks of the lower clergy. Basically then, European secondary schools reinforced the class hierarchy of Europe rather than creating avenues for social mobility. In fact, most of the philosophes reinforced the belief that education should function to keep people in their own social class. Baron d'Holbach said, "Education should teach princes to reign, the ruling classes to distinguish themselves by their merit and virtue, the rich to use their riches well, the poor to live by honest industry."

The curriculum of these secondary schools still largely concentrated on the Greek and Latin classics with little attention paid to mathematics, the sciences, and modern languages. Complaints from philosophe-reformers, as well as from merchants and other middle-class people who wanted their sons to have a more practical education, led to the development of new schools designed to provide a broader education. In Germany, the first *Realschule* was opened in Berlin in 1747 and offered modern languages, geography, and bookkeeping to prepare boys for careers in business. New schools of this kind were also created for upper-class girls although they placed most of their emphasis on religion and domestic skills.

The most common complaint about universities, especially from the philosophes, was the old-fashioned curriculum that focused on the classics and Aristotelian philosophy and left out training in the sciences and modern languages. Before the end of the century, this criticism led to reforms that introduced new ideas in the areas of physics, astronomy, and even mathematics into the universities. It is significant, however, that very few of the important scientific discoveries of the eighteenth century occurred in the universities. Most universities produced little intellectual growth and scholarship, although there were exceptions, such as Göttingen and Edinburgh. The University of Göttingen in Hanover, founded in 1737, emphasized the physical sciences. Although a new institution, it had the greatest university library in Europe by the end of the century. Newtonian science was introduced at the University of Edinburgh in the 1730s, and its scientists and philosophers became well known in Europe.

Crime and Punishment

By the eighteenth century, most European states had developed a hierarchy of courts to deal with crimes. Except in England, judicial torture remained an important means of obtaining evidence before a trial. Courts used the rack, thumbscrews, and other instruments to obtain confessions in criminal cases. Punishments for crimes were often cruel and even spectacular. Public executions were a basic part of traditional punishment and were regarded as a neces-

The Punishment of Crime

Torture and capital punishment remained common features of European judicial systems well into the eighteenth century. Public spectacles were especially gruesome as this excerpt from the Nocturnal Spectator *of Restif de la Bretonne demonstrates.*

Restif de la Bretonne, *Nocturnal Spectator*

The Broken Man

I went home by way of rue Saint-Antoine and the Place de Gréve. Three murderers had been broken on the wheel there, the day before. I had not expected to see any such spectacle, one that I had never dared to witness. But as I crossed the square I caught sight of a poor wretch, pale, half dead, wracked by the pains of the interrogation inflicted on him twenty hours earlier; he was stumbling down from the Hôtel de Ville supported by the executioner and the confessor. These two men, so completely different, inspired an inexpressible emotion in me! I watched the latter embrace a miserable man consumed by fever, filthy as the dungeons he came from, swarming with vermin! And I said to myself, "O Religion, here is your greatest glory! . . . "

I saw a horrible sight, even though the torture had been mitigated. . . . The wretch had revealed his accomplices. He was garroted before he was put to the wheel. A winch set under the scaffold tightened a noose around the victim's neck and he was strangled; for a long while the confessor and the hangman felt his heart to see whether the artery still pulsed, and the hideous blows were dealt only after it beat no longer. . . . I left, with my hair standing on end in horror.

sary means of deterring potential offenders in an age when a state's police arm was too weak to assure the capture of criminals. Although nobles were executed by simple beheading, lower-class criminals condemned to death were tortured, broken on the wheel, or drawn and quartered (see the box above). The death penalty was still commonly used in property as well as criminal cases. By 1800, more than 200 crimes were subject to the death penalty in England. In addition to executions, European states resorted to forced labor in mines, forts, and navies. England also sent criminals as indentured servants to colonies in the New World and, after the American Revolution, to Australia.

Appalled by the unjust laws and brutal punishments of their times, some philosophes sought to create a new approach to justice. The most notable effort was made by the Italian philosophe, Cesare Beccaria (1738–1794). In his essay, *On Crimes and Punishments,* written in 1764, Beccaria argued that punishments should serve only as deterrents, not as exercises in brutality: "Such punishments . . . ought to be chosen as will make the strongest and most lasting impressions on the minds of others, with the least torment to the body of the criminal."[11] Beccaria was also opposed to the use of capital punishment. It was spectacular, but failed to stop others from committing crimes. Imprisonment, the deprivation of freedom, made a far more lasting impression. Moreover, capital punishment was harmful to society because it set an example of barbarism: "Is it not absurd, that the laws, which detest and punish homicide, should, in order to prevent murder, publicly commit murder themselves?"

By the end of the eighteenth century, a growing sentiment against executions and torture led to a decline in both corporal and capital punishment. A new type of prison, in which criminals were placed in cells and subjected to discipline and regular work to rehabilitate them, began to replace the public spectacle of barbarous punishments.

The World of Medicine

In the eighteenth century, medicine was practiced by a hierarchy of practitioners. At the top stood the physicians, who were university graduates and enjoyed a high social status. Despite the scientific advances of the seventeenth and eighteenth centuries, however, university medical education was still largely conducted in Latin and was based primarily on Galen's work. New methods emphasizing clinical experience did begin to be introduced at the University of Leiden, which replaced Padua as the foremost medical school of Europe in the first half of the seventeenth century, only to be surpassed in the last half of that century by Vienna. A graduate with a doctorate in medicine from a university needed to receive a license before he could be a practicing member of the physicians' elitist corporate body. In England the Royal College of Physicians licensed only 100 physicians in the early eighteenth century. Only officially licensed physicians could hold regular medical consultations with patients and receive payments, already regarded in the eighteenth century as outrageously high.

Below the physicians were the surgeons, who were still known as barber-surgeons well into the eighteenth century from their original dual occupation. Their primary functions were to bleed patients and perform surgery; the latter was often done in a crude fashion since it was performed without painkillers and in filthy conditions because there was no understanding of bacteria and infection. Bleeding was widely believed to be efficacious as this doctor reported in 1799:

> Bleeding is proper at the beginning of all inflammatory fevers, as pleurisies. . . . It is likewise proper in all topical inflammations, as those of the intestines, womb, bladder, stomach, kidneys, throat, eyes, etc. as also in the asthma, sciatic pains, coughs, head-aches, rheumatisms, the apoplexy, epilepsy, and bloody flux. After falls, blows, bruises, or any violent hurt received either externally or internally, bleeding is necessary.[12]

The surgeons underwent significant changes in the course of the eighteenth century. In the 1740s, they began to separate themselves from the barbers and organize their own guilds. At the same time, they started to undergo additional training by dissecting corpses and studying anatomy more systematically. As they became more effective, the distinction between physicians and surgeons began to break down, and surgeons were examining patients in a fashion similar to physicians by the end of the century. Moreover, surgeons also began to be licensed. In England the Royal College of Surgeons required clinical experience before granting the license.

Other medical practitioners, such as apothecaries, midwives, and faith healers, primarily served the common people in the eighteenth century. Although their primary function was to provide herbs and potions as recommended by physicians, apothecaries or pharmacists also acted independently in diagnosing illnesses and selling remedies. In the course of the eighteenth century, male doctors increasingly supplanted midwives in delivering babies. However, the tradition of faith healing, so prominent in medieval medicine, continued to be practiced, especially in the rural areas of Europe.

Hospitals in the eighteenth century seemed more a problem than an aid in dealing with disease and illness. That conditions were bad is evident in this description by the philosophe Denis Diderot, who characterized the Hôtel-Dieu in Paris, France's "biggest, roomiest, and richest" hospital, in these words:

> Imagine a long series of communicating wards filled with sufferers of every kind of disease who are sometimes packed three, four, five or even six into a bed, the living alongside the dead and dying, the air polluted by this mass of unhealthy bodies, passing pestilential germs of their afflictions from one to the other, and the spectacle of suffering and agony on every hand. That is the Hôtel-Dieu.
>
> The result is that many of these poor wretches come out with diseases they did not have when they went in, and often pass them on to the people they go back to live with. Others are half-cured and spend the rest of their days in an invalidism as hard to bear as the illness itself; and the rest perish, except for the fortunate few whose strong constitutions enable them to survive.[13]

Despite appeals, reform efforts for hospitals in the eighteenth century remained in an infantile stage.

Popular Culture

Popular culture refers to the often unwritten and unofficial culture passed down orally that was fundamental to the lives of most people. The distinguishing characteristic of popular culture is its collective and public nature. Group activity was especially evident in the festival, a broad name used to cover a variety of celebrations: family festivals, such as weddings; community festivals in Catholic Europe that celebrated the feastday of the local patron saint; annual festivals, such as Christmas and Easter that go back to medieval Christianity; and Carnival, the most spectacular form of festival, which was celebrated in the Mediterranean world of Spain, Italy, and France as well as in Germany and Austria. All of these festivals shared common characteristics. While having a spiritual function, they were celebrated in a secular fashion. They were special occasions on which people ate, drank, and celebrated to excess. In traditional societies, festival was a time of play because much of the rest of the year was a time of unrelieved work. As the poet Thomas Gray said of Carnival in Turin in 1739: "This Carnival lasts only from Christmas to Lent; one half of the remaining part of the year is passed in remembering the last, the other in expecting the future Carnival."[14]

"The example par excellence of the festival" was Carnival, which started in January and lasted until the beginning of Lent, traditionally the forty-day period of fasting and purification leading up to Easter. Carnival was a time of great indulgence, just the reverse of Lent when people were expected to abstain from meat, sex, and most recreations. A heavy consumption of food, especially meat and other delicacies, and heavy drinking were the norm: "they drink as if they were never to drink more." Carnival was a time of intense sexual activity as well. Songs with double meanings could be sung publicly at this time of year whereas otherwise they would be considered offensive to the community. A float of Florentine "key-makers," for example, sang this ditty to the ladies: "Our tools are fine, new and useful; We always carry them with us; They are good for anything, If you want to touch them, you can."[15] Finally, it was a time of aggression, a time to release pent-up feelings. Most often this took the form of verbal aggression since people could openly insult other people and were even allowed to criticize their social superiors and authorities. But other acts of violence were also permitted. People pelted each other with apples, eggs, flour, and pig's bladders filled with water. This limited and sanctioned violence also led to unplanned violence. All contemporaries observed that Carnival was a time when the incidence of murder increased dramatically.

The same sense of community evident in festival was also present in the chief gathering places of the common people, the local taverns or cabarets. Taverns were supposedly for travelers but functioned more frequently as a regular gathering place for neighborhood men to talk, play games, conduct small business matters, and, of course, to drink. In some countries, the favorite drinks of poor people, such as gin in England and vodka in Russia, proved devastating as poor people regularly drank themselves into oblivion. Gin was cheap; the classic sign in English taverns, "Drunk for a penny, dead drunk for two pence," was literally true. In England the consumption of gin rose from two to five million gallons between 1714 and 1733 and only declined when complaints finally led to strict laws to restrict sales in the 1750s. Of course, the rich drank too. Samuel Johnson once remarked: "All the decent people in Lichfield got drunk every night and were not the worse thought of." But unlike the poor, the rich drank port and brandy, usually in large quantities.

This difference in drinking habits between rich and poor reminds us of the ever-widening separation between the elite and poor in the eighteenth century. In 1500, popular culture was for everyone; a second culture for the elite, it was the only culture for the rest of society. But between 1500 and 1800, the nobility, clergy, and bourgeoisie had abandoned popular culture to the lower classes. This was, of course, a gradual process, and in abandoning the popular festivals, the upper classes were also abandoning the popular worldview as well. The new scientific outlook had brought a new mental world for the upper classes, and they now viewed such things as witchcraft, faith healing, fortune telling, and prophecy as the beliefs of "such as are of the weakest judgment and reason, as women, children, and ignorant and superstitious persons."

Despite this growing gulf between elite and common people, there were still some forms of entertainment that occasionally brought them together. Most common were the urban fairs, a product of what some historians now call the "commercialization of leisure," or the attempt by businesses to turn leisure activities into a good investment. The three fairs in Paris provided entertainment—farcical theater, magic shows, circus performers, or freak shows—as well as food booths and popular wares for purchase. Both the privileged and unprivileged classes were still attracted to boxing matches and horse races as well as the bloodier spectacles of bullbaiting, bearbaiting, and cockfighting.

Popular culture had always included a vast array of traditional songs and stories that were passed down from generation to generation. But popular culture was not entirely based on an oral tradition; a popular literature existed as well. So-called chapbooks, printed on cheap paper, were short brochures sold by itinerant peddlers to the lower classes. They contained both spiritual and secular material; lives of saints and inspirational stories competed with crude satires and adventure stories.

It is apparent from the chapbooks that popular culture did not have to remain primarily oral. Its ability to change was dependent upon the growth of literacy. There is still considerable uncertainty about literacy in early modern Europe because of the difficulty in measuring it. Some reasonable estimates based on studies in France indicate that literacy rates for men increased from 29 percent in the late seventeenth century to 47 percent in the late eighteenth century; for women, the increase was from 14 to 27 percent during the same period. Of course, certain groups were more likely to be literate than others. Upper-class elites as well as the upper middle classes in the cities were mostly all literate. However, the figures also indicate dramatic increases for lower-middle-class artisans in urban areas. Recent research in the city of Marseilles, for example, indicates that literacy of male artisans and workers increased from 28 percent in 1710 to 85 percent in 1789, though the rate for women remained at 15 percent. Peasants, who constituted as much as 75 percent of the French population, remained largely illiterate.

The spread of literacy was closely connected to primary education. In Catholic Europe, primary education was largely a matter of local community effort, leading to little real growth. Only in the Habsburg Austrian Empire was a system of state-supported primary schools (*Volkschulen*) established. Although attendance was supposedly compulsory, a 1781 census revealed that only one in four school-age children was actually attending.

The emphasis of the Protestant reformers on reading the Bible had led Protestant states to take greater interest in primary education. Some places, especially the Swiss cantons, Scotland, and the German states of Saxony and Prussia, witnessed the emergence of universal primary schools that provided a modicum of education for the masses. An edict of the Prussian king Frederick II (see Chapter 18) in 1763 made the schooling of children compulsory. But effective systems of primary education were hindered by the attitudes of the ruling classes, who feared the consequences of any education beyond teaching the lower classes the virtues of hard work and deference to their superiors. Hannah More, an English writer who set up a network of Sunday schools, made clear the philosophy of her charity school for poor children: "My plan of instruction is extremely simple and limited. They learn on weekdays such coarse work as may fit them for servants. I allow of no writing for the poor. My object is to train up the lower classes in habits of industry and piety."

◆ Religion and the Churches

The music of Bach and the pilgrimage and monastic churches of southern Germany and Austria make us aware of a curious fact. Though much of the great art and music of the time was religious, the thought of the time was antireligious as life became increasingly secularized and men of reason attacked the established churches. And yet most Europeans were still Christians. Even many of those most critical of the churches accepted that society could not function without religious faith.

The Institutional Church

In the eighteenth century, the established Catholic and Protestant churches were basically conservative institutions that upheld society's hierarchical structure, privileged classes, and traditions. Although churches experienced change because of new state policies, they did not sustain any dramatic internal changes. Whether in Catholic or Protestant countries, the parish church run by priest or pastor remained the center of religious practice. In addition to providing religious services, the parish church kept records of births, deaths, and marriages, provided charity for the poor, supervised whatever primary education there was, and cared for orphans.

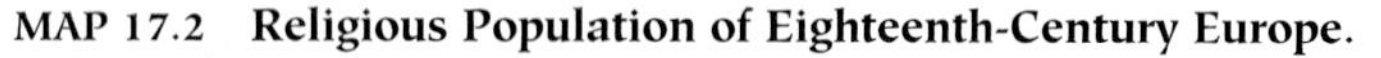

CHURCH-STATE RELATIONS

Early on, the Protestant Reformation had solved the problem of the relationship between church and state by establishing the principle of state control over the churches. In the eighteenth century, Protestant state churches flourished throughout Europe: Lutheranism in Scandinavia and the north German states; Anglicanism in England; and Calvinism (or Reformed churches) in Scotland, the United Provinces, and some of the Swiss cantons and German states. There were also Protestant minorities in other European countries.

In 1700, the Catholic church still exercised much power in Catholic European states: Spain, Portugal, France, Italy, the Habsburg Empire, Poland, and most of southern Germany. The church also continued to possess enormous wealth. In Spain, 3,000 monastic institutions housing 100,000 men and women controlled enormous landed estates.

The Catholic church remained hierarchically structured. In most Catholic countries, the highest clerics, such as bishops, archbishops, abbots, and abbesses, were members of the upper class, especially the landed nobility, and received enormous revenues from their landed estates and tithes from the faithful. A wide gulf existed between the upper and lower clergy. While the French bishop of Strasbourg, for example, received 100,000 livres a year, parish priests were paid only 500.

In the eighteenth century, the governments of many Catholic states began to seek greater authority over the churches in their countries. This "nationalization" of the

MAP 17.2 Religious Population of Eighteenth-Century Europe.

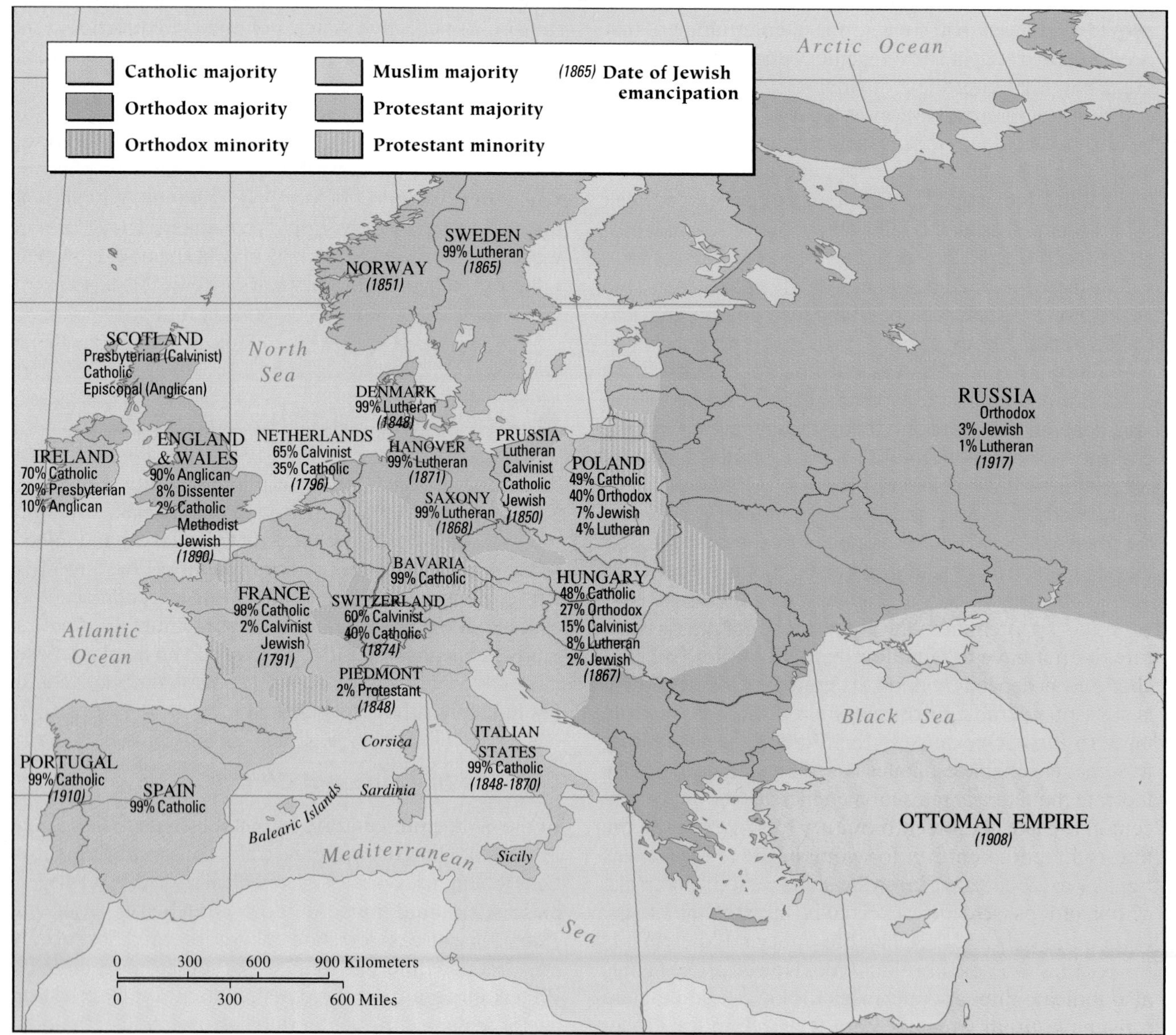

Catholic church meant controlling the papacy and in turn the chief papal agents, the Society of Jesus. The Jesuits had proved extremely successful, perhaps too successful for their own good. They had created special enclaves, virtually states-within-states, in the French, Spanish, and Portuguese colonies in the New World. Through their excellent secondary schools, they directed the education of the sons of Catholic aristocrats. As advisers to Catholic rulers, they exercised considerable political influence. But the high profile the Jesuits achieved through their successes led to a wide range of enemies, and a series of actions soon undermined Jesuit power. The Portuguese monarch destroyed the powerful Jesuit state in Paraguay and then in 1759 expelled the Jesuits from Portugal and confiscated their property. In 1764, they were expelled from France and three years later from Spain and the Spanish colonies. In 1773, when Spain and France demanded that the entire society be dissolved, Pope Clement XIV reluctantly complied. The dissolution of the Jesuit order, the pillar of Catholic fanaticism and strength, was yet another victory for Catholic governments determined to win control over their churches.

The end of the Jesuits was paralleled by a decline in papal power. Already by the mid-eighteenth century, the papacy played only a minor role in diplomacy and international affairs. The nationalization of the churches by the states meant the loss of the papacy's power to appoint high clerical officials.

Another aspect of state control over the Catholic church involved the regulation and suppression of monastic orders. The most radical program was carried out in the Austrian Empire. By the Edict on Idle Institutions in 1782, Emperor Joseph II suppressed all the contemplative monastic orders, allowing only those that provided charitable or educational services to survive. The number of monks in the Austrian Empire was cut in half, and the confiscated monastic properties were used to extend education.

TOLERATION AND RELIGIOUS MINORITIES

One of the chief battle cries of the philosophes had been a call for religious toleration. Out of political necessity, a certain level of tolerance of different creeds had occurred in the seventeenth century in such places as Germany after the Thirty Years' War and France after the divisive religious wars. But many rulers still found it difficult to accept. Louis XIV had turned back the clock in France at the end of the seventeenth century, insisting on religious uniformity and suppressing the rights of the Huguenots (see Chapter 15). Some devout rulers, such as Maria Theresa of Austria, continued to believe that there was only one path to salvation; it was the true duty of a ruler not to allow subjects to be condemned to hell by being heretics. Catholic minorities in Protestant countries and Protestant minorities in Catholic countries did not enjoy full civil or political rights. Persecution of heretics continued; the last burning of a heretic took place in 1781.

Nevertheless, some progress was made toward the principle of religious toleration. No ruler was more interested in the philosophes' call for religious toleration than Joseph II of Austria. His Toleration Patent of 1781, while recognizing Catholicism's public practice, granted Lutherans, Calvinists, and Greek Orthodox the right to worship privately. In all other ways, all subjects were now equal: "Non-Catholics are in future admitted under dispensation to buy houses and real property, to practice as master craftsmen, to take up academic appointments and posts in public service, and are not to be required to take the oath in any form contrary to their religious tenets."[16]

TOLERATION AND THE JEWS

The Jews remained the despised religious minority of Europe. The largest number of Jews (known as the Ashkenazic Jews) lived in eastern Europe. Except in relatively tolerant Poland, Jews were restricted in their movements, forbidden to own land or hold many jobs, forced to pay burdensome special taxes, and also subject to periodic outbursts of popular wrath. The resulting pogroms in which Jewish communities were looted and massacred made Jewish existence precarious and dependent upon the favor of their territorial rulers.

Another major group was the Sephardic Jews who had been expelled from Spain in the fifteenth century. Although many had migrated to Turkish lands, some of them had settled in cities, such as Amsterdam, Venice, London, and Frankfurt, where they were relatively free to participate in the banking and commercial activities that Jews had practiced since the Middle Ages. The highly successful ones came to provide valuable services to rulers, especially in central Europe where they were known as the court Jews. But even these Jews were insecure since their religion set them apart from the Christian majority and served as a catalyst to social resentment.

Some Enlightenment thinkers in the eighteenth century favored a new acceptance of Jews. They argued that Jews and Muslims were all human and deserved the full rights of citizenship despite their religion. Many philosophes denounced persecution of the Jews but made no attempt to hide their hostility and ridiculed Jewish customs. Diderot, for example, said that the Jews had "all the defects peculiar to an ignorant and superstitious nation." Many Europeans favored the assimilation of the Jews into the mainstream of society, but only by the conversion of Jews to Christianity as the basic solution to the "Jewish problem." This, of course, was not acceptable to most Jews.

The Austrian emperor Joseph II attempted to adopt a new policy toward the Jews, although it too was limited. It freed Jews from nuisance taxes and allowed them more freedom of movement and job opportunities, but they were still restricted from owning land and worshiping in public. At the same time, Joseph II encouraged Jews to learn German and work toward greater assimilation into Austrian society. Joseph's policy was but a small step in the liberation of the Jews as it took a moderate position between toleration and assimilation.

Popular Religion in the Eighteenth Century

Despite the rise of skepticism and the intellectuals' belief in deism and natural religion, it would appear that religious devotion remained strong in the eighteenth century. Catholic popular piety continued to be strong, and within Protestantism the desire for more direct spiritual experience actually led to religious revivalism, especially in Germany and England.

CATHOLIC PIETY

It is difficult to assess the religiosity of Europe's Catholics precisely. The Catholic parish church remained an important center of life for the entire community. How many people went to church regularly cannot be known exactly, but it has been established that 90 to 95 percent of Catholic populations did go to mass on Easter Sunday, one of the church's most special celebrations. Confraternities, which were organizations of laypeople dedicated to good works and acts of piety, were especially popular with townspeople. Each confraternity honored its patron saint by holy processions in which members proudly wore their special robes.

Catholic religiosity proved highly selective, however. Despite the Reformation, much popular devotion was still directed to an externalized form of worship focusing on prayers to saints, pilgrimages, and devotion to relics and images. The latter bothered many clergymen who felt that their parishioners were "more superstitious than devout," as one Catholic priest remarked. Many common people continued to fear witches and relied on the intervention of the saints and the Virgin Mary to save them from personal disasters caused by the devil.

PROTESTANT REVIVALISM

After the initial century of religious fervor that created Protestantism in the sixteenth century, Protestant churches in the seventeenth century had settled down into well-established patterns controlled by state authorities and served by a well-educated clergy. Protestant churches became bureaucratized and bereft of religious enthusiasm. In Germany and England, where rationalism and deism had become influential and moved some theologians to a more "rational" Christianity, the desire of ordinary Protestant churchgoers for greater depths of religious experience led to new and dynamic religious movements.

Pietism in Germany was a response to this desire for a deeper personal devotion to God. Begun in the seventeenth century by a group of German clerics who wished their religion to be more personal and transformative of daily experience, Pietism was spread by the teachings of Count Nikolaus von Zinzendorf (1700–1760). To Zinzendorf and his Moravian Brethren, as his sect was called, it was the mysticial dimensions—the personal experience of God—in one's life that constituted true religious experience. He was utterly opposed to what he perceived as the rationalistic approach of orthodox Lutheran clergy who were being educated in new "rational" ideas. As Zinzendorf commented: "He who wishes to comprehend God with his mind becomes an atheist."

After the civil wars of the seventeenth century, England too had arrived at a respectable, uniform, and complacent state church. While local Anglican parish rectors were under the control of neighboring landholding nobles and reflected their social prejudices, higher members of the clergy—the bishops—were appointed by the crown, most often for political reasons. A pillar of the establishment, the Anglican church seemed to offer little spiritual excitement, especially to the masses of people. The dissenting Protestant groups—the Puritans, Quakers, Baptists—were relatively subdued while the growth of deism seemed to challenge Christianity itself. The desire

JOHN WESLEY. In leading a deep spiritual revival in Britain, John Wesley founded a religious movement that came to be known as Methodism. He loved to preach to the masses, and this 1766 portrait by Nathaniel Hope shows him as he might have appeared before a crowd of people.

The Conversion Experience in Wesley's Methodism

After his own conversion experience, John Wesley traveled extensively to bring the "glad tidings" of Jesus to other people. It has been estimated that he preached over 40,000 sermons, some of them to audiences numbering 20,000 listeners. Wesley gave his message wherever people gathered—in the streets, hospitals, private houses, and even pubs. In this selection from his journal, Wesley describes how emotional and even violent conversion experiences could be.

❋ *The Works of the Reverend John Wesley*

Sunday, May 20 [1759], being with Mr. B—11 at Everton, I was much fatigued, and did not rise: but Mr. B. did, and observed several fainting and crying out, while Mr. Berridge was preaching: afterwards at Church, I heard many cry out, especially children, whose agonies were amazing: one of the eldest, a girl of ten or twelve years old, was full in my view, in violent contortions of body, and weeping aloud, I think incessantly, during the whole service. . . . The Church was equally crowded in the afternoon, the windows being filled within and without, and even the outside of the pulpit to the very top; so that Mr. B. seemed almost stifled by their breath; yet feeble and sickly as he is, he was continually strengthened, and his voice, for the most part, distinguishable; in the midst of all the outcries. I believe there were present three times more men than women, a great part of whom came from far; thirty of them having set out at two in the morning, from a place thirteen miles off. The text was, *Having a form of godliness, but denying the power thereof.* When the power of religion began to be spoken of, the presence of God really filled the place: and while poor sinners felt the sentence of death in their souls, what sounds of distress did I hear! The greatest number of them who cried or fell, were men: but some women, and several children, felt the power of the same almighty Spirit, and seemed just sinking into hell. This occasioned a mixture of several sounds; some shrieking, some roaring aloud. The most general was a loud breathing, like that of people half strangled and gasping for life: and indeed almost all the cries were like those of human creatures, dying in bitter anguish. Great numbers wept without any noise: others fell down as death: some sinking in silence; some with extreme noise and violent agitation. I stood on the pew-seat, as did a young man in the opposite pew, an able-bodied, fresh, healthy countryman: but in a moment, while he seemed to think of nothing less, down he dropped with a violence inconceivable. The adjoining pews seemed to shake with his fall: I heard afterwards the stamping of his feet; ready to break the boards, as he lay in strong convulsions, at the bottom of the pew. Among several that were struck down in the next pew, was a girl, who was as violently seized as he. . . . Among the children who felt the arrows of the Almighty, I saw a sturdy boy, about eight years old, who roared above his fellows, and seemed in his agony to struggle with the strength of a grown man. His face was as red as scarlet: and almost all on whom God laid his hand, turned either very red or almost black. . . .

The violent struggling of many in the above-mentioned churches, has broken several pews and benches. Yet it is common for people to remain unaffected there, and afterwards to drop down on their way home. Some have been found lying as dead on the road: others, in Mr. B.'s garden; not being able to walk from the Church to his house, though it is not two hundred yards.

for deep spiritual experience seemed unmet until the advent of John Wesley (1703–1791).

An ordained Anglican minister, John Wesley took religion very seriously, experienced a deep spiritual crisis, and underwent a mystical experience: "I felt I did trust in Christ alone for salvation; and an assurance was given me, that He had taken away my sins, even mine, and saved me from the law of sin and death. I felt my heart strangely warmed." To Wesley, "the gift of God's grace" assured him of salvation and led him to become a missionary to the English people, bringing the "glad tidings" of salvation to all people, despite opposition from the Anglican church, which criticized this emotional mysticism or religious enthusiasm as superstitious nonsense. To Wesley, all could be saved by experiencing God and opening the doors to his grace.

In taking the Gospel to the people, Wesley preached to the masses in open fields, appealing especially to the lower classes neglected by the socially elitist Anglican church. He tried, he said, "to lower religion to the level of the lowest people's capacities." Wesley's charismatic preaching often provoked highly charged and even violent conversion experiences (see the box above). Afterward, converts were organized into so-called Methodist societies or chapels in which they could aid each other in doing the good works that Wesley considered a component of salvation. A Central Methodist Conference supervised new lay preachers from Methodist circles. Controlled by Wesley, it enabled him to dominate the evangelical movement he had created. Although Wesley sought to keep Methodism within the Anglican church, after his death it became a separate and independent sect. Methodism was an important revival of Christianity and proved that the need for spiritual experience had not been expunged by the eighteenth-century search for reason.

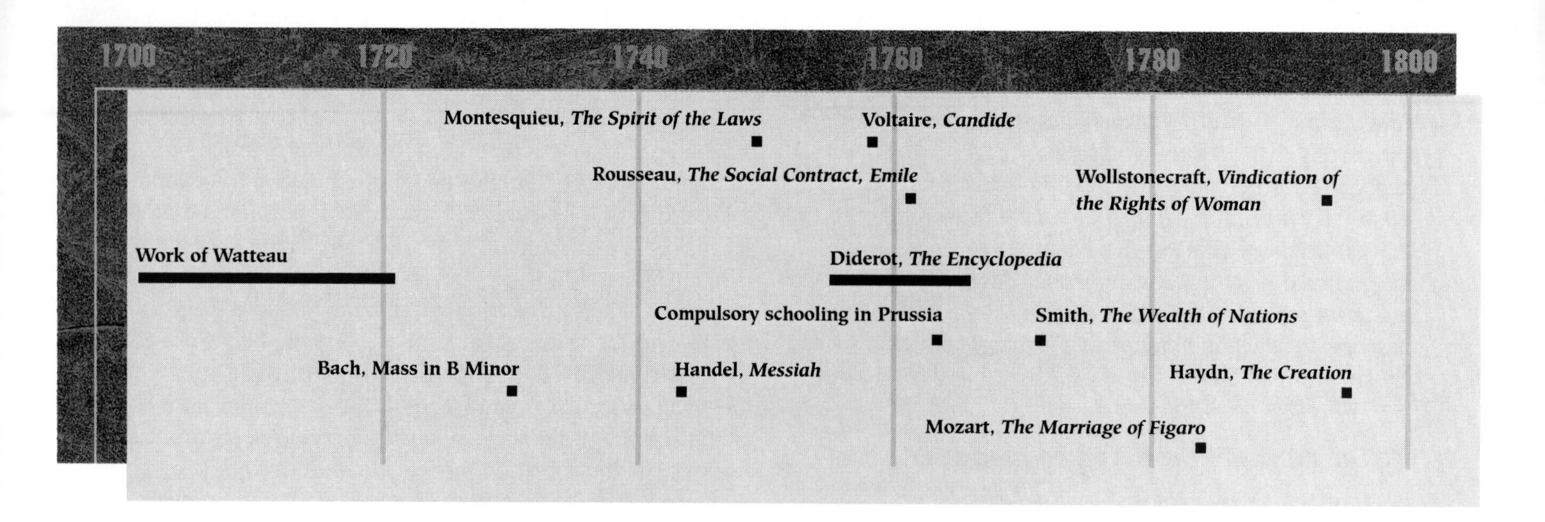

CONCLUSION

One prominent historian of the eighteenth century has appropriately characterized it as a century of change and tradition. Highly influenced by the new worldview created by the Scientific Revolution and especially the ideas of Locke and Newton, the philosophes hoped that they could create a new society by using reason to discover the natural laws that governed it. Like the Christian humanists of the fifteenth and sixteenth centuries, they believed that education could create better human beings and a better human society. By attacking traditional religion as the enemy and creating the new "sciences of man" in economics, politics, justice, and education, the philosophes laid the foundation for a modern worldview based on rationalism and secularism.

But it was also an age of tradition. Although secular thought and rational ideas began to pervade the mental world of the ruling elites, most people in eighteenth-century Europe still lived by seemingly eternal verities and practices—God, religious worship, and farming. The most brilliant architecture and music of the age were religious. And yet, the forces of secularization were too strong to stop. In the midst of intellectual change, economic, political, and social transformations of great purport were taking shape and, by the end of the eighteenth century, were to lead to both political and industrial revolutions. It is time now to examine the political, economic, and social traditions and changes of the century.

NOTES

1. Quoted in Paul Hazard, *The European Mind, 1680–1715* (New York, 1963), pp. 304–305.
2. Ibid., p. 12.
3. John Locke, *An Essay Concerning Human Understanding* (New York, 1964), pp. 89–90.
4. Baron d'Holbach, *Common Sense,* as quoted in Frank E. Manuel, ed., *The Enlightenment* (Englewood Cliffs, N.J., 1965), p. 62.
5. Jean-Jacques Rousseau, *A Discourse on Inequality,* trans. Maurice Cranston (Harmondsworth, 1984), p. 109.
6. Jean-Jacques Rousseau, *The Social Contract,* trans. Maurice Cranston (Harmondsworth, 1968), p. 141.
7. *A Serious Proposal to the Ladies,* in Moira Ferguson, ed., *First Feminists: British Women Writers, 1578–1799* (Bloomington, Ind., 1985). p. 190.
8. Ibid., p. 193.
9. Kenneth Clark, *Civilisation* (New York, 1969), p. 231.
10. Voltaire, *The Age of Louis XIV,* trans. Martyn P. Pollack (New York, 1961), p. 1.
11. Cesare Beccaria, *An Essay on Crimes and Pubishments,* trans. E. D. Ingraham (Philadelphia, 1819), pp. 59–60.
12. Quoted in Lester S. King, *The Medical World of the Eighteenth Century* (Chicago, 1958), pp. 318–319.
13. Quoted in Rene Sand, *The Advance to Social Medicine* (London, 1952), pp. 86–87.
14. Quoted in Peter Burke, *Popular Culture in Early Modern Europe* (New York, 1978), p. 179.
15. Quotations (in order of appearance) are from ibid., pp. 183, 186.
16. Quoted in C. A. Macartney, *The Habsburg and Hohenzollern Dynasties in the Seventeenth and Eighteenth Centuries* (New York, 1970), p. 157.

SUGGESTIONS FOR FURTHER READING

Two sound, comprehensive surveys of eighteenth-century Europe are I. Woloch, *Eighteenth-Century Europe* (New York, 1982); and M. S. Anderson, *Europe in the Eighteenth Century* (London, 1987). See also R. Birn, *Crisis, Absolutism, Revolution: Europe 1648–1789,* 2d ed. (Fort Worth, Tex., 1992).

Good introductions to the Enlightenment can be found in N. Hampson, *A Cultural History of the Enlightenment* (New York, 1968); U. Im Hof, *The Enlightenment* (Oxford, 1994); D. Goodman, *The Republic of Letters: A Cultural History of the French Enlightenment* (Ithaca, N.Y., 1994); and D. Outram,

The Enlightenment (Cambridge, 1995). A more detailed synthesis can be found in P. Gay, *The Enlightenment: An Interpretation,* 2 vols. (New York, 1966–69). For a short, popular survey on the French philosophes, see F. Artz, *The Enlightenment in France* (Kent, Ohio, 1968). Also of value are E. J. Wilson and P. H. Reill, *Encyclopedia of the Enlightenment* (New York, 1996); and J. W. Yolton, ed., *The Blackwell Companion to the Enlightenment* (Cambridge, Mass., 1995). Studies of the major Enlightenment intellectuals include J. Sklar, *Montesquieu* (Oxford, 1987); H. T. Mason, *Voltaire: A Biography* (Baltimore, 1981); P. N. Furbank, *Diderot: A Critical Biography* (New York, 1992); and M. Cranston, *The Noble Savage: Jean-Jacques Rousseau* (New York, 1991). Specialized studies on various aspects of the Enlightenment include M. W. Cranston, *Philosophers and Pamphleteers: Political Theorists of the Enlightenment* (London, 1986); M. C. Jacob, *The Radical Enlightenment: Pantheists, Freemasons and Republicans* (London, 1981); and J. Censer, *The French Press in the Age of Enlightenment* (New York, 1994). On women in the eighteenth century, see N. Z. Davis and A. Farge, eds., *A History of Women: Renaissance and Enlightenment Paradoxes* (Cambridge, Mass., 1993); C. Lougee, *Le Paradis des Femmes: Women, Salons, and Social Stratification* (Princeton, N.J., 1976); O. Hufton, *The Prospect before Her: A History of Women in Western Europe, 1500–1800* (New York, 1998); and B. S. Anderson and J. P. Zinsser, *A History of Their Own,* vol. 2 (New York, 1988).

Two readable general surveys on the arts and literature are M. Levy, *Rococo to Revolution* (London, 1966); and H. Honour, *Neo-classicism* (Harmondsworth, 1968). On the eighteenth-century novel, see G. J. Barker-Benfield, *The Culture of Sensibility: Sex and Society in the Eighteenth Century English Novel* (Chicago, 1992). On Gibbon, see W. B. Carnuchan, *Gibbon's Solitude: The Inward World of the Historian* (London, 1987). On the growth of literacy, see R. A. Houston, *Literacy in Early Modern Europe: Culture and Education, 1500–1800* (New York, 1988). Different facets of crime and punishment are examined in the important works by M. Foucault, *Discipline and Punish: The Birth of the Prison* (New York, 1977); and J. Langbein, *Torture and the Law of Proof* (Chicago, 1977). On the medical profession, see L. King, *The Medical World of the Eighteenth Century* (Chicago, 1958); and A. Cunningham and R. French, eds., *The Medical Enlightenment of the Eighteenth Century* (New York, 1990).

Important studies on popular culture include P. Burke, *Popular Culture in Early Modern Europe* (New York, 1978); and R. Darnton, *The Great Cat Massacre and Other Episodes in French Cultural History* (New York, 1984). Recreational activities are covered in R. Malcolmson, *Popular Recreation in English Society, 1700–1850* (Cambridge, 1973); and R. Isherwood, *Farce and Fantasy: Popular Entertainment in Eighteenth-Century Paris* (New York, 1986).

A good introduction to the religious history of the eighteenth century can be found in G. R. Cragg, *The Church and the Age of Reason, 1648–1789* (London, 1966). The problem of religious toleration is examined in J. I. Israel, *European Jewry in the Age of Mercantilism, 1550–1750,* 2d ed. (New York, 1989). On Pietism, see R. Gawthorp, *Pietism and the Making of Eighteenth-Century Prussia* (New York, 1993). On John Wesley, see H. Rack, *Reasonable Enthusiast: John Wesley and the Rise of Methodism* (New York, 1989).

For additional reading, go to InfoTrac College Edition, your online research library at http://web1.infotrac-college.com

Enter the search term *Enlightenment* using the Subject Guide.

Enter the search term *Voltaire* using Key Terms.

Enter the search term *Diderot* using Key Terms.

Enter the search term *Rousseau* using Key Terms.

CHAPTER

18

The Eighteenth Century: European States, International Wars, and Social Change

CHAPTER OUTLINE

- The European States
- Wars and Diplomacy
- Economic Expansion and Social Change
- The Social Order of the Eighteenth Century
- Conclusion

FOCUS QUESTIONS

- What do historians mean by the term *enlightened absolutism,* and to what degree did eighteenth-century Prussia, Austria, and Russia exhibit its characteristics?
- How did the concepts of "balance of power" and "reason of state" influence international relations in the eighteenth century?
- What were the causes and results of the Seven Years' War?
- What changes occurred in agriculture, finance, industry, and trade during the eighteenth century?
- Who were the main groups making up the European social order in the eighteenth century, and how did the conditions in which they lived differ both between groups and between different parts of Europe?

HISTORIANS HAVE OFTEN DEFINED the eighteenth century chronologically as spanning the years from 1715 to 1789. Politically, this makes sense since 1715 marks the end of the age of Louis XIV and 1789 was the year in which the French Revolution erupted. This period has often been portrayed as the final phase of Europe's old order, before the violent upheaval and reordering of society associated with the French Revolution. Europe's old order, still largely agrarian, dominated by kings and landed aristocrats, and grounded in privileges for nobles, clergy, towns, and provinces, seemed to continue a basic pattern that had prevailed in Europe since medieval times. But new ideas and new practices were also beginning to emerge. Just as a new intellectual order based on rationalism and secularism was emerging from the intellectual revolution of the Scientific Revolution and Enlightenment, demographic, economic, and social patterns were beginning to change in ways that represent the emergence of a modern new order.

For some, the ideas of the Enlightenment seemed to herald the possibility of a new political age as well. Catherine the Great, who ruled Russia from 1762 to 1796, wrote to Voltaire: "Since 1746 I have been under the greatest obligations to you. Before that period I read nothing but romances, but by chance your works fell into my hands, and ever since then I have never ceased to read them, and have no desire for books less well written than yours, or less instructive." The empress of Russia also invited Diderot to Russia and, when he arrived, urged him to speak frankly "as man to man." Diderot did, offering her advice for a far-ranging program of political and financial reform. But Catherine's apparent eagerness to make enlightened reforms was tempered by skepticism. She said of Diderot: "If I had believed him everything would have been turned upside down in my kingdom; legislation, administration, finance—all would have been turned topsy-turvy to make room for impractical theories." For Catherine, enlightened reform remained more a dream than a reality, and in the end, the waging of wars to gain more power was more important.

In the eighteenth century, the process of centralization that had characterized the growth of states since the Middle Ages continued as most European states enlarged their bureaucratic machinery and consolidated their governments in order to collect the revenues and build the armies they needed to compete militarily with the other European states. International competition continued to be the favorite pastime of eighteenth-century rulers. Within the European state system, the nations that would dominate Europe until World War I—Britain, France, Austria, Prussia, and Russia—emerged as the five great powers of Europe. Their rivalries led to major wars, which some have called the first "world wars" because they were fought outside as well as inside Europe. In the midst of this state building and war making, dramatic demographic, economic, and social changes heralded the emergence of a radical transformation in the way Europeans would raise food and produce goods.

◆ The European States

Most European states in the eighteenth century were ruled by monarchs. Few people questioned either the moral or practical superiority of hereditary monarchy as the best form of government, especially in the large and successful states. As Catherine II wrote in 1764: "The Russian Empire is so large that apart from the Autocratic Sovereign every other form of government is harmful to it, because all others are slower in their execution and contain a great multitude of various horrors, which lead to the disintegration of power and strength more than that of one Sovereign."[1]

Although the seventeenth-century justification for strong monarchy on the basis of divine right continued into the succeeding century, as the eighteenth century became increasingly secularized, divine-right assumptions were gradually superseded by influential utilitarian arguments. The Prussian king Frederick II expressed these well when he attempted to explain the services a monarch must provide for his people:

> These services consisted in the maintenance of the laws; a strict execution of justice; an employment of his whole powers to prevent any corruption of manners; and defending the state against its enemies. It is the duty of this magistrate to pay attention to agriculture; it should be his care that provisions for the nation should be in abundance, and that commerce and industry should be encouraged. He is a perpetual sentinel, who must watch the acts and the conduct of the enemies of the state. . . . If he be the first general, the first minister of the realm, it is not that he should remain the shadow of authority, but that he should fulfill the duties of such titles. He is only the first servant of the state.[2]

This utilitarian argument was reinforced by the praises of the philosophes.

Enlightened Absolutism?

There is no doubt that Enlightenment thought had some impact on the political development of European states in the eighteenth century. Closely related to the Enlightenment idea of natural laws was the belief in natural rights, which were thought to be inalienable privileges that ought not to be withheld from any person. These natural rights included equality before the law, freedom of religious worship, freedom of speech and press, and the right to assemble, hold property, and pursue happiness. The American Declaration of Independence summarized the Enlightenment concept of natural rights in its opening paragraph: "We hold these truths to be self-evident, that all men are created equal; that they are endowed by their creator with certain unalienable rights; that among these are life, liberty and the pursuit of happiness."

But how were these natural rights to be established and preserved? In *The Spirit of the Laws,* Montesquieu had argued for constitutional guarantees achieved by a separation of powers. Rousseau had advocated a democratic society as the ideal path to maintain people's natural rights. Most philosophes, however, did not trust the "people." "It must please the animals," Voltaire said, "when they see how foolishly men behave." In the opinion of the philosophes, most people needed the direction provided by an enlightened ruler. What, however, made rulers enlightened? They must allow religious toleration, freedom of speech and press, and the right to hold private property. They must foster the arts, sciences, and education. Above all, they must not be arbitrary in their rule; they must obey the laws and enforce them fairly for all subjects. To

Voltaire, only strong monarchs seemed capable of overcoming vested interests and effecting the reforms society needed. Reforms then should come from above—from the rulers rather than from the people. Distrustful of the masses, the philosophes believed that absolute rulers, swayed by enlightened principles, were the best hope of reforming their societies.

The extent to which rulers actually did so is frequently discussed in political histories of the eighteenth century. Many historians once assumed that a new type of monarchy emerged in the later eighteenth century, which they called "enlightened despotism" or "enlightened absolutism." Monarchs such as Frederick II of Prussia, Catherine the Great of Russia, and Joseph II of Austria supposedly followed the advice of the philosophes and ruled by enlightened principles, establishing a path to modern nationhood. Recent scholarship, however, has questioned the usefulness of the concept of "enlightened absolutism." We can best determine the extent to which it can be applied by surveying the development of the European states in the eighteenth century and then making a judgment about the "enlightened absolutism" of the later eighteenth century.

The Atlantic Seaboard States

As a result of overseas voyages in the sixteenth century, the European economic axis began to shift from the Mediterranean to the Atlantic seaboard. In the seventeenth century, the English and Dutch expanded as Spain and Portugal declined. By the eighteenth century, Dutch power had waned, and it was left to the English and French to build the commercial empires that presaged the growth of a true global economy.

FRANCE: THE LONG RULE OF LOUIS XV

In the eighteenth century, France experienced an economic revival while the movement of the Enlightenment gained strength. The French monarchy, however, was not overly influenced by the philosophes and resisted reforms as the French aristocracy grew stronger.

Louis XIV had left France with enlarged territories but also an enormous debt, an unhappy populace, and a five-year-old great-grandson as his successor. The governing of France fell into the hands first of the regent, the duke of Orléans, whose good intentions were undermined by his drunken and immoral behavior, and later of Cardinal Fleury, the king's minister. France pulled back from foreign adventures while commerce and trade expanded and the government promoted the growth of industry, especially in coal and textiles. The budget was even balanced for a while. When Fleury died in 1743, Louis XV (1715–1774) decided to rule alone. But Louis was both lazy and weak, and ministers and mistresses soon began to influence the king, control the affairs of state, and undermine the prestige of the monarchy. One mistress—probably the most famous of eighteenth-century Europe—was Madame de Pompadour. An intelligent and beautiful woman, she charmed Louis XV and gained both wealth and power, often making important government decisions and giving advice on appointments and foreign policy. The loss of an empire in the Seven Years' War, accompanied by burdensome taxes, an ever-mounting public debt, more hungry people, and a court life at Versailles that remained frivolous and carefree, forced even Louis to realize the growing disgust with his monarchy. "Things will last my time at any rate," he remarked myopically and prophetically.

Perhaps all might not have been in vain if Louis had been succeeded by a competent king. But the new king, Louis's twenty-year-old grandson who became Louis XVI (1774–1792), knew little about the operations of the French government and lacked the energy to deal decisively with state affairs (see the box on p. 519). His wife, Marie Antoinette, was a spoiled Austrian princess who devoted much of her time to court intrigues. As France's financial crises worsened, neither Louis nor his queen seemed able to fathom the depths of despair and discontent that soon led to violent revolution (see Chapter 19).

GREAT BRITAIN: KING AND PARLIAMENT

The success of the Glorious Revolution in England had prevented absolutism without clearly inaugurating constitutional monarchy. The eighteenth-century British political system was characterized by a sharing of power between king and Parliament, with Parliament gradually gaining the upper hand. (The United Kingdom of Great Britain came into existence in 1707 when the governments of England and Scotland were united; the term *British* came into use to refer to both English and Scots.) The king chose ministers responsible to himself who set policy and guided Parliament; Parliament had the power to make laws, levy taxes, pass the budget, and indirectly influence the king's ministers. The eighteenth-century British Parliament was dominated by a landed aristocracy that historians usually divide into two groups: the peers, who sat in the House of Lords and served as lord lieutenants controlling the appointment of the justices of the peace; and the landed gentry, who sat in the House of Commons and served as justices of the peace in the counties. There is much historical debate over whether it makes sense to distinguish between the aristocracies because the two groups had much in common. Both were landowners with similar economic interests, and they frequently intermarried.

Although the British monarchy was faced with a powerful aristocracy that monopolized Parliament and held most of the important governing posts locally (as justices of the peace in the counties) and nationally, it still exercised considerable power. Because the aristocracy was divided by factional struggles based on family rivalries, the kings could take advantage of the divisions to win aristocratic supporters through patronage, awarding them titles, government posts, and positions in the church and household staff.

The French King's Bedtime

Louis XIV had used court etiquette to magnify the dignity of kingship. During the reign of Louis XVI (1774–1792), however, court etiquette degenerated to ludicrous depths. This excerpt from the Memoirs of the Comtesse de Boigne *describes the king's* coucher, *the formal ceremony in which the king retired for the night.*

❊ Comtesse de Boigne, *Memoirs*

The king [Louis XVI] went to his *coucher*. The so-called *coucher* took place every evening at half past nine. The gentlemen of the court assembled in the bedroom of Louis XVI (but Louis XVI did not sleep there). I believe that all those who had been presented at court were permitted to attend.

The king came in from an adjoining room, followed by his domestic staff. His hair was in curlers, and he was not wearing his decorations. Without paying attention to anybody, he stepped behind the handrail surrounding the bed, and the chaplain on duty was given the prayer book and a tall taperstand with two candles by one of the valets. He then joined the king behind the handrail, handed him the book, and held the taperstand during the king's prayer, which was short. The king then went to the part of the room where the courtiers were, and the chaplain gave the taperstand back to the first valet who, in turn, took it over to a person indicated by the king. This person held it as long as the *coucher* lasted. This distinction was very much sought after. . . .

The king had his coat, vest and finally shirt removed. He was naked to the waist, scratching and rubbing himself as if alone, though he was in the presence of the whole court and often a number of distinguished foreigners.

The first valet handed the nightshirt to the most qualified person. . . . If it was a person with whom the king was on familiar terms, he often played little tricks before donning it, missed it, passed it, and ran away, accompanying this charming nonsense with hearty laughter, making those who were sincerely attached to him suffer. Having donned the nightshirt, he put on his robe and three valets unfastened the belt and the knee buckles of his trousers, which fell down to his feet. Thus attired, hardly able to walk so absurdly encumbered, he began to make the round of the circle.

The duration of this reception was by no means fixed; sometimes it lasted only a few minutes, sometimes almost an hour; it depended on who was there. . . . When the king had enough, he dragged himself backward to an easy chair which had been pushed to the middle of the room and fell heavily into it, raising both legs. Two pages on their knees seized his shoes, took them off, and dropped them on the floor with a thump, which was part of the etiquette. When he heard it, the doorman opened the door and said, "This way, gentlemen." Everybody left, and the ceremony was over. However, the person who held the taperstand was permitted to stay if he had anything special to say to the king. This explains the high price attached to this strange favor.

What enabled the British system of political patronage to work was the structure of parliamentary elections. The deputies to the House of Commons were chosen from the boroughs and counties but not by popular vote and hardly in any equitable fashion. Of the almost 500 deputies in the House of Commons, about 400 were chosen from the boroughs. Past history rather than population determined the number of delegates from each borough, however, so in one borough six people might choose two representatives whereas new cities like Manchester had no delegates at all despite their growing populations. Who could vote also varied wildly, enabling wealthy landed aristocrats to gain support by patronage and bribery; the result was a number of "pocket boroughs" controlled by a single person (hence "in his pocket"). The duke of Newcastle, for example, controlled the representatives from seven boroughs. It has been estimated that out of 405 borough deputies, 293 were chosen by fewer than 500 voters. This aristocratic control also extended to the county delegates, two from each of England's forty counties. Although all holders of property worth at least forty shillings a year could vote, members of the leading landed gentry families were elected over and over again. Parliament then was an institution largely dominated by the landed aristocracy, but their factional struggles enabled the monarchy still to exercise some power by its control of patronage.

Since the ministers were responsible for exercising the king's patronage, who became his chief ministers took on great political significance. In 1714, a new dynasty—the Hanoverians—was established when the last Stuart ruler, Queen Anne (1702–1714), died without an heir. The crown was offered to the Protestant rulers of the German state of Hanover. Both George I (1714–1727) and George II (1727–1760) relied on Robert Walpole as their chief or prime minister and the duke of Newcastle as their main dispenser of patronage, putting the latter at the center of British politics. Since the first Hanoverian king did not speak English and neither the first nor the second George had much familiarity with the British system, the chief ministers were allowed to handle Parliament and dispense patronage. Many historians feel that this exercise of ministerial power was an important step in the development of the modern cabinet system in British government.

CHRONOLOGY

The European States: The Atlantic Seaboard States

France	
Louis XV	1715–1774
Louis XVI	1774–1792
Great Britain	
The Stuarts	
Queen Anne	1702–1714
The Hanoverians	
George I	1714–1727
George II	1727–1760
Robert Walpole	1721–1742
William Pitt the Elder	1757–1761
George III	1760–1820
William Pitt the Younger	1783–1801

Robert Walpole served as prime minister from 1721 to 1742 and pursued a peaceful foreign policy to avoid new land taxes. But new forces were emerging in eighteenth-century Britain as growing trade and industry led an ever-increasing middle class to favor expansion of trade and world empire. The exponents of empire found a spokesman in William Pitt the Elder, who became prime minister in 1757 and furthered imperial ambitions by acquiring Canada and India in the Seven Years' War (see The Seven Years' War later in this chapter).

Despite his successes, however, Pitt the Elder was dismissed by the new king George III (1760–1820) in 1761 and replaced by the king's favorite, Lord Bute. Although characterized as a rather stupid person, George III was not the tyrant he is often portrayed as being. Determined to strengthen monarchical authority, his desire to wield the power of patronage personally led to the ouster of Pitt. At the same time, however, as a growing number of newspapers spread Enlightenment ideas to an expanding reading public, the clamor for the reform of both patronage and the electoral system began to increase. The saga of John Wilkes soon intensified the public outcry.

An ambitious middle-class member of the House of Commons, John Wilkes was an outspoken journalist who publicly criticized the king's ministers. Arrested and soon released, Wilkes was expelled from his seat in Parliament. When he persevered and won another parliamentary seat from the county of Middlesex near London, he was again denied the right to take his place in Parliament. The cause of John Wilkes quickly became identified with liberty, and the slogan "Wilkes and Liberty" was frequently used by his supporters who came from two major social groups: the common people of London, who had no voting rights, and a middle element of voting freeholders, such as guild masters and small merchants in London and the surrounding counties. The cry for liberty soon spilled over into calls for the reform of Parliament and an end to parliamentary privileges. In 1780, the House of Commons affirmed that "the influence of the crown has increased, is increasing, and ought to be diminished." At the same time, criticism at home was exacerbated by criticism abroad, especially by the American colonists whose discontent with the British system had led to rebellion and separation (see Chapter 19). Although minor reforms of the patronage system were made in 1782, King George III managed to avoid more drastic change by appointing William Pitt the Younger (1759–1806), son of William Pitt the Elder, as prime minister in 1783. Supported by the merchants,

THE BRITISH HOUSE OF COMMONS. A sharing of power between king and Parliament characterized the British political system in the eighteenth century. Parliament was divided into the House of Lords and House of Commons. This painting shows the House of Commons in session in 1793 during a debate over the possibility of war with France. William Pitt is addressing the House.

MAP 18.1 Europe in 1763.

industrial classes, and the king, who used patronage to gain support for Pitt in the House of Commons, the latter managed to stay in power through the French revolutionary and Napoleonic eras. George III, however, remained an uncertain supporter because of periodic bouts of insanity (he once thought a tree in Windsor Park was the king of Prussia). With Pitt's successes, serious reform of the corrupt parliamentary system was avoided for another generation.

THE DECLINE OF THE DUTCH REPUBLIC

After its century in the sun, the Dutch Republic or United Netherlands suffered a decline in economic prosperity. Both local and national political affairs were dominated by the oligarchies that governed the Dutch Republic's towns. In the eighteenth century, the struggle continued between these oligarchs (or regents as they were called from their governing positions) and the house of Orange, who as stadholders headed the executive branch of government. The regents sought to reduce the power of the Orangists but soon became divided when Dutch burghers who called themselves the Patriots (artisans, merchants, shopkeepers) began to agitate for democratic reforms that would open up the municipal councils to greater participation than that of the oligarchs. The success of the Patriots, however, led to foreign interference when the Prussian king sent troops to protect his sister, wife of the Orangist stadholder. The Patriots were crushed, and both Orangists and regents reestablished the old system. The intervention by Prussia serves to remind us of the growing power of the central European states.

Absolutism in Central and Eastern Europe

Of the five major European states, three were located in central and eastern Europe and came to play an increasingly important role in European international politics.

PRUSSIA: THE ARMY AND THE BUREAUCRACY

Two able Prussian kings in the eighteenth century, Frederick William I and Frederick II, further developed the two major institutions—the army and the bureaucracy—that were the backbone of Prussia. Frederick William I (1713–1740) promoted the evolution of Prussia's highly efficient civil bureaucracy by establishing the General Directory. It served as the chief administrative agent of the central government, supervising military, police, economic, and financial affairs. Because Prussia's disjointed territories could hardly have been preserved without a centralized administrative machine, Frederick William strove to maintain a highly efficient bureaucracy of civil service workers. It became a special kind of organization with its own code in which the supreme values were obedience,

FREDERICK II AT SANS-SOUCI. Frederick II was one of the most cultured and well-educated European monarchs. In this painting, he is shown visiting the building site of his residential retreat of Sans-Souci at Potsdam.

honor, and service to the king as the highest duty. As Frederick William asserted: "One must serve the king with life and limb, with goods and chattels, with honor and conscience, and surrender everything except salvation. The latter is reserved for God. But everything else must be mine."[3] For his part, Frederick William personally kept a close watch over his officials to ensure that they performed their duties. As the Saxon minister at Berlin related:

> Every day His Majesty gives new proofs of his justice. Walking recently at Potsdam at six in the morning, he saw a post-coach arrive with several passengers who knocked for a long time at the post-house which was still closed. The King, seeing that no one opened the door, joined them in knocking and even knocked in some window-panes. The master of the post then opened the door and scolded the travelers, for no one recognized the King. But His Majesty let himself be known by giving the official some good blows of his cane and drove him from his house and his job after apologizing to the travelers for his laziness. Examples of this sort, of which I could relate several others, make everybody alert and exact.[4]

Close, personal supervision of the bureaucracy became a hallmark of the eighteenth-century Prussian rulers.

Under Frederick William I, the rigid class stratification that had emerged in seventeenth-century Brandenburg-Prussia persisted. The nobility or landed aristocracy known as Junkers, who owned large estates with many serfs, still played a dominating role in the Prussian state. The Junkers held a complete monopoly over the officer corps of the Prussian army, which Frederick William passionately continued to expand. By the end of his reign, the army had grown from 45,000 to 83,000 men. Though tenth in physical size and thirteenth in population among the European states, Prussia had the fourth largest army after France, Russia, and Austria.

While nobles served as officers, rank-and-file soldiers were usually peasants who served a long number of years. Discipline in the army was extremely rigid and even cruel—so cruel, in fact, that desertion was common. The king advised his generals not to take troops through a forest on maneuvers because it offered too many opportunities for running away. By using nobles as officers, Frederick William ensured a close bond between the nobility and the army and, in turn, the loyalty of the nobility to the absolute monarch.

As officers, the Junker nobility became imbued with a sense of service to the king or state. All the virtues of the Prussian nobility were, in effect, military virtues: duty, obedience, sacrifice. At the same time, because of its size and reputation as one of the best armies in Europe, the Prussian army was the most important institution in the state. "Prussian militarism" became synonymous with the extreme exaltation of military virtues. Indeed, one Prussian minister remarked around 1800 that "Prussia was not a country with an army, but an army with a country which served as headquarters and food magazine."[5]

The remaining classes in Prussia were considerably less important than the nobility. The peasants were born

Frederick the Great and His Father

As a young man, the future Frederick the Great was quite different from his strict and austere father, Frederick William I. Possessing a high regard for French culture, poetry, and flute playing, Frederick resisted his father's wishes that he immerse himself in governmental and military affairs. Eventually, Frederick capitulated to his father's will and accepted the need to master affairs of state. These letters, written when Frederick was sixteen, illustrate the difficulties in their relationship.

Frederick to His Father, Frederick William I (September 11,1728)

I have not ventured for a long time to present myself before my dear papa, partly because I was advised against it, but chiefly because I anticipated an even worse reception than usual and feared to vex my dear papa still further by the favor I have now to ask; so I have preferred to put it in writing.

I beg my dear papa that he will be kindly disposed toward me. I do assure him that after long examination of my conscience I do not find the slightest thing with which to reproach myself; but if, against my wish and will, I have vexed my dear papa, I hereby beg most humbly for forgiveness, and hope that my dear papa will give over the fearful hate which has appeared so plainly in his whole behavior and to which I cannot accustom myself. I have always thought hitherto that I had a kind father, but now I see the contrary. However, I will take courage and hope that my dear papa will think this all over and take me again into his favor. Meantime I assure him that I will never, my life long, willingly fail him, and in spite of his disfavor I am still, with most dutiful and childlike respect, my dear papa's

Most obedient and faithful servant and son,
Frederick

Frederick William to His Son Frederick

A bad, obstinate boy, who does not love his father; for when one does one's best, and especially when one loves one's father, one does what he wishes not only when he is standing by but when he is not there to see. Moreover you know very well that I cannot stand an effeminate fellow who has no manly tastes, who cannot ride or shoot (to his shame be it said!), is untidy about his person, and wears his hair curled like a fool instead of cutting it; and that I have condemned all these things a thousand times, and yet there is no sign of improvement. For the rest, haughty, offish as a country lout, conversing with none but a favored few instead of being affable and popular, grimacing like a fool, and never following my wishes out of love for me but only when forced into it, caring for nothing but to have his own way, and thinking nothing else is of any importance. This is my answer.

Frederick William

on their lords' estates and spent most of the rest of their lives there or in the army. They had few real rights and even needed their Junker's permission to marry. For the middle class, the only opportunity for any social prestige was in the Prussian civil service where the ideal of loyal service to the state became a hallmark of the middle-class official. Frederick William allowed and even encouraged men of nonnoble birth to serve in important administrative posts. When he died in 1740, only three of his eighteen privy councillors were of noble birth.

Frederick the Great (1740–1786) was one of the best educated and most cultured monarchs in the eighteenth century. He was well versed in Enlightenment thought and even invited Voltaire to live at his court for several years. His intellectual interests were despised by his father who forced his intelligent son to prepare for a career in ruling (see the box above). A believer in the king as the "first servant of the state," Frederick the Great became a conscientious ruler who made few innovations in the administration of the state. His diligence in overseeing its operation, however, made the Prussian bureaucracy well known for both its efficiency and its honesty.

For a time, Frederick seemed quite willing to follow the philosophes' recommendations for reform. He established a single code of laws for his territories that eliminated the use of torture except in treason and murder cases. He also granted a limited freedom of speech and press as well as complete religious toleration, no difficult task since he had no strong religious convictions anyway. Although Frederick was well aware of the philosophes' condemnation of serfdom, he was too dependent on the Prussian nobility to interfere with it or with the hierarchical structure of Prussian society. In fact, Frederick II was a social conservative who made Prussian society even more aristocratic than it had been before. Frederick reversed his father's policy of allowing commoners to rise to power in the civil service and reserved the higher positions in the bureaucracy for members of the nobility. The upper ranks of the bureaucracy came close to constituting a hereditary caste over time.

Like his predecessors, Frederick the Great took a great interest in military affairs and enlarged the Prussian army (to 200,000 men). Unlike his predecessors, he had no objection to using it. Frederick did not hesitate to take advantage of a succession crisis in the Habsburg monarchy to seize the Austrian province of Silesia for Prussia. This act aroused Austria's bitter hostility and embroiled Frederick in two major wars, the War of the Austrian

MARIA THERESA AND HER FAMILY. Maria Theresa governed the vast possessions of the Austrian Empire from 1740 to 1780. Of her ten surviving children, Joseph II succeeded her; Leopold became grand-duke of Tuscany and the ruler of Austria after Joseph's death; Ferdinand was made duke of Modena; and Marie Antoinette became the bride of King Louis XVI of France.

Succession and the Seven Years' War (see Wars and Diplomacy later in this chapter). Although the latter war left his country exhausted, Frederick succeeded in keeping Silesia. After the wars, the first partition of Poland with Austria and Russia in 1772 gave him the Polish territory between Prussia and Brandenburg and created greater unity for the scattered lands of Prussia. By the end of his reign, Prussia was recognized as a great European power.

THE AUSTRIAN EMPIRE OF THE HABSBURGS

The Austrian Empire had become one of the great European states by the beginning of the eighteenth century. The city of Vienna, center of the Habsburg monarchy, was filled with magnificent palaces and churches built in the Baroque style and became the music capital of Europe. And yet Austria, by its very nature as a sprawling empire composed of many different nationalities, languages, religions, and cultures, found it difficult to provide common laws and a centralized administration for its people.

Empress Maria Theresa (1740–1780), however, stunned by the loss of Austrian Silesia to Prussia in the War of the Austrian Succession, resolved to reform her empire in preparation for the seemingly inevitable next conflict with rival Prussia. Although Maria Theresa was forced to accept the privileges of the Hungarian nobility and the right of her Hungarian subjects to have their own laws, she did abolish the Austrian and Bohemian chancelleries and replaced them with departments of foreign affairs, justice, war, commerce, and internal affairs that functioned for both territories. Maria Theresa also curtailed the role of the diets or provincial assemblies in taxation and local administration. Now clergy and nobles were forced to pay property and income taxes to royal officials rather than the diets. The Austrian and Bohemian lands were divided into ten provinces and subdivided into districts, all administered by royal officials rather than representatives of the diets, making part of the Austrian Empire more centralized and more bureaucratic. But these administrative reforms were done for practical reasons—to strengthen the power of the Habsburg state—and were accompanied by an enlargement and modernization of the armed forces. Maria Theresa remained staunchly Catholic and conservative and was not open to the wider reform calls of the philosophes. But her successor was.

From 1765 to 1780, Maria Theresa had allowed her son Joseph II to share rule with her, although Joseph felt restrained by his mother's lack of interest in the reform ideas of the Enlightenment that greatly appealed to him. When he achieved sole power in 1780, he was determined to make changes; at the same time, he carried on his mother's chief goal of enhancing Habsburg power within the monarchy and Europe. Joseph II was an earnest man who believed in the need to sweep away anything standing in the path of reason. As Joseph expressed it: "I have made Philosophy the lawmaker of my empire, her logical applications are going to transform Austria."

Joseph's reform program was far-reaching. He abolished serfdom and tried to give the peasants hereditary rights to their holdings. An exponent of Physiocratic ideas (see Chapter 17), he abandoned economic restraints by eliminating internal trade barriers, ending monopolies, and removing guild restrictions. A new penal code was instituted that abrogated the death penalty and established the principle of equality of all before the law. Joseph introduced drastic religious reforms as well, including complete religious toleration and restrictions on the Catholic church. Altogether, Joseph II issued 6,000 decrees and 11,000 laws in his effort to transform Austria.

Joseph's reform program proved overwhelming for Austria, however. He alienated the nobility by freeing the

The Proposals of Catherine II for a New Law Code

Catherine II the Great of Russia appeared for a while to be an enlightened ruler. In 1767, she convened a legislative commission to prepare a new code of laws for Russia. In her famous Instruction, *she gave the delegates a detailed guide to the principles they should follow. Although the guidelines were obviously culled from the liberal ideas of the philosophes, the commission itself accomplished nothing, and Catherine's* Instruction *was soon forgotten.*

Catherine II, Proposals for a New Law Code

13. What is the true End of Monarchy? Not to deprive People of their natural Liberty; but to correct their Actions, in order to attain the supreme good.
33. The Laws ought to be so framed, as to secure the Safety of every Citizen as much as possible.
34. The Equality of the Citizens consists in this; that they should all be subject to the same Laws.
38. A Man ought to form in his own Mind an exact and clear Idea of what Liberty is. Liberty is the Right of doing whatsoever the Laws allow: And if any one Citizen could do what the Laws forbid, there would be no more Liberty; because others would have an equal Power of doing the same.
123. The Usage of Torture is contrary to all the Dictates of Nature and Reason; even Mankind itself cries out against it, and demands loudly the total Abolition of it.
180. That Law, therefore, is highly beneficial to the Community where it is established, which ordains that every Man shall be judged by his Peers and Equals. For when the Fate of a Citizen is in Question, all Prejudices arising from the Difference of Rank or Fortune should be stifled; because they ought to have no Influence between the Judges and the Parties accused.
194. No Man ought to be looked upon as guilty, before he has received his judicial Sentence; nor can the Laws deprive him of their Protection, before it is proved that he has forfeited all Right to it. What Right therefore can Power give to any to inflict Punishment upon a Citizen at a Time, when it is yet dubious, whether he is Innocent or guilty?
270. It is highly necessary that the Law should prescribe a Rule to the Lords, for a more judicious Method of raising their Revenues; and oblige them to levy such a Tax, as tends least to separate the Peasant from His House and Family; this would be the Means by which Agriculture would become more extensive, and Population be more increased in the Empire.

serfs and alienated the church by his attacks on the monastic establishment. Even the serfs were unhappy, unable to comprehend the drastic changes inherent in Joseph's policies. His attempt to rationalize the administration of the empire by imposing German as the official bureaucratic language alienated the non-German nationalities. As Joseph complained, there were not enough people for the kind of bureaucracy he needed. His deep sense of failure is revealed in the epitaph he wrote for his gravestone: "Here lies Joseph II who was unfortunate in everything that he undertook." His successors undid many of his reform efforts.

RUSSIA UNDER CATHERINE THE GREAT

Peter the Great was followed by a series of six successors who were made and unmade by the palace guard. The last of these six was Peter III, whose German wife Catherine learned Russian and won the favor of the palace guard. Peter was murdered by a faction of nobles, and Catherine II the Great (1762–1796) emerged as autocrat of all the Russias.

Catherine was an intelligent woman who was familiar with the works of the philosophes. Voltaire and Diderot were among her correspondents, although some historians believe she corresponded with philosophes simply to improve her image abroad. Catherine claimed that she wished to reform Russia along the lines of Enlightenment ideas, but she was always shrewd enough to realize that her success depended upon the support of the palace guard and the gentry class from which it stemmed. She could not afford to alienate the Russian nobility.

Initially, Catherine seemed eager to pursue reform. She called for the election of an assembly in 1767 to debate the details of a new law code. In her *Instruction,* written as a guide to the deliberations, Catherine questioned the institution of serfdom, torture, and capital punishment and even advocated the principle of the equality of all people in the eyes of the law (see the box above). But one and one-half years of negotiation produced little real change.

In fact, Catherine's subsequent policies had the effect of strengthening the landholding class at the expense of all others, especially the Russian serfs. In order to reorganize local government, Catherine divided Russia into fifty provinces, each of which in turn was subdivided into districts whose ruling officials were chosen by the nobles. In this way, the local nobility became responsible for the day-to-day governing of Russia. Moreover, the

CATHERINE THE GREAT. Autocrat of Russia, Catherine was an intelligent ruler who favored reform. She found it expedient, however, to retain much of the old system in order to keep the support of the landed nobility. In this portrait by Dmitry Levitsky, she is shown in legislative regalia in the Temple of Justice in 1783.

CHRONOLOGY

The European States: Absolutism in Central and Eastern Europe

Prussia	
Frederick William I	1713–1740
Frederick II the Great	1740–1786
The Austrian Empire	
Maria Theresa	1740–1780
Joseph II (co-rule with Maria Theresa)	1765–1780
Joseph II	1780–1790
Russia	
Peter III	1762
Catherine II the Great	1762–1796
Pugachev's rebellion	1773–1775
Charter of the Nobility	1785
Poland	
First partition	1772
Second partition	1793
Third partition	1795

gentry were now formed into corporate groups with special legal privileges, including the right to trial by peers and exemption from personal taxation and corporal punishment. A Charter of the Nobility formalized these rights in 1785.

Catherine's policy of favoring the landed nobility led to even worse conditions for the Russian peasantry. In 1767, serfs were forbidden to appeal to the state against their masters. The attempt of the Russian government to impose restrictions upon free peasants in the border districts of the Russian Empire soon led to a full-scale revolt that spread to the Volga valley. It was intensified by the support of the Cossacks, independent tribes of fierce warriors who had at times fought for the Russians against the Turks but now resisted the government's attempt to absorb them into the empire.

An illiterate Cossack, Emelyan Pugachev, succeeded in welding the disparate elements of discontent into a mass revolt. Beginning in 1773, Pugachev's rebellion spread across southern Russia from the Urals to the Volga River. Initially successful, Pugachev won the support of many peasants when he issued a manifesto in July 1774, freeing all peasants from oppressive taxes and military service. Encouraged to seize their landlords' estates by Pugachev, the peasants responded by killing more than 1,500 estate owners and their families. The rebellion soon faltered, however, as government forces rallied and became more effective. Betrayed by his own subordinates, Pugachev was captured, tortured, and executed. The rebellion collapsed completely, and Catherine responded with even greater repression of the peasantry. All rural reform was halted; serfdom was expanded into newer parts of the empire, and peasants on crown land were also reduced to serfdom.

Above all, Catherine proved a worthy successor to Peter the Great by expanding Russia's territory westward (into Poland) and southward (to the Black Sea). Russia spread southward by defeating the Turks. In the Treaty of Kuchuk-Kainarji in 1774, the Russians gained some land, the privilege of protecting Greek Orthodox Christians in the Ottoman Empire, and the right to sail in Turkish waters. Russian expansion westward occurred at the expense of neighboring Poland. In the three partitions of Poland, Russia gained about 50 percent of Polish territory.

THE DESTRUCTION OF POLAND

Poland was an excellent example of why a strong monarchy was needed in early modern Europe. The failure to develop the machinery of state building because of the excessive powers of the aristocracy proved disastrous. The Polish king was elected by the Polish nobles and forced to accept drastic restrictions upon his power, including limited revenues, a small bureaucracy, and a standing army of no more than 20,000 soldiers. For Polish nobles, these

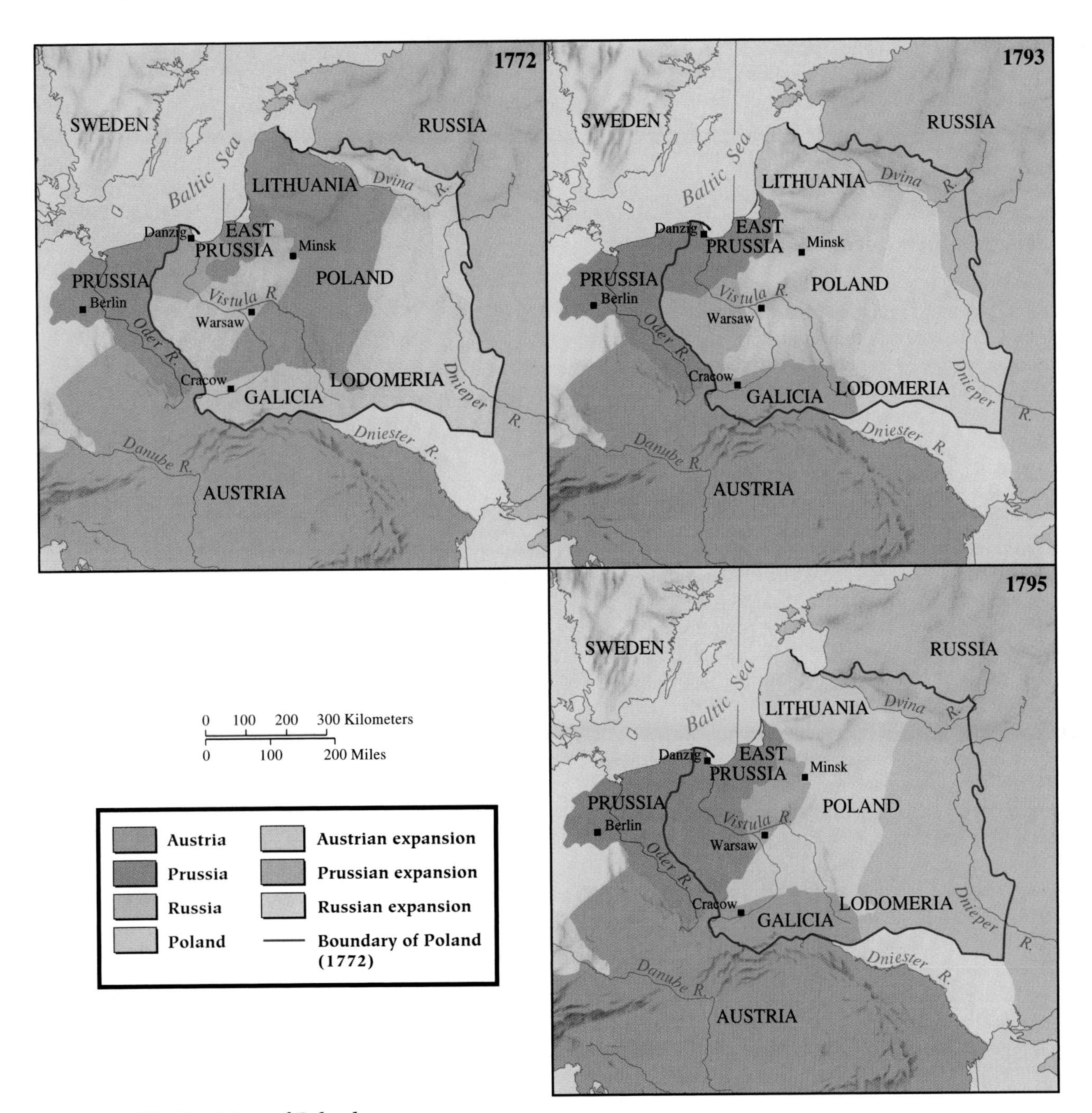

MAP 18.2 The Partitions of Poland.

limitations eliminated an absolute king; for Poland's powerful neighbors, they were an invitation to meddle in its affairs.

The total destruction of the Polish state in the eighteenth century arose out of the rivalries of its three great neighbors, Austria, Russia, and Prussia. To avoid war, the leaders of these powers decided to compensate themselves by dividing Poland. To maintain the balance of power in central and eastern Europe, the three great powers cynically agreed to the acquisition of roughly equal territories at Poland's expense.

In 1772, Poland lost about 30 percent of its land and 50 percent of its population. Austria gained the agriculturally rich district of Galicia, Russia took the largest slice of land in eastern Poland, and Prussia acquired West Prussia, the smallest but most valuable territory because it united two of the chief sections of Prussia.

The remaining Polish state was supposedly independent; in truth, it was dominated by the Russians who even kept troops on Polish territory. After the Poles attempted to establish a stronger state under a hereditary monarchy in 1791, the Russians gained the support of Austria and Prussia and intervened militarily in May 1792. In the following year, Russia and Prussia undertook a second partition of Polish territory. Finally, after a heroic but hopeless rebellion in 1794–1795 under the General

Thaddeus Kosciuszko, the remaining Polish state was obliterated by Austria, Prussia, and Russia in the third partition of Poland (1795). Many historians have pointed to Poland's demise as a cogent example of why building a strong, absolutist state was essential to survival in the seventeenth and eighteenth centuries.

The Mediterranean World

At the beginning of the eighteenth century, Spain experienced a change of dynasties from the Habsburgs to the Bourbons. Bourbon rule temporarily rejuvenated Spain and at least provided an opportunity to centralize the institutions of the state. Under Philip V (1700–1746), the laws, administrative institutions, and language of Castile were established in the other Spanish kingdoms, making the king of Castile truly the king of Spain. Moreover, French-style ministries replaced the old conciliar system of government, and officials similar to French intendants were introduced into the various Spanish provinces.

Since the Treaty of Utrecht in 1713 had taken the Italian territories and Netherlands away from Spain, the latter now had fewer administrative problems and less drain on its already overtaxed economic resources. In the second half of the eighteenth century, especially during the reign of Charles III (1759–1788), the Catholic church was also brought under control when the king banished the Jesuits and circumscribed the activities of the Inquisition. The landed aristocracy continued to exercise substantial power throughout the eighteenth century, however.

Portugal had experienced decline since the glorious days of empire in the sixteenth century. Nevertheless, during the long ministry of the marquis of Pombal (1699–1782), who served as chief minister to a series of Portuguese kings, the nobility and Catholic church were curtailed and the Portuguese empire temporarily revived. After Pombal was removed from office, the nobility and church regained much of their power.

After the Treaty of Utrecht, Austria had replaced Spain as the dominant force in Italy in the eighteenth century. The duchy of Milan, Sardinia, and the kingdom of Naples were all surrendered to the Habsburg emperors, and Sicily was given to the northern Italian state of Savoy, which was slowly emerging as a state with "an appetite for territorial expansion." In 1734, the Bourbons of Spain reestablished control over Naples and Sicily. Though some Italian states, such as Venice and Genoa, remained independent, they grew increasingly impotent in international affairs.

The Scandinavian States

In the seventeenth century, Sweden had become the dominant power in northern Europe, but after the Battle of Poltava in 1709, Swedish power declined rapidly. Following the death of the powerful Charles XII in 1718, the Swedish nobility, using the Swedish diet as its instrument, gained control of public life and reduced the monarchy to puppet status. But the division of the nobility into pro-French and pro-Russian factions eventually enabled King Gustavus III (1771–1792) to reassert the power of the monarchy. Gustavus proved to be one of the "most enlightened monarchs of his age." By decree, he established freedom of religion, speech, and press and instituted a new code of justice that eliminated the use of torture. Moreover, his economic reforms smacked of laissez-faire: he reduced tariffs, abolished tolls, and encouraged trade and agriculture. In 1792, however, a group of nobles, incensed at these reforms and their loss of power, assassinated the king, but they proved unable to fully restore the rule of the aristocracy.

Denmark also saw an attempt at enlightened reforms by King Christian VII (1766–1808) and his chief minister, John Frederick Struensee. Aristocratic opposition stymied their efforts, however, and led to Struensee's death in 1772.

CHRONOLOGY

The European States: The Mediterranean World and Scandinavia

Spain	
Philip V, the first Bourbon king	1700–1746
Charles III	1759–1788
Portugal	
Marquis of Pombal	1699–1782
Sweden	
Charles XII	1697–1718
Gustavus III	1771–1792
Denmark	
Christian VII	1766–1808

Enlightened Absolutism Revisited

The subject of enlightened absolutism revolves around the relationship between "an intellectual movement and the actual practice of government." The ideas of the Enlightenment did have an impact on rulers after 1750. Almost every European ruler in the second half of the eighteenth century pursued some enlightened reforms, be they reform of laws, the development of secondary education, or religious tolerance. Few rulers, however, felt compelled to make the state an experimental lab for a set of political principles. Of the three major rulers traditionally associated most closely with enlightened absolutism—Joseph II, Frederick II, and Catherine the Great—only Joseph II sought truly radical changes based on Enlightenment ideas. Both Frederick and Catherine liked to be cast as disciples of the Enlightenment, expressed interest in enlightened reforms, and even attempted some, but the policies of neither seemed seriously affected by Enlightenment thought. Necessities of state and maintenance of the existing system took precedence over reform. Indeed, many historians feel that Joseph, Frederick, and Catherine were all primarily guided by a concern for the power and well-being of their states and that their policies were not all that different from those of their predecessors. In the final analysis, heightened state power was used to amass armies and wage wars to gain more power. Nevertheless, in their desire to build stronger state systems, these rulers did pursue such enlightened reforms as legal reform, religious toleration, and the extension of education because these served to create more satisfied subjects and strengthened the state in significant ways.

It would be foolish, however, to overlook the fact that political and social realities limited the ability of enlightened rulers to make reforms. Everywhere in Europe the hereditary aristocracy was still the most powerful class in society. Enlightened reforms were often limited to changes in the administrative and judicial systems that did not seriously undermine the powerful interests of the European nobility. Although aristocrats might join the populace in opposing monarchical extension of centralizing power, as the chief beneficiaries of a system based on traditional rights and privileges for their class, they were certainly not willing to support a political ideology that trumpeted the principle of equal rights for all.

◆ Wars and Diplomacy

The philosophes had denounced war as a foolish waste of life and resources in stupid quarrels of no value to humankind. Rulers, however, paid little attention to these comments and continued their costly struggles. By the eighteenth century, the European system of self-governing, individual states was grounded largely in the principle of self-interest. Because international relations were based on considerations of power, the eighteenth-century concept of a "balance of power" was predicated on how to counterbalance the power of one state by another to prevent any one power from dominating the others. This balance of power, however, did not imply a desire for peace. Large armies created to defend a state's security were often used for offensive purposes as well. As Frederick the Great of Prussia remarked: "The fundamental rule of governments is the principle of extending their territories." Nevertheless, the regular use of diplomacy served at times to lead to compromise.

The diplomacy of the eighteenth century still focused primarily on dynastic interests or the desire of ruling families to provide for their dependents and extend their dynastic holdings. But the eighteenth century also saw the emergence of the concept of "reason of state," on the basis of which a ruler such as Frederick II and a minister such as William Pitt the Elder looked beyond dynastic interests to the long-term future of their states.

International rivalry and the continuing centralization of the European states were closely related. The need for taxes to support large armies and navies created its own imperative for more efficient and effective control of power in the hands of bureaucrats who could collect taxes and organize states for the task of winning wars. At the same time, the development of large standing armies ensured that political disputes would periodically be resolved by armed conflict rather than diplomacy. Between 1715 and 1740, it had seemed that Europe preferred peace. But in 1740, a major conflict erupted over the succession to the Austrian throne.

The War of the Austrian Succession (1740–1748)

Unable to produce a male heir to the Austrian throne, the Habsburg emperor Charles VI (1711–1740) so feared the consequences of the succession of his daughter Maria Theresa that he spent much of his reign negotiating the Pragmatic Sanction by which different European powers agreed to recognize his daughter as his legal heir.

Charles, however, failed to foresee the faithlessness and duplicity of Europe's rulers. After his death, the Pragmatic Sanction was conveniently pushed aside, especially by Frederick II who had just succeeded to the throne of Prussia. The new Prussian ruler took advantage of the new empress to invade Austrian Silesia. At the same time, the ruler of the south German state of Bavaria seized some Habsburg territory and had himself chosen as the new Holy Roman Emperor. The vulnerability of Maria Theresa encouraged France to enter the war against its traditional enemy Austria; in turn, Maria Theresa made an alliance with Great Britain who feared French hegemony over continental affairs. All too quickly, the Austrian succession had produced a worldwide conflagration. The war was fought not only in Europe where Prussia seized Silesia, and France occupied the Austrian Netherlands, but in the East where France took Madras in India from the British and in North America where the British captured the French fortress of Louisbourg at the entrance to the St. Lawrence River. By 1748, all parties were exhausted and agreed to stop. The peace treaty of Aix-la-Chapelle promised the return of all occupied territories except Silesia to their original owners. Prussia's refusal to return Silesia guaranteed another war, at least between the two hostile central European powers of Prussia and Austria.

The Seven Years' War (1756–1763)

Maria Theresa refused to accept the loss of Silesia and prepared for its return by rebuilding her army while working diplomatically through her able foreign minister, Count

Wenzel von Kaunitz, to separate Prussia from its chief ally, France. In 1756, Austria achieved what was soon labeled a diplomatic revolution. Bourbon-Habsburg rivalry had been a fact of European diplomacy since the late sixteenth century. But two new rivalries made this old one seem superfluous: Britain and France over colonial empires, and Austria and Prussia over Silesia. France now abandoned Prussia and allied with Austria. Russia, which saw Prussia as a major hindrance to Russian goals in central Europe, joined the new alliance. In turn, Great Britain allied with Prussia. This diplomatic revolution of 1756 now led to another worldwide war.

There were three major areas of conflict: Europe, India, and North America. Europe witnessed the clash of the two major alliances: the British and Prussians against the Austrians, Russians, and French. With his superb army and military prowess, Frederick the Great was able for some time to defeat the Austrian, French, and Russian armies. He won a spectacular victory at the Battle of Rossbach in Saxony (1757) over combined French-Austrian forces that far outnumbered his own troops. Under attack from three different directions, however, the forces of Frederick II were gradually worn down and faced utter defeat when they were saved by the death of Tsarina Elizabeth of Russia, which brought her nephew Peter III to power. A great admirer of Frederick the Great, Peter withdrew the Russian troops from the conflict and from the Prussian lands that they had occupied. His withdrawal guaranteed a stalemate and led to a desire for peace. The European conflict was ended by the Peace of Hubertusburg in 1763. All occupied territories were returned, and Austria officially recognized Prussia's permanent control of Silesia.

The Anglo-French struggle in the rest of the world had more decisive results. Known as the Great War for Empire, it was fought in India and North America. The French had returned Madras to Britain after the War of the Austrian Succession, but jockeying for power continued as the French and British supported opposing native Indian princes. The British under Robert Clive (1725–1774) ultimately won out, not because they had better forces but because they were more persistent. By the Treaty of Paris in 1763, the French withdrew and left India to the British.

By far, the greatest conflicts of the Seven Years' War took place in North America. There were two primary areas of contention. One consisted of the waterways of the Gulf of St. Lawrence, guarded by the fortress of Louisbourg and by forts near the Great Lakes and Lake Champlain that protected French Quebec and French traders. The other was the unsettled Ohio River valley. As the French moved south from the Great Lakes and north from their forts on the Mississippi, they began to establish forts from the Appalachians to the Mississippi River. To the British settlers in the thirteen colonies to the east, this French activity threatened to cut off a vast area from British

MAP 18.3 The Seven Years' War.

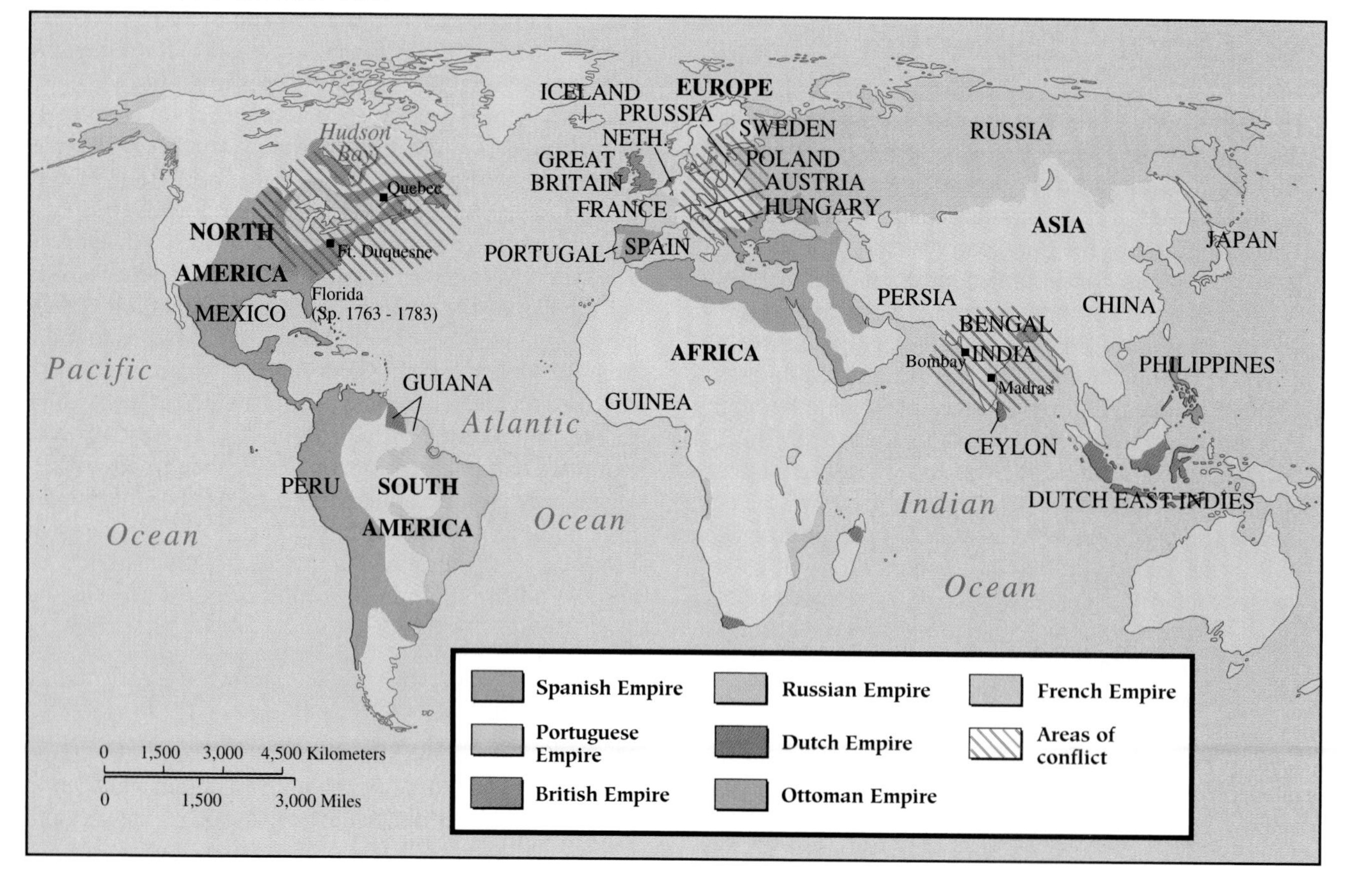

British Victory at Quebec

One of the major battles of the Seven Years' War in North America occurred in Canada in 1759 when British forces under General James Wolfe defeated the French under General Louis-Joseph Montcalm outside Quebec. This description of the important battle is taken from a detailed account of the British campaign in North America by Captain John Knox, an experienced soldier.

John Knox, *Historical Journal of the Campaign in North America*

Before daybreak this morning [September 13, 1759] we made a descent upon the north shore, about half a quarter of a mile to the eastward of Sillery. . . . We had in this debarkation thirty flat-bottomed boats, containing about sixteen hundred men. This was a great surprise on the enemy, who from the natural strength of the place did not suspect, and consequently were not prepared against so bold an attempt. The chain of sentries which they had posted along the summit of the heights galled us a little, and picked off several men and some officers before our light infantry got up to dislodge them. This great enterprise was conducted and executed with great good order and discretion.

As fast as we landed the boats put off for reinforcements, and the troops formed with much regularity. General Wolfe . . . was ashore with the first division. We lost no time here, but clambered up one of the steepest precipices that can be conceived, being almost a perpendicular, and of an incredible height. As soon as we gained the summit all was quiet, and not a shot was heard, owing to the excellent conduct of the light infantry under Colonel Howe. It was by this time clear daylight. Here we formed again . . . and halted a few minutes. . . . We then faced to the right, and marched toward the town by files till we came to the Plains of Abraham, an even piece of ground which Mr. Wolfe had made choice of, while we stood forming upon the hill. Weather showery. About six o'clock the enemy first made their appearance upon the heights between us and the town, whereupon we halted and wheeled to the right, thereby forming the line of battle. . . .

About ten o'clock the enemy began to advance briskly in three columns, with loud shots and recovered arms . . . from the distance of one hundred and thirty, until they came within forty yards, which our troops withstood with the greatest firmness, still reserving their fire and paying the strictest obedience to their officers. This uncommon steadiness, together with the havoc which the grape-shot from our field-pieces made among them, threw them into some disorder and was most critically maintained by a well-timed, regular, and heavy discharge of our small arms, such as they could no longer oppose. Hereupon they gave way, and fled, so that by the time the cloud of smoke was vanished our men were again over them, pursued them almost to the gates of the town and the bridge over the little river, making many officers and men prisoners. . . .

Our joy at this success is inexpressibly damped by the loss we sustained of one of the greatest heroes which this or any other age can boast of—General James Wolfe. . . . After [he] was carried off wounded to the rear of the front line, he desired those who were about him to lay him down. Being asked if he would have a surgeon, he replied, "It is needless: it is all over with me." One of them cried out, "They run, see how they run!" "Who runs?" demanded our hero with great earnestness, like a person roused from sleep. The officer answered: "The enemy, sir. Egad, they give way everywhere." Thereupon the general rejoined: "Go, one of you, my lads, to Colonel Burton; tell him to march Webb's regiment with all speed down to Charles River, to cut off the retreat of the fugitives from the bridge." Then, turning on his side, he added, "Now, God be praised, I will die in peace!" and thus expired.

exploitation. The French found allies among the Indians, who considered the French traders less threatening than the British settlers.

Despite initial French successes, British fortunes were revived by the efforts of William Pitt the Elder who was convinced that the destruction of the French colonial empire was a necessary prerequisite for the creation of Britain's own colonial empire. Accordingly, Pitt decided to make a minimal effort in Europe while concentrating resources, especially the British navy, on the colonial war. Although French troops were greater in number, the ability of the French to use them in the New World was contingent upon naval support. The defeat of French fleets in major naval battles in 1759 gave the British an advantage since the French could no longer easily reinforce their garrisons. A series of British victories soon followed. In 1758, Forts Louisbourg and Duquesne were captured. On the night of September 13, 1759, British forces led by General James Wolfe scaled the heights outside Quebec and defeated the French under General Louis-Joseph Montcalm on the Plains of Abraham (see the box above). Both generals died in the battle. The British went on to seize Montreal, the Great Lakes area, and the Ohio valley. The French were forced to make peace. By the Treaty of Paris, they ceded Canada and the lands east of the Mississippi to Britain. Their ally Spain transferred Spanish Florida to British control; in return, the French gave their Louisiana territory to the Spanish. By 1763, Great Britain had become the world's greatest colonial power.

THE DEATH OF WOLFE. The great powers of Europe fought the Seven Years' War in Europe, India, and North America. Despite initial French successes in North America, the British went on to win the war. This painting by Benjamin West presents a heroic rendering of the death of General James Wolfe, the British commander who defeated the French forces at the Battle of Quebec.

European Armies and Warfare

The professional standing army, initiated in the seventeenth century, became a standard feature of eighteenth-century Europe. Especially noticeable was the increase in the size of armies, which paralleled the development of absolutist states. Between 1740 and 1780, the French army grew from 190,000 to 300,000 men; the Prussian from 83,000 to 200,000; the Austrian from 108,000 to 282,000; and the Russian from 130,000 to 290,000.

The composition of these armies reflected the hierarchical structure of European society and the great chasm that separated the upper and lower classes. Officers were primarily from the landed aristocracy, which had for centuries regarded military activity as one of its major functions. Prussia made military service compulsory for its nobles and forced the teenage sons of aristocrats to attend a military academy in Berlin for training as officers. Middle-class individuals were largely kept out of the higher ranks of the officer corps while being admitted to the middle ranks. A prejudice against commoners in the officer corps remained a regular feature of military life in the eighteenth century.

Rank-and-file soldiers came mostly from the lower classes of society. Some states, such as Prussia and Russia, conscripted able-bodied peasants. But many states realized that this was counterproductive since they could not afford to waste their farmers. For that reason, eighteenth-century armies were partially composed of foreign troops, many from Switzerland or the petty German states. Of the great powers, Britain alone had no regular standing army and relied on mercenaries, evident in its use of German troops in America. Most troops in European armies, especially the French and Austrian, were natives who enlisted voluntarily for six-year terms. Some were not exactly volunteers; often vagabonds and the unemployed were pressed into service. Most, however, came from the lower classes—peasants and also artisans from the cities—who saw the military as an opportunity to escape from hard times or personal problems.

The maritime powers, such as Britain and the Dutch Republic, regarded navies as more important than armies. In the second half of the eighteenth century, the British possessed 174 warships manned by 80,000 sailors. Conditions on these ships were often poor. Diseases such as scurvy and yellow fever were rampant, and crews were frequently press-ganged into duty.

The dramatic increase in the size of armies and navies did not necessarily result in more destructive warfare in eighteenth-century Europe. For one thing, warfare was no longer driven by ideology as the religious wars of the sixteenth and seventeenth centuries had been. By their very nature, ideological wars are often violent and destructive. Moreover, since the larger armies depended upon increased tax revenues, rulers regarded the wanton destruction of civilian taxpayers as foolish. Finally, the costliness of eighteenth-century armies as well as the technology and tactical traditions of the age created a system of warfare based on limited objectives.

Since generals were extremely reluctant to risk the destruction of their armies in pitched battles, clever and elaborate maneuvers, rather than direct confrontation, became fashionable. A system of formalities accepted by all sides allowed defeated opponents to withdraw without being captured or destroyed. This mentality also encouraged the construction of vast fortresses to secure major roads and the enormous quantities of supplies needed by eighteenth-century armies. With its own set patterns of tactics, siege warfare often became, as one French critic said disgustedly, "the art of surrendering strongholds honorably after certain conventional formalities." Nevertheless, despite the maneuvering and the sieges, European

CHRONOLOGY

The Mid-Century Wars

War of the Austrian Succession	1740–1748
Peace of Aix-la-Chapelle	1748
The Seven Years' War	1756–1763
Diplomatic revolution	1756
Battle of Rossbach	1757
British capture of Forts Duquesne and Louisbourg	1758
Battle of Quebec	1759
Peace of Hubertusburg	1763
Peace of Paris	1763

warfare in the eighteenth century also involved many battles and considerable risk.

◆ Economic Expansion and Social Change

The economic depression that had characterized the seventeenth century began to end in the early eighteenth century. Rapid population growth, expansion in banking and trade, an agricultural revolution (at least in Britain), the beginnings of a new pattern of industrialization, and an increase in worldwide trade characterized the economic patterns of the eighteenth century.

Growth of the European Population

The cycles of population growth and decline that had characterized Europe since the Middle Ages came to an end in the eighteenth century. Despite regional variations, Europe's population began to grow around 1750 and continued a "slow but irreversible upward movement." It has been estimated that the total European population was around 120 million in 1700, expanded to 140 million by 1750, and then grew to 190 million by 1790; thus, the growth rate in the second half of the century was double that of the first half. Individual states also experienced rapid growth between 1700 and 1790: Russia's population went from 14 million to 28 million (much of it due to territorial expansion); France from 20 to 26 or 27 million; Spain from 6 to 10 million; Brandenburg-Prussia from 1.5 to 5.5 million (over half of this came from territorial acquisition); and Britain from 5 or 6 to 9 million. These increases occurred during the same time that several million Europeans were going abroad as colonists.

Historical demographers are not sure of the causes of this population growth. Enough statistical studies have been done, however, to show that a falling death rate was perhaps most important, especially the decline in infant mortality rates. One study of several French parishes reveals that in the first part of the century the mortality rate for infants under one year was 29 percent and the rate for all children from birth to nineteen years was 51 percent, compared to 20 and 42 percent, respectively, in the 1780s. Although the percentage of decrease seems small, it is statistically significant enough to cause a noticeable increase in population.

But why the decline in the death rate? Historians are not sure. Certainly, it was not from improved health care since little change occurred in that area until the end of the eighteenth century. No doubt, more plentiful food and better transportation of available food supplies led to some improvement in diet and relief from devastating famines. Also of great significance was the lowering of death rates that accompanied the end of the bubonic plague. The last great outbreak in western Europe occurred in 1720 in southern France. Nevertheless, despite the increase in population, death was still a ubiquitous feature of everyday life. Other diseases, such as typhus, smallpox, influenza, and dysentery, were rampant, especially since hygienic conditions remained poor—little bathing, dirty clothes, and no systematic elimination of human wastes. Despite the improved transportation, famine and hunger could still be devastating. As a small textile merchant in Germany wrote in 1770: "And the misery grew so much that poor people could only hope for spring when they could find roots and herbs. And I had to cook that sort of stuff."[6]

Family, Marriage, and Birthrate Patterns

The family, rather than the individual, was still at the heart of Europe's social organization. For the most part, people still thought of the family in traditional terms, as a patriarchal institution with the husband dominating his wife and children. The upper classes in particular were still concerned for the family as a "house," an association whose collective interests were more important than those of its individual members. Parents (especially the fathers) still generally selected marriage partners for their children based on the interests of the family. One French noble responded to his son's inquiry about his upcoming marriage: "Mind your own business."

At the beginning of the eighteenth century, traditional attitudes also prevailed in the care of children. Generally, lower-class women breast-fed their own children because it provided the best nourishment. Moreover, since there were strong taboos in various parts of Europe against sexual intercourse while one was breast-feeding, mothers might also avoid another immediate pregnancy; if the infant died, they could then have another child. Lower-class women, however, also served as wet nurses for children of the aristocratic and upper middle classes. Mothers from these higher social strata considered breast-feeding undignified and hired wet nurses instead. Even urban mothers, the wives of artisans, for economic reasons sent their babies to wet nurses in the countryside if

CHILDREN OF THE UPPER CLASSES. This painting of John Bacon and his family illustrates an important feature of upper-class family life in Great Britain in the first half of the eighteenth century. The children appear as miniature adults, dressed in clothes modeled after the styles of their parents.

they could, making the practice widespread in the eighteenth century.

In the second half of the eighteenth century, traditional attitudes began to alter, especially in western Europe. The impact of Enlightenment thought, such as Rousseau's *Emile,* and the increasing survival of more infants led to new attitudes toward children. Childhood was more and more viewed as a phase in human development. One result was a shift to dressing children in more comfortable clothes appropriate to their age rather than dressing them in clothes modeled after adult styles. Shops for children's clothes appeared for the first time. Primogeniture or the practice of treating the first son as the favorite also came under attack. All children, it was argued, deserve their parents' attention. Appeals for women to breast-feed their own children rather than use wet nurses soon followed. In England, games and toys specifically for children now appeared. The jigsaw puzzle was invented in the 1760s, and books, such as *Little Pretty Pocket-Book* (1744), aimed to please as well as teach children. These changes, however, were limited mostly to the upper classes of western European society and did not extend to the peasants. For most Europeans, children were still a source of considerable anxiety. They represented more mouths to feed and in times of economic crisis proved such a liability that infanticide was practiced and foundling homes were overcrowded.

Despite being punishable by death, infanticide remained a solution to the problem of too many children. So many children were being "accidentally" suffocated while in their parents' bed that in Austria in 1784 a law was enacted that forbade parents to place children under five years old in bed with them. More common than infanticide was the placement of unwanted children in foundling homes or hospitals, which became a favorite charity of the rich in eighteenth-century Europe. The largest of its kind, located in St. Petersburg, Russia, was founded by members of the nobility. By the end of the century, it was taking in 5,000 new babies a year and caring for 25,000 children at one time.

But severe problems arose as the system became overburdened. One historian has estimated that in the 1770s one-third of all babies born in Paris were taken to foundling institutions by parents or desperate unmarried mothers, creating serious overcrowding. Foundling institutions often proved fatal for infants. Mortality rates ranged from 50 to as high as 90 percent (in a sense making foundling homes a legalized form of infanticide). Those who survived were usually sent to miserable jobs. The suffering of poor children was one of the blackest pages of eighteenth-century European history.

In most of Europe, newly married couples established their own households independent of their parents. This nuclear family, which had its beginning in the Middle Ages, had become a common pattern, especially in northwestern Europe. In order to save what they needed to establish their own households, both men and women (outside the aristocracy) married quite late; the average

age for men in northwestern Europe was between twenty-seven and twenty-eight, for women between twenty-five and twenty-seven.

Late marriages imposed limits on the birthrate; in fact, they might be viewed as a natural form of birth control. But was this limitation offset by the number of babies born illegitimately? From the low illegitimacy rate of 1 percent in some places in France and 5 percent in some English parishes, it would appear that it was not, at least in the first half of the eighteenth century. After 1750, however, illegitimacy appears to have increased. Studies in Germany, for example, show that rates of illegitimacy increased from 2 percent in 1700 to 5 percent in 1760 and to 10 percent in 1800, followed by an even more dramatic increase in the early nineteenth century.

For married couples, the first child usually appeared within one year of marriage, and additional children came at intervals of two or three years, producing an average number of five births per family. It would appear then that the birthrate had the potential of creating a significant increase in population. This possibility was restricted, however, because 40 to 60 percent of European women of childbearing age (between fifteen and forty-four) were not married at any given time. Moreover, by the end of the eighteenth century, especially among the upper classes in France and Britain, birth control techniques were being used to limit the number of children. Figures for the French aristocracy indicate that the average number of children declined from six in the period between 1650 and 1700 to three between 1700 and 1750 and to two between 1750 and 1780. These figures are even more significant when one considers that aristocrats married at younger ages than the rest of the population. Coitus interruptus remained the most commonly used form of birth control.

Among the working classes, whether peasants or urban workers, the contributions of women and children to the "family economy" were often crucial. In urban areas, both male and female children either helped in the handicraft manufacturing done in the home or were sent out to work as household servants. In rural areas, children worked on the land or helped in the activities of cottage industry. Married women grew vegetables in small plots, tended livestock, and sold eggs, vegetables, and milk. Wives of propertyless agricultural workers labored in the fields or as textile workers, spinning or knitting. In the cities, wives of artisans helped their husbands at their crafts or worked as seamstresses. The wives of unskilled workers labored as laundresses and cleaners for the rich or as peddlers of food or used clothing to the lower classes. But the family economy was often precarious.

THE PRACTICE OF INFANTICIDE. Infanticide remained one of the solutions to the problem of too many children in the eighteenth century. This engraving recounts the story of one infanticide in Germany. *Top left:* the infant is discovered, smothered under a mattress. *Bottom left:* the mother is taken from prison to be executed. *Right:* a large crowd observes the execution of the mother for her crime.

Bad harvests in the countryside or a downturn in employment in the cities often reduced people to utter poverty and a life of begging.

An Agricultural Revolution?

Did improvements in agricultural practices and methods in the eighteenth century lead to an agricultural revolution? The topic is much debated. Some historians have noted the beginning of agrarian changes already in the seventeenth century, especially in the Low Countries. Others, however, have questioned the use of the term, arguing that significant changes occurred only in England and noting that even there the upward trend in agricultural production was not maintained after 1750.

Eighteenth-century agriculture was characterized by increases in food production that can be attributed to four interrelated factors: more land under cultivation, increased yields per acre, healthier and more abundant livestock, and an improved climate. Climatologists believe that the "little ice age" of the seventeenth century declined in the eighteenth, especially evident in the moderate summers that provided more ideal growing conditions.

The amount of land under cultivation was increased by abandoning the old open field system in which part of the land was left to lie fallow to renew it. New crops, such as alfalfa, turnips, and clover, which stored nitrogen in their roots and helped to restore the soil's fertility, were planted in England, parts of France, and the Low Countries. These crops not only renewed the soil but also provided winter fodder for livestock, enabling landlords to maintain an ever-larger number of animals; some enterprising landlords also engaged in scientific breeding and produced stronger and more productive strains of animals.

The more numerous livestock increased the amount of meat in the European diet and enhanced food production by making available more animal manure, which was used to fertilize fields and produce better yields per acre. Increased yields were also encouraged by landed aristocrats who shared in the scientific experimentation of the age. In England, Jethro Tull (1674–1741) discovered that using a hoe to keep the soil loose allowed air and moisture to reach plants and enabled them to grow better. He also used a drill to plant seeds in rows instead of scattering them by hand, a method that had lost much seed to the birds.

The eighteenth century witnessed greater yields of vegetables, including two important American crops, the potato and maize (Indian corn). Although they were not grown in quantity until after 1700, both had been brought to Europe from America in the sixteenth century and were part of what some historians have called the Columbian exchange—a reciprocal exchange of plants and animals between Europe and America. The potato became a staple in Germany, the Low Countries, and especially Ireland, where repression by English landlords forced large numbers of poor peasants to survive on small pieces of marginal land. The potato took relatively little effort to produce in large quantities. High in carbohydrates and calories, rich in vitamins A and C, it could be easily stored for winter use.

The new agricultural techniques were considered best suited to large-scale farms. Consequently, a change in landholding accompanied the increase in food production. Large landowners or yeomen farmers enclosed the old open fields, combining the many small holdings that made up the fields into larger units. The end of the open field system led to the demise of the cooperative farming of the village community. In England, where small landholders resisted this process, Parliament, dominated by the landed aristocracy, enacted legislation allowing agricultural lands to be legally enclosed. As a result of these enclosure acts, England gradually became a land of large estates, and many small farmers were forced to become wage laborers or tenant farmers working farms of 100–500 acres. Although some historians have emphasized the advantages of enclosures in enabling large landowners to practice new agricultural techniques and increase food production, the enclosure movement and new agricultural practices also effectively destroyed the traditional patterns of English village life.

In the eighteenth century, the English were the leaders in adopting the new techniques that have been characterized as an agricultural revolution (see the box on p. 538). This early modernization of English agriculture with its noticeable increase in productivity made possible the feeding of an expanding population about to enter a new world of industrialization and urbanization.

New Methods of Finance and Industry

The decline in the available supply of gold and silver in the seventeenth century had created a chronic shortage of money that undermined the efforts of governments to meet their needs. The creation of new public and private banks and the acceptance of paper notes made possible an expansion of credit in the eighteenth century.

Perhaps the best example of this process can be observed in England where the Bank of England was founded in 1694. Unlike other banks accustomed to receiving deposits and exchanging foreign currencies, the Bank of England also made loans. In return for lending money to the government, the bank was allowed to issue paper "bank notes" backed by its credit. These soon became negotiable and provided a paper substitute for gold and silver currency. In addition, the issuance of government bonds paying regular interest, backed by the Bank of England and the London financial community, created the notion of a public or "national debt" distinct from the monarch's personal debts. This process meant that capital for financing larger armies and other government undertakings could be raised in ever-greater quantities.

These new financial institutions and methods were not risk-free, however. In both Britain and France in the early eighteenth century, speculators provided opportunities for people to invest in colonial trading companies. The French company under John Law was also tied to his

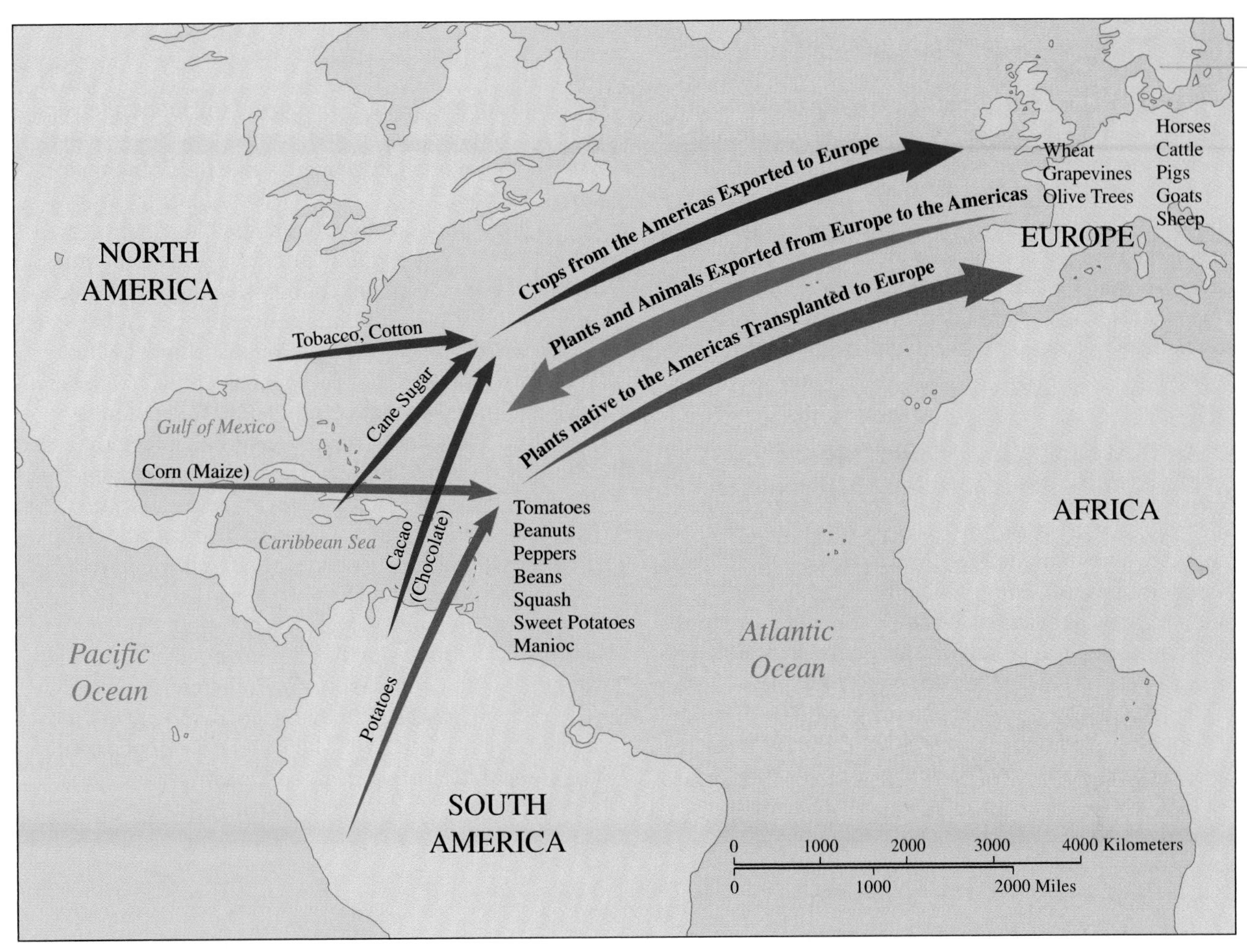

MAP 18.4 The Columbian Exchange.

attempt to create a national bank and paper currency for France. When people went overboard and drove the price of the stock to incredibly high levels, the bubble burst. Law's company and bank went bankrupt, leading to a loss of confidence in paper money that prevented the formation of a French national bank. Consequently, French public finance developed slowly in the eighteenth century.

This was not the case in Britain, however. Despite crises, public confidence in the new financial institutions enabled the British government to borrow large sums of money at relatively low rates of interest, giving it a distinct advantage in the struggle with France. According to a contemporary observer, Britain's public credit was "the permanent miracle of her policy, which has inspired both astonishment and fear in the States of Europe."[7] Despite Britain's growing importance in finance, however, the Dutch Republic remained the leader in Europe's financial life, and Amsterdam continued to be the center of international finance until London replaced it in the nineteenth century. One observer noted in 1769:

> If ten or twelve businessmen of Amsterdam of the first rank meet for a banking operation, they can in a moment send circulating throughout Europe over two hundred million florins in paper money, which is preferred to cash. There is no Sovereign who could do as much. . . . This credit is a power which the ten or twelve businessmen will be able to exert over all the States of Europe, in complete independence of any authority.[8]

The decline of Dutch trade, industry, and power meant that Dutch capitalists were inclined to lend money abroad because they had fewer opportunities at home.

The most important product of European industry in the eighteenth century was textiles. Woolen cloth made up 75 percent of Britain's exports in the early eighteenth century. France, too, was a leader in the production of woolen cloth, and other major states emulated both France and Britain by encouraging the development of their own textile industries.

Most textiles were still produced by traditional methods. In cities that were textile centers, master artisans employed timeworn methods to turn out finished goods in their guild workshops. But by the eighteenth century textile production was beginning to shift to the countryside in parts of Europe. In the countryside, textiles were produced by the "putting-out" or "domestic" system in which a merchant-capitalist entrepreneur bought the raw materials, mostly wool and flax, and "put them out" to rural workers who spun the raw material into yarn and

Propaganda for the New Agriculture

Enthusiastic supporters of the new English agricultural practices went to the continent to examine less efficient kinds of farming. One of these Englishmen, Arthur Young, wrote an account of his travels in which he blamed the low yields of French farmers on the old system of allowing part of the land to lie fallow and the small size of the farms. The latter factor was especially important to English aristocratic landholders who wished to justify the enclosure movement. This selection is taken from Young's account.

Arthur Young, *Travels during the Years, 1787, 1788, and 1789 . . . in the Kingdom of France*

The Englishman, in eleven years, gets three bushels more of wheat than the Frenchman. He gets three crops of barley, tares, or beans, which produce nearly twice as many bushels per acre, as what the three French crops of spring corn produce. And he farther gets, at the same time, three crops of turnips, and two of clover, the turnips worth 40s. the acre, and the clover 60s. That is 121 for both. What an enormous superiority. More wheat; almost double of the spring corn; and above 20s. per acre per annum in turnips and clover. But farther; the Englishman's land, by means of the manure arising from the consumption of the turnips and clover is in a constant state of improvement, while the Frenchman's farm is stationary.

The great populousness of France, I attribute very much to the division of the lands into small properties, which takes place in that country to a degree of which we have in England but little conception. . . . it has been said to me in France, "Would you leave uncultivated lands wastes, rather than let them be cultivated in small portions, through a fear of population?" I certainly would not: I would, on the contrary, encourage their culture; but I would prohibit the division of small farms, which is as mischievous to cultivation, as it is sure to be distressing to the people. . . . Go to districts where the properties are minutely divided, and you will find (at least I have done it) universally, great distress, and even misery, and probably very bad agriculture. Go to others, where such sub-division has not taken place, and you will find a better cultivation, and infinitely less misery. When you are engaged in this political tour, finish it by seeing England, and I will show you a set of peasants well clothed, well nourished, and tolerably drunken from superfluity, well-lodged, and at their ease.

then wove it into cloth on simple looms. Capitalist-entrepreneurs sold the finished product, made a profit, and used it to manufacture more. This system became known as the "cottage industry," because spinners and weavers did their work on spinning wheels and looms in their own cottages. Cottage industry was truly a family enterprise since women and children could spin while men wove on the looms, enabling rural people to earn incomes that supplemented their pitiful wages as agricultural laborers.

The cottage system utilized traditional methods of manufacturing and spread to many areas of rural Europe in the eighteenth century. But significant changes in industrial production also began to occur in the second half of the century, pushed along by the introduction of cotton, originally imported from India. The importation of raw cotton from slave plantations encouraged the production of cotton cloth in Europe where a profitable market developed because of the growing demand for lightweight cotton clothes that were less expensive than linens and woolens. But the traditional methods of the cottage industry proved incapable of keeping up with the growing demand, leading English cloth entrepreneurs to develop new methods and new machines. The flying shuttle sped up the process of weaving on a loom, thereby increasing the need for large quantities of yarn. In response, Richard Arkwright (1732–1792) invented a "water frame," powered by horse or water, which turned out yarn much faster than cottage spinning wheels. This abundance of yarn, in turn, led to the development of mechanized looms, invented in the 1780s but not widely adopted until the early nineteenth century. By that time Britain was in the throes of an industrial revolution, but already at the end of the eighteenth century, rural workers, perceiving that the new machines threatened their traditional livelihood, had begun to call for the machines' destruction (see the box on p. 539).

Toward a Global Economy: Mercantile Empires and Worldwide Trade

Though bankers and industrialists came to dominate the economic life of the nineteenth century, in the eighteenth century merchants and traders still reigned supreme. Trade within Europe still dominated total trade figures as wheat, timber, and naval stores from the Baltic, wines from France, wool and fruit from Spain, and silk from Italy were exchanged along with a host of other products. But the eighteenth century witnessed only a slight increase in this trade while overseas trade boomed. From 1716 to 1789, total French exports quadrupled; intra-European trade, which constituted 75 percent of these exports in 1716, constituted only 50 percent of the total in 1789. This increase in overseas trade has led some historians to speak of the emergence of a truly global economy in the eighteenth century. By the beginning of the century, Spain, Portugal, and the Dutch Republic, which had earlier monopolized over-

The Beginnings of Mechanized Industry: The Attack on New Machines

Already by the end of the eighteenth century, mechanization was beginning to bring changes to the traditional cottage industry of textile manufacturing. Rural workers who depended on the extra wages earned in their own homes often reacted by attacking the machinery that threatened their livelihoods. This selection is a petition that English wool workers published in their local newspapers asking that machines no longer be used to prepare wool for spinning.

The Leeds Woolen Workers' Petition (1786)

To the Merchants, Clothiers and all such as wish well to the Staple Manufactory of this Nation.

The Humble ADDRESS and PETITION of Thousands, who labor in the Cloth Manufactory.

The Scribbling-Machines have thrown thousands of your petitioners out of employ, whereby they are brought into great distress, and are not able to procure a maintenance for their families, and deprived them of the opportunity of bringing up their children to labor: We have therefore to request, that prejudice and self-interest may be laid aside, and that you may pay that attention to the following facts, which the nature of the case requires.

The number of Scribbling-Machines extending about seventeen miles southwest of LEEDS, exceed all belief, being no less than *one hundred and seventy!* and as each machine will do as much work in twelve hours, as ten men can in that time do by hand (speaking within bounds) and they working night and day, one machine will do as much work in one day as would otherwise employ twenty men.

As we do not mean to assert any thing but what we can prove to be true, we allow four men to be employed at each machine twelve hours, working night and day, will take eight men in twenty-four hours; so that, upon a moderate computation twelve men are thrown out of employ for every single machine used in scribbling; and as it may be supposed the number of machines in all the other quarters together, nearly equal those in the South-West, full four thousand men are left to shift for a living how they can, and must of course fall to the Parish, if not time relieved. Allowing one boy to be bound apprentice from each family out of work, eight thousand hands are deprived of the opportunity of getting a livelihood.

We therefore hope, that the feelings of humanity will lead those who have it in their power to prevent the use of those machines, to give every discouragement they can to what has a tendency so prejudicial to their fellow-creatures. . . .

We wish to propose a few queries to those who would plead for the further continuance of these machines:

How are those men, thus thrown out of employ to provide for their families; and what are they to put their children apprentice to, that the rising generation may have something to keep them at work, in order that they may not be like vagabonds strolling about in idleness? Some day, Begin and learn some other business.—Suppose we do, who will maintain our families, whilst we undertake the arduous task; and when we have learned it, how do we know we shall be any better for all our pains; for by the time we have served our second apprenticeship, another machine may arise, which may take away that business also. . . .

But what are our children to do; are they to be brought up in idleness? Indeed as things are, it is no wonder to hear of so many executions; for our parts, though we may be thought illiterate men, our conceptions are, that bringing children up to industry, and keeping them employed, is the way to keep them from falling into those crimes, which an idle habit naturally leads to.

seas trade, found themselves increasingly overshadowed by France and Britain. The rivalry between these two great western European powers was especially evident in the Americas and the East.

COLONIAL EMPIRES

Both the French and British colonial empires in the New World included large parts of the West Indies and the North American continent. In the former, the British held Barbados, Jamaica, and Bermuda, and the French possessed Saint Dominique, Martinique, and Guadeloupe. On these tropical islands, both the British and the French had developed plantation economies, worked by African slaves, which produced tobacco, cotton, coffee, and sugar, all products increasingly in demand in Europe.

The French and British colonies on the North American continent were structured in different ways. French North America (Canada and Louisiana) was run autocratically as a vast trading area, where valuable furs, leather, fish, and timber were acquired. However, the inability of the French state to get its people to emigrate to these North American possessions left them thinly populated.

British North America had come to consist of thirteen colonies on the eastern coast of the present United States. They were thickly populated, containing about 1.5 million people by 1750, and were also prosperous. Supposedly run by the British Board of Trade, the Royal Council, and Parliament, these thirteen colonies had legislatures that tended to act independently. Merchants in such port cities as Boston, Philadelphia, New York, and Charleston resented and resisted regulation from the British government.

Both the North American and West Indian colonies of Britain and France were assigned roles in keeping with mercantilist theory. They provided raw materials for the mother country while buying the latter's manufactured goods. Navigation acts regulated what could be taken from and sold to the colonies. Theoretically, the system was supposed to provide a balance of trade favorable to the mother country.

British and French rivalry was also evident in the Spanish and Portuguese colonial empires in Latin America. The decline of Spain and Portugal had led these two states to depend even more on resources from their colonies, and they imposed strict mercantilist rules to keep others out. Spain, for example, tried to limit all trade with its colonies to Spanish ships. But the British and French were too powerful to be excluded. The British cajoled the Portuguese into allowing them into the lucrative Brazilian trade. The French, however, were the first to break into the Spanish Latin American market when the French Bourbons became kings of Spain. Britain's entry into Spanish American markets first came in 1713, when the British were granted the privilege, known as the *asiento,* of transporting 4,500 slaves a year into Spanish Latin America.

The rivalry also extended to the East where Britain and France competed for the tea, spices, cotton, hard woods, and luxury goods of India and the East Indies. The rivalry between the two countries was played out by their state-backed national trading companies. In the course of the eighteenth century, the British defeated the French, and by the mid-nineteenth century, they had assumed control of the entire Indian subcontinent.

THE SALE OF SLAVES. In the eighteenth century, the slave trade was one of the more profitable commercial enterprises. This painting shows a Western slave merchant negotiating with a local African leader over slaves at Goree, Senegal, in West Africa in the late eighteenth century.

GLOBAL TRADE

To justify the term *global economy,* historians have usually pointed to the patterns of trade that interlocked Europe, Africa, the East, and the American continents. In an example of triangular trade, British merchant ships carried British manufactured goods to Africa, where they were traded for a cargo of slaves, which were then shipped to Virginia and paid for by tobacco, which in turn was shipped back to England where it was processed and then sold in Germany for cash.

Of all the goods traded in the eighteenth century, perhaps the most profitable and certainly the most infamous were African slaves. Of course, the slave trade was not new; the Spanish and Portuguese had introduced black slaves into America in the sixteenth century. But the need for slaves on the plantations where they produced the lucrative sugar, tobacco, rice, and cotton made the eighteenth century the high point of the Atlantic slave trade. It has been estimated that of the total 9.3 million slaves transported from Africa, almost two-thirds were taken in the eighteenth century. Between 75,000 and 90,000 Africans were transported annually, 50 percent in British ships, with the rest divided among French, Dutch, Portuguese, Danish, and American ships.

Slaving ships sailed from a European port to the African coast where Europeans had established bases where merchants could trade manufactured goods, rum, and brandy for blacks captured by African intermediaries. The captives were then closely packed into cargo ships, 300 to 450 per ship, and chained in holds without sanitary facilities or enough space to stand up; there they remained during the voyage to America, which took at least 100 days (see the box on p. 541). Mortality rates averaged 10 percent except when longer journeys due to storms or adverse winds resulted in even higher death rates.

As soon as the human cargoes arrived in the New World, they entered the plantation economy. Here the "sugar factories," as the sugar plantations in the Caribbean were called, played an especially prominent role. By the last two decades of the eighteenth century, the British colony of Jamaica, one of Britain's most important, was producing 50,000 tons of sugar annually with the slave labor of 200,000 blacks. The French colony of Saint Dominique (later Haiti) had 500,000 slaves working on 3,000 plantations at the same time. This colony produced

The Atlantic Slave Trade

One of the most odious practices of early modern Western society was the Atlantic slave trade, which reached its height in the eighteenth century. Blacks were transported in densely packed cargo ships from the western coast of Africa to the Americas to work as slaves in the plantation economy. Not until late in the eighteenth century did a rising chorus of voices raise serious objections to this trade in human beings. This excerpt presents a criticism of the slave trade from an anonymous French writer.

Diary of a Citizen

As soon as the ships have lowered their anchors off the coast of Guinea, the price at which the captains have decided to buy the captives is announced to the Negroes who buy prisoners from various princes and sell them to Europeans. Presents are sent to the sovereign who rules over that particular part of the coast, and permission to trade is given. Immediately the slaves are brought by inhuman brokers like so many victims dragged to a sacrifice. White men who covet that portion of the human race receive them in a little house they have erected on the shore, where they have entrenched themselves with two pieces of cannon and twenty guards. As soon as the bargain is concluded, the Negro is put in chains and led aboard the vessel, where he meets his fellow sufferers. Here sinister reflections come to his mind; everything shocks and frightens him and his uncertain destiny gives rise to the greatest anxiety. . . .

The vessel sets sail for the Antilles, and the Negroes are chained in a hold of the ship, a kind of lugubrious prison where the light of day does not penetrate, but into which the air is introduced by means of a pump. Twice a day some disgusting food is distributed to them. Their consuming sorrow and the sad state to which they are reduced would make them commit suicide if they were not deprived of all the means for an attempt upon their lives. Without any kind of clothing it would be difficult to conceal from the watchful eyes of the sailors in charge any instrument apt to alleviate their despair. The fear of a revolt, such as sometimes happens on the voyage from Guinea, is the basis of a common concern and produces as many guards as there are men in the crew. The slightest noise or a secret conversation among two Negroes is punished with utmost severity. All in all, the voyage is made in a continuous state of alarm on the part of the white men, who fear a revolt, and in a cruel state of uncertainty on the part of the Negroes, who do not know the fate awaiting them.

When the vessel arrives at a port in the Antilles, they are taken to a warehouse where they are displayed, like any merchandise, to the eyes of buyers. The plantation owner pays according to the age, strength, and health of the Negro he is buying. He has him taken to his plantation, and there he is delivered to an overseer who then and there becomes his tormentor. In order to domesticate him, the Negro is granted a few days of rest in his new place, but soon he is given a hoe and a sickle and made to join a work gang. Then he ceases to wonder about his fate; he understands that only labor is demanded of him. But he does not know yet how excessive this labor will be. As a matter of fact, his work begins at dawn and does not end before nightfall; it is interrupted for only two hours at dinnertime. The food a full-grown Negro is given each week consists of two pounds of salt beef or cod and two pots of tapioca meal. . . . A Negro of twelve or thirteen years or under is given only one pot of meal and one pound of beef or cod. In place of food some planters give their Negroes the liberty of working for themselves every Saturday; others are even less generous and grant them this liberty only on Sundays and holidays.

100,000 tons of sugar a year but at the expense of a high death rate from the brutal treatment of the slaves. It is not surprising that Saint Dominique saw the first successful slave uprising in 1793.

Despite a rising chorus of humanitarian sentiments from the philosophes, the use of black slaves remained acceptable to Western society. By and large, Europeans continued to view blacks as inferior beings fit primarily for slave labor. Not until the Society of Friends or Quakers began to criticize slavery in the 1770s and exclude from their church any member adhering to slave trafficking, did European sentiment against slavery begin to build. Even then it was not until the radical stage of the French Revolution in the 1790s that the French abolished slavery. The British followed suit in 1807. Despite the elimination of the African source, slavery continued in the newly formed United States until the Civil War of the 1860s.

The Social Order of the Eighteenth Century

The pattern of Europe's social organization, first established in the Middle Ages, continued well into the eighteenth century. Social status was still largely determined not by wealth and economic standing but by the division into the traditional "orders" or "estates" determined by heredity and quality. This divinely sanctioned division of society into traditional orders was supported by Christian teaching, which emphasized the need to fulfill the responsibilities of one's estate. Although Enlightenment intellectuals attacked these traditional distinctions, they did not die easily. In the Prussian law code of 1794, marriage between noble males and middle-class females was forbidden without a government dispensation. Even without government regulation, however, different social groups remained easily distinguished everywhere in Europe by the distinctive, traditional clothes they wore.

Nevertheless, some forces of change were at work in this traditional society. The ideas of the Enlightenment made headway as reformers argued that the idea of an unchanging social order based on privilege was hostile to the progress of society. Moreover, especially in some cities, the old structures were more difficult to maintain as new economic structures, especially the growth of larger industries, brought new social contrasts that destroyed the old order. Despite these forces of change, however, it would take the revolutionary upheavals at the end of the eighteenth century before the old order would finally begin to disintegrate.

The Peasants

Since society was still mostly rural in the eighteenth century, the peasantry constituted the largest social group, making up as much as 85 percent of Europe's population. The conditions of peasant life differed significantly from area to area, however. The most important distinction—at least legally—was between the free peasant and the serf. Peasants in Britain, northern Italy, the Low Countries, Spain, most of France, and some areas of western Germany shared freedom despite numerous regional and local differences. Legally free peasants, however, were not exempt from burdens. Some free peasants in Andalusia in Spain, southern Italy, Sicily, and Portugal lived in a poverty more desperate than that of many serfs in Russia and eastern Germany. In France, 40 percent of free peasants owned little or no land whatever by 1789.

Small peasant proprietors or tenant farmers in western Europe were also not free from compulsory services. Most owed tithes, often one-third of their crops. Although tithes were intended for parish priests, in France only 10 percent of the priests received them. Instead the tithes wound up in the hands of towns and aristocratic landowners. Moreover, peasants could still owe a variety of dues and fees. Local aristocrats claimed hunting rights on peasant land and had monopolies over the flour mills, community ovens, and wine and oil presses needed by the peasants. Hunting rights, dues, fees, and tithes were all deeply resented.

Eastern Europe continued to be dominated by large landed estates owned by powerful lords and worked by serfs. Serfdom had come late to the east, having largely been imposed in the sixteenth and seventeenth centuries. Peasants in eastern Germany were bound to the lord's estate, had to perform labor services on the lord's land, and could not marry or move without permission and payment of a tax. By the eighteenth century, landlords also possessed legal jurisdiction, giving them control over the administration of justice. Only in the Habsburg empire had a ruler attempted to improve the lot of the peasants through a series of reforms. With the exception of the clergy and a small merchant class, eighteenth-century Russia, unlike the rest of Europe, was still largely a society of landlords and serfs. Russian peasants were not attached to the land but to the landlord and thus existed in a condition approaching slavery. In 1762, landowners were given the right to transfer their serfs from one estate to another.

The local villages in which they dwelt remained the centers of peasants' social lives. Villages, especially in western Europe, maintained public order; provided poor relief, a village church, and sometimes a schoolmaster; collected taxes for the central government; maintained roads and bridges; and established common procedures for sowing, plowing, and harvesting crops. But villages were often dominated by richer peasants and proved highly resistant to innovations, such as new crops and agricultural practices.

The diet of the peasants in the eighteenth century did not vary much from that of the Middle Ages. Dark bread, made of roughly ground wheat and rye flour, remained the basic staple. It was quite nourishing and high in vitamins, minerals, and even proteins since the bran and germ were not ground out. Peasants drank water, wine, and beer and ate soups and gruel made of grains and vegetables. Especially popular were peas and beans, eaten fresh in summer but dried and used in soups and stews in winter. The new foods of the eighteenth century, potatoes and American corn, added important elements to the peasant diet. Of course, when harvests were bad, hunger and famine became the peasants' lot in life, making them even more susceptible to the ravages of disease.

The Nobility

The nobles, who constituted about 2 or 3 percent of the European population, played a dominating role in society. Being born a noble automatically guaranteed a place at the top of the social order with all of its attendant special privileges and rights. The legal privileges of the nobility included judgment by their peers, immunity from severe punishment, exemption from many forms of taxation, and rights of jurisdiction. Especially in central and eastern Europe, the rights of landlords over their serfs were overwhelming. In Poland until 1768, the nobility even possessed the right of life or death over their serfs.

In many countries, nobles were self-conscious about their unique style of life that set them apart from the rest of society. This did not mean, however, that they were unwilling to bend the conventions of that lifestyle if there were profits to be made. For example, by convention nobles were expected to live off the yields of their estates. But although nobles almost everywhere talked about trade as being beneath their dignity, many were not averse to mercantile endeavors. Many were also only too eager to profit from industries based on the exploitation of raw materials found on their estates; as a result, many nobles were involved in mining, metallurgy, and glassmaking.

Their diet also set them off from the rest of society. Aristocrats consumed enormous quantities of meat and fish dishes accompanied by cheeses, nuts, and a variety of sweets.

Nobles also played important roles in military and government affairs. Since medieval times, landed aristocrats had functioned as military officers. Although monarchs found it impossible to exclude commoners from the ranks of officers, tradition maintained that nobles made the most natural and hence the best officers. Moreover, the eighteenth-century nobility played a significant role in the administrative machinery of state. In some countries, such as Prussia, the entire bureaucracy reflected aristocratic values. Moreover, in most of Europe, the landholding nobility controlled much of the local government in their districts.

The nobility or landowning class was not a homogeneous social group. Landlords in England leased their land to tenant farmers while those in eastern Europe used the labor services of serfs. Nobles in Russia and Prussia served the state, but those in Spain and Italy had few official functions. Differences in wealth, education, and political power also led to differences within countries as well. In France, where there were about 350,000 nobles, only 4,000 noble families had access to the court. The gap between rich and poor nobles could be enormous. According to figures for the poll tax in France, the richest nobles were assessed 2,000 livres a year while some nobles, because of their depressed economic state, paid only 6. Both groups were legally nobles. As the century progressed, poor nobles sometimes sank into the ranks of the unprivileged masses of the population. It has been estimated that the number of European nobles declined by one-third between 1750 and 1815.

Although the nobles clung to their privileged status and struggled to keep others out, almost everywhere a person with money found it possible to enter the ranks of the nobility. Rights of nobility were frequently attached to certain lands, so purchasing the lands made one a noble; the acquisition of government offices also often conferred noble status.

THE ARISTOCRATIC WAY OF LIFE: THE COUNTRY HOUSE

One aristocrat who survived the French Revolution once commented that "no one who did not live before the Revolution" could know the real sweetness of living. Of course, he spoke not for the peasants whose labor maintained the system, but for the landed aristocrats. For them the eighteenth century was a final century of "sweetness" before the Industrial Revolution and bourgeois society diminished their privileged way of life.

In so many ways, the court of Louis XIV had provided a model for other European monarchs who built palaces and encouraged the development of a court society as a center of culture. As at Versailles, these courts were peopled by members of the aristocracy whose income from rents or officeholding enabled them to participate in this lifestyle. This court society, whether in France, Spain, or Germany, manifested common characteristics: participation in intrigues for the king's or prince's favor, serene walks in formal gardens, and duels to maintain one's honor.

The majority of aristocratic landowners, however, remained on their country estates and did not participate in court society; their large houses continued to give witness to their domination of the surrounding countryside. This was especially true in England where the court of the Hanoverian kings (Georges I–III from 1714 to 1820) made little impact on the behavior of upper-class society. English landed aristocrats invested much time, energy, and money in their rural estates, giving the English country house an important role in English social life. One American observer remarked: "Scarcely any persons who hold a leading place in the circles of their society live in London. They have houses in London, in which they stay while Parliament sits, and occasionally visit at other seasons; but their homes are in the country."[9]

After the seventeenth century, the English referred to their country homes, regardless of size, not as chateaus or villas but merely houses. Although there was much variety in country houses, many in the eighteenth century were built in the Georgian style named after the Hanoverian kings. This style was greatly influenced by the classical serenity and sedateness of the sixteenth-century Venetian architect Andrea Palladio, who had specialized in the design of country villas. The Georgian country house combined elegance with domesticity, and its interior was often characterized as possessing a comfort of home that combined visual delight and usefulness.

The country house also fulfilled a new desire for greater privacy that was reflected in the growing separation between the lower and upper floors. The lower floors were devoted to public activities—dining, entertaining, and leisure. A central entrance hall provided the setting for the ceremonial arrival and departure of guests on formal occasions. From the hall, guests could proceed to a series of downstairs common rooms. The largest was the drawing room (larger houses possessed two), which contained musical instruments and was used for dances or card games, a favorite pastime. Other common rooms included a formal dining room, informal breakfast room, library, study, gallery, billiard room, and conservatory. The entrance hall also featured a large staircase that led to the upstairs rooms, which consisted of bedrooms for husbands and wives, sons, and daughters. These rooms were used not only for sleeping but also for private activities, such as playing for the children and sewing, writing, and reading for wives. This arrangement reflected the new desire for privacy. "Going upstairs" literally meant leaving the company of others in the downstairs common rooms to be alone in the privacy of one's bedroom. This eighteenth-century desire for privacy also meant keeping servants at a distance. They were now

THE ARISTOCRATIC WAY OF LIFE. The eighteenth-century country house in Britain fulfilled the desire of aristocrats for both elegance and greater privacy. The painting above by Richard Wilson shows a typical English country house of the eighteenth century surrounded by a simple and serene landscape. Thomas Gainsborough's *Conversation in the Park*, shown at right, captures the relaxed life of two aristocrats in the park of their country estate.

housed in their own wing of rooms and alerted to their employers' desire for assistance by a new invention—long-distance cords connected to bells in the servants' quarters.

Although the arrangement of the eighteenth-century Georgian house originally reflected male interests, the influence of women was increasingly evident by the second half of the eighteenth century. Already in the seventeenth century, it had become customary for the sexes to separate after dinner; while the men preoccupied themselves with brandy and cigars in the dining room, women would exit to a "withdrawing room" for their own conversation. In the course of the eighteenth century, the drawing room became a larger, more feminine room with comfortable furniture grouped casually in front of fireplaces to create a cozy atmosphere.

Aristocratic landowners, especially in Britain, also sought to expand the open space around their country houses to separate themselves from the lower classes in the villages and to remove farmland from their view. Often these open spaces were then enclosed by walls to create parks (as they were called in England) to provide even more privacy. Sometimes entire villages were destroyed to create a park, causing one English poet to lament the social cost:

The man of wealth and pride
Takes up the space that many poor supplied;
Space for his lake, his park's extended bounds,
Space for his horses, equipage and hounds.[10]

Along with a sense of privacy, parks gave landed aristocrats the ability to reshape their property to meet their leisure needs.

THE ARISTOCRATIC WAY OF LIFE: THE GRAND TOUR

One characteristic of the high culture of the Enlightenment was its cosmopolitanism, reinforced by education in the Latin classics and the use of French as an international language. Travel was another manifestation of the Enlightenment's cosmopolitanism and interest in new vistas. One important aspect of eighteenth-century travel was the Grand Tour in which the sons of aristocrats completed their educations by making a tour of Europe's major cities. The English aristocracy in particular regarded the Grand Tour as crucial to their education. The great-aunt of Thomas Coke wrote to him upon his completion of school: "Sir, I understand you have left Eton and probably intend to go to one of those Schools of Vice, the Universities. If, however, you choose to travel I will give you 500 pounds [about $12,500] per annum."[11] Coke was no fool and went on the Grand Tour, along with many others. In one peak year alone, 40,000 Englishmen were traveling in Europe.

Travel was not easy in the eighteenth century. Crossing the English Channel could be difficult in rough seas and might take anywhere from three to twelve hours. The trip from France to Italy could be made by sea, where the traveler faced the danger of pirates, or overland by sedan chair

A MARKET IN TURIN. Below the wealthy patrician elites who dominated the towns and cities were a number of social groups with a wide range of incomes and occupations. This remarkable diversity is evident in this view of a market square in the Italian city of Turin.

over the Alps, where narrow passes made travel an adventure in terror. Inns, especially in Germany, were populated by thieves and the ubiquitous bed bugs. The English in particular were known for spending vast sums of money during their travels; as one observer recounted: "The French usually travel to save money, so that they sometimes leave the places where they sojourn worse off than they found them. The English, on the other hand, come over with plenty of cash, plenty of gear, and servants to wait on them. They throw their money about like lords."[12]

Since the trip's purpose was educational, young Englishmen in particular were usually accompanied by a tutor who ensured that his charges spent time looking at museum collections of natural history and antiquities. But tutors were not able to stop young men from also pursuing wine, women, and song. After crossing the Channel, English visitors went to Paris for a cram course on how to act sophisticated. They then went on to Italy, where their favorite destinations were Florence, Venice, and Rome. In Florence, the studious and ambitious studied art in the Uffizi Gallery. The less ambitious followed a less vigorous routine; according to the poet Thomas Gray, they "get up at twelve o'clock, breakfast till three, dine till five, sleep till six, drinking cooling liquors till eight, go to the bridge till ten, sup till two, and so sleep till twelve again." In Venice, where sophisticated prostitutes had flourished since Renaissance times, the chief attraction for young English males was women. As Samuel Johnson remarked: "If a young man is wild, and must run after women and bad company, it is better this should be done abroad." Rome was another "great object of our pilgrimage," where travelers visited the "modern" sights, such as Saint Peter's and, above all, the ancient ruins. To a generation raised on a classical education, souvenirs of ruins and Piranesi's etchings of classical ruins were required purchases. The accidental rediscovery of the ancient Roman towns of Herculaneum and Pompeii made them a popular eighteenth-century tourist attraction.

The Inhabitants of Towns and Cities

The social importance of towns differed significantly between eastern and western Europe. In eastern Europe, cities were generally smaller and had little real autonomy. In western Europe, they were larger and frequently were accustomed to municipal self-government and municipal privileges.

Except in the Dutch Republic, Britain, and parts of Italy, townspeople were still a distinct minority of the total population. At the end of the eighteenth century, about one-sixth of the French population lived in towns of 2,000 or more. The biggest city in Europe was London with its 1 million inhabitants while Paris numbered between 550,000 and 600,000. Altogether, Europe had at least twenty cities in twelve countries with populations over 100,000, including Naples, Lisbon, Moscow, St. Petersburg, Vienna, Amsterdam, Berlin, Rome, and Madrid.

Although urban dwellers were vastly outnumbered by rural inhabitants, towns played an important role in Western culture. The contrasts between a large city with its education, culture, and material consumption and the surrounding, often poverty-stricken countryside were striking, evident in this British traveler's account of Russia's St. Petersburg in 1741:

> The country about Petersburg has full as wild and desert a look as any in the Indies; you need not go above 200 paces out of the town to find yourself in a wild wood of firs, and

Poverty in France

Unlike the British, who had a system of public-supported poor relief, the French responded to poverty with ad hoc policies when conditions became acute. This selection is taken from an intendant's report to the controller-general at Paris describing his suggestions for a program to relieve the grain shortages expected for the winter months.

❋ M. de la Bourdonnaye, Intendant of Bordeaux, to the Controller-General, September 30, 1708

Having searched for the means of helping the people of Agen in this cruel situation and having conferred with His Eminence, the Bishop, it seems to us that three things are absolutely necessary if the people are not to starve during the winter.

Most of the inhabitants do not have seed to plant their fields. However, we decided that we would be going too far if we furnished it, because those who have seed would also apply [for more]. Moreover, we are persuaded that all the inhabitants will make strenuous efforts to find some seed, since they have every reason to expect prices to remain high next year. . . .

But this project will come to nothing if the collectors of the taille continue to be as strict in the exercise of their functions as they have been of late and continue to employ troops [to force collection]. Those inhabitants who have seed grain would sell it to be freed from an oppressive garrison, while those who must buy seed, since they have none left from their harvest and have scraped together a little money for this purchase, would prefer to give up that money [for taxes] when put under police constraint. To avoid this, I feel it is absolutely necessary that you order the receivers-general to reduce their operations during this winter, at least with respect to the poor. . . .

We are planning to import wheat for this region from Languedoc and Quercy, and we are confident that there will be enough. But there are two things to be feared: one is the greed of the merchants. When they see that general misery has put them in control of prices, they will raise them to the point where the calamity is almost as great as if there were no provisions at all. The other fear is that the artisans and the lowest classes, when they find themselves at the mercy of the merchants, will cause disorders and riots. As a protective measure, it would seem wise to establish two small storehouses. . . . Ten thousand ecus [30,000 livres] would be sufficient for each. . . .

A third point demanding our attention is the support of beggars among the poor, as well as of those who have no other resources than their wages. Since there will be very little work, these people will soon be reduced to starvation. We should establish public workshops to provide work as was done in 1693 and 1694. I should choose the most useful kind of work, located where there are the greatest number of poor. In this manner, we should rid ourselves of those who do not want to work and assure the others a moderate subsistence. For these workshops, we would need about 40,000 livres, or altogether 100,000 livres. The receiver-general of the taille of Agen could advance this sum. The 60,000 livres for the storehouses he would get back very soon. I shall await your orders on all of the above.

❋ Marginal Comments by the Controller-General

Operations for the collection of the taille are to be suspended. The two storehouses are to be established; great care must be taken to put them to good use. The interest on the advances will be paid by the king. His Majesty has agreed to the establishment of the public workshops for the able-bodied poor and is willing to spend up to 40,000 livres on them this winter.

> such a low, marshy, boggy country that you would think God when he created the rest of the world for the use of mankind had created this for an inaccessible retreat for all sorts of wild beasts.[13]

Peasants often resented the prosperity of towns and their exploitation of the countryside to serve urban interests. Palermo in Sicily used one-third of the island's food production while paying only one-tenth of the taxes. Towns lived off the countryside not by buying peasant produce, but by acquiring it through tithes, rents, and dues.

Many cities in western and even central Europe had a long tradition of patrician oligarchies that continued to control their communities by dominating town and city councils. Despite their domination, patricians constituted only a small minority of the urban population. Just below the patricians stood an upper crust of the middle classes: nonnoble officeholders, financiers and bankers, merchants, wealthy rentiers who lived off their investments, and important professionals, including lawyers. Another large urban group was the petty bourgeoisie or lower middle class made up of master artisans, shopkeepers, and small traders. Below them were the laborers or working classes. Much urban industry was still carried on in small guild workshops by masters, journeymen, and apprentices. Apprentices who acquired the proper skills became journeymen before entering the ranks of the masters, but increasingly in the eighteenth century, guilds became closed oligarchies as membership was restricted to the relatives of masters. Many skilled artisans were then often forced to become low-paid workers. Urban communities also had a large group of unskilled workers who served as servants, maids, and cooks at pitifully low wages. One study of a pre-industrial French city found that two married workers with one child received a family income of 380 livres; basic necessities for the family cost 336 livres, leaving very little for extra expenses.

Despite an end to the ravages of plague, eighteenth-century cities still experienced high death rates, especially among children, because of unsanitary living conditions, polluted water, and a lack of sewerage facilities. One observer compared the stench of Hamburg to an open sewer that could be smelled for miles around. Overcrowding also exacerbated urban problems as cities continued to grow from an influx of rural immigrants. But cities proved no paradise for them as unskilled workers found few employment opportunities. The result was a serious problem of poverty in the eighteenth century.

THE PROBLEM OF POVERTY

Poverty was a highly visible problem in the eighteenth century both in cities and in the countryside (see the box on p. 546). In Venice licensed beggars made up 3 to 5 percent of the population, and unlicensed beggars may have constituted as much as 13 to 15 percent. Beggars in Bologna, Italy, were estimated at 25 percent of the population; in Mainz figures indicate that 30 percent of the people were beggars or prostitutes. Prostitution was often an alternative to begging. In France and Britain by the end of the century, an estimated 10 percent of the people depended on charity or begging for their food.

Earlier in Europe the poor had been viewed as blessed children of God; assisting them was a Christian duty. A change of attitude that had begun in the latter part of the sixteenth century became even more apparent in the eighteenth century. Charity to poor beggars, it was argued, simply encouraged their idleness and led them to vice and crime. A French official stated: "Beggary is the apprenticeship of crime; it begins by creating a love of idleness which will always be the greatest political and moral evil. In this state the beggar does not long resist the temptation to steal."[14] Although private charitable institutions such as the religious Order of Saint Vincent de Paul and the Sisters of Charity had been founded to help such people, they were soon overwhelmed by the increased numbers of indigent in the eighteenth century.

Although some "enlightened" officials argued that the state should become involved in the problem, mixed feelings prevented concerted action. Since the sixteenth century, vagrancy and begging had been considered crimes. In the eighteenth century, French authorities attempted to round up vagrants and beggars and incarcerate them for eighteen months to act as a deterrent. This effort accomplished little, however, since the basic problem was socioeconomic. These people had no work. In the 1770s, the French tried to use public works projects, such as road building, to give people jobs, but not enough funds were available to accomplish much. The problem of poverty remained as another serious blemish on the quality of eighteenth-century life.

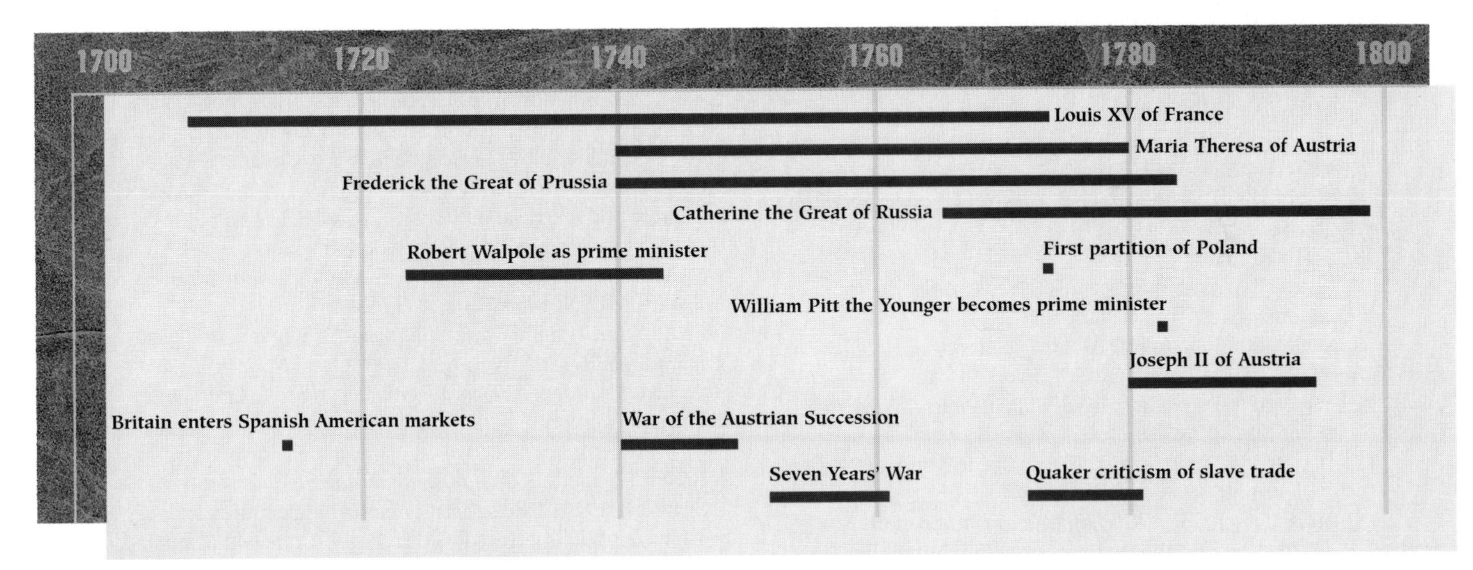

CONCLUSION

Everywhere in Europe at the beginning of the eighteenth century, the old order remained strong. Nobles, clerics, towns, provinces all had privileges, some medieval in origin, others the result of the attempt of monarchies in the sixteenth and seventeenth centuries to gain financial support from their subjects. Everywhere in the eighteenth century, monarchs sought to enlarge their bureaucracies to raise taxes to support the new large standing armies that had originated in the seventeenth century. The existence of these armies made wars more likely. The existence of five great powers, with two of them (France and Britain) in conflict in the East and the New World, initiated a new scale of conflict; the Seven Years' War could legitimately be viewed as the first world war. The wars altered some boundaries on the European continent, but were perhaps most significant for the British victories that marked the emergence of Great Britain as the world's greatest naval and colonial power. Everywhere in Europe, increased demands for taxes to support these conflicts led to attacks on the privileged orders and a desire for change not met by the ruling monarchs.

At the same time, sustained population growth, dramatic changes in finance, trade, and industry, and the growth of poverty created tensions that undermined the traditional foundations of European society. The inability of the old order to deal meaningfully with these changes led to a revolutionary outburst at the end of the eighteenth century that brought the beginning of the end for that old order.

NOTES

1. Quoted in Paul Dukes, *The Making of Russian Absolutism, 1613–1801* (London, 1982), pp. 144–145.
2. Frederick II, *Forms of Government,* in Eugen Weber, *The Western Tradition* (Lexington, Mass., 1972), pp. 538, 544.
3. Quoted in Reinhold A. Dorwart, *The Administrative Reforms of Frederick William I of Prussia* (Cambridge, Mass., 1953), p. 36.
4. Quoted in Sidney B. Fay, *The Rise of Brandenburg-Prussia to 1786,* rev. Klaus Epstein (New York, 1964), p. 92.
5. Quoted in Hans Rosenberg, *Bureaucracy, Aristocracy, and Autocracy: The Prussian Experience, 1660–1815* (Cambridge, Mass., 1958), p. 40.
6. Quoted in W. Abel, "Die Landwirtschaft 1648–1800," in *Handbuch der deutschen Wirtschafts-und Sozialgeschichte,* eds. H. Aubin and W. Zorn (Stuttgart, 1971), 1:524–525.
7. Quoted in Fernand Braudel, *Civilization and Capitalism* (London, 1981–84), 3:378.
8. Quoted in ibid., 3:245.
9. Quoted in Witold Rybczynski, *Home: A Short History of an Idea* (New York, 1986), p. 105.
10. Quoted in Jonathan Dewald, *The European Nobility, 1400–1800* (Cambridge, 1996), pp. 91–92.
11. Quoted in Peter Gay, *Age of Enlightenment* (New York, 1966), p. 87.
12. Quoted in Paul Hazard, *The European Mind, 1680–1715* (Cleveland, 1963), pp. 6–7.
13. Igor Vinogradoff, "Russian Missions to London, 1711–1789: Further Extracts from the Cottrell Papers," *Oxford Slavonic Papers,* New Series (1982), 15:76.
14. Quoted in Jeffrey Kaplow, *The Names of Kings: The Parisian Laboring Poor in the Eighteenth Century* (New York, 1972), p. 134.

SUGGESTIONS FOR FURTHER READING

For a good introduction to the political history of the eighteenth century, see the relevant chapters in the general works by Woloch, Anderson, and Birn listed in Chapter 17. See also G. Treasure, *The Making of Modern Europe, 1648–1780* (London, 1985); W. Doyle, *The Old European Order, 1660–1800* (Oxford, 1978); and O. Hufton, *Europe: Privilege and Protest, 1730–1789* (London, 1980). On enlightened Absolutism, see H. M. Scott, ed., *Enlightened Absolutism: Reform and Reformers in Later Eighteenth-Century Europe* (Ann Arbor, Mich., 1990). Good studies of individual states include J. B. Owen, *The Eighteenth Century, 1714–1815* (London, 1975), on England; S. Schama, *Patriots and Liberators: Revolution in the Netherlands, 1780–1813* (New York, 1977); P. R. Campbell, *The Ancien Régime in France* (Oxford, 1988); E. Wangermann, *The Austrian Achievement, 1700–1800* (London, 1973); R. Vierhaus, *Germany in the Age of Absolutism* (Cambridge, 1988); J. Gagliardo, *Germany under the Old Regime* (London, 1991); J. Lynch, *Bourbon Spain, 1700–1808* (Oxford, 1989); H. W. Koch, *A History of Prussia* (London, 1978); P. Dukes, *The Making of Russian Absolutism, 1613–1801,* 2d ed. (London, 1990); and D. Kirby, *Northern Europe in the Early Modern Period* (London, 1991). Good biographies of some of Europe's monarchs include R. Asprey, *Frederick the Great, The Magnificent Enigma* (New York, 1986); I. De Madariaga, *Catherine the Great: A Short History* (New Haven, Conn., 1990); the first volume of a major new work on Joseph II by D. Deales, *Joseph II* (Cambridge, 1987); T. C. W. Blanning, *Joseph II* (New York, 1994); and J. Brooke, *King George III* (London, 1972).

The warfare of this period is examined in J. Childs, *Armies and Warfare in Europe, 1648–1789* (Manchester, 1982); and M. S. Anderson, *War and Society in Europe of the Old Regime, 1615–1789* (New York, 1988). On the social composition of European armies, see A. Corvisier, *Armies and Society in Europe, 1494–1789* (Bloomington, Ind., 1978). For a study of one of the wars, see R. S. Browning, *The War of Austrian Succession* (London, 1995).

A good introduction to European population can be found in M. W. Flinn, *The European Demographic System, 1500–1820* (Brighton, 1981). Although historians now disagree with many of his conclusions, still worthwhile is the pioneering study of childhood by P. Aries, *Centuries of Childhood: A Social History of Family Life* (New York, 1965). One of the best works on family and marriage patterns is L. Stone, *The Family, Sex, and Marriage in England, 1500–1800* (New York, 1977). On wet nurses and infanticide, see G. Sussman, *Selling Mother's Milk: The Wet-Nursing Business* (Bloomington, Ind., 1982); N. Hull, *Murdering Mothers: Infanticide in England and New England, 1558–1803* (New York, 1981); and M. Jackson, *New-Born Child Murder: Women, Illegitimacy, and the Courts in Eighteenth-Century England* (New York, 1996).

A different perspective on economic history can be found in F. Braudel's *Capitalism and Material Life, 1400–1800* (New York, 1973). The subject of mercantile empires and worldwide trade is covered in J. H. Parry, *Trade and Dominion: European Overseas Empires in the Eighteenth Century* (London, 1971); D. K. Fieldhouse, *The Colonial Empires* (New York, 1971); P. K. Liss, *Atlantic Empires: The Network of Trade and Revolution, 1713–1826* (Baltimore, 1983); and R. Davis, *The Rise of the Atlantic Economies* (Ithaca, N.Y., 1973). On the problem of slavery, see H. Thomas, *The Slave Trade: The Story of the Atlantic Slave Trade, 1440–1870* (New York, 1997); and J. Walvin, *Black Ivory: A History of British Slavery* (Washington, D.C., 1994). On England's agricultural revolution, see J. D. Chambers and G. E. Mingay, *The Agricultural Revolution, 1750–1880* (London, 1966). Eighteenth-century cottage industry and the beginnings of industrialization are examined in the early chapters of D. Landes, *The Unbound Prometheus: Technological Change and Industrial Development in Western Europe from 1750 to the Present* (New York, 1969); and M. Berg, *The Age of Manufactures: Industry, Innovation, and Work in Britain, 1700–1820* (Oxford, 1985).

On the European nobility, see J. Dewald, *The European Nobility, 1400–1800* (Cambridge, 1996); and H. M. Scott, *The European Nobility in the Seventeenth and Eighteenth Centuries* (London, 1995). On the peasantry, see J. Blum, *The End of the Old Order in Rural Europe* (Princeton, N.J., 1978); and R. Evans, ed., *The German Peasantry* (New York, 1986). On European cities, see J. de Vries, *European Urbanization, 1500–1800* (Cambridge, Mass., 1984). On the lower urban classes, see J. Kaplow, *The Names of Kings: The Parisian Laboring Poor in the Eighteenth Century* (New York, 1972); R. M. Schwartz, *Policing the Poor in Eighteenth-Century France* (Chapel Hill, N.C., 1988); and B. Hill, *Servants: English Domestics in the Eighteenth Century* (New York, 1996). There is no better work on the problem of poverty than O. Hufton, *The Poor of Eighteenth-Century France* (Oxford, 1974).

For additional reading, go to InfoTrac College Edition, your online research library at http://web1.infotrac-college.com

Enter the search terms *William Pitt* using Key Terms.

Enter the search terms *Frederick II or Frederick the Great* using Key Terms.

Enter the search terms *Joseph II* using Key Terms.

Enter the search terms *Catherine the Great* using Key Terms.

CHAPTER

19

A Revolution in Politics: The Era of the French Revolution and Napoleon

CHAPTER OUTLINE

FOCUS QUESTIONS

- What were the causes and results of the American Revolution, and what impact did it have on Europe?
- What were the long-range and immediate causes of the French Revolution?
- What were the main events of the French Revolution between 1789 and 1799?
- What role did each of the following play in the French Revolution: lawyers, peasants, women, the clergy, the Jacobins, the sans-culottes, the French Revolutionary Army, and the Committee of Public Safety?
- What aspects of the French Revolution did Napoleon preserve, and which did he destroy?

ON THE MORNING of July 14, 1789, a Parisian mob of some 8,000 people in search of weapons streamed toward the Bastille, a royal armory filled with arms and ammunition. The Bastille was also a state prison, and, although it now contained only seven prisoners, in the eyes of these angry Parisians it was a glaring symbol of the government's despotic policies. The armory was defended by the marquis de Launay and a small garrison of 114 men. The attack began in earnest in the early afternoon, and after three hours of fighting, de Launay and the garrison surrendered. Angered by the loss of ninety-eight of their members, the victorious mob beat de Launay to death, cut off his head, and carried it aloft in triumph through the streets of Paris. When King Louis XVI was told the news of the fall of the Bastille by the duc de La Rochefoucauld-Liancourt, he exclaimed, "Why, this is a revolt." "No, Sire," replied the duc, "It is a revolution."

Historians have long assumed that the modern history of Europe began with two major transformations—the French Revolution and the Industrial Revolution (on the latter, see Chapter 20). Accordingly, the

French Revolution has been portrayed as the major turning point in European political and social history when the institutions of the "old regime" were destroyed and a new order was created based on individual rights, representative institutions, and a concept of loyalty to the nation rather than the monarch. This perspective does have certain limitations, however.

France was only one of a number of areas in the Western world where the assumptions of the old order were challenged. Although some historians have used the phrase "democratic revolution" to refer to the upheavals of the late eighteenth and early nineteenth centuries, it is probably more appropriate to speak not of a "democratic movement," but of a liberal movement to extend political rights and power to the bourgeoisie "possessing capital," namely, those besides the aristocracy who were literate and had become wealthy through capitalist enterprises in trade, industry, and finance. The years preceding and accompanying the French Revolution included attempts at reform and revolt in the North American colonies, Britain, the Dutch Republic, some Swiss cities, and the Austrian Netherlands. The success of the American and French Revolutions makes them the center of attention for this chapter.

Not all of the decadent privileges that characterized the old European regime were destroyed in 1789, however. The revolutionary upheaval of the era, especially in France, did create new liberal and national political ideals, summarized in the French revolutionary slogan, "Liberty, Equality, and Fraternity," that transformed France and were then spread to other European countries through the conquests of Napoleon. After Napoleon's defeat, however, the forces of reaction did their best to restore the old order and resist pressures for reform.

◆ The Beginnings of the Revolutionary Era: The American Revolution

The revolutionary era began in North America when the thirteen British colonies along the eastern seaboard revolted against their mother country. Despite their differences, the colonists found ways to create a new government based on liberal principles that made an impact on the "old world" European states.

Reorganization, Resistance, and Rebellion

The immediate causes of the American Revolution stemmed from Great Britain's response to its victory over France in the Seven Years' War (1756–1763), known as the French and Indian War in the American colonies. The colonists were not pleased when British policymakers asked them to contribute new revenues to pay the expenses the British army incurred in defending the colonies. In 1765, the British Parliament enacted the Stamp Act, which attempted to levy new taxes on the colonies, but riots quickly led to the statute's repeal.

The immediate crisis had ended, but the fundamental cause of the dispute had not been resolved. In the course of the eighteenth century, significant differences had arisen between the American and British political worlds. The property requirement for voting—voters had to possess property that could be rented for at least forty shillings a year—was the same in both areas, but the number of voters differed markedly. In Britain, fewer than one in five adult males had the right to vote. In the colonies, where a radically different economic structure led to an enormous group of independent farmers, the property requirement allowed over 50 percent of adult males to vote.

Although both the British and Americans had representative governments, different systems had evolved. Representation in Britain was indirect; the members of Parliament did not speak for local interests but for the entire kingdom. In the colonies representation was direct; representatives were expected not only to reside in and own property in the communities electing them, but also to represent the interests of those local districts.

This divergence in political systems was paralleled by conflicting conceptions of the British Empire. The British envisioned the empire as a single unit with Parliament as the supreme authority throughout. All the people in the empire, including the American colonists, were represented indirectly by members of Parliament, whether they were from the colonies or not. Colonial assemblies in the British perspective were only committees that made "temporary by-laws"; the real authority to make laws for the empire resided in London.

The Americans had developed their own peculiar view of the British Empire. To them, the empire was composed of self-regulating parts. Though they conceded that as British subjects they owed allegiance to the king and that Parliament had the right to make laws for the peace and prosperity of the whole realm, they argued, nevertheless, that neither king nor Parliament had any right to interfere in the internal affairs of the colonies since they had their own representative assemblies. American colonists were especially defensive about property and believed strongly that no tax could be levied without the consent of an assembly whose members actually represented the people.

By the 1760s, the American colonists had developed a sense of a common identity. It was not unusual for American travelers to Britain in the eighteenth century to see British society as old and decadent in sharp contrast to the youthfulness and vitality of their own. This sense of superiority made Americans resentful of British actions that seemed to treat them like children. Resentment eventually led to a desire for independence.

Crisis followed crisis in the early 1770s. The Tea Act of 1773, which was an attempt by Parliament to help the financially hard-pressed East India Company by allowing it to bypass American wholesalers and sell its tea directly to distributors, was roundly denounced by Americans as an attempt to ruin colonial businesses. In Boston, protest took a destructive turn when 150 Americans dressed as Indians dumped the East India Company's tea into Boston harbor. Parliament responded vigorously with the Coercive Acts, which closed the port of Boston until compensation for the destroyed tea was paid, restricted town meetings, and strengthened the power of the royal governor of Massachusetts. Designed to punish radical Massachusetts as an example to the other colonies, the Coercive Acts backfired. Colonial assemblies everywhere denounced the British action, and the colonies' desire to take collective action led to the First Continental Congress, which met at Philadelphia in September 1774. The more militant members refused to compromise and urged the colonists to "take up arms and organize militias." When the British army under General Gage attempted to stop rebel mobilization in Massachusetts, fighting between colonists and redcoats erupted at Lexington and Concord in April 1775.

The War for Independence

Despite the outbreak of hostilities, the colonists did not rush headlong into rebellion and war. After Lexington and Concord, more than a year passed before the colonists decided to declare their independence from the British Empire. An important factor in mobilizing public pressure for that decision was *Common Sense,* a pamphlet published in January 1776 by Thomas Paine, a recently arrived English political radical. Within three months, it had sold 120,000 copies. Paine's pamphlet argued that it was ridiculous for "a continent to be perpetually governed by an island." On July 4, 1776, the Second Continental Congress approved a Declaration of Independence written by Thomas Jefferson (see the box on p. 553). A stirring political document, the Declaration of Independence affirmed the Enlightenment's natural rights of "life, liberty, and the pursuit of happiness" and declared the colonies to be "free and independent states absolved from all allegiance to the British crown." The war for American independence had formally begun.

The war against Great Britain was a great gamble. Britain was a strong European military power with enormous financial resources; by 1778 Britain had sent 50,000 regular British troops and 30,000 German mercenaries to America. The Second Continental Congress had authorized the formation of a Continental Army under George Washington as commander-in-chief. Washington, who had political experience in Virginia and military experience in the French and Indian War, was a good choice for the job. As a southerner, he brought balance to an effort that up to now had been led by New Englanders. Nevertheless, compared to the British forces, the Continental Army consisted of undisciplined amateurs whose terms

THE DECLARATION OF INDEPENDENCE. John Trumbull's famous painting, *The Signing of the Declaration,* shows members of the committee responsible for the Declaration of Independence (from left to right, John Adams, Roger Sherman, Robert Livingston, Thomas Jefferson, and Benjamin Franklin) standing before John Hancock, president of the Second Continental Congress.

The Argument for Independence

On July 2, 1776, the Second Continental Congress adopted a resolution declaring the independence of the American colonies. Two days later the delegates approved the Declaration of Independence, which gave the reasons for their action. Its principal author was Thomas Jefferson who basically restated John Locke's theory of revolution (see Chapter 15).

The Declaration of Independence

When in the course of human events it becomes necessary for one people to dissolve the political bands which have connected them with another, and to assume among the Powers of the earth, the separate and equal station to which the Laws of Nature and of Nature's God entitle them, a decent respect to the opinions of mankind requires that they should declare the causes which impel them to the separation.

We hold these truths to be self-evident, that all men are created equal, that they are endowed by their Creator with certain unalienable Rights, that among these are Life, Liberty and the pursuit of Happiness. That to secure these rights, Governments are instituted among Men, deriving their just powers from the consent of the governed, That whenever any Form of Government becomes destructive of these ends, it is the Right of the People to alter or to abolish it and to institute new Government, laying its foundation on such principles and organizing its powers in such form, as to them shall seem most likely to effect their Safety and Happiness. Prudence, indeed, will dictate that Governments long established should not be changed for light and transient causes; and accordingly all experience has shown, that mankind are more disposed to suffer, while evils are sufferable, than to right themselves by abolishing the forms to which they are accustomed. But when a long train of abuses and usurpations, pursuing invariably the same Object evinces a design to reduce them under absolute Despotism, it is their right, it is their duty, to throw off such Government, and to provide new Guards for their future security.—Such has been the patient sufferance of these Colonies; and such is now the necessity which constrains them to alter their former Systems of government. The history of the present King of Great Britain is a history of repeated injuries and usurpations, all having in direct object the establishment of an absolute Tyranny over these States.

of service were usually very brief. The colonies also had militia units, but they likewise tended to be unreliable. Although 400,000 men served in the Continental Army and the militias during the course of the war, Washington never had more than 20,000 troops available for any single battle.

Of great importance to the colonies' cause was the assistance provided by foreign countries that were eager to gain revenge for their defeats in earlier wars at the hands of the British. The French were particularly generous in supplying arms and money to the rebels from the beginning of the war. French officers also served in Washington's army. Uncertain of the military outcome, however, France was at first unwilling to recognize the new republic. The defeat of the British at Saratoga in October 1777 finally led the French to grant diplomatic recognition to the American state. When Spain and the Dutch Republic entered the war against Great Britain in 1779 and 1780, respectively, and Russia formed the League of Armed Neutrality in 1780 to protect neutral shipping from British attacks, the British were faced with war against much of Europe as well as the Americans. Despite having won most of the battles, the British were in danger of losing the war. When the army of General Cornwallis was forced to surrender to a combined American and French army and French fleet under Washington at Yorktown in 1781, the British decided to call it quits. After extensive negotiations, complicated by French and Spanish aims that often conflicted with American desires, the Treaty of Paris was signed in 1783. It recognized the independence of the American colonies and granted the Americans control of the western territory from the Appalachians to the Mississippi River. By playing off the mutual fears of the European powers, the Americans had cleverly gained a peace settlement that stunned the Europeans. The Americans were off to a good start but soon showed signs of political disintegration.

Toward a New Nation

Although the thirteen American colonies agreed to "hang together" to gain their independence from the British, a fear of concentrated power and concern for their own interests caused them to have little enthusiasm for establishing a united nation with a strong central government. The Articles of Confederation, proposed in 1777 but not completely ratified until 1781, did little to provide for a strong central government. A series of economic, political, and international problems soon led to a movement for a different form of national government. In the summer of 1787, fifty-five delegates attended a convention in Philadelphia that was authorized by the Confederation Congress "for the sole and express purpose of revising the

CHRONOLOGY

The American Revolution

Stamp Act	1765
Tea Act—Boston Tea Party	1773
First Continental Congress	1774
Battle at Lexington and Concord	1775
Second Continental Congress	1775
Declaration of Independence	1776
Battle of Saratoga	1777
Battle of Yorktown	1781
Ratification of the Articles of Confederation	1781
Treaty of Paris	1783
Constitutional Convention	1787
Ratification of the Constitution	1788
Bill of Rights adopted	1791

Articles of Confederation." The convention's delegates—wealthy, politically experienced, well educated, and nationalistically inclined—rejected revision and decided to devise a new constitution.

The proposed Constitution created a central government distinct from and superior to the governments of the individual states. The national government was given the power to levy taxes, raise a national army, regulate domestic and foreign trade, and establish a national currency. Though the states were not eliminated, their powers were noticeably diminished. Following Montesquieu's principle of a "separation of powers" to provide a system of "checks and balances," the central or federal government was divided into three branches, each with some power to check the functioning of the others. A president, elected by the indirect system of an electoral college, would serve as the chief executive with the power to execute laws, veto the legislature's acts, make judicial and executive appointments, supervise foreign affairs, and direct military forces. Legislative power was vested in the second branch of government, a bicameral legislature composed of a Senate elected by the state legislatures and a House of Representatives elected directly by the people. The federal judiciary, embodied in a Supreme Court and other courts "as deemed necessary" by Congress, provided the third branch of government. With judges nominated by the executive and approved by the legislative branch, the federal judiciary would enforce the Constitution as the "supreme law of the land."

The Constitutional Convention stipulated that the new Constitution would have to be ratified by popularly chosen conventions in nine of the thirteen states before it would take effect. After fierce contests, the Federalists, who favored the new Constitution, won, although the margin of victory was quite slim. Important to their success was a promise to add a Bill of Rights to the Constitution as the new government's first piece of business. Accordingly, in March of 1789, the new Congress proposed the first ten amendments to the Constitution; they went into effect in 1791 after ratification by the states. Ever since known as the Bill of Rights, these amendments guaranteed freedom of religion, speech, press, petition, and assembly, as well as the right to bear arms, protection against unreasonable searches and arrests, trial by jury, due process of law, and the protection of property rights. Although many of these guarantees had their origins in English law, others were derived from the natural rights philosophy of the eighteenth-century philosophes and American experience. Is it any wonder that many European intellectuals saw the American Revolution as the embodiment of the Enlightenment's political dreams?

The Impact of the American Revolution on Europe

The year 1789 witnessed two far-reaching events, the beginning of a new United States of America and the eruption of the French Revolution. Was there a connection between the two great revolutions of the last half of the eighteenth century?

There is no doubt that the American Revolution had an important impact on Europeans. Books, newspapers, and magazines provided a newly developing reading public with numerous accounts of American events. To many in Europe, it seemed to portend an era of significant changes, including new arrangements in international politics. The Venetian ambassador to Paris astutely observed in 1783 that "if only the union of the [American] provinces is preserved, it is reasonable to expect that, with the favorable effects of time, and of European arts and sciences, it will become the most formidable power in the world."[1] But the American Revolution also meant far more than that. It proved to many Europeans that the liberal political ideas of the Enlightenment were not merely the vapid utterances of intellectuals. The rights of man, ideas of liberty and equality, popular sovereignty, freedom of religion, thought, and press, and the separation of powers were not merely utopian ideals. The Americans had created a new social contract, embodied it in a written constitution, and made concepts of liberty and representative government a reality. The premises of the Enlightenment seemed confirmed; a new age and a better world could be achieved. As a Swiss philosophe expressed it: "I am tempted to believe that North America is the country where reason and humanity will develop more rapidly than anywhere else."[2]

Europeans obtained much of their information about America from returning soldiers, especially the hundreds of French officers who had served in the American war. One of them, the aristocratic marquis de Lafayette, had

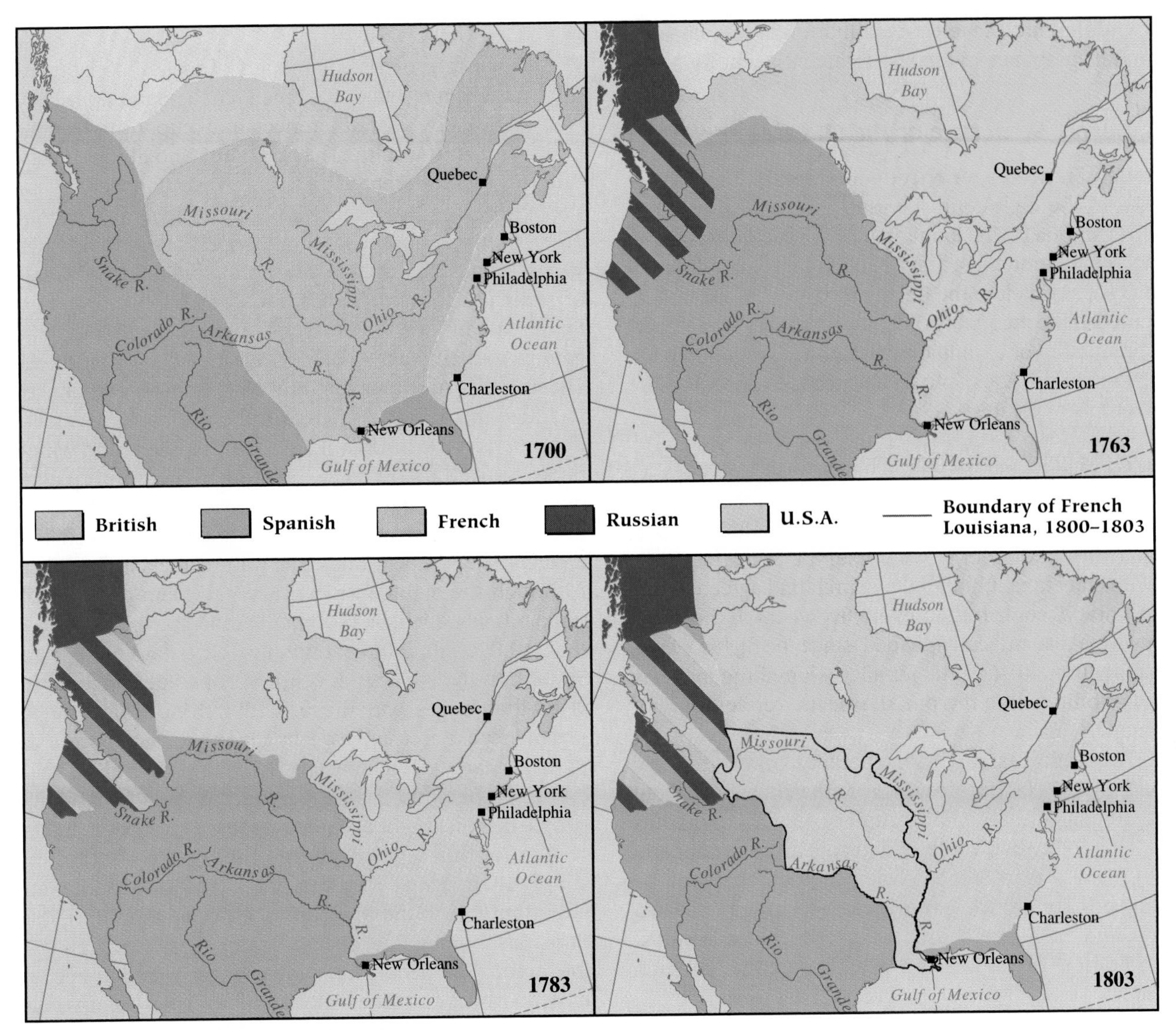

MAP 19.1 **North America, 1700–1803.**

volunteered for service in America in order to "strike a blow against England," France's old enemy. Closely associated with Washington, Lafayette returned to France with ideas of individual liberties and notions of republicanism and popular sovereignty. He became a member of the Society of Thirty, a club composed of people from the Paris salons. These "lovers of liberty" were influential in the early stages of the French Revolution. The Declaration of the Rights of Man and the Citizen (see The Destruction of the Old Regime later in this chapter) showed unmistakable signs of the influence of the American Declaration of Independence as well as the American state constitutions. Yet, for all of its obvious impact, the American Revolution proved in the long run to be far less important to Europe than the French Revolution. The French Revolution was more complex, more violent, and far more radical with its attempt to construct both a new political order and a new social order. The French Revolution provided a model of revolution for Europe and much of the rest of the world; to many it has remained the political movement that truly inaugurated the modern political world.

◆ Background to the French Revolution

Although we associate events like the French Revolution with sudden changes, the causes of such events involve long-range problems as well as immediate, precipitating forces. Revolutions, as has been repeatedly shown, are not necessarily the result of economic collapse and masses of impoverished people hungering for change. In fact, in the fifty years before 1789, France had experienced a period of economic growth due to an expansion of foreign trade and an increase in industrial production, although many people, especially peasants, no doubt failed to share in the prosperity. Thus, the causes of the French Revolution must be found in a multifaceted examination of French society and its problems in the late eighteenth century.

Social Structure of the Old Regime

Although France experienced an increase in economic growth in the eighteenth century, the wealth was not evenly distributed. The long-range or indirect causes of the French Revolution must first be sought in the condition of French society. Before the Revolution, French society was grounded in the inequality of rights or the idea of privilege. The population of 27 million was divided, as it had been since the Middle Ages, into legal categories known as the three orders or estates.

THE FIRST AND SECOND ESTATES

The first estate consisted of the clergy and numbered about 130,000 people. The church owned approximately 10 percent of the land. Clergy were exempt from the *taille*, France's chief tax, although the church had agreed to pay a "voluntary" contribution every five years to the state. Clergy were also radically divided, since the higher clergy, stemming from aristocratic families, shared the interests of the nobility while the parish priests were often poor commoners.

The second estate was the nobility, composed of no more than 350,000 people who nevertheless owned about 25 to 30 percent of the land. Under Louis XV and Louis XVI, the nobility had continued to play an important and even crucial role in French society, holding many of the leading positions in the government, the military, the law courts, and the higher church offices. Much heavy industry in France was controlled by nobles, either through investment or by ownership of mining and metallurgical enterprises. The French nobility was also divided. The nobility of the robe derived their status from officeholding, a pathway that had often enabled commoners to attain noble rank. These nobles now dominated the royal law courts and important administrative offices. The nobility of the sword claimed to be descendants of the original medieval nobility. As a group, the nobles sought to expand their privileges at the expense of the monarchy—to defend liberty by resisting the arbitrary actions of monarchy, as some nobles asserted—and to maintain their monopolistic control over positions in the military, church, and government. In 1781, in reaction to the ambitions of aristocrats newly arrived from the bourgeoisie, the Ségur Law attempted to limit the sale of military officerships to fourth-generation nobles, thus excluding newly enrolled members of the nobility.

Although there were many poor nobles, on the whole the fortunes of the wealthy aristocrats outstripped those of most others in French society. Generally, the nobles tended to marry within their own ranks making the nobility a fairly closed group. Although their privileges varied from region to region, the very possession of privileges remained a hallmark of the nobility. Common to all were tax exemptions, especially from the *taille*.

THE THIRD ESTATE

The third estate, or the commoners of society, constituted the overwhelming majority of the French population. They were divided by vast differences in occupation, level of education, and wealth. The peasants who alone constituted 75 to 80 percent of the total population were by far the largest segment of the third estate. They owned about 35 to 40 percent of the land, although their landholdings varied from area to area and over half had no or little land on which to survive. Serfdom no longer existed on any large scale in France, but French peasants still had obligations to their local landlords that they deeply resented. These "relics of feudalism," survivals from an earlier age, included the payment of fees for the use of village facilities, such as the flour mill, community oven, and winepress, as well as tithes to the clergy. The nobility also maintained the right to hunt on peasants' land.

Another part of the third estate consisted of skilled artisans, shopkeepers, and other wage earners in the cities. Although the eighteenth century had been a period of rapid urban growth, 90 percent of French towns had fewer than 10,000 inhabitants; only nine cities had more than 50,000. In the eighteenth century, consumer prices rose faster than wages, with the result that these urban groups experienced a noticeable decline in purchasing power. In Paris, for example, income lagged behind food prices and especially behind a 140 percent rise in rents for working people in skilled and unskilled trades. The economic discontent of this segment of the third estate—and often simply their struggle for survival—led them to play an important role in the Revolution, especially in the city of Paris. Insubordination, one observer noted, "has been visible among the people for some years now and above all among craftsmen." One historian has charted the ups and downs of revolutionary riots in Paris by showing their correlation to changes in bread prices. Sudden increases in the price of bread, which constituted three-fourths of an ordinary person's diet and cost one-third to one-half of his or her income, immediately affected public order. People expected bread prices to be controlled. They grew desperate when prices rose, and their only recourse was mob action to try to change the situation. The towns and cities were also home to large groups of unskilled workers. One magistrate complained that "misery ... has thrown into the towns people who overburden them with their uselessness, and who find nothing to do, because there is not enough for the people who live there."[3]

About 8 percent or 2.3 million people constituted the bourgeoisie or middle class who owned about 20 to 25 percent of the land. This group included merchants, industrialists, and bankers who controlled the resources of trade, manufacturing, and finance and benefited from the economic prosperity after 1730. The bourgeoisie also included professional people—lawyers, holders of public offices, doctors, and writers. Many members of the bourgeoisie sought security and status through the purchase of land. They had their own set of grievances because they were often excluded from the social and political privileges monopolized by the nobles. These resentments of the middle class were for a long time assumed to be a major cause of the French Revolution. But although these tensions existed, the situation was not a simple case of a unified bourgeoisie against a unified noble class. As is evident, neither group was monolithic. Nobles were separated by vast differences in wealth and importance. A similar gulf separated wealthy financiers from local lawyers in French provincial towns.

Remarkable similarities existed at the upper levels of society between the wealthier bourgeoisie and the nobility. It was still possible for wealthy middle-class individuals to enter the ranks of the nobility by obtaining public offices and entering the nobility of the robe. In fact, between 1774 and 1789, the not insignificant number of 2,500 wealthy bourgeoisie entered the ranks of the nobility. Over the century as a whole, 6,500 new noble families were created. In addition, as we saw in Chapter 18, the aristocrats were also engaging in capitalist activities on their landed estates, such as mining, metallurgy, and glassmaking, and were even investing in foreign trade. Viewed in terms of economic function, many members of the bourgeoisie and nobility formed a single class. Finally, the new and critical ideas of the Enlightenment proved attractive to both aristocrats and bourgeoisie. Members of both groups shared a common world of liberal political thought. The old view that the French Revolution was the result of the conflict between two rigid orders, the bourgeoisie and nobility, has been enlarged and revised. Both aristocratic and bourgeois elites, long accustomed to a new socioeconomic reality based on wealth and economic achievement, were increasingly frustrated by a monarchical system resting on privileges and on an old and rigid social order based on the concept of estates. The opposition of these elites to the old order ultimately led them to take drastic action against the monarchical regime, although they soon split over the question of how far to proceed in eliminating traditional privileges. In a real sense, the Revolution had its origins in political grievances.

Other Problems Facing the French Monarchy

Although the long-range causes of the French Revolution can thus be found in part in the growing frustration at the monarchy's inability to deal with new social realities and problems, other factors were also present. The failure of the French monarchy was exacerbated by specific problems in the 1780s. Although the country had enjoyed fifty years of growth overall, periodic economic crises still occurred. Bad harvests in 1787 and 1788 and the beginnings of a manufacturing depression resulted in food shortages, rising prices for food and other necessities, and unemployment in the cities. The number of poor, estimated by some at almost one-third of the population, reached crisis proportions on the eve of the Revolution. An English traveler noted the misery of the poor in the countryside: "All the country girls and women are without shoes or stockings; and the plowmen at their work have neither sabots nor stockings to their feet. This is a poverty that strikes at the root of national prosperity."[4]

Increased criticism of existing privileges as well as social and political institutions also characterized the eighteenth century. Although the philosophes did not advocate revolution, their ideas were widely circulated among the literate bourgeois and noble elites of France. The actual influence of the ideas of the philosophes is difficult to prove, but once the Revolution began, the revolutionary leaders frequently quoted Enlightenment writers, especially Rousseau.

The French Parlements often frustrated efforts at reform. Responsible for registering royal decrees, these thirteen law courts could block royal edicts by not registering them. Although Louis XIV had forced them into submission, the Parlements had gained new strength in the eighteenth century as they and their noble judges assumed the role of defenders of "liberty" against the arbitrary power of the monarchy. As noble defenders, however, they often pushed their own interests as well, especially by blocking new taxes. This last point reminds us that one of the fundamental problems facing the monarchy was financial.

The immediate cause of the French Revolution was the near collapse of government finances. French governmental expenditures continued to grow due to costly wars and royal extravagance. Since the government responded by borrowing, by 1788 the interest on the debt alone constituted half of the government's spending. The king's finance ministry wrestled with the problem but met with resistance. In 1786, Charles de Calonne, the controller-general of finance, proposed a complete revamping of the fiscal and administrative system of the state. To gain support, Calonne convened an Assembly of Notables early in 1787. This gathering of nobles, prelates, and magistrates refused to cooperate, and the government's attempt to go it alone brought further disaster. On the verge of a complete financial collapse, the government was finally forced to call a meeting of the Estates-General, the French parliamentary body that had not met since 1614. By calling the Estates-General, the government was virtually admitting that the consent of the nation was required to raise taxes.

◆ The French Revolution

In summoning the Estates-General, the government was merely looking for a way to solve the immediate financial crisis. Certainly, the monarchy had no wish for a major reform of the government. Nor did the delegates who arrived at Versailles come with plans for the revolutionary changes that ultimately emerged. Yet, over the next years, through the interplay of the deputies meeting in various legislative assemblies, the common people in the streets of Paris and other cities, and the peasants in the

THE TENNIS COURT OATH. Finding themselves locked out of their regular meeting place on June 20, 1789, the deputies of the Third Estate met instead in the nearby tennis courts of the Jeu de Paume and committed themselves to continue to meet until they established a new constitution for France. In this painting, the Neoclassicist Jacques-Louis David presents a dramatic rendering of the Tennis Court Oath.

countryside, much of the old regime would be destroyed, and Europe would have a new model for political and social change.

From Estates-General to a National Assembly

The Estates-General consisted of representatives from the three orders of French society. In the elections for the Estates-General, the government had ruled that the Third Estate should get double representation (it did, after all, constitute 97 percent of the population). Consequently, while both the First Estate (the clergy) and the Second (the nobility) had about 300 delegates each, the commoners had almost 600 representatives. Two-thirds of the latter were people with legal training, and three-fourths were from towns with over 2,000 inhabitants, giving the Third Estate a particularly strong legal and urban representation. Of the 282 representatives of the nobility, about 90 were liberal minded, urban oriented, and interested in the enlightened ideas of the century; half of them were under forty years of age. The activists of the Third Estate and reform-minded individuals among the First and Second Estates had common ties in their youth, urban background, and hostility to privilege. The *cahiers de doléances,* or statements of local grievances, which were drafted throughout France during the elections to the Estates-General, advocated a regular constitutional government that would abolish the fiscal privileges of the church and nobility as the major way to regenerate the country.

The Estates-General opened at Versailles on May 5, 1789. It was divided from the start over the question of whether voting should be by order or by head (each delegate having one vote). The Parlement of Paris, consisting of nobles of the robe, had advocated voting by order according to the form used in 1614. Each order would vote separately; each would have veto power over the other two, thus guaranteeing aristocratic control over reforms. But opposition to the Parlement of Paris's proposal had arisen from a group calling themselves the patriots or "lovers of liberty." Although they claimed to be the nation, they consisted primarily of bourgeoisie and nobles. One group of patriots known as the Society of Thirty drew most of its members from the salons of Paris. Some of this largely noble group had been directly influenced by the American Revolution, but all had been affected by the ideas of the Enlightenment and favored reforms made in the light of reason and utility.

THE NATIONAL ASSEMBLY

The failure of the government to assume the leadership at the opening of the Estates-General created an opportunity for the Third Estate to push its demands for voting by head. Since it had double representation, with the assistance of liberal nobles and clerics, it could turn the three estates into a single-chamber legislature that would reform France in its own way. One representative, the Abbé Sieyès, issued a pamphlet in which he asked, "What is the third estate? Everything. What has it been thus far in the political order? Nothing. What does it demand? To become something." Sieyès's sentiment, however, was not representative of the general feeling in 1789. Most delegates still wanted to make changes within a framework of respect for the authority of the king; revival or reform did not mean the overthrow of traditional institutions. When the First Estate declared in favor of voting by order, the Third Estate felt compelled to respond in a significant fashion. On June 17, 1789, the Third Estate voted to constitute itself a "National Assembly" and decided to draw up a constitution. Three days later, on June 20, the deputies of the Third Estate arrived at their meeting place, only to find the doors locked; thereupon they moved to a nearby indoor tennis court and swore (hence, the Tennis Court Oath) that they would continue to meet until they had produced a French

The Fall of the Bastille

On July 14, 1789, Parisian crowds in search of weapons attacked and captured the royal armory known as the Bastille. It had also been a state prison, and its fall marked the triumph of "liberty" over despotism. This intervention of the Parisian populace saved the Third Estate from Louis XVI's attempted counterrevolution.

A Parisian Newspaper Account of the Fall of the Bastille

First, the people tried to enter this fortress by the Rue St.—Antoine, this fortress, which no one has even penetrated against the wishes of this frightful despotism and where the monster still resided. The treacherous governor had put out a flag of peace. So a confident advance was made; a detachment of French Guards, with perhaps five to six thousand armed bourgeois, penetrated the Bastille's outer courtyards, but as soon as some six hundred persons had passed over the first drawbridge, the bridge was raised and artillery fire mowed down several French Guards and some soldiers; the cannon fired on the town, and the people took fright; a large number of individuals were killed or wounded; but then they rallied and took shelter from the fire . . . meanwhile, they tried to locate some cannon; they attacked from the water's edge through the gardens of the arsenal, and from there made an orderly siege; they advanced from various directions, beneath a ceaseless round of fire. It was a terrible scene. . . . The fighting grew steadily more intense; the citizens had become hardened to the fire; from all directions they clambered onto the roofs or broke into the rooms; as soon as an enemy appeared among the turrets on the tower, he was fixed in the sights of a hundred guns and mown down in an instant; meanwhile cannon fire was hurriedly directed against the second drawbridge, which it pierced, breaking the chains; in vain did the cannon on the tower reply, for most people were sheltered from it; the fury was at its height; people bravely faced death and every danger; women, in their eagerness, helped us to the utmost; even the children, after the discharge of fire from the fortress, ran here and there picking up the bullets and shot; [and so the Bastille fell and the governor, de Launey, was captured]. . . . Serene and blessed liberty, for the first time, has at last been introduced into this abode of horrors, this frightful refuge of monstrous despotism and its crimes.

Meanwhile, they get ready to march; they leave amidst an enormous crowd; the applause, the outbursts of joy, the insults, the oaths hurled at the treacherous prisoners of war; everything is confused; cries of vengeance and of pleasure issue from every heart; the conquerors, glorious and covered in honor, carry their arms and the spoils of the conquered, the flags of victory, the militia mingling with the soldiers of the fatherland, the victory laurels offered them from every side, all this created a frightening and splendid spectacle. On arriving at the square, the people, anxious to avenge themselves, allowed neither de Launey nor the other officers to reach the place of trial; they seized them from the hands of their conquerors, and trampled them underfoot one after the other. De Launey was struck by a thousand blows, his head was cut off and hoisted on the end of a pike with blood streaming down all sides. . . . This glorious day must amaze our enemies, and finally usher in for us the triumph of justice and liberty. In the evening, there were celebrations.

constitution. These actions of June 17 and June 20 constitute the first step in the French Revolution since the Third Estate had no legal right to act as the National Assembly. This revolution, largely the work of the lawyers of the Third Estate, was soon in jeopardy, however, as the king sided with the First Estate and threatened to dissolve the Estates-General. Louis XVI now prepared to use force. The revolution of the lawyers appeared doomed.

THE COMMON PEOPLE INTERVENE

The intervention of the common people, however, in a series of urban and rural uprisings in July and August of 1789 saved the Third Estate from the king's attempt to stop the revolution. From now on, the common people would be mobilized by both revolutionary and counterrevolutionary politicians and used to support their interests. The common people had their own interests as well and would use the name of the Third Estate to wage a war on the rich, claiming that the aristocrats were plotting to destroy the Estates-General and retain its privileges. This war was not what the deputies of the Third Estate had planned.

The most famous of the urban risings was the fall of the Bastille (see the box above). The king's attempt to take defensive measures by increasing the number of troops at the arsenals in Paris and along the roads to Versailles served not to intimidate but rather to inflame public opinion. Increased mob activity in Paris led Parisian leaders to form a Permanent Committee to keep order. Needing arms, they organized a popular force to capture the Invalides, a royal armory, and on July 14 attacked the Bastille, another royal armory. But the Bastille had also been a state prison, and though it now contained only seven prisoners (five forgers and two insane people), its fall quickly became a popular symbol of triumph over despotism. Paris was abandoned to the insurgents, and Louis XVI was soon informed that the royal troops were unreliable. Louis's acceptance of that reality signaled the collapse of royal authority; the king could no longer

STORMING OF THE BASTILLE. Louis XVI planned to use force to dissolve the Estates-General, but a number of rural and urban uprisings by the common people prevented this action. The fall of the Bastille, pictured here in an anonymous painting, is perhaps the most famous of the urban risings.

enforce his will. Louis then confirmed the appointment of the marquis de Lafayette as commander of a newly created citizens' militia known as the National Guard. The fall of the Bastille had saved the National Assembly.

At the same time, independently of what was going on in Paris, popular revolutions broke out in numerous cities. In Nantes, Permanent Committees and National Guards were created to maintain order after crowds had seized the chief citadels. This collapse of royal authority in the cities was paralleled by peasant revolutions in the countryside.

A growing resentment of the entire seigneurial system with its fees and obligations, greatly exacerbated by the economic and fiscal activities of the great estate holders—whether noble or bourgeois—in the difficult decade of the 1780s, created the conditions for a popular uprising. The fall of the Bastille and the king's apparent capitulation to the demands of the Third Estate now encouraged peasants to take matters into their own hands. From July 19 to August 3, peasant rebellions occurred in five major areas of France. Patterns varied. In some places, peasants simply forced their lay and ecclesiastical lords to renounce dues and tithes; elsewhere they burned charters listing their obligations. The peasants were not acting in blind fury; they knew what they were doing. Many also believed that the king supported their actions. As a contemporary chronicler wrote: "For several weeks, news went from village to village. They announced that the Estates-General was going to abolish tithes, quitrents and dues, that the King agreed but that the peasants had to support the public authorities by going themselves to demand the destruction of titles."[5]

The agrarian revolts served as a backdrop to the Great Fear, a vast panic that spread like wildfire through France between July 20 and August 6. Fear of invasion by foreign troops, aided by a supposed aristocratic plot, encouraged the formation of more citizens' militias and permanent committees. The greatest impact of the agrarian revolts and Great Fear was on the National Assem-

Declaration of the Rights of Man and the Citizen

One of the important documents of the French Revolution, the Declaration of the Rights of Man and the Citizen, was adopted in August 1789 by the National Assembly. The declaration affirmed that "Men are born and remain free and equal in rights," that governments must protect these natural rights, and that political power is derived from the people.

Declaration of the Rights of Man and the Citizen

The representatives of the French people, organized as a national assembly, considering that ignorance, neglect, and scorn of the rights of man are the sole causes of public misfortunes and of corruption of governments, have resolved to display in a solemn declaration the natural, inalienable, and sacred rights of man, so that this declaration, constantly in the presence of all members of society, will continually remind them of their rights and their duties. . . . Consequently, the National Assembly recognizes and declares, in the presence and under the auspices of the Supreme Being, the following rights of man and citizen:

1. Men are born and remain free and equal in rights; social distinctions can be established only for the common benefit.
2. The aim of every political association is the conservation of the natural and imprescriptible rights of man; these rights are liberty, property, security, and resistance to oppression.
3. The source of all sovereignty is located in essence in the nation; no body, no individual can exercise authority which does not emanate from it expressly.
4. Liberty consists in being able to do anything that does not harm another person. . . .
6. The law is the expression of the general will; all citizens have the right to concur personally or through their representatives in its formation; it must be the same for all, whether it protects or punishes. All citizens being equal in its eyes are equally admissible to all honors, positions, and public employments, according to their capabilities and without other distinctions than those of their virtues and talents.
7. No man can be accused, arrested, or detained except in cases determined by the law, and according to the forms which it has prescribed. . . .
10. No one may be disturbed because of his opinions, even religious, provided that their public demonstration does not disturb the public order established by law.
11. The free communication of thoughts and opinions is one of the most precious rights of man: every citizen can therefore freely speak, write, and print. . . .
12. The guaranteeing of the rights of man and citizen necessitates a public force; this force is therefore instituted for the advantage of all, and not for the private use of those to whom it is entrusted. . . .
14. Citizens have the right to determine for themselves or through their representatives the need for taxation of the public, to consent to it freely, to investigate its use, and to determine its rate, basis, collection, and duration.
15. Society has the right to demand an accounting of his administration from every public agent.
16. Any society in which guarantees of rights are not assured nor the separation of powers determined has no constitution.
17. Property being an inviolable and sacred right, no one may be deprived of it unless public necessity, legally determined, clearly requires such action, and then only on condition of a just and prior indemnity.

bly meeting in Versailles. We will now examine its attempt to reform France.

The Destruction of the Old Regime

One of the first acts of the National Assembly, which was also called the Constituent Assembly because from 1789 to 1791 it was writing a new constitution, was to destroy the relics of feudalism or aristocratic privileges. To some deputies, this measure was necessary to calm the peasants and restore order in the countryside, although many urban bourgeoisie were willing to abolish feudalism as a matter of principle. On the night of August 4, 1789, the National Assembly in an astonishing session voted to abolish seigneurial rights as well as the fiscal privileges of nobles, clergy, towns, and provinces.

THE DECLARATION OF THE RIGHTS OF MAN AND THE CITIZEN

On August 26, the assembly provided the ideological foundation for its actions and an educational device for the nation by adopting the Declaration of the Rights of Man and the Citizen (see the box above). This charter of basic liberties reflected the ideas of the major philosophes of the French Enlightenment and also owed much to the American Declaration of Independence and American state constitutions. The declaration began with a ringing affirmation of "the natural and imprescriptible rights of man" to "liberty, property, security and resistance to oppression." It went on to affirm the destruction of aristocratic privileges by proclaiming an end to exemptions from taxation, freedom and equal rights for all men, and access to public office based on talent. The monarchy was restricted, and all citizens were to have the right to take part in the legislative process. Freedom of speech and press were coupled with the outlawing of arbitrary arrests.

The Declaration also raised another important issue. Did the proclamation's ideal of equal rights for all men also include women? Many deputies insisted that it did, at least in terms of civil liberties, provided that, as one said, "women do not aspire to exercise political rights and functions." Olympe de Gouges, a playwright and pamphleteer, refused to accept this exclusion of women from political rights. Echoing the words of the official declaration, she penned a Declaration of the Rights of Woman and the Female Citizen, in which she insisted that women should have all the same rights as men (see the box on p. 563). The National Assembly ignored her demands.

THE KING AND THE CHURCH

In the meantime, Louis XVI had remained inactive at Versailles. He did refuse, however, to promulgate the decrees on the abolition of feudalism and the Declaration of Rights, but an unexpected turn of events soon forced the king to change his mind. On October 5, after marching to the Hôtel de Ville, the city hall, to demand bread, crowds of Parisian women numbering in the thousands set off for Versailles, twelve miles away, to confront the king and the National Assembly. One eyewitness was amazed at the sight of "detachments of women coming up from every direction, armed with broomsticks, lances, pitchforks, swords, pistols and muskets." After meeting with a delegation of these women, who tearfully described how their children were starving from a lack of bread, Louis XVI promised them grain supplies for Paris, thinking that this would end the protest. But the women's action had forced the Parisian National Guard under Lafayette to follow their lead and march to Versailles. The crowd now insisted that the royal family return to Paris. On October 6, the king complied. As a goodwill gesture, he brought along wagonloads of flour from the palace stores. All were escorted by women armed with pikes (some of which held the severed heads of the king's guards) singing, "We are bringing back the baker, the baker's wife, and the baker's boy" (the king, queen, and their son). The king now accepted the National Assembly's decrees; it was neither the first nor the last occasion when Parisian crowds would affect national politics. The king was virtually a prisoner in Paris, and the National Assembly, now meeting in Paris, would also feel the influence of Parisian insurrectionary politics.

The Catholic church was viewed as an important pillar of the old order, and it soon also felt the impact of reform. Because of the need for money, most of the lands of the church were confiscated, and assignats, a form of paper money, were issued based on the collateral of the newly nationalized church property. The church was also secularized. In July 1790, a new Civil Constitution of the Clergy was put into effect. Both bishops and priests of the Catholic church were to be elected by the people and paid by the state. All clergy were also required to swear an oath of allegiance to the Civil Constitution. Since the pope forbade it, only 54 percent of the French parish clergy took the oath, and the majority of bishops refused. This was a critical development because the Catholic church, still an important institution in the life of the French people, now became an enemy of the Revolution. The Civil Constitution has often been viewed as a serious tactical blunder on the part of the National Assembly for, by arousing the opposition of the church, it gave counterrevolution a popular base from which to operate.

A NEW CONSTITUTION

By 1791, the National Assembly had finally completed a new constitution that established a limited, constitutional

THE WOMEN'S MARCH TO VERSAILLES. On October 5, 1789, thousands of Parisian women marched to Versailles to confront King Louis XVI and to demand bread for their starving children. This contemporary print shows a group of dedicated marchers armed with pikes and other weapons and pulling an artillery piece.

Declaration of the Rights of Woman and the Female Citizen

Olympe de Gouges (a pen name for Marie Gouze) was a butcher's daughter who wrote plays and pamphlets. She argued that the Declaration of the Rights of Man and the Citizen did not apply to women and composed her own Declaration of the Rights of Woman in 1791.

Declaration of the Rights of Woman and the Female Citizen

. . . Mothers, daughters, sisters and representatives of the nation demand to be constituted into a national assembly. Believing that ignorance, omission, or scorn for the rights of woman are the only causes of public misfortunes and of the corruption of governments, the women have resolved to set forth in a solemn declaration the natural, inalienable, and sacred rights of woman in order that this declaration, constantly exposed before all the members of the society, will ceaselessly remind them of their rights and duties. . . .

Consequently, the sex that is as superior in beauty as it is in courage during the sufferings of maternity recognizes and declares in the presence and under the auspices of the Supreme Being, the following Rights of Woman and of Female Citizens.

1. Woman is born free and lives equal to man in her rights. Social distinctions can be based only on the common utility.
2. The purpose of any political association is the conservation of the natural and imprescriptible rights of woman and man; these rights are liberty, property, security, and especially resistance to oppression.
3. The principle of all sovereignty rests essentially with the nation, which is nothing but the union of woman and man; no body and no individual can exercise any authority which does not come expressly from it [the nation].
4. Liberty and justice consist of restoring all that belongs to others; thus, the only limits on the exercise of the natural rights of woman are perpetual male tyranny; these limits are to be reformed by the laws of nature and reason.
6. The law must be the expression of the general will; all female and male citizens must contribute either personally or through their representatives to its formation; it must be the same for all: male and female citizens, being equal in the eyes of the law, must be equally admitted to all honors, positions, and public employment according to their capacity and without other distinctions besides those of their virtues and talents.
7. No woman is an exception; she is accused, arrested, and detained in cases determined by law. Women, like men, obey this rigorous law.
10. No one is to be disquieted for his very basic opinions; woman has the right to mount the scaffold; she must equally have the right to mount the rostrum, provided that her demonstrations do not disturb the legally established public order.
11. The free communication of thought and opinions is one of the most precious rights of woman, since that liberty assured the recognition of children by their fathers. . . .
12. The guarantee of the rights of woman and the female citizen implies a major benefit; this guarantee must be instituted for the advantage of all, and not for the particular benefit of those to whom it is entrusted.
14. Female and male citizens have the right to verify, either by themselves or through their representatives, the necessity of the public contribution. This can only apply to women if they are granted an equal share, not only of wealth, but also of public administration, and in the determination of the proportion, the base, the collection, and the duration of the tax.
15. The collectivity of women, joined for tax purposes to the aggregate of men, has the right to demand an accounting of his administration from any public agent.
16. No society has a constitution without the guarantee of rights and the separation of powers; the constitution is null if the majority of individuals comprising the nation have not cooperated in drafting it.
17. Property belongs to both sexes whether united or separate; for each it is an inviolable and sacred right; no one can be deprived of it, since it is the true patrimony of nature, unless the legally determined public need obviously dictates it, and then only with a just and prior indemnity.

monarchy. There was still a monarch (now called king of the French), but he enjoyed few powers not subject to review by the new Legislative Assembly. The Legislative Assembly, in which sovereign power was vested, was to sit for two years and consist of 745 representatives chosen by an indirect system of election that preserved power in the hands of the more affluent members of society. A distinction was drawn between active and passive citizens. Although all had the same civil rights, only active citizens (those men over the age of twenty-five paying taxes equivalent in value to three days' unskilled labor) could vote. The active citizens probably numbered 4.3 million in 1790.

These citizens did not elect the members of the Legislative Assembly directly, but voted for electors (those men paying taxes equal in value to ten days' labor). This relatively small group of 50,000 electors chose the deputies. To qualify as a deputy, one had to pay at least a "silver mark" in taxes, an amount equivalent to fifty-four days' labor.

The National Assembly also undertook an administrative restructuring of France. In 1789, it abolished all the old local and provincial divisions and divided France into eighty-three departments, roughly equal in size and population. In turn, departments were divided into districts and communes, all supervised by elected councils and officials who oversaw financial, administrative, judicial, and ecclesiastical institutions within their domains. Although both bourgeoisie and aristocrats were eligible for offices based on property qualifications, few nobles were elected, leaving local and departmental governments in the hands of the bourgeoisie, especially lawyers of various types.

By 1791, France had moved into a revolutionary reordering of the old regime that had been achieved by a revolutionary consensus that was largely the work of the wealthier bourgeoisie. By mid-1791, however, this consensus faced growing opposition from clerics angered by the Civil Constitution of the Clergy, lower classes hurt by the rise in the cost of living resulting from the inflation of the assignats, peasants who remained opposed to dues that had still not been abandoned, and political clubs offering more radical solutions to the nation's problems. The most famous were the Jacobins, who first emerged as a gathering of more radical deputies at the beginning of the Revolution, especially during the events of the night of August 4, 1789. After October 1789, they occupied the former Jacobin convent in Paris. Jacobin clubs also formed in the provinces where they served primarily as discussion groups. Eventually, they joined together in an extensive correspondence network and, by spring 1790, were seeking affiliation with the Parisian club. One year later, there were 900 Jacobin clubs in France associated with the Parisian center. Members were usually the elite of their local societies, but they also included artisans and tradespeople.

In addition, by mid-1791, the government was still facing severe financial difficulties due to massive tax evasion. Despite all of their problems, however, the bourgeois politicians in charge remained relatively unified on the basis of their trust in the king. But Louis XVI disastrously undercut them. Quite upset with the whole turn of revolutionary events, he sought to flee France in June 1791 and almost succeeded before being recognized, captured at Varennes, and brought back to Paris. Though radicals called for the king to be deposed, the members of the National Assembly, fearful of the popular forces in Paris calling for a republic, chose to ignore the king's flight and pretended that he had been kidnapped. In this unsettled situation, with a discredited and seemingly disloyal monarch, the new Legislative Assembly held its first session in October 1791.

Because the National Assembly had passed a "self-denying ordinance" that prohibited the reelection of its members, the composition of the Legislative Assembly tended to be quite different from that of the National Assembly. The clerics and nobles were largely gone. Most of the representatives were men of property; many were lawyers. Although lacking national reputations, most had gained experience in the new revolutionary politics and prominence in their local areas through the National Guard, the Jacobin clubs, and the many elective offices spawned by the administrative reordering of France. The king made what seemed to be a genuine effort to work with the new Legislative Assembly, but France's relations with the rest of Europe soon led to Louis's downfall.

OPPOSITION FROM ABROAD

Over a period of time, some European countries had become concerned about the French example and feared that revolution would spread to their countries. On August 27, 1791, Emperor Leopold II of Austria and King Frederick William II of Prussia issued the Declaration of Pillnitz, which invited other European monarchs to take "the most effectual means . . . to put the king of France in a state to strengthen, in the most perfect liberty, the bases of a monarchical government equally becoming to the rights of sovereigns and to the wellbeing of the French Nation."[6] But European monarchs were too suspicious of each other to undertake such a plan, and in any case French enthusiasm for war led the Legislative Assembly to declare war on Austria on April 20, 1792. But why take such a step in view of its obvious dangers? Many people in France wanted war. Reactionaries hoped that a preoccupation with war would cool off the Revolution; French defeat, which seemed likely in view of the army's disintegration, might even lead to the restoration of the old regime. Leftists hoped that war would consolidate the Revolution at home and spread it to all of Europe.

The French fared badly in the initial fighting, and loud recriminations were soon heard in Paris. A frantic search for scapegoats began; as one observer noted: "Everywhere you hear the cry that the king is betraying us, the generals are betraying us, that nobody is to be trusted; . . . that Paris will be taken in six weeks by the Austrians . . . we are on a volcano ready to spout flames."[7] Defeats in war coupled with economic shortages in the spring reinvigorated popular groups that had been dormant since the previous summer and led to renewed political demonstrations, especially against the king. Radical Parisian political groups, declaring themselves an insurrectionary commune, organized a mob attack on the royal palace and Legislative Assembly in August 1792, took the king captive, and forced the Legislative Assembly to suspend the monarchy and call for a National Convention, chosen on the basis of universal male suffrage, to decide on the future form of government. The French Revolution was about to enter a more radical stage as power passed from the assembly to the new Paris Commune, composed of many who proudly called themselves the sans-culottes, ordinary patriots without fine clothes. Although it has become customary to equate the more radical sans-culottes with working people or the poor, many were merchants and better-off artisans who were often the elite of their neighborhoods and trades.

The Radical Revolution

Before the National Convention met, the Paris Commune dominated the political scene. Led by the newly appointed minister of justice, Georges Danton (1759–1794), the sans-culottes sought revenge on those who had aided the king and resisted the popular will. Thousands of presumed traitors were arrested and then massacred as ordinary Parisian tradespeople and artisans solved the problem of overcrowded prisons by mass executions of their inmates. In September 1792, the newly elected National Convention began its sessions. Although it was called to draft a new constitution, it also acted as the sovereign ruling body of France.

Socially, the composition of the National Convention was similar to its predecessors. Dominated by lawyers, professionals, and property owners, it also included for the first time a handful of artisans. Two-thirds of the deputies were under age forty-five, and almost all had had political experience as a result of the Revolution. Almost all were also intensely distrustful of the king and his activities. It was therefore no surprise that the convention's first major step on September 21 was to abolish the monarchy and establish a republic. But that was about as far as members of the convention could agree, and the National Convention soon split into factions over the fate of the king. The two most important were the Girondins and the Mountain. Both were members of the Jacobin club.

Representing primarily the provinces, the Girondins came to fear the radical mobs in Paris and were disposed to keep the king alive as a hedge against future eventualities. The Mountain, on the other hand, represented the interests of the city of Paris and owed much of its strength to the radical and popular elements in the city, although the members of the Mountain themselves were middle class. The Mountain won out at the beginning of 1793 when they passed a decree condemning Louis XVI to death, although by a very narrow margin. On January 21, 1793, the king was executed and the destruction of the old regime was complete. Now there could be no turning back. But the execution of the king produced new challenges by creating new enemies for the Revolution both at home and abroad while strengthening those who were already its enemies.

Factional disputes between Girondins and the Mountain were only one aspect of France's domestic crisis in 1792 and 1793. Within Paris the local government was controlled by the Commune, which drew a number

EXECUTION OF THE KING. **At the beginning of 1793, the National Convention decreed the death of the king, and on January 21 of that year, Louis XVI was executed. As seen in this engraving by Carnavalet, the execution of the king was accomplished by the new revolutionary device of the guillotine.**

of its leaders from the city's artisans and shopkeepers. The Commune favored radical change and put constant pressure on the National Convention, pushing it to ever more radical positions. As one man warned his fellow deputies: "Never forget that you were sent here by the sans-culottes."[8] At the end of May and the beginning of June 1793, the Commune organized a demonstration, invaded the National Convention, and forced the arrest and execution of the leading Girondins, thus leaving the Mountain in control of the convention. The National Convention itself still did not rule all France. The authority of the convention was repudiated in western France, particularly in the department of the Vendée, by peasants who revolted against the new military draft (see A Nation in Arms later in this chapter). The Vendéan rebellion soon escalated into a full-blown counterrevolutionary appeal: "Long live the king and our good priests. We want our king, our priests and the old regime." Some of France's major provincial cities, including Lyons and Marseilles, also began to break away from the central authority. Arguing as Marseilles did that "it is time for the anarchy of a few men of blood to stop,"[9] these cities favored a decentralized republic to free themselves from the ascendancy of Paris. In no way did they favor breaking up the "indivisible Republic."

CHRONOLOGY

The French Revolution

The National Assembly (Constituent Assembly)	**1789–1791**
Meeting of Estates-General	May 5, 1789
Formation of National Assembly	June 17, 1789
Tennis Court Oath	June 20, 1789
Fall of the Bastille	July 14, 1789
Great Fear	Summer 1789
Abolition of feudalism	August 4, 1789
Declaration of the Rights of Man and the Citizen	August 26, 1789
Women's march to Versailles; the king's return to Paris	October 5–6, 1789
Civil Constitution of the Clergy	July 12, 1790
Flight of the king	June 20–21, 1791
Declaration of Pillnitz	August 27, 1791
The Legislative Assembly	**1791–1792**
France declares war on Austria	April 20, 1792
Attack on the royal palace	August 10, 1792
The National Convention	**1792–1795**
Abolition of the monarchy	September 21, 1792
Execution of the king	January 21, 1793
Universal mobilization of the nation	August 23, 1793
Execution of Robespierre	July 28, 1794
The Directory	**1795–1799**
Constitution of 1795 is adopted	August 22, 1795

Domestic turmoil was paralleled by a foreign crisis. By the beginning of 1793, after the king had been executed, much of Europe—an informal coalition of Austria, Prussia, Spain, Portugal, Britain, and the Dutch Republic—was pitted against France. Carried away by initial successes and their own rhetoric, the French welcomed the struggle. Danton exclaimed to the convention: "They threaten you with kings! You have thrown down your gauntlet to them, and this gauntlet is a king's head, the signal of their coming death."[10] Grossly overextended, the French armies began to experience reverses, and by late spring some members of the anti-French coalition were poised for an invasion of France. If successful, both the Revolution and the revolutionaries would be destroyed and the old regime reestablished. The Revolution had reached a decisive moment.

To meet these crises, the program of the National Convention became one of curbing anarchy and counterrevolution at home while attempting to win the war by a great national mobilization. To administer the government, the convention gave broad powers to an executive committee known as the Committee of Public Safety, which was dominated initially by Danton. Maximilien Robespierre (1758–1794) eventually became one of its most important members. For a twelve-month period, from 1793 to 1794, virtually the same twelve members were reelected and gave the country the leadership it needed to weather the domestic and foreign crises of 1793.

A NATION IN ARMS

To meet the foreign crisis and save the Republic from its foreign enemies, the Committee of Public Safety decreed a universal mobilization of the nation on August 23, 1793:

> Young men will fight, young men are called to conquer. Married men will forge arms, transport military baggage and guns and will prepare food supplies. Women, who at long last are to take their rightful place in the revolution and follow their true destiny, will forget their futile tasks: their delicate hands will work at making clothes for soldiers; they will make tents and they will extend their tender care to shelters where the defenders of the Patrie [nation] will receive the help that their wounds require. Children will make lint of old cloth. It is for them that we are fighting: children, those beings destined to gather all the fruits of the revolution, will raise their pure hands toward the skies. And old men, performing their missions again, as of yore, will be guided to the public squares of the cities where they will kindle the courage of young warriors and preach the doctrines of hate for kings and the unity of the Republic.[11]

In less than a year, the French revolutionary government had raised an army of 650,000; by September 1794, it numbered 1,169,000. The Republic's army was the largest ever seen in European history. It now pushed the allies back across the Rhine and even conquered the Austrian Netherlands. By May 1795, the anti-French coalition of 1793 was breaking up.

Historians have focused on the importance of the French revolutionary army in the creation of modern nationalism. Previously, wars had been fought between governments or ruling dynasties by relatively small armies of professional soldiers. The new French army, however, was the creation of a "people's" government; its wars were now "people's" wars. The entire nation was to be involved in the war. But when dynastic wars became people's wars, warfare increased in ferocity and lack of restraint. Although innocent civilians had suffered in the earlier struggles, now the carnage became appalling at times. The wars of the French revolutionary era opened the door to the total war of the modern world.

THE COMMITTEE OF PUBLIC SAFETY AND THE REIGN OF TERROR

To meet the domestic crisis, the National Convention and the Committee of Public Safety established the "Reign of Terror." Revolutionary courts were organized to protect the revolutionary Republic from its internal enemies, those "who either by their conduct, their contacts, their words

CITIZENS ENLIST IN THE NEW FRENCH ARMY. To save the Republic from its foreign enemies, the National Convention created a new revolutionary army of unprecedented size. In this painting, citizens joyfully hasten to sign up at the recruitment tables set up in the streets. On this occasion, officials are distributing coins to those who have enrolled.

or their writings, showed themselves to be supporters of tyranny or enemies of liberty," or those "who have not constantly manifested their attachment to the revolution."[12] Victims of the Terror ranged from royalists, such as Queen Marie Antoinette, to former revolutionary Girondins, including Olympe de Gouges, the chief advocate for political rights for women, and even included thousands of peasants. Many victims were persons who had opposed the radical activities of the sans-culottes (see the box on p. 568). In the course of nine months, 16,000 people were officially killed under the blade of the guillotine, the latter a revolutionary device for the quick and efficient separation of heads from bodies. But the true number of the Terror's victims was probably closer to 50,000. The bulk of the Terror's executions took place in the Vendée and in cities such as Lyons and Marseilles, places that had been in open rebellion against the authority of the National Convention.

Military force in the form of Revolutionary Armies was used to bring recalcitrant cities and districts back under the control of the National Convention. Marseilles fell to a Revolutionary Army in August. Starving Lyons surrendered early in October after two months of bombardment and resistance. Since Lyons was France's second city after Paris and had defied the National Convention during a time when the Republic was in peril, the Committee of Public Safety decided to make an example of it. By April 1794, 1,880 citizens of Lyons had been executed. When guillotining proved too slow, cannon fire and grape shot were used to blow condemned men into open graves. A German observed:

> . . . whole ranges of houses, always the most handsome, burnt. The churches, convents, and all the dwellings of the former patricians were in ruins. When I came to the guillotine, the blood of those who had been executed a few hours beforehand was still running in the street . . . I said to a group of sansculottes that it would be decent to clear away all this human blood. Why should it be cleared? one of them said to me. It's the blood of aristocrats and rebels. The dogs should lick it up.[13]

In the Vendée, Revolutionary Armies were also brutal in defeating the rebel armies. After destroying one army on December 12, the commander of the Revolutionary Army ordered that no quarter be given: "The road to Laval is strewn with corpses. Women, priests, monks, children, all have been put to death. I have spared nobody." The Terror was at its most destructive in the Vendée. Forty-two percent of the death sentences during the Terror were passed in territories affected by the Vendée rebellion. Perhaps the most notorious act of violence occurred in Nantes where victims were executed by sinking them in barges in the Loire River.

Contrary to popular opinion, the Terror demonstrated no class prejudice. Estimates are that the nobles constituted 8 percent of its victims; the middle classes, 25 percent; the clergy, 6; and the peasant and laboring classes, 60. To the Committee of Public Safety, this bloodletting was only a temporary expedient. Once the war and domestic emergency were over, "the republic of virtue" would ensue, and the Declaration of the Rights of Man and the Citizen would be fully established. Although theoretically a republic, the French government during the Terror was led by a group of twelve men who ordered the execution of people as enemies of the Republic. But how did they justify this? Louis Saint-Just, one of the younger members of the Committee of Public Safety, explained their rationalization in a speech to the

A Victim of the Reign of Terror

The Reign of Terror created a repressive environment in which even quite innocent people could be accused of crimes against the Republic. As seen in this letter by Anne-Félicité Guinée, wife of a wig maker, merely insulting an official could lead to arrest and imprisonment.

Letter of Anne-Félicité Guinée

Citizen Anne-Félicité Guinée, twenty-four years old . . . informs you that she was arrested at the Place des Droits de l'Homme, where I had gone to get butter. I point out to you that for a long time I have had to feed the members in my household on bread and cheese and that, tired of complaints from my husband and my boys, I was compelled to go wait in line to get something to eat. For three days I had been going to the same market without being able to get anything, despite the fact that I had waited from 7 or 8 A.M. until 5 or 6 P.M. After the distribution of butter on the twenty-second, . . . a citizen came over to me and said that I was in a very delicate condition. To that I answered, "You can't be delicate and be on your legs for so long. I wouldn't have come if there were any other food." He replied that I needed to drink milk. I answered that I had men in my house who worked and that I couldn't nourish them with milk, that I was convinced that if he, the speaker, was sensitive to the difficulty of obtaining food, he would not vex me so, and that he was an imbecile and wanted to play despot, and no one had that right. Here, on the spot, I was arrested and brought to the guard house. I wanted to explain myself. I was silenced and dragged off to prison. . . . About 7 P.M., I was led to the Revolutionary Committee [of the section], where I was called a counterrevolutionary and was told I was asking for the guillotine because I told them I preferred death to being treated ignominiously the way he was treating me. . . . I was asked if I knew whom I had called a despot. I answered, "I didn't know him," and I was told that he was the commander of the post. I said that he was more [a commander] beneath his own roof than anyone, given that he was there to maintain order and not to provoke bad feelings. . . . I was told that I had done three times more than was needed to get the guillotine and that I would be explaining myself before the Revolutionary Tribunal. The next day, I was taken to the Revolutionary Committee, which, without waiting to hear me, had me taken to the Mairie, where I stayed for nine days without a bed or a chair with vermin and with women addicted to all sorts of crimes. . . .

On the ninth day I was transferred to the prison of La Force. . . . In the end I can give you only the very slightest idea of all the horrors that are committed in these terrible prisons. . . . I was thrown together not with women but with monsters who gloried in all their crimes and who gave themselves over to all the most horrible excesses. One day, two of them fought each other with knives. Day and night I lived in mortal fear. The food that was sent in to me was grabbed away immediately. That was my cruel situation for seventeen days. My whole body was swollen from . . . the poor treatment I had endured. . . . [Anne-Félicité Guinée was discharged provisionally after the authorities realized that she was pregnant.]

convention: "Since the French people has manifested its will, everything opposed to it is outside the sovereign. Whatever is outside the sovereign is an enemy."[14] Clearly, Saint-Just was referring to Rousseau's concept of the general will, but it is equally apparent that these twelve men, in the name of the Republic, had taken to themselves the right to ascertain the sovereign will of the French people (see the box on p. 569) and to kill their enemies as "outside the sovereign."

THE "REPUBLIC OF VIRTUE"

Along with the Terror, the Committee of Public Safety took other steps both to control France and to create a new republican order and new republican citizens. By spring 1793, they were sending "representatives on mission" as agents of the central government to all departments to explain the war emergency measures and to implement the laws dealing with the wartime emergency.

The committee also attempted to provide some economic controls, especially since members of the more radical working class were advocating them. They established a system of requisitioning food supplies for the cities enforced by the forays of Revolutionary Armies into the countryside. The Law of the General Maximum established price controls on goods declared of first necessity ranging from food and drink to fuel and clothing. The controls failed to work very well because the government lacked the machinery to enforce them.

Women continued to play an active role in this radical phase of the French Revolution. As spectators at sessions of revolutionary clubs and the National Convention, women made the members and deputies aware of their demands. When on Sunday, February 25, 1793, a group of women appealed formally to the National Convention for lower bread prices, the convention reacted by adjourning until Tuesday. The women

Robespierre and Revolutionary Government

In its time of troubles, the National Convention, under the direction of the Committee of Public Safety, instituted a Reign of Terror to preserve the Revolution from its internal enemies. In this selection, Maximilien Robespierre, one of the committee's leading members, tries to justify the violence to which these believers in republican liberty resorted.

Robespierre, Speech on Revolutionary Government

The theory of revolutionary government is as new as the Revolution that created it. It is as pointless to seek its origins in the books of the political theorists, who failed to foresee this revolution, as in the laws of the tyrants, who are happy enough to abuse their exercise of authority without seeking out its legal justification. And so this phrase is for the aristocracy a mere subject of terror or a term of slander, for tyrants an outrage and for many an enigma. It behooves us to explain it to all in order that we may rally good citizens, at least, in support of the principles governing the public interest.

It is the function of government to guide the moral and physical energies of the nation toward the purposes for which it was established.

The object of constitutional government is to preserve the Republic; the object of the revolutionary government is to establish it.

Revolution is the war waged by liberty against its enemies; a constitution is that which crowns the edifice of freedom once victory has been won and the nation is at peace.

The revolutionary government has to summon extraordinary activity to its aid precisely because it is at war. It is subjected to less binding and less uniform regulations, because the circumstances in which it finds itself are tempestuous and shifting above all because it is compelled to deploy, swiftly and incessantly, new resources to meet new and pressing dangers.

The principal concern of constitutional government is civil liberty; that of revolutionary government, public liberty. Under a constitutional government little more is required than to protect the individual against abuses by the state, whereas revolutionary government is obliged to defend the state itself against the factions that assail it from every quarter.

To good citizens revolutionary government owes the full protection of the state; to the enemies of the people it owes only death.

responded bitterly by accosting the deputies: "We are adjourned until Tuesday; but as for us, we adjourn ourselves until Monday. When our children ask us for milk, we don't adjourn them until the day after tomorrow."[15] In 1793, two women—an actress and a chocolate manufacturer—founded the Society for Revolutionary Republican Women. Composed largely of working-class women, this Parisian group viewed themselves as a "family of sisters" and vowed "to rush to the defense of the Fatherland."

Despite the importance of women to the revolutionary cause, male revolutionaries reacted disdainfully to female participation in political activity. In the radical phase of the Revolution, the Paris Commune outlawed women's clubs and forbade women to be present at its meetings. One of its members explained why:

> It is horrible, it is contrary to all laws of nature for a woman to want to make herself a man. The Council must recall that some time ago these denatured women, these viragos, wandered through the markets with the red cap to sully that badge of liberty and wanted to force all women to take off the modest headdress that is appropriate for them [the bonnet]. . . . Is it the place of women to propose motions? Is it the place of women to place themselves at the head of our armies?[16]

WOMEN PATRIOTS. Women played a variety of roles in the events of the French Revolution. This picture shows a women's patriotic club discussing the decrees of the National Convention, an indication that some women had become highly politicized by the upheavals of the Revolution.

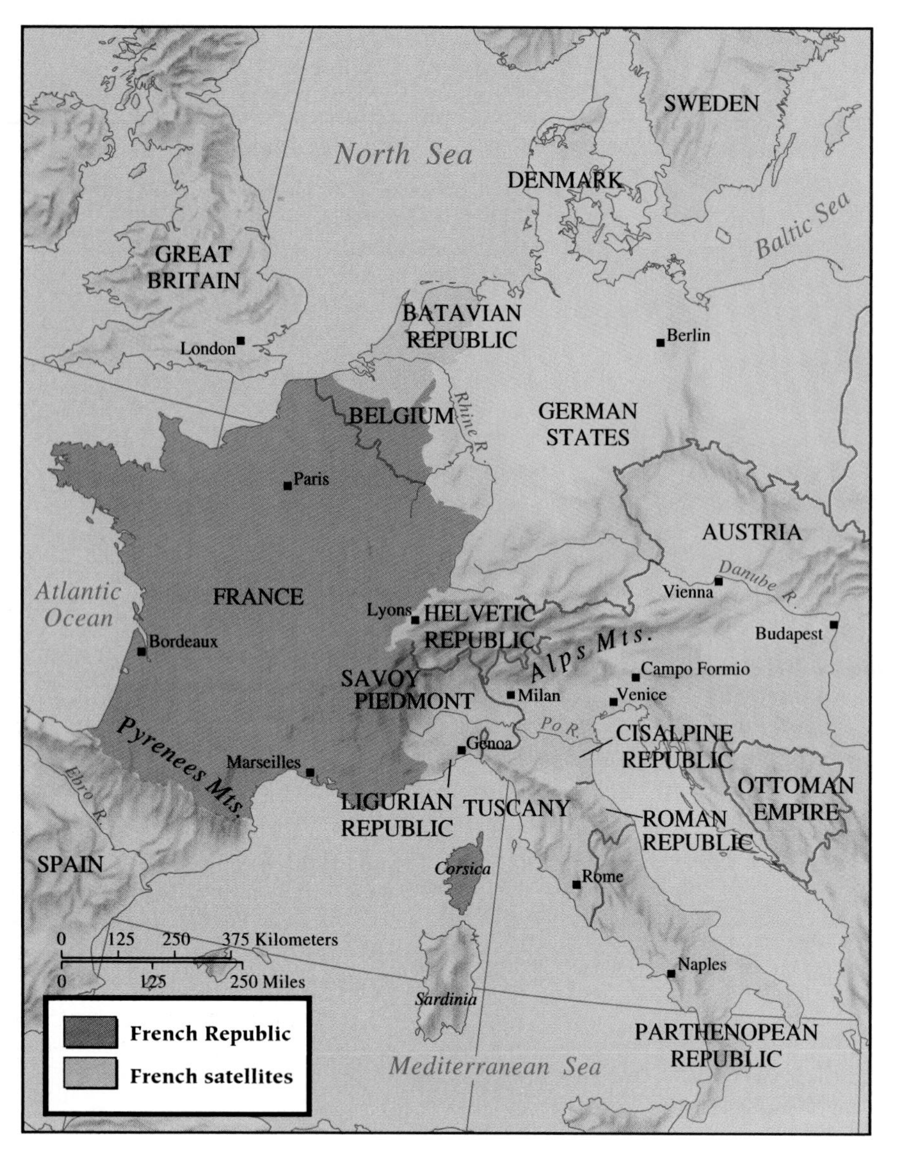

MAP 19.2 French Conquests during the Revolutionary Wars.

Most men—whether radical or conservative—agreed that a woman's place was in the home and not in military or political affairs. As one man asked: "Since when is it considered normal for a woman to abandon the pious care of her home, the cradle of her children, to listen to speeches in the public forum?"[17]

In its attempt to create a new order, the National Convention also pursued a policy of dechristianization. The word "saint" was removed from street names, churches were pillaged and closed by Revolutionary Armies, and priests were encouraged to marry. In Paris, the cathedral of Notre Dame was designated a Temple of Reason. In November 1793, a public ceremony dedicated to the worship of reason was held in the former cathedral; patriotic maidens adorned in white dresses paraded before a temple of reason where the high altar once stood. At the end of the ceremony, a female figure personifying Liberty rose out of the temple. As Robespierre came to realize, dechristianization backfired because France was still overwhelmingly Catholic. In fact, dechristianization created more enemies than friends.

Yet another manifestation of dechristianization was the adoption of a new republican calendar on October 5, 1793. Years would no longer be numbered from the birth of Jesus but from September 22, 1792, the day the French Republic was proclaimed. Thus, at the time the calendar was adopted, the French were already living in year two. The calendar contained twelve months; each month consisted of three ten-day weeks (*décades*) with the tenth day of each week a rest-day (*décadi*). This eliminated Sundays and Sunday worship services and put an end to the ordering of French lives by a Christian calendar that emphasized Sundays, saints' days, and church holidays and festivals. The latter were to be replaced by revolutionary festivals. Especially important were the five days (six in leap years) left over in the calendar at the end of the year. These days were to form a half-week of festivals to celebrate the revolutionary virtues—Virtue, Intelligence, Labor, Opinion, and Rewards. The sixth extra day in a leap year would be a special festival day when French citizens would "come from all parts of the Republic to celebrate liberty and equality, to cement by their embraces the national fraternity." Of course, ending church holidays also reduced the number of nonworking holidays from fifty-six to thirty-two, a goal long recommended by eighteenth-century economic theorists.

The anti-Christian purpose of the calendar was reinforced in the naming of the months of the year. The months were given names that were supposed to evoke the seasons, the temperature, or the state of the vegetation: Vendémiaire (harvest—the first month of thirty days beginning September 22), Brumaire (mist), Frimaire (frost), Nivôse (snow), Pluviôse (rain), Ventôse (wind), Germinal (seeding), Floréal (flowering), Prairial (meadows), Messidor (wheat harvest), Thermidor (heat), and Fructidor (ripening).

The new calendar faced intense popular opposition, and the revolutionary government relied primarily on coercion to win its acceptance. Journalists, for example, were commanded to use republican dates in their newspaper articles. But many people refused to give up the old calendar, as one official reported:

> Sundays and Catholic holidays, even if there are ten in a row, have for some time been celebrated with as much pomp and splendor as before. The same cannot be said of *décadi,* which is observed by only a small handful of citizens. The first to disobey the law are the wives of public officials, who dress up on the holidays of the old calendar and abstain from work more religiously than anyone else.[18]

The government could hardly expect peasants to follow the new calendar when government officials were ignoring it. Napoleon later perceived that the revolutionary calendar was politically unpopular, and he simply abandoned it on January 1, 1806.

In addition to its anti-Christian function, the revolutionary calendar had also served to mark the Revolution as a new historical beginning, a radical break in time. Revolutionary upheavals often project millenarian expectations, the hope that a new age is dawning. The revolutionary dream of a new order presupposed the creation of a new human being freed from the old order and its symbols, a new citizen surrounded by a framework of new habits. Restructuring time itself offered the opportunity to forge new habits and create a lasting new order.

But maintaining the revolutionary ideals was not easy. By the Law of 14 Frimaire (passed on December 4, 1793), the Committee of Public Safety sought to centralize the administration of France more effectively and to exercise greater control in order to check the excesses of the Reign of Terror. The activities of both the representatives on mission and the Revolutionary Armies were scrutinized more carefully, and the campaign against Christianity was also dampened. Finally, in 1794, the Committee of Public Safety turned against its radical Parisian supporters, executed the leaders of the revolutionary Paris Commune, and turned it into a docile tool. This might have been a good idea for the sake of order, but in suppressing the people who had been its chief supporters, the National Convention alienated an important group. At the same time, the French had been successful against their foreign foes. The military successes meant that the Terror no longer served much purpose. But the Terror continued because Robespierre, now its dominant figure, had become obsessed with purifying the body politic of all the corrupt. Only then could the Republic of Virtue follow. Many deputies in the National Convention

ROBESPIERRE. Maximilien Robespierre eventually came to exercise much control over the Committee of Public Safety. Robespierre and the committee worked to centralize the administration of France and curb the excesses of the Reign of Terror. However, fear of Robespierre led many in the National Convention to condemn him, and on July 28, 1794, he was executed.

feared, however, that they were not safe while Robespierre was free to act. An anti-Robespierre coalition in the National Convention, eager now to destroy Robespierre before he destroyed them, gathered enough votes to condemn him. Robespierre was guillotined on July 28, 1794, beginning a reaction that brought an end to this radical stage of the French Revolution.

The National Convention and its Committee of Public Safety had accomplished a great deal. By creating a nation in arms, they preserved the French Revolution and prevented it from being destroyed by its foreign enemies, who, if they had been successful, would have re-established the old monarchical order. Domestically, the Revolution had also been saved from the forces of counterrevolution. The committee's tactics, however, provided an example for the use of violence in domestic politics that has continued to bedevil the Western world until this day.

Reaction and the Directory

After the death of Robespierre on July 28, 1794, revolutionary fervor began to give way to the Thermidorean Reaction, named after the month of Thermidor. The Terror began to abate. The National Convention curtailed the power of the Committee of Public Safety, shut down the Jacobin club, and attempted to provide better protection for its deputies against the Parisian mobs. Churches were allowed to reopen for public worship, and a decree of February 21, 1795, gave freedom of worship to all cults. Economic regulation was dropped in favor of laissez-faire policies, another clear indication that moderate forces were again gaining control of the Revolution. In addition, a new constitution was created in August 1795 that reflected this more conservative republicanism or a desire for a stability that did not sacrifice the ideals of 1789.

To avoid the dangers of another single legislative assembly, the Constitution of 1795 established a national legislative assembly consisting of two chambers: a lower house, known as the Council of 500, whose function was to initiate legislation, and an upper house of 250 members, the Council of Elders, composed of married or widowed members over age forty, which accepted or rejected the proposed laws. The 750 members of the two legislative bodies were chosen by electors who had to be owners or renters of property worth between 100 and 200 days' labor, a requirement that limited their number to 30,000, an even smaller base than the Constitution of 1791 had provided. The electors were chosen by the active citizens, now defined as all male taxpayers over twenty-one. The Council of Elders elected five directors from a list presented by the Council of 500 to act as the executive authority or Directory. To ensure some continuity from the old order to the new, the members of the National Convention ruled that two-thirds of the new members of the National Assembly must be chosen from their ranks. This decision produced disturbances in Paris and an insurrection at the beginning of October that was dispersed after fierce combat by an army contingent under the artillery general Napoleon Bonaparte. This would be the last time in the great French Revolution that the city of Paris would attempt to impose its wishes on the central government. Even more significant and ominous was this use of the army, which made it clear that the Directory from the beginning had to rely upon the military for survival.

The period of the Directory was an era of stagnation, corruption, and graft, a materialistic reaction to the sufferings and sacrifices that had been demanded in the Reign of Terror and the Republic of Virtue. Speculators made fortunes in property by taking advantage of the government's severe monetary problems. Elaborate fashions, which had gone out of style because of their identification with the nobility, were worn again. Gambling and roulette became popular once more.

The government of the Directory was faced with political enemies from both the left and the right of the political spectrum. On the right, royalists who dreamed of restoring the monarchy continued their agitation; some still toyed with violent means. On the left, Jacobin hopes of power were revived by continuing economic problems, especially the total collapse in the value of the assignats. Some radicals even went beyond earlier goals, especially Gracchus Babeuf who raised the question "What is the French Revolution? An open war between patricians and plebeians, between rich and poor." Babeuf, who was appalled at the misery of the common people, wanted to abolish private property and eliminate private enterprise. His Conspiracy of Equals was crushed in 1796, and he was executed in 1797.

New elections in 1797 created even more uncertainty and instability. Battered by the left and right, unable to find a definitive solution to the country's economic problems, and still carrying on the wars left from the Committee of Public Safety, the Directory increasingly relied on the military to maintain its power. This led to a coup d'etat in 1799 in which the successful and popular general Napoleon Bonaparte was able to seize power.

◆ The Age of Napoleon

Napoleon dominated both French and European history from 1799 to 1815. The coup d'etat that brought him to power occurred exactly ten years after the outbreak of the French Revolution. In a sense, Napoleon brought the Revolution to an end in 1799, but Napoleon was also a child of the Revolution; he called himself the son of the Revolution. The French Revolution had made possible his rise first in the military and then to supreme power in France. Even beyond this, Napoleon had once said, "I am the revolution," and he never ceased to remind the French that they owed to him the preservation of all that was beneficial in the revolutionary program.

NAPOLEON AS A YOUNG OFFICER. Napoleon had risen quickly through the military ranks, being promoted to the rank of brigadier general at the age of twenty-five. This painting of Napoleon by the Romantic painter Baron Gros presents an idealized, heroic image of the young Napoleon.

The Rise of Napoleon

Napoleon was born in Corsica in 1769, only a few months after France had annexed the island. The son of a lawyer whose family stemmed from the Florentine nobility, the young Napoleon obtained a royal scholarship to study at a military school in France. His education in French military schools led to his commission in 1785 as a lieutenant, although he was not well liked by his fellow officers because he was short, spoke with an Italian accent, and had little money. For the next seven years, Napoleon spent much of his time reading the works of the philosophes and educating himself in military matters by studying the campaigns of great military leaders from the past. The French Revolution and the European war that followed broadened his sights and presented him with new opportunities.

Napoleon rose quickly through the ranks. In 1792, he became a captain and in the following year performed so well as an artillery commander that he was promoted to the rank of brigadier general in 1794, when he was only twenty-five. In October 1795, he saved the National Convention from the Parisian mob and in 1796 was made commander of the French army in Italy (see the box on p. 574). There he turned a group of ill-disciplined soldiers into an effective fighting force and, in a series of stunning victories, defeated the Austrians and dictated peace to them in 1797. Throughout his Italian campaigns, Napoleon won the confidence of his men by his energy, charm, and ability to comprehend complex issues quickly and make decisions rapidly. These qualities, combined with his keen intelligence, ease with words, and supreme confidence in himself, enabled him throughout the rest of his life to influence people and win their firm support (see the box on p. 575).

In 1797, Napoleon returned to France as a conquering hero and was given command of an army in training to invade England. Believing that the French were unready for such an invasion, he proposed instead to strike indirectly at Britain by taking Egypt and threatening India, a major source of British wealth. But the British controlled the seas and, by 1799, had cut off supplies from Napoleon's army in Egypt. Seeing no future in certain defeat, Napoleon did not hesitate to abandon his army and return to Paris where he participated in the coup d'etat that ultimately led to his virtual dictatorship of France. He was only thirty years old at the time.

With the coup d'etat of 1799, a new form of the Republic was proclaimed with a constitution that established a bicameral legislative assembly elected indirectly

Napoleon and Psychological Warfare

In 1796, at the age of twenty-seven, Napoleon Bonaparte was given command of the French army in Italy where he won a series of stunning victories. His use of speed, deception, and surprise to overwhelm his opponents is well known. In this selection from a proclamation to his troops in Italy, Napoleon also appears as a master of psychological warfare.

Napoleon Bonaparte, Proclamation to the French Troops in Italy (April 26, 1796)

Soldiers:

In a fortnight you have won six victories, taken twenty-one standards, fifty-five pieces of artillery, several strong positions, and conquered the richest part of Piedmont [in northern Italy]; you have captured 15,000 prisoners and killed or wounded more than 10,000 men. . . . You have won battles without cannon, crossed rivers without bridges, made forced marches without shoes, camped without brandy and often without bread. Soldiers of liberty, only republican troops could have endured what you have endured. Soldiers, you have our thanks! The grateful Patrie [nation] will owe its prosperity to you. . . .

The two armies which but recently attacked you with audacity are fleeing before you in terror; the wicked men who laughed at your misery and rejoiced at the thought of the triumphs of your enemies are confounded and trembling.

But, soldiers, as yet you have done nothing compared with what remains to be done. . . . Undoubtedly the greatest obstacles have been overcome; but you still have battles to fight, cities to capture, rivers to cross. Is there one among you whose courage is abating? No. . . . All of you are consumed with a desire to extend the glory of the French people; all of you long to humiliate those arrogant kings who dare to contemplate placing us in fetters; all of you desire to dictate a glorious peace, one which will indemnify the Patrie for the immense sacrifices it has made; all of you wish to be able to say with pride as you return to your villages, "I was with the victorious army of Italy!"

to reduce the role of elections. Executive power in the new government was vested in the hands of three consuls although as Article 42 of the constitution said, "The decision of the First Consul shall suffice." As first consul, Napoleon directly controlled the entire executive authority of government. He had overwhelming influence over the legislature, appointed members of the bureaucracy, controlled the army, and conducted foreign affairs. In 1802, Napoleon was made consul for life and in 1804 returned France to monarchy when he crowned himself as Emperor Napoleon I. This step undoubtedly satisfied his enormous ego but also stabilized the regime and provided a permanency not possible in the consulate. The revolutionary era that had begun with an attempt to limit arbitrary government had ended with a government far more autocratic than the monarchy of the old regime. As his reign progressed and the demands of war increased, Napoleon's regime became ever more dictatorial.

The Domestic Policies of Emperor Napoleon

Napoleon often claimed that he had preserved the gains of the Revolution for the French people. The ideal of republican liberty had, of course, been destroyed by Napoleon's thinly disguised autocracy. But were revolutionary ideals maintained in other ways? An examination of his domestic policies will enable us to judge the truth or falsehood of Napoleon's assertion.

In 1801, Napoleon made peace with the oldest and most implacable enemy of the Revolution, the Catholic church. Napoleon himself was devoid of any personal faith; he was an eighteenth-century rationalist who regarded religion at most as a convenience. In Egypt, he called himself a Muslim; in France, a Catholic. But Napoleon saw the necessity to come to terms with the Catholic church in order to stabilize his regime. In 1800, he had declared to the clergy of Milan: "It is my firm intention that the Christian, Catholic, and Roman religion shall be preserved in its entirety. . . . No society can exist without morality; there is no good morality without religion. It is religion alone, therefore, that gives to the State a firm and durable support."[19] Soon after making this statement, Napoleon opened negotiations with Pope Pius VII to reestablish the Catholic church in France.

Both sides gained from the Concordat that Napoleon arranged with the pope in 1801. Although the pope gained the right to depose French bishops, this gave him little real control over the French Catholic church since the state retained the right to nominate bishops. The Catholic church was also permitted to hold processions again and reopen the seminaries. But Napoleon gained more than the pope. Just by signing the Concordat, the pope acknowledged the accomplishments of the Revolution. Moreover, the pope agreed not to raise the question of the church lands confiscated during the Revolution. Contrary to the pope's wishes, Catholicism was not reestablished as the state religion; Napoleon was only willing to recognize

The Man of Destiny

Napoleon possessed an overwhelming sense of his own importance. Among the images he fostered, especially as his successes multiplied and his megalomaniacal tendencies intensified, were those of the man of destiny and the great man who masters luck.

Selections from Napoleon

When a deplorable weakness and ceaseless vacillations become manifest in supreme councils; when, yielding in turn to the influences of opposing parties, making shift from day to day, and marching with uncertain pace, a government has proved the full measure of its impotence; when even the most moderate citizens are forced to admit that the State is no longer governed; when, in fine, the administration adds to its nullity at home the gravest guilt it can acquire in the eyes of a proud nation—I mean its humiliation abroad—then a vague unrest spreads through the social body, the instinct of self-preservation is stirred, and the nation casts a sweeping eye over itself, as if to seek a man who can save it.

This guardian angel a great nation harbors in its bosom at all times; yet sometimes he is late in making his appearance. Indeed, it is not enough for him to exist: he also must be known. He must know himself. Until then, all endeavors are in vain, all schemes collapse. The inertia of the masses protects the nominal government, and despite its ineptitude and weakness the efforts of its enemies fail. But let that impatiently awaited savior give a sudden sign of his existence, and the people's instinct will divine him and call upon him. The obstacles are smoothed before his steps, and a whole great nation, flying to see him pass, will seem to be saying: "Here is the man!"

. . . A consecutive series of great actions never is the result of chance and luck; it always is the product of planning and genius. Great men are rarely known to fail in their most perilous enterprises. . . . Is it because they are lucky that they become great? No, but being great, they have been able to master luck.

Catholicism as the religion of a majority of the French people. The clergy would be paid by the state, but to avoid the appearance of a state church, Protestant ministers were also put on the state payroll. As a result of the Concordat, the Catholic church was no longer an enemy of the French government. At the same time, the agreement reassured those who had acquired church lands during the Revolution that they would not be stripped of them, an assurance that obviously made them supporters of the Napoleonic regime.

Before the Revolution, France did not have a single set of laws, but rather virtually 300 different legal systems. During the Revolution, efforts were made to prepare a codification of laws for the entire nation, but it remained for Napoleon to bring the work to completion in seven codes of law, of which the most important was the Civil Code (or Code Napoléon). This preserved most of the revolutionary gains by recognizing the principle of the equality of all citizens before the law, the right of individuals to choose their professions, religious toleration, and the abolition of serfdom and feudalism. Property rights continued to be carefully protected while the interests of employers were safeguarded by outlawing trade unions and strikes. The Civil Code clearly reflected the revolutionary aspirations for a uniform legal system, legal equality, and protection of property and individuals.

But the rights of some people were strictly curtailed by the Civil Code. During the radical phase of the French Revolution, new laws had made divorce an easy process for both husbands and wives, restricted the rights of fathers over their children (they could no longer have their children put in prison arbitrarily), and allowed all children (including daughters) to inherit property equally. Napoleon's Civil Code undid most of this legislation. The control of fathers over their families was restored. Divorce was still allowed, but made more difficult for women to obtain. A wife caught in adultery, for example, could be divorced by her husband and even imprisoned. A husband, on the other hand, could only be accused of adultery if he moved his mistress into his home. Women were now "less equal than men" in other ways as well. When they married, their property was brought under the control of their husbands. In lawsuits they were treated as minors, and their testimony was regarded as less reliable than that of men.

Napoleon also worked on rationalizing the bureaucratic structure of France by developing a powerful, centralized administrative machine. During the Revolution, the National Assembly had divided France into eighty-three departments and replaced the provincial estates, nobles, and intendants with self-governing assemblies. Napoleon kept the departments but eliminated the locally elected assemblies and instituted new officials, the most important of which were the prefects. As the central government's agents, appointed by the first consul (Napoleon), the prefects were responsible for supervising all aspects of local government. Yet they were not local men and their careers depended on the central government.

As part of Napoleon's overhaul of the administrative system, tax collection became systematic and efficient

THE CORONATION OF NAPOLEON. In 1804, Napoleon restored monarchy to France when he crowned himself as emperor. In the coronation scene painted by Jacques-Louis David, Napoleon is shown crowning the empress Josephine while the pope looks on. Shown seated in the box in the background is Napoleon's mother, even though she was not at the ceremony.

(which it had never been under the old regime). Taxes were now collected by professional collectors employed by the state who dealt directly with each individual taxpayer. No tax exemptions due to birth, status, or special arrangement were granted. In principle these changes had been introduced in 1789, but not until Napoleon did they actually work. In 1802, the first consul proclaimed a balanced budget.

Administrative centralization required a bureaucracy of capable officials, and Napoleon worked hard to develop one. Early on, the regime showed its preference for experts and cared little whether that expertise had been acquired in royal or revolutionary bureaucracies. Promotion, whether in civil or military offices, was to be based not on rank or birth but only on demonstrated abilities. This was, of course, what many bourgeoisie had wanted before the Revolution. Napoleon, however, also created a new aristocracy based on merit in the state service. Napoleon created 3,263 nobles between 1808 and 1814; nearly 60 percent were military officers, and the remainder came from the upper ranks of the civil service and other state and local officials. Socially, only 22 percent of Napoleon's aristocracy came from the nobility of the old regime; almost 60 percent were bourgeois in origin.

In his domestic policies, then, Napoleon both destroyed and preserved aspects of the Revolution. Although equality was preserved in the law code and the opening of careers to talent, the creation of a new aristocracy, the strong protection accorded to property rights, and the use of conscription for the military make it clear that much equality had been lost. Liberty had been replaced by an initially benevolent despotism that grew increasingly arbitrary. Napoleon shut down sixty of France's seventy-three newspapers and insisted that all manuscripts be subjected to government scrutiny before they were published. Even the mail was opened by government police. One prominent writer—Germaine de Staël—refused to accept Napoleon's growing despotism. Educated in Enlightenment ideas, Madame de Staël wrote novels and political works that denounced Napoleon's rule as tyrannical. Napoleon banned her books in France and exiled her to the German states, where she continued to write.

Napoleon's Empire and the European Response

When Napoleon became consul in 1799, France was at war with a second European coalition of Russia, Great Britain, and Austria. Napoleon realized the need for a pause. He remarked to a Prussian diplomat "that the French Revolution is not finished so long as the scourge of war lasts. . . . I want peace, as much to settle the present French government, as to save the world from chaos."[20] The peace he sought was achieved at Amiens in March 1802 and left France with new frontiers and a number of client territories from the North Sea to the Adriatic. But the peace did not last because the British and French both regarded it as temporary and had little inten-

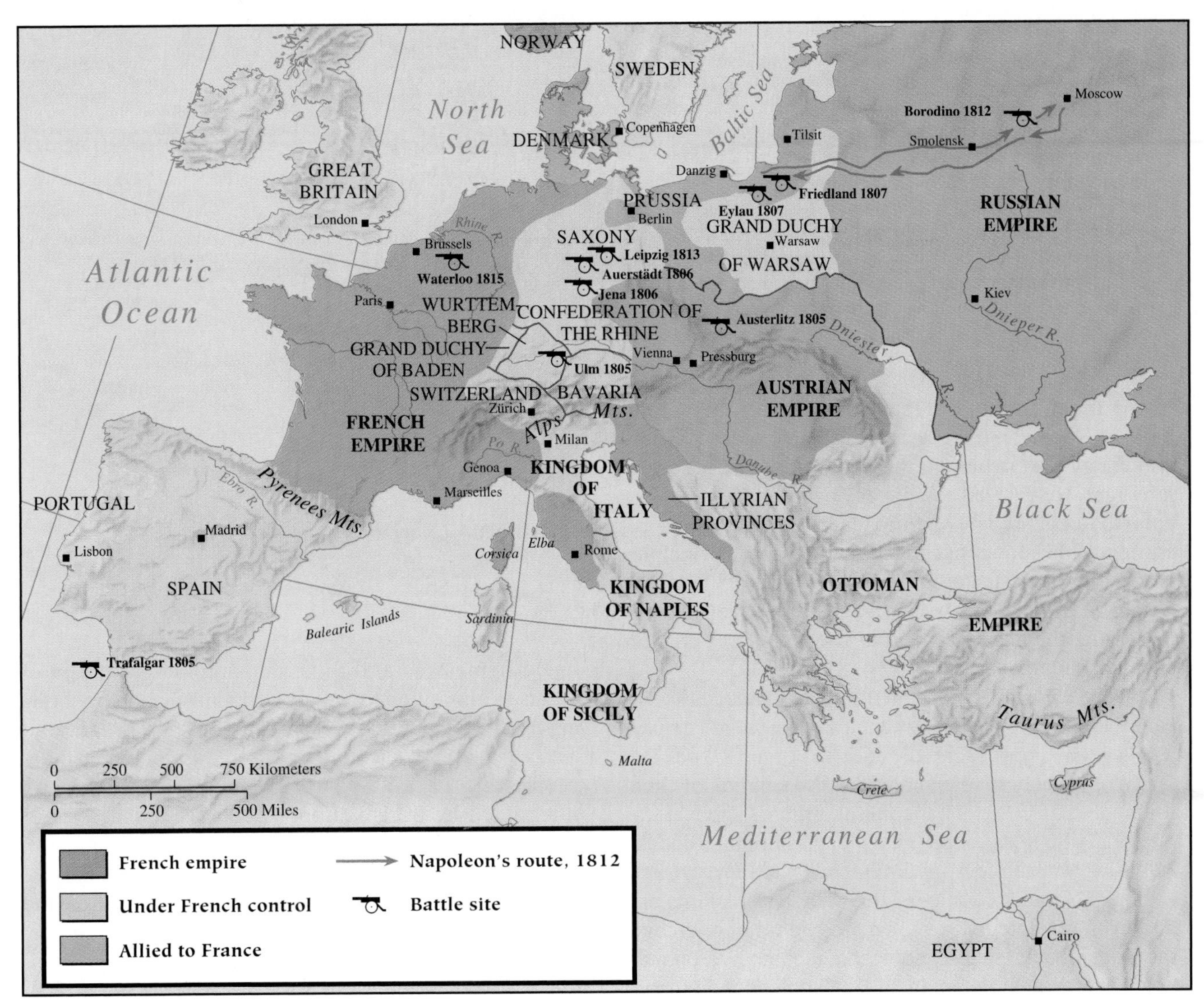

MAP 19.3 Napoleon's Grand Empire.

tion of adhering to its terms. In 1803, war was renewed with Britain, which was soon joined by Austria, Russia, and Prussia in the Third Coalition. In a series of battles at Ulm, Austerlitz, Jena, and Eylau from 1805 to 1807, Napoleon's Grand Army defeated the continental members of the coalition, giving him the opportunity to create a new European order. The Grand Empire was composed of three major parts: the French empire, a series of dependent states, and allied states. The French empire, the inner core of the Grand Empire, consisted of an enlarged France extending to the Rhine in the east and including the western half of Italy north of Rome. Dependent states included Spain, Holland, the kingdom of Italy, the Swiss Republic, the Grand Duchy of Warsaw, and the Confederation of the Rhine, the latter a union of all German states except Austria and Prussia. Allied states were those defeated by Napoleon and forced to join his struggle against Britain; they included Prussia, Austria, and Russia. Although the internal structure of the Grand Empire varied outside its inner core, Napoleon considered himself leader of the whole: "Europe cannot be at rest except under a single head who will have kings for his officers, who will distribute his kingdom to his lieutenants."

Within his empire, Napoleon demanded obedience, in part because he needed a common front against the British and in part because his growing egotism required obedience to his will. But as a child of the Enlightenment and Revolution, Napoleon also sought acceptance everywhere of certain revolutionary principles, including legal equality, religious toleration, and economic freedom. As he explained to his brother Jerome after he had made him king of the new German state of Westphalia:

> What the peoples of Germany desire most impatiently is that talented commoners should have the same right to your esteem and to public employments as the nobles,

that any trace of serfdom and of an intermediate hierarchy between the sovereign and the lowest class of the people should be completely abolished. The benefits of the Code Napoléon, the publicity of judicial procedure, the creation of juries must be so many distinguishing marks of your monarchy. . . . What nation would wish to return under the arbitrary Prussian government once it had tasted the benefits of a wise and liberal administration? The peoples of Germany, the peoples of France, of Italy, of Spain all desire equality and liberal ideas. I have guided the affairs of Europe for many years now, and I have had occasion to convince myself that the buzzing of the privileged classes is contrary to the general opinion. Be a constitutional king.[21]

In the inner core and dependent states of his Grand Empire, Napoleon tried to destroy the old order. Nobility and clergy everywhere in these states lost their special privileges. He decreed equality of opportunity with offices open to talent, equality before the law, and religious toleration. This spread of French revolutionary principles was an important factor in the development of liberal traditions in these countries. These reforms have led some historians to view Napoleon as the last of the enlightened absolutists.

Like Hitler 130 years later, Napoleon hoped that his Grand Empire would last for centuries; like Hitler's empire, it collapsed almost as rapidly as it had been formed. Two major reasons help to explain this, the survival of Great Britain and the force of nationalism. Britain's survival was primarily due to its seapower. As long as Britain ruled the waves, it was almost invulnerable to military attack. Although Napoleon contemplated an invasion of England and even collected ships for it, he could not overcome the British navy's decisive defeat of a combined French-Spanish fleet at Trafalgar in 1805. Napoleon then turned to his Continental System to defeat Britain. Put into effect between 1806 and 1807, it attempted to prevent British goods from reaching the European continent in order to weaken Britain economically and destroy its capacity to wage war. But the Continental System failed. Allied states resented the ever-tightening French economic hegemony; some began to cheat and others to resist, thereby opening the door to British collaboration. New markets in the Levant and in Latin America also provided compensation for the British. Indeed, by 1809–1810 British overseas exports were at near-record highs.

A second important factor in the defeat of Napoleon was nationalism. This political creed had arisen during the French Revolution in the French people's emphasis on brotherhood (*fraternité*) and solidarity against other peoples. Nationalism involved the unique cultural identity of a people based on common language, religion, and national symbols. The spirit of French nationalism had made possible the mass armies of the revolutionary and Napoleonic eras. But Napoleon's spread of the principles of the French Revolution beyond France inadvertently brought a spread of nationalism as well. The French aroused nationalism in two ways: by making themselves hated oppressors and thus arousing the patriotism of others in opposition to French nationalism, and by showing the people of Europe what nationalism was and what a nation in arms could do. The lesson was not lost on other peoples and rulers. A Spanish uprising against Napoleon's rule, aided by British support, kept a French force of 200,000 pinned down for years.

CHRONOLOGY

The Napoleonic Era, 1799–1815

Napoleon as first consul	1799–1804
Concordat with Catholic church	1801
Peace of Amiens	1802
Emperor Napoleon I	1804–1815
Battles of Austerlitz; Trafalgar; Ulm	1805
Battle of Jena	1806
Continental System established	1806
Battle of Eylau	1807
Invasion of Russia	1812
War of liberation	1813–1814
Exile to Elba	1814
Battle of Waterloo; exile to Saint Helena	1815
Death of Napoleon	1821

The beginning of Napoleon's downfall came in 1812 with his invasion of Russia. The latter's defection from the Continental System left Napoleon with little choice. Although aware of the risks in invading such a large country, he also knew that if the Russians were allowed to challenge the Continental System unopposed, others would soon follow suit. In June 1812, a Grand Army of more than 600,000 men entered Russia. Napoleon's hopes for victory depended on quickly meeting and defeating the Russian armies, but the Russian forces refused to give battle and retreated for hundreds of miles while torching their own villages and countryside to prevent Napoleon's army from finding food and forage. When the Russians did stop to fight at Borodino, Napoleon's forces won an indecisive and costly victory. When the remaining troops of the Grand Army arrived in Moscow, they found the city ablaze. Lacking food and supplies, Napoleon abandoned Moscow late in October and made the "Great Retreat" across Russia in terrible winter conditions. Only 40,000 out of the original army managed to straggle back to Poland in January 1813. This military disaster then led to a war of liberation all over Europe, culminating in Napoleon's defeat in April 1814.

The defeated emperor of the French was allowed to play ruler on the island of Elba, off the cost of Tuscany, while the Bourbon monarchy was restored to France in the person of Louis XVIII, brother of the executed king. But the new king had little support, and Napoleon, bored on the island of Elba, slipped back into France. The troops sent to capture him went over to his side, and Napoleon entered Paris in triumph on March 20, 1815. The powers that had defeated him pledged once more to fight this person they called the "Enemy and Disturber of the Tranquility of the World." Having decided to strike first at his enemies, Napoleon raised yet another army and moved to attack the nearest allied forces stationed in Belgium. At Waterloo on June 18, Napoleon met a combined British and Prussian army under the duke of Wellington and suffered a bloody defeat. This time the victorious allies exiled him to Saint Helena, a small and forsaken island in the South Atlantic. Only Napoleon's memory would continue to haunt French political life.

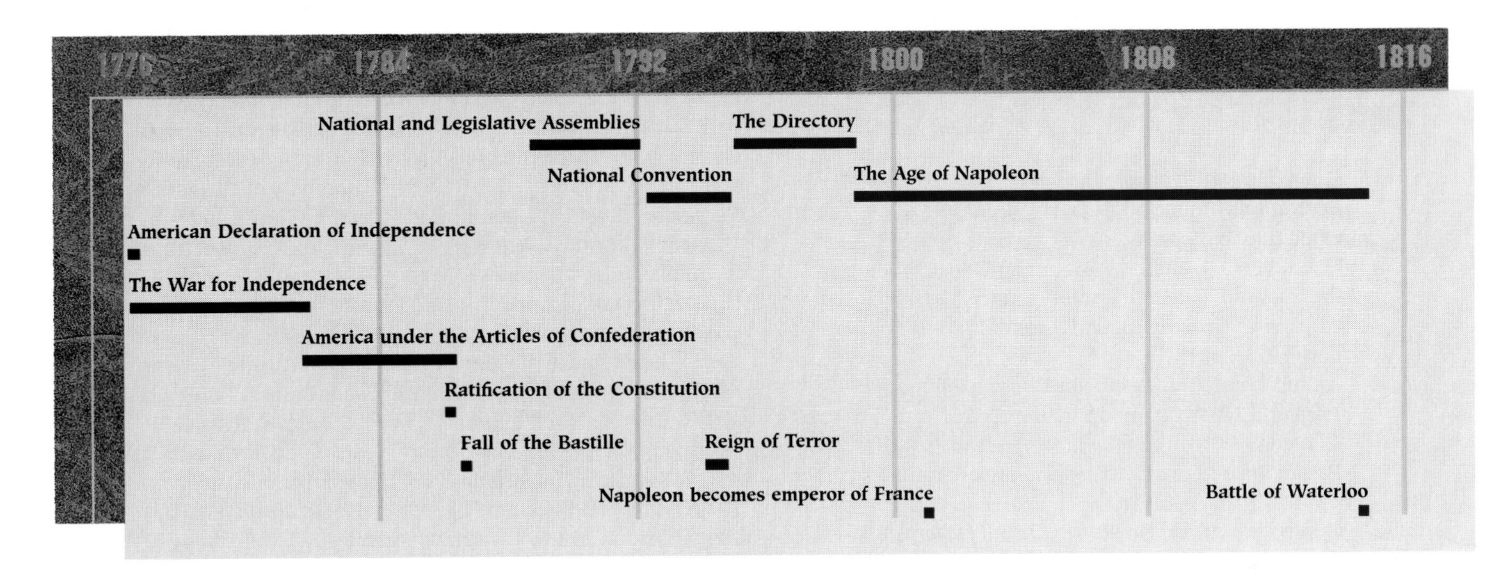

CONCLUSION

The revolutionary era of the late eighteenth century witnessed a dramatic political transformation. Revolutionary upheavals, beginning in North America and continuing in France, produced movements for political liberty and equality. The documents created by these revolutions, the Declaration of Independence and the Declaration of the Rights of Man and the Citizen, embodied the fundamental ideas of the Enlightenment and set forth a liberal political agenda based on a belief in popular sovereignty—the people are the source of political power—and the principles of liberty and equality. Liberty, frequently limited in practice, meant, in theory, freedom from arbitrary power as well as the freedom to think, write, and worship as one chose. Equality meant equality in rights and equality of opportunity based on talent rather than birth. In practice, equality remained limited; those who owned property had greater opportunities for voting and office-holding, and there was certainly no equality between men and women.

The leaders of France's liberal revolution, achieved between 1789 and 1791, were men of property, both bourgeois and noble, but they were assisted by commoners, both sans-culottes and peasants. Yet the liberal revolution, despite the hopes of the men of property, was not the end of the Revolution. The decision of the revolutionaries to go to war "revolutionized the Revolution," opening the door to a more radical, democratic, and violent stage. The excesses of the Reign of Terror, however, led to a reaction, first under the Directory and then under Napoleon, when men of property were willing to give up liberty in exchange for order, security, and economic opportunity. Napoleon, while diminishing freedom by establishing order and centralizing the government, shrewdly preserved equality of rights and the opening of careers to talent and integrated the bourgeoisie and old nobility into a new elite of property owners. For despite the anti-aristocratic revolutionary rhetoric and the loss of their privileges, nobles remained important landowners. Though the nobles lost some of their lands during the Revolution, they were still the largest proprietors in the early 1800s. The great gainers from the redistribution of clerical and noble property, however, had been the bourgeoisie, who also gained dramatically when important government and military positions were opened to men of talent. After 1800, an elite group of property owners, both noble and middle class, dominated French society.

The French Revolution created a modern revolutionary concept. No one had foreseen or consciously planned the upheaval that began in 1789, but after 1789 "revolutionaries" knew that the proper use of mass uprisings could succeed in overthrowing unwanted governments. The French Revolution became the classical political and social model for revolution. At the same time, the liberal and national political ideals created by the Revolution and spread through Europe by Napoleon's conquests dominated the political landscape of the nineteenth and early twentieth centuries. A new European era had begun and Europe would never again be the same.

NOTES

1. Quoted in R. R. Palmer, *The Age of the Democratic Revolutions* (Princeton, N.J., 1959), 1:239.
2. Quoted in ibid., p. 242.
3. Quoted in O. J. Hufton, "Toward an Understanding of the Poor of Eighteenth Century France," in J. F. Bosher, ed., *French Government and Society, 1500–1850* (London, 1973), p. 152.
4. Arthur Young, *Travels in France during the Years 1787, 1788 and 1789* (Cambridge, 1929), p. 23.
5. Quoted in D. M. G. Sutherland, *France 1789–1815: Revolution and Counter-Revolution* (New York, 1986), p. 74.
6. Quoted in William Doyle, *The Oxford History of the French Revolution* (Oxford, 1989), p. 156.
7. Quoted in ibid., p. 184.
8. Quoted in J. Hardman, ed., *French Revolution Documents* (Oxford, 1973), 2:23.
9. Quoted in W. Scott, *Terror and Repression in Revolutionary Marseilles* (London, 1973), p. 84.
10. Quoted in H. Morse Stephens, *The Principal Speeches of the Statesmen and Orators of the French Revolution* (Oxford, 1892), 2:189.
11. Quoted in Leo Gershoy, *The Era of the French Revolution* (Princeton, N.J., 1957), p. 157.
12. Quoted in J. M. Thompson, *French Revolution Documents* (Oxford, 1933), pp. 258–259.
13. Quoted in Doyle, *The Oxford History of the French Revolution*, p. 254.
14. Quoted in R. R. Palmer, *Twelve Who Ruled* (New York, 1965), p. 75.
15. Quoted in Darline Gay Levy, Harriet Branson Applewhite, and Mary Durham Johnson, eds., *Women in Revolutionary Paris, 1789–1795* (Urbana, Ill., 1979), p. 132.
16. Ibid., pp. 219–220.
17. Quoted in Elizabeth G. Sledziewski, "The French Revolution as the Turning Point," in Geneviève Fraisse and Michelle Perrot, eds., *A History of Women in the West* (Cambridge, 1993), 4:39.
18. Quoted in François Furet and Mona Ozouf, *A Critical Dictionary of the French Revolution*, trans. Arthur Goldhammer (Cambridge, Mass., 1989), p. 545.
19. Quoted in Felix Markham, *Napoleon* (New York, 1963), pp. 92–93.
20. Quoted in Doyle, *The Oxford History of the French Revolution*, p. 381.
21. Quoted in J. Christopher Herold, ed., *The Mind of Napoleon* (New York, 1955), pp. 74–75.

SUGGESTIONS FOR FURTHER READING

A well-written, up-to-date introduction to the French Revolution can be found in W. Doyle, *The Oxford History of the French Revolution* (Oxford, 1989). For the entire revolutionary and Napoleonic eras, see O. Connelly, *The French Revolution and Napoleonic Era*, 2d ed. (Fort Worth, 1991); and D. M. G. Sutherland, *France 1789–1815: Revolution and Counter-Revolution* (New York, 1986). Two brief works are A. Forrest, *The French Revolution* (Oxford, 1995); and J. M. Roberts, *The French Revolution*, 2d ed. (New York, 1997). A different approach to the French Revolution can be found in E. Kennedy, *A Cultural History of the French Revolution* (New Haven, Conn., 1989). Three comprehensive reference works are S. F. Scott and B. Rothaus, eds., *Historical Dictionary of the French Revolution*, 2 vols. (Westport, Conn., 1985); F. Furet and M. Ozouf, *A Critical Dictionary of the French Revolution*, trans. A. Goldhammer (Cambridge, Mass., 1989); and O. Connelly, et al., *Historical Dictionary of Napoleonic France, 1799–1815* (Westport, Conn., 1985).

The origins of the French Revolution are examined in W. Doyle, *Origins of the French Revolution* (Oxford, 1988). See also R. Chartier, *The Cultural Origins of the French Revolution* (Durham, N.C., 1991). On the early years of the Revolution, see M. Kennedy, *The Jacobin Clubs in the French Revolution: The First Years* (Princeton, N.J., 1982); N. Hampson, *Prelude to Terror* (Oxford, 1988); T. Tackett, *Becoming a Revolutionary* (Princeton, N.J., 1996), on the deputies to the National Assembly; and J. Markoff, *The Abolition of Feudalism: Peasants, Lords, and Legislators in the French Revolution* (University Park, Pa., 1996). Important works on the radical stage of the French Revolution include N. Hampson, *The Terror in the French Revolution* (London, 1981); A. Soboul, *The Sans-Culottes* (New York, 1972); R. R. Palmer, *Twelve Who Ruled* (New York, 1965); and R. Cobb, *The People's Armies* (London, 1987). For a biography of Robespierre, one of the leading figures of this period, see N. Hampson, *The Life and Opinions of Maximilien Robespierre* (London, 1974). The importance of the revolutionary wars in the radical stage of the Revolution is underscored in T. C. W. Blanning, *The French Revolutionary Wars, 1787–1802* (New York, 1996). The importance of the popular revolutionary crowds is examined in the classic work by G. Rudé, *The Crowd in the French Revolution* (Oxford, 1959); and D. Roche, *The People of Paris: An Essay in Popular Culture* (Berkeley, 1987). On the Directory, see M. Lyons, *France under the Directory* (Cambridge, 1975); and R. B. Rose, *Gracchus Babeuf* (Stanford, 1978).

The religious history of the French Revolution is covered in J. McManners, *The French Revolution and the Church* (London, 1969). On the Great Fear, there is the classic work by G. Lefebvre, *The Great Fear of 1789: Rural Panic in Revolutionary France* (London, 1973). On the role of women in revolutionary France, see O. Hufton, *Women and the Limits of Citizenship in the French Revolution* (Toronto, 1992); J. Landes, *Women and the Public Sphere in the Age of the French Revolution* (Ithaca, N.Y., 1988); and the essays in G. Fraisse and M. Perrot, eds., *A History of Women in the West*, vol. 4 (Cambridge, Mass., 1993). There is a good collection of essays in S. E. Melzer and L. Rabine, eds., *Rebel Daughters: Women and the French Revolution* (New York, 1992).

The best, brief biography of Napoleon is F. Markham, *Napoleon* (New York, 1963). Also valuable are G. J. Ellis,

Napoleon (New York, 1997); M. Lyons, *Napoleon Bonaparte and the Legacy of the French Revolution* (New York, 1994); and the recent massive biographies by F. J. McLynn, *Napoleon: A Biography* (London, 1997); and A. Schom, *Napoleon Bonaparte* (New York, 1997). On Napoleon's wars, see S. J. Woolf, *Napoleon's Integration of Europe* (New York, 1991).

A history of the revolutionary era in America can be found in R. Middlekauff, *The Glorious Cause: The American Revolution, 1763–1789* (New York, 1982); and C. Bonwick, *The American Revolution* (Charlottesville, Va., 1991). The importance of ideology is treated in G. Wood, *The Radicalism of the American Revolution* (New York, 1992). A comparative study that puts the American Revolution into a larger context is R. R. Palmer, *The Age of the Democratic Revolutions: A Political History of Europe and America, 1760–1800,* 2 vols. (Princeton, N.J., 1959–64).

For additional reading, go to InfoTrac College Edition, your online research library at http://web1.infotrac-college.com

Enter the search terms *French Revolution* using Key Terms.

Enter the search terms *American Revolution* using Key Terms.

Enter the search term *Napoleon* using Key Terms.

Enter the search terms *Napoleonic Wars* using Key Terms.

Glossary

absolutism a form of government where the sovereign power or ultimate authority rested in the hands of a monarch who claimed to rule by divine right and was therefore responsible only to God.

Agricultural (Neolithic) Revolution the shift from hunting animals and gathering plants for sustenance to producing food by systematic agriculture that occurred gradually between 10,000 and 4000 B.C. (the Neolithic or "New Stone" Age).

agricultural revolution the application of new agricultural techniques that allowed for a large increase in productivity in the eighteenth century.

anarchism a political theory that holds that all governments and existing social institutions are unnecessary and advocates a society based on voluntary cooperation.

anti-Semitism hostility toward or discrimination against Jews.

appeasement the policy, followed by the European nations in the 1930s, of accepting Hitler's annexation of Austria and Czechoslovakia in the belief that meeting his demands would assure peace and stability.

Arianism a Christian heresy that taught that Jesus was inferior to God. Though condemned by the Council of Nicaea in 325, Arianism was adopted by many of the Germanic peoples who entered the Roman Empire over the next centuries.

aristocracy a class of hereditary nobility in medieval Europe; a warrior class who shared a distinctive lifestyle based on the institution of knighthood, although there were social divisions within the group based on extremes of wealth.

Ausgleich the "Compromise" of 1867 that created the dual monarchy of Austria-Hungary. Austria and Hungary each had its own capital, constitution, and legislative assembly, but were united under one monarch.

authoritarian state a state that has a dictatorial government and some other trappings of a totalitarian state, but does not demand that the masses be actively involved in the regime's goals as totalitarian states do.

auxiliaries troops enlisted from the subject peoples of the Roman Empire to supplement the regular legions composed of Roman citizens.

balance of power a distribution of power among several states such that no single nation can dominate or interfere with the interests of another.

benefice in the Christian church, a position, such as a bishopric, that consisted of both a sacred office and the right of the holder to the annual revenues from the position.

bicameral legislature a legislature with two houses.

Black Death the outbreak of plague (mostly bubonic) in the mid-fourteenth century that killed from 25 to 50 percent of Europe's population.

Blitzkrieg "lightning war." A war conducted with great speed and force, as in Germany's advance at the beginning of World War II.

Bolsheviks a small faction of the Russian Social Democratic Party who were led by Lenin and dedicated to violent revolution; seized power in Russia in 1917 and were subsequently renamed the Communists.

boyars the Russian nobility.

Brezhnev Doctrine the doctrine, enunciated by Leonid Brezhnev, that the Soviet Union had a right to intervene if socialism was threatened in another socialist state; used to justify the use of Soviet troops in Czechoslovakia in 1968.

caliph the secular leader of the Islamic community.

capital material wealth used or available for use in the production of more wealth.

cartel a combination of independent commercial enterprises that work together to control prices and limit competition.

Cartesian dualism Descartes's principle of the separation of mind and matter (and mind and body) that enabled scientists to view matter as something separate from themselves that could be investigated by reason.

chansons de geste a form of vernacular literature in the High Middle Ages that consisted of heroic epics focusing on the deeds of warriors.

chivalry the ideal of civilized behavior that emerged among the nobility in the eleventh and twelfth centuries under the influence of the church; a code of ethics knights were expected to uphold.

Christian (northern) humanism an intellectual movement in northern Europe in the late fifteenth and early sixteenth centuries that combined the interest in the classics of the Italian Renaissance with an interest in the sources of early Christianity, including the New Testament and the writings of the church fathers.

civic humanism an intellectual movement of the Italian Renaissance that saw Cicero, who was both an intellectual and a statesman, as the ideal and held that humanists should be involved in government and use their rhetorical training in the service of the state.

civil rights the basic rights of citizens including equality before the law, freedom of speech and press, and freedom from arbitrary arrest.

Cold War the ideological conflict between the Soviet Union and the United States after World War II.

collective farms large farms created in the Soviet Union by Stalin by combining many small holdings into one large farm worked by the peasants under government supervision.

collective security the use of an international army raised by an association of nations to deter aggression and keep the peace.

coloni free tenant farmers who worked as sharecroppers on the large estates of the Roman Empire (singular: *colonus*).

common law law common to the entire kingdom of England; imposed by the king's courts beginning in the twelfth century to replace the customary law used in county and feudal courts that varied from place to place.

commune in medieval Europe, an association of townspeople bound together by a sworn oath for the purpose of obtaining basic liberties from the lord of the territory in which the town was located; also, the self-governing town after receiving its liberties.

conciliarism a movement in fourteenth- and fifteenth-century Europe that held that final authority in spiritual matters resided with a general church council, not the pope; emerged in response to the Avignon papacy and the Great Schism and used to justify the summoning of the Council of Constance (1414–1418).

condottieri leaders of bands of mercenary soldiers in Renaissance Italy who sold their services to the highest bidder.

conquistadors "conquerors." Leaders in the Spanish conquests in the Americas, especially Mexico and Peru, in the sixteenth century.

conscription a military draft.

conservatism an ideology based on tradition and social stability that favored the maintenance of established institutions, organized religion, and obedience to authority and resisted change, especially abrupt change.

consuls the chief executive officers of the Roman Republic. Two were chosen annually to administer the government and lead the army in battle.

consumer society a term applied to Western society after World War II as the working classes adopted the consumption patterns of the middle class and installment plans, credit cards, and easy credit made consumer goods such as appliances and automobiles widely available.

Continental System Napoleon's effort to bar British goods from the Continent in the hope of weakening Britain's economy and destroying its capacity to wage war.

cosmopolitanism the quality of being sophisticated and having wide international experience.

cottage industry a system of textile manufacturing in which spinners and weavers worked at home in their cottages using raw materials supplied to them by capitalist entrepreneurs.

cultural relativism the belief that no culture is superior to another because culture is a matter of custom, not reason, and derives its meaning from the group holding it.

cuneiform "wedge-shaped." A system of writing developed by the Sumerians that consisted of wedge-shaped impressions made by a reed stylus on clay tablets.

decolonization the process of becoming free of colonial status and achieving statehood; occurred in most of the world's colonies between 1947 and 1962.

deism belief in God as the creator of the universe who, after setting it in motion, ceased to have any direct involvement in it and allowed it to run according to its own natural laws.

demesne the part of a manor retained under the direct control of the lord and worked by the serfs as part of their labor services.

depression a very severe, protracted economic downturn with high levels of unemployment.

destalinization the policy of denouncing and undoing the most repressive aspects of Stalin's regime; begun by Nikita Khrushchev in 1956.

détente the relaxation of tension between the Soviet Union and the United States that occurred in the 1970s.

dialectic logic, one of the seven liberal arts that made up the medieval curriculum. In Marxist thought, the process by which all change occurs through the clash of antagonistic elements.

Diaspora the scattering of Jews throughout the ancient world after the Babylonian captivity in the sixth century B.C.

dictator in the Roman Republic, an official granted unlimited power to run the state for a short period of time, usually six months, during an emergency.

diocese the area under the jurisdiction of a Christian bishop; based originally on Roman administrative districts.

direct representation a system of choosing delegates to a representative assembly in which citizens vote directly for the delegates who will represent them.

divination the practice of seeking to foretell future events by interpreting divine signs, which could appear in various forms, such as in entrails of animals, in patterns in smoke, or in dreams.

divine-right monarchy a monarchy based on the belief that monarchs receive their power directly from God and are responsible to no one except God.

domino theory the belief that if the Communists succeeded in Vietnam, other countries in Southeast and East Asia would also fall (like dominoes) to communism; a justification for the U.S. intervention in Vietnam.

dualism the belief that the universe is dominated by two opposing forces, one good and the other evil.

dynastic state a state where the maintenance and expansion of the interests of the ruling family is the primary consideration.

economic imperialism the process in which banks and corporations from developed nations invest in underdeveloped regions and establish a major presence there in the hope of making high profits; not necessarily the same as colonial expansion in that businesses invest where they can make a profit, which may not be in their own nation's colonies.

empiricism the practice of relying on observation and experiment.

enclosure movement in the eighteenth century, the fencing in of the old open fields, combining many small holdings into larger units that could be farmed more efficiently.

encyclical a letter from the pope to all the bishops of the Roman Catholic church.

enlightened absolutism an absolute monarchy where the ruler follows the principles of the Enlightenment by introducing reforms for the improvement of society, allowing freedom of speech and the press, permitting religious toleration, expanding education, and ruling in accordance with the laws.

Enlightenment an eighteenth-century intellectual movement, led by the philosophes, that stressed the application of reason and the scientific method to all aspects of life.

entrepreneur one who organizes, operates, and assumes the risk in a business venture in the expectation of making a profit.

Epicureanism a philosophy founded by Epicurus in the fourth century B.C. that taught that happiness (freedom from emotional turmoil) could be achieved through the pursuit of pleasure (intellectual rather than sensual pleasure).

equestrians a group of extremely wealthy men in the late Roman Republic who were effectively barred from high office, but sought political power commensurate with their wealth; called equestrians because many had gotten their start as cavalry officers (*equites*).

ethnic cleansing the policy of killing or forcibly removing people of another ethnic group; used by the Serbs against Bosnian Muslims in the 1990s.

eucharist a Christian sacrament in which consecrated bread and wine are consumed in celebration of Jesus' Last Supper; also called the Lord's Supper or communion.

evolutionary socialism a socialist doctrine espoused by Eduard Bernstein who argued that socialists should stress cooperation and evolution to attain power by democratic means rather than by conflict and revolution.

fascism an ideology or movement that exalts the nation above the individual and calls for a centralized government with a dictatorial leader, economic and social regimentation, and forcible suppression of opposition; in particular, the ideology of Mussolini's Fascist regime in Italy.

feminism the belief in the social, political, and economic equality of the sexes; also, organized activity to advance women's rights.

fief a landed estate granted to a vassal in exchange for military services.

Final Solution the physical extermination of the Jewish people by the Nazis during World War II.

folk culture the traditional arts and crafts, literature, music, and other customs of the people; something that people make, as opposed to modern popular culture, which is something people buy.

free trade the unrestricted international exchange of goods with low or no tariffs.

general strike a strike by all or most workers in an economy; espoused by Georges Sorel as the heroic action that could be used to inspire the workers to destroy capitalist society.

gentry well-to-do English landowners below the level of the nobility; played an important role in the English Civil War of the seventeenth century.

geocentric theory the idea that the earth is at the center of the universe and that the sun and other celestial objects revolve around the earth.

glasnost "openness." Mikhail Gorbachev's policy of encouraging Soviet citizens to openly discuss the strengths and weaknesses of the Soviet Union.

good emperors the five emperors who ruled from 96 to 180 (Nerva, Trajan, Hadrian, Antoninus Pius, and Marcus Aurelius), a period of peace and prosperity for the Roman Empire.

Great Schism the crisis in the late medieval church when there were first two and then three popes; ended by the Council of Constance (1414–1418).

guest workers foreign workers working temporarily in European countries.

guild an association of people with common interests and concerns, especially people working in the same craft. In medieval Europe, guilds came to control much of the production process and to restrict entry into various trades.

gymnasium in classical Greece, a place for athletics; in the Hellenistic Age, a secondary school with a curriculum centered on music, physical exercise, and literature.

heliocentric theory the idea that the sun (not the earth) is at the center of the universe.

Hellenistic literally, "to imitate the Greeks"; the era after the death of Alexander the Great when Greek culture spread into the Near East and blended with the culture of that region.

helots serfs in ancient Sparta, who were permanently bound to the land that they worked for their Spartan masters.

heresy the holding of religious doctrines different from the official teachings of the church.

Hermeticism an intellectual movement beginning in the fifteenth century that taught that divinity is embodied in all aspects of nature; included works on alchemy and magic as well as theology and philosophy. The tradition continued into the seventeenth century and influenced many of the leading figures of the Scientific Revolution.

hetairai highly sophisticated courtesans in ancient Athens who offered intellectual and musical entertainment as well as sex.

hieroglyphics a highly pictorial system of writing used in ancient Egypt.

high culture the literary and artistic culture of the educated and wealthy ruling classes.

Holocaust the mass slaughter of European Jews by the Nazis during World War II.

hoplites heavily armed infantry soldiers used in ancient Greece in a phalanx formation.

Huguenots French Calvinists.

humanism an intellectual movement in Renaissance Italy based upon the study of the Greek and Roman classics.

iconoclasm an eighth-century Byzantine movement against the use of icons (pictures of sacred figures), which was condemned as idolatry.

ideology a political philosophy such as conservatism or liberalism.

imperium "the right to command." In the Roman Republic, the chief executive officers (consuls and praetors) possessed the *imperium;* a military commander was an *imperator.* In the Roman Empire, the title *imperator,* or emperor, came to be used for the ruler.

indirect representation a system of choosing delegates to a representative assembly in which citizens do not choose the delegates directly but instead vote for electors who choose the delegates.

individualism emphasis on and interest in the unique traits of each person.

indulgence the remission of part or all of the temporal punishment in purgatory due to sin; granted for charitable contributions and other good deeds. Indulgences became a regular practice of the Christian church in the High Middle Ages, and their abuse was instrumental in sparking Luther's reform movement in the sixteenth century.

infanticide the practice of killing infants.

inflation a sustained rise in the price level.

intendants royal officials in seventeenth-century France who were sent into the provinces to execute the orders of the central government.

intervention, principle of the idea, after the Congress of Vienna, that the great powers of Europe had the right to send armies into countries experiencing revolution to restore legitimate monarchs to their thrones.

isolationism a foreign policy in which a nation refrains from making alliances or engaging actively in international affairs.

jihad "striving in the way of the Lord." In Islam, the practice of conducting raids against neighboring peoples, which was an expansion of the Arab tradition of tribal raids against their persecutors.

joint-stock company a company or association that raises capital by selling shares to individuals who receive dividends on their investment while a board of directors runs the company.

joint-stock investment bank a bank created by selling shares of stock to investors. Such banks potentially have access to much more capital than do private banks owned by one or a few individuals.

justification of faith the primary doctrine of the Protestant Reformation; taught that humans are saved not through good works, but by the grace of God, bestowed freely through the sacrifice of Jesus.

laissez-faire "to let alone." An economic doctrine that holds that an economy is best served when the government does not interfere but allows the economy to self-regulate according to the forces of supply and demand.

latifundia large landed estates in the Roman Empire (singular: *latifundium*).

lay investiture the practice in which a layperson chose a bishop and invested him with the symbols of both his temporal office and his spiritual office; led to the Investiture Controversy, which was ended by compromise in the Concordat of Worms in 1122.

Lebensraum "living space." The doctrine, adopted by Hitler, that a nation's power depends on the amount of land it occupies; thus, a nation must expand to be strong.

legitimacy, principle of the idea that after the Napoleonic wars peace could best be reestablished in Europe by restoring legitimate monarchs who would preserve traditional institutions; guided Metternich at the Congress of Vienna.

Leninism Lenin's revision of Marxism that held that Russia need not experience a bourgeois revolution before it could move toward socialism.

liberal arts the seven areas of study that formed the basis of education in medieval and early modern Europe. Following Boethius and other late Roman authors, they consisted of grammar, rhetoric, and dialectic or logic (the *trivium*) and arithmetic, geometry, astronomy, and music (the *quadrivium*).

liberalism an ideology based on the belief that people should be as free from restraint as possible. Economic liberalism is the idea that the government should not interfere in the workings of the economy. Political liberalism is the idea that there should be restraints on the exercise of power so that people can enjoy basic civil rights in a constitutional state with a representative assembly.

limited liability the principle that shareholders in a joint-stock corporation can be held responsible for the corporation's debts only up to the amount they have invested.

limited (constitutional) monarchy a system of government in which the monarch is limited by a representative assembly and by the duty to rule in accordance with the laws of the land.

mandates a system established after World War I whereby a nation officially administered a territory (mandate) on behalf of the League of Nations. Thus, France administered Lebanon and Syria as mandates, and Britain administered Iraq and Palestine.

manor an agricultural estate operated by a lord and worked by peasants who performed labor services and paid various rents and fees to the lord in exchange for protection and sustenance.

Marshall Plan the European Recovery Program, under which the United States provided financial aid to European countries to help them rebuild after World War II.

Marxism the political, economic, and social theories of Karl Marx, which included the idea that history is the story of class struggle and that ultimately the proletariat will overthrow the bourgeoisie and establish a dictatorship en route to a classless society.

mass education a state-run educational system, usually free and compulsory, that aims to ensure that all children in society have at least a basic education.

mass leisure forms of leisure that appeal to large numbers of people in a society including the working classes; emerged at the end of the nineteenth century to provide workers with amusements after work and on weekends; used during the twentieth century by totalitarian states to control their populations.

mass politics a political order characterized by mass political parties and universal male and (eventually) female suffrage.

mass society a society in which the concerns of the majority—the lower classes—play a prominent role; characterized by extension of voting rights, an improved standard of living for the lower classes, and mass education.

materialism the belief that everything mental, spiritual, or ideal is an outgrowth of physical forces and that truth is found in concrete material existence, not through feeling or intuition.

mercantilism an economic theory that held that a nation's prosperity depended on its supply of gold and silver and that the total volume of trade is unchangeable; therefore, advocated that the government play an active role in the economy by encouraging exports and discouraging imports, especially through the use of tariffs.

Mesolithic Age the period from 10,000 to 7000 B.C., characterized by a gradual transition from a food-gathering/hunting economy to a food-producing economy.

metics resident foreigners in ancient Athens; not permitted full rights of citizenship but did receive the protection of the laws.

militarism a policy of aggressive military preparedness; in particular, the large armies based on mass conscription and complex, inflexible plans for mobilization that most European nations had before World War I.

ministerial responsibility a tenet of nineteenth-century liberalism that held that ministers of the monarch should be responsible to the legislative assembly rather than to the monarch.

Modernism the new artistic and literary styles that emerged in the decades before 1914 as artists rebelled against traditional efforts to portray reality as accurately as possible (leading to Impressionism and Cubism) and writers explored new forms.

monotheistic/monotheism having only one god; the doctrine or belief that there is only one god.

mutual deterrence the belief that nuclear war could best be prevented if both the United States and the Soviet Union had sufficient nuclear weapons so that even if one nation launched a preemptive first strike, the other could respond and devastate the attacker.

mystery religions religions that involve initiation into secret rites that promise intense emotional involvement with spiritual forces and a greater chance of individual immortality.

nationalism a sense of national consciousness based on awareness of being part of a community—a "nation"—that has common institutions, traditions, language, and customs and that becomes the focus of the individual's primary political loyalty.

nationalities problem the dilemma faced by the Austro-Hungarian Empire in trying to unite a wide variety of ethnic groups including, among others, Austrians, Hungarians, Poles, Croats, Czechs, Serbs, Slovaks, and Slovenes in an era when nationalism and calls for self-determination were coming to the fore.

nationalization the process of converting a business or industry from private ownership to government control and ownership.

nation in arms the people's army raised by universal mobilization to repel the foreign enemies of the French Revolution.

nation-state a form of political organization in which a relatively homogeneous people inhabits a sovereign state, as opposed to a state containing people of several nationalities.

NATO the North Atlantic Treaty Organization; a military allianced formed in 1949 in which the signatories (Belgium, Canada, Denmark, France, Great Britain, Iceland, Italy, Luxembourg, the Netherlands, Norway, Portugal, and the United States) agreed to provide mutual assistance if any one of them was attacked; later expanded to include other nations.

natural laws a body of laws or specific principles held to be derived from nature and binding upon all human society even in the absence of positive laws.

natural rights certain inalienable rights to which all people are entitled; include the right to life, liberty, and property, freedom of speech and religion, and equality before the law.

natural selection Darwin's idea that organisms that are most adaptable to their environment survive and pass on the variations that enabled them to survive, while other, less adaptable organisms become extinct; "survival of the fittest."

Nazi New Order the Nazis' plan for their conquered territories; included the extermination of Jews and others considered inferior, ruthless exploitation of resources, German colonization in the east, and the use of Poles, Russians, and Ukrainians as slave labor.

Neoplatonism a revival of Platonic philosophy. In the third century A.D., a revival associated with Plotinus; in the Italian Renaissance, a revival associated with Marsilio Ficino who attempted to synthesize Christianity and Platonism.

New Economic Policy a modified version of the old capitalist system introduced in the Soviet Union by Lenin in 1921 to revive the economy after the ravages of the civil war and war communism.

new imperialism the revival of imperialism after 1880 in which European nations established colonies throughout much of Asia and Africa.

new monarchies the governments of France, England, and Spain at the end of the fifteenth century, where the rulers were successful in reestablishing or extending centralized royal authority, suppressing the nobility, controlling the church, and insisting upon the loyalty of all peoples living in their territories.

nobiles "nobles." The small group of families from both patrician and plebeian origins who produced most of the men who were elected to office in the late Roman Republic.

nominalism a school of thought in medieval Europe that, following Aristotle, held that only individual objects are real and that universals are only names created by humans.

nuclear family a family group consisting only of father, mother, and children.

old regime/old order the political and social system of France in the eighteenth century before the Revolution.

oligarchy rule by a few.

optimates "best men." Aristocratic leaders in the late Roman Republic who generally came from senatorial families and wished to retain their oligarchical privileges.

orders/estates the traditional tripartite division of European society based on heredity and quality rather than wealth or economic standing, first established in the Middle Ages and continuing into the eighteenth century; traditionally consisted of those who pray (the clergy), those who fight (the nobility), and those who work (all the rest).

organic evolution Darwin's principle that all plants and animals have evolved over a long period of time from earlier and simpler forms of life.

Paleolithic Age the period of human history when humans used simple stone tools (c. 2,500,000–10,000 B.C.).

pantheism a doctrine that equates God with the universe and all that is in it.

paterfamilias the dominant male in a Roman family whose powers over his wife and children were theoretically unlimited, though they were sometimes circumvented in practice.

patriarchal/patriarchy a society in which the father is supreme in the clan or family; more generally, a society dominated by men.

patriarchal family a family in which the husband/father dominates his wife and children.

patricians great landowners who became the ruling class in the Roman Republic.

patronage the practice of awarding titles and making appointments to government and other positions to gain political support.

Pax Romana "Roman peace." A term used to refer to the stability and prosperity that Roman rule brought to the Mediterranean world and much of western Europe during the first and second centuries A.D.

Pentateuch the first five books of the Hebrew Bible (Genesis, Exodus, Leviticus, Numbers, and Deuteronomy).

perestroika "restructuring." A term applied to Mikhail Gorbachev's economic, political, and social reforms in the Soviet Union.

permissive society a term applied to Western society after World War II to reflect the new sexual freedom and the emergence of a drug culture.

Petrine supremacy the doctrine that the bishop of Rome—the pope—as the successor of Saint Peter (traditionally considered the first bishop of Rome) should hold a preeminent position in the church.

phalanx a rectangular formation of tightly massed infantry soldiers.

philosophes intellectuals of the eighteenth-century Enlightenment who believed in applying a spirit of rational criticism to all things, including religion and politics, and who focused on improving and enjoying this world, rather than on the afterlife.

plebeians the class of Roman citizens who included nonpatrician landowners, craftspeople, merchants, and small farmers in the Roman Republic. Their struggle for equal rights with the patricians dominated much of the Republic's history.

pluralism the practice in which one person holds several church offices simultaneously; a problem of the late medieval church.

pogroms organized massacres of Jews.

polis an ancient Greek city-state encompassing both an urban area and its surrounding countryside; a small but autonomous political unit where all major political and social activities were carried out in a central location.

political democracy a form of government characterized by universal suffrage and mass political parties.

politiques a group who emerged during the French Wars of Religion in the sixteenth century; placed politics above religion and believed that no religious truth was worth the ravages of civil war.

polytheistic/polytheism having many gods; belief in or the worship of more than one god.

popular culture as opposed to high culture, the unofficial, written and unwritten culture of the masses, much of which was passed down orally; centers on public and group activities such as festivals. In the twentieth century, refers to the entertainment, recreation, and pleasures that people purchase as part of mass consumer society.

populares "favoring the people." Aristocratic leaders in the late Roman Republic who tended to use the people's assemblies in an effort to break the stranglehold of the *nobiles* on political offices.

popular sovereignty the doctrine that government is created by and subject to the will of the people, who are the source of all political power.

praetorian guard the military unit that served as the personal bodyguard of the Roman emperors.

predestination the belief, associated with Calvinism, that God, as a consequence of his foreknowledge of all events, has predetermined those who will be saved (the elect) and those who will be damned.

price revolution the dramatic rise in prices (inflation) that occurred throughout Europe in the sixteenth and early seventeenth centuries.

primogeniture an inheritance practice in which the eldest son receives all or the largest share of the parents' estate.

principate the form of government established by Augustus for the Roman Empire; continued the constitutional forms of the Republic and consisted of the *princeps* ("first citizen") and the senate, although the *princeps* was clearly the dominant partner.

proletariat the industrial working class. In Marxism, the class who will ultimately overthrow the bourgeoisie.

Puritans English Protestants inspired by Calvinist theology who wished to remove all traces of Catholicism from the Church of England.

querelles des femmes "arguments about women." A centuries-old debate about the nature of women that continued during the Scientific Revolution as those who argued for the inferiority of women found additional support in the new anatomy and medicine.

rationalism a system of thought based on the belief that human reason and experience are the chief sources of knowledge.

realism in medieval Europe, the school of thought that, following Plato, held that the individual objects we perceive are not real but merely manifestations of universal ideas existing in the mind of God. In the nineteenth century, a school of painting that emphasized the everyday life of ordinary people, depicted with photographic realism.

Realpolitik "politics of reality." Politics based on practical concerns rather than theory or ethics.

real wages/income/prices wages/income/prices that have been adjusted for inflation.

reason of state the principle that a nation should act on the basis of its long-term interests and not merely to further the dynastic interests of its ruling family.

relativity theory Einstein's theory that holds, among other things, that (1) space and time are not absolute but are relative to the observer and interwoven into a four-dimensional space-time continuum and (2) matter is a form of energy ($E = mc^2$).

relics the bones of Christian saints or objects intimately associated with saints that were considered worthy of veneration.

Renaissance the "rebirth" of classical culture that occurred in Italy between c. 1350 and c. 1550; also, the earlier revivals of classical culture that occurred under Charlemagne and in the twelfth century.

rentier a person who lives on income from property and is not personally involved in its operation.

reparations payments made by a defeated nation after a war to compensate another nation for damage sustained as a result of the war; required from Germany after World War I.

revisionism a socialist doctrine that rejected Marx's emphasis on class struggle and revolution and argued instead that workers should work through political parties to bring about gradual change.

revolution a fundamental change in the political and social organization of a state.

revolutionary socialism the socialist doctrine espoused by Georges Sorel who held that violent action was the only way to achieve the goals of socialism.

rhetoric the art of persuasive speaking; in the Middle Ages, one of the seven liberal arts.

sacraments rites considered imperative for a Christian's salvation. By the thirteenth century consisted of the eucharist or Lord's Supper, baptism, marriage, penance, extreme unction, holy orders, and confirmation of children; Protestant reformers of the sixteenth century generally recognized only two—baptism and communion (the Lord's Supper).

salons gatherings of philosophes and other notables to discuss the ideas of the Enlightenment; so-called from the elegant drawing rooms (salons) where they met.

sans-culottes the common people who did not wear the fine clothes of the upper classes (sans-culottes means "without breeches") and played an important role in the radical phase of the French Revolution.

satrap/satrapy a governor with both civil and military duties in the ancient Persian Empire, which was divided into satrapies, or provinces, each administered by a satrap.

scholasticism the philosophical and theological system of the medieval schools, which emphasized rigorous analysis of contradictory authorities; often used to try to reconcile faith and reason.

scientific method a method of seeking knowledge through inductive principles; uses experiments and observations to develop generalizations.

Scientific Revolution the transition from the medieval worldview to a largely secular, rational, and materialistic perspective; began in the seventeenth century and was popularized in the eighteenth.

secularization the process of becoming more concerned with material, worldly, temporal things and less with spiritual and religious things.

self-determination the doctrine that the people of a given territory or a particular nationality should have the right to determine their own government and political future.

senate/senators the leading council of the Roman Republic; composed of about 300 men (senators) who served for life and dominated much of the political life of the Republic.

serf a peasant who is bound to the land and obliged to provide labor services and pay various rents and fees to the lord; considered unfree but not a slave because serfs could not be bought and sold.

skepticism a doubtful or questioning attitude, especially about religion.

Social Darwinism the application of Darwin's principle of organic evolution to the social order; led to the belief that progress comes from the struggle for survival as the fittest advance and the weak decline.

socialism an ideology that calls for collective or government ownership of the means of production and the distribution of goods.

social security/social insurance government programs that provide social welfare measures such as old age pensions and sickness, accident, and disability insurance.

Socratic method a form of teaching that uses a question-and-answer format to enable students to reach conclusions by using their own reasoning.

Sophists wandering scholars and professional teachers in ancient Greece who stressed the importance of rhetoric and tended toward skepticism and relativism.

soviets councils of workers' and soldiers' deputies formed throughout Russia in 1917; played an important role in the Bolshevik Revolution.

sphere of influence a territory or region over which an outside nation exercises political or economic influence.

Stoicism a philosophy founded by Zeno in the fourth century B.C. that taught that happiness could be obtained by accepting one's lot and living in harmony with the will of God, thereby achieving inner peace.

subinfeudation the practice in which a lord's greatest vassals subdivided their fiefs and had vassals of their own, and those vassals, in turn, subdivided their fiefs and so on down to simple knights whose fiefs were too small to subdivide.

suffrage the right to vote.

suffragists those who advocate the extension of the right to vote (suffrage), especially to women.

surplus value in Marxism, the difference between a product's real value and the wages of the worker who produced the product.

syncretism the combining of different forms of belief or practice, as, for example, when two gods are regarded as different forms of the same underlying divine force and are fused together.

tariffs duties (taxes) imposed on imported goods; usually imposed both to raise revenue and to discourage imports and protect domestic industries.

tetrarchy rule by four; the system of government established by Diocletian (284–305) in which the Roman Empire was divided into two parts, each ruled by an "Augustus" assisted by a "Caesar."

theocracy a government ruled by a divine authority.

three-field system in medieval agriculture, the practice of dividing the arable land into three fields so that one could lie fallow while the others were planted in winter grains and spring crops.

tithe a tenth of one's harvest or income; paid by medieval peasants to the village church.

Torah the body of law in Hebrew Scripture, contained in the Pentateuch (the first five books of the Hebrew Bible).

totalitarian state a state characterized by government control over all aspects of economic, social, political, cultural, and intellectual life, the subordination of the individual to the state, and insistence that the masses be actively involved in the regime's goals.

total war warfare in which all of a nation's resources, including civilians at home as well as soldiers in the field, are mobilized for the war effort.

trade union an association of workers in the same trade, formed to help members secure better wages, benefits, and working conditions.

transubstantiation a doctrine of the Roman Catholic church that teaches that during the eucharist the substance of the bread and wine is miraculously transformed into the body and blood of Jesus.

trench warfare warfare in which the opposing forces attack and counterattack from a relatively permanent system of trenches protected by barbed wire; characteristic of World War I.

trivium* and *quadrivium together formed the seven liberal arts that were the basis of medieval and early modern education. Grammar, rhetoric, and dialectic or logic made up the *trivium;* arithmetic, geometry, astronomy, and music made up the *quadrivium.*

Truman Doctrine the doctrine, enunciated by Harry Truman in 1947, that the United States would provide economic aid to countries that said they were threatened by Communist expansion.

tyrant/tyranny in an ancient Greek *polis* (or an Italian city-state during the Renaissance), a ruler who came to power in an unconstitutional way and ruled without being subject to the law.

uncertainty principle a principle in quantum mechanics, posited by Heisenberg, that holds that one cannot determine the path of an electron because the very act of observing the electron would affect its location.

unconditional surrender complete, unqualified surrender of a belligerent nation.

utopian socialists intellectuals and theorists in the early nineteenth century who favored equality in social and economic conditions and wished to replace private property and competition with collective ownership and cooperation; deemed impractical and "utopian" by later socialists.

vassal a person granted a fief, or landed estate, in exchange for providing military services to the lord and fulfilling certain other obligations such as appearing at the lord's court when summoned and making a payment on the knighting of the lord's eldest son.

vernacular the everyday language of a region, as distinguished from a language used for special purposes. For example, in medieval Paris, French was the vernacular, but Latin was used for academic writing and for classes at the University of Paris.

volkish thought the belief that German culture is superior and that the German people have a universal mission to save Western civilization from inferior races.

war communism Lenin's policy of nationalizing industrial and other facilities and requisitioning the peasants' produce during the civil war in Russia.

War Guilt Clause the clause in the Treaty of Versailles that declared that Germany (and Austria) were responsible for starting World War I and ordered Germany to pay reparations for the damage the Allies had suffered as a result of the war.

Warsaw Pact a military alliance, formed in 1955, in which Albania, Bulgaria, Czechoslovakia, East Germany, Hungary, Poland, Romania, and the Soviet Union agreed to provide mutual assistance.

welfare state a social/political system in which the government assumes the primary responsibility for the social welfare of its citizens by providing such things as social security, unemployment benefits, and health care.

wergeld "money for a man." In early Germanic law, a person's value in monetary terms, which was paid by a wrongdoer to the family of the person who had been injured or killed.

world-machine Newton's conception of the universe as one huge, regulated, and uniform machine that operated according to natural laws in absolute time, space, and motion.

ziggurat a massive stepped tower upon which a temple dedicated to the chief god or goddess of a Sumerian city was built.

Zionism an international movement that called for the establishment of a Jewish state or a refuge for Jews in Palestine.

Zoroastrianism a religion founded by the Persian Zoroaster in the seventh century B.C.; characterized by worship of a supreme god Ahuramazda who represents the good against the evil spirit, identified as Ahriman.

Pronunciation Guide

al-Abbas, Abu al-AH-bus, AH-boo
Abbasid AB-uh-sid *or* a-BA-sid
Adenauer, Konrad AD-n'our-er
aediles EE-diles
Aeolians ee-OH-lee-uns
Aeschylus ESS-kuh-lus
Afrikaners a-fri-KAH-ners
Agincourt AJ-in-kor
Ahuramazda ah-HOOR-ah-MAHZ-duh
Akhenaton ah-kuh-NAH-tun
Akkadians a-KAY-dee-uns
Albigensians al-bi-GEN-see-uns
d'Albret, Jeanne dahl-BRAy, ZHAHN
Albuquerque, Afonso de AL-buh-kur-kee, ah-FON-soh d'
Alcibiades al-suh-BY-uh-deez
Alcuin AL-kwin
Aliz, Ramiz AL-ee-uh, ra-MEEZ
Allah AH-luh *or* AL-uh
Amenhotep ah-mun-HOE-tep
Andreotti, Giulio ahn-dray-AH-tee, JOOL-yoh
Andropov, Yuri an-DROP-ov, YOOR-ee
Anjou AN-joo
Antigonid an-TIG-oh-nid
Antigonus Gonatus an-TIG-oh-nus goh-NAH-tus
Antiochus an-TIE-uh-kus
Antonescu, Ion An-tuh-NES-koo, YON
Antoninus Pius an-toh-NIGH-nus PIE-us
apella a-PELL-uh
Apollonius ap-uh-LOH-nee-us
Aquinas, Thomas uh-KWIGH-nus
aratrum a-RA-trum
Archimedes are-kuh-MEE-deez
Argonautica ARE-guh-NOT-i-kuh
Aristarchus ar-is-TAR-kus
Aristotle ar-i-STAH-tul
Arsinoë ar-SIN-oh-ee
artium baccalarius are-TEE-um back-uh-LAR-ee-us
artium magister are-TEE-um ma-GIS-ter
Ashkenazic ash-kuh-NAH-zic
Ashurnasirpal ah-shoor-NAH-suh-pul
asiento a-SEE-en-toh
assignat as-seen-YAH *or* AS-sig-nat
Assyrians uh-SEER-ee-uns
Atahualpa ah-tuh-WALL-puh
Attalid AT-a-lid
audiencias ah-DEE-en-CEE-ahs
Augustine AW-gus-STEEN
Avicenna av-i-SEN-uh
Avignon ah-veen-YONE
Auschwitz-Birkenau OUSH-vitz-BUR-kuh-now
Ausgleich OUS-glike
Babeuf, Gracchus bah-BUHF, GRAK-us
Bach, Johann Sebastian BAHK, yoh-HAHN suh-BASS-chen
Bakunin, Michael ba-KOO-nin
Balboa, Vasco Nuñez de bal-BOH-uh, VASH-koh NOON-yez duh
Ballin, Albert BAHLL-een
Barbarossa bar-buh-ROH-suh
Bastille ba-STEEL
Bayle, Pierre BAYL, PYER
Beauvoir, Simone de boh-VWAH, see-MOAN duh
Bebel, August BAY-bul
Beccaria, Cesare bek-KAH-ree-uh, CHAY-zahr-ay
Beguines bi-GEENS
Belisarius bell-i-SAR-ee-us
benefice BEN-uh-fiss
Bergson, Henri BERG-son, AWN-ree
Bernini, Gian Lorenzo bur-NEE-nee, JAHN loh-RENT-soh
Bernstein, Eduard BURN-stine, AY-doo-art
Blitzkrieg BLITZ-kreeg
Blum, Léon BLOOM, LAY-OHN
Boccaccio, Giovanni boh-KAH-chee-oh, joe-VAHN-nee
Bodichon, Barbara BOH-duh-chon
Boer BOHR
Boethius boh-EETH-ee-us
Boleyn, Anne BUH-lin
Bólivar, Simón BOH-luh-VAR, see-MOAN
Bologna buh-LOHN-yuh
Bossuet, Jacques baw-SWAY, ZHAHK
Bottai, Giuseppe BOT-tah, joo-ZEP-pay
Boticelli, Sandro BOT-i-CHELL-ee, SAHN-droh
Boulanger, Georges boo-lahn-ZHAY, ZHORZH
Bracciolini, Poggio braht-choh-LEE-nee, POD-joh
Brahe, Tycho BRAH, TIE-koh
Bramante, Donato brah-MAHN-tee, doe-NAY-toe
Brandt, Willy BRAHNT, VIL-ee

Brétigny bray-tee-NYEE
Brezhnev, Leonid BREZH-nef, lyi-on-YEET
Briand, Aristide bree-AHN, a-ree-STEED
Brunelleschi, Filippo BROO-nuh-LES-kee, fee-LEEP-poe
Brüning, Heinrich BROO-ning, HINE-rik
Bulganin, Nilolai bul-GAN-in, nyik-uh-LYE
Bund deutscher Mädel BUNT DOICHer MAIR-del
Burschenschaften BOOR-shen-shaft-un
Calais ka-LAY
Caligula ka-LIG-yuh-luh
caliph/caliphate KAY-lif/KAY-li-FATE
Calonne, Charles de kah-LAWN, SHARL duh
Cambyses kam-BY-seez
Camus, Albert kuh-MOO, al-BEAR
Canaanites KAY-nuh-nites
Capet/Capetian ka-PAY *or* KAY-put/kuh-PEE-shun
Caraffa, Gian Pietro kah-RAH-fuh, JAHN PYEE-troh
carbonari kar-buh-NAH-ree
Carolingian kar-oh-LIN-jun
carruca ca-ruh-kuh
Carthage/Carthaginian KAR-thij/KAR-thuh-JIN-ee-un
Cassiodorus kass-ee-oh-DOR-us
Castlereagh, Viscount KAS-ul-RAY
Catharism KA-tha-ri-zem
Catullus ka-TULL-us
Cavendish, Margaret KAV-un-dish
Cavour, Camillo di ka-VOOR, kah-MIL-oh
Ceausescu, Nicolai chow-SHES-koo, nee-koh-LYE
cenobitic sen-oh-BIT-ik
Cèzanne, Paul say-ZAN
Chaeronea ker-oh-NEE-uh
Chaldean kal-DEE-un
chanson de geste shahn-SAWN duh ZHEST
Charlemagne SHAR-luh-mane
Chateaubriand, François-René de shah-TOH-bree-AHN, FRAN-swah-ruh-NAY duh
Chernenko, Konstantin cher-NYEN-koh, kon-stunTEEN
Chiang Kai-Shek CHANG KIGH-shek
Chrétien de Troyes KRAY-tee-ahn duh TRWAH
Cicero SIS-uh-roh
ciompi CHOM-pee
Cistercians si-STIR-shuns
Claudius KLAW-dee-us
Cleisthenes KLISE-thuh-neez
Clemenceau, Georges klem-un-SOH, ZHORZH
Clovis KLOH-vis
Codreanu, Corneliu kaw-dree-AH-noo, kor-NELL-yoo
colonus kuh-LOH-nus
Columbanus kol-um-BAHN-us
comitia centuriata kuh-MISH-ee-uh sen-TYOO-ree-ah-tuh
Commodus KOM-uh-dus
Comnenus kom-NEE-nus
Comte, Auguste KOHNT
concilium plebis con-CIL-ee-um PLE-bis
Concordat of Worms kon-KOR-dat of WURMZ *or* VAWRMZ
Condorcet, Marie-Jean de kawn-dar-SAY, mur-REE-ZHAHN duh
condottieri kon-dah-TEE-AIR-ee
consul KON-sul
Contarini, Gasparo kahn-tuh-REE-nee, GAHS-pah-roh
conversos kon-VAIR-sohs
Copernicus, Nicolaus koh-PURR-nuh-kus, nee-koh-LAH-us
Corinth KOR-inth
corregidores kor-REG-uh-DOR-ays
Cortés, Hernán kor-TEZ, er-NAHN
Corvinus, Matthias kor-VIE-nus, muh-THIGH-us
Courbet, Gustave koor-BAY, guh-STAWV
Crassus KRASS-us
Crécy kray-SEE
Crédit Mobilier kred-EE mohb-eel-YAY
Croesus KREE-sus
Danton, Georges dahn-TAWN, ZHORZH
Darius duh-RYE-us
dauphin DAW-fin
David, Jacques-Louis dah-VEED, ZHAHK-LWEE
Debussy, Claude de-BYOO-see, KLODE
Decameron di-KAM-uh-run
Deffand, marquise du di-FAHN, mar-KEEZ doo
de Gaulle, Charles duh GOLL, SHARL
Delacroix, Eugène del-uh-KWAW, yoo-ZHAHN
Demosthenes di-MOSS-thuh-neez
Denikin, Anton dyi-NYEE-kin, an-TAWN
Descartes, René day-KART, ruh-NAY
Diaghilev, Sergei dee-AHG-uh-lef, syir-GYAY
Dias, Bartholomeu DEE-us, bar-too-loo-MAY
Diaspora die-AS-pur-uh
Diderot, Denis DEE-duh-roh, duh-NEE
Diocletian die-uh-KLEE-shun
Disraeli, Benjamin diz-RAY-lee
Dollfuss, Engelbert DOLL-foos
Domesday Book DOOMZ-day
Domitian doh-MISH-un
Donatus/Donatist doh-NAY-tus/DOH-nuh-tist
Dorians DOR-ee-uns
Dostoevsky, Fyodor DOS-tuh-YEF-skee, FYOD-ur
Douhet, Giulio doo-EE, JOOL-yoh
Dreyfus, Alfred DRY-fus
Dubcek, Alexander DOOB-chek
Duma DOO-muh
Dürer, Albrecht DOO-er, AWL-brekt
ecclesia eh-KLEE-zee-uh
Eckhart, Meister EK-hart, MY-ster
encomienda en-koh-mee-EN-dah
Engels, Friedrich ENG-ulz, FREE-drik

Entente Cordiale ahn-TAHNT kor-DYALL
Epaminondas i-PAM-uh-NAHN-dus
ephor EF-or
Epicurus/Epicureanism EP-i-KYOOR-us/EP-i-kyoo-REE-uh-ni-zem
equestrians i-KWES-tree-uns
equites EK-wuh-tays
Erasistratus er-uh-SIS-truh-tus
Erasmus, Desiderius i-RAZZ-mus, des-i-DIR-ee-us
Eratosthenes er-uh-TOSS-thuh-neez
eremitical air-uh-MITT-i-cul
d'Este, Isabella ES-tay
Erhard, Ludwig AIR-hart
Etruscans i-TRUSS-kuhns
Euclid YOO-klid
Euripides yoo-RIP-i-deez
exchequer EX-chek-ur
fasces FASS-eez
Fascio di Combattimento FASH-ee-oh di com-BATT-ee-men-toh
Fatimid FAT-i-mid
Fedele, Cassandra FAY-del-ee
Feltre, Vittorino da FELL-tree, vee-tor-EE-noh dah
Ficino, Marsilio fee-CHEE-noh, mar-SIL-ee-oh
Flaubert, Gustave floh-BEAR, guh-STAWV
Fleury, Cardinal floe-REE
Fontainebleau FAWN-tin-BLOW
Fontenelle, Bernard de fawnt-NELL, BER-nar duh
Fouquet, Nicolas foo-KAY, nee-KOH-lah
Frequens FREE-kwens
Friedan, Betty fri-DAN
Frimaire free-MARE
Fronde FROND
Führerprinzip FYOOR-ur-PRIN-tseep
gabelle gah-BELL
Gama, Vasco da GAM-uh, VASH-koh duh
Gamond, Zoé Gatti de gah-MAHN, zaw-ay GAHT-tee duh
Garibaldi, Giuseppe gar-uh-BAWL-dee, joo-ZEP-pay
Gasperi, Alcide de GAHS-pe-ree, awl-CHEE-day de
Gaugamela gaw-guh-MEE-luh
Gentileschi, Artemisia jen-tul-ESS-kee, are-tee-MISS-ee-uh
gerousia juh-ROO-see-uh
Gierek, Edward GYER-ek
Gilgamesh GILL-guh-mesh
Giolitti, Giovanni joh-LEET-tee, joe-VAHN-nee
Giotto JAW-toh
Girondins juh-RAHN-dins
glasnost GLAZ-nohst
Gleichschaltung GLIKE-shalt-ung
Goebbels, Joseph GUHR-bulz
Gomulka, Wladyslaw goh-MOOL-kuh, vla-DIS-lawf
gonfaloniere gon-fa-loh-NEE-ree
Gorbachev, Mikhail GOR-buh-chof, meek-HALE
Gracchus, Tiberius and Gaius GRAK-us, tie-BIR-ee-us and GAY-us *or* GUY-us
grandi GRAHN-dee
Grieg, Edvard GREEG, ED-vart
Groote, Gerard GROH-tuh
Gropius, Walter GROH-pee-us, VAHL-ter
Grossdeutsch gross-DOICH
Guicciardini, Francesco gwee-char-DEE-nee, frahn-CHASE-koh
Guizot, François gee-ZOH, FRAN-swah
Gustavus Adolphus gus-STAY-vus a-DOLF-us
Guzman, Gaspar de goos-MAHN, gahs-PAR day
Habsburg HAPS-burg
Hadrian HAY-dree-un
Hagia Sophia HAG-ee-uh soh-FEE-uh
hajj HAJ
Hammurabi ham-uh-RAH-bee
Handel, George Friedrich HAN-dul
Hannibal HAN-uh-bul
Hanukkah HAH-nuh-kuh
Hardenberg, Karl von HAR-d'n-burg
Harun al-Rashid huh-ROON al-ra-SHEED
Hatshepsut hat-SHEP-soot
Haussmann, Baron HOUS-mun
Havel, Vaclav HAH-vuhl, VAHT-slaf
Haydn, Franz Joseph HIDE-n, FRAHNTS
hegemon HEJ-uh-mon
Heisenberg, Werner HIGH-zun-burg, VUR-nur
Hellenistic hell-uh-NIS-tik
helots HELL-uts
hermandades er-mahn-DAHDH-ays
Herodotus hi-ROD-oh-tus
Herophilus hi-ROF-uh-lus
Herzen, Alexander HER-tsun
Herzl, Theodor HERT-sul, TAY-oh-dor
Hesiod HEE-see-ud
Heydrich, Reinhard HIGH-drik, RINE-hart
hieroglyph HIGH-ur-oh-glif
Hildegard of Bingen HILL-duh-gard of BING-en
Hitler Jugend JOO-gunt
Ho Chi Minh HOE CHEE MIN
Höch, Hannah HOKH
Hohenstaufen HOE-un-SHTAU-fun
Hohenzollern HOE-un-ZAHL-lurn
d'Holbach, Paul awl-BAHK
Honecker, Erich HOE-nuh-ker
hoplites HOP-lites
Horace HOR-us
Horthy, Miklós HOR-tee, MIK-lohsh
Hoxha, Enver HAW-jah
Huguenots HYOO-guh-nots
Husák, Gustav HOO-sahk, guh-STAHV
Ibn Sina ib-en SEE-nuh

Ignatius of Loyola ig-NAY-shus of loi-OH-luh
Il Duce eel DOO-chay
imperator im-puh-RAH-tor
imperium im-PIER-ee-um
intendant in-TEN-duhnt
Isis EYE-sis
Issus ISS-us
ius gentium YOOS GEN-tee-um
Jacobin JAK-uh-bin
Jacquerie zhah-KREE
Jagiello yah-GYELL-oh
Jahn, Friedrich Ludwig YAHN, FREE-drik
Jaruzelski, Wojciech yahr-uh-ZEL-skee, VOI-chek
Jaurés, Jean zhaw-RESS, ZHAHN
jihad ji-HAHD
Judaea joo-DEE-uh
Judas Maccabaeus JOO-dus mak-uh-BEE-us
Jung, Carl YOONG
Junkers YOONG-kers
Jupiter Optimus Maximus JOO-pi-ter OPP-tuh-mus MAK-suh-mus
Justinian juh-STIN-ee-un
Juvenal JOO-vuh-nul
Kádár, János KAY-dahr, YAHN-us
Kadinsky, Vasily kan-DIN-skee, vus-YEEL-yee
Karlowitz KARL-oh-vitz
Kaunitz, Wenzel von KOU-nits, VENT-sul
Kerensky, Alexander kuh-REN-skee
Keynes, John Maynard KAYNZ
Khrushchev, Nikita KROOSH-chef, nuh-KEE-tuh
Kleindeutsch kline-DOICH
Kohl, Helmut KOLE, HELL-mut
koiné koi-NAY
Kolchak, Alexander KAWL-chok
Kollantai, Alexandra kawl-un-TIE
Kosciuszko, Thaddeus kos-ee-US-koh, tah-DE-us
Kossuth, Louis KOSS-ooth
kouros KOO-raws
Kraft durch Freude CRAFT durch FROI-duh
Kristallnacht KRIS-tal-NAHCHT
Krupp, Alfred KROOP
Kuchuk-Kainarji koo-CHOOK-kigh-NAR-jee
kulaks koo-LAKS
kulturkampf kool-TOOR-kahmf
Kun, Béla KOON, BAY-luh
Lafayette, marquis de lah-fee-ETTE, mar-KEE duh
laissez-faire les-ay-FAIR
Lamarck, Jean-Baptiste luh-MAHRK, ZHAHN-buh-TEEST
Lancaster LAN-kas-ter
latifundia lat-uh-FUN-dee-uh
Latium LAY-shee-um
Laurier, Wilfred LAWR-ee-ay
Lebensraum LAY-benz-roum
Lespinasse, Julie de les-peen-AHS
Le Tellier, François Michel luh tel-YAY, FRAN-swah-mee-SHELL
Lévesque, René luh-VEK, ruh-NAY
Leyster, Judith LE-ster
Liebenfels, Lanz von LEE-bun-felz, LAHNZ
Liebknecht, Karl LEEP-knekt
Liebknecht, Wilhelm LEEP-knekt, VIL-helm
Lionne, Hugues de LYAWN, UGH
List, Friedrich LIST, FREE-drik
Liszt, Franz LIST, FRAHNZ
Livy LIV-ee
Lucretius loo-KREE-shus
Luddites LUD-ites
Ludendorff, Erich LOOD-un-dorf
Lueger, Karl LOO-ger
Luftwaffe LUFT-vaf-uh
Luxemburg, Rosa LUK-sum-burg
Machiavelli, Niccolò mak-ee-uh-VELL-ee, nee-koh-LOH
Magna Graecia MAG-nuh GREE-shuh
Magyars MAG-yars
Maistre, Joseph de MES-truh
Malleus Maleficarum mall-EE-us mal-uh-FIK-ar-um
al-Ma'mun al-MAH-moon
Manetho MAN-uh-THOH
Mao Zedong mau zee-DONG
Marcus Aurelius MAR-kus au-REE-lee-us
Marcuse, Herbert mar-KOO-zuh
Marie Antoinette muh-REE an-twuh-NET
Marius MAR-ee-us
Marsiglio of Padua mar-SIL-ee-oh of PA-juh-wuh
Masaryk, Thomas MAS-uh-rik
Matteotti, Giacomo mat-ee-OH-tee, JAHK-oh-moh
Mazarin maz-uh-RAN
Mazzini, Giuseppe maht-SEE-nee, joo-ZEP-pay
Meiji MAY-jee
Mein Kampf mine KAHMF
Melanchthon, Philip muh-LANGK-thun
Menander me-NAN-der
Mendeleyev, Dmitri men-duh-LAY-ef, di-MEE-tri
Merian, Maria Sibylla MARE-ee-un
Mesopotamia mess-oh-poh-TAME-ee-uh
Messiaen, Olivier me-SYAHN, 0-LEEV-yay
Metaxas, John me-TAK-sus
Metternich, Klemens von MET-er-nik, KLAY-mens
Michel, Louise mee-SHELL
Michelangelo my-kell-AN-juh-loh
Mieszko MYESH-koh
Millet, Jean-François mi-LAY, ZHAHN-FRAN-swah
Milošević, Slobodan mi-LOH-suh-vik, SLOW-buh-dan
Miltiades mil-TIE-uh-deez
Mirandola, Pico della muh-RAN-duh-luh, PEE-koh DELL-uh
missi dominici MISS-ee doe-MIN-ee-chee

Moctezuma mahk-tuh-ZOO-muh
Mohács MOH-hach
Moldavia mahl-DAY-vee-uh
Molière, Jean-Baptiste mole-YAIR, ZHAHN-buh-TEEST
Moltke, Helmuth von MOLT-kuh, HELL-mut fahn
Monet, Claude moh-NAY, KLODE
Montaigne, Michel de mahn-TANE, mee-SHELL duh
Montefeltro, Federigo da mahn-tuh-FELL-troh, fay-day-REE-goh dah
Montesquieu MONT-ess-skyoo
Montessori, Maria mon-ti-SOR-ee
Morisot, Berthe mor-ee-ZOH, BERT
Muawiyah moo-AH-wee-yah
Mühlberg mool-BERK
Muhammad moe-HA-mud
Müntzer, Thomas MOON-tsur
Muslim MUZ-lum
Mutsuhito moo-tsoo-HEE-toe
Mycenaean my-suh-NEE-un
Nabonidas na-bun-EYE-dus
Nagy, Imry NAHJD, IM-re
Navarre nuh-VARR
Nebuchadnezzar neb-uh-kad-NWZZ-ar
Nero NEE-roh
Nerva NUR-vuh
Neumann, Balthasar NOI-mahn, BAHL-tah-zar
Neumann, Solomon NOI-mahn
Nevsky, Alexander NEW-skee
Newcomen, Thomas new-KUH-mun
Ngo Dinh Diem NGOH din dee-EM
Nietzsche, Friedrich NEE-chuh, FREE-drik
Nimwegen NIM-vay-gun
Ninhursaga nin-HUR-sah-guh
Nogaret, William de noh-guh-RAY
Nogarola, Isotta NOH-guh-roll-uh, eye-SOT-tuh
Novalis, Friedrich noh-VAH-lis, FREE-drik
Novotny, Antonin noh-VOT-nee, AN-ton-yeen
Nystadt nee-STAHD
Octavian ok-TAY-vee-un
Odoacer oh-doh-AY-ser
optimates opp-tuh-MAH-tays
Osiris oh-SIGH-ris
Ovid OV-id
Paleologus pay-lee-OHL-uh-gus
papal curia PAY-pul KOOR-ee-uh
Papen, Franz von PAH-pun, FRAHNTZ fahn
Paracelsus par-uh-SELL-sus
Parlement par-luh-MAHN
Pascal, Blaise pass-KAL, BLEZ
paterfamilias pay-ter-fuh-MILL-ee-us
Pentateuch PEN-tuh-tuke
Pepin PEP-in
perestroika pair-ess-TROY-kuh
Pergamum PURR-guh-mum
Pericles PER-i-kleez
perioeci per-ee-EE-sie
Pétain, Henri pay-TAN, AHN-ree
Petrarch PE-trark
Petronius pi-TROH-nee-us
philosophe fee-luh-ZAWF
Phoenicians fi-NISH-uns
Photius FOH-shus
Picasso, Pablo pi-KAW-soh
Pilsudski, Joseph peel-SOOT-skee
Pisistratus pi-SIS-truh-tus
Pissaro, Camille pi-SARR-oh, kah-MEEYL
Pizarro, Francesco pi-ZARR-oh, frahn-CHASE-koh
Planck, Max PLAHNK
Plantagenet plan-TA-juh-net
Plato PLAY-toe
Plautus PLAW-tus
Poincaré, Raymond pwan-kah-RAY, re-MOAN
polis POE-lis
politiques puh-lee-TEEKS
Polybius poe-LIB-ee-us
Pombal, marquis de pom-BAHL, mar-KEE duh
Pompadour, madame de POM-puh-door, muh-DAM duh
Pompey POM-pee
pontifex maximus PON-ti-feks MAK-suh-mus
populares POP-yoo-lar-ays
populo grasso POP-uh-loh GRAH-soh
Poussin, Nicholas poo-SAN, NEE-kaw-lah
Praecepter Germaniae PREE-sep-ter ger-MAN-ee-eye
praetor PREE-ter
princeps PRIN-seps
Procopius proh-KOH-pee-us
procurator PROK-yuh-ray-ter
Ptolemy/Ptolemaic TOL-uh-mee/TOL-uh-MAY-ik
Pugachev, Emelyan POO-guh-choff, yim-yil-YAHN
Punic PYOO-nik
Pyrrhus/Pyrrhic PIR-us/PIR-ik
quaestors KWES-ters
Quetzelcoatl ket-SAHL-koh-ATE-ul
Quran kuh-RAN
Racine, Jean-Baptiste ra-SEEN, ZHAHN-buh-TEEST
al-Rahman, Abd al-RAH-mun, abd
Ramesses RAM-i-seez
Raphael RAFF-ee-ul
Rasputin rass-PYOO-tin
Realpolitik ray-AHL-poe-li-teek
Reichsrat RIKES-raht
Rembrandt van Rijn REM-brant vahn RINE
Renan, Ernst re-NAHN
Ricci, Matteo REECH-ee, mah-TAY-oh
Richelieu RISH-uh-loo
Rilke, Rainer Maria RILL-kuh, RYE-ner
risorgimento ree-SOR-jee-men-toe

Robespierre, Maximilien ROHBZ-pee-air, mak-SEE-meel-yahn
Rococo ro-KOH-koh
Röhm, Ernst RURM
Roon, Albrecht von ROHN AHL-brekt
Rousseau, Jean-Jacques roo-SOH ZHAHN-ZHAHK
Rurik ROOR-ik
Ryswick RIZ-wik
Sacrosancta sak-roh-SANK-tuh
Saint-Just san-ZHOOST
Saint-Simon, Henri de san-see-MOAN, AHN-ree duh
Sakharov, Andrei SAH-kuh-rof, ahn-DRAY
Saladin SAL-uh-din
Sallust SALL-ust
Samnites SAM-nites
San Martín, José de san mar-TEEN, hoe-SAY day
Sartre, Jean-Paul SAR-truh, ZHAHN-PAUL
satrap/satrapy SAY-trap/SAY-truh-pee
Satyricon SAY-tir-ee-kon
Schaumburg-Lippe SHAHM-berkh-LI-puh
Schleswig-Holstein SCHLES-vig-HOLE-stine
Schlieffen, Alfred von SHLEE-fun
Schmidt, Helmut SHMIT, HELL-mut
Schönberg, Arnold SHURN-burg, ARR-nawlt
Schönerer, George von SHURN-er-er, ZHORSH
Schuschnigg, Karl von SHOOSH-nik
Schutzmannschaft SHOOTS-mun-shaft
Scipio Africanus SI-pee-oh af-ri-KAY-nus
Scipio Aemilianus SI-pee-oh i-mill-ee-AY-nus
scriptoria skrip-TOR-ee-uh
Sejm SAME
Seleucus/Seleucid si-LOO-kus/si-LOO-sid
Seljuk Turks SELL-juke
Seneca SEN-i-kuh
Sephardic suh-FAR-dik
Septimius Severus sep-TIM-ee-us se-VIR-us
Sforza, Ludovico SFORT-zuh, loo-doe-VEE-koh
Sieveking, Amalie SEEVE-king
Sieyès, Abbé sye-YES, a-BAY
signoria seen-YOOR-ee-uh
Socrates SOK-ruh-teez
Solon SOH-lun
Solzhenitsyn, Alexander SOLE-zhuh-NEET-sin
Sophocles SOF-uh-kleez
Sorel, Georges sah-RELL, ZHORZH
Spartacus SPAR-tuh-kus
Speer, Albert SHPIER
Speransky, Michael spyuh-RAHN-skee
Spinoza, Benedict de spi-NOH-zuh
squadristi sqah-DREES-tee
Staël, Germaine de STAWL, ZHER-men duh
Stein, Heinrich von STINE, HINE-rik
Stoicism STOH-i-siz-um
Stolypin, Peter stuh-LEE-pyin
Stravinsky, Igor struh-VIN-skee, EE-gor
Stresemann, Gustav SHTRAY-zuh-mahn, GUS-tahf
Struensee, John Frederick SHTROO-un-zay
Sulla SULL-uh
Sumerians soo-MER-ee-uns
Suppiluliumas suh-pil-oo-LEE-uh-mus
Suttner, Bertha von ZOOT-ner
Taafe, Edward von TAH-fuh
Tacitus TASS-i-tus
taille TAH-yuh *or* TIE
Talleyrand, Prince TAL-ee-ran
Tauler, Johannes TOU-ler, yoh-HAHN-us
Tenochtitlán tay-NAWCH-teet-LAWN
Tertullian tur-TULL-yun
Theocritus thee-OCK-ri-tus
Theodora thee-uh-DOR-uh
Theognis thee-OGG-nus
Thermidor ter-mee-DOR
Thermopylae thur-MOP-uh-lee
Thiers, Adolphe tee-ER, a-DOLF
Thucydides thoo-SID-uh-deez
Thutmosis thoot-MOH-sus
Tiberius tie-BIR-ee-us
Tiepolo, Giovanni Battista tee-AY-puh-loh, joe-VAHN-ee baht-TEES-tah
Tiglath-pileser TIG-lath-puh-LEE-zur
Tirpitz, Admiral von TUR-puts
Tito TEE-toh
Tlaxcala tlah-SKAHL-uh
Torah TOR-uh
Tordesillas tor-duh-SEE-yus
Trajan TRAY-jun
Trevithick, Richard TREV-uh-thik
Tristan, Flora TRIS-tun
Tyche TIE-kee
Ulbricht, Walter UL-brikt, VAHL-ter
Umayyads oo-MY-ads
Unam Sanctam OON-ahm SANK-tahm
universitas yoo-ni-VER-si-tahs
Valois VAL-wah
van Eyck, Jan van IKE
van Gogh, Vincent van GOE
Vasa, Gustavus VAH-suh, gus-STAY-vus
Vega, Lope de VAY-guh, LOH-pay day
Vendée vahn-DAY
Venetia vuh-NEE-shee-uh
Vesalius, Andreas vi-SAY-lee-us, ahn-DRAY-us
Vespasian ves-PAY-zhun
Vespucci, Amerigo ves-POO-chee, ahm-ay-REE-goe
Vichy VISH-ee
Vierzenheiligen feer-tsun-HILE-i-gun
Virchow, Rudolf FEER-koh, roo-DOLF

Virgil VUR-jul
Volkschulen FOLK-shool-un
Voltaire vole-TAIR
von Bora, Katherina BOR-uh
Wagner, Richard VAHG-ner, RIK-art
Walesa, Lech va-WENZ-uh, LEK
Wallachia wah-lay-KEE-uh
Wallenstein, Albrecht von WOLL-un-stine, AWL-brekt
Watteau, Antoine wah-TOE, AHN-twahn
Wannsee VAHN-say
Weizsäcker, Richard von VITS-zek-er, RIK-art
wergeld wur-GELD
Windischgrätz, Alfred vin-dish-GRETS
Winkelmann, Maria VING-kul-mun
Witte, Sergei VIT-uh, syir-GYAY
Worms, Edict of WURMZ *or* VAWRMZ
Wyclif, John WIK-lif
Xavier, Francis ZAY-vee-ur
Xerxes ZURK-seez
Xhosa KOH-suh
Ximenes hee-MAY-nus
Yahweh YAH-wah
Yeats, William Butler YATES
Yeltsin, Boris YELT-sun
yishuv YISH-uv
Zemsky Sobor ZEM-skee SOH-bur
zemstvos ZEMPST-voh
Zeno ZEE-noh
Zeus ZOOS
Zhivkov, Todor ZHEV-kof, toh-DOR
ziggurat ZIG-guh-rat
Zimmermann, Domenikus TSIM-ur-mahn, doe-MEE-nee-kus
Zinzendorf, Nikolaus von ZIN-zun-dorf, nee-koh-LAH-us
Zola, Emile ZOH-luh, ay-MEEL
zollverein TSOL-fuh-rine
Zoroaster ZOR-oh-as-ter

Photo Credits

FRONTMATTER ESSAY

xx (left) © Will and Deni McIntyre/Photo Researchers, Inc.; **xx** (right) Art Resource, NY; **xxi** (left) © Michael Holford, London; **xxi** (right) Photo, Vatican Museums; **xxii** (left) Bibliotheque Nationale, Paris, Ms. Nouv. Acq. Fr. 1098; **xxii** (right) *Statue of Charlemagne,* Musee du Louvre, © Photo R.M.N.; **xxiii** (left) Bibliotheque Nationale, Paris; **xxiii** (right) G. Dagli Orti

CHAPTER 11

296 Bibliotheque Nationale, Paris; **298** © Bibliotheque royale Albert ler, Bruxelles (Ms. 13076–77, f. 12v); **301** © Bibliotheque royale Albert ler, Bruxelles (Ms. 13076–77, f. 16v); **303** Bibliotheque Nationale, Paris; **304** Staatliche Landesbildstelle Hamburg; **306** *Battle of Crecy from the Hundred Years War, 24th August 1346, showing the English and French Armies. Froissart's Chronicle,* (late 15th century) Bibliotheque Nationale, Paris, France/Bridgeman Art Library; **308** Giraudon/ Art Resource, NY; **310** The Granger Collection; **313** British Library, London, Ms. Add. 23923,f.2; **319** British Library, London, folio 290, Harley ms. 4431; **320** Scala/Art Resource, NY; **322** Meister des Marienlebens, *"Geburt Mariae,"* Alte Pinakothek, Munich, Photo © Artothek; **323** British Library, London, Ms. Sloane 1977, f.7

CHAPTER 12

326 Photo, Vatican Museums; **332** *The Wedding Feast* by Sandro Botticelli (1444/5-1510) Private Collection/Bridgeman Art Library, London/New York; **336** Scala/Art Resource, NY; **338** © ARCHIV/Photo Researchers, Inc.; **345** Scala/Art Resource, NY; **346** Erich Lessing/Art Resource, NY; **346** Scala/Art Resource, NY; **347** Scala/Art Resource, NY; **347** Scala/Art Resource, NY; **348** Erich Lessing/Art Resource, NY; **349** Photo, Vatican Museums; **349** Scala/Art Resource, NY; **350** Art Resource, NY; **351** Jan van Eyck, *Giovanni Arnolfini and His Bride,* reproduced by Courtesy of the Trustees, The National Gallery, London; **351** Alinari/Art Resource, NY ; **356** Kunsthistorisches Museum, Vienna; **359** Photo, Vatican Museums

CHAPTER 13

362 Scala/Art Resource, NY; **364** Oeffentliche Kunstsammlung Basel, Kunstmuseum: Colorphoto Hans Hinz; **368** Scala/Art Resource, NY ; **370** Staatliche Museen Preussischer Kulturbesitz, Kupferstichkabinett, Berlin, Photo: Jorg P. Anders; **373** Jean Clouet, *Francis I,* Musee du Louvre, © Photo R.M.N.; **374** Alte Pinakothek, Munich; **376** Hans Asper, Zwingli, Kunstmuseum Winterthur; **378** © British Museum; **380** The Royal Collection © Her Majesty Queen Elizabeth II; **382** © Bibliotheque Publique et Universitaire, Geneva; **385** Oeffentliche Kunstsammlung Basel, Kunstmuseum: Colorphoto Hans Hinz; **388** Scala/Art Resource, NY

CHAPTER 14

392 *The Massacre of Indian at Cholula on the orders of Cortes, 1519* William Clements Library, University of Michigan, USA/Bridgeman Art Library, London/New York; **394** North Wind Picture Archives; **397** The Metropolitan Museum of Art, Gift of J. Pierpont Morgan, 1900 (00.18.2); **399** *The Massacre of Indian at Cholula on the orders of Cortes, 1519* William Clements Library, University of Michigan, USA/Bridgeman Art Library, London/New York; **402** Francois Dubois D'Amiens, *The St. Bartholomew's Day Massacre,* Musee Cantonal des Beaux-Arts, Lausanne; **405** Derechos Reservados, © Museo del Prado, Madrid; **407** Private Collection; **410** Herzog Anton Ulrich Museum, Braunschweig; **413** Giraudon/Art Resource, NY; **416** Kunsthistorisches Museum, Vienna; **419** (top) Laocoon, *El Greco,* National Gallery of Art, Washington: Samuel H. Kress Collection; **419** (bottom) Scala/Art Resource, NY; **420** Peter Paul Rubens, *The Landing of Marie de Medicis at Marseilles,* Musee du Louvre, © Photo R.M.N.; **421** (left) Scala/Art Resource, NY; **421** (right) Giraudon/ Art Resource; **422** John Taylor, *William Shakespeare,* By courtesy of the National Portrait Gallery, London, England

CHAPTER 15

426 Jacob van der Ulft, *The Square of the Dam at Amsterdam,* 1659, Musee Conde, Chantilly, Photo Giraudon/Art Resource, NY; **428** Reproduced by Courtesy of the Trustees, The National Gallery, London; **430** Hyacinthe Rigaud, *Louis XIV,* Musee du Louvre © Photo R.M.N.; **431** Giraudon/Art Resource, NY; **433** Giraudon/Art Resource, NY; **440** Russian School, Czar Peter the Great, Rijksmuseum, Amsterdam; **445** Jacob van der Ulft, *The Square of the Dam at Amsterdam,* 1659, Musee Conde, Chantilly, Photo Giraudon/Art Resource, NY; **448** Robert Walker, *Oliver Cromwell,* 1649, By Courtesy of the National Portrait Gallery; **453** H. V. Schuylenburgh, *Head Office of the Dutch East India Company at Hugly in Bengal, 1665,* Rijksmuseum, Amsterdam; **455** Nicholas Poussin, Landscape with the Burial of the Phocion, Musee du Louvre, © Photo R.M.N.; **456** Rembrandt Van Rijn , *Syndics of the Cloth Guild,* Rijksmuseum, Amsterdam; **456** Leyster, Judith (Dutch, 1609–1660) *Self-Portrait,* c. 1630, oil on canvas, (29 3/8 x 25 5/8"); National Gallery of Art, Washington, Gift of Mr. and Mrs. Robert Woods Bliss

CHAPTER 16

460 Dumesnil, *Queen Christina of Sweden with Descartes,* Musee du Louvre, © Photo R.M.N.; **464** Courtesy of the Lilly Library, Indiana University, Bloomington, Indiana; **465** Courtesy of the Lilly Library, Indiana University, Bloomington, Indiana; **468** (left) Deutsches Museum, Munich; **468** (right) Biblioteca Nazionale Centrale, Firenze;

470 National Portrait Gallery, London; **474** Corbis; **477** Dumesnil, *Queen Christina of Sweden with Descartes,* Musee du Louvre, © Photo R.M.N.; **480** Ecole francaise (17e siecle), *Blaise Pascal,* Versailles et Trianon, © Photo R.M.N.; **482** Giraudon/Art Resource, NY; **482** Reproduced by Courtesy of the Science Museum, (neg. 4534)

CHAPTER 17

486 Photo © Michael Holford; **488** By permission of the Houghton Library, Harvard University; **491** Mary Evans Picture Library; **493** J. Honore Fragonard, *Diderot,* Musee du Louvre, © Photo R.M.N.; **495** Allan Ramsay, *Jean-Jacques Rousseau,* National Gallery of Scotland; **498** Giraudon/Art Resource, NY; **500** Antoine Watteau, *The Pilgrimage to Cythera,* Musee du Louvre, © Photo R.M.N.; **501** (top) Courtesy of James R. Spencer; **501** (bottom) Scala/Art Resource, NY; **502** Louis David, *The Oath of the Horatii,* Musee du Louvre, © Photo R.M.N.; **503** Musee Conde, *Chantilly,* Photo Giraudon/Art Resource, NY; **506** Photo © Michael Holford; **512** Nathaniel Hone, *John Wesley,* c. 1766, By courtesy of the National Portrait Gallery, London

CHAPTER 18

516 Erich Lessing/Art Resource, NY; **520** National Portrait Gallery; **522** Giraudon/Art Resource, NY; **524** Kunsthistorisches Museum, Vienna; **526** Scala/Art Resource, NY; **532** Benjamin West, *The Death of General Wolfe,* Transfer from the Canadian War Memorial, 1921, Gift of the second Duke of Westminster, Eaton Hall, Cheshire, 1918, National Gallery of Canada, Ottawa; **534** Arthur Devis, *The John Bacon Family,* c. 1742–3, Yale Center for British Art, Paul Mellon Collection; **535** Germanisches Nationalmuseum; **540** Bibliotheque des Arts Decoratifs, Photo © J.L. Charmet; **544** (right) Erich Lessing/Art Resource, NY; **544** (left) Wilton House, *East View Showing the Old Entrance* by Richard Wilson (1714–82) Collection of the Earl of Pembroke, WIlton House, Wilts., UK/Bridgeman Art Library, London/ New York; **545** Giovanni Michele Graneri, *Market in Piazza San Carlo,* 1752, Museo Civico di Torino

CHAPTER 19

550 Anonymous, *Fall of the Bastille,* (detail) Musee National des Chateay de Versailles, © Photo R.M.N.; **552** John Trumbull, *The Declaration of Independence, 4 July, 1776,* Yale University Art Callery, Trumbull Collection; **558** Giraudon/ Art Resource, NY; **560** Anonymous, *Fall of the Bastille,* (detail) Musee National des Chateay de Versailles, © Photo R.M.N.; **562** Photo Bulloz; **565** ET Archive; **567** Giraudon/ Art Resource, NY; **569** Giraudon/Art Resource, NY; **571** Giraudon/Art Resource, NY; **573** Antoine Jean Gros, *Napoleon Crossing the Bridge at Arcola,* Musee du Louvre, © Photo R.M.N.; **576** Louis David, *Sacre de l'empereur* (detail), Musee du Louvre, © Photo R.M.N.

Documents

The Trial of Michael Sattler 379
From *Spiritual and Anabaptist Writers in Volume XXV of The Library of Christian Classics,* edited by G. H. Williams, copyright © 1957 by SCM Press, Ltd.

The Role of Discipline in the "Most Perfect School of Christ on Earth" 383
From *The Reformation: A Narrative History Related by Contemporary Observers and Participants* by Hans J. Hillerbrand. Copyright © 1964 by Harper & Row, Publishers. Reprinted with permission of Hans J. Hillerbrand.

A Protestant Woman 385
Excerpt from *Not in God's Image* by Julia O'Faolain and Lauro Martines. Copyright © 1973 by Julia O'Faolain and Lauro Martines. Reprinted by permission of Harper & Row, Publishers, Inc.

Loyola and Obedience to "Our Holy Mother, the Hierarchical Church" 389
From *Spiritual Exercises of St. Ignatius,* translated by Louis J. Puhl, copyright © 1951 by Newman Press. Used with permission of the publisher, Loyola University Press.

CHAPTER 14

The Spanish Conquistador: Cortes and the Conquest of Mexico 398
Excerpt from *The European Reconnaissance: Selected Documents* edited by John H. Parry. Copyright © 1968 by John H. Parry. Reprinted by permission of HarperCollins Publishers Inc.

Las Casas and the Spanish Treatment of the American Natives 400
From *The Tears of the Indians,* Bartolome de Las Casas. Copyright © 1970 by The John Lilburne Company Publishers.

Philip II, the Most Catholic King of Spain 404
From *Readings in European History,* James Harvey Robinson (Lexington, Mass.: Ginn and Co., 1934).

Queen Elizabeth Addresses Parliament (1601) 408
From *Elizabeth I and Her Parliaments* by John E. Neale. Copyright © 1958. Reprinted with permission of Jonathan Cape, Publisher.

The Face of War in the Seventeenth Century 414
From *Simplicius Simplicissimus* by Jacob von Grimmelshausen, translated byGeorge Schulz-Behrend, copyright © 1965 by Bobbs-Merrill. Translation © Camden House, Inc. Columbia, SC. Used with permission.

A Witchcraft Trial in France 417
From *Witchcraft in Europe, 1100–1700: A Documentary History,* by Alan C. Kors and Edward Peters (Philadelphia: University of Pennsylvania Press, 1972), pp. 266–275.

William Shakespeare: In Praise of England 423
Excerpt from *Richard II* in *Shakespeare, The Complete Works* by G. B. Harrison, copyright © 1968 by Harcourt Brace & Company.

CHAPTER 15

Louis XIV: Kingly Advice 429
Reprinted with the permission of Macmillan Publishing Company from *From Absolutism to Revolution 1648–1848* by Herbert H. Rowen. Copyright © 1963 by Macmillan Publishing Company.

Travels with the King 432
From *The Age of Magnificence,* Sanche de Gramont, ed. Copyright © 1964 Capricorn Books. Reprinted with permission of The Putnam Publishing Group.

Peter the Great Deals with a Rebellion 439
From, *Readings in European History,* James Harvey Robinson (Lexington, Mass.: Ginn and Co., 1934).

The Economic Superiority of the Dutch 446
From "Observations Touching Trade and Commerce with the Hollanders, and Other Nations," in J.R. McCulloch, ed. *A Select Collection of Scarce and Valuable Tracts on Commerce* (1859; reprinted 1966 by A.M. Kelley, Publishers).

The Bill of Rights 450
From *The Statutes: Revised Edition* (London: Eyre and Spottiswoode, 1871), Vol. 2, pp. 10–12.

Hobbes and Locke:
Two Views of Political Authority 451
From *Leviathan* by Thomas Hobbes. Copyright © 1968 by Penguin Books; from *The Second Treatise of Government,* by John Locke, ed. Thomas Peardon (New York: The Liberal Arts Press, 1952), pp. 123–124.

West Meets East: An Exchange of Royal Letters 454
From *The World of Southeast Asia: Selected Historical Readings,* Harry J. Benda and John A. Larkin, eds. Copyright © 1967 by Harper & Row, Publishers. Used with permission of the author.

French Comedy: The Would-Be Gentleman 457
From Moliere, *The Would-Be Gentleman,* in Mary A.F. Witt, Charlotte V. Brown, Robert A. Dunbar, Frank Tirro, and Ronald G. Witte, *The Humanities: Cultural Roots and Continuities.* Copyright © (1980) by D.C. Heath and Co.

CHAPTER 16

Magic and Science: The Case of Girolamo Cardano 463
From Jerome Cardan, *The Book of My Life,* Jean Stoner, trans. Copyright © 1930 by E.P. Dutton. Reprinted by permission of Penguin Books USA Inc.

On the Revolutions of the Heavenly Spheres 466
From *On the Revolutions* by Nicholaus Copernicus, pp. 4–5, 20. Copyright © 1978 by The Johns Hopkins University Press. Reprinted with permission of the publisher.

Kepler and the Emerging Scientific Community 467
From *Johannes Kepler, Life and Letters* by Carola Baumgardt, copyright © 1951 by the Philosophical Library. Used by permission.

The Starry Messenger 469
From *Discoveries and Opinions of Galileo,* Stillman Drake, ed., trans. Copyright © 1957 by Doubleday and Co. Reprinted with permission of the publisher.

CHAPTER 17

CHAPTER 18

CHAPTER 19

Declaration of the Rights of Woman and the Female Citizen 563
From *Women in Revolutionary Paris 1789–1795* by Darleen Gay Levy, Harriet Branson Applewhite, and Mary Durham Johnson. Copyright © 1979 by University of Illinois Press. Used with permission of the publisher.

A Victim of the Reign of Terror 568
From *Women in Revolutionary Paris 1789–1795* by Darleen Gay Levy, Harriet Branson Applewhite, and Mary Durham Johnson. Copyright © 1979 by University of Illinois Press. Used with permission of the publisher.

Robespierre and Revolutionary Government 569
From Robespierre, *Speech on Revolutionary Government* by George Rude, editor, © 1967. Reprinted by permission of the publisher, Prentice Hall/A Division of Simon & Schuster, Prentice Hall, N.J.

Napoleon and Psychological Warfare 574
Reprinted with the permission of Macmillan Publishing Company from *A Documentary Survey of the French Revolution* by John Hall Stewart. Copyright © 1951 by Macmillan Publishing Company, renewed 1979 by John Hall Stewart.

The Man of Destiny 575
From *The Mind of Napoleon* by J. Christopher Herold. Copyright © 1955 by Columbia University Press. Reprinted with the permission of the publisher.

Index

Note: Page references in italics indicate map or figure.

S

W

X

Y

Z